Anything
of which a
Woman is capable

Cover Design by Carol L. Smith, CSJ

Preface

When the Federation of the Sisters of St. Joseph was created in 1966 there were 24 distinct congregations in the United States. Mary McGlone has done a masterful job tracing the growth of the Sisters of St. Joseph from their French beginnings in the Seventeenth Century, to their humble beginnings in the United States in 1836 and their spread throughout the country by the time the Federation formed.

As with any project of this scope, the author stands of the shoulders of those who came before. All who trace the history of religious congregations owe a huge debt of gratitude to Evangeline Thomas whose Women Religious History Sources: A Guide to Repositories in the United States (1983) laid the foundation for studies that enrich our understanding today.

Much is owed, also, to the Federation-sponsored research teams which translated and published documents relating to the French beginnings of the Sisters of St. Joseph. The illuminating publication on French roots by Marguerite Vacher, so ably translated by Patricia Byrne, has proved vital to later research, as has also Patricia Byrne's work on the Sisters' American developments.
Carol Coburn and Martha Smith's Spirited Lives: How Nuns Shaped Catholic Culture and American Life, 1836-1920 (1999) made an invaluable contribution to the literature. Barbara Baer and Patricia Byrne carried out interviews that constitute an oral history archive to complement published accounts.

The Conference on the History of Women Religious begun in the 1980s can be credited with awakening researchers in the United States and Europe to the importance of women religious in shaping culture and furthering the work of the church. Mary McGlone explores the fascinating history of the women who led the Sisters of St. Joseph to establish themselves in this country, their interactions with bishops during decades when the independence of religious congregations vis a vis bishops was ill-defined in canon law, and their role in defusing prevalent anti-Catholicism throughout in Nineteenth and early Twentieth centuries.

Readers of Mary's volume one tracing the growth of the Sisters of St. Joseph in the United States 1836-1920 can look forward to a great read, rich in personalities and the drama of beginnings. A second volume promises to describe the multiple and varied ministries carried out by Sisters of St. Joseph in the field of education, health care and social services, individuals distinguished for their work as artists, social activists, and theologians; and the founding of international missions beginning with the Sisters of St. Joseph of Baden in China in the 1920s.

Karen M. Kennelly
St. Paul, Minnesota

Acknowledgements

This project began long before I came on the scene. It started with the dream of Sisters Barbara Baer and Patricia Byrne and leaders of the U. S. Federation of the Sisters of St. Joseph who gave it the necessary support so that Barbara Baer could spend years gathering what is literally tons of research to begin the project. We would not have this work today had it not been for all of them.

In more recent years, the Federation gathered a committee to oversee and encourage the work. That group, headed by Sister Karen Kennelly included Sisters Marcia Allen, Anne Hennessy and Theresa Kvale and Dr. Carol Coburn of Avila University. Their help, encouragement and direction has been both generous and invaluable to me as has been the ongoing support and help of Sister Patty Johnson, the Executive Director of the Federation of the Sisters of St. Joseph in the United States.

The research in this volume has been completed with the immense and big-hearted help of many people, most particularly the archivists of the CSSJ communities and the sisters who so patiently proof read every page over and over. At the risk of missing a name, for which I offer my sincere apologies, I want to thank Sisters Mary Salvaterra of Albany, Mary Rita Grady of Boston, Eva Amadori of Buffalo, Carol Marie Wildt of the Carondelet Congregation, Bernadine Pachta of Concordia, Judi Keehnen, June Hanson, Mary Palmer, Ursula Fotovich, Marty McEntee and Janet Roesener of the Congregation of St. Joseph, Patricia Rose Shanahan of Los Angeles, Adele Marie Korhummel and Patricia Haley of Orange, Patricia Annas of Philadelphia, Catherine Bitzer of St. Augustine, Mary Kraft of St. Paul, Mary Jane Garry of West-Hartford, and Norma Bryant of Watertown, Ms. Kathleen Washy of Baden, Ms. Virginia Dowd of Brentwood, Ms. Jessica Anderson-Rath of Buffalo, Ms. Lisa Gibbons and Ms. Lisa Murphy of the Congregation of St. Joseph, Ms. Kathleen Urbanic of Rochester, Ms. Sherry Enserro of Springfield and Mr. Leo Catahan of Orange. Special thanks to Adonna Thompson, the archivist at the Martha Smith Archives and Research Center at Avila University who bent over backwards to help me sort through Barbara Baer's research. To each of you professionals I express my deep thanks for your help and patience with me as I learned more about your congregations and archives. I also thank each of our CSSJ congregations who received me with such warmth and cordial charity, fed and housed me and encouraged this project in word and deed and prayer.

I could not have done this without the help of patient and picky proof-readers, Sisters Ann Pace, Margaret Schulz, Joanne Gallagher, Lisa Lazio, Monica Kleffner, Ida Robertine Berresheim, Mary Hugh McGowan, Rita Louise Huebner, Barbara

Jennings, Barbara Moore, Loretta Costa, Kathleen Crowley, Laura Ann Grady, Audrey Olson, and Janet Kuciejczyk. They have done their best to correct my errors and give me good suggestions. On the other side of the ocean, Sister Simone Saugues of the Institut des Soeurs de Saint-Joseph in France helped me in many ways, especially in pointing out resources, understanding something of helping me understand a little about French history and arranging for me to meet with Sister Terese Vacher, the author of Nuns Without Cloister. Like her, Bénédicte de Vaublanc of the Chambéry Congregation introduced me to the Sisters of St. Joseph in Chambéry and the area of Moutiers from where so many of our early French missionaries came to serve in the United States. In a very special way I express my gratitude to Sr. Jane Behlmann of Carondelet who not only answered every question I could come up with and listened to my ideas but also shared my enthusiasm for little facts that would make most ordinary people go glassy-eyed. Of course, the beauty of the design we hold in our hands comes from the artistry and hard work of Sister Carol Louise Smith of Carondelet's Los Angeles Province.

Most of all, and in the name of every Sister of St. Joseph in the United States, I express our gratitude to the sisters who have gone before us and brought us to this moment of our history. May we have the grace and strength to live up to the legacy you have left us!

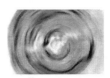

INTRODUCTION

No one is born of her own power or volition; we enter the world as the fruit of a history of human relations and the long course of ongoing creation. Not only do we evolve from the life of our ancestors, but from the moment of our birth, we are conditioned by the environment in which we live. Our environment, beginning with our families, our mother tongue and our communities, teach us how to understand the world and our place in it. Our biography is simply the history of our relationships with the people, the cultures, and the world that surround us. At one and the same moment, we are created by and creators of history. This is our collaboration in God's ongoing creation.

The history of the Sisters of St. Joseph is a story of relationships. Born in seventeenth century France, the life of the Congregation was interwoven with the Spirit's movement in the Tridentine Reformation and its French expressions. Through the course of more than three and a half centuries, following the inspiration of the Spirit, the Sisters of St. Joseph have grown in relationship with their neighbors in diverse historical and religious contexts. We cannot fully appreciate who we are today without an awareness of the travelers and trajectories that have brought us to this moment.

The consensus statement of the Sisters of St. Joseph says, "Stimulated by the Holy Spirit of Love and receptive to the Spirit's inspiration, the Sister of St. Joseph moves always toward profound love of God and love of neighbor without distinction..." We believe firmly that the Holy Spirit played the major role in inspiring the hearts of our sisters and their collaborators in the activities that have created this moment of our history. This story is about thousands of individuals, Sisters of St. Joseph, their collaborators, church leaders, and the ordinary People of God who called them forth. We know the names of many of our founders and their first collaborators. They and some other sisters who played an outsized role in our history are among the people whose names are listed in the "Cast of Characters" that begins each chapter of this book. A large part of the importance of their story derives from the fact that others were attracted to join with them because they shared their passion for God and neighbor. Therefore, as we get to know our founders and other "famous characters" we are somehow also getting to know thousands of others who didn't bequeath us diaries or documents.

In East of Eden, Ernest Hemingway tells us, "No story has power, nor will it last, unless we feel in ourselves that it is true and true of us." This story is about us – as Sisters of St. Joseph, as women of the Church, as part of the long procession of saints and sinners who strive to collaborate with God's great design for the life of the world. This story is true as far as the facts can be verified. It is also true insofar as we recognize ourselves and others who share this charism in the love and the humble audacity that made our predecessors capable of doing anything necessary to serve their neighbor.

The more I have delved into this story, the more I have been inspired and have felt proud to be a part of it. I hesitate to call this book the history of the Sisters of St. Joseph in the United States. Our history does not fit in books but it can be glimpsed in the multiple ways through which our sisters have carried forward what Father Médaille called the Little Design. Our history lives in each person our sisters have touched, taught, healed and loved. I hope this volume helps us deepen our understanding of who we are called to be by introducing us to the women who were called forth by their times and circumstances to undertake all the spiritual and corporal works of mercy of which women are capable and thus to further God's work of bringing all into one. This book is written for Sisters of St. Joseph and everyone who shares our passion for weaving unity of neighbor with neighbor and the entire universe with God.

We may have once thought that the task of the historian is simply to relate what happened in the past, more or less reporting the on past as an objective journalist reports on current events. Today we are aware that what one sees depends on where one stands; one's point of view or vantage point determines what she can see and what remains invisible. A Marxist writes history very differently from a monarchist. A Sister of St. Joseph will understand this story differently than will a scholar of feminist studies or a sociologist of religion. I have approached the task of telling this story as a Sister of St. Joseph and a historical theologian.

Historical theology, as I have used it to produce this work, includes serious research and contemplation. Historical theology is not dogmatic; while it understands reality through a lens of faith, it makes no proclamation about God's will or the ultimate meaning of events. It tries to discover the theological-historical context in which things happened and to describe how spiritualties and movements of grace have created the unique texture of events. It seeks to capture what was evolving in the complex interactions of peoples and their environment, all oriented and flavored by grace and faith in God. It assumes faith rather than professing it. This is not a book about our spirituality, but about how sisters lived our spirituality in service of God and the dear neighbor. It describes some of the mission journeys, bedside care, educational and other works that expressed these women's love of God, the daily activities that incarnated God's great love.

As I worked through our foundation stories, it became clear that they constituted a story in themselves. Thus, what was planned as one book that could be completed in three years has become Volume 1 of a two-volume work. The second volume will narrate ways in which the members of our congregations have participated in the mission of building up the People of God in the United States and how our vision has been stretched beyond our borders and boundaries. The stories of our foundations are not presented here in equal length. That is not because of any favoritism, but because of the wealth of the material available. Additionally, some communities continue to play a role in the stories of others, most particularly Brooklyn (Brentwood) Carondelet, and Philadelphia. Their histories weave through the rest rather than being told discreetly in only one section.

I have done my best to find credible resources to tell us what Sisters of St. Joseph were doing at a given time and place. When there have been conflicting opinions or reports, I have tried to represent the different points of view. I have endeavored to frame the events of our sisters' lives within the setting of larger stories, sketching the context within which various episodes took place so that we can recognize the larger movements of grace, the sinful social structures and the institutional, social and spiritual currents that gave shape or direction to events in which individuals and groups exercised their own creative influence. This is an attempt to describe something of the tangible reality that has housed particular dimensions of the in-breaking of the kingdom of God during the past three and a half centuries. I hope this work makes a contribution not only to our history, but to the study of the Catholic Church in the United States and the history of women religious.

Not surprisingly, the contexts that have shaped us as Sisters of St. Joseph are quite diverse. We first came together in France in the mid-1600s, a time of suffering for the poor and an era of great spiritual dynamism demonstrated by the enormously energetic mission of the Society of Jesus and the influences of saintly personalities including Francis de Sales and Jane de Chantal, Vincent de Paul and Louise de Marillac, John Francis Regis and Jean Pierre Médaille. All of them were shaped by and contributed to the spiritual currents of their day. This historical and spiritual atmosphere gave birth to the Little Design that blossomed into congregations of Sisters of St. Joseph throughout the world.

When the violence and chaos of the French Revolution endangered individual lives and the very existence of our congregations, there were women whose passion for God and neighbor could not be extinguished. Inspired by belief in their unique style of religious life, they were energized to reinstate and restructure their communities to serve the changing needs of their times.

The missionary zeal of the Church in France sent religious and priests throughout the world in the early 19th century. Under that influence, and with the help of the Countess de Rochejacquelein, Mother St. John Fontbonne sent the first eight Sisters of St. Joseph to America. They and the sisters from Moutiers, Bourg, and Le Puy who followed them in the mid-nineteenth century, were the first wave of missionary Sisters of St. Joseph to establish themselves in the United States. Toward the end of the nineteenth century, other sisters would respond to persecution of the Church in France and rejection of their own ministries by becoming missionary-exiles. French anti-clericalism turned out to be the precipitating cause of an ever greater spread of the mission of the Sisters of St. Joseph in other parts of Europe as well as in America and India. That wave brought sisters from Chambéry and second waves from Le Puy and Lyon.

Sisters from the United States, almost all from immigrant backgrounds, built on what the French missionaries began and formed a total of at least twenty-eight diverse congregations or provinces of Sisters of St. Joseph in the U.S.A. The congregations of Sisters of St. Joseph grew and extended their presence in response to the requests of bishops and pastors desperate for the indispensable contributions women religious would make to the building up of the educational, healing, and social mission of the Church in a country with an influx of poor, Catholic immigrants such as had never been seen in history. These sisters had to find their way through the labyrinths of diverse cultural settings, mistrust of women's leadership, anti-Catholicism, the vagaries of Church authorities, and multi-cultural religious communities. Through it all, whether in partnership with collaborating clergy and laity or struggling with dictatorial priests or bishops, Sisters of St. Joseph maintained amazingly strong ties among themselves across the country as they met the demands of each situation. Following the pattern of Father Médaille's Little Design, they usually established their ministries in response to the needs of their neighbors rather than from a preconceived apostolic plan. Their preparation for ministry was often based more in their willingness to respond than in formal education or training.

While we have drawn genealogical trees to neatly illustrate the relationships among the communities of St. Joseph throughout the world, a more apt symbol may be a web through which we discover that the relationships among us are so interwoven that we not only share the same spirit and spirituality, but we have been far more interconnected throughout the course of our history than we have generally realized. From our earliest days on American soil, interrelationship and mutual support have been our lifeblood; that connection has sometimes come to concrete expression through the sharing of personnel and amalgamation of communities. The world of the 21st century will surely call forth much greater interrelationship as we become intentionally global rather than merely national. There are many unsolved mysteries between the lines of this narrative and many stories yet to be discovered. They go beyond the scope of this work, but what we have here offers hints to others who want to dig into the intricacies of our historical relationships and unearth more about the ways we have grown together since 1650. The task I have attempted in this volume is to tell the story of our origins from Le Puy, France in 1650 to Eureka, California in 1912.

Much of the information here can be gleaned from our various histories, but we have never before put it all together. In addition to congregational resources, I have relied on common references such as histories of the Church in the United States and diocesan histories. The annual editions of the Catholic Directory provide excellent background information and inadvertently demonstrate that through the years, our dioceses maintained and published careful records of the number of parishes, schools, institutions, the names of clergy, and the number of seminarians in their jurisdiction, but they rarely mentioned even the number of women religious serving in their dioceses and the institutions they proudly listed. Other very helpful sources of information I have found are various dissertations, interviews, encyclopedia entries, and Wikipedia's reporting of U.S. census records for the various cities in which we have served. I have tried as much as possible to include footnotes that can not only lead scholars to rich sources of information, but may also add some depth, breadth and enjoyment to the text.

This story is written primarily for Sisters of St. Joseph and others who share our life and vision. It speaks from the inside, presuming a familiarity with the milieu of religious life, and therefore I do not bother to explain vocabulary and concepts that are basic to Catholicism or this life-style and its history. Those who are not familiar with those elements can gain the necessary understanding from the context and a simple dictionary.

There is much left untold in this volume. I have simply tried to introduce each of our congregations and the people and circumstances that called them into being. There is much more to do even to continue to discover and narrate the stories of our earliest days. As mentioned in the acknowledgements, I am most grateful to the archivists of our various congregations. They have saved me from many mistakes, but I am sure some have remained. For those, I apologize; it was never my intention to misinterpret, skip, or gloss over anyone's story. I hope that this general work will inspire more in-depth study of how our history and spirituality have evolved on the soil of this unique place we call the United States of America.

Most of all, I hope that this story will be a source of inspiration, joy, and pride in those women who gave us our start in this country. I hope and pray that the spirit of our pioneer sisters will inspire us, today's Sisters of St. Joseph, to ever widen our vision and go beyond our boundaries as they did. Stimulated by the Holy Spirit of Love and continually receptive to inspiration, they didn't hesitate to venture into the unknown. They simply trusted that God would accomplish in them far more than they could ask or imagine. That faith led them to believe in themselves and one another; such faith and God's grace made them capable of doing anything that would be asked of them for the sake of the dear neighbor. In the end, that is their legacy to us.

Mary M. McGlone, CSJ
October 15, 2017

Anything

of which a
Woman is capable

*A History of the Sisters
of St. Joseph in the United States*

VOLUME 1- The Foundations

MARY M MCGLONE, CSJ

TABLE of CONTENTS

Chapter One: The Little Design Takes Shape in France

Chapter Two: Adjusting The Design

Chapter Three: The Little Design Goes to America

Chapter Ten: French Communities Continue
to Bring the Little Design to the U.S.   447

∾

Chapter One: Beginnings in France

THE LITTLE DESIGN TAKES SHAPE IN FRANCE

Cast of Characters

Precursors And Co-Founders	Founding Sisters Of Le Puy
Francis de Sales: 1567 – 1622	Françoise Eyraud
Jane de Chantal: 1572 – 1641	Claudia Chastel
Vincent de Paul 1581 - 1660	Marguerite Burdier
Louise de Marillac 1591 - 1660	Anna Chaleyer
Jean Pierre Médaille 1610 - 1669	Anna Vey
Bishop Henri de Maupas 1604 - 1680	Anna Brun

THE SOCIO-POLITICAL CONTEXT

In 1644 René Descartes published his most famous phrase: "I think, therefore I am." That declaration came from his search for philosophical certainty unconstrained by the truth claims of theologians. While his thinking has been called the inauguration of modern Western philosophy, few people who lived during his era could enjoy the leisure of philosophical pursuits. The ideas of the Enlightenment would take time to filter down to ordinary people. Meanwhile, as is always the case, the miseries of mid-seventeenth century France had their most devastating effects among the poor and included ongoing religious and political wars which gave marauding armies the opportunity to have their way with local populations and their goods. Even nature seemed to punish the people by sending both famine and plague.

When the Reformation brought Calvinism to France, its theology which questioned the Tradition of the church and promoted the idea of individual salvation quickly attracted the least religiously sophisticated segments of society. With time, Protestant spirituality gained such power that some of its adherents withstood Catholic censure and even bloody persecution rather than give it up. The spiritual chaos of the age was such that diverse popular preachers could move the population of entire villages to change their religious denomination various times in a single week.[1] Over time, a significant proportion of the nobility accepted the Calvinist or "Huguenot" faith.[2] Because of their antagonism toward the Catholic

---

1 See Andre Dodin, C.M.: Vincent de Paul and Charity: *A Contemporary Portrait of his Life and Apostolic Spirit* (New Rochelle, N.Y.: New City Press, New Rochelle, 1993), 15.
2 The name Huguenot comes from French, and implies that a person is a sworn confederate of a movement that began with Besancon Hugues. Eventually, it came to refer to any French Protestant of the 16th or 17th Century. See Joseph Lortz, Historia de la Iglesia en la Perspectiva de la Historia del Pensamiento Tomo II, Edad Moderna y Contemporanea, Traducido por J. Rey Marcos, (Madrid: Ediciones Cristiandad, 1982.) 146.

Church and their influence over the peasantry, what had been labeled religious discord can be understood just as well as political struggles. Henry of Navarro, the future King Henry IV of France (1533-1610), was baptized a Catholic but raised as a Protestant. Before ascending the throne he participated in the religious wars and barely escaped death in the so-called St. Bartholomew's massacre which killed more than 10,000 Huguenots.[3] In 1593 King Henry IV returned to the Catholic Church and the bloodshed began to decrease. It diminished even more in 1598 when he proclaimed the Edict of Nantes, conceding freedom of religion to the Huguenots and thereby legalizing freedom of conscience. [4]

Henry's son, King Louis XIII reigned from 1610 to 1643, ascending to the throne at the age of nine under the regency of his mother, Marie de Medici. His reign was as turbulent as his father's and he abdicated great authority to others, including the infamous Cardinal Richelieu who destroyed the power and even the castles of much of the nobility and doubled the taxes on the lower classes. He attained the rare distinction of being reviled among wealthy and poor alike.[5]

THE ECCLESIAL CONTEXT
Conditions in the Catholic Church in France mirrored the turmoil of the political situation. Under the influence of Cardinal Richelieu (1585-1643), the Church in France took on an ever-stronger Gallican position.[6] This nationalistic ecclesiology had strong roots in the 16th century when the French monarchy prohibited the publication of the decrees of the Council of Trent (1545-63) in French territory. Individual diocesan synods gradually promulgated the results of Trent in France, a process which took more than 50 years following the close of the Council.
In counterpoint to Gallican resistance to Roman authority, a broad mixture of people including theologians, members of traditional and new religious orders, and active laity brought about a reforming religious renaissance. A movement known as "the French School" made tremendous pastoral contributions by trying to teach and stimulate the practice of the faith among people of every social class.

---

3 Lortz, 147. The "massacre" actually went on for several weeks.
4 The popular belief is that Henry returned to the Church for reasons more political than religious. In order to pressure him, Spanish and papal troops had occupied Paris. Henry is said to have returned to the Church because he finally decided that "Paris is worth a Mass." Lortz, 147. In 1685, King Louis XIV rescinded the Edict of Nantes, setting off another wave of cruel persecution of Protestants.
5 See William Stearns Davis, *A History of France, from the Earliest Times to the Treaty of Versailles*, Boston: Houghton and Mifflin, 1919, Kindle Edition: locations 2021 – 2079.
6 Gallicanism refers to the attempts made by French royalty to subordinate the papacy to the authority of ecumenical councils and to reserve certain ecclesial powers to the monarchy. The movement began forcefully in 1438 and rose and fell until the First Vatican Council (1869-70) defined papal power.

While some civil and religious leaders attached themselves to the Church for reasons of personal gain, many of the people engaged in these movements were on fire with the love of God and the spirit of the reformed Church. With a lively memory of saints like Teresa of Avila, John of the Cross, Ignatius of Loyola and Charles Borromeo, advocates of the renewed spirituality inherited new models of sanctity and great religious energy from the preceding century and neighboring countries. Nevertheless, they were not content merely to imitate previous reforms. The French movement gave special attention to the laity. Thus leaders such as Pierre de Bérulle, Jane de Chantal, Francis de Sales and Vincent de Paul promoted new currents of spirituality, giving birth to new experiments including that which led to the Congregation of the Sisters of St. Joseph. In order to understand the religious context of seventeenth century France, one must know at least a little about these people and the way in which their ideas changed the Church of their time.

PIERRE DE BÉRULLE AND THE FRENCH SCHOOL

Pierre de Bérulle (1575 - 1629), the father of the "French School," was a close friend of three saints, John Eudes (+1680), Francis de Sales (+1622), and Vincent de Paul (+1660). His circle of friends included his cousin, Madame Acarie, famous in her time for hosting leading men and women in her home for spiritual discussions that not only edified the participants, but led them to great works of charity. The theology Bérulle shared with these groups emerged from extensive meditation on the mystery of the Trinity and the two natures of Christ. In contemplating Jesus in the light of the life of the Trinity, he concluded that Jesus had to make an act of total submission of his human person to enter into union with God. From de Bérulle's point of view, Christ's real sacrifice was the self-emptying that characterized his life, culminating at the Last Supper and on the Cross. Pierre de Bérulle taught that the way to union with God was imitation of Christ's self-emptying. Following this intuition, he believed that the Eucharist was the privileged activity through which the faithful, beginning with the priests, could unite themselves with the self-emptying sacrifice of Christ.

We can easily recognize the seeds of four dimensions of the spirituality of the Sisters of Saint Joseph in the traditions of de Bérulle and the French School: an emphasis on the Trinity, self-emptying, the preeminence of the Eucharist and a growing intellectual and spiritual role for women. These four emphases would go through a process of Ignatian and Salesian evolution before they would assume their particular character as a part of the spirituality of the Sisters of St. Joseph.

FRANCIS DE SALES

One modern author characterizes Francis de Sales by saying that the essence of his spirituality can be summed up in the phrase "MORE JOY!"[7] Perhaps better than any others, those two words synthesize the quality of douceur, a key characteristic of Salesian spirituality[8] At the same time, it would be too easy to lose sight of the depth of the quality of douceur by allowing any two words to interpret it. Salesian douceur is the fruit of a life of study, prayer and loving service, and thus is best understood in light of the life of the saint who promoted it.

1567~1622

Francis de Sales studied under the Jesuits in Paris and then at the University of Padua. While he specialized in law, he also studied theology. As a student, he suffered a few short but extreme crises of faith.[9] When he had come through the crises, he had learned something that would serve him for the rest of his life. The experience of having gone through serious doubt convinced him that only the love of God could sustain and perfect human love and efforts. This simple idea seasoned the Ignatian maxim "All for the greater honor and glory of God" with a uniquely Salesian flavor. While he shared the Ignatian spirit of orienting all of one's strength to the glory of God, Francis de Sales put great, conscious emphasis on humanity's dependence on God.

He insisted that we must constantly remember and celebrate the reality

---

7 Lortz (286) says, "No one before or after him has given such emphasis to the idea of joy. No one has approached his brilliance in giving the religion of the cross the role of enriching the human person. His secret, surpassed by no one in history, resided in the art of manifesting the richness of the faith and at the same time taking advantage of its mild but effective conquering force."

8 Because the French word *douceur*, referred to in the CSJ Consensus Statement as "gentleness, peace and joy," defies adequate English translation, the original French will be used here.

9 The first crisis emerged as a result of the Protestant/Catholic debates over grace. Francis believed that it was possible that he might be among those predestined to eternal condemnation. He conquered the temptation to despair with "a heroic act of the will," abandoning himself to the mercy of God, at which time he prayed: Will I be deprived of the grace of the One who has so kindly let me experience his delights, and who has shown himself so loving to me?...However that may be, Lord, at least let me love you in this life if I am not to be able to love you in eternal life, for no one praises you in hell. (Ps. 6:5)

The grace that came from this crisis led him to recognize and value his own capacity to love everything he encountered in life as an integral part of his love of God. From the moment he overcame this test, he felt free to express his immense capacity to love. See Francis de Sales, *Jane de Chantal Letters of Spiritual Direction*, Translated by Peronne Marie Thibert, V.H.M., Selected and introduced by Wendy M. Wright and Joseph F. Power, O.S.F.S. (N.Y., Paulist Press, 1988) 19-20 and Lortz, 284

that God alone is the source, energy and destiny of every action that gives God glory.

At the age of thirty-seven, Francis de Sales was named bishop of Geneva, with a residence in Annecy because Geneva was thoroughly Calvinist.[10] He would spend the next eighteen years in a ministry that included the implementation of the Tridentine reforms, diplomatic service, catechetics and the preaching of missions. He dedicated his "free time" to the ministry that made him most famous: spiritual direction. It was this latter that led him to a career as the cofounder of a religious congregation, the author of books and a partner in extraordinary exchanges of correspondence about spirituality. His letters, even more than his books, offer a privileged view of the ideal of douceur that the Sisters of St. Joseph inherited from him.

In his ministry as a spiritual director, de Sales manifested a predilection for working with women – or perhaps they chose him above others because of his ability to fathom the feminine spirit. Doubtless he was rowing against the current in the attention and respect he gave to women. In his society, women, particularly the upper classes, were considered perpetual minors in the eyes of the law. While a peasant woman could work alongside her husband and lower class women could participate in artisan groups, the social status of women of the upper class prevented them from exercising any type of profession. No matter their class, women's narrow prospects were summarized by the adage "aut maritus, aut murus," either to a husband or to the cloister.[11]

Francis de Sales accepted neither the practice nor the theory of such denigration of women. He expressed his posture quite clearly when writing to Bishop Denis-Simon de Marquemont, the bishop of Lyon. Citing the Book of Genesis, de Sales said:

> God created the human person in the divine image and likeness, the person was created in the image of God, created as man and woman.

---

10 The city of Annecy is less than 30 miles from Geneva. When Francis de Sales was ordained, the Diocese of Geneva had its center in Annecy, and the bishop, Claude de Granier, gave Francis the highest office in the diocesan chapter. Francis' ministry of preaching and hearing confessions brought about a great number of conversions, gave witness to his charismatic leadership and led the bishop to have him named as his coadjutor. The diocese of Geneva, like those of Annecy and Chambery, were suffragan dioceses of the Archdiocese of Lyon.

11 See Elizabeth Rapley; *The Dévotees: Women and Church in Seventeenth Century France* (Montreal: McGill-Queen's University Press, 1990) 40-42. At the same time, their intellectual and spiritual energy found outlets in the "salon" gatherings in which people would gather to discuss the theological and spiritual currents of the day. One of the most famous was that of Madame Acarie who enjoyed the company of well-known ladies of the day as well as the Jesuit Peter Coton (spiritual director to Henry IV), Vincent de Paul and Francis de Sales.

Because of this, the woman, no less than the man, enjoys the favor of having been created in the image of God. The same honor is given to both genders, their virtues are equal, each is offered the same reward; and if they sin, they receive the same punishment. I don't want the woman to say, "I am fragile, my condition is weak." She may be weak in the flesh, but virtue, which resides in the soul, is strong and powerful.

We see the divine image glorified in both genders, and both demonstrate their virtue when they do good works.[12]

St. Jane Francis
de Chantal
1572~1641

De Sales expressed his esteem for women not only by accepting so many under his guidance as a spiritual director, but even more by joining with his friend Saint Jane de Chantal in the work of the foundation of "The Visitation."[13] The inspiration for the name of the Congregation came from Mary's visit to her cousin Elizabeth when they were both pregnant. While traditional images of Mary in the Annunciation and the Presentation in the Temple were contemplative, the Visitation portrayed Mary as an evangelized and evangelizing woman. The Visitation presented an image of Mary wholly active and fully capable of composing a canticle of contemplative love.[14] Emulating that image, the Sisters of The Visitation dedicated themselves to the practice the two arms of charity: expressing love of God in prayer and love of neighbor through service to others. Founded in 1610,

---

12 Francis de Sales, Oeuvres Completes (Annecy, 1892-1908), vol. 25: 291 ff.) De Sales wrote this when Bishop Marquemont of Lyon withdrew the permission he had given for the Sisters of the Visitation to live outside the cloister in his diocese. Characteristically, de Sales did not write simply on his own authority but cited St. Basil the Great as an ancient authority who agreed with his own point of view.

13 In Francis' day, religious life was not an option open for women who lacked a good dowry or good health. Nuns had no real sources of income and therefore had to live with what the sisters brought when they came to the community, supplemented by public charity. Because of this, it was a great risk to accept an older woman or one with health problems. The fact that The Visitation was open to women who were not considered apt for the religious life led some people to criticize Francis de Sales for wasting his time and founding an asylum for the handicapped instead of building a genuine religious congregation. See *Letters of Spiritual Direction*, 67.

14 The seventeenth century witnessed what might seem a competition among images of the Virgin Mary. Diverse groups chose Marian feasts and adapted her image to their own preferences. Thus, Mary in the Temple was envisioned as the contemplative or as the promoter of education for women. The Visitation became the icon for the missionary work of the Church. The image of Mary, Queen of the Apostles, illustrated the importance of Mary in the primitive Church and was used to support Catholic doctrine in debates with Protestants and as a defense for a more active role for Christian women. In addition, women's religious role was promoted by the religious art of the epoch which went beyond simple representations of Mary, including additional women as a sign that Mary was an example for all rather than the only woman capable of being genuinely apostolic. See Rapley, 170 - 173.

their plan functioned successfully for only five years before Archbishop Denis-Simon de Marquemont of Lyon ordered the Visitation Sisters to observe strict enclosure. Short-lived as it was, the Visitation's original plan expressed and encouraged an apostolic spirituality shared by committed women of the era. The religious energy that had been generated by the Catholic Reform had awakened a popular religiosity as active as it was pious. In full harmony with the teachings of the Council of Trent, women wanted to express their faith in works as well as in a life of prayer.

The life of apostolic faith animated by Francis de Sales could be assumed by lay and religious alike. Underneath it all lay that quality of douceur which could be summarized with Francis' call to "live joyously and courageously."[15] That phrase encourages the love of God and neighbor that springs from a joy based on humble gratitude. Living in that joy will demand courage: the courage required by ongoing self-giving, the courage to be patient and understanding of self and others.[16]

SAINT VINCENT DE PAUL AND THE APOSTOLATE OF WOMEN

Vincent de Paul
1581-1660

As mentioned earlier, the role of French women in the seventeenth century was quite restricted and at the same time, new spiritual movements and women's desire to be more active in living the faith combined to give birth to new opportunities. The Protestant Reformation, with the individualism expressed in the dogma of personal salvation, attracted a good number of women because it offered them a new but still limited level of autonomy and self-esteem.[17] Among the many Catholic movements that grew up in the seventeenth century, those sponsored by Vincent de Paul (1581-1660) were among the most influential and had the greatest long-term success.

France, as Vincent de Paul knew it from his mission work, was characterized by a tragic impoverishment. Poor harvests had forced hungry peasants to migrate to the cities where they found neither work nor decent shelter. One writer of that epoch, painting conditions with a rather broad brush, described the urban

---

15 Francis de Sales, *(Letters of Spiritual Direction*, op. cit., 149).
16 See essay on Douceur, Mary M. McGlone, CSJ, *Comunidad para el Mundo*, 495-510 (Lima: CEP, 2004).
17 Throughout the Christian era, the freedom and equality promoted by various novel religious movements, some of which were labeled as heresies, have been especially attractive to women. The more egalitarian the sect, the more women were attracted to it. See Rapley, 16.

situation as follows:

> One saw wandering troops of vagrants, without religion and without discipline, begging with more obstinacy than humility, often stealing what they could not otherwise get by pretended infirmities, coming even to the foot of the altars gaining the public's attention by devotions of the faithful.[18]

In the face of the material and spiritual poverty of the day, Vincent developed a passion for the poor and was determined to entice others to share it. Preaching to people who had sufficient means, he pointed them toward the poor with the admonition: "If you don't feed them, you are murdering them."[19] At the same time, Vincent learned that awakening consciences was not enough to create an adequate response to the needs of the day. It would happen that, after he preached, women could be so moved that they brought an overabundance of food all at once; it would spoil before it could be consumed, leaving an indigent family no better off in the long run. Vincent realized that in order to be effective, charity had to be organized and that the women of the parish could best take charge of this apostolate.[20] This is the origin of the Ladies of Charity, local groups who organized to care for the poor.[21]

Between 1620 and 1650, France witnessed an upsurge of Church-based social action leading to the establishment of orphanages, refuges, workshops and asylums for the poor. In order to respond to the needs of the times, women organized themselves in a broad variety of groupings. Although the Council of Trent had reiterated the prohibition of non-cloistered women's religious communities, around the second half of the century groups of women, well-organized and dedicated to apostolic work, began to come into existence. One type that would enjoy success, but was susceptible to a limited life-span was the "confraternity," one of which was founded in Le Puy in 1635 by St. John Francis

---

18 See Rapley, 78.
19 Dodin 15. See also, Mary Purcell, *The World of Monsieur Vincent*, (Chicago, Loyola University Press, 1989). Purcell writes: "...the poor of the countryside...Tenant-farmers, share-croppers, agricultural laborers or journeymen – all lived at bare subsistence level. On them fell the major portion of the taxes, the entire economic structure depending on their contribution, in toil, time, money and produce...Poor, illiterate, oppressed, unorganized, it was an easy matter to fleece them. [115]
20 See Rapley 81.
21 Vincent explained his preference for having women lead the way in charity saying:
Men and women do not get along together at all in matters of administration; the former want to take it over entirely and the latter will not allow it. We charged the men with the care of the healthy poor and the women with the sick; but because there was a shared purse, we had to get rid of the men. And I can bear this witness in favor of the women, that there is no fault to find in their administration, so careful and accurate are they.

Regis to carry out works of charity and deepen the spiritual life of the members.[22]

The most successful and long-lived of these was the Daughters of Charity of St Vincent de Paul. In order to assure that there would be a stable group in the service of the poor, Vincent and his friend Louise de Marillac founded the Daughters of Charity in 1635. Because their purpose was to serve the poor and sick, they avoided being identified as a religious congregation; they placed more value on the ability to serve than on a canonical classification. Replacing the characteristics of a traditional order

Louise deMarillac with their particular charism, Vincent described their life in the
1591~1660 following way:

> They will have for a monastery the houses of the sick and the house where their superior lives. For a cell, a rented room. For a chapel, the parish church. For a cloister, the streets of the city. For an enclosure, obedience. For a grate, the fear of God. For a veil, holy modesty. For profession, continual confidence in Providence and the offering of all that they are.[23]

Vincent understood canon law and could avoid the traps that had forced the Ursulines and the Sisters of the Visitation into the cloister. After 1640, the Daughters took private annual vows which were enough to express their spirituality of self-giving and maintain their freedom from the restrictions canon law could impose if they were considered members of a religious order.[24]

SUMMARY OF THE CONTEXT

In mid-seventeenth century France, all the circumstances were ripe for new birth in the Church. The material and spiritual needs of the people were obvious to everyone who had eyes to see. The conflicts of the Protestant Reformation and the

---

Purcell, citing Vincent de Paul, Correspondence, 4:11.

22 See Marie Louise Gondal, Les Origines des soeurs de Saint-Joseph au XVIIe : *Histoire oubliée d'une fondation. Saint-Flour-Le Puy* (1641-1650-1661) (Paris: Les Éditions Cerf, 2000) 132. The two French scholars who had done recent work on the origins of the Sisters of St. Joseph are Marguerite Vacher and Marie-Louise Gondal. There are various ways in which the two do not fully agree. Because Vacher's work Nuns Without Cloister has been translated into English and is generally available and Gondal's is available only in French with very few copies available in the U.S., Gondal's ideas will be presented here, knowing that other interpretations are easily accessible to the English speaking reader.

23 Dodin, 33.

24 By 1660, there were 800 Daughters of Charity working in France under a centralized authority. They wore distinctive clothing, but due to the adroit thinking of their founders, they were officially lay women rather than members of an Order. When the experiments of the Visitation and Ursulines attempted to modify the structures

Catholic Reform had given rise to waves of renewed Catholic spirituality and a new level of activity among the laity. Under the influence of spiritual guides like Pierre de Bérulle, Francis de Sales, and Vincent de Paul, the laity had begun to live a depth and intensity of spirituality previously reserved to the members of religious orders. With models like Teresa of Avila, Jeanne de Chantal and Louise de Marillac, women were no longer content with the ideal of staying in the house - whether it be the home of their husbands or the monastery. All of the conditions were right - or in the words of Vincent de Paul, "Divine Providence had everything prepared" for the dreams of a Jesuit missionary and a group of women who desired to dedicate themselves to the love of God and neighbor.

THE SISTERS OF ST. JOSEPH AND THE LITTLE DESIGN

The foundation of the Sisters of St. Joseph is a product of a largely hidden evolution; almost no records exist to outline their precise origins. What do exist are various documents that hint at Jesuit Father Jean Pierre Médaille's activities with groups of women beginning in 1646 or earlier. Those documents include Règlements (a rule), *Constitutions* used by a group founded in 1650 and a letter variously called "The Eucharistic Letter" or "The Letter about the Little Design."[25] Other documentary sources regarding Father Médaille and his activities come from the archives of The Society of Jesus.[26]

Since at least 1693, Sisters of St. Joseph have formally recognized Father Médaille as their "founder" in the sense that he gathered the first women who formed a community of St. Joseph in Le Puy in 1650 under the approval of Bishop Henri de Maupas of that diocese. It is a generally accepted theory that the Le Puy community was preceded by informal groupings known by diverse names and very likely by one or more formal "congregations" begun under the direct influence of Father Médaille. After an overview of what we know about Father Médaille, we will see a summary of the results of diverse research about the earliest communities that flowed from Médaille's "Little Design."

JEAN PIERRE MÉDAILLE

The data it has been possible to collect about Jean Pierre Médaille includes

---

of religious life, they were viewed as threatening or disobedient to hierarchical authority. The Daughters took the opposite tack, not claiming to modify religious life, but rather to adapt the secular life of women to make it "more devout and more ordered." (Rapley, 93)25 Marie Louise Gondal insists that the letter should properly be called "The Letter About the Little Design," recognizing that it uses the Eucharist as a symbol to illuminate its real subject, the group of women founded at Saint Flour in 1646. See Gondal, 164-190.

26 Marius Nepper, Origins : The Sisters of St. Joseph, translated from *AUX ORIGINES DES FILLES DE*

the following:

- ❖ 1610, October 6, Jean Pierre Médaille is born in Carcassonne;
- ❖ October 10, he is baptized in the Cathedral on Saint-Michel;
- ❖ 1625, September 16, he enters the Jesuit novitiate and studies until 1632 or 1633 in Toulouse;
- ❖ 1633-35, he is missioned to the Jesuit school at Carcassonne;
- ❖ 1635-37, he studies theology;
- ❖ 1637, he is ordained and sent to the school in Aurillac as Assistant to the rector;
- ❖ 1637-42, he is missioned to the school at Aurillac;
- ❖ 1642-43, he completes his year of tertainship at Toulouse;
- ❖ 1643, October 11 he makes his 4 solemn vows;
- ❖ 1643-49, he is missioned to the school at Saint Flour;[27]
- ❖ 1650-54, he is missioned to the school at Aurillac;
- ❖ 1654-62, he is missioned to the school at Montferrand;
- ❖ 1662-69, he is missioned to the school at Billom;
- ❖ 1669, December 30, Jean Pierre Médaille dies at Billom [28.]

It should not escape notice that even though his older confrere, St. John Francis Regis, served in Le Puy, Father Médaille was never missioned there. When Jean Pierre Médaille entered the Jesuit novitiate in 1625, the Company of Jesus had been in existence for sixty-five years and had approximately 13,112 members in thirty-two provinces.[29] The first indication that we have about Father Médaille's abilities comes from Father Verthamont his novice director. Among the 25 novices in his class, Médaille was one of only two that Father Verthamont classified as having exceptional intellectual capacity.[30] The novice master's assessment was reiterated when the superiors allowed Father Médaille to be ordained and make solemn vows after having completed only two of the usual four years of studies.

SAINT-JOSEPH, (Le Puy en Velay) Translation commissioned by the Federation of the Sisters of St. Joseph, U.S.A., Third Printing, 1981) 15-18.

27 There is a lack of information about his activities between 1647 and 48.

28 Toulouse is northwest of Carcassonne; Aurillac is almost directly west of Le Puy with Saint Flour almost half-way between them; Montferrand is the area now called Clermont-Ferrand. For reference, on today's roads the distance from Le Puy to Saint Flour is about 110 Kilometers (68 miles).

29 See: In Search of a Founder: The Life and Spiritual Setting of Jean-Pierre Médaille, S.J., Founder of the Sisters of St. Joseph, (A Dissertation by Anne Hennessy, CSJ, Orange, California) 34. In 2014, the website Jesuit.org stated that with a membership of nearly 17,000 men, the Jesuits were the most numerous male religious order in the world.

30 See Marguerite Vacher, *Des Régulières dans le siècle: Les soeurs de Saint-Joseph du Père Médaille aux XVII et XVIII siècles* (Clermont-Ferrand, Édiciones Adosa: 1991) 61. (English translation: *Nuns Without Cloister, Sisters of St. Jospeh in the Seventeenth and Eighteenth Centuries* (Lanham: University Press of America, 2010). Future references will be to Vacher, Soeurs or Vacher, Nuns.

Another indication of Father Médaille's outstanding aptitude is the list of ministries in which he served over the years. In the 32 years of his priesthood he almost always held a position of great responsibility. Those included:

- ❖ Consulter or a member of the superior's advisory council;
- ❖ Prefect of "The Great Congregation" - a Marian sodality for youth;
- ❖ Confessor for the community and the public;
- ❖ Companion to the preacher of missions in Saint-Flour;
- ❖ Procurator (who visited the public to collect debts owed the Jesuits or to ask for donations);
- ❖ Admonisher (the priest who cautions the superior about his errors).

Each of these roles demonstrates that Father Médaille enjoyed great respect from his superiors; he would not have been given such roles of responsibility if this had not been true.[31] In addition, when his superiors wrote their regular reports to Rome, they described Médaille with phrases such as even-tempered, melancholic, balanced, peaceful, penetrating, sublime and intellectually superior. They also mentioned that he had a great aptitude for all the works of the Society, and especially for spiritual direction.[32] From what we know, he taught little and was never a superior.[33] Interestingly, the superiors' acclamations for Father Médaille became more measured after 1646. It seems that the new attitude had something to do with his missionary activities.

JEAN PIERRE AND THE MISSIONS

According to seventeenth-century Jesuit practice, each priest was to have an "external" ministry to complement his office or his work as a teacher. For Médaille, who was famous as a preacher, that external ministry included time dedicated to the missions in the dioceses of Saint-Flour, Le Puy, Vienne, and Clermont-Ferrand.[34]

Area of France in which Médaille preached and the Sisters of St. Joseph made their early foundations

---

31 For a fuller description of these roles, see Hennessy, 103-115.
32 Father Nepper discovered these facts in the Archives of the Society of Jesus in Rome. They are published in Origins, 5-6. It is quite feasible that the term "melancholy" refers to a seriousness of character more than to the current interpretation as sadness.
33 Gondal, 43.

The purpose of the missions was to educate those who knew little about their faith, enliven the faith of the faithful, and convert Protestants. The missionaries went to rural and urban parishes, offering an irreplaceable service to the Church in France which badly needed formation and renewal. Two important characteristics of the Jesuit missions were that the missionaries normally went out in pairs and in each place where they gave a mission they gave extra attention and formation to leaders who would be able to share with others the grace that they had received in the mission.

Father Médaille and his companion would have spent weeks or even months in rural areas, preaching, catechizing, hearing confessions and forming leaders in towns that lacked adequate spiritual attention.[35] In each mission site, the priests would gather information about local sodalities; if they needed encouragement, they were to give it, and if there were none, they could form one or more.[36] The Jesuits had the permission of the local bishops to carry out the work of the missions; when they had to make prudential decisions, their instructions indicated that "the superior of the mission could make decisions after consultation with his companions, but matters of importance should be referred to the rector."[37]

MÉDAILLE AND THE "PIOUS WOMEN"

In 1646, Father Médaille took the initiative to communicate directly with Father Vincent Caraffa, the Jesuit Superior General. Although his original letter has not been found, a letter Caraffa wrote to Médaille's superior, the rector at Saint-Flour, refers to what Médaille had written him:

> As regards the grouping of pious women which he reports he has founded, I can only reply that it should not have been begun without the approval of the Provincial. Much less should rules have been prescribed for them unless he approved. Both could lead to idle talk, perhaps even dangers. And so you are to take care that I am informed more fully

---

34 Origins, 36. The French Jesuits dedicated themselves to both home and foreign missions. Their local ministry took them to areas that had been underserved by the Church for more than a hundred years. The map copied here is from the Barbara Baer collection.

35 One of the major problems of the day was the lack of good pastoral leadership. In order to avoid conflicts that could have lost them the privilege of preaching throughout the area, Jesuits were instructed not to ask questions about the moral conduct of the local priests. (See Hennessy, 131.)

36 The sodalities were a special apostolate among the Jesuits. They formed them with groups of their students or alumni as well as among some of the most suitable people they met in the missions. See Hennessy, 169-186 and John W. O'Malley, *The First Jesuits* John W. O'Malley, (Cambridge U. Press, Cambridge Ma. London England, 1993) 194-198.

37 O'Malley, 131-2, 142

through the Provincial, so that if this is for the glory of God, it may be carried on with all the more effectiveness as it is seen to be well-grounded. I want to know the nature of his plan and from whom he obtained permission to busy himself with such matters which are hardly in accordance with our Institute...[38]

Because Father Médaille's side of the correspondence is not available, the only thing we know for certain is that he went beyond the activities prescribed for the Jesuits on mission by "founding" a group of women. While they could have thought of themselves as a type of sodality or confraternity, it seems that they were more than that.[39] According to Father Marius Nepper, S.J., one of the first to research Médaille's history, we have in the Superior General's letter the first partial evidence of the existence of the "Little Design," or one of the earliest foundations leading to the Sisters of St. Joseph.[40] Others think that the Superior General's letter simply refers to women's groups founded by Father Médaille, and that the first foundation leading to the Congregation of St. Joseph began at Dunières in 1649.[41] Whichever of those opinions is closer to the reality, it is clear that Médaille was willing to risk supporting the growth of groups of women who wanted more in their apostolic and spiritual life than contemporary possibilities allowed.

The name The Little Design is found in a letter from Father Médaille often called "The Eucharistic Letter." * In that letter he frequently referred to the littleness of the project he and the sisters had begun. The name, The Little Design, captures the humility of the great dreams Father Médaille and the early sisters shared. In contrast to the great designs of the king, this group intended to serve God in littleness, in imitation of Christ who emptied himself for the sake of the divine mission of salvation. The letter uses the word "little" no fewer than thirteen times in the course of reflecting on the vocation of the members of the community. Father Médaille's Little Design began as a secret project, so it is difficult to describe it with great precision. Nevertheless, the "Eucharistic Letter" or "Letter about the Little Design," one of the few documents he left for posterity, gives us interesting evidence about the projects he began and the spirituality he and the first sisters developed.

---

38 Nepper, Origins, 15-18.
39 The Jesuits had a practice of founding sodalities, groups founded for piety and service to the poor. These would help people prolong and deepen the conversion or commitment that resulted from the missions. See O'Malley,
40 O'Malley, 11.
41 See Vacher, Soeurs, 45.
*For a full text of the "Eucharistic Letter" see csjcarondelet.org/about-us/our-history/

Sister Marie Louise Gondal, a French Sister of St. Joseph of the Institute and historical theologian presents evidence of Father Médaille's influence on the foundation of a "congregation" for apostolic women "religious" in Saint-Flour as early as 1646. Originally called the Congregation of Widows and Daughters of Jesus and Mary, this group had a stable residence and way of life and had received episcopal approval.[42] On January 25, 1646, Madame Gabrielle de Foix made a restricted donation of the considerable sum of 12,000 livres to buy a house from which this congregation could serve the sick. The amount was also to endow a chapel where perpetual Masses would be celebrated for the repose of the soul of the donor.[43]

In June of that same year, Madame de Foix added a codicil to the will. She indicated that if the bishop or councilors of Saint-Flour no longer wanted these "Daughters" in the city, they could take the sum and install the foundation in some other place they would find acceptable.[44]

While there is really very little information about this group, public records attest to their existence. There are two primary reasons for the dearth of information about them and similar groups: first, a royal decree of March 27, 1646, forbad the foundation of new religious establishments without the permission of the bishop, the people and the king; second, the rampant destruction of records in the French Revolution obliterated many records.[45]

Unfortunately the new group in Saint-Flour soon faced major problems. First, their bishop-protector, Charles de Noailles, received an appointment to the see of Rodez in September of 1646, and his replacement did not arrive for more than a year, leaving the local Church with a lack of leadership and rife with conflicts of interest. Secondly, the sisters' inheritance was contested by Gabriel de Foix's family and creditors, all of whom enjoyed significant social status and power, making it easy for them to expropriate the community's property. Additionally since there was no local bishop at the moment, the sisters' very existence had fallen into a "juridical vacuum" and they became subject to menace from civil as well as religious authorities who did not approve of them and their style of life. In sum, as a result of the ecclesial situation and the family's opposition, the "congregation" lost everything.[46]

---

42 Gondal, 25-28.
43 At that time the annual salary of a servant was 100 livres. Of the 12,000 livres, 10,000 was to buy a house and 2,000 to endow the Masses. The gift implied the construction of a chapel. (Gondal, 25)
44 Gondal, 27-28.
45 Gondal, 80.
46 Gondal, 86-88.

Their situation was hardly unique; there were many similar groups coming into existence with and without episcopal approval, with and without formal structures, patrimony or organized ministry. However, this group has particular importance for the Sisters of St. Joseph because of their probable link to Father Médaille and the influence of their history on the foundation in Le Puy in 1650.

Sister Marie Louise Gondal makes a case for the idea that Father Médaille's famous Letter was written to the community at Saint-Flour while they were in the throes of the loss described above. She bases this on an analysis of the Letter that can be summarized in very broad strokes as follows.[47]

Father Médaille addressed the Letter to someone he called "sister" who found herself in an extreme situation known to both herself and to him, a situation he interpreted with a prophetic vision for both of them as well as for others implicated in what he called "our cherished association." The Letter refers to external events he interpreted and believed could be lived as "events of faith." It is as if in the midst of their loss, Médaille discerned the genuine meaning and potential of their foundation; the Savior had given him the vision of the "Little Design" as an institute invited to imitate Christ even more closely in the very circumstances that stripped them as Christ had been stripped. In this interpretation, the Letter is a meditation in the mode of prophecy: it speaks of what has happened, what it means and what can come about under the influence of grace.

According to Gondal, the situation of the group Father Médaille addresses is that of the congregation of Saint-Flour. They are without a father in the person of the absent bishop and they have no charismatic founding mother in the group. Jean-Pierre Médaille who so freely spoke of "our association" did not assume the title of founder and the only person who might have earned that title, Gabrielle de Foix, had died and her founding donation was in jeopardy if not already gone.[48] After the Daughters of Jesus and Mary had lost their home in the legal battles, according to Sister Marie Louise Gondal, "We see here a situation which could be an exact representation of the Congregation of Jesus and Mary in December 1646: a group in existence, but denuded of everything, that is, of all appearances and social support."[49] Gondal posits that the Letter can be taken as a foundational text for the group, a description of what Médaille saw God doing in the events of the gathering, organization, stripping and hope-against-hope endurance of the

---

47 Gondal, 164-175.
48 In the sense of the day, Médaille was not a "founder" because he neither provided the material needs of the foundation nor did he have the ecclesial power to establish it legally in the Church.
49 Gondal, 171.

group he identified in the Letter as the participants in God's "Little Design."[50]

This interpretation sheds a different light on a text that has been treasured by Sisters of St. Joseph since the 1960s. If we understand the Letter as directed to the Saint-Flour community, it becomes for the Sisters of Saint Joseph a model of how to live Ignatian indifference and discernment. It demonstrates faith in God's presence in the most devastating circumstances and the trust that no matter how other powers may be manipulating events, God's design has its own methods and trajectory. The Letter is not then so much a call to seek nothingness as an exhortation to discernment of God's will in every situation. In its own historical circumstances, the Letter gives testament to a well-constituted community founded under Médaille's influence previous to 1649. It also offers a spirituality of discernment and imitation of Christ available to every Sister of Saint Joseph from those days forward.[51]

FROM SAINT-FLOUR TO LE PUY

Le Puy en Velay,
Twentieth Century View

Médaille's Little Design was secret, and thus impossible to describe with great precision. Nevertheless, the Règlements which Médaille wrote for a small community which preceded the official foundation in Le Puy reveal something of

---

50 That name may have had some connection to the popularity of the idea of the Great Design (grand dessein) which was popularized by Louis XIV referring to his hopes to reunite Protestants with the Church. See Gondal, 169, footnote 1.

51 Of the "Letter," Gondal (190) says:

The letter that has come to us remains a unique testimony to his insight and his broad vision of the main spiritual problem that his time had to confront with the reform begun by Trent, which was essentially clerical and masculine. The interior way attracted many laity, especially women, but the institutional face of the Church was often opaque. The Letter about the Design testifies to a balanced attempt, perhaps without equal in those years, to guard the mystical river that irrigated the Church from [the influence of] a half-century in which the ecclesial institution was constantly menaced by a meaningless exteriorization and a masculine exclusivity. The Church of Father Médaille is a universal Church more than cultic; it moves out to the ends of the earth. A holy church, going to the heart of the human condition, a Church where reciprocity among the members, men or women, is realized because the Gospel continually confronts its aspirations and the limits of a time, a universal Church which results from its very particularity.

the life of those little groups hidden in the pre-history of the Sisters of St. Joseph. The Règlements give a good picture of the ideals of their common life and ample evidence that these women wanted something distinct from the ordinary life of laywomen of their time. In Father Nepper's opinion:

> It is a group of active religious, not cloistered, taking on, without making mention of it, the attempt of Saint Francis de Sales for his first Visitandines (1610-1618), "visitors" of the poor and the sick. This attempt of Saint Francis de Sales is surpassed here by the number and the variety of activities as well as the manner of exercising them.[52]

The unknown women who formed the secret communities could not help but realize that they were innovators; in spite of official restrictions, they had decided to live as religious with an apostolate outside their house. The Règlements goes on to describe the purpose of the foundation saying "This association is established to provide for many young women or widows not called to the cloister or who have not the means to enter it, and who, nevertheless, wish to live chastely in the world."[53]

When the document indicates that the members are "not called to the cloister" the meaning is quite precise. They are not called to monastic life which was the only style of religious life available to women of that day. The women who formed the communities of the Little Design had no intention of living in a cloister. Additionally they avoided language that would cause them to suffer the same fate as their near contemporaries whose desire for a new style of religious life had been thwarted.

Other parts of the Règlements give ample evidence that the women of the Little Design did in fact aspire to a formal type of consecrated life. Although the document does not speak specifically of vows, it does specify that the women who joined the community would "make profession of poverty, chastity, and obedience, and will have these virtues, as far as they are able, with the working of grace, in a rather great degree of perfection." Unlike traditional nuns, they did not wear a habit, but "their clothing, dress and standard of living will be appropriate to their social class and the background from which they come." Without specifying a "vow" of obedience, they were to "have one superior for all, a mistress and spiritual directress, and such other officers customary in religious orders as will be necessary for operation in keeping with their number and [the number of the]

---

52 Origins, 44.
53 Règlements, opening paragraph.

houses." They had no monastery with enclosure but rather structured a common life in which "the number of associates will normally be three."[54] Finally, the Règlements describes a structure for the day, the week, the month, and the year that could be adapted but was very similar to the structure found in religious congregations of that time. One example of the creative and open-ended adaptations of the Règlements to the particularities of the new group is found in the paragraph referring to comings and goings in the house. The Règlements states:

> They will maintain in their house a kind of cloister never open to men; and they will leave only to go to the churches, to visit the sick, hospitals, prisons, and to perform other exercises of charity.[55]

In other words, the sisters should go out whenever necessary. In this, we have a rule that, beginning with an "appropriately restrictive" tone, effectively opens the door to any and every real need. Reminiscent of Vincent de Paul's community that found its cloister in the city streets, it suggests that Médaille borrowed liberally from Vincent - his only successful predecessor in helping women develop and maintain a form of apostolic religious life.

With the Règlements, Médaille created a rule for women who were not nuns but who made a commitment to living the essential content of religious vows in community. Médaille outlined a life of community and service structured to support apostolic and spiritual growth. In effect, he and the women of his early groupings designed structures that would enhance living their charism. Rather than push for official Church recognition, they could wait until the official structures relaxed sufficiently to open space for new models.

The danger of falling under the restrictions of church law is one part of the rationale behind the secret character of the new institute. If the women who came together in this new community wanted to continue without problems with authority, secrecy served a clear purpose.[56] That would have been even more understandable if they found themselves under the jurisdiction of someone like Bishop Marquemont of Lyon who had insisted that the Sisters of The Visitation accept the cloister, or if they were subject to the whims of a bishop like the one

---

54 All of these citations come from the opening paragraphs of the Règlements.
55 Règlements.
56 Civil authorities were opposed to new religious foundations because if the religious couldn't sustain themselves, the responsibility fell on the municipal government. The situation was difficult because while many nuns ran schools, they were not allowed to charge for their services.

Vincent de Paul described as having "more interest in hunting rabbits than souls."[57]

The other motive for secrecy, more mystical than practical, came from currents of popular spirituality in seventeenth century France. Between 1630 and 1660, a religious movement called "The Company of the Blessed Sacrament" became the largest and most powerful grouping of its kind in France. Founded in Paris, The Company grew rapidly, forming secret groups in cities throughout the country. The members of the movement, influenced by the charity of Vincent de Paul, had a special dedication to the Blessed Sacrament and to the works of mercy. Their secret character had a double purpose. First, in a culture characterized by ambition for "honor," secrecy about devotions and works of charity was a practical way to grow in humility. In the second place, it seems that the secret served a political purpose by preventing outsiders from knowing too much about the finances and the activities of the Company. In the beginning, secrecy served to enhance the efficacy of the Company's works. As time went on, the members of the Company developed a mysticism of the secret, looking to the self-emptying Christ in the Eucharist as their model.

When Father Médaille was in Toulouse for his tertianship, it is nearly impossible that he would not have had contact with the group of the Company of the Blessed Sacrament active in that city. His writings echo much of their vocabulary and mystique. If he had known them, it is also very probable that he came to know some of the women of Toulouse who were anxious to become members of the Company or to form a feminine branch of the organization. Because of this, Father Médaille would have been familiar with the obstacles that impeded the women from attaining their goal. Would it not also be possible that the experience of knowing good women, thwarted in their desire to become active in the apostolate, intensified his sensitivity to women and their capacity?

There are details that cannot be known with certainty. Nevertheless, it is possible to affirm that Father Médaille knew The Company of the Blessed Sacrament and it is clear that his writings reflect and even go beyond the spirituality of that dynamic movement in French Catholic history. It is not difficult to believe that he learned much about the political and spiritual utility of secrecy from them. With all of that in mind, when Father Médaille says "The Blessed Sacrament is the origin of our very little congregation," it is entirely possible that he is referring to

---

57 Vincent was referring to Bishop de la Rouge. We have little information about the bishops in the dioceses where Father Médaille preached his mission, but it is certain that not all of them were as open or supportive of apostolic women as Henri de Maupas.

the devotional movement rather than directly to the Sacrament of the Eucharist.[58] In the end, in spite of all that remains unknown, it is possible to conclude that the women who took part in the Little Design created a new model of consecrated life and thus opened the way for the foundation of the Sisters of St. Joseph. They accepted a rule that structured a religious life, all the while assuring the necessary freedom to respond fully to their apostolic calling. Secrecy helped them to protect the vulnerable novelty of their project as well as to nurture a spirituality characterized by the self-emptying ideal that typified their epoch.

THE SISTERS OF ST. JOSEPH
DUNIÈRES

The first house of the Sisters of St. Joseph about which we have certifiable documentation is that established in Dunières in 1649. According to the official records, on September 29, 1649, Sister Anna Deschaux was the first to take the habit and also the first superior of a group founded "at the request of Reverend Father Médaille of the Company of Jesus." The documents continue, saying that Sister Anna was followed by many others, including Sisters Catherine Gagnaire and Marie Blanc.[59] It seems that these sisters formed a parish community with the purpose of working for the spiritual and temporal welfare of the neighbor in the immediate area. Unfortunately we know little more about them. Nevertheless, recalling that the communities described in Médaille's *Règlements* were formed by groups of three, it would seem reasonable that in this community we see one more step in the evolution toward Church recognition of women's apostolic life.

THE COMMUNITY AT LE PUY IN 1650

The community of Le Puy, recognized by the Sisters of St. Joseph as their official foundation, was also the product of a process of evolution. The best evidence that we have about that community comes from the preface to the *Constitutions* of the Sisters of St. Joseph of Vienne published in 1694. The history recounted in that preface says that on the 15th of October, 1650, when everything was prepared

---

58 This is the opinion of Marguerite (Sr. Terese) Vacher. She says that it can be shown via letters exchanged between Médaille and his superiors in Rome that some sisters had received a rule in 1646, almost at the same time that women were rejected as members of the Company. She hypothesizes that the first Sisters of St. Joseph, desiring membership in the Company of the Blessed Sacrament, were willing to adapt their aspiration and deepen their desire through a total offering of themselves to God and neighbor. This idea is further supported with the knowledge that Marguerite Burdier, one of the first Sisters of St. Joseph, had been in relation with the Company throughout her whole life and that all of the first sisters came from regions where the Company had had a great influence in the preaching of missions. See Vacher, Soeurs, 95.
59 Vacher, Soeurs, 98

for the realization of the Little Design, His Excellency Henri de Maupas called together all of the Daughters of the Hospital for Orphans and delivered:

> ...an exhortation, filled with the unction of the Spirit of God by which he encouraged all of them to the great Love of God and the most perfect Charity for the neighbor; at the end he gave his blessing, with extraordinary testimonies, speaking paternally and cordially about the Congregation. He put them directly under the protection of Saint Joseph, and ordered that their Congregation should be called the Congregation of the Sisters or the Daughters of Saint Joseph; he gave the Rule for their conduct and stipulated a form of habit; at the end, he confirmed the establishment of the Congregation and the Rules that he gave by his Lettres Patentes, given on March 10, 1651.[60]

We know the names of the first sisters of Le Puy only because on December 13, 1651, they signed a contract of association, legalizing the vows that they took that day. The newly vowed sisters were:

❖ Françoise Eyraud, 39 years old, from Saint-Privat in the diocese of Le Puy;
❖ Claudia Chastel, a widow since 1647, from Langogne, in the Diocese of Mende;
❖ Marguerite Burdier, 26 years old, from Saint-Julien, in the diocese of Vienne;
❖ Anna Chaleyer, 46 years old, from Saint-Finey-Malafau, in the diocese of Lyon;
❖ Anna Vey de Saint-Jeure, 15 years old, from the diocese of Le Puy;
❖ Anna Brun, 15 years old, from Saint-Victor, in the diocese of Le Puy.

The ages listed for the sisters are approximations based on baptismal or death certificates. Given the age of the last two, it is quite possible that they had been children residing in the sisters' orphanage who wanted to join in community with the women who cared for them. It would seem that Françoise Eyraud and Anna Chaleyer at the other end of the age spectrum could well have been living a form of their apostolic life for some time previous to the legal formation of the community.

It is obvious that this foundation went through a process of preparation, but the question of how is not quite so clear. The history behind the scenes

---

60 Vacher 64. Abbe Rivaux clarifies this statement, explaining that Bishop de Maupas gave the community "authority...by an episcopal ordinance, dated March 10, 1651," and that his successor, Armand de Bethune confirmed it on September 23, 1665 and that the community received the "letters patent of King Louis XIV...1666, authorizing and confirming the first establishments in the cities of Puy, St. Didier and several other places of Velay." See Abbe Rivaux, *History of The Reverend Mother Sacred Heart of Jesus*, Translated by the Sisters of St. Joseph, (Lindsay, Ontario, Canada: Montreal, Messenger Press, 1910) 14-15.
Lettres Patentes are civil rather than Church documents that give legal recognition to an institution.

would probably reveal that Françoise Eyraud and others among the six, perhaps with Father Médaille's collaboration, had obtained positions in the Hospital for Orphans and Widows called Montferrand in Le Puy. The hospital archives show that Françoise Eyraud had been the director of the hospital since 1646. Those same archives indicate that in the hospital, Françoise was in charge of thirty-nine orphans and two servants. Reading between the lines, one sees here another community of three sisters. Nevertheless, the size of the community was not rigidly established; in fact, another report indicates that a few days later a somewhat mysterious fourth woman named Marguerite arrived to join the group.

Sister Marie Louise Gondal presents evidence that before the orphanage community was established, Françoise Eyraud and other women gathered in the home of a local laywoman, Lucrèce de la Planche. According to the French historian, Crétineau-Joly, Lucrèce de la Planche brought some women to Le Puy whom Father Médaille thought were destined for that type of life. There is also evidence that Marguerite de Saint-Laurans visited Le Puy a few times in those years, and may therefore have been a mentor to them. Because this Marguerite was connected with the Saint-Flour community, it seems probably that there was communication among the communities, even if there were no official ties. Whether or not Marguerite came to Le Puy to help the new community, there remains the strong possibility that many of these women initiating a new experiment in religious life at least knew of one another if they did not have much direct contact. What is certain is that Bishop Henri de Maupas of Le Puy had the authority to decide who would administer the hospital. Because the women who arrived to take charge were part of a group formed by Father Médaille, it appears likely that the bishop and the Jesuit had made a plan together and that sometime before 1650 the bishop allowed the women to begin to experiment with their new lifestyle in the public atmosphere of the local hospital.

If all this is true, the evolution of the project begun by Father Médaille and

Parish Church in Dunières

groups of women begins to become clear. He began supporting the communities as early as 1646, if not earlier. One of those communities established itself in the orphans' hospital at Montferrand while another had begun in the parish at Dunières early enough to formalize its structure in 1649.[61]

From what is known about the hospital community between 1646 and 1650, it appears that there was a period of experimentation in apostolic and communal life before they formalized their association. Bishop de Maupas gave his approval on March 10, 1651 and after more than a year of formation, they made vows on December 13, 1651. The permission for establishment, Bishop de Maupas' legal document, makes it clear that the bishop expected the group to grow. The text reads:

> We, Henry de Maupas...desiring to enhance the Glory of God and the salvation of souls and the service of charity in our diocese, knowing that some good widows and young women desired to consecrate themselves to the admirable exercise of charity, in the service of the great hospital for the poor sick of our community as well as in education and the orientation of orphan girls from our hospital of Montferrand, and so that they might dedicate themselves with more energy to those exercises they have wanted, under our acquiescence, to institute a society and congregation in which, living in Community, it would be possible without any impediment to dedicate themselves to those exercises; this design has appeared to us to be so admirable that we have accepted it with great affection, we have permitted and we permit these widows and young women to create a Congregation under the name and title of the Daughters of St. Joseph; to meet and live in community in one or various houses, according to what seems necessary to best distribute the fruit of their charity and to be able to multiply said houses in all parts of our diocese where they think it adequate; and so that everything be done with good order, so that the new congregation may prosper, we have redacted and given these daughters and widow a rule that they dedicate themselves to the greater glory of God and attention to their neighbor, just as they have begun to do in the above mentioned hospital of Montferrand; from this moment we take said widows and young women under our protection and we order our vicars and ecclesiastical judges to support them so that their admirable undertaking will always receive new impulses and so that no one come to bother these widows and young women, to whom we give our blessing all the fullness of our affection and we desire with all that affection that they receive the

---

61 Picture of Dunières from Barbara Baer Collection – Federation of the Sisters of St. Joseph.

blessing of God the Father, Son and Holy Spirit.
Given at Le Puy, March 10, 1651. Henry C. of Puy and Count of Velay. [62]

When Bishop de Maupas wrote this document, the "congregation" had six members who had not yet pronounced vows. Obviously, he believed there could be more in the future. His openness to their expansion provided the space for growth he never would have imagined.

TOWARD THE FUTURE

In the beginning Bishop de Maupas acted as the father protector of the community. After two years, when he was no longer able to do so, he appointed his vicar, the

Henri de Maupas
1606-1680

Sulpician Monsieur Charles Louis de Lantages to take over that responsibility. It seems that de Lantages, who was also the protector of the Sisters of the Visitation in Le Puy and the founder of the seminary, was a specialist in formation. Without a doubt, he too had great influence in the early days of the new congregation as did the next bishop, Armand de Béthune, who served as Bishop of Le Puy from 1661 to 1703, a time of immense expansion for the community of St. Joseph.[63]

As we noted in the list of Father Médaille's assignments, he was never missioned to Le Puy. Because of this, it is obvious that he could not have been involved in the daily life of the sisters. While Father Médaille fulfilled his responsibilities in Aurillac, he also wrote *Constitutions* and *avis* (counsels) for some of his communities. But even so, he was not in charge of his Little Design. A note that he wrote with the avis gives a glimpse into his feelings when he found himself so far from the congregation. In a letter which has no date he wrote:

---

62 This is a translation of the Spanish version of the document as it is published in Fin y Carácter, published by the Sisters of St. Joseph of Argentina in 1968.
63 Sister Terese Vacher suggests that neither Bishop de Maupas nor Lantages grasped the spirituality that Father Médaille had developed in the Sisters, most particularly, the devotion to the two trinities with all the implications that brings for a charism of unity and a practice of loving the neighbor in God. (Personal interview of Sr. Terese Vacher, by Mary McGlone with Sr. Simone Saugues, September, 2015.)

My very dear Sisters,
I hope that if your superiors are in agreement, that each of your houses
might have a copy of this document [avis] and that it be read now and
then, either in chapter or in the refectory. The desire that I have for the
perfection of your Congregation leads me to take the liberty of sending
you this reminder.[64]

Obviously, the "founder" no longer had direct authority over the evolution
of the Congregation. It is uncertain whether that was a result of his own choice
or due to decisions that came from Jesuit or diocesan authorities. What is sure
is that the moment had come for Jean Pierre Médaille to live the maxim he had
written down for others: "Advance good works until near completion; and then,
whenever possible, let them be completed by someone else who will receive the
honor."[65]

While Father Médaille may not have been present to influence the daily
life and growth of the communities that carried The Little Design forward, the
influence of his spirit and spirituality would touch Sisters of St. Joseph for centuries
to come. Although he left no corpus of writings comparable to those of Francis
de Sales or Vincent de Paul, Father Médaille's Ignatian spirituality permeates his
maxims, the Constitutions, Règlements and Avis. Put most clearly in the Eucharistic
Letter, Father Médaille set the sisters on the Ignatian foundation of contemplation
in action, a way of living that combines the mysticism of seeing God in all things
with the practical response of being ready to do anything of which a woman is
capable to serve God in the Dear Neighbor.

When Father Médaille died in 1669, there were more than thirty
communities of Saint Joseph in the region and they included Le Puy, Lyon,
Grenoble, d'Embrun, Gap, Sisternon, Vivarais, Uses, Clermont, Vienne, Viviers,
and Mende.[66] Each community was independent. New communities were formed
when sisters from an established community received the request to extend the
movement to a new place. In this way the Congregation grew, extending itself
throughout the region of the original foundation in Le Puy, and then later Lyon.

The proliferation of communities of Saint Joseph, together with their
characteristic openness to diversity, left ample space for differing opinions about
the structure of their life. Even before the end of the seventeenth century, there were
diverse ideas and practices among the Sisters. Some sisters wanted to emphasize

---

64 Nepper, Origins, 25-26.
65 J. P. Médaille, Maxims of the Little Institute "Maxim # 85".
66 Rivaux, *Rev. Mother Sacred Heart*, 15.

and reinforce the structures of the Congregation similar to a religious order while others wanted the Congregation to develop and adapt its structures more freely in response to the needs to which they were called to respond. A few examples will suffice to demonstrate the ways in which those tensions manifested themselves.

The preface to the *Constitutions* of Vienne, supposedly published in 1693, says that when Bishop de Maupas met with the first sisters, he "gave them the rule and he prescribed the kind of habit" they should wear. The *Constitutions* of 1694, considered the original edition, said that the bishop "gave them the rule and prescribed a form of a habit." With the change of one word, the whole idea of "dressing modestly" could be changed to insist that the sisters wear a particular kind of habit which would distinguish them as women with a special status.[67]

Another example of the tension caused by distinct interpretations of the community's life comes from what different documents say about the purpose of the Congregation. According to Father Médaille, the purpose of the Congregation is similar to that of the Society of Jesus: to attain one's own salvation and perfection through the exercise of the works of mercy and, by means of those exercises to procure the salvation and the perfection of others.[68] According to the project designed by Father Médaille, the sisters were to undertake all the works of mercy of which they were capable, in whatever place to which they might be sent. It was by means of the apostolate that they would grow in holiness. They received the same apostolic mandate given to the great missionaries.

Other texts which present a much more restricted vision suggest that the Sisters should work for their own perfection and serve the neighbor through the observance of all of the prescribed rules. Later, the same document cited in this paragraph states: "There are two principal ends for the stability of the Congregation. The first is that all the Sisters work for their sanctification and advance in the most sublime perfection. The second is that the dear neighbor be helped and served by means of all the works of charity." Although it may appear subtle, the difference is between having two goals which can be separate and unequal (personal salvation followed by charity for the neighbor), or one goal which understands that salvation of both self and neighbor are achieved by means of service.[69]

In reality, such tension and difference of opinion should hardly be a surprise. The Congregation of the Sisters of St. Joseph began as an experiment.

---

67 There is great debate about these *Constitutions*. Historical research points to the idea that the edition favoring a stricter interpretation of the habit and rule were written later, but given an earlier date so as to appear to be more official. See Vacher, Nuns, 141-168.

68 Vacher, Nuns, 167

69 Vacher, Soeurs, 202-203.

Chapter Two: Mother St. John Adjusting Her Designs
DRAWN BY THE SPIRIT -- ADJUSTING PLANS

Cast of Characters

Mother St. John Fontbonne – First Superior General in Lyon after the Revolution
Mother Anne-Marie Grand – First Superior General in Le Puy after the Revolution
Mother St. Francis Fontbonne – Superior in Bas and Monistrol, Aunt to Mother St. John
Sister St. John Marcoux – originally of the Black Sisters, Founder: Chambéry 1812
Mother St. John Chanay – Founder of Bourg Congregation, 1823

Bishop Marie-Joseph de Galard – Bishop of Le Puy, 1774-1804
Monsignor Claude Cholleton – Founder of the "Black Sisters," Vicar General of Lyon
Cardinal Joseph Fesch – Cardinal-Archbishop of Lyon, 1802-1815,
Uncle of Napoleon Bonaparte

MOTHER ST. JOHN FONTBONNE AND COMPANIONS
IN THE LITTLE DESIGN AT 150
THE POLITICAL SOCIAL WORLD OF PRE-REVOLUTIONARY FRANCE:
THE RULING CLASSES AND THE POOR

The Sisters of St. Joseph were founded and grew out of a particular context. They were French women whose ancient culture was being challenged by new ideas that would underpin a revolution after which neither Church nor state nor Western civilization itself would ever be the same. Through most of the eighteenth century, France was a monarchy with the population divided into three "estates:" the clergy, the nobility and the common people. The monarchy was understood under the rubric of "the divine right of kings" which is succinctly portrayed in a description of King Louis XIV (1638-1715):

> From infancy he had been told that he was a "visible divinity," a "Vice-God." The first copy-book set for him to learn writing read "Homage is due to kings. They do that which they please." He was penetrated with this dogma – which said he was a being set apart, holding his crown by the divine will, King by the grace of God, His lieutenant upon the earth. To God, but to God alone, he must someday render account for his deeds.[1]

Practically all Europeans of the seventeenth and eighteenth centuries lived

---

1 William Stearns Davis, *A History of France from the Earliest Times to the Treaty of Versailles*, (Boston & New York: Houghton Mifflin Co. 1919, Kindle Edition), location 2350. Davis adds that there developed a royal "cult" such that "each of the King's ordinary acts of daily life, arising, dining, taking a walk, hunting, having supper, going to bed, became a public ceremony with minutely regulated details."

unquestioningly out of this mindset. The nobility, if they hoped for any privileges, had to render proper deference to the king. The peasants, comprising the vast majority of the population, bore the real burden of supporting the king and nobility in the style to which they felt entitled.

By the eve of the Revolution, France's national finances were in chaos.[2] The burden of taxes fell on the peasants, craftsmen and bourgeois, first of all through the taille, an onerous tax which had no rational basis for assessment, but depended solely on the whim of the assessor. According to historian W. S. Davis, "The sight of a few hen feathers at a wretched peasant's door, implying that he was acquiring more than a starving living, was in itself enough sometimes to increase the poor wight's taille." [3] While up to fifty-percent of the meager earnings of the lower classes were collected in the *taille tax*, the upper classes were exempt from the taille and even other taxes they might have paid were more real on paper than in practice.[4]

"You should hope this game will soon be over." 1789 French Political Cartoon

The lower classes, most of them subsistence farmers whose landholdings were too small to support even their own families, formed the majority of the population. Of the approximately 25,000,000 inhabitants of France in the eighteenth century, the total number of clergy and nobles was something under 275,000, with another 300,000 bourgeois, all of whom enjoyed tax exemptions and privileges. The peasant population, numbering over 24,000,000 were stereotyped as undereducated and often superstitious, commonly inclined to drink away their troubles – and their cash. "Frequently they lived under the same roof with their barnyard animals in what must have been appalling squalor and filth. Their diet, made up mainly of rye

2 Davis, loc. 3789. In another place Davis describes the lavish living at court: the food budget was over the equivalent $1,400,000 per year, Queen Marie Antoinette required four new pair of shoes per week and "the first waiting-women between them added fully $30,000 per year to their incomes by disposing of the partly burned candles used in lighting the palace." (loc. 3710)
3 Davis, loc. 3796.
4 The gabelle was another economic burden that required every subject over the age of seven to purchase at least seven pounds of salt from the overpriced government salt monopoly. In 1787, it was reported that 30,000 people had been arrested annually for breaking salt laws, and "500 were condemned to the galleys or gallows for contraband salt running. Davis, loc. 3820-3828.

bread, gruel, and dairy products, was meager and monotonous."[5] Unsurprisingly, there was little love lost between the peasants and upper classes. While the peasants chafed, defenseless under economic oppression, they were disparaged by the upper classes. One nobleman, the Duke de Deux-Ponts, expressed the opinion of many of his peers saying "The villages are the natural enemies of their seigneurs…It is in our interest to feed them, but it would be dangerous to fatten them."[6]

In spite of the all-pervasive class system, the royal court and the universality of taxes on the poor, France was a "nation" in notion more than in fact. Provinces, while formally a part of the same realm, enjoyed independent status with the power to tax goods from other provinces; the residents of many provinces spoke their own dialect and used their own systems of measurements. Voltaire once quipped that traveling through France, "one changed the laws as one changed post-horses."[7] Education, of course, brought more unity; the privileged learned Latin and standard French, the languages of philosophy and theology, the two key branches of knowledge.[8] Nevertheless, there was no such thing as universal education; the availability of formal education was stratified by both class and gender, although religious men and women did provide educational opportunities to all classes to the measure that they were able.[9]

THE RELIGIOUS WORLD

Since making a Concordat with the Vatican in 1516, the Kings of France, like the Kings of Spain, had enjoyed the right to control the national hierarchy by sending nominations of prospective bishops to Rome for a nearly-assured ratification. According to historian W. S. Davis,

---

5 *The European Peasantry From the Fifteenth to the Nineteenth Century*, Jerome Blum, (Princeton University Service Center for Teachers of History, A Service of the American Historical Association: the American Historical Society, 1960) 21. (The public domain cartoon can be found at Wikipedia/commons/8/8e/troisordres.jpg) "You should hope this game will soon be over." 1789 French Political Cartoon
6 Georges Lefebvre, *The Great Fear of 1789*, (NY: Schocken Books, a Division of Random House, 1989) 36.
7 Davis, (loc. 3745), adds the great province of Aubergne was split in twain…one city, Aurillac, being under the civil law of the South and the next, Clermont, under the customary law, both…subject to the jurisdiction of the Parlement [sic] of Paris as their high court."
8 The course of study in the Jesuit college at Saint-Flour in the time of Fr. Médaille included grammar, humanities, and rhetoric. Gondal, 57.
9 Robert Darnton, explains that in the mid-18th century the idea that the Christian Brothers would educate the Third Estate (the common people) brought serious criticism, saying that the other classes saw that some wanted "to close the schools and to abolish instruction in reading among the pauper children in the Hôpital Général… Only by keeping learned culture closed to the "Third Estate" could society save itself from having to support a population of unemployed intellectuals, who ought to be walking behind plays or laboring…in workshops." *(The Great Cat Massacre*, Kindle Edition, loc. 2228-2232.)10 Davis, loc. 1804 and 3858.

They were...in theory subject to the Pope, but actually – in view of the Concordat of Francis I and the vigorous assertion of the "Gallican liberties" under Louis XIV – a wise Pontiff would let the affairs of the French Church pretty strictly alone; and the King was more influentialin most ecclesiastical matters than the Holy Father."[10]

It was assumed that nearly every clergyman of rank would come from the nobility. In aristocratic families a younger son was expected to choose either the military or the Church as his career, and if the latter he might prepare for his role through education and time spent as vicar to a bishop.[11]

The "lower clergy," the poor curés and vicars came from the "Third Estate," or non-noble classes. The pay received by local pastors was 875 francs ($350) per year, and their less powerful assistants received about half of that – when their salaries were actually paid. Because advancement in Church office had little or nothing to do with holiness or ability, the lower clergy shared many of the grievances of the powerless classes from which they came; their ordination hardly increased their importance in the eyes of their "betters."

In the world of theological ideas two popular extremes were represented by the Jansenists and the Jesuits. Jansenism minimized belief in humanity's freedom to do good and kindled scrupulosity and the fear of hell. Although it was condemned by the Vatican more than once, its adherents persisted in their rigorist teaching and in the 1730s a popular movement strengthened its appeal by

---

10 Davis, loc. 1804 and 3858. Even the King was not always free from outside influence in the nomination of hierarchy. It is said that at one time Louis XVI protested against court pressure to name a certain bishop explaining that he thought that at the very least "a bishop should really believe in God." (Davis, loc. 3896.)
11 John McManners writes: In practice, young men of these families had a choice between two main careers, the Church and the armed forces. A stock figure in eighteenth-century literature is the younger son of a penurious noble house having to choose between them. An unpleasant mother in one of Monmontel's Contes moraux tells her second son, "Your father's fortune was not so considerable as was imagined; it will scarce suffice to settle your elder brother. For your part, you have simply to decide whether you will follow the career of benefices or of arms, whether you will have your head shaved or broken, whether you will take [holy] orders or a lieutenancy of infantry." See John McManners, *Church and Society in Eighteenth Century France: Volume I, The Clerical Establishment and its Social Ramifications*, (Oxford: Clarendon Press, 1998), 223.
12 See Davis, loc. 3273. The Catholic Encyclopedia explains the latter saying that when their theological arguments lost, the Jansenists invoked the direct testimony of God."They pretended that at his tomb in the little cemetery of Saint-Médard marvelous [sic] cures took place. A case alleged as such was examined by de Vintimille, Archbishop of Paris...declared it false and superstitious (1731). But other cures were claimed by the party...They fell into violent transports... as the convulsionaries of Cévennes...denounced the papacy and the Mass. In the excited crowd women were especially noticeable, screaming, yelling, throwing themselves about, sometimes assuming the most astounding and unseemly postures." See: "Jansenius and Jansenism." *The Catholic Encyclopedia* (http://newadvent.org/cathen/). (Hereafter, The Catholic Encyclopedia)

broadcasting the word that miracles were occurring at the tomb of a prominent Jansenist deacon. Church officials vigorously denied the validity of the miracles, but the movement was so popular that the government finally shut down the cemetery leading to the satirical refrain "By order of the King: It is forbidden to God to work miracles in this place!"[12] In spite of official censure, Jansenism continued to influence Catholicism through the early twentieth century.[13]

Voltaire's philosophy offers a snapshot of the Enlightenment ideas that flooded France in the eighteenth century. Seen by some as the Church's most fearsome foe, Voltaire (1694-1788) wanted to replace theology with reason and philosophy as the essential guides for human life. Rejecting the Church on the basis of what he saw in France, Voltaire judged Catholicism as the source of the medievalism, intolerance and absolutism that maintained the divine privileges of the King and clergy. Notably, Voltaire's goal for society was not democracy but rather "enlightened despotism." He assumed that intellectual elites would govern their underlings in the spirit of philosophy, saying: "We have never pretended to enlighten the shoemakers and servants…What the populace wants is guidance and not instruction." Voltaire also promoted questioning all authority. [14]
An ironic dimension of Voltaire's thinking was his opinion of the service of apostolic women religious. Rather than write them off along with the "superstitious" and power-hungry clergy, he is quoted as saying:

> The religious institutions devoted to succouring the poor and serving the sick are amongst those most commanding of respect. There is perhaps nothing greater on this earth than the sacrifice that the delicate sex makes of its beauty and its youth in caring within hospitals for every kind of wretched human suffering, the very sight of which is so humiliating to mankind's pride and so offensive to our sensibilities.[15]

Somewhat more constructive than Voltaire was Jean-Jacques Rousseau (1712-1778). His passion was human freedom and the social contract: the free relinquishment of some individual liberty for the sake of the community.

---

13 At the time of the suppression, John Carroll of Maryland (1735-1815) was a Jesuit priest teaching in Europe. He returned to America and worked as a missionary where his fellow priests nominated him as superior of the Maryland missions until, in 1789, they elected him as the first bishop in the United States. "John Carroll" in The Catholic Encyclopedia. 14 Davis, 102, loc. 3430
15 Olwen H. Hufton, *Women and the Limits of Citizenship in the French Revolution* (Toronto: University of Toronto Press, 1992) 53, citing *Voltaire Oeuvres Complètes*, 52 Vol. (Paris 1877-85) xii, p 344.
16 Davis, loc. 3438-3443.

Obviously this undermined the "divine" authority of both king and church. To replace organized religion, he proposed a civil religion which recognized a deity who had little to do with earthly realities.[16] These currents of "enlightened" philosophy grew increasingly popular throughout France and, while they offered hope for change, their proponents never imagined what horrific violence would be employed to bring it about.

Often overlooked in eighteenth-century European religious and secular history are the influences coming from the west side of the Atlantic. Beginning in the seventeenth century, Europe, particularly Spain, France, Great Britain and Portugal had cast an eye on the possibilities offered by the uncharted territories of America. From Quebec to New Orleans and Haiti the French left their mark on the land and people they colonized. They organized agriculture and fur-trapping export ventures and sent Catholic missionaries to care for indigenous peoples as well as the immigrant settlers. The stories recounted by zealous missionaries fired the imagination of the French faithful and inspired many to support the missions or even to exotic dreams of evangelizing American natives who had never known Christ.

In the late eighteenth century, the world known by the Sisters of St. Joseph was entering into unpredictable and irreversible change. As the Church wavered between allegiance to Rome and national loyalties, dreams of America proffered heroic missionary possibilities. The hardships suffered by the poor on one hand and the novelty of Enlightenment thinking on the other, the ineptitude of King Louis XVI and the unpopularity of his queen, Marie Antoinette, and even the successful revolution and democracy in America coalesced to promote previously unimaginable questions about religious and political authority. Those disparate cultural, political and religious factors would combine in 1789, shaking France and the Catholic Church, causing reverberations from Europe through America, with echoes that would resound for hundreds of years.

THE LITTLE DESIGN AFTER 140 YEARS

The available sources reveal relatively little about the history of the first century of the Sisters of St. Joseph. The story of unpretentious women who served the neighbor in simplicity did not appear important enough to enter into the official historical annals of the nation or the Church.[17] What is clear is that following the

---

17 In recent years there have been multiple scholarly attempts to recover women's history. Vacher and Rapley's works offer ample bibliographies for additional information about women's contribution to Church and society in recent centuries.

inspiration of their foundation, in mid-eighteenth century France there existed a variety of groupings of Sisters of St. Joseph in well over 150 communities concentrated in the dioceses of Le Puy, Lyon, Clermont, and Vienne.[18] Many foundations were independent, under the authority of the local bishop and the clerical superior he appointed. New foundations were typically begun by sisters who went from an established community to found another or even by local clerics who wanted sisters and gathered women borrowing and sometimes freely adapting the *Constitutions* from established groups. Some groups organized themselves with a city "center house" and semi-dependent country houses related to them as Father Médaille had envisioned. The ministries of the Sisters included education of girls, care and education of orphans, care for the sick, and other services as needed locally.

These communities were far from uniform. The *Constitutions* emphasize such a great respect for diversity that one could say that they make it a key characteristic of the Congregation. Thus, the Constitutions say that:

> In order to be of better service to others, [the sisters] will have three types of association: The first will be demoiselles de service, that is, widows and single women of the nobility who will have sufficient means to be free to devote themselves completely to the direction of works of charity. The second will consist of demoiselles de travail, that is, widows and single women of the nobility who, having insufficient means will compensate for this lack by earnest labor. The third (will be) widows and single women of the lower class who, being poorer than those of the second type, will have a life entailing more labor and a less costly manner of living. The same Institute will serve, nevertheless, for everyone with exception only in food, clothing, the time spent in prayer and daily occupations.[19]

Clearly the *Constitutions* provide for diversity among the sisters and encourage each community to adopt the lifestyle most appropriate to its members and the context in which they find themselves. The *Constitutions* make it clear that the rationale for such diversity was "in order to be of better service to others." Such diversity could be both a strength and a weakness. The strength of diversity is

---

18 See Vacher, "Annexe 5" for a chart of the foundations from 1649 to 1789. This includes the Sisters of St. Joseph of Saint-Vallier whose motherhouse is now in Quebec.
19 *Constitutions* First Part, (Primitive Documents, 80). This diversity in membership may help explain the disagreements exposed in the different editions of the *Constitutions* of Vienne in 1693 and 1694. It appears that some of the higher-class women collaborated with their ecclesiastical superior to "regularize" the life of the community, in other words, to make it more monastic. See Vacher, 177-251.

precisely its openness. The Sisters of St. Joseph did not define themselves in terms of one special apostolate or a particular style of life; they organized themselves to be able to respond to any need in any place. Because of that in the course of the first one hundred years of their history they could be found in cities, small towns, and in rural areas. They ministered in parishes and cared for orphans; they sheltered abandoned women and opened schools; they administered hospitals, visited the jails, and taught manual arts to women and children in order to help them become financially independent. The reality is that no one knows how many ministries they carried out because they did not publish their activities and many parish archives that could have provided some information about their labor disappeared during the Revolution.

The debility of diversity and independent foundations becomes evident in the inevitable inequality among communities well-endowed with vocations and/ or financial means and those that lacked one or both. One community could have more vocations than necessary to serve an area while another would lack the minimum number to form community or carry on a ministry. The same could be true of their material resources. Additionally, the independence of each foundation allowed for the possibility that a community could be subordinated to the vision of an ecclesiastical superior who did not understand the charism of the community or who was interested in nothing more than laborers for his ministry. A cleric like that could interfere with the normal life of the community and limit their expression of the charism. In this regard, we should note that although the early *Constitutions* clearly state that the bishop is the religious superior of a community in his diocese, the only thing said about obedience to the bishop is that the sisters will receive from him a confessor and director.[20] According to the *Constitutions*, everything that had to do with the internal life of the community fell under the authority of the sister superior. The role of the ecclesiastical superior was to be an official liaison with the Church; he had no authorized role in the internal life of the community.

It is clear that from 1650 to 1789, the communities grew, spread and adapted to the needs of the people and places where they were established. The *Constitutions* offer a general panorama of the spirit of the group, so that, even without knowing the details of the sisters' daily life, it is possible to decipher the

---

20 *Primitive Constitutions*, part 1. The responsibilities of the sister superior are found in the fourth part of the *Constitutions*. (The translation of *Constitutions* used in reference here is the version published in 1984 for the Federation of Sisters of St. Joseph under the title The Congregation of the Daughters of St. Joseph: Primitive Texts. Page numbers will refer to that edition.)

main lines of their corporate personality.[21]

The *Constitutions* explain the end of the Congregation in four short, clear articles:

> First, the end of this little Congregation is to unite in a body of religious or of associées and agrégées the holiest persons whom God has in the world who lack the means to enter religion or who are not called to it, and to perfect these persons more and more in the exercise of the holy service of God.
>
> Secondly, that through the zeal of these same persons, it aspires to provide for all the spiritual and temporal needs of the dear neighbor.
>
> Thirdly, that in order the better to succeed in this holy enterprise, it aspires also to establish or to direct everywhere holy congregations of mercy capable of bringing great good to the Church of God if they are maintained in fervor and in the exact observance of their laudable exercises.
>
> Fourthly, that it intends, in particular through these activities, to distribute, when the opportunity is present, well organized directives for the spiritual life of all classes of women, so that, through their efforts, all families and all classes of people may be gently led to a holy fear and love of God, to the cherished virtues of the Gospel, to a courageous and cordial charity, humility, simplicity, and gentleness which in many areas seem to be banished from Christianity.[22]

The first idea that stands out from this selection is that the Sisters of St. Joseph live in community precisely for the benefits that communal life offer to their apostolic service. Secondly, while they are carrying out any and every apostolate, the purpose of their service is to bring all, including themselves, to the love of God and the practice of virtue. It is noteworthy that in the four articles that speak of the end of the Congregation two of them refer to the formation of "congregations" or groups that the sisters should form and advise. This demonstrates the strong emphasis they put on developing the spirit and the reality of community among their neighbors. Because of this, it is possible to deduce that the religious communities were designed to be schools in which the sisters themselves would learn to form community and continually develop in the spiritual life – not just for themselves but also as a part of their core service to the dear neighbor. Additionally,

---

21 The *Primitive Constitutions* are divided in six parts: 1) the nature of the Congregation, 2) its end and the means to that end, 3) the qualities required in persons to be admitted, 4) the various offices and officers, rules, 5) their exercises, 6) the means appropriate to…make it grow. According to the studies, the hand of Father Médaille is more evident in some parts than in others.

22 *Primitive Constitutions*, Second Part, page 84.

the description of their service in forming congregations indicates that the sisters should present "well organized directives for the spiritual life" of their neighbor. This indicates that as an essential part of their ministry, the sisters were acting as spiritual directors for the people and groups they formed. No matter what might be her particular ministry, the mission of the Sister of St. Joseph was to form community and, in the process, to help others deepen their own spirituality individually and collectively.

Speaking of the qualities required in the women who would form part of the institute, the *Constitutions* indicate that they need to have extraordinary aptitudes to be able to maintain the delicate balance required of a ministerial religious. This is not to diminish a spirit of humility, but rather, according to the text, it is because community life without a cloister demands "certain conditions and qualities of spirit and of body more advanced than in those who enter religion since the latter are not in direct contact with nor openly engaged in the use of zeal for the assistance of the neighbor as are our Daughters of St. Joseph."[23] Added to the ordinary requirements for living religious life, the Constitutions say that a suitable candidate for this congregation should demonstrate particular qualities:

> ...regarding qualities of mind, it is expedient for God's greater glory that no one be accepted who is not basically sound, humanly speaking, that is, having rather good judgment...indeed, were it possible, it would be fitting that no one be accepted who did not have the qualities appropriate for being the superior of the entire community.[24]

If the woman called to enter this community is expected to be extraordinary, that does not imply that she be perfect nor attempt to appear so. When the *Constitutions* speak of not accepting candidates who are advanced in age or whose personality does not exhibit the qualities of douceur and joy, they specify that if the candidate is apt for the apostolate and seems to be able to overcome her limitations, she can be admitted.[25]

In some ways, all of the aspirations of the *Constitutions* are summarized in the instructions for the director of novices because she is responsible to help

---

23 *Constitutions*, Third Part (Primitive Documents, 95).
24 *Constitutions*, Third Part, (Primitive Documents 96). Before this paragraph, the *Constitutions* repeat the common requisites for any religious congregation: that the candidate be of good moral standing, with mental and physical health, etc.
25 Primitive Documents, 96.

new members recognize their unique gifts and graces and to help them to develop those in communal life. Among the rules for the director of novices, we read:

> ...she will have special care for the novices and as far as possible, thanks to divine grace, she will form them in the desire for and the effective pursuit of the greatest holiness.
>
> ...she will take pains to point out to them little by little the path to the perfection proper to the Institute, and she will be convinced that they cannot become holy all at once and practice the most sublime maxims of this virtue. She will consider carefully the nature of each sister in order to correct what could be lacking and, for the profession and perfection of the pure love of God, be attentive to all that can be useful and serve as an instrument of grace. Let her also seek to know the attraction of the Holy Spirit and the way by which (the Spirit) wants to draw each of the sisters in order to help them follow this divine attraction without any desire of obliging them to follow her way of virtue and to pattern themselves on her ideas or her practice of it. She will be gentle and affable to all her daughters and, by this gentleness and affability, endeavor to win their hearts in order to be able with greater facility to point out to them the path to the virtue characteristic of their Institute.
>
> ...she will endeavor, by her conversation and by proposing to them the examples of their predecessors...to understand that the characteristic of the daughters of St. Joseph is to profess in all things and everywhere, in a great joy and gentleness of heart, the greatest perfection with as much exactitude as if they had vowed it.[26]

These lines demonstrate that the director's task is to encourage each novice in the pursuit of perfection, which is another way of saying in continual growth. The director does not hide the candidates' failings, but she is called to highlight the gifts of each one. When this section speaks of perfection, it is not a dry, prefabricated perfection – a universal concept of holiness. The role of the director is to help each candidate discern the movement of the Holy Spirit in her own life, and in this Institute; there is no way that can be accomplished without joy and douceur. Here, in Médaille's words we have a simple, clear articulation of the Ignatian spirit expressed in Salesian douceur. No one who has experienced religious life would believe that the ideals expressed in the *Constitutions* portray each moment of the everyday life of all of the communities. At the same time, one would hope that no one would enter the Institute if she did not have the desire to live those ideals.

---

26 Primitive Documents, 102

Because of that, the *Constitutions* allow us to describe the general characteristics of the corporate personality of the Sisters of St. Joseph.

According to the ideals to which they have committed themselves and dependent on the grace of God, the Sisters of St. Joseph are faithful daughters of the Church – careful to maintain an official tie to the hierarchy without allowing

Le Puy - Monistrol 28 Miles

undue interference in the interior life of the Congregation. They not only accept diversity but also proclaim it a value. This value leads them to seek and appreciate the particular way in which the Holy Spirit moves in the life of each person. In addition, the value they put on diversity encourages them to respect different expressions of communal life and to adapt their style of life and their ministry to the particular needs of the people among whom they find themselves. For the sisters of this apostolic movement, communal life is essential because it prepares them to foster community among all the people and groups with whom they are in contact. This is the Congregation in which Jeanne Fontbonne received the habit on December 17, 1778.

MOTHER SAINT JOHN FONTBONNE

Jeanne Fontbonne was born on March 31, 1759, in the town of Bas-en-Basset in Haute-Loire.[27] According to her biographers, Jeanne showed qualities of leadership from an early age.[28]

---

27 Bas-en-Basset is a small village about 60 miles south of Lyon and 31 miles north of Le Puy. Today, Le Puy is the capital of department of Haute-Loire. The Sisters of St. Joseph first established a community in Bas-en-Basset in 1687. (See Vacher, 453.)

28 The majority of what is known about Mother St. John comes from Abbe Rivaux whose work has been reproduced in two books with various translations. I am using two editions of her major biography: Abbé Rivaux, *Life of Mother Saint John Fontbonne*: (Translated from the French of Abbé Rivaux, (N.Y.: Benzinger Bros.) 1887, and *Sencilla y Grande Madre San Juan Fontbonne, Fundadora de la Congregación de San José de Lyón, Restauradora de Instituto* (Por el autor de ¡EL! [desconocida]) Traducido por una religiosa de San José de Buenos Aires, (Buenos Aires: 1944) The second, the Spanish version of a French original, is a translation; the English version, *Mother Saint John Fontbonne:* A Biography, (N.Y.: Kennedy and Sons, 1935) is "adapted from the original French edition by a Sister of Saint Joseph, Brentwood," and is a slight abridgement of the French original. Here, the first of the sources will be referred to as "Rivaux," the second as *Sencilla* and the third as Life of Mother Saint John. Facts about the Fontbonne family can be found in *Sencilla*, 11-14. In regard to primary sources, Patricia Byrne, CSJ, explains that Mother St. John's correspondence disappeared in a fire while it was in the possession of her first biographer, Abbe Rivaux. (See "Sisters of St. Joseph: The Americanization of a French Tradition," (U.S. Catholic Historian 5 (1986):241-72). Most of the published biographies of Mother St.

Street in Bas-en-Basset

She also gave early evidence of having a strong will and discerning judgment. As one story goes, when her elder sister Marie was preparing for First Communion, the sister catechist strove to impress the child with the holiness of the sacrament and her own unworthiness. She was so successful that Marie became scrupulously afraid to approach the altar. It was the younger sister, Jeanne, who encouraged Marie, telling her to put more confidence in the goodness of God than in the opinion of the religious. Not only was the child a good little theologian, but audacious enough to dispute the opinion of the sister catechist who was none other than the director of their school and their paternal aunt. That aunt, Sister St. Francis, together with her half-sister, Sister of the Visitation, were among the hundreds of French women who, captivated by Médaille's dream for the Little Design, had dedicated themselves to serving the dear neighbor in that part of France since 1650.[29]

In 1778, the 19 year old Jeanne Fontbonne and her sister Marie told Mother Saint Francis that they wanted to enter the congregation of the Sisters of St. Joseph in Bas. Instead of rejoicing, Mother St. Francis painted a harsh picture

---

John lack citations to verify their content. There are numerous traditions about Mother St. John, but Abbe Rivaux was the one biographer who had the opportunity to converse with people who had known her personally. Much of what follows in this chapter comes from oral tradition, with all the advantages and disadvantages it offers. Parish archives indicate that her father Michel Fontbonne, a shoemaker, was born in 1726. On January 13, 1756, he married the 25-year-old Benoîte Theillière. Of their eight children, three died as infants.

29 *Sencilla*, 23-24. While there are various opinions on the foundation year of the Sisters of St. Joseph, we will use 1650 as the most widely accepted.

30 *Sencilla*, 33-35. The author mentions that Mother St. Francis had a "strong, righteous, brave, and generous heart" and also "an austere piety. She had entered the community at Le Puy before coming to the convent at Bas-en-Basset. Mother Saint Francis Fontbonne seems to have been well respected yet strict if not rigid. Abbe Rivaux mentions that Sister St. John avoided allowing her aunt to catch her showing her sense of humor. Rivaux attributes Mother St. Francis' severity to a desire to infuse her niece with a strong character – a goal that was seemingly unnecessary. (Sencilla, 79)

31 Marie-Joseph de Galard de Terraube was bishop of Le Puy from 1774–1790 and died in 1801. He seemed to have taken note of Jeanne Fontbonne from the time she was a student, recognizing her capacity and taking care to provide her with opportunities to fulfill it. Monistrol was the summer residence of the bishops of Le Puy. Interestingly, de Galard's predecessor, J.G. Le Franc de Pompignan became Archbishop of Vienne and later sided with the juring clergy in the Revolution. Uniting with the Third Estate, he served as the Minister of Public at the time when the Civil Constitution of the Clergy was forced on the French clergy.

of religious life, suggesting that they did not possess the strength and virtue necessary to live it. In spite of her warnings, or perhaps in reaction to them, the two sisters only intensified their resolve.[30] What they did not anticipate was that, just before the date of their entrance into the postulate, Bishop de Galard of Le Puy, would ask Mother St. Francis to go to Monistrol, just a few miles from their hometown of Bas-en-Basset, to found a new community in that city. He instructed her that it would be a good idea to have her two nieces go with her to found the new community.[31] Thus, even before beginning religious life, the two sisters had to adjust their dreams and leave their hometown. There is evidence that Bishop de Galard had already recognized Jeanne Fontbonne as an unusually gifted and graced young woman. His hopes for her would be more than fulfilled in the six decades of her religious life.

In July of 1778, when the founders of the new community arrived in Monistrol, the group included four relatives: Mother Saint Francis and Sister of the Visitation, and their postulant nieces, Jeanne and Marie Fontbonne. The two young women received the habit on December 17 of that same year.[32] Seven years later, in 1785, with the Monistrol community well established, Mother St. Francis returned to her community in Bas. Bishop de Galard made it known that he hoped that Sister Saint John would replace her aunt as superior.[33] The sisters of the community elected Sister St. John superior of the Monistrol community when she was 26 years of age. That was the beginning of what would be a very long experience of leadership.

THE SISTERS OF ST. JOSEPH AND THE REVOLUTION

While the seeds of the French Revolution were germinating, Mother St. John and her sisters continued in their mission. In Monistrol where their labor now included the administration of a hospital, Mother St. John wanted to amplify the sisters' ministry by establishing a workshop of sorts. Unfortunately she lacked sufficient funds. She took her case to Bishop de Galard and he put her in contact with Madame de Chantemule, "a noble lady" of the region. Not only did this woman provide funds for the workshop, but she became Mother St. John's close friend and supported many of the community's projects.[34]

---

32 Rivaux states that the year was 1779. (77)
33 It is said that when the bishop indicated his hope that Sister Saint John be named superior, Mother St. Francis tried to dissuade him by saying that she was one of the youngest in the community and she lacked experience. It seems quite possible that Sister Saint John also lacked the strict spirit cultivated by her aunt. Sencilla, 40.
34 See Rivaux, *Mother of the Sacred Heart*, 23.

The workshop functioned as a creative expression of the charism and mission of the Sisters of St. Joseph. It was founded to provide a place "in which pious persons could meet to work together, whether on behalf of the poor, for their families, or for their own sustenance. The Sisters would offer them help in

Monistrol Convent and the twice Blessed Stone

their work and, if necessary, instruct them."[35] Here we see Mother St. John's mission in action. She gathered women "without distinction," bringing different ages and classes together under one roof; the workshop included women whose resources permitted them to work on behalf of the poor, mothers who needed to work for their children and finally, young women who were apparently on their own.[36] With such diversity, this group not only produced artisan goods but also brought together people who, given their social differences, would rarely gather socially. Thus, while the nation was feeling the tensions of class divisions and increasing poverty, the Sisters of St. Joseph in Monistrol were forging community among representatives of groups that would soon regard one another as bitter enemies.

One anecdote from this period brings to light Mother St. John's reputation. When the cornerstone of the new institution was being blessed, Bishop de Galard invited Mother St. John to bless it after him. She was reputedly embarrassed, but did his bidding. His invitation and her acquiescence to perform what seemed to be a clerical function formed part of the lore around the impressive but unassuming young superior.[37]

It is impossible to know the opinions and feelings of the Sisters of St. Joseph regarding the political agitation of their day. It is likely that because of their contacts with people of the upper class and the clergy, some of the sisters knew about the new philosophies becoming the rage. In conversations and homilies they could have heard criticism of the Enlightenment ideas that promoted the

---

35 *Sencilla*, 42-44 36 The plight of women on their own was so serious that after the Revolution Cardinal Fesch called for Sisters of St. Joseph from Lyon to come to Aix les Bains to help rescue them. (Bouchage, 107)
37 See Rivaux, *Mother of the Sacred Heart*, 24. Even into the 21st century the cornerstone has been preserved by the Sisters at Monistrol.

individualism, questioning of traditional authority and other ideas that formed the intellectual basis of the Revolution. According to some critics, the liberal philosophers of the day were promulgating the idea that "it was impossible to recognize any authority beyond that of individual reason."[38] With all of its new expressions, this philosophy still had much in common with the individualism fomented by the Protestant Reformation with its questioning of authority, faith in personal interpretation and emphasis on individual salvation. To people not caught up in it, the new philosophy could well have appeared to be nothing more than the old Protestant wolf in a new sheepskin.

Even if the sisters were not in touch with the intellectual currents of the day, their encounters with the needy kept them aware of the suffering of the poor. They knew that the people could not withstand the burden of their excessive taxation. They also knew that rampant corruption benefited many civil and even Church leaders while class divisions escalated in a system that continually increased the misery of the poor. No matter what the level of their intellectual and political

---

The French Revolution and the Sisters of St. Joseph

1789 June 17, Third Estate declares itself the "National Assembly"
    July 14, The storming of the Bastille
    August, Abolition of Tithes, Declaration of the Rights of Man
1790 February: Religious Orders dissolved, religious vows
    declared illicit
    April: Church property transferred to State
    July: Civil Constitution of the Clergy
    November: Priests required to swear oath of allegiance
1791 April: Pope Pius VI condemns the Constitutional Oath
1792 August: Religious forbidden to administer public institutions
    September: Massacre of prisoners, priests, sisters, bishops
    in Paris, Lyon, etc.
    September 29: Mother St. John ordered to vacate Monistrol
    October 2: Father Ollier demands sisters' presence at Mass
    October 14: Three remaining Sisters forced to abandon
        Monistrol
1793 January 21: Execution of King Louis XVI
    September 5: Beginning of the Reign of Terror
1794 July 28: Robespierre executed.

awareness the sisters would have had daily contact with people who needed their material help.

The French Revolution affected the sisters where they lived, prayed, and worked, attacking their moral sensibilities before it began to threaten their physical well-being. The Catholic Church and the monarchy were the institutions most aggressively attacked by the Revolutionaries. In August of 1789, the clergy were forced to renounce their privileges;[39] in October, the National Assembly stripped the Church of its material goods; and in February of 1790, all the religious orders were suppressed.[40] However, by an exception clause, the congregations that served the common good in hospitals and schools were allowed to remain in existence.

Radical changes for the Sisters of St. Joseph began with the promulgation of the Civil Constitution of the Clergy on July 12, 1790. With the intention of nationalizing the Church, the Constitution revised the structures of dioceses and parishes, and replaced the authority of the pope and bishops with a democratic system of appointments in which every citizen, Catholic or not, had the right to vote in the election of the bishop and the pastor of the region. In November 1790, a law was passed requiring all priests to swear allegiance to the Civil Constitution. "Non-juring" or "refractory" priests, those who refused to take the oath, lost their positions and their means of support.[41]

At first, it was far from easy to discern how to respond to the new laws. To some clerics, the oath appeared to be a matter more patriotic than religious, so it did not bother them to take it. After the Pope denounced it, the faithful saw the oath as the Revolution's attempt to break all ties between the Church in France and the Roman Catholic Church. As time went on, the division between the revolutionary governments and the Church became ever clearer; the government would stop at nothing less than the abolition of Roman Catholicism in France, allowing some

---

38 See Francisco Montalban, S.J., *Historia de la Iglesia Católica en sus cuatro grandes edades*, Tomo IV, Edad Moderna (Madrid: Biblioteca de Autores Cristianos, 1963) 355.
Monistrol Convent and the twice Blessed Stone
39 The upper clergy, like the nobles, were exempt from taxes and enjoyed incomes for which they exerted no labor.
40 According to Hufton, at the time of the Revolution, there were approximately 55,000 women religious in France, serving in some 2,000 establishments. Fifteen percent of those were Daughters of Charity who received an individual recompense of 75 livres per year. The services they offered included helping the sick in their homes, soup kitchens, teaching basic literacy or skills to young women or even finding shoes, clothing and layettes for poor women and their children. Their commitment ranged from help for the domiciled sick, layettes for nursing mothers, provision of shoes, soup kitchens…teaching basic literacy or vocational skills to young girls. (Hufton, 57-60)
41 While up to 45% of the priests took the oath, many retracted publicly after Pope Pius VI published the encyclical Charitas, condemning it as schismatic. See *The Guillotine and the Cross*, (Warren H. Carroll, Front Royal, VA , Christendom Press, 1991) 30.

vestige of the faith to remain only insofar as the government acted as the supreme religious authority. The power-hungry inflexibility of the revolutionaries served only to strengthen the resolve of those who remained faithful to their traditional Catholic faith. By forcing separation from Rome, the revolutionaries created a schism and unwittingly watered the growing seeds of heroic resistance, especially among the religious and clergy who valued faith in Catholicism over loyalty to France. With the execution of King Louis XVI in January of 1793 and the September inauguration of the Reign of Terror, the Revolution earned its reputation as a demonic and demented movement.

In Monistrol, when the National Assembly imposed the oath of fidelity to the Civil Constitution of the Clergy, Father Ollier, the pastor of the Sisters of St. Joseph, used his pulpit to swear the constitutional oath while Bishop de Galard refused, lost his position and went into exile.[42] The sisters considered Father Ollier as an apostate and so refused to attend any event or liturgy in his parish. When he came to their hospital during the Corpus Christi procession, not one of them could be found on the property to participate in the ceremony.

The sisters' resistance provoked their pastor to seek retaliation; he became obstinately determined to impose his will and authority on them. On September 12, 1791, at his instigation, the sisters were denounced for incompetent administration of the hospital. The official document against them read in part:

> The poor of this house have fallen under the direction of the Sisters of St. Joseph who instruct them in such a manner as to keep them from going to Mass or parish catechism. Behold to what they expose these miserable victims who instead of being brought up in Christianity are in the greatest danger of falling into fanaticism! What a horror for this city and what reproaches would it not deserve if, after receiving so much praise for patriotism and zeal everywhere, you neglect to organize that administration now?[43]

In spite of being accused of being poor administrators and fanatics, the sisters were not expelled from the hospital. In reality their service was too important to the town and there was no one to replace them.

Meanwhile Father Ollier decided that if public humiliation did not bring them to collaborate with him, he would try intimidation. Once again he found allies ready to help him:

---

42 *Sencilla*, 55.
43 *Life of Mother St. John*, 30. The note in the text cites "M. Fraisse, Manuscrit: L'Hôpital de Monistrol."

One day they went armed with hatchets, ready to break down the doors if they were refused admittance. Mother Saint John kept them from having to go to that much trouble. She appeared alone and met the excited mob. They asked her to swear that for the future the Sisters would obey the Constitution and assist at Mass. Neither their cries nor their threats frightened her. She remained calm and firm in her refusal. When the fanatics tried to advance into the house to see the Sisters and obtain from them what their Mother refused, she placed herself at the door and with great dignity and coolness said:
"It is useless to present yourselves to the community.
Here, the head answers for the body."
The men withdrew saying, "What a woman that is! There is nothing to gain from her!"[44]

Although the local priest was unable to depose the sisters, the progress of the Revolution made their exile inevitable. On August 18, 1792, a decree was promulgated prohibiting religious from administering public institutions. At first the sisters thought that they could take advantage of a clause of the law that left open one possibility. That clause said that the same people could continue in their service to the poor and the care of the sick if they did it as private citizens and under the vigilance of the municipal corporation. But even after abandoning the habit to dress as lay women, not all the sisters were able to remain in their ministry. The hospital records indicate that on September 29, 1792, the Sisters of St. Joseph departed from their home at the hospital and returned to their families. However, that statement passed over one detail: three "unmarried women" dressed as lay women (Martha, Jeanne and Marie) remained to serve the residents.

Although the three sisters did not maintain any outward trappings of religious life, they continued to be a thorn in the side of the pastor who seemed incapable of retreating from the private vendetta he had declared on them. On October 2, only days after the other sisters had left the hospital, there was to be a Mass in honor of the new Republic. Father Ollier "invited" the sisters with the fervid intention of compelling their presence. Staging a public display of his power, he prepared kneelers for them in full view of the congregation. Before the Mass, he sent a group of men accompanied by drummers to convey the sisters to the church. The scene took on the character of a theatrical performance:

The mob went to the hospital beating the drums. The men rang the bell

---

44 *Life of Mother St. John*, 30-31

and asked for Jeanne Fontbonne and her Sisters. Without any hesitation, all presented themselves. "What do you want, my friends?" she asked. "We want to take you and your companions to the Mass which the patriot priest is going to say in the parish church." "Never," replied Mother Saint John in a dignified, confident manner; "never will we consent to communicate with an apostate priest." "We would rather die than renounce the Faith," added the Sisters unanimously.

Upon this refusal, they were seized and dragged by force to the church. The men, continuing to beat the drums, cried out, "Make way for these three citizenesses whom we are leading to church..."
All resistance was useless. The Sisters, calm and dignified, allowed themselves to be led to the kneeling benches, but these strong Christians refused to kneel. They stood erect during the entire ceremony giving no sign of participation in the sacrilegious service.

Leaving the church, Mother Saint John protested aloud against the violence which they had suffered. "Know well," she said, "that by force alone, have we been led to the sacrilegious Mass of an apostate priest. Our hearts and wills had no part therein. We remain inviolably attached and faithful to the true Catholic Faith, and no violence shall ever be able to separate us from it."[45]

Mother Saint John succeeded in undermining Ollier's drama. She and her sisters won that battle, but he had more political power than they did. On October 14, 1792, the three remaining sisters were forced to leave the hospital in Monistrol. The Fontbonnes together with Sister Martha returned to the family home in Bas.

In terms of the general situation of women religious and the Revolutionary government, some revolutionary officials honestly believed that women religious had been incompetent to run charitable institutions. At the same time, avaricious authorities set their sights on the donations sisters received and their desirable land and buildings. The Revolutionaries decided that they could find a better solution than hospitals and orphanages for the sick and abandoned, many of whom they accused of seeking public help out of laziness.[46] In spite of it all, very few women abandoned their religious life when forced out of their convents or institutions. The revolutionaries knew not with whom they were dealing. Instead of weaning faithful women away from their commitments, persecution, especially of priests and sisters, only strengthened their counter-revolutionary sentiments and activity. Historian Olwen Hufton explains:

---

45 *Life of Mother St. John*, 33-34.
46 Hufton, 63.

The failure of the real nun to disband as the Assembly thought they should involved a fervent and stolid support of the non-juring priesthood. This found expression in the women making available to the non-jurors convent and hospital chapels for the saying of mass, thus robbing the constitutional priesthood of its clientele… There was public humiliation of religious women – other women could punish them, publicly beating their bare buttocks with brooms – and the scene would then be reported by the gutter press…

In actual assaults on houses, rather than on individuals, gangs of youths were usually involved…The Sisters of Saint Joseph du Puy, for example, who made no bones about their hostility to the legislation, experienced severe threats to person and property in some of the bourgs of the Haute Loire. Windows were smashed and tiles torn off roofs and tethered animals released.[47]

As has happened through history, persecution reinforced the commitment of the faithful and called forth an underground church made up of congregations who were nothing short of heroic.

A RETREAT: AT HOME AND IN PRISON -
CHAPTER TWO OF THE REVOLUTION

It would not be an exaggeration to say that the Fontbonne home in Bas became a convent in those days. When Jeanne and Marie arrived from Monistrol, they found Mother St. Francis and her exiled sisters already there. For a little over a year, they lived in relative tranquility. Then the government promulgated a new law requiring all those who had retired from religious life to take the oath of fidelity to the state. Those who did not do so could be arrested.[48]

It became dangerous to remain in the family home and the sisters, like many "non-juring" priests, hid in the woods during the day returning to sleep in the homes of their family or other collaborators. In those precarious conditions, faithful Catholics created an underground Church; they celebrated the Eucharist in secret and the bravest among them guarded consecrated hosts in their homes. The inevitable finally happened in 1793 when Jeanne, Marie, and their companion Martha were arrested. They did not resist the guards who came for them, because to do so could have triggered a house search which would have given away the

---

47 Hufton, 72-75. For a first-hand account of a religious community during the Revolution, see *I Leave You My Heart: A Visitandine Chronicle of the French Revolution*, Mère Marie-Jéronyme Vérot's Letter of 15 May, 1794, (Translated and Edited by Péronne-Marie Thibert, V.H.M. (Philadelphia: St. Joseph's University Press, 2000)
48 An unpublished manuscript in the Barbara Baer research collection, notes that in the diocese of Viviers, whose bishop was one of the seven who took the oath, between 14 and 16 Sisters of St. Joseph took it as well.

priests hiding in the Fontbonne home.[49]

At that moment, only the sisters from Monistrol were taken, Mother St. Francis and her companions were not discovered.

Because the jails of France were insufficient to hold the number of prisoners being taken, buildings that had been confiscated from the Church were used to hold the overflow.[50] The Fontbonne sisters were taken 25 kilometers from their home and jailed in the former convent of the Augustinians in Saint-Didier, known under the revolutionary government as Montfranc. Inside the prison everyone was a "citizen;" there were no titles or professions, but this was hardly sufficient to strip the inmates of their innate dignity.

REVOLUTIONARY TIME

The revolutionaries, interpreting their epoch as the fulcrum of history, established the year 1792 as the first year of a new era. They renamed the months according to their characteristics (rainy, snowy, fruitful, etc.) and eliminated the 7 day week, replacing it with the numbered days of the "decade" making the tenth day a day of relaxation. To rid their world of religious memories, anything called by a saint's name was renamed: Saint-Didier became Montfanc, etc.

Among the many examples of courage and resistance by the prisoners, we hear that Mother Saint John actually dominated the jailers by her calm, serene manner. At one point the guards ordered her to respect the "decade" – the 10-day system that had replaced the 7-day week. She took that order as an opportunity to demonstrate the futility of threatening prisoners of conscience:

> When they ordered her to work on Sunday she answered very simply:
> "If I had been willing to do that, I wouldn't be in prison."
> When they threatened her with solitary confinement, she replied: "How do we get there?"[51]

---

49 *Sencilla*, 64-65.
50 During the Revolution the Sisters of St. Joseph's home in Le Puy became a garrison, leading to great destruction of the property.
51 *Sencilla*, 69.

Already in prison with the shadow of the guillotine hanging over her, what had she to fear?

The families of prisoners were permitted to visit them and the officials counted on the food friends and relatives brought to supplement the small amount allotted to keep the prisoners alive. The visitors also slipped contraband mail to the inmates, allowing them to know what was happening on the outside. Those messages often provided nourishment as vital as the food that came with them.

The prisoners of faith developed a strong solidarity among themselves even when they were not incarcerated in the same location. Many considered those who sacrificed their freedom for the faith to be saints – and Mother Saint John herself kept a notebook listing the names of the martyrs whose intercession she sought. Among themselves the captives never knew how many of them would give their lives, nor when their day might come. One letter the sisters secretly shared reveals the communion shared among the prisoners of conscience. The letter came from Father Clavel, the brother of a Sister of St. Joseph and friend of Mother Saint John. Writing to his sister while awaiting his encounter with the guillotine he invited her to share his words with carefully chosen people. Reflecting on his own experience he encouraged the sisters in with the following letter.[52]

This depiction of Marie Antoinette on the way to the guillotine shows how every woman prisoner, noble, peasant or religious, would have been attired. Her hair cut short, a simple cap and white shift equalized them all as they were taken to the scaffold.

Do not be surprised if, on the evening of your captivity, you were seized with a secret trouble, the cause of which you did not know. Human nature being terrified, the demon made a last effort to force you to take the oath, which, apparently, would have brought peace to your troubled soul, but which would have caused real sorrow after the return of your reason.

---

52 Both images are from the public domain.
53 The letter is translated from *Sencilla*, 49-50.

In the garden, Jesus Christ felt a fear which made Him tremble and beg His Father not to compel Him to drink the chalice of His passion, but after having given human nature a little of what it demanded, recovering Himself, He cried out: "Father, not my will, but Thine be done." This submission brought an angel who consoled Him. The day after your imprisonment, your trouble ceased and peace took its place. It is the reward of the sacrifice you made to God in refusing to take the oath, preferring captivity to the advantages which the world offered you, had you adored at the altar of the fatherland.

Do not seek any occasion for martyrdom; that would be presumption. If God sends it to you, do not fly from it; that would be apostasy. Martyrdom is the most signal grace that you could receive from your Spouse. Do not cast frightened glances at the future, 'for sufficient for the day is the evil thereof,' but pray every morning to the God of mercy to give you each day, what is necessary to love Him and please Him in all your actions. All the profanations that you have seen during the week show you God's anger toward His people and call you to redouble your fervor and mortification and to draw to you His loving regard...

I send you a letter in common, which I have written hastily. If you judge proper to read it to your companions, you may do so, under the express prohibition that you tell no one its author. Make no mention of me unless to my two sisters, members of your community, and to Mother Saint John. Eventually you will have the kindness to note for me what impression it made. If you do not find it convenient to communicate it, burn it...

I beg of you by the tenderness of Jesus Christ to pray for the Church and above all, for me that the Lord have mercy on me and that He cast a favorable glance upon His people and that He have mercy on all.

I am, with all possible reverence,
Your very humble and obedient servant
Clavel

As in the days of the catacombs, faithful Catholics treasured the testimony of the martyrs. Two days after writing this letter, Father Clavel was decapitated.

The Fontbonne sisters, later accompanied by their aunt, Mother St. Francis, survived long months in prison while chaos and cruelty reigned throughout the country. In three unforgettable days, September 2-5, 1792, more than a thousand prisoners went to their death, among them, more than three hundred priests and three bishops. The government published pamphlets advertising the news about how the guillotine was accomplishing its bloody purpose. Little by little the sisters learned the names of Sisters of St. Joseph and other friends who had fallen victim to the dementia reigning in the country. They believed their day would come soon.

According to tradition, when one of the guards addressed Mother Saint John saying, "Citizen, tomorrow for you," the sisters believed that their date with the guillotine had arrived: the day when they would be taken from St. Didier to Le Puy for trial, followed by execution within 24 hours. Thinking about their last tomorrow, the sisters decided to spend the little money they had to wash and prepare their clothes as if they were going to a gala event.[53] Thus, ready to celebrate the last day of their lives, they received the news that Robespierre had fallen and the day would herald their freedom rather than death.[54]

When they returned to Bas, Mother St. Francis recovered her convent and was able to reestablish community life there. Mother Saint John did not enjoy the same success. When she attempted to recuperate the sisters' property in Monistrol, she found that it had been sold to a revolutionary patriot who would not even consider selling it to a group of religious. Because of that, she and Sister Teresa remained in the home of their parents where they spent the next years in a life of prayer and service.[55]

Martyrs Among the Sisters of St. Joseph

Among the Sister martyrs whose names we know are:

❖ Sister Marie Aubert of Argentière, 38 years old, arrested for hiding non-juring priests.

❖ Sister Marie Anne Garnier, arrested for the same, apparently after she turned herself in to accompany Sister Marie Aubert and the priests, both were executed at Craponne on June 15, 1794.

❖ Mother Sainte Croix, 63 years old, Sister Madeline 40 years old and Sister Toussaint, 31 years old, all of Vernosc Ardèche, martyred with five priests on August 4, 1794 for refusing to take the oath to the Civil Constitution and hiding priests. They lost their lives after the death of Robespierre under the bloody rule of the revolutionary Marcon who prolonged the Reign of Terror in Ardèche.

In addition to these, the oral tradition remembers others who were arrested, subjected to cruelty and condemned without judicial procedures.

---

53 No note is made of the dress of the sisters, but we know that from at least 1792, they could not use the habit and would not have done so in hiding. Prisoners taken to the guillotine were robed simply and their hair was cut short. No one would have been executed garbed as a cleric or religious.

54 *Sencilla*, 121. Robespierre was guillotined on July 28, 1794. We do not know the date of the sisters' arrest or their release from prison, but there is evidence that they were free by November, 1794. *(Sencilla*, 125.)

55 *Sencilla*,126-127.

THE CARDINAL, THE VICAR AND THE NEW COMMUNITY

The chaos of the Revolution disrupted the life of almost every faithful French Catholic. Most of the priests and religious who refused to take the oath lost their homes and had to go into exile or be deported. After the fall of Robespierre, many religious were released from prison, but as late as 1799, some were still being imprisoned or exiled to Guinea. In 1801, Napoleon negotiated a Concordat with Pope Pius VII which recognized Catholicism as the religion of the majority of the population and allowed for freedom of worship. The Concordat favored the government, including granting it the royalty's traditional right to name prelates who would be almost compulsorily approved by the papacy.

The 1801 Concordat brought peace between the Church and the state. It assured freedom of worship, realigned dioceses, required clerics to take an oath of loyalty, removed many bishops from their sees, agreed that the government would pay clerical salaries and gave the Republic the rights to name bishops. Traditional religious orders remained officially suppressed, although Napoleon eventually authorized more than two hundred women's congregations because of the useful services they offered in nursing, social work and teaching.

Father Claude Cholleton was among the thousands of French priests who had accepted exile rather than swear the Constitutional oath. When he was allowed to return to France he resumed his ministry in Saint-Etienne.[56] There he brought together a group of pious women who wanted to become nuns. He himself took on the task of their formation, He wanted to reinforce in them a life of contemplation and extraordinary sacrifice.[57] Given their practice of dressing in black, they were known as "The Black Daughters." Needing to provide for their own sustenance, the Black Daughters "slept little, worked much and prayed even more." Servants of the common people, they were engaged in works of charity visiting the sick and dying, for which they also came to be called the "Sisters of a Good Death" even while they thought of themselves as called to the contemplative life.[58]

---

56 In 1801, Napoleon made a Concordat with the Vatican that recognized the Catholic Church as the religion of the majority of the French people. Although the arrangement maintained the government's right to name bishops, it admitted that the papacy would have limited power to confirm the nomination.

57 Father Cholleton took charge of their direction and with the zeal of an apostle and the austerity of an anchorite he prepared them. He formed his spiritual daughters in his own likeness...In order to teach them to avoid looking for human respect he had them dress in a costume that was not a religious habit, but neither was it worldly."O," he would say to them, "how happy I would be if I learned that...you were found worthy of not only being covered with derision...but also of having mud and stones showered upon you." Although they did much to serve others, those sisters apparently also received a share of the ridicule Cholleton wished or them. Sencilla, 141.

58 Sencilla, 142.

Before the first Black Sisters had completed their time of formation, Cardinal Joseph Fesch of Lyon named Father Cholleton as his vicar. At that time, Cardinal Fesch was the most powerful prelate in France, largely because he was Napoleon's maternal uncle. [59] It was not a good idea to ignore a request from Cardinal Fesch; Father Cholleton had to leave his community in the hands of another director so that he could move to Lyon.

The trajectory that brought Father Cholleton, Cardinal Fesch, and Mother Saint John into collaboration is so contorted that it would be difficult to deny that Providence played a role in it. In Lyon, Father Cholleton spoke to the Cardinal about his concern for the fledgling community. The Cardinal had known Sisters of St. Joseph and he suggested that their congregation might be able to help. Father Cholleton accepted the proposal, but neither of them knew to whom to turn. At this point Father Imbert, a Capuchin from Monistrol, entered the picture. He knew Mother Saint John and had heard about the Vicar's plan. When he suggested that Mother Saint John take responsibility for the community, the Cardinal and Father Cholleton accepted the idea. Thus, seemingly out of nowhere, a messenger from Cardinal Fesch arrived at the Fontbonne home to ask that Mother Saint John return with him to St. Etienne in the Diocese of Lyon. She accepted and arrived to stay with her new sisters on August 14, 1807.[60]

This new stage in life could not have been easy for anyone involved. Father Cholleton had accepted the idea that a religious whom he had never met and who had never lived in the cloister would take charge of his little group. At the age of 49, Mother Saint John left her hometown after 15 years and set down roots in a new location with a group of would-be Sisters of St. Joseph whom she had neither received nor tested. For their part, the "Black Daughters" accepted an unknown sister from a different tradition as their novice director.

Mother Saint John instilled a new spirit in the group. In the beginning, it was difficult for them to understand and accept the practical type of self-emptying endorsed by their director. In the tradition of the Sisters of St. Joseph, penance was not seen as a good in itself but as a means and more often than not,

---

59 Cardinal Fesch was the half-brother of Napoleon's mother, Maria Letizia Buonaparte née Ramolino. As a non-juring priest, he had to abandon priestly work during the Revolution, but his star rose with Napoleon. He helped negotiate the 1801 Concordat between France and the papacy and in 1802, he was named Archbishop of Lyon and soon thereafter to be made a Cardinal. See Montalban, *Historia*, 396-405. For additional information about the 1801 Concordat see Controversial Concordats: The Vatican's Relations with Napoleon, Mussolini, and Hitler, Frank J. Coppa, ed. (Washington D.C., the Catholic University Press of America, 1999)
60 According to Mother Saint John's biographer, her mother did not want to lose her daughter again and so protested with the warning, "She has no good sense!" Nevertheless, Mother Saint John went, leaving her sister, Sister Teresa, at home with their parents. *Sencilla*, 146. See also *Mother Sacred Heart*, 37-38.

a difficult experience to be accepted rather than a freely chosen practice. Contending with the Jansenistic mortification that seemed to characterize their spirituality, Mother Saint John challenged her new sisters with the idea that mortifications like mutual tolerance, weariness from work and care for the sick could be more demanding and efficacious than any penance or suffering they would decide to impose upon themselves.[61] Little by little, the Black Daughters came to appreciate the spirit of the Institute that Mother Saint John represented, and on July 14, 1808, twelve postulants received the habit. They were:

❖ Anne Matrat – Sister St. Francis Regis, (from La Valla, Loire)
❖ Jeanne Marie Matrat - Sister St. Clare (from La Valla, Loire)
❖ Anne Amrie Didier - Sister St. Paul (from La Valla, Loire)
❖ Suzanne Marcoux - Sister St. John Baptist (from Firminy, Loire)
❖ Jeanne Poitrasson-Gonnet – Sister St. Francis de Sales (from Chessy)
❖ Philippine Ménard – Sister St. Teresa (from Saint-Victor)
❖ Benoît Perrin – Sister Marie (from Saint-Victor)
❖ Antoinette Montiellier – Sister St. Michel (from Saint-Julien)
❖ Marie Anne Pitiot – Sister St. Augustine (from Saint-Just)
❖ Antoinette Cessier – Sister Marie Joseph (from Saint-Etienne)
❖ Marie Louise Foret – Sister Saint Madeleine (from Saint-Etienne)
❖ Elisabeth Plason - Sister St. Agnes (from Saint-Etienne). [62]

Under Mother Saint John's guidance these sisters reestablished a community of St. Joseph in the Diocese of Lyon. They identified themselves as "The Society of Saint Joseph" because the political climate still did not allow them to call themselves a Congregation.[63]

The first group was followed by others, and the Society grew rapidly. According to Abbe Rivaux, in the beginning, the little group sustained itself by taking in work from the manufacturing establishments of the city, but even with that, they were so poor that Mother Saint John had to forego her snuff.[64]

---

61 Jansenism was an extreme movement in the sixteenth century. Based on a theology of predestination and the human incapacity to do any good on one's own, Jansenist morality promoted rigor, a renewal of penitential practices, and a reverent distancing from the Eucharist. Even after it was condemned as a heresy, Jansenist ideas had a great deal of influence in post- Tridentine spirituality. The Jansenists and the Jesuits were vociferous ideological enemies as the latter promoted a far more positive theological anthropology.
62 Life of Mother St. John, 96.
63 Somewhat later, in 1815, the Sisters of St. Joseph in Le Puy recovered their property on the rue Montferrand and reconstituted their community under the leadership of Sister Anne-Marie Grand. As would happen with Lyon, dispersed local communities joined in a congregation with Le Puy as the motherhouse. The Le Puy community, like Lyon, would eventually found multiple communities in France and abroad.
64 Rivaux Mother Sacred Heart, 38-39 and Mother Saint John Fontbonne, 112 (including the 6 course meal).

In 1814, Mother Saint John began to make arrangements to move the community from St. Etienne to Lyon where they would have more space and more direct contact with the seat of the Archdiocese. The move would allow sisters scattered in various novitiates to come together for one formation program that would eventually be a key part of the evolution of a centralized Congregation.[65] In 1816, she bought a ruined castle and began a seven-year process of overseeing the renovations necessary to make of it a motherhouse.

While they were in the midst of the process of construction, the pastor of a neighboring parish brought some orphan girls who needed care, and the new building became an orphanage as well as a convent. Adjusting plans to meet the needs of the neighbor would never be an insurmountable problem for Mother Saint John.

> The community's poverty was apparently public knowledge. A concerned pastor asked postulants from his parish if they had enough to eat. They told him not to worry, that they generally had a dinner of five courses. What they did not explain was that those five were broth, vegetables, a piece of cheese, a piece of bread and watered-down milk. When they got home and accidently spilled ashes on their dinner they decided that they should let him know that they really enjoyed six courses.

A different kind of challenge arose when the renovated convent was ready for its formal opening on November 28, 1823. The new vicar of the archdiocese, Father Brouchard, came to inspect the construction and was scandalized by the large windows that the superior had ordered. From her perspective, the large windows promoted the physical and emotional health of the inhabitants. In his opinion, they were a luxury opposed to the spirit of poverty. Exercising his

---

65 *Mother Sacred Heart*, 134.

authority as ecclesiastical superior, he said he would not permit the novices to reside in the house until the windows were changed.[66] Mother Saint John accepted the imposition of his authority but, instead of remodeling the house, she waited for the arrival of the new apostolic administrator, Bishop Jean-Paul Gaston de Pins. There is no record of how she explained the problem to him, but after a little more than three months in which the novices could not reside in the house, the bishop revoked the restrictions and on March 5, 1824, all the sisters began to stay under one roof in a house bright with sunlight.[67]

THE LE PUY RESTORATION AND THE ESTABLISHMENT OF CENTRALIZED RELIGIOUS CONGREGATIONS
LE PUY

Le Puy to St. Etienne~ 48 Miles
Le Puy to Lyon~82 Miles

The community at Bas-en-Basset, like every other community of the Sisters of St. Joseph, had its origins in Le Puy. Like the hundreds of other communities throughout France, it would have been a small congregation under the authority of the bishop of Le Puy, usually receiving and training its own new members while maintaining relationship with the other congregations of the diocese and giving special recognition to the founding community of Le Puy. The rule and customs under which Mother St. John was received were those developed in Le Puy and there is every reason to believe that the sisters belonging to distinct communities

---

66 It is an interesting concept of poverty that demands costly renovations to simplify the sisters' lifestyle.
67 *Sencilla*, 216-218, Rivaux, 130. There seems to be some confusion among the different sources about the dates of these incidents. When Napoleon lost power, Cardinal Fesch left France, but retained his title as Archbishop of Lyon. In 1823, Bishop de Pins replaced him to administer the Archdiocese of Lyon, serving in that post until 1840. 45-46 The dates come from Sisters Dolorita Dougherty, Helen Angela Hurley, Emily Joseph Daly and St. Claire Coyne, The Sisters of St. Joseph of Carondelet (St. Louis: Herder, 1966), 45-46. Hereafter referred to as Dougherty.

collaborated to the extent that circumstances would allow. At the time of the Revolution, the sisters in Le Puy lost their motherhouse and formal ministries; the sisters were dispersed and as we have seen, some of them were martyrs.[68]

After the trauma of the Revolution, beginning around 1807, Mother Anne Marie Grand and her companions, Sisters Antoinette Marie Tallogros and Anne Marie Robert began a long process of negotiations with civil and military authorities to recuperate their property in Le Puy. Although they eventually succeeded, it took a royal decree to achieve the return the property to the sisters in a manner that was not only legally binding but supposedly "amicable" as the "residents" returned the keys to the superior.[69] Except for its location in the city, the recovered motherhouse property bore precious little resemblance to the well cared for institution the sisters had built up over the course of more than 150 years.

In the time of its occupation by the military, the Montferrand property had housed far more people than it was meant for, at one point using seventeen rooms to hold forty beds serving eighty men.[70] The remains of the chapel were a disaster. Having served for a time as a stable, most of the removable wood had been utilized for heating such that when the sisters first returned to it "a glacial wind blew through the holes in the walls and broken windows."[71] But the sisters' zealous determination proved more than a match for the Revolutionary destruction.

It was not until 1814 that the Sisters of St. Joseph in Le Puy, commonly known as "hospitalières of Montferrand," received formal title to their former home. Even then, their legal struggles were not over. In order to be officially authorized, every religious congregation had to file formal papers to both religious and civil authorities explaining their goals and the means they would use to reach them. With preliminary approval, they were then to reorganize their rules in accordance with Napoleonic legislation. For the Sisters of St. Joseph of Le Puy, as for those of Lyon, this entailed a revision of their congregational organization. Whereas the superior at Le Puy had traditionally held a primacy of honor as the superior of the original foundation, the new legislation would extend and formalize her authority over the communities in the diocese. In April, 1827, a royal ordinance authorized the Montferrand house in Le Puy as a Motherhouse. By October of that year, sixty individual communities were united under the authority of that center,

---

68 For the history of the Le Puy congregation and the martyrs see F. Gouit, *Une Congrégation Salésienne, Les Soeurs de Saint Joseph du Puy-en-Velay*, 1648-1915 (Le Puy, Imprimerie de la Haute-Loire, 1930).
69 Gouit, 245.
70 The property had been commandeered as a residence for indigent veterans.
71 Gouit, 246.

each retaining a local superior, but all subject to the Superior at Le Puy in the motherhouse, Montferrand. Over the course of more than two decades the sisters would experiment with their organization until in 1852 their bishop approved an ordinance with nineteen statutes regulating the governance of the community. That new rule reflected the *Primitive Constitutions* of the Sisters of St. Joseph while organizing the sisters into a single Congregation under the leadership of a general superior and with a common novitiate.[72]

LYON EXTENDS HER INFLUENCE WITHIN AND BEYOND THE ARCHDIOCESE

The Lyon house was not renovated and furnished simply because the community needed more space. In accord with the Napoleonic legislation, Mother Saint John planned it to be the "mother house" of many communities. Over time, she had come to see the logic of uniting dispersed communities in a single congregation with numerous houses. She had various reasons for reaching that conclusion.

As described above, communities of St. Joseph had multiplied in various dioceses in France. Some of those communities lacked the basic human and material resources to be able to carry out their ministries or have a quality community life. Additionally conducting a formation program in each community was a duplication of effort and ran the risk of having formation programs too diverse to maintain fidelity to the foundational charism of the institute. Finally the new laws of the Republic of France promoted the centralization of congregations of religious.[73]

In addition, the sisters' organization as fully independent communities suffered from an institutionalized flaw. Although the Cardinal was the ecclesiastical superior of all of the communities of St. Joseph in his archdiocese, each of those communities remained independent of the others with local superiors answerable to the bishop. Over time, the sisters began to recognize this as a weakness because it allowed the Cardinal (or the bishop of any diocese in which they lived) to make changes in the communities while the sisters themselves had no broad unifying structure or levels of internal appeal. For the sisters, congregational unity offered them better structures for formation and service. In the mind of the Cardinal and his uncle Napoleon, the motive for union was the efficacy of unified governance.

---

72 The Lyon Congregation's revised *Constitutions* of 1858 were similar and may have been based on Le Puy's.
73 A note in the Rivaux text Life of Mother St. John, says, "Until their dispersion in 1793, the different houses of our congregation had been independent like those of The Visitation. But after the restoration of peace, Napoleon permitted the sisters to return to communal life under the condition that there would be a motherhouse, responsible for the affiliated houses. This mandate together with practical reasons led our communities dispersed throughout France, to form diocesan Congregations, of which Lyon, Bourg, Le Puy, Clermont, Aix Vams, Saint-Fervaise-sur-Marc and Annecy have come to be the most important." (Rivaux, 127, note 1.)

The organization of a congregation with centralized governance was truly an immense change, a radical reformation of Medaille's "Little Design." At the same time, it conformed perfectly to Medaille's inspiration in that it was a response to the needs of the time.[74] That reorganization took place in both Le Puy and Lyon at different times.

The new union of communities under Lyon took in more than established communities of St. Joseph. One example of the Congregation's openness to a diversity of membership and ministry is the group called the "Charlottes." Their community began with the work of a woman named Charlotte Dupin, a "popular saint" who, after having been jailed during the Reign of Terror, began her own pastoral ministry to prisoners. She brought them everything she could to alleviate their suffering and she also evangelized them. For those sentenced to death, she discovered the details of their planned execution and arranged for their families to stand in a predetermined place along the route to the execution site in order to be able to bid farewell to the condemned, at least by way of gestures. She made a similar arrangement with priests who would give absolution to the condemned as they passed by.[75]

Charlotte's ministry attracted followers. After her death, some of the fifty women who shared her mission decided to found a congregation to assure the continuity of the apostolate. The bishop approved their idea, but instead of permitting them to found a new congregation, he recommended that they unite with the Sisters of St. Joseph. Thus, in 1819, a woman named Jeanne Juliand and a companion presented themselves to Mother Saint John Fontbonne and were accepted into the novitiate with the understanding that, once professed, they would continue in their distinctive ministry. The prison apostolate continued to attract vocations and became a specialty within the congregation. As years passed, the sisters began to realize that this apostolate was so specialized that it could be better carried out by a separate congregation. In 1841, the sisters who wished to do so founded the Congregation of Mary and Joseph to continue the apostolate begun by Charlotte Dupin. When this group separated from the Sisters of St. Joseph,

---

74 The 1801 Concordat brought France peace with Rome. As the product of long negotiations and concessions, it was an exceptionally decisive action on the part of the Vatican, allowing the diocesan structure of the Church in France to be radically reorganized. According to Montalban (*Historia* 394) the pope, using the plenitude of his powers, on November 19, 1801, promulgated the Bull of Suppression of the old dioceses of France, authorizing his legate to institute the new bishops. "Never in the history of the Church of God has there been seen a similar exercise of the plenitude of papal power: the deposition of such a large number of bishops without any canonical process, and only because it was demanded for the good of the Church." With many of the non-jurors summarily removed by Rome,there must have been great confusion if not real bitterness.

75 *Sencilla* 239.

Mother St. John insisted that each sister in the congregation be permitted to choose to which of the two groups she felt most called, thus allowing approximately 200 sisters to form a new specialized congregation.[76]

While the "Charlottes" were integrating themselves in the congregation, another unique situation came to Mother Saint John's attention. This had to do with a 52-year-old woman named Reina Françon who asked to be admitted to the congregation. Her history offers a window through which to observe various facets of life in the post-Revolutionary era.

Reina Françon was born in 1770, one of eleven children of peasant parents. When Reina was four years old, their home burned and the family had to migrate to the city. Their poverty was such that when she was ten, Reina's parents were compelled to send her to live with a woman who had promised to teach her to weave. Tragically, it turned out that the woman treated Reina almost like a slave. Unable to escape, Reina lived like Cinderella except that she was not the only child in the house who suffered like that - the woman had numerous children under her dominion. During the years that she spent under those circumstances, Reina sustained her hope with the dream that she would one day consecrate her life to the rescue of children who suffered her same fate.

When she finally escaped from her servitude, she found the needs of her family so desperate that she spent the next twenty years working to provide for her elderly parents. In 1820, at the age of 50, she was finally free to pursue her dream. Within one year, she acquired a house to shelter 20 orphans and also obtained the help of other women who were moved by her zeal and helped her found a well-organized orphanage. Before long, Reina realized that she needed more support to assure the longevity of her project. With that, she turned to Mother Saint John.

Although her age was against her, her spirit of service to the neighbor fit in perfectly with the mission of the Congregation. Because of that, Mother St. John accepted her into the novitiate. After making vows, Reina returned to her orphanage which had come under the sponsorship of the Sisters of St. Joseph. She lived there until her death, spending the last nineteen years of her life as a member of a local community of Sisters of St. Joseph dedicated to the care of girls.

While Mother St. John's new congregation received vocations, some smaller communities continued to resist the movement toward participating in a congregation which would unify the diverse communities of St. Joseph in the diocese. They feared that union entailed a loss of independence and they were not sure about accepting an unknown superior general.

---

76 *Sencilla*, 239-264

In one legendary case, it seems that Mother Saint John went to visit one of those resistant communities without their knowing who she was. She presented herself among them as a sister from the Lyon community who needed a place to stay while she attended to some affairs in their town. She spent time conversing with the sisters and they thoroughly enjoyed their visitor from Lyon. Some of them took advantage of conversation to make subtle inquiries about the motherhouse in Lyon and relationships within the growing congregation. Nobody suspected why their visitor was so well informed about the state of the congregation until she was preparing to return to Lyon. Then one of the local sisters announced, "I think that the woman about to take her leave is Mother Saint John." She could not deny it. Instead of leaving, she remained with them and dispersed their fears. Before long, that community joined the congregation.[77]

That was not the last time that Mother Saint John would pass unperceived in the midst of a group. One day, after having conversed with the postulants about the vow of obedience, she accompanied them to the kitchen. When they left, she had not properly closed the door. From inside the kitchen, without knowing who had accompanied the young people, the sister-cook shouted: "Whoever left the door open, kneel down, and kiss the floor!" When the cook came out to see who had responded to her order, she was mortified to find the superior general on her knees with her head touching the floor. Then the guilty party stood and said nothing more than "I am the one who committed the infraction.[78]

Just as she could show a sense of humor, she could also stand up for her sisters when necessary, and she knew how to choose her battles. One time, at the request of the Vicar, Father Cholleton, the sisters accepted the ministry of running a house for the chronically ill poor in Ainay. Before long, they discovered that the lay people who formed the administrative council of the house, refused to give them the power necessary to organize the institution. Experience quickly proved that the dissension perturbing the administrators, the families, and the patients themselves was more than enough to obstruct a successful ministry. Seeing that, Mother Saint John supported the sisters' decision to leave the institution. They were replaced by the Daughters of Charity who were similarly unable to bring order to the house and stayed less than six months. Father Cholleton returned to ask Mother Saint John's help. She accepted his request, but only after being assured that very clear conditions would have to be met before the sisters would return. While Mother St. John tried to respond to every request for sisters, she

---

77 *Sencilla*, 436-437.
78 *Sencilla*, 280.

knew there would never be enough sisters to mission any of them to impossible situations.[79]

On another occasion, Father Charles Cholleton made the mistake of getting too involved in the affairs of the sisters.[80] He had sent a very intelligent young woman to enter the congregation. He suggested that, even before she made vows, she should take the role of director of studies for the novices. Mother Saint John agreed, but problems quickly arose. When the young woman presented herself to ask to make vows, the council and the directors of novices decided that she should wait until she had developed more humility and simplicity. When the Vicar heard this, he acted with all the power he had as ecclesiastical superior. He accused the directors of novices of acting out of envy and ordered them to leave their post. It reached the extreme that he took the liberty to decide where the sisters would be sent on mission. With that, Mother Saint John refused to accept any more of his authoritarianism. One of the novice directors was her niece and Father Cholleton had tried to assign her to a ministry thoroughly out of keeping with her personality and her capabilities. When faced with the resolution of the Superior General, the Vicar backed down.[81]

THE BIRTH OF NEW CONGREGATIONS
Bourg, Gap and Bordeaux
In addition to her work of uniting Sisters of St. Joseph in Lyon, Mother St. John Fontbonne also played a role in the establishment of a number of Congregations of Sisters of St. Joseph. Among the first were those established successively in Belley, Gap and Bordeaux under Mother St. Joseph Chanay who had made her novitiate in Lyon. Mother St. John sent Mother St. Joseph Chanay to found the community at Belley, a town of approximately 4,000 inhabitants about 60 miles east of Lyon. The community became independent of Lyon after 1823 when Belley was made a diocese. The motherhouse eventually moved to Bourg where the community became known as the Sisters of St. Joseph of Bourg, a congregation that would found a mission in Bay St. Louis, Louisiana in 1854.

---

79 *Sencilla*, 345 - 358. An apocryphal detail about this story says that when the Daughters of Charity arrived, they had arranged for the delivery of an image of St. Vincent de Paul for the convent. When the package arrived, the image was not of Vincent, but rather of St. Joseph. The sisters returned the image, clarifying that they were asking for a statue of Vincent. The second package arrived, and again it contained an image of Joseph. With that, the sisters decided that they could not overcome fate and they put the image in their house.

80 This was most likely Father Charles Cholleton, the nephew of Father Claude Cholleton who had brought the Black Sisters to Mother St. John. He also represented Bishop Rosati's interests with the Propagation of the Faith in Lyon.

81 *Sencilla*, 362 - 364. The text adds the detail that after the death of Mother Saint John, the sister protégé of the Vicar left the congregation.

Mother St. Joseph Chaney
1795-1853
Foundress of Bourg, Gap & Bordeaux.

Nearly fifteen years after the foundation of the Congregation of Bourg, the Vicar General from Bourg, Nicolas-Augustin de la Croix D`Azolette, was named bishop of Gap which is situated some 140 miles southeast of Lyon. The new bishop quickly invited Mother St. Joseph to return to that place where Sisters of St. Joseph had served from 1671 until they were dispersed by the Revolution. Although her health prevented her from staying more than three years, the Gap community established in 1837 flourished.[82] Mother St. Joseph's final foundation was at Bordeaux, nearly 350 miles to the southwest of Lyon. There, on December 10, 1840, she established the congregation of the Sisters of St. Joseph of Bordeaux.[83]

Chambery, Turin, Pignorol, Annecy, Cuneo

One of Mother St. John Fontbonne's first postulants at St. Etienne, Sister St. John (Suzanne) Marcoux (1785-1855), not only became one of her most trusted companions, but also a leader to whom the elder Mother St. John would confide the first mission of the sisters outside of the Archdiocese of Lyon.[84] It was an interesting assignment in that Cardinal Fesch, concerned about the situation of young women in Aix-les-Baix, specifically asked for the help of Sister St. John Marcoux, but he neglected to let the bishop of nearby Chambéry know that she and two companions were being sent. After some uncomfortable confusion upon their arrival, the sisters took up residence in the ruins of a chateau where they began to nurse the wounded soldiers residing in the house. Before long they opened a school, keeping for their "convent" an attic large enough to house their three cots.[85]

---

82 These foundations are described in Rivaux, 177-181. Rivaux mentions that when Mother St. Joseph went to the hot springs at Aix to recover her health, she unexpectedly met Mother St. John Fontbonne there, giving the two the opportunity to share their joys and concerns about the growing congregations.
83 In 1996, the congregations of Bourg and Bordeaux merged with their founding congregation, the Sisters of St. Joseph of Lyon.
84 The post-Revolution Archdiocese of Lyon was officially established in 1801. Its history reaches back to the second century when Saints Pothinus and Irenaeus served successively as its first bishops
85 According to Sister Benedict De Vaublanc of Chambery, when the Cardinal came to visit the sisters his surprise at not being invited to sit down was compounded by the discovery that the sisters had no furniture at all. (Essay: Mother St. John Marcoux, available on the web (sistersofstjosephfederation.org).

Lyon continued to send sisters to Chambéry until 1816, when the fall of Napoleon made the territory of Savoy, including the city of Chambery, independent of France. With that, the Sisters of St. Joseph in Chambéry established their own novitiate and became independent of the Lyon Congregation. Having survived an epidemic in 1815, and famine in 1817, Mother St. John Marcoux did not hesitate to send sisters over the Alps so that in 1821, they established a community in Turin and in 1828, in Pinerolo, both now part of Italy.[86] In 1833, the sisters in Pignerol founded a community in Annecy (now in France), and the sisters from Turin established a community in Navarre (Italy) in 1826. During that same time period, the Congregation of Cuneo (Italy) was established by the Italian priest, Giovanni Manassero who obtained the *Constitutions* from the community at Lyon.[87]

In 1822, only a year after the foundation in Turin, a priest from Saint Jean-de-Maurienne asked for sisters to take over a poorly managed and run-down hospital in that town. Willing to have her sisters accept the mission but wary of the extent of the challenge, Mother St. John Marcoux herself accompanied the sisters to the village on June 2, 1822. In 1826, the community became independent of the Chambéry motherhouse and in 1882, they extended their mission to America by founding the Sisters of St. Joseph of Buenos Aires, Argentina.

In 1824, while he was exiled in Rome, Cardinal Fesch obtained papal support in asking that fourteen sisters from Lyon, including Mother St. John Marcoux, found a community in that city. Having no will to reject such an authoritative request, Mother St. John Marcoux secretly left Chambéry and went to Lyon to choose thirteen companions. When political problems prevented the foundation from taking place, Mother St. John Fontbonne hoped that her former novice and companion could remain with her as a much needed assistant, but the sisters in Lyon protested, fearing that Mother St. John Marcoux would introduce a regime stricter than they wanted. Mother St. John Fontbonne, reluctant to cause division, abandoned the plan and Mother St. John Marcoux returned to Chambéry. By 1828, with changes in the local church, the community established its own novitiate and became independent of Chambéry.[88]

---

86 Pinerolo was founded at the request of Bishop Rey who had been Vicar General in Chambéry. The history of Chambéry recounts the anecdote that Bishop Rey had a difficult time learning the language of Pinerolo, while Mother Espérance, the superior had great facility for it. The bishop had a practice of inviting the poor for a meal and religious instruction. Given the circumstances, the bishop decided to wait on tables and asked Mother Espérance to give the instructions. (Bouchage, 276)

87 In the 21st century, the Cuneo community has members in Italy, the Democratic Republic of Congo, Cameroon, Argentina and Brazil.

88 Additional information about the Chambéry foundations is found in Bouchage, 199-286.

In 1825, Mother St. John Marcoux accompanied two of her community, Sisters Constance and Victoire, to Moutiers, a small city about fifty miles east of Chambery. Beginning in 1854, the Moutiers community would send sisters to the United States. By 1867, a total of thirty-nine Moutiers missionaries arrived to minister with the Carondelet sisters and also establishing a short-lived, independent French mission in Oconto, Wisconsin.[89]

FORTY YEARS AFTER THE REVOLUTION

In 1830, Mother Saint John Fontbonne was seventy years old and had been a Sister of St. Joseph since the age of eighteen. Her years had been among the most turbulent in Western history. The story of her life summarized the experience of many people of her era. Far from being a lone heroine, she was one of a number of saints and leaders in an era of great faith. Among the saints, the most well-known was St. John Vianney, a collaborator, friend and advisor to Mother St. John and other Sisters of St. Joseph. Among the outstanding leaders of Sisters of St. Joseph were Mother Anne Marie Grand of Le Puy whose experience paralleled her own in so many ways and her protégé, Mother St. John Marcoux who was second only to her mentor in spreading the charism and expanding the horizons of the Sisters of St. Joseph. Among them these three women set a course for the post-Revolutionary Sisters of St. Joseph that would continue for centuries to come.

The chaos and suffering caused by the Revolution had led the faithful of France to clarify and deepen their commitment. Aggression against the Church forced those who persevered to discern and discover how the deep meaning of Christianity stood in contrast to the factions, philosophies and political movements that presented themselves as omniscient. Facing the risk of martyrdom had shed laser-like light on the difference between events of passing importance and commitments that cannot be broken or brokered. For Mother Saint John Fontbonne and many of her generation, the tragedy of the Revolution was transformed into the grace that helped them develop a deeper faith and genuine holiness.

From the first days of her religious life, Mother Saint John had learned to adjust her plans and dreams to respond to the needs that surrounded her. She was a woman of strong will and willing obedience. In Salesian terms, she embraced

---

89 The sisters in Oconto decided to join with Carondelet and maintained a long-term presence in Oconto.

the need to continually adapt herself, ceding her personal desire and following God's will as it became manifest through the signs of the times.[90]

In addition to preparing her for martyrdom, the conflicts and theological confusion engendered by the Revolution helped her develop a critical consciousness. While the apostasy of her pastor taught her to beware of blind confidence in people who occupied positions of authority, she was still capable of collaborating with a powerful Cardinal who called her to begin a project she had never imagined. Following along that path, she was able to open that project to such new expressions that it would spread from Europe to India, Africa, the Americas and Australia.

Before she died, Mother Saint John had founded or reorganized more than 240 houses of the Congregation, not to mention those that came to life in foreign lands after her death. Like the Black Daughters, some of the communities who joined with her came from traditions that had little in common with the Little Design. As Superior General, she led her sisters in such a way that they allowed themselves to be in a continual process of reform as they responded to the needs of the times or, in the words of the *Primitive Constitutions*, so that they would always "be of better service to others."

The figure of Mother Saint John Fontbonne whom we meet in the traditions is a holy and wise woman. Instead of conceiving a plan and making it happen, she opened herself so that the plan of God could take flesh and become history – in her and in the neighbor. This is the woman who, in the third decade of the nineteenth century, when she was 77 years old, opened the congregation to a new expression of its Catholicism: a foundation in America.

---

90 St. Francis de Sales made a distinction between what a person or community discerned to be the will of God and what he called the "will of God's good pleasure." The first is known through prayer, tradition and discerning decision, the latter is manifest in the events and realities of the world that surrounds us. One of the greatest sacrifices a person can make is to let go of the first in order to respond faithfully to the second. (See Letters, 41-42).

ಚಿ
Chapter Three: Little Design Goes to America

Cast of Characters

Mother St. John Fontbonne – Lyon (1759 – 1843)
Bishop Joseph Rosati – Bishop of St. Louis (1827-1843)
Father Charles Cholleton – Lyon
Countess Felicité De La Rochejacquelein – Lyon
Pauline Jaricot - The Society for the Propagation of the Faith – Lyon
Rev. John Timon, C.M. – accompanied Bishop Rosati in New Orleans

THE FIRST FRENCH MISSIONARIES:
Sisters

Febronie Fontbonne	Delphine Fontbonne
Saint Protais Deboille	Philoméne Vilaine
Febronie Chapellon	M. Felicité Bouté
Celestine Pommerel	St. John Fournier

The unprecedented decision of the Sisters of St. Joseph of Lyon to establish a mission in America can be compared to Mother Saint John's decision to receive Father Claude Cholleton's "Black Daughters" as Sisters of St. Joseph. Once again something never dreamed of came into being through relationships among people who did not originally know one another and who had not planned to work together. Around the year 1835, the Countess de la Rochejacquelein, influenced by The Society for the Propagation of the Faith, brought the Sisters of St. Joseph into contact with Father Charles Cholleton and Bishop Rosati of St. Louis.

THE SOCIETY FOR THE PROPAGATION OF THE FAITH

The Society for the Propagation of the Faith began with the dream of Pauline Jaricot, a nineteen-year-old woman from Lyon. In 1818, moved by hearing stories of the poverty of missionaries, she decided to do something for them. She organized groups of friends and friends of friends who gave a penny a week for the missions and eventually found that they were amassing a substantial collection. Between 1820 and 1822, Blessed Pauline's organization sent over 7,500 francs to the missions.[1] In 1823, a group of clerics and laymen who wanted to help Bishop DuBourg of Louisiana organized and called themselves The Society for the

---

1 Pauline and her work received a good share of criticism; some priests even called it schismatic. It seems that their real problem was jealousy and the fear that their preferred missions would lose out because of the work of Jaricot's organization. See Edward Hickey, *The Society for The Propagation of the Faith: Its Foundation, Organization, Success* (1822-1922), The Catholic University of America Studies in American Church History, no. 3, (Washington, 1922, reprint, New York, 1974).

Propagation of the Faith and persuaded Pauline to bring her groups into their society. By 1825, the Society had spread throughout France and become an international organization. In the year 1836, the members collected 727,000 francs, a third of which was destined for French missioners working in the territory of the United States.[2]

As part of their fundraising efforts the Society began to publish official "Annals" which highlighted mission stories designed to touch the heart and open the purses of potential benefactors. The Annals effectively exposed a great many people to heroic stories previously heard only from itinerant missionaries making parish visits. Lyon, the city in which the Society was founded, remained the center of its activities and therefore became a preferred stopping place for foreign missionaries looking for support.

BISHOP ROSATI AND FATHER CHARLES CHOLLETON
In 1826, Father Joseph Rosati was named the first bishop of the diocese of St. Louis. His territory included the state of Missouri, western Illinois and all of the U.S. territory north of Louisiana and west to the Rocky Mountains. Rosati wasted no time before turning to the Society for help. He asked Reverend Charles Cholleton, the Vicar General of Lyon and an active member of the Society, to serve as his Vicar in relation to the Society.[3] Father Cholleton accepted the request and promised to do all that was possible to secure funds for the mission.[4] The relationship between Bishop Rosati and Reverend Cholleton opened a door for the noblewoman Félicité de Duras to act on her enormous enthusiasm for sending Sisters of St. Joseph to America as missionaries.

THE COUNTESS FELICITÉ DE LA ROCHEJACQUELEIN
Félicité de Duras, the Countess de la Rochejacquelein, experienced the aftermath of the French Revolution from the vantage point of

Félicité de Duras
1789 - 1883

---

2 France's mission history in North America began before the foundation of the Sisters of St. Joseph with heroic efforts like that of Isaac Jogues (+1646) and his companions. The French evangelized in Canada, what became the Northeast of the U.S. and the Louisiana territory. With the exile resulting from the French Revolution and later Church-State problems, French missionaries also emigrated to areas of America that were not traditionally under French influence, including the southwestern territories ceded to the U.S. from Mexico (Texas, New Mexico, Arizona, Colorado).
3 Father Charles Cholleton was nephew of Father Claude Cholleton who introduced Mother Saint John to the Black Daughters.
4 A translation of that letter can be found in the CSJ Congregational archives (Archives, Carondelet).

the nobility. The daughter of the Duchess of Duras, she married the Prince of Talmont, was widowed at the age of seventeen and later married the Count de la Rochejacquelein and was again widowed. This combination of family relations connected her to nobility throughout Europe and provided her with a significant fortune that included extensive landholdings.

The Countess came to know the Sisters of St. Joseph in 1812, when they established a school and a hospital in Aix-les Bains, near one of her estates.[5] In 1824, she asked Mother Saint John Fontbonne to open a school near her property in Saint Aubin and Tuerna in the southwest of France.[6]

The pious Countess belonged to the Third Order of St. Francis and gave generously to the Society for the Propagation of the Faith. Her reading of the stories published by the Society for the Propagation of the Faith kindled her great enthusiasm for the missions in America and led her to dream of sending Sisters of St. Joseph to Missouri, a locale frequently featured in the Annals. She knew Father Cholleton and through that connection began to correspond with Bishop Rosati. This correspondence reveals her desire to send missionaries, and also her strong personality and unflagging initiative. Writing to the bishop of St. Louis on June 10, 1835, she expressed her respect as well as her impatience at not having received a response to her offer to sponsor Sisters of St. Joseph as missionaries in Missouri. Carefully explaining her motives, her concrete hopes and her deep esteem for the Sisters of Saint Joseph, she assured the bishop of their readiness to serve any need. She wrote:

> I think the excellent Father Odin and the Vicar General of Lyon have written to you several times on the subject of the desire I have to send Sisters of St. Joseph to America. Your silence on this subject proves either that the letters did not reach you or that you are not anxious for this establishment.[7] If, indeed, you have any objections to it, I wonder what they may be.

Bishop Guiseppe Rosati, CM
1789-1843

---

5 The sisters went to Aix-les-Bains at the request of Cardinal Fesch, but unbeknownst to the local bishop. This mission became the founding mission for the Congregation of the Sisters of St. Joseph of Chambery.
6 *Sencilla*, 311-312. Her estates in Southwestern France were significantly distant from the majority of the missions of the Sisters of St. Joseph.
7 Bishop Rosati did not seem to be actively seeking missionary sisters, at least for the city of St. Louis. In 1832, he told the Sisters of the Visitation that the educational needs of St. Louis were well cared for, but they could open a school in Kaskaskia Illinois. The Sisters of Loretto had already established a school in The Barrens (Perryville, Missouri) in 1828.

It is not a vague idea to do a good work in America which has made me propose them to you…

These incomparable Sisters, once they are established, could be sent two by two into little villages, and there prepare the way for Baptism, First Communion and Confirmation…

My Lord, perhaps you do not know the Sisters of St. Joseph…They work in free schools, paid boarding houses, great hospitals, hospices for the elderly or abandoned children, jails, refuges for the poor, home care for the sick, the care of people with scabies and ringworm; in pharmacies, at manual labor, sewing and weaving.

If you had seen, as I, their spirit of poverty and humility; it is evangelical…The East of France is alive with the activity of these Sisters. I have sent them to the West. They are not numerous enough for the demands…I know a foundation which began in a stable and with only six cents…

My Lord, the spirit of the Congregation of Saint Joseph is something without precedent….if I succeed in establishing the Sisters of St. Joseph in your America…I shall have done, during my life, something pleasing to God to win His mercy for my sins. ..

I pray you to answer as soon as possible. I am anxious that the work be accomplished…I am imposing on your time which is so valuable. Permit me to ask you to remember me to Madame Henrietta Kersaint, my cousin, a Religious of the Sacred Heart in Saint Louis. I ask her prayers and yours particularly, while begging you to accept my sentiments of respectful consideration and devotion in Our Lord.

I have the honor of being your very humble and very obedient servant, Félicité de Duras, Countess de la Rochejacquelein.[8]

In that long letter the Countess might have imposed on the bishop's time, but she was passionate about her plan and refused to let it die of inertia. Knowing that she already had a cousin who was a Religious of the Sacred Heart missioned in Missouri, one might wonder why the Countess wanted to send the Sisters of St. Joseph. Her explanation was that she had seen their service, appreciated their religious spirit and most particularly she believed in their freedom and ability to take on any work of charity, including that of being itinerant missionaries. Even if the early sisters did not take on the tasks the Countess envisioned, the Sisters of St. Joseph's willingness to assume any ministry of which a woman is capable has made it possible for the Congregation to grow in unexpected ways. Obviously, the first missionary Sisters of St. Joseph went to Missouri primarily due to the tenacity

---

8 Excerpted and translated from *Sencilla* 522-525.

of the Countess Félicité de Duras.

Bishop Rosati's overriding concern was that his immense diocese lacked funds and priests. If he sought sisters at all, tradition says that he wanted sisters who were prepared to teach the deaf, a specialty that did not exist among the Sisters of St. Joseph in Lyon in 1836.[9] Although the Sisters of St. Joseph did accept the invitation Father Cholleton extended in the name of the bishop, there is no indication that Mother Saint John or her sisters

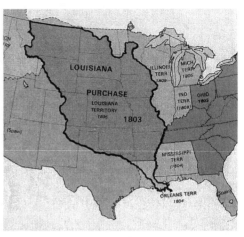

THE DIOCESE OF ST. LOUIS

In 1815, Louis DuBourg was appointed bishop of Louisiana and the Floridas. He made St. Louis his provisional episcopal city in an area that stretched from the Gulf of Mexico to the Canadian border and from the territory of the Louisiana Purchase to the Rocky Mountains. DuBourg resigned his see in 1826 while visiting Europe, leaving Joseph Rosati, his coadjutor, to inherit the vast diocese. In 1826, the diocese of St. Louis was separated from Louisiana and the new diocese included Missouri, the western half of Illinois and all the American territory west of the Mississippi and north of the State of Louisiana, making its territory equal to that of the other nine U.S. dioceses existing at that time.

In 1827, the diocese had 14 priests, and in 1828, Rosati reported that there were seven communities of women religious running schools. In 1832, Bishop Rosati invited the Sisters of the Visitation to open a school in the area of Kaskaskia, about 70 miles south of St. Louis, because he felt that the educational needs of the City were well met.

had previously considered overseas mission a part of their ministry. There is not even evidence that the Sisters of St. Joseph were involved with the Society for the Propagation of the Faith. It was the Countess who forged the connections among all of the principal characters. It was she whose zeal prompted her to use her web of relationships to create something new. Weaving together the diverse threads

---

9 Bishop Rosati's concern for the deaf is unexplained, especially in light of the fact that in 1837, there were apparently no deaf children in the area near Carondelet or the city of St. Louis. The sisters' first deaf pupil came from 75 miles south of St. Louis. In 1836, the only religious congregation in Lyon which specialized in the teaching of the deaf was the Sisters of St. Charles, but they were unable to accept a mission in Saint Louis. See Sister Dolorita Dougherty, CSJ, et al., *The Sisters of St. Joseph of Carondelet*, (St. Louis: The Herder Book Company, 1966) 53.

of her esteem for the Congregation, her generosity and her missionary spirit, she inspired and funded a radically new missionary outreach on the part of the Sisters of St. Joseph. It appears that only at her insistence did Bishop Rosati accept the plan to send six sisters to St. Louis – with the promise that two others would follow when they had prepared for ministry to the deaf.[10]

MOTHER ST. JOHN SENDS MISSIONARIES FROM LYON :
THE 1836 FOUNDATION

Under Mother Saint John's leadership in Lyon, the Congregation had enjoyed continual growth and Sisters of St. Joseph were invited to serve in more and more areas of France. There was no lack of opportunities to serve the neighbor and it seemed there were never enough sisters to meet the needs. Nevertheless, in spite of the requests that poured in from different areas in France, at the insistence of their patroness and with the support of Father Cholleton, Mother Saint John Fontbonne accepted the proposition to send a group of missionaries to the diocese of Saint Louis.

When she asked for volunteers, her own two nieces figured among the many sisters who offered themselves.[11] When it came time to name the missionaries, Mother St. John absented herself from the council meeting in order to avoid prejudicing the decision. The council chose six Sisters: Delphine and Febronie Fontbonne, Febronie Chapellon, Saint Protais Débiolle, Philomène Vilaine and Marguerite-Félicité Bouté.[12] Father Cholleton named Sister Febronie Fontbonne as the superior of the group.[13] In addition, Sister Celestine Pommerel and a postulant, Julie Fournier, were sent to St. Etienne to study sign language.[14]

We know little about the missionaries' hopes and expectations or how the

---

10 Bishop Rosati's response to the Countess was either immediate or his correspondence crossed hers in transit. The Countess wrote her complaint in May of 1835, and the first group of Sisters of St. Joseph left for America in January of 1836. Given the slowness of mail between the two continents, the preparations were made with notable velocity. The information with the map comes from "The Life of Rt. Rev. Joseph Rosati, C.M. (Dissertation for PhD Rev. Frederick Kohn Easterly C.M. 1942 CUA Press, 1942), 110, 146, 149.

11 Whether they knew it or not, the Fontbonnes were not leaving all well at home. Their father, Claude, died within a few months of their departure for America.

12 When they began the mission, Sr. Marguerite took the name Félicité in honor of the Countess.

13 Sister Febronie Fontbonne was born at Bas on February 11, 1806, and made vows at the age of 16. Febronie Chapellon, her friend, was born in Valbenoite in 1810. Sister Delphine Fontbonne was born in 1810. Sister Félicité was born in Le Puy in 1804, and made vows in 1827; Sister St. Protais was born in 1814, and made vows in 1836, and Sister Philomène, born in 1811, also made vows in 1836. (Data from the Profession Book, Carondelet Generalate.)

14 *Sencilla,* 529. Julie Fournier transferred to the Sisters of St. Joseph from a contemplative community because she had heard of the mission and wished to participate.

other sisters felt as the six prepared for their mission across the ocean. One anecdote hints at the mixed feelings surrounding the missionaries and their venture. According to Mother St. John's biography

> One of the sisters prepared a performance of the biblical scene of the father preparing for the immolation of his son. The novices acted out the sacrifice of Abraham. The allusion was too much and many tears were shed.[15]

While the obvious comparison in the play referred to the superior's sacrifice of her two nieces, a more subtle one can be seen with Abraham's readiness to go wherever God would lead him. At this moment we see the 77 year-old Mother Saint John adopting a plan that, although it was not hers, had appeared in her path with undeniable signs of being the will of God.

THE MISSION IN THE WORDS OF SISTER ST. PROTAIS
THE MISSION JOURNEY

The best record we have of the missionaries' adventures comes from the hand of Sister St. Protais whose memoir is preserved in the Carondelet archives.[16] Her account begins with the mission journey from Lyon to St. Louis.

In Sister St. Protais' own words, words that give witness to the struggle of learning a new language,

> The third of January we went at Archbishop palace to ask the benediction of Archbishop Monseigneur of Pins who had the administration of the Diocese. Cardinal Fesch, uncle of Napoleon, was exiled in Rome…[17]
> On 4 January 1836 early in morning they went at Fourvière before they depart for America. [18] The little brave and valiant Colony descended the Hill of Chartreux. At some little distance, the last contour or crescent, they turn to take the last Glance of the convent.

---

15 *Sencilla*, 529

16 Sister St. Protais wrote the memoir at the request of Sister Monica Corrigan who was collecting documentation for a history of the sisters around 1890. Sister St. Protais was born in 1814, to a prosperous family of Genas, about nine miles Southeast of Lyon. She received the habit on October 5, 1835, and participated in the founding of Cahokia, Carondelet, the St. Louis school for Negro children, and Wheeling, West Virginia. She served in many other communities until her death among the Native Americans in the Upper Peninsula of Michigan in 1892. Hereafter this will be cited as "St. Protais, Letter."

17 Jean-Paul-Gaston de Pins (b 1766) was ordained a priest in 1788, and ordained a bishop in 1817. He served as Ordinary of Béziers and of Limoges before being named Apostolic Administrator of the Archdiocese of Lyon in 1823, where he died in 1850. (Cardinal Fesch had been banished from France in 1815.)

18 Fourvière was a Marian shrine in Lyon to which Mother St. John was known to walk in the early mornings to pray before joining the community in Morning Prayer.

From the Hill of the Chartreux the Colony go to the Hill of Fourvière. They wish…to consacret themselves and to pray her to bless the mission that they go to establish.

Revd Mother John had preceded her daughters. They find their Mother prostrated at the foot of the Altar praying our blessed Lady to give her benediction to the Sisters and to be for them the Star of the Sea. Father Fontbonne offered the Holy Sacrifice of the Mass at Notre Dame of Fourviére…

When come down they had a modest breakfast at the Sisters of Apothecary of dispensary on Tupin Street to mitigate Mother St. John sorrow. The Superior of the dispensary procures with dexterity a conversation of a moment with a priest and the Superioress General during this time. The little Caravan coming out furtively to take the diligence for Paris. But what was their astonishment to see their Revd. Mother who had come to the diligence to say a last Adieu and to have a glance more of her dear children.

When they were leaving Lyons some turn. Soon the departure was accomplish back, crying and saying "Adieu city, we will see you no more", but one sister told others "Do not cry, we are going to take a little ride…[19]

In arriving in the Havre embark on the Sea; 17 January we came… They remain 49 days on the ocean. Some were very sick but others were able to wait on the sick…

Some time they had nice pleasant moment during recreation. Once a Sister say that she could not live without her Mass prayer book. Then the Supr. say -- Why Sister, could you not live without your missal? She answer - No Mother. Then she said - give it to me. It was pretty old. She took it, put fire on, burn the book, throw the ashes in the ocean. The Sister feel pretty bad. They had a good recreation on it. They say to the Sister - now you must use some other books. But when Father Fontbonne heard it he go down and bring a nice prayer book to the Sister of some kind. A grand new one. You may think how the Sister was glad to receive it…

Before they arrived on the Gulf of Mexico the vessel was taken by violent storm that the ship was most submerge and after it was so foggy and the mist was so thick that they could see nothing… They had to wait until the steamer come to bring the ship on Mississippi…

When they arrived in New Orleans they were so glad, but Father Fontbonne would not let come out until he had see the Bishop. He came

---

19 Sister St. Protais does not say how long it took their "diligence" (horse drawn carriage) to travel the 300 plus miles to Paris. The trip to La Havre port involved an additional 125 miles. According to her report, the missionaries spent two weeks in travel from the time they left Lyon until they embarked on the ocean, implying that they traveled at a reasonably rigorous pace.

Ship's Manifest with Passenger List including the Sisters

back with a carriage to take the Sisters to the Ursuline Nuns where Bishop Blanc and Bishop Rosati come to see them.[20]

By the time the Sisters arrived in St. Louis, they had been "on the way" for almost 12 weeks. They had bidden farewell to everything familiar, journeyed forty-nine days at sea and disembarked on foreign soil where they were met by their Italian missionary bishop and his U.S. born vicar, both of whom knew much more than they probably told the sisters about the hardships awaiting them. The end of the sea journey was hardly a propitious time to speak of the challenges of frontier life!

The homey report Sister St. Protais bequeathed us describes details of the journey as well as some of the feelings and values of the group. One thing that stands out is the priority the group put on prayer. Of course, private and communal prayer was the norm for the sisters, but her specific mention of visits to the Blessed Sacrament underlines the community's Eucharistic piety and the key role of prayer as a part of their journey. They were letting go of everything that they had known; they could cling to nothing other than their faith in God and their relationships with one another.

---

20 The Ursuline nuns were the first women religious to serve in what would become U.S. territory. The original group came from France in 1727, nine years after the city was founded. They arrived 98 years after the first French Ursuline missionaries had founded their congregation in Quebec. Bishop Antoine Blanc was named to New Orleans in July, 1835. The Diocese of St. Louis had been separated from New Orleans in 1825. It is likely that Bishop Rosati and Fr. Timon passed the winter there because of cold and ice that would make the River impassable.

The topic of their relationships prompts a closer look at an incident that has entered the folklore of the community, the episode of the raggedy old prayer book. At first glance this incident seems to portray an unfeeling or aloof superior, but it comes off differently when we focus on just how Sister St. Protais recalls the story. First, she puts the tale in the context of the time of recreation. Without changing her theme or tone, she relates the anecdote about the "pretty old" prayer book. Narrating the precise dialogue between the superior and the unidentified sister, she then says the book was burned and the ashes spread on the ocean. Her two final details clarify the group's feelings about the event: first she says, "They had a good recreation on it" and quotes the sisters saying "now you must use some other books." The second detail is that Father Fontbonne gave the sister a new book and she was very happy with it.[22]

This story helps us to imagine how, in an adventure that included at least two weeks of travel over land and 49 long and sometimes dangerous days on the ocean, the sisters forged unique communal bonds including the vibrant memories and inside jokes that grow out of such an intense experience. If they had lacked a sense of humor and the ability to laugh together, the journey could well have seemed interminable. In that light, instead of being an example of the callousness of a superior, the book incident appears to recall the type of joking they did together, highlighted in the spirited teasing of a sister who would not let go of a book in shambles. That interpretation gains support by recalling that Sister Febronie, the superior on the journey, was reputedly the less austere of the two Fontbonne sisters. This seems to be a celebrated story about mischievousness on the ship deck when Sister Febronie Fontbonne got carried away. If that is true, it opens a window through which to watch the group of young sisters as they laughed together and learned not to take themselves, or even their sacrifices, too seriously.

BEGINNINGS ARE HARD

Sister St. Protais' memoirs go on to chronicle the sisters' beginnings in St. Louis, sometimes providing telling details and other times only hinting at all that was entailed in their adjustment to life in America. We pick up her narrative as Bishop Rosati and Father Timon took them to a New Orleans convent. With sparse detail, she recounts the early days in America, from landing in New Orleans to the opening of the convents at Cahokia and Carondelet.

---

22 It seems likely that Sister St. Protais herself was the sister in question. She recounts vivid details and more than once in this letter she refers to herself in the third person while generally referring to others by name.

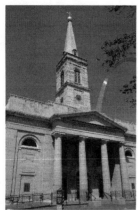

Bishop Rosati's Cathedral in St. Louis

They remain some days with the Ursulines to take little repose after the fatigue of so long voyage. The Ursulines not like to see the Sisters with their habit as they had been in ship. They said that people would think that some Nuns had escape from the convent. Before they could go in City they had to put on a cape and mourning veil. They had to go on the Mississippi in same way. The Sisters do not like it very…They were look like beggars…

When everything was ready the little caravan conducted by Rt. Rev. Bishop Rosati, Father Fontbonne and Father Timon, they ascended the Mississippi. At last they arrived in St. Louis, the Episcopal City of Bishop Rosati, March 25, 1836.

IN ST. LOUIS

When they arrived the Bishop was in hope that he been in time to say Mass, but it was too late. They go first to the Cathedral to thank God for their happy voyage. Then the Bishop sent them to the Sisters of St. Vincent Hospital. The Sisters put them in little house that they had on Third Street in the end of their garden…They try to see who could pronounce best the English. [23]

CAHOKIA

A holy priest, Father Doutreluigue, CM, Parish priest in Cahokia 3 miles from St. Louis, ardently desire to have Sisters of St. Joseph's instruct the children of this parish, compose in great part of Canadian. During two years this good priest eat only corn bread and often deprive himself of nourishment that he might found an establishment that could assist him in his holy ministry. The Bishop Rosati touch his zeal and charity decide to give him the Sisters.[24]

Then he select Mother Febronie Fontbonne that was nominate our Superieuress in Lyons was to continue and go to Cahokia. Sister Mary Febronie Chapellon and Sister St. Protais Deboille would go to Cahokia.

---

23 The Sisters of Charity arrived in St. Louis in 1829 to staff a hospital underwritten by John Mullanphy. Other women religious had preceded them in the diocese, including five Religious of the Sacred Heart who settled in St. Charles in 1818, twelve Sisters of Loretto from Kentucky who began teaching at "The Barrens," and the Sisters of the Visitation who had been at Kaskaskia since 1833.

24 Bishop Rosati had not sought teaching sisters for the city of St. Louis, but responded to Cahokia's need and then sent sisters to open a school in Carondelet.

"The Arrival," depiction of the sisters'
first experiences, by Rudy Torini,
Chapel Hall, Carondelet

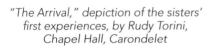

Sister M. Delphine Fontbonne, Sister Felicity Bouté and Sister Philoméne Devilaine would remain in St. Louis to learn English. The day of the depart had arrived...When they had cross the Mississippi they find number of people that had come from Cahokia with their little carts. They were waiting on shore, then everyone go on carts and started in woods. They arrived about at noon. Their first visit was in Church to adore Our Lord in Blessed Sacrament. When they had their dinner in priest house, the Priest had only two rooms, one for himself, the other his housekeeper and family, and for the cooking they had a little passage between. They had nice corn bread -- some like it very much and some not like it. After dinner the Bishop and Father Fontbonne went to the convent to fix the cooking stove.

The population of Cahokia speak a kind of French Canadian, less difficult to comprehend and to learn than the English.

Sister St. Protais (b 1814) ministered
in America for 56 years before dying
among her beloved Native Americans
on April 12, 1892.

They were all so glad and happy to receive the Sisters and with joy they prove for what they think they need.

One day a Lady send to them a large bowl of pottage of rice gombeau [gumbo] and chicken. They put it on Sisters table. But looking at it they said we could not eat for it was Friday. They told it to the Lady, who said that it had no meat, she had only boiled the chicken in it. They had grand laugh at her simplicity.

Madame Turgon, a rich lady, had built for the Sisters pretty nice Chapel close to the Convent, and the Sisters could decorate it with the ornaments that they brought from France. Immediately they open their School they had great number of children, and boarders that they were oblige to enlarge the house. Those brave Canadiens love that French establishment and the sound of the Convent bell of the little Chapel of the Sisters...They venerated the Sisters as saints and charitable country women [who] come from the same Mother as their Catholic France to have care of their sick, their poor, their children. For them they think of them as their Mothers... Bishop Rosati send them a young French priest Father Condamine in the month of August. He fell sick with bilious fever. He was on point of death...

Some of the Sisters had been very sick already, they were little better but they would not let them go to Mass and funeral...

As the Sisters were sick, Sister Philomine had to come from St. Louis to Cahokia to take care of them but one could not be cure[d]...

Mother Delphine and Sister Félicité had come to establish Carondelet Academy, that was September 12th, 1836, then Bishop Rosati send word to the Sisters of Cahokia to send the sick Sister to Carondelet...The Sister soon get well and she remain in Carondelet all the winter.[25]

While Sister St. Protais retained vivid memories of the sisters' early days, she recounted their difficulties in a decidedly understated manner. Her writing reveals that English remained challenging, but she barely alludes to the struggle of learning the new language. She tells us that the sisters did not like the fact that they had to dress in civilian clothing, but makes no point of explaining that it was necessary because of the potential perils caused by Protestant prejudice. She speaks with compassion about the death of the priest at Cahokia and mentions the illnesses of the sisters but avoids dwelling on the conditions and unhealthy climate that caused those problems. Nevertheless, reading between the lines, it is clear that the sisters' lives were in danger as they contended with the vagaries of flood-bred diseases. It was Sister St. Protais herself who fell ill and was replaced by Sister Philomène in Cahokia.

Sister St. Protais was taken to a St. Louis hospital thereby leaving Sisters Delphine and Félicité to begin the mission at Carondelet alone. In speaking of their early days, Sister St. Protais stressed the great welcome that helpful families gave the sisters from their first moments in Cahokia. She highlighted their neighbors' care for them by recalling Sister Febronie Fontbonne's near brush with death in the

---

25 St. Protais, Letter.

woods. As she told the story,

> One winter day Mother Delphine come to visit her Sister, Mother Febronie, in Cahokia and the latter accompanied Mother Delphine to Carondelet, but in going back she misly [lost] her way wandering in forest. When the Sisters find that she had not come home in the beginning of cold and severe night, all the inhabitants was moved and alarmed as well as the Sisters. They ring the alarm bell. They all came together in public place. The chief of the village said - my friends, our Sisters are in great affliction. Their Superior is lost in large forest of the pointe. We must find her whatever it may cost us. You will take torches to guide you in obscurity and your Carabins [rifles] in case of bad accident... And you will shout out [from] time to time. Have fear, [sic] Mother of Cahokia, your children are looking for you. As soon as this was given it was executed. The forest was searched in all its depth and extent.
>
> Mother Febronie, after having wandered and followed hundreds of little paths that all put her out of the way, she stopped, exhausted with hunger and fatigue. She took shelter in the hole of an old tree recommending herself to God. Sighing, groaning and praying, she had no more strength, no more hope. She prepared herself to die. Happily her groans were heard by one of the good and brave Canadians; he blew the horn and they all ran to the place where they heard the sound. The good Mother was soon surrounded with care in middle of most sensible joy...Everyone wished to carry her but one of the ancien observed to them that as she was almost frozen with cold and fright they must make her walk to reanimate and revive the heat. We will sustain and help and if it be necessary we will carry her from time to time in our arms.
>
> It is thus that the good and dear Mother was restored to her spiritual family who could not thank God enough and the good people of Cahokia for it.
>
> Mother St. John [Fontbonne] was informed of all this. She united herself to her dear Daughters to bless and thank God and the excellent population where her good children were...[26]

Maintaining her narrative restraint, Sister St. Protais let her readers know that the sisters faced very real dangers in the forests surrounding their villages. She continued with that unassuming tone as she described the Carondelet mission.

CARONDELET

The Sisters of St. Vincent of Paul were in Carondelet before the Sisters of St. Joseph with few orphans and when the Asylum near the Cathedral

---

26 Ibid.

finished they took the orphans to St. Louis.[27] They left one old cot bed and it was the bed that sick Sister had, and one night she break it. She feel very bad for the bed was not belong to them.

The difference of Cahokia [is] that the marsh swampy climate was unwholesome. Carondelet situated six miles from St. Louis on a little hill inaccessible to inundation. The air is healthy and pure.

But at the epoch when Mother Mary Delphine arrive in it with her little colony Carondelet was a small place, few houses or, rather little huts of log. The inhabitants were poor. They live on the product of wood. After they had cut it they put it on a little cart and carry it to St. Louis. After they cut the wood, grub and clear the ground and make a little garden and field. It was a hard work, the misery, and with little hope.

The Sisters had log house, two rooms and little passage, two little sheds, one for cooking, the other for the orphans when the summer came. But in the beginning they had the children in Sisters' room when they were not in school. The Sisters' room was use for oratory, dormitory, sitting room and parlor. They eat in passage.[28]

The children slept in school room. They keep their beds in garret during the day and bring them down in the evening and bring them up in morning. Often in morning their beds were cover with snow through the crevices of the roof of their habitation for the planks were not very close. When it rain they were oblige to keep an umbrella over the cooking stove in the shed.

In leaving St. Louis they had at the example of St. Theresa bring with them some covering sheets, two straw beds that they fill it up as soon as they arrive. The straw was damp. They spread it on the floor. It was their beds. The Sisters had no Chapel, not even a corner to say their prayers. They had to say them in Sisters rooms with the children and they had to go hear Mass about a square in little old wood Church. Father Saulnier

---

27 The log cottage at Carondelet had been built in 1833 for the Sisters of Charity who cared for orphan boys. In July, 1836, they moved to a new orphanage, leaving the log cabin for the Sisters of St. Joseph. (Savage,45)
28 Savage (45) describes the cabin saying: "The convent faced the river, and from the front door a passage-way extended between two rooms each fifteen by twenty-four feet. An attic was reached by a ladder from the outside. Two sheds, one containing a single large room which had served as a boy's classroom, and the other used for a storeroom and kitchen completed the convent buildings. With the exception of one cot, a table and a few chairs, the rooms were destitute of furniture. Two ticks [feather mattresses] which the sisters filled with straw and laid on the floor provided them with beds, and the cot they reserved for Sister St. Protais."

had but a small log house contigu to the Church for himself. He built a stone Church close to the convent. The Sisters had to fix it - they make curtains with calico to make a partition to separate the sanctuary from the sacristy and thus Father Saulnier said first Masses on Christmas day 1836.

Such was the privations that Mother Delphine and her Sisters had to pass first winter in Carondelet amidst a population so poor they had neither taste for Religion or Instruction. But they were happy in their poverty, the providence not let them without consolation. Father Fontbonne had remain in St. Louis to be parish priest at the Cathedral. He came some time to visit them for he love his own Sister tenderly. He sold even some of ornaments of the Church that he had brought from France to supply their want.

The first they [the Sisters] came [to Carondelet] Father Saulnier gave to them a little supper and in the morning their breakfast and told them that he was poor (that this was true, for one day the Sisters go to see him, he was at supper, he had nothing but pieces of cheese on bare table and bread.)...

Father Saulnier, Missionary and parish priest in Carondelet, hard to himself. When he had some things he bring to the Sisters, even the few cents of the collection of the Mass on Sunday. He often give it to the Sisters, and he was happy when by his economy he could buy a small cow to procure them some milk.

The Sisters deprive themselves of many things and work as the poorest servant. They try to grub their field but they were not strong enough...They had diverse industry, they make sacs for powder...at a cent a sac, but God bless and make fruitful their poverty. As soon as they had means they raise the roof of the two rooms and made a dormitory for the children.

As Mr. Judge John Mullanphy for charitable use gave the land, Madame Mullanphy, his widow, come some time to visit the Sisters. One day she came and bring two orphan girls. She give to the Sisters some means to help them to build the first brick house [1840]. They had three rooms in first floor, the refectory, parlour and little room use for the sick. On second floor school and Chapel and in third a little dormitory for the children.

The Sisters had another benefactress, Miss Eliza Soulard, who has given the ground on 8th Street and Marion to the Sisters for school. She come some time to visit the Sisters and bring with her calico and other things to make clothes for the orphans and remain with the Sisters one or two weeks to make them.[29]

Sister St. Protais explained well some of the significant differences between Cahokia and Carondelet. Without a doubt the sisters would have felt more at home in the organized francophone village of Cahokia. Carondelet was quite different. In the midst of people whose language and culture were unfamiliar, the sisters found the people so poverty-stricken that they could not even think about religion. Nevertheless, in spite of all the problems, on both sides of the river the sisters began their educational labors immediately. In each place they opened their schools, the one in Cahokia better equipped than the one in Carondelet. In less than a month,

Holy Family Church, Cahokia, IL

the Carondelet cabin had also become an orphanage. This was the beginning of a ministry Sisters of St. Joseph would continue until the late twentieth century.

Although Sister St. Protais neglects mentioning it, conditions at Carondelet were strained almost to the point of breaking. The combination of adjusting to a new language and culture, poor housing, four orphans, twenty day students and one ailing sister among them was more than three young sisters should have had to cope with. We know from Sister St. Protais that Mother St. John Fontbonne was concerned about them but, hard-pressed to meet demands in her own part of the world, she did not feel that she had the ability to send more help than she had promised originally.

Mother St. John Fournier (b. 1814) who had made vows in the contemplative Sisters of the Immaculate Conception in 1832, transferred to the Sisters of St. Joseph because she wanted to be a missionary. She was received in 1836 in Lyon, trained to teach the deaf and went to St. Louis in 1837. She made vows Dec. 27, 1838, the first sister to profess vows at Carondelet. In addition to her ministries in St. Louis, she was a founder of the Chestnut Hill Congregation and the St. Paul Province of Carondelet.

---

29 St. Protais, Letter. In spite of their poverty, the sisters were quickly introduced to some of St. Louis' major Catholic philanthropists. The Mullanphys were major benefactors to Catholic causes in St. Louis' early days. Miss Soulard was probably related to Antoine Soulard, a French immigrant who fled the French Revolution, developed a farm in Carondelet (Vide Poche) and became a wealthy landowner in St. Louis.

Lyon's final sacrifice for St. Louis had been the preparation and missioning of two sisters to teach the deaf. In May, 1837, the sisters in St. Louis received word from Lyon that Sisters Celestine Pommerel and St. John Fournier had completed their studies and had begun their journey to St. Louis.[32]

Sister St. John Fournier, a novice at the time of her departure from France, narrated their adventure in a letter she wrote for the community in Lyon in 1873.

> Good Mother Celestine and I left Lyons on April 7, 1837. We arrived at Brest the 17th of the same month, stayed with the Sisters of Wisdom at the expense of the government (the government also paid our passage), until the 5th of June when we embarked on the frigate Hermione; we stopped for four days at Fort Royale, then set sail for Havana, which we reached at the end of July. We were obliged to stay there for seventeen days, waiting for the French consul's boat which was to take us to New Orleans.
>
> Yellow fever had broken out in that city, and our Commander, who was a real father to us, did not want to let us leave the frigate. Every morning he sent two officers in uniform to take us to Holy Mass, and at five in the evening he would take us in his row boat to the consul's house or to the home of some of his French friends. He would bring us back at ten or eleven o'clock. A fine Religious life!
>
> ...Finally we left Havana for New Orleans. There the Vicar General, Father Jeanjean, fearing the fever, accompanied us next day on the boat to St. Louis, which we reached on the 4th of September, the same year. When we arrived, Bishop Rosati received us with open arms, saying he believed we had run away with the soldiers. (We had 400 on board besides the forty Officers, all of whom treated us with the greatest respect.) The bishop placed us with the Sisters of Charity at the asylum, where we stayed for five days because of the continued rain. Finally, on the 9th of September, we left for Carondelet, which is only five or six miles from St. Louis. Our good sisters came half way to meet us. The bishop, in telling us he did not want us to lose our rosy cheeks, had not told us the real reason he was lodging us in St. Louis. The poor house was too small, he was having it raised one story, and there was no roof; but the weather was good.
>
> We opened our trunks and were distributing the little presents sent to our sisters, when all of a sudden, the rain fell in torrents on us, on our beds, on our books, on everything. Good Mother Delphine had foreseen that, and had hired a cabin not far from our garden, a cabin which had been vacant for three years. We had to run there, but with mud up to our knees, we did not run very fast.

---

32 Savage, 48.

They brought us some mattresses which we stretched out on the floor, and we tried to take a little rest in our wet habits, but alas, who could sleep with rats, mice and numberless little insects not only as companions but walking over us all night and for ten or twelve nights in succession? The house was finally covered with a roof, and we left our famished companions to feed themselves as best they could.[33]

The young missionaries recorded no comments about the difference between their new home and the Lyon motherhouse, but a log cabin with no roof and the vermin infested short-term shelter could well have exceeded their expectations about being missionaries who would have to sacrifice some creature comforts. While

Sister Febronie Fontbonne, (b. 1806) received the habit in 1820 and made vows in 1822. She was the first superior at Cahokia, returned to France in 1844 and died in 1881 in Changy, France.

they may have been ready for physical inconveniences, other challenges were less expected and more perilous to the success of their mission.

At Carondelet, even more than the poverty, there had developed a situation that Father Médaille had foreseen as a serious danger to community: a multiplicity of superiors. When the sisters left France, Father Cholleton had named Sister Febronie Fontbonne as superior. At the same time Father James Fontbonne acted as their ecclesiastical superior until they arrived in the diocese of Saint Louis. In Saint Louis, the sisters were under the authority of Bishop Rosati. In each of the parishes, the sisters respected the authority of the pastors who were also their confessors. In January, 1837, Bishop Rosati named Father Fontbonne as the ecclesiastical superior of the two houses of sisters while each house also had its own local superior. With all of this, the number of individuals who could call themselves superiors for the group was equal to the number of sisters in the group itself - a situation ripe for the generation of problems.

---

33 The English translation of the letter quoted here, comes from Sister Maria Kostka Logue, *Sisters of St. Joseph of Philadelphia: A Century of Growth and Development, 1847 - 1947* (Westminster, Maryland: The Newman Press, 1950), appendix II, 327-329. Hereafter, "Fournier, Letter." Another version of the sisters' arrival says that Bishop Rosati liked surprises and therefore did not send word to Carondelet that the sisters had arrived. Then, on September 10, he procured a carriage from a doctor and sent the sisters in it, guided by a Black servant named Margaret. Margaret spoke French and told the sisters many stories about the area as they traveled along. They arrived at the convent during the afternoon recreation period and the sisters at Carondelet were astounded to see their "lost sisters" - and the astonishment grew greater as they realized that the new arrivals knew more about the area than they did. (See Savage, 49)

Although we have little information from the sisters themselves, the priests left ample evidence of the conflicts that arose in the communities and with their superiors.[34] On one side is the opinion of Father John Fontbonne. In 1837, he wrote to Bishop Rosati saying:

Your Excellency,
During the time of your absence, I found it necessary to transfer my elder sister, Sister Febronie, from Cahokia and to replace her with my younger sister, Sister Delphine from Carondelet. My two sisters obeyed me, but Sister Marie Febronie and Sister St. Protais appealed to your Vicar General who confirmed my decision.

Sister Delphine Fontbonne, the first superior at Carondelet, was born in 1813, received into the community in 1832, and made vows in 1835. After serving in St. Louis and Philadelphia, she founded the Congregation in Toronto in 1851 where she died in 1856.

Because Sisters Marie Febronie and St. Protais continually refused to obey Sister Delphine, my younger sister, I found myself obliged to order her to return to Carondelet. Father St. Cyr accused me of lacking tact in this affair, and, concerned that this could damage my reputation, I returned things to their original state.

For some time, Your Excellency, I have felt obliged to warn you that I have noted some disorder in the community of Cahokia. Today again I feel obliged to explain that the illnesses there are not the cause of this disorder, but rather they serve as a pretext.

I put at the foot of the Cross all the confusion that can originate from such a stubborn resistance to my orders, but you should know that I can have nothing more to do with the Sisters at Cahokia. I leave everything in hands of Your Excellency.

---

34 Mother St. John Fournier is the only one of the early sisters who left any commentary about Father James Fontbonne. In her memoir letter she stated "Reverend J. Fontbonne went away to New Orleans, but he came to Philadelphia as soon as he found out that his sister Mother Delphine had gone there, and Bishop Kenrick [Francis Patrick] did not know him as well as his brother...[Peter Richard of St. Louis] and appointed him chaplain of the hospital. (Logue, 331)

I have the honor of being, Monsignor, Your Excellency's humble and
obedient servant.
Fontbonne
May 28, 1837[35]

While Father Fontbonne alleged that communal life at Cahokia was too lax,
Father Edmund Saulnier, the pastor at Carondelet, thought that the Carondelet
community suffered from excessive rigor. In a letter dated February 9, 1838, he
wrote the following to Bishop Rosati.

Monsignor,
It appears that in the house of the Sisters there is something that is not
going right in terms of charity. Almost all the sisters are against Sister
Delphine. According to the conversations that I have had with them, I
can see that the superior wants to enjoy all the advantages of superiority,
and that she wants to drive all the others in a rough way, without any
condescension to her inferiors, wanting the sisters to comply with
everything very strictly, and, on her side, wanting to avoid everything
that might offend her superiority. In front of her, all the sisters move like
slaves or Negroes. She orders, but with the rule in her hand, without
any consideration of its weakness or of her own weakness as a superior.

According to my perception the worst is that according to their
Constitutions, she should have an admonitrix to counsel her, but the
superior thinks she is above all that and wants to rule alone, with
nothing more than the help of the Holy Spirit. That is what I understand
from what I have been able to see.

Although she is a good religious and strict in her observance, Sister
Delphine asks more of the sisters than God Himself asks. She has the
same character as her brother, rustic.[36]

While Father Saulnier could have been exaggerating, the communities obviously
had interpersonal problems. It appears that Sister Delphine lacked the wisdom

---

35 The translation of this letter is in the Carondelet archives (Archives, Carondelet). From the existing
correspondence, it is clear that there was no love lost between Fathers Fontbonne and Saulnier. While Father
Saulnier may have had a problem with alcohol, Father Fontbonne did not fit well into the diocese. In fact, on
October 28, 1838, he wrote to Bishop Rosati and said: "Finally, the greatest favor that Your Excellency could
do for me would be to send me out of your episcopal town as quickly as possible." According to reports, he was
not the only one who hoped for that outcome. Rev. James Fontbonne eventually tried unsuccessfully to join the
order of Clerics of St. Viator, served in New Orleans and went to Philadelphia after Sister Delphine had been
missioned there. Most of the correspondence dealing with him indicates that he was a demanding person who
frequently fomented division among the religious with whom he dealt. (See correspondence from the Society of
St. Viator and other letters in the Carondelet archives.)
36 Letter from Father Saulnier to Bishop Rosati, February 9, 1838, (Archives, Carondelet).

and douceur that characterized her aunt, Mother St. John. To sympathize with her, one should recall that she was only twenty-three years old when she was given responsibility for leadership in the new foundation. The circumstances of the new mission offered a combination of challenges to the missionary sisters who, along with material privations, also bore the emotional strain of being far from home and adjusting to a new language and culture. It would be easy to understand that some resisted Sister Delphine's austere authority, even considering it unjust or imprudent to have named her as superior -- perhaps more for her family name than for her natural gifts or competence. The priests' correspondence leaves no doubt that there was a significant difference in spirit and customs between the two houses. In December of 1838, Fr. Saulnier wrote directly to Mother Delphine, calling her attention to a series of complaints that he had and that he had heard from the sisters. He said:

> My Sister in Jesus Christ,
> I am leaving my breviary to tell you my feelings about various things…
> It is good to keep the Constitutions. I approve everything that you do in that…Nevertheless, we have to respond in everything to our superiors, and your superior is the Bishop, as he is also mine. Thus, you should talk to him about what I am going to say…

Father Saulnier went on to list six specific questions concerning Sister Delphine's decisions about what the sisters could and could not do. They included the question of why the sisters at Carondelet lived so differently from those at Cahokia and why they could not participate more fully in parish life by being godmothers and by singing at the liturgy. The gist of his questions comes down to the fifth on his list: "Why do you make life so difficult when it should be easy?" He ended his letter saying:

> Thus, Sister, I am talking about your conduct and mine, everything is at the disposition of the Bishop…The Bishop's response will leave me tranquil. It is he who must respond, not I…
> Pray for him who is your servant,
> Edm. Saulnier[37]

Combining the information from the priests' letters we might conclude that at Carondelet, Mother Delphine may have tried to reproduce French religious life,

---

37 Saulnier to Delphine, December, 1838, (Archives, Carondelet).

while at Cahokia, Mother Febronie adapted to local circumstances.

The diverse approaches of the two Fontbonne sisters reflect both personality and context. The sisters at Cahokia settled very quickly and this demanded a rapid adaptation to their new surroundings. They went almost from the boat to the village school. Meanwhile, the sisters who went to Carondelet spent six months studying in St. Louis before going to their mission, time during which it would have been natural to follow the customs of French communal life, slowing down and obscuring the need for significant adaptation. In addition, the warm welcome and relatively comfortable house provided for the sisters in Cahokia allowed them to enjoy conditions propitious for creating a new life in the midst of a French speaking community. In contrast, there was nothing easy or comfortable about life at Carondelet: their house was ramshackle, the people of the area spoke English and had neither the interest nor the ability to give them a warm welcome. The sisters at Cahokia saw their first pastor as a model of missionary holiness and they related well with his successors. At Carondelet, Mother Delphine and Father Fontbonne seemed to lean on each other while they experienced friction in their relationship with Father Saulnier and the other sisters. Finally, there is the difference in the personalities of the two young superiors. Sister Febronie appears to have been easy-going and adaptable to new circumstances, whereas Sister Delphine, with the encouragement of her brother, seemed to rely on a strict observance of the rule to mitigate the difficulties of adjustment to foreign circumstances.

The tensions of those first years were not sufficient to thwart the development of the apostolate. The school at Cahokia attracted so many students that in 1837, they had to build a second classroom. In 1838, they celebrated the blessing of a chapel built with the help of one of their neighbors, Madame Turgon.[38] The school at Carondelet was so successful that at the end of their first year, the municipality established it as a free school for the girls of the village, promising to pay the sisters an annual salary of $375.[39] The following spring, Sisters Celestine and St. John, arrived and began to teach deaf children.

In addition to serving as a convent, school and orphanage, when Miss Eliza Dillon asked to enter the community, the house at Carondelet became a novitiate as well. Eliza was a native of St. Louis who had been educated in the convent of the Religious of the Sacred Heart where she learned French. While

---

38 This detail comes from Sister St. Protais' Letter.
39 Dougherty, 64. Savage (95) explains that the sisters taught classes from a manual that had been published in Lyon. This book of 300 pages provides a model of the course of studies with precise instructions about the themes and the methodology to be used. When Sisters Celestine and St. John arrived, they brought French manuals for the instruction of the deaf.

studying at the convent school, she met Sisters Delphine and Félicité who were studying English. On January 3, 1838, at the age of eighteen, Eliza was received into the Congregation and received the name Sister Mary Francis Joseph.

For three years, she was the only American in the Congregation. It is hard to know exactly why there was only one vocation in the first five years of the mission, but there is evidence that Sister Mary Joseph's life was less than easy. A letter she wrote to Bishop Rosati on March 22, 1838 opens a window on the tensions at Carondelet. She had been a novice for only a few months when she wrote:

> Rev. Father and Honoured Bishop,
> You will permit me to reveal to you in quality of Superior and director the sentiments which I at present feel; for a long time I have desired to do so, but always hoping to have the honor of seeing you, I deferred writing until at present I find myself constrained to do so.
> To begin, I do not fulfill the ends for which I embraced the congregation of St. Joseph which were - for God's glory by rendering myself useful to the congregation and my own salvation. But notwithstanding my good will, I cannot succeed in pleasing the Superior who requires me to do work, for which I have not strength sufficient. I have never refused to do the work which was allotted to me; although, frequently through fatigue I have been obliged to rest. My health is not very good and at times I have severe pains in my breast and side. Mother is forever scolding me, she says as a Novice I ought to be employed in the kitchen and that it is an honor for me to teach…
> If you were once convinced of the necessity of your presence here, you would not, I believe, defer visiting us. The disagreements which at present disturb the peace of the community are a source of great trouble for me.
> Pardon me the liberty which I have taken to write to you and believe that I still desire to become a true Sister of St. Joseph. I find nothing in the rules which I cannot fulfill with the assistance of God, but the manner in which they are enforced is not only detrimental to me, but also to the congregation.
> My best respects to Father Jameson,
> I remain, Rev. Father, your humble servant,
> Sister Mary Francis Joseph[40]

Between Father Saulnier and Sister Mary Francis Joseph, the evidence on Bishop

---

40 Sister Monica Corrigan copied this letter from the St. Louis Archdiocesan archives. (Archives, Carondelet)

Rosati's desk was beginning to pile up. Eventually he took action. Sister St. Protais' Memoirs explain:

> Mother Delphine was Superioress in Carondelet from Sept. 12 1836 to August 10, 1839. At her request Bishop Rosati discharge her from Supr and he appoint Sister Celestine in her place.
> Mother Delphine retire in Cahokia with her sister Mother Febronie. She remain three years in Cahokia and she came back in Carondelet where she was teaching French until Spring, 1846, when she go to establish a school in St. Vincent Parish.[41]

Mother Delphine Fontbonne went to Cahokia in August of 1839 when the 26 year old Sister Celestine Pommerel was named superior at Carondelet. Less than two years later, Elizabeth Marsteller and Maria Kinkaid entered the Carondelet community.[42] Although the precise details are impossible to ascertain, we note that under the leadership of Mother Celestine, communal life became more attractive to American women. Beginning in 1844, the community grew continuously.

Sister Celestine Pommerel (1813-1857) studied deaf education before beginning her missionary life in America. Named superior at Carondelet in 1839, she founded multiple missions in the diocese and opened houses in Philadelphia, St. Paul, Wheeling, Canandaigua and Brooklyn in the U.S. as well as Toronto, Hamilton and Ontario in Canada. She died before she could implement her plans for a Congregational union of the foundations.

By 1860, 128 women had joined the Congregation in America and a total of 46 had come as missionaries from France.[43] American-born sisters played an important role in helping the community to establish itself and learn how best to serve

---

41 St. Protais, Letter.
42 The new superior, Mother Celestine Pommerel, was born on April 7, 1813 in Ain, France. She was educated by the Sisters of St. Charles in Macon, but when she decided to follow a religious vocation, she chose to enter the Sisters of St. Joseph in Lyon, distant from her paternal home. She received the habit on May 19, 1831. (Savage, 55).
43 These figures have been culled from the Reception Book, at the Congregational Center. That book records data about each sister who has been received into the Congregation since 1836. According to that book, by 1866, 314 women had become a part of the Congregation in America, 47 of whom came from France. These numbers include only those whose professions were recorded for the Carondelet Congregation.

in the new environment.[44] The native sisters knew the people and their customs and they could teach in English. As they became the majority, they helped the community become more American than French.[45] The school at Carondelet grew and served as the original site for St. Joseph's Academy, Fontbonne College and St. Joseph Institute for the Deaf, three institutions still functioning in the 21st century. The Cahokia mission fell victim to environmental conditions. After floods forced the sisters to suspend classes numerous times, it stopped functioning entirely between 1844 and 1848 and in 1855 it closed for the last time.

The third mission of the Sisters of St. Joseph in America was St. Joseph's School for Negro Girls. On February 5, 1845, Father Augustus Paris founded this school with the full approval of Bishop Peter Kenrick who was by then bishop of St. Louis. At St. Joseph's, Sisters St. John Fournier, Antoinette Kincaid and St. Protais taught the basic course as well as French and embroidery.[46] They eventually had a hundred students, without counting the children of slaves who came in the afternoons and on weekends for catechetical instruction. Sister St. John Fournier described the tragically brief history of the school.

> The first mission in St. Louis [was] a school for liberated Negroes. Obedience sent me there with two other sisters. We also prepared slaves for the reception of the sacraments, and this displeased the whites very much.

Peter Richard Kenrick, the first Archbishop of St. Louis, succeeded Bishop Rosati in 1841. He was a strong supporter of the Sisters of St. Joseph, helping them solidify the community as a congregation of papal right, a status fully achieved in 1877.

---

44 A fact that should not be overlooked is that a good number of the women who entered the Congregations of St. Joseph during their first 100 years in America were themselves immigrants. Young immigrants have a tendency to adapt themselves to the customs of their new country while the missionary sisters who came after they had gone through religious formation would more easily tend to transplant their French style to the new environment. For a study of the inculturation of the congregation see Patricia Byrne, "Sisters of St. Joseph, The Americanization of a French Tradition" (*U.S. Catholic Historian*, 5, 1986: 241-72).

45 One of the early students, Eliza McKenney Brouillet, shared her memories of school days with Sister Monica Corrigan and mentioned the special love the students had for Mother Celestine and the French sisters. The document is available in the Carondelet archives.

46 Sister Antoinette Kincaid was one of the first American women to join the Congregation. Born in St. Louis in 1822, she entered the congregation at Cahokia on March 6, 1842 and made vows at Carondelet on March 19, 1844. (Details from the Congregational Archives, thanks to Sister Patricia Kelly, former archivist.)

After some time, they threatened to have us put out by force. The threats were repeated every day. Finally, one morning as I was leaving the church, several people called out to me and told me that they were coming that night to put us out of the house. I said nothing to the sisters, and was not afraid, so great confidence had I in the Blessed Virgin! I put some miraculous medals on the entrance gate and on the fences (we already had them on all doors and windows of the house). At eleven o'clock, the sisters woke with a start when they heard a loud noise. Out in the street was a crowd of people crying out and cursing. We recited together the Memorare and other prayers.

Suddenly, the police patrol came and scattered those villains who were trying to break open the door. They returned three times that same night, but our good Mother protected us and they were not able to open the door from the outside nor to break it down.

The day after our adventure, the Mayor of St. Louis advised Bishop Kenrick to close that school for a time and he did so.[47]

So ended the Sisters of St. Joseph's first ministry to African-Americans. The school for African Americans was the sisters' first mission in the city of St. Louis and their first experience of service to people of a non-European culture in the U.S.

In that same year, the sisters opened a parish school, St. Vincent de Paul. In 1844, the community had also seen two of their original missionaries return to France; Sister Febronie Chapellon accompanied Sister Febronie Fontbonne who had to return for reasons of health.[48] Meanwhile, the motherhouse at Carondelet had been enlarged with the construction of a three-story brick building to house the convent, novitiate, school for the deaf, and academy. From those beginnings the community branched forth in ways the first eight missionaries could never have imagined, and they were unexpectedly on the brink of expansion far beyond the diocese of St. Louis.

Sisters Febronie Chapellon
and Febronie Fontbonne

---

47 Fournier, Letter
48 Sister Febronie Fontbonne could not recover her health and returned to France in 1844 accompanied by Sister Febronie Chapellon as her companion. They were the only sisters among the original eight to see their homeland again.

ಐ

Chapter Four: Little Design Moves Beyond St. Louis

Cast of Characters

M. St. John Fournier: Founding Superior in Philadelphia & St. Paul
M. Delphine Fontbonne: Founder Carondelet, Novice
Director, Philadelphia, Founder Toronto
M. Martha Von Bunning: Carondelet, Philadelphia, Toronto, Hamilton (Canada)
M. Agnes Spencer: Carondelet, Philadelphia, Founder: Canandaigua/Buffalo
M. Francis Joseph Ivory: Chronicler, Carondelet, St. Paul, Canandaigua/Buffalo
M. Stanislaus Leary: First to receive the habit in the State of New York, 1857,
Founding Superior, Rochester (1868)
M. Agnes Hines: Second Superior General of Rochester
M. Austin Kean: Founder Brooklyn, Baden, Rutland
M. de Chantal Keating: Brooklyn, Superior in Wheeling
Sister Baptista Hanson; Received in Philadelphia, Missioned in Buffalo,
Founder in Brooklyn
Sister Antoinette Cuff: Received in Rochester,
Second Superior General of Concordia

Bishops Peter Richard Kenrick of St. Louis and
Francis Patrick Kenrick of Philadelphia
Bishop Saint John Neumann. C.SS.R. of Philadelphia
Bishop Joseph Cretin – St. Paul
Bishop John Loughlin – Brooklyn
Bishop John Timon, C.M., St. Louis, Buffalo
Bishop Bernard McQuaid: Bishop of Rochester, 1868-1909

THE PROGRESS OF A DECADE

In 1846, when the Sisters of St. Joseph completed their first decade in the Diocese of St. Louis, the motherhouse at Carondelet was serving as a novitiate, public school, orphanage and school for the deaf. All of that activity required that it be enlarged and with the help of the Mullanphy family, the wealthiest Catholics in St. Louis, the sisters added a three-story brick building to the Motherhouse.1 By 1845, the sisters had opened two missions in the City of St. Louis. The first, St. Joseph School for the Colored, functioned for less than two years, its closure brought on by the violence of local brigands. The next, St. Vincent de Paul School, served children of German and Irish immigrants as well as "native born families," meaning those who had been in the country for a generation or more. In 1846, the community

---

1 Savage tells us that by spring, 1838 the log cabin had been remodeled, giving it the dignified designation of being a frame house. It was home to "four mutes and five orphans" and a girl boarder whose fur-trapper father had left her with the sisters after her mother had died. (Mary Lucida Savage, 52) John Mullanphy earned a fortune in the cotton market and real estate.

took over a boys' orphanage in St. Louis because the Sisters of Charity, by then affiliated with the Daughters of Charity, could no longer care for boys.[2] By 1847, twenty-nine women had entered the community, more than tripling the original community of French missionaries. The first of the new members, Sr. Mary Francis Joseph (Eliza) Dillon, died in 1842.[3] In 1844, two of the original missionaries, Sisters Febronie Fontbonne and Febronie Chapellon, returned to France due to the former's illness.[4] The women who entered the congregation in the first decade brought a challenging diversity to the congregation. They ranged in age from 18 to 36; ten of them were born in France, four in Germany, two in Ireland, one in Prussia, one in England, five in the eastern US (Virginia, Pennsylvania and New York) and five in Missouri. Of the sisters born in Europe, the majority listed St. Louis as their place of residence before entering the congregation as did the sisters born in the Eastern U.S. The only members who came to the congregation directly from Europe in that period were the original French missionaries from Lyon and Margaret Fitzsimmons whose residence previous to entering the community was listed as Ireland. We have very little evidence about how these women came to know the Sisters of St. Joseph but can assume that they may have heard about the sisters' schools (Carondelet, St. Joseph School for Colored and St. Vincent's) or they were directed to the community by friendly priests who knew of the sisters. In the ten years since the Sisters of St. Joseph had arrived in the U.S., the population of St. Louis had doubled to 16,500 residents. Beyond the city, the diocesan boundaries which had stretched from St. Louis to Quebec were gradually redrawn. In 1837, the Diocese of Dubuque which included territory in Iowa, Minnesota and the Dakotas was created from St. Louis. With the creation of the Diocese of Little Rock in 1843, the Indian Territories and state of Arkansas no longer belonged to the Diocese of St. Louis, but even so the diocese remained exceedingly large and understaffed. In 1846, the Catholic Directory reported that the diocese of St. Louis had 43 parishes, 25 other active mission stations, 44 priests active in ministry,

---

2 Dougherty, 132. This was apparently the orphanage built by the Mullanphy family for the Sisters of Charity. Those sisters moved from the Carondelet log cabin to this orphanage in 1836.
3 According to Savage, Sister Mary Joseph Dillon died of consumption on Sunday, October 30, 1842: "Sister Mary Joseph was always delicate...The village carpenter made her pine coffin...After Vespers on a Sunday afternoon, the sisters followed by her white-haired , sorrow-stricken father and her young sister, bore her to ... the little cemetery beside the village church." (Savage, 61)
4 Sister Febronie Fontbonne had to return to France in 1844, and Sister Febronie Chapellon accompanied her. They were the only sisters among the original eight to see their homeland again.

at least 65 women religious, 7 charitable institutions, 9 schools, 9 academies for young ladies and 1 academy for boys.[5]

In 1839, immediately after the close of the Fourth Provincial Council of Baltimore, Bishop Rosati traveled to Europe. Among other reasons for the trip, he felt compelled to visit the Society for the Propagation of the Faith in Lyon to disabuse them of the rumor that the diocese of St. Louis enjoyed significant wealth and therefore no longer needed assistance. While that idea may have been based on the amount of construction Rosati had undertaken in building a cathedral and seminary as well as parishes and schools, the expense of all that was precisely the reason that the diocese was desperate for help. We might wonder if the rumored prosperity of St. Louis influenced Mother St. John Fontbonne's decision not to send additional sisters to the diocese. In any case, Bishop Rosati left the diocese in 1840 without anyone imagining that he would never return. When he arrived in Europe, Pope Gregory XVI gave him a diplomatic mission to Haiti. By the time he concluded that work, he was a spent man who returned to his Vincentian community in Rome where he died on September 25, 1843.

While Bishop Rosati was in Rome, his insistence on his need for help bore fruit and Peter Richard Kenrick was named his coadjutor. Peter Kenrick, the younger brother of Bishop Francis P. Kenrick of Philadelphia, had served in Philadelphia as seminary president, rector of the cathedral and Vicar General.[6] In 1841, Father Peter Richard Kenrick went to Rome seeking to join the Society of Jesus. He was not accepted but was instead singled out by Bishop Rosati who had known him from his work in Philadelphia. Bishop Rosati arranged to have him named his coadjutor and Peter Richard Kenrick was consecrated bishop in 1841 by Bishop Flaget of Kentucky under whom he had begun his missionary career in the U.S. as a seminary instructor.[7] From the moment Bishop P.R. Kenrick arrived in St. Louis, he had to assume leadership of the diocese, a mission he continued until his death in 1895. When St. Louis was made an Archdiocese in 1847, Peter Kenrick became the third archbishop in the United States, having received that title four years before his elder brother Francis Patrick Kenrick became the Archbishop of

---

5 References to the Catholic Directory throughout the work are to the Official Catholic Directory, an annual publication of Sadlier, many volumes of which are available online.

6 Executive Committee of Clergymen, *Life of the Most Reverend Peter Richard Kenrick, D.D., Archbishop of St. Louis* (St. Louis, Catholic Publishing Co. of St. Louis, 1891), 9. Bishop Rosati's first choice for a coadjutor was John Timon who refused the appointment. (ibid. 11)

7 Flaget who had sought instructors for the seminary and also as missionaries said he had cried when the Urban College of Rome sent him Kenrick because he was an Irishman. He admitted to crying even more when the Irishman was taken away from him for Philadelphia. (Ibid. 7)

Baltimore.[8]

CATHOLICS IN THE U.S.A. IN MID-NINETEENTH CENTURY
FACING ANTI-CATHOLIC AND ANTI-IMMIGRANT PREJUDICE

When the first missionary Sisters of St. Joseph arrived in New Orleans and St. Louis, the Ursulines and the Sisters of Charity cautioned them against wearing the religious habit in public. Even among the French Catholic population of New Orleans, the sisters encountered enough anti-Catholic prejudice that wearing religious garb in public was as likely to arouse suspicion as to garner appreciation. The sisters would soon learn that the religious freedom espoused by the young nation did not indicate a lack of religious prejudice among its predominantly Protestant citizens.

Anti-Catholicism held sway as one of U.S. citizens' most acceptable prejudices through the nineteenth century and into the twentieth. The historical basis of such prejudice could be found in the bigotry inherited from England's history of conflict with the Catholic Church and the bitterness left by the Reformation and wars of religion in other parts of Europe. Added to that, in the U.S. there were the problems caused by an immense influx of poor, Catholic immigrants in the mid-nineteenth century. The U.S. population in 1820, counted 190,000 Catholics in the total white population of 7.8 million. By 1879, the total population had risen to 33.5 million with 4.5 million Catholics, most of whom were poor, and thus a double affront to the U.S. self-image.[9] In the 1830s, the Reverend Lyman Beecher, a renowned anti-Catholic orator, published and promulgated "A Plea for the West," a classic tirade warning of the dangers of allowing Catholic immigration to the U.S.[10] Cautioning naïve citizens about the danger of tolerance, his lengthy screed included the following warnings about the Church and Catholic immigrants:

The conflict which is to decide the destiny of the West, will be a conflict

---

8 Francis Patrick Kenrick was nine years older than Peter Richard. They maintained a strong relationship as brothers and fellow scholar-prelates who carried on their personal correspondence in Latin. The decision to make the twenty-year old diocese of St. Louis an archdiocese was not universally well received. Some bishops assumed that the bishop of Philadelphia had lobbied Rome on his brother's behalf, while it was known that Bishop Chanche of Natchez went to Rome to lobby against it. See Hugh J. Nolan, *Francis Patrick Kenrick, Bishop of Philadelphia, 1830-1851* (Philadelphia, American Catholic Historical Society of Philadelphia,1948) 362. The second archdiocese in the U.S. was Oregon City in OR which was made an archdiocese in 1846.
9 H. Jedin and J. Dolan, eds. *Church in the Industrial Age – Vol. IX of History of the Church* (NY: Crossroads1981), 150. (The figures available mention only the "white" portion of the population.)
10 Lyman Beecher (1775-1863) was a Presbyterian minister, an outspoken advocate of temperance, an abolitionist and President of Lane Theological Seminary, an institution founded to prepare ministers to save the West for Protestantism. Among his 13 children were the famous abolitionists Henry Ward Beecher and Harriet Beecher Stowe.

of institutions for the education of her sons, for purposes of superstition, or evangelical light; of despotism, or liberty...

[S]ince the irruption of the northern barbarians, the world has never witnessed such a rush of dark minded population from one country to another, as is now leaving Europe, and dashing upon our shores...

Assuring his audiences that the Catholic immigrants were being sent with a well-defined purpose, he went on:

Clouds like the locusts of Egypt are rising from the hills and plains of Europe, and on the wings of every wind, are coming over to settle down upon our fair fields; while millions, moved by the noise of their rising and cheered by the news of their safe arrival and green pastures, are preparing for flight in an endless succession...

Our unoccupied soil is coming fast into the European market, and foreign capitalists and speculators are holding competition with our own. So that, were there no political and no ecclesiastical ends to be accomplished, the rapid influx upon us of such masses of uneducated mind of other tongues and habits would itself alone demand an immediate and earnest national supervision, on the same principles of self-preservation that would dyke out the ocean...

Beecher reminded his audience of Catholic-Protestant disagreements over Scripture and made no secret of his opinion of Catholic intellectual life:

If they could read the Bible, and might and did, their darkened intellect would brighten, and their bowed down mind would rise. If they dared to think for themselves, the contrast of Protestant independence with their thralldom, would awaken the desire of equal privileges, and put an end to an arbitrary clerical dominion over trembling superstitious minds. If the pope and potentates of Europe held no dominion over ecclesiastics here, we might trust to time and circumstances to mitigate their ascendency and produce assimilation.

Focusing on the particular dangers presented by women religious and their ministries he explained how sisters were subverting the faith of the country:

Mr. Flaget [the first bishop in Kentucky] has established in his diocese many convents of nuns devoted to the education of young females. These establishments do wonderful good. Catholics and Protestants are admitted indiscriminately. The latter, after having finished their education, return to the bosom of their families, full of esteem and veneration for their instructresses. They are ever ready to refute the calumnies, which the jealousy of heretics loves to spread against the religious communities: and often, when they have no longer any opposition of their relations to fear, they embrace the Catholic religion.[11]

Beecher designed that last sentence to plant holy terror in the hearts of good protestant parents. Reverend Beecher may have been unusually articulate in speech and writing, but significant segments of the population shared his opinion and not only promoted anti-Catholic prejudice but incited violence, the most egregious example of which was burning of the Ursuline convent/school in Charlestown, Massachusetts in 1832.[12]

As Bishop of Philadelphia, Francis P. Kenrick had seen ethnic/religious unrest since the 1830s. In the 1840s, Philadelphia experienced full scale "nativist" (anti-Catholic) riots which were directly tied to the question of denominational education. Speaking for his Catholic

Anti-Catholic sensationalism reached a high point with the 1836 publication of The Awful Disclosures of Maria Monk, a scurrilous fiction about life in a Canadian convent where "Maria" had been kept against her will and subjected to cruelty and sexual exploitation. The book sold 300,000 copies before the Civil War.

population, Bishop Kenrick protested the sectarian practices in public schools which included the "daily singing of Protestant hymns in the classroom and more seriously the use of anti-Catholic texts and reference books and 'ungracious' treatment of the Irish children by their teachers and fellow students."[13] Bishop Kenrick focused his protest on the required use of the King James Bible in the public schools. Reacting to Kenrick and his allies, Protestant clergy formed anti-Catholic organizations including American Protestant Association (APA) and the American Republican Party which won local elections in New York and Philadelphia in 1844. In May, 1844, tensions in Philadelphia came to a head with rioting that resulted in the death of a number of "nativists" or anti-immigrant activists. The following July violence broke out again leaving at least four militiamen and a dozen or more nativists dead and two Catholic churches burned. Although the riots were quelled and many Philadelphians denounced the violence, nativist candidates received

---

11 Lyman Beecher, "A Plea for the West" For Maria Monk see https://espanol.search.yahoo.com search?p=maria+monk&fr=yfp-t-406.

12 John Tracy Ellis attributes the convent burning to a mob incited by Beecher, adding that one of the Catholic responses was to strengthen their own press as a source of true information about the Church. By 1842, there were about 20 Catholic weekly papers being published in English as well as at least one German paper. (American Catholicism...) 64-65.

13 M. Jane Coogan, The Price of Our Heritage, Vol. 1: 1839-1869 (Dubuque, IA.: Mt. Carmel Press, 1975), 106.

more support than ever in the following October elections.[14]

Although other eastern cities such as New York and Boston also experienced their share of inter-religious violence and anti-Catholicism, Philadelphia is singled out because it was the first city where the Sisters of St. Joseph would encounter this degree of civic/religious dissension.[15] It is worth noting that religion was not the only cause of mob violence in this era. Religious conflict actually played a secondary role compared with labor disputes even though those too had religious undertones as they pitted ethnic groups which were traditionally denominational against one another.

MISSION TO PHILADELPHIA

While it seems unusual that the first Sisters of St. Joseph missioned outside the Diocese of St. Louis should go east to Philadelphia rather than west with the pioneer flow, that logic does not take the brothers Kenrick into account. The diocese of Philadelphia had enjoyed the services of the Sisters of Charity, the Religious of the Sacred Heart and the newly founded Sisters of Charity of the Blessed Virgin Mary (BVM), but by the time of the arrival of the Sisters of St. Joseph only the Sisters of Charity remained.[16] Bishop Francis Patrick Kenrick of Philadelphia was anxious to have more teaching sisters and while visiting his brother in St. Louis in 1846, he learned of the work of the Sisters of St. Joseph. According to his biographer, while Bishop Francis Kenrick was visiting St. Louis,

> ...the bishop immediately went to Carondelet...and begged Mother Celestine...to send some sisters to Philadelphia to take charge of St. John's Male Orphanage. At first Mother Celestine declined saying it was impossible to spare sisters...But after listening to the prelate's pleading she agreed to put the matter before a council of sisters in the morning. So anxious was Kenrick to procure these sisters for Philadelphia that he stayed all night at Carondelet as a guest of...Father Edmund Saulnier. The bishop hoped his presence might influence the decision of the

---

14 See Zachary M. Schrag, "Nativist Riots of 1844" http://philadelphiaencyclopedia.org/archive/nativist-riots-of-1844.

15 Racial conflict and labor riots frequently made for a violent atmosphere with minimal civic control. See Noel Ignatiev, *How the Irish Became White* (NY: Routledge), especially chapter 5 "The Tumultuous Republic." At the same time, the missionary sisters were already familiar with violent civic unrest; in 1834, Lyon had been the site of silk-workers strikes that resulted in great bloodshed and the imprisonment of 10,000 insurgents.

16 The Sisters of Charity of the Blessed Virgin Mary (B.V.M.) were founded in Philadelphia in 1833 and opened a school there. By 1843, they left Philadelphia for Dubuque in part because of the hostility of the neighborhood. Likewise, the Sisters of St. Clare decided to abandon their Philadelphia mission and return to Europe. The Religious of the Sacred Heart had opened a school at McSherrystown but when a number of their sisters there died, they decided that the area was harmful to health and they left (Logue, 69). Much of the problem for

council. He was successful. The council agreed that four sisters should be given the work: Mother St. John Fournier, Sister Mary Magdalen Weber, Sister Mary Joseph Clark, and Sister Mary Elizabeth Kinkaid. The latter two were only lately professed.[17]

Mother St. John Fournier described the foundation of the mission in Philadelphia saying,

On the 6th of May, 1847, after repeated requests from the Bishop of Philadelphia, F. Patrick Kenrick of happy memory, four sisters arrived in Philadelphia to take charge of the orphanage which for two years had been entrusted to ladies and servants who received their salaries and took little care of the orphans so that we found them covered with vermin and in rags. We had to get to work immediately and with courage, even though we were quite disgusted.[18]

St. John's Orphanage had been founded in 1830 as an emergency measure when the other Catholic orphanage in Philadelphia was so overcrowded that "the public almshouse [became] the only refuge for four small children orphaned by the death of their [Irish immigrant] parents."[19] In response, a group of people with hearts larger than their incomes sought a solution with the help of Father John Hughes.[20] Hughes obtained a house and with the help of his own sister, a Sister of Charity from Emmitsburg, they opened St. John's orphanage with donated furniture and the promise of support from a large group of people who pledged to sacrifice $1.50 per year to support the work.[21]

When the Sisters of St. Joseph arrived in Philadelphia, the Catholic community seemed delighted to see St. John's Orphanage come under their direction. The diocesan paper, the *Catholic Herald*, published the news saying:

---

all of these communities was the anti-Catholicism which demoralized them and threatened their institutions. See Hugh Nolan, *Francis Patrick Kenrick, Bishop of Philadelphia 1830-1851* (Philadelphia: American Catholic Historical Society of Philadelphia, 1948), 292-3.

17 Nolan, 386. According to Carondelet records, Sister Magdalen Weber who was received into the community in 1845, was originally from Adams County in Southcentral Pennsylvania. She remained a part of the Philadelphia community until her death in 1876.

18 In 1873, Mother St. John Fournier wrote to the Superior General of Lyon, giving her an account of her experiences since leaving Lyon on April 7, 1837. The letter is one of the few primary sources we have of our earliest history. (Logue, 327-353) Hereafter referred to as "Fournier Letter."

19 Logue, 18.

20 John Hughes (b. 1797) would be named bishop and then archbishop of New York (1842-1864) and was a moving force in convincing Rome to create the dioceses of Buffalo and Albany and thereby reducing the size of the New York diocese.

21 Logue, 18. The needs were so great that Bishop John Hughes of New York persuaded the Sisters of Charity

The friends of the orphans will be happy to hear that the Asylum has been placed under the direction of the "Sisters of St. Joseph" who arrived within the last week…There is every reason to hope that this valuable institution will again be as flourishing as in its best days…The zeal and skill of the Sisters of St. Joseph whose institute embraces every form of charity – the success with which God has blessed their labors in the West, cheers us with the hope that they will have no reason to repent that they have traveled so many hundreds of miles…[22]

Although the sisters were well welcomed by church and public officials, not everyone was prepared to trust them as much as Bishop Kenrick did.

The bishop seemed to have his own plan, and while he supported the sisters very well in theory, he may not have appreciated their day-to-day needs or the outside pressures they faced as newcomers to the city. As if the pitiful conditions suffered by the orphans were not difficult enough, Bishop Kenrick insisted that the sisters almost immediately accept new members. Meanwhile, some suspicious souls questioned the sisters' motives and seemed ready to criticize them on any pretext. Mother St. John explained the situation saying:

St. John's Orphanage

In the month of June after our arrival Bishop Kenrick asked me to receive several good subjects. Quite against my will we received four who were soon as busy with the children as we. Soon they said everywhere (even the priests) that our postulants were eating the orphans' bread. At first we did not receive any salary, then we kept our own money separate, which was not very easy. With the postulants' money we bought all the necessities of life for the postulants. I explained everything to Bishop Kenrick who told me not to pay any attention to such nonsense.[23]

It would take a decade for the sisters to get the orphanage and community on stable financial footing as they received more candidates for the community and

---

in his diocese to break from their Emmitsburg community in 1846 so that they could continue caring for male orphans. The group who accepted his request became the Sisters of Charity of New York.
22 Catholic Herald, May 13, 1847, cited in Logue, 31.
23 "Fournier Letter," (Logue, 335). Photo of the orphanage: http://www.archives.upenn.edu/histy/features/wphila

the bishop continued to find ministries in need of their service. The bishop apparently had a better grasp of their generosity and ingenuity than their need. Soon after the sisters began their ministry in Philadelphia Bishop Francis Kenrick wrote to his brother, Bishop Peter Richard Kenrick, summing up the spirit and ability of the sisters saying: "The arrival of the Sisters of St. Joseph has given us all great joy. They have indeed a generous spirit ready for any good work."[24] The sisters coming from St. Louis found themselves in a surprisingly unstable situation. Philadelphia was larger and better established than St. Louis and at the same time its citizens were attempting to deal with an influx of immigrants that would have been hard to imagine. At that time, tens of thousands of Catholic immigrants were arriving in Philadelphia, a great number of whom were Irish fleeing the famine of 1846.[25] Sister M. Jane Coogan, B.V.M., describes Philadelphia of the 1840s as follows:

> The poor and distressed were beginning to pour into it. Weather-racked and unseaworthy sailing vessels were disgorging daily from their steerage decks hundreds of soiled, ragged, half-starved families from the sod houses of the Irish countrysides and the crowded slums of Ireland's cities. The sick, the old, the orphaned would soon be city charges. Even relatively strong and healthy immigrants came with empty pockets and with a debt of service to pay for their passage. Largely unprepared for the amenities of urban life and untrained for any but unskilled labor or domestic service, they showed themselves often a reckless and turbulent element in a staid, self-conscious city.[26]

That scene of displacement and human need must have been a shock to the four sisters from St. Louis. Mother St. John Fournier had extensive experience from the time of her transfer to the Sisters of St. Joseph in Lyon, her preparation in deaf education, her missionary venture and the positions she held in St. Louis before going to Philadelphia, but even she had never witnessed anything like the constant influx of the poor into Philadelphia. Sisters Magdalen Weber, Antoinette Kinkaid and Mary Joseph Clark, all from St. Louis, may have heard stories, but they grew up far from the ports of entry and were unlikely to have ever seen anything comparable to the desperate conditions of newly arrived immigrants.

For a time, the small community of Sisters of St. Joseph that opened the

---

24 Logue, 30.
25 The Irish were often very poorly received. Coogan explains that to be called Irish had come to be a great insult. She quotes a slave who complained, "My Master is a great tyrant. He treats me as badly as if I were a common Irishman." (op cit. 102)
26 Coogan, 93.

mission in Philadelphia would be joined by other missionaries from St. Louis including Sister Delphine Fontbonne, but the community quickly began to be self-sustaining, accepting a fast-growing number of new members, primarily from the Irish residents of the area. According to Sister Mary Helen Bierne, "A list of fifty-four professed sisters [in Philadelphia] dating from 1857, shows thirty-five born in Ireland, three in Germany, and the remainder in America, with most of these from Philadelphia. Virtually all of the American born sisters had Irish surnames."[27] Clearly, it did not take long for English to become the dominant language in the community, especially with Mother St. John's encouragement as she herself developed an expertise for translating French literature into English.[28] In Philadelphia as in St. Louis and the other foundations of the mid-nineteenth century, the sisters' need to adapt to the diverse cultures of the community would have given them practical insight and sensitivity to the struggles of their immigrant students and their families. Community living gave them a first-hand awareness of the cultural conflicts and misunderstandings that are inevitable as diverse groups learn to live together.

The sisters had arrived in Philadelphia in May of 1847 to care for orphans, but within two years their expanding ministries stretched their capacities in terms of personnel as well as in preparation. Mother St. John described their new missions in education and healthcare saying:

Pottsville was our first mission. It was founded the 28th of August 1848. As in Philadelphia, the Sisters of Charity had given up the charge of the orphans, who were all scattered before the arrival of the sisters. The bishop did not plan to reopen the asylum but he did want the sisters to open the parochial school [at St. Patrick Parish]...

On June 18, 1849, five sisters opened the hospital dedicated to St. Joseph under the auspices of His Excellency, Bishop Kenrick...Three patients entered with us. We had only five beds; three of them we gave to the hospital, and for nearly three weeks two of us had a bed and the other three slept crosswise on a mattress. Our sisters were so afraid of the dying that I had to stay with them during the night. If there was a festering sore to dress, the sister would faint. Little by little these poor children got accustomed to working for the sick and the dying.[29]

---

27 Mary Helen Bierne, Ready for Any Good Work, *History of the Sisters of St. Joseph*, Chestnut Hill, Philadelphia, 1944-1999, (Lanham MD: University Press of America, 2015) 7-8.
28 Logue (359) lists the works Mother St. John translated.
29 "Fournier Letter," (Logue, 335). Mother St. John goes on to explain that in 1859, the hospital came under the care of the Sisters of Charity because the Sisters of St. Joseph could not afford to take it over from the gentlemen of the board of directors whom the bishop wanted to replace. The loss of this, the first hospital in

Mother St. John paints a vivid picture of the movement and growth of the community. Her letter also subtly notes how the Sisters of St. Joseph were beginning to make a habit of following in the wake of the Sisters of Charity. As the community grew in Philadelphia, Mother St. John explained how others came to their aid as they encountered and overcame obstacles even more worrisome than their poverty. Here she also introduces Bishop (Saint) John Neumann who would prove to be her great friend even though she was in St. Paul at the time he assumed leadership in Philadelphia.[30]

Bishop Kenrick had been transferred to the Archdiocese of Baltimore [1851] and…Bishop Neumann had his place in Philadelphia. That worthy bishop was full of zeal for religious communities and the education of children. He advised us to go to McSherrystown and establish our novitiate there…

On May 2, 1854, we left eight sisters at the asylum, and seven sisters and two postulants set out for McSherrystown. The house there had been given for a school, and the Sisters of Charity had left it twice because of the poverty of the place. The Madams of the Sacred Heart had replaced the Sisters of Charity, and they left it also. When we arrived, the house had been closed for two years…Through oversight or the permission of God, we had no provisions. McSherrystown is a little village where each family has five acres of ground, which provides them with all they need for the year. So when we arrived…there was no baker nor any kind of shopkeeper…

The few provisions we had brought with us were gone…About six in the evening, good Mrs. Lilly brought us our supper, and our poor children, although they had not had too much to eat, were able to sleep, a thing they had not been able to do the night before…We had brought with us a ham, and the bone served us for soup for a whole week…our sisters were happy and contented.

Since McSherrystown was too far from Philadelphia for the novitiate (140 miles) the bishop told us to get a place in the suburbs of the city… we decided to buy the house where we are now, ten miles from

---

the United States under the care of Sisters of St. Joseph, was a source of great sorrow to the sisters involved. With the exception of nursing service during the Civil War and a large infirmary at the motherhouse, the Philadelphia community would have little involvement in the ministry of health care after the early years.

30 John N. Neumann came to the U.S. as an immigrant seminarian hoping to become a missionary. Ordained in June, 1836, by Bishop Du Bois of New York he ministered alone for a few years before deciding he would do better as a member of the Congregation of the Most Holy Redeemer (Redemptorists). As pro-tem superior of the U.S. Redemptorists he became confessor to Archbishop F. P. Kenrick of Philadelphia who was instrumental in having Neumann named as his successor in Philadelphia. (See themissionchurch.com/stjohnneumann.htm and cssr.com)

Philadelphia...We left eight sisters at McSherrystown and took possession of what the bishop wants us to call St. Joseph's Convent on August 16, 1858...Here we were installed without food, without beds, without chairs, with nothing but the four walls and a staircase on which we could sit. A storm came up, and there was no way of getting out until after six in the evening.

We were all prepared to go to bed without supper, when after six o'clock we saw a poor woman crossing the fields...She asked if she could do anything to help us. We begged our supper from her; she brought it as well as our breakfast for the next morning. But where would we lie down? It occurred to us to go to the stable where we found a little straw. This we...used to make our beds. The next day our bones were broken and we could scarcely walk. We had told the pastor (an Augustinian father) that we would go to Mass and he said he would wait for us. He is still waiting...

I do not know whether, when we sang our Lady's hymn on the river bank, we chased the devil up to the house, but it is a fact that he tormented us for several months. Every night at eleven o'clock, there was a loud knocking at the door, and at the same time you could hear knocking on the furnace in the cellar. That lasted until after midnight and no one could sleep. Neither postulants nor novices wanted to stay, and I could not blame them...I spoke about it to the bishop who came himself to watch all night, but he heard nothing. The next morning the bishop blessed the cellar again...and he threw the rest of the holy water into the furnace saying: "Burn in hell, and don't come back here anymore." From that day to this we have never been bothered. That holy Bishop Neumann told us that he had no doubt that the devil did not want us here and that he was doing all in his power to make us leave the place where he had reigned for so long. With this trouble over we could continue the novitiate...[31]

Once the new novitiate was established on the outskirts of Philadelphia, the sisters opened Mount St. Joseph Academy boarding school on the same campus. Education quickly became the sisters' main ministry as they opened free parish schools as well as the academies from which the tuition provided some financial sustenance for the community.

FROM ST LOUIS TO PHILADELPHIA TO TORONTO

In 1850, Mother Celestine at Carondelet sent Sisters Delphine Fontbonne and Martha Bunning to Philadelphia to help Mother St. John.

---

31 "Fournier Letter," (Logue 339-341).

Sister Delphine became the superior in the orphanage and novitiate, allowing Mother St. John the freedom to go to St. Louis for a rest in 1851. But neither Sister Delphine's leadership nor Mother St. John's respite lasted long. In 1850, Toronto's Bishop Armand de Charbonnel, originally of Monistrol-sur-Loire, France, visited Bishop Kenrick in Philadelphia, heard of the work of the Sisters of St. Joseph and learned that Sister Delphine Fontbonne was the superior of the orphanage there.

Because their families had long known one another, Bishop de Charbonnel requested that Mother Celestine allow Sister Delphine to found a mission in his diocese.[32]

In 1851, Mother Delphine and Sisters Martha von Bunning, Alphonsus Margerum and Bernard Dinan opened the mission that became the Congregation of the Sisters of St. Joseph of Toronto. The following year, Sister Martha von Bunning opened a mission in Hamilton, Ontario. That community evolved to become an independent congregation when Hamilton became a diocese in 1856.[33]

Mother Delphine

On January 18, 1856, nearly five years after leaving Philadelphia, Mother Delphine wrote a letter to her missionary companion Sister Félicité Bouté. She said:

> Twenty years yesterday, the feast of St. Anthony, we embarked at Havre du Grâce. Who could tell then that that in twenty years we would all be living still and separated from each other by such great distances? We indeed would not have believed it. How we ought to admire the Providence of God which has protected us until now. Think of me

---

32 Bishop Armand François-Marie, Comte de Charbonnel, was born in 1802 of a noble family. According to Logue (41), Bishop Charbonnel's father had been a major benefactor to Mother St. John Fontbonne when she reorganized her community after the Revolution. After joining the Society of St. Sulpice and teaching in Lyon, Versailles, and Bordeaux, Fr. Charbonnel volunteered for the missions in Montreal. He was named bishop of Toronto in 1850. (*The Congregation of the Sisters of St. Joseph, Le Puy, Lyon, St. Louis, Toronto*, Sister Mary Agnes, CSJ (Toronto: University of Toronto Press, 1951), 76-80. For additional information see Murray W. Nicholson, "Bishop Charbonnel, The Beggar Bishop and the Origins of Catholic Social Action," (*CCHA Historical Studies*, vol. 52, 1885, 51-66).

33 Sister Martha von Bunning (her name appears in different records with and without the "von") was born in 1824 in Hanover, Germany and was received into the congregation at Carondelet in 1845. More of her story can be found below in relation to Mother Agnes Spencer. The Hamilton Congregation was one of the four founding congregations of the Sisters of St. Joseph in Canada. (The other founding congregations are London, Peterborough and Pembroke.)

sometimes in your prayers. Give my love to all our dear Sisters.[34]

Less than a month later, on February 8, 1856, Mother Delphine died of cholera which she contracted while nursing the victims of an epidemic in Toronto. At the age of 43 Mother Delphine Fontbonne was the first of the French missionary sisters to die. She is greatly revered by the Canadian congregations who regard her as a martyr of charity. At her death, Bishop Charbonnel took it upon himself to send the news to France via the auspices of the Society for the Propagation of the Faith. His letter, a copy of which is preserved in the Toronto Sisters' archives, begins with a request to give the news to Father Fontbonne:

Sister Félicité Bouté ~ 1804-1881
1804 – Born in Le Puy
1825 – Received into the community in Lyon
1836 – Mission to Carondelet
1837– 47 Teacher/Infirmarian, Carondelet
1847– 70 St. Joseph Home for Boys – Superior/
    Childcare
1866 – 72 General Councilor
1870 – 73 Superior in St. Louis
1873 – 81 Retirement at Nazareth Convent

It is my sad duty to announce to him that his sister, Mother Delphine Fontbonne, Foundress and Superior of the Religious of St. Joseph in Canada, entered into her reward February 7, 1856...
This excellent and worthy niece of the saintly Mother St. John had, in five years, established in Toronto, a Novitiate, an Orphan Asylum, a House of Providence, which affords to the poor every spiritual and temporal succor, and several other houses...This holy Superior enforced the rule with sweetness and firmness. Her judgment was solid, her mind clear and penetrating and her prudence enlightened and far-seeing. She was laborious, energetic and provident...Her robust health promised her a long life, but she has fallen a victim to her charity while attending some of her Sisters and Novices stricken with fever.
    Will you be kind enough to transmit this communication to her Reverend brother, and inform also the Reverend Superior General of the Mother House at Lyon...[35]

---

34 Mother Delphine Fontbonne to Sister Félicité Bouté, January 18, 1856. (Archives, Carondelet)
35 Bishop Charbonnel to the Director of the Grand Seminary of Lyon, February, 1856. (Archives, Sisters of St. Joseph of Toronto)

THE SISTERS OF ST. JOSEPH IN PHILADELPHIA
AND CATHOLIC EDUCATION

From the time of the First Plenary Council of Baltimore in 1852, U.S. Catholic Bishops strongly promoted the establishment of parochial schools. In 1884, at the Third Plenary Council, they intensified that support by obliging parish priests to establish schools and parents to send their children to them. Catholic education became a cause célèbre for the bishops because they considered it essential to the preservation of the faith of the immigrants. Situations like that of the public schools in Philadelphia in the 1840s provided the rationale for that movement. According to historian Hugh Nolan:

> Catholic children…were suffering many abuses in public schools because of their religion. The flood of vile and oftentimes obscene anti-Catholic literature, mostly cheap pamphlets and the denunciatory sermons and speeches cascading in the 1830's from so many pulpits and platforms against the Catholic Church had not been without its effect. Biased by what they heard and read, several of the poorly trained teachers in the public schools decided to deliver their Catholic pupils…from the priestly superstitions that threatened to mislead them. Others of these teachers, aroused by bigoted contemporary accounts of the pope and his "plots" were determined to punish his followers for his great iniquities. The majority of the Protestant teachers in the public schools were not anti-Catholic…but the number of anti-Catholic teachers in the public schools did mount in the wave of anti-Catholicism that swept over the country (1835-1845), and they became more militant. [36]

The social reality of the immigrants with their need to preserve the faith in the face of discrimination called forth sister-educators across the country. From very early on Bishop John Neumann, Bishop Kenrick's successor in Philadelphia, did everything he could to promote Catholic education as well as the professional education of the teaching sisters who would carry it out.[37] Sister Assisium McEvoy of Philadelphia (1843-1939) recalled that when she was but a postulant she had heard Bishop Neumann say, "He would need for the schools all the sisters he could get – and that they must be prepared." Bishop Neumann also assured the

---

36 Hugh J. Nolan, *Francis Patrick Kenrick, Bishop of Philadelphia, 1830-1851* (Philadelphia: American Catholic Historical Society of Philadelphia, 1948) 289-90.

37 The Brentwood archives include Sister Alphonsa Maria Molloy's memories of Mother Austin and Bishop Neumann. She said that Mother Austin called him "the homeliest man that God ever made, and the holiest." Sister Alphonsa adds that he was called the "horseback priest because he would travel from Philadelphia to

sisters of an annual $50 stipend for their teaching services.[38] In spite of the bishop's priorities, Sister Assisium admitted that in the early years the sisters' education was not always a top priority. She wrote:

> Class, as class, was but sporadic, owing to building operations; there was no place to have class, even had it not been as was the case, that the students were engaged in avocations far from literacy, such as weeding, attending to dairy-farm work, and so on. . . . Studies were held in the Community room, the professed and others not studying being in the same room, and the machines and sometimes the piano being very much in evidence…
>
> To tell the truth, there seemed something of a fear of allowing a Sister to devote much time to study, lest religious humility and simplicity be injured. Time and experience, however, proved that lack of wider knowledge was no safeguard of humility, and that the modern requirements called for more strenuous preparation.[39]

If reticence about higher education characterized the community in the early years, that attitude soon lost out to a determination to prepare sisters to offer the best education possible to their students. Sister Assisium herself became a key force in promoting the education of the sisters as she worked with novices from 1868 until 1913, first teaching in the novitiate and as novice director. By 1885, three sisters were appointed to arrange a common course of studies for the sisters and four years later the congregation named a supervisor of schools. With those moves the community had taken decisive steps toward assuring the intellectual preparation necessary for excellence in the ministry of education which would be their primary service for generations to come.

THE FOUNDATION IN ST. PAUL

After a few years of constant activity and administration, Mother St. John Fournier needed a rest. In 1850, Mother Celestine Pommerel sent Sister Delphine Fontbonne to take over Mother St. John's responsibilities in the orphanage and with the novices, but that did not provide sufficient relief. As Mother St. John described the situation:

Buffalo [nearly 400 miles] to administer the sacraments, a trip which would take him a week. ("Bishop Neumann" ACSJB)
38 See Sister Mary Helen Kashuba, "Bridge" unpublished manuscript, (50)
39 Bierne e al, 10. See also Kashuba, 46 and footnote 146

The doctors insisted that I take a little rest. I decided to go and stay for a while with Mother Celestine.[40]

Upon arrival in St. Louis, she found Mother Celestine, her good friend, even more inundated with work than she herself was. At the same time, the Rt. Rev. Joseph Cretin, newly named as Bishop of St. Paul, had asked the Sisters of St. Joseph for help in his new diocese. His request was no great surprise as he had known the Sisters of St. Joseph since 1838, when he and Mathias Loras, the first bishop of Dubuque, spent the winter 1838-39 at Carondelet because ice on the Mississippi made it impossible for them to travel north.[41] The two clerics had given a mission at Carondelet followed by a retreat for the sisters just before Sister St. John Fournier pronounced her vows. Because Father Saulnier at the Carondelet parish had no room for them in the rectory, the two clerics lodged in a cabin on the sisters' property and shared meals with the sisters at Carondelet. Bishop Loras even helped in the kitchen and shared recipes with Sister Philomène, the cook.[42] Thirteen years later, after he was named the first bishop of the new Diocese of St. Paul, Joseph Cretin remembered the sisters. Although other communities had refused his request for sisters, he had success when he turned to Mother Celestine. Mother St. John Fournier described these events as follows:

> Shortly after my arrival at Carondelet, Bishop Cretin came to ask for some sisters for his Diocese of St. Paul. Seeing our poor Mother in a great quandary because the classes and different missions had all been arranged, I offered to accompany the sisters and help the young superior a little. This consoled our dear Mother very much but caused me many secret tears.
>
> Four of us...sailed up the Mississippi. When we arrived at Lake Pepin, almost a hundred miles from St. Paul, the ice was so thick you could scarcely move. Finally we arrived on November 24, 1851, and

Bishop Joseph Cretin

---

40 "Fournier Letter." (Logue 337)
41 Mathias Loras (1792-1858) was from a noble Lyon family that lost 17 members to the guillotine during the Revolution. Ordained by Cardinal Fesch, he became a missionary to Mobile, Alabama in 1829 and was named first bishop of Dubuque in 1837. He immediately traveled to France to recruit missionaries. Joseph Cretin (1799-1857) was born in Ain, about 90 kilometers north of Lyon. After ordination he hoped to become a missionary to China but instead accepted Loras' invitation. The lore is that he was so well loved that he had to leave his parish secretly in the night lest the parishioners try to stop him. After accompanying Loras to the U.S. and serving in Dubuque, he took over in St. Paul on July 2, 1851, where he took possession of the log cabin that served as his first cathedral and rectory. (Savage, 53-54)
42 Savage, 53-54 and Logue 43.

Bishop Cretin, that dear, good bishop, took us ashore and housed us in his palace which was nothing but a log cabin, consisting of one room and an attic open on all sides. So our room served us as chapel, refectory, community room, parlor, and dormitory. In the evening we would bring out mattresses and put two of them on the table (when it was made) and two on the floor.

We began school in the old church near us. The following spring the bishop built a fine brick school which served us also as a dormitory for the boarders.[43]

The sisters who founded the mission in St. Paul included two Frenchwomen, Mother St. John and Sister Philomène Vilaine from Lyon, Sister Scholastica Vasques, a "creole" from Saint Louis, and Sister Francis Joseph Ivory who was born in Pennsylvania. It would have been difficult to assemble a more diverse group of U.S. Sisters of St. Joseph. Mother St. John was 37 years old and an experienced superior. The 39 year old Sister Philomène had come to Carondelet in 1836, may have been a lay sister who, in spite of that designation, ministered as a teacher and superior in St. Louis and St. Paul.[44] The youngest among them, the 17 year old Sister Scholastica, came from a family whose ethnic background probably included French and Spanish members. Sister Francis Joseph Ivory, 21 years old, was the daughter of Irish immigrants from Loretto County, Pennsylvania and had received the habit three years previous, in 1847.

The primitive conditions the sisters experienced in St. Paul were similar to those at Carondelet in the early years with the addition of frigid winters and the meager number of residents in the region. According to Bishop Cretin, the population of the entire diocese included 3,000 Catholics, 1,000 heretics (Protestants) and 27,000 infidels (Native Americans). Three foreign-born priests served the entire area. The bishop also reported that "two kinds of stables actually serve for the celebration of the sacred mysteries, meriting neither the name of

---

43 "Fournier Letter," (Logue, 337)
44 Sister Philomène is the only Carondelet foundress of whom there is no extant photograph. That has led to the speculation that she was a lay sister. On the other hand, she had just made vows when the missionaries departed for New Orleans and the list of her ministries does not sound like that of a lay sister.
The tradition of designating some members as "lay sisters" was common in religious communities that came from France where the division of classes was accepted as normal. Lay sisters wore a distinctive habit and did not receive the same education as the "choir sisters." According to the research done by Coburn and Smith, Bishop Rosati counseled the first sisters that it would be better if the sisters all dressed in the same style of habit in order to avoid offending the democratic sensibilities of the people of the United States. See Carol Coburn and Martha Smith, *Spirited Lives, How Nuns Shaped Catholic Culture and American Life, 1836-1920.* (Chapel Hill: University of North Carolina Press) 84 and 253. Sister Scholastica was "a young Sister of French-

churches or chapels."[45] Sister Francis Joseph described the state of affairs in those days saying:

> To understand the position of the young Community our first year, you must know (at that time) Minnesota was an Indian Camping grounds. The chief settlers were Indian traders. No farms had yet been planted, no public conveyance. (Winter) The only roadway to settlement below was the Miss. River which was then frozen and the wolves often attacked travelers as they traveled over the ice. The nearest place to procure provision was Dubuque, Iowa, 500 miles away. So very often others were as bad off as ourselves, nothing could be procured for Love nor Money. This was the state of things, from Nov. to about the last of May -- when an Event occurred that changed all for the better up to this time. This was the arrival of the first Steamer after the ice had broken. As the Steamer, the City of St. Paul, came steaming up, the excitement was intense. Every individual in town was on the river bank, with a loud Welcome for the friend who brought them all comfort. All temporal difficulty vanished with this event.[46]

Writing about those days, Mother St. John shared her wry humor as she filled out some details about their first year in St. Paul.

> We were quite far from the church and there were not as yet any streets or roads in St. Paul. All they had done was to cut down trees in a row and leave all the stumps. Every morning that winter, before the snow came, when we were going to church, we would make a number of genuflections and finally would kiss the ground. Once the snow came we would sink in two or three feet, or we would walk over it, if it were ice. It was on one of these mornings that the hungry wolf tried to get a piece or all of my body. The next day, and all the rest of the winter, the bishop came to say Mass on the table in our old palace.[47]

After spending but a few days settling in their rustic surroundings, the sisters opened a school in the vestibule of the church. Less than a year later, in autumn, 1852, classes began in the new brick school house that Bishop Cretin had built. Regarding that house, Bishop John Ireland, the third bishop of St. Paul, wrote:

Spanish descent...a native of St. Louis." (Monograph: "History of the St. Paul Province, 1851-1943," Sister Marie du Rosaire Coloumbe. Archives Carondelet 1.)
45 "Fournier Letter" (Logue, 337).
46 Letter from Sister Francis Joseph Ivory, September 10, 1890, written at the request of Sister Monica Corrigan (Generalate Archives: Carondelet). Hereafter: "Ivory, "Letter."
47 "Fournier Letter," (Logue, 337-339)

Mean of proportion and of form this building seemed in the eyes of the later generation that doomed it to demolition; but in 1852 it was the wonder of the village, and its construction was taken by the settlers as an indubitable sign of rapidly-coming prosperity and civilization in the Northwest.[48]

The new building was large enough for 87 students and also served as a dormitory for the 17 boarders among them. It was from there in 1852, sixteen years after the the first sisters arrived in the U.S., that the Sisters of St. Joseph initiated their first mission to the Native American population in Long Prairie in central Minnesota.[49] According to Sister Francis Joseph:

> Sister Scholastica Vasques, went alone up to the Long Prairie, amongst the Chippawey [sic] Indians, remained one winter instructing, aiding an enthusiastic Italian Priest, Pere de Vivaldi, who afterward became a fugitive from the Church. Poor Sister told us thrilling tales...in her school were grown up men and women. Sometimes the men would drink and then she was obliged to hide.[50]

Serving alone on that mission, Sister Scholastica lived with a French and Indian family whose daughter helped her prepare the indigenous people to receive the sacraments. The following year additional sisters were missioned to the reservation to teach in a school sponsored by the federal government.[51] According to Father Vivaldi's reports, the school served more than 60 children. Commenting on the children, he said:

> The little girls in particular behave in a remarkable way. Almost all of them have learned to read, write and sing. Many have embraced the Christian religion and are advancing rapidly in becoming civilized: all

---

48 Helen Angela Hurley, CSJ, *On Good Ground, The Story of the Sisters of St. Joseph in St. Paul*, (St. Paul: University of Minnesota Press, 1951) 32.

49 The Long Prairie area had been inhabited by Native American peoples (Sioux/Dakota and later Anishinaabe/Ojibwe) long before settlers of European heritage came to the area. In 1845, the area was designated as a site for a U.S. Indian Agency and then a school. In the early 21st century the town encompassed less than 3 square miles and had a population of just under 3,500. Prior to opening this mission, Sisters of St. Joseph had probably taught a few Native American children in the schools in Philadelphia and St. Paul, but this was the first time they ministered to a community of Native Americans.

50 Ivory, "Letter."

51 The sisters' mission in Long Prairie was affected by the ongoing competition between Catholic and Protestant missionaries for rights and funds to serve the Native Americans. Bishop Cretin had a strong desire to serve the people, but his efforts were frustrated by government agents who were slow to provide the financing that had been promised for the maintenance of the school and faculty. See Hurley, 32 - 41 and Dougherty, 432.

because of the zeal and the love of the Sisters.[52]

Sister Ursula Murphy, one of the sisters later assigned to the school, wrote a long letter to a friend describing her experience. She included the tale of her adventure with a kind Protestant who helped her on her journey and the way she was able to stand up to Father Vivaldi, a man generally determined to have his own way.

> I was sent to Long Prairie Jan. 3, 1854. Sister Scholastica was recalled to St. Paul. I found Sister Cesarine and Simeon there...Sr. C. was put in Sr. Scholastica's place as Superior, I remained there until the Indians were removed to Blue Earth [1855]...
>
> According to their Treaty, each pupil received a certain amount of flour, pork, blankets, and everything needed for food and raiment. Each of us received $40 per month...everything had to be brought from St. Paul and hauled in wagons to the Mission. It was in one of those trips that I was hauled up there.
>
> You know dear Bishop Cretin was fond of sending Sisters off alone... The weather was extremely severe, and I was not well provided for such a journey in an open wagon loaded with barrels of flour & pork, etc. After riding all day we arrived late in the evening at a little log house, occupied by an old couple & their son. They had no accommodations – however we were glad to get shelter for the night...The old woman fell in love with me – she tried every way she could think of to have me stay with her. She seemed almost heartbroken next morning when I was leaving her.
>
> The next day we were overtaken by a man by the name of Moran, with a team loaded with provisions going to the pineries above Long Prairie...Mr. Moran...asked where I was going, how I came to be alone – he said: I see those men have no judgment or no care for your safety – you will never get there alive traveling in this way. I will take you in my sleigh and try to get you there safe. You will perish if you remain as you are...
>
> I consented to travel in his sleigh – he deprived himself of his Buffalo robes, blankets, etc. for my comfort. At night wherever we put up the best accommodations had to be for me, the rest might be satisfied with anything they could get.
>
> When we arrived at Long Prairie, Rev. de Vivaldi met us. After Mr. Moran had left he showed some displeasure and asked me why I was with that Orangeman. I told him how and why. I had been sent out

---

52 Hurley, 49.

without robes or blankets and the men had kept theirs for themselves & I was very cold, when that man took me and gave me his robes and took good care of me all the way. It seemed not to satisfy Rev. F. de V. He said "That is an Orangeman of the worst kind." But I did not think so.[53]

Problems with the wily Father Vivaldi combined with the government's decision to move the native people of Long Prairie to a reservation called Blue Earth led the sisters to return to St. Paul in 1855, bringing to an end the community's first ministry with Native Americans. Nevertheless, Father Vivaldi's influence continued in that he persuaded one of the sisters, Sister Cesarine, to go with him as the superior of a congregation he decided to found to serve as missionaries to indigenous people.[54]

The St. Paul community grew with local vocations as well as additional sisters sent from Carondelet. Louisa (Sister Mary Gregory) LeMay, St. Paul's first postulant was a French Canadian who entered the community in 1854, at the age of 22. Eventually fifteen members of her extended family would become members of the Congregation.[55] Louisa must have been remarkably mature – or the community felt a dire need for workers – as she received the habit within twelve weeks of becoming a postulant. Sister Marie Rosaire tells the story of her reception as follows:

The ceremony took place in the Cathedral on Wabasha Street. Bishop Cretin presided and Mother Celestine came from Carondelet...There was so much excitement attending this first ceremony that the young novice left the church without being given a name. She was obliged to repair to the sacristy to inform the Bishop. Opening his ordo to the Saint

---

53 Hurley (50 - 52), notes that Sister Ursula had written all of this to Sister Ignatius Cox, "a stately Bostonian" who later commented that during the War Between the States, Sister Ursula, an impetuous Irish woman, had been expelled from the community in St. Paul "for her too open expression of southern sympathies, on account of which the work of the mission was threatened. Sister [Ursula] went to Wheeling, West Virginia and was received by the Sisters of St. Joseph, then an independent foundation." After a short period of poor adjustment to that group, she finally settled down to a peaceful life with the Sisters of St. Joseph in Buffalo, New York, where she died in 1916." The government salary would have been a great boon to the community. In that same era, the Philadelphia sister teachers were receiving $50 per year, which was certainly more typical of what bishops and parishes could offer.
54 In spite of the bishop's refusal to give him permission to do so, Father Vivaldi founded The Sisters of the Love of God, a congregation for women from European-Native families. When Sister Cesarine joined that community as its first superior, the bishop excommunicated her. According to Vivaldi, the Congregation of the Love of God was ten times more perfect than the Sisters of St. Joseph, about whom he began to speak very disparagingly. The Congregation of the Love of God community did not flourish and Sister Cesarine later moved to another community of Sisters of St. Joseph. (Hurley 58.)
55 Coloumbe, 6-7.

of the day, the Bishop gave her the name of Gregoire.[56]

Another sister from the St. Paul Province filled out the story with details that included including the participation of the whole community in the reception ceremony and the unusual way in which Sister M. Louisa's parents learned of her entry into the Congregation.

> Louise LeMay was the first postulant received into the community in St. Paul and her reception was altogether unique in the history of the sisterhood. It was on the occasion of Mother Celestine's second visit to Minnesota. Another missionary was needed for the Long Prairie Mission, so Bishop Cretin and Mother Celestine on May 26th decided to give the habit to one of the two postulants then on probation. The retreat ordained by the rule was dispensed with and the following day...the ceremony was to take place.
>
> We had no sewing machines then, and you can easily imagine how all hands were pressed into service to prepare the postulant's outfit. At the cathedral on Sunday morning at the six o'clock Mass the ceremony was performed...
>
> Owing to the confusion and hurry incident to time and place, the ringlets severed from the head of the postulant were forgotten in the sacristy, where they were afterwards found and sent, by the order of the bishop, to her parents. This was the first intimation they received of the reception of their daughter.[57]

After two years at Long Prairie, Sister Mary Gregory ministered in health care in what became the St. Paul and St. Louis provinces.

The next sister to be received in St. Paul was Sister Mary Gregory's nineteen year old sister Justine (Julia) who was received on June 10, 1854, and made vows on November 20, 1856. She was followed by her cousin, Sister Pauline LeMay. Between 1851 and 1861, thirteen women entered the congregation in St. Paul, of those, five were born in Canada, four in Ireland, one in St. Paul, one in Maine and the birthplace of two was unrecorded. Their ages at reception ranged from sixteen (Sister Seraphine Ireland and her cousin Sister Celestine Howard) to twenty-three (Sister Peter Richard Grace).

------

56 Columbe, 5-6. According to congregational records, Sister "Mary Gregory" LeMay entered the congregation on February 28, 1854, and received the habit on May 25th of the same year. She made vows on August 4, 1856, and died on July 17, 1894, at St. Joseph Hospital, Kansas City, Missouri.
57 From "A Diary of a Sister of St. Joseph Written in the Period 1852-1905 (Excerpts read by Sister Mary William to a Group of Sisters on March 9, 1977." Transcriber Ida Darsow.) Archives Carondelet.

By August, 1853, Mother Saint John Fournier had returned to Philadelphia at the request of Bishop Neumann and the sisters there. Sister Seraphine Coughlin became the next superior in St. Paul.[58] At the time of that transition, Sister Francis Joseph Ivory returned to St. Louis, and Mother Celestine had sent five more sisters to St. Paul so that there were a total of seven sisters serving in two local schools and Long Prairie. Sister Seraphine Coughlin would remain in St. Paul as superior until her untimely death in 1861.

THE COMMUNITY AT AGE 18

In 1853 more than 80 Sisters of St. Joseph could be found in the dioceses of St. Louis, Philadelphia and St. Paul and there was no dearth of requests for their services.[59] The Philadelphia community had already opened its own novitiate with Mother St. John Fournier as the first novice director, followed by Sister Delphine Fontbonne in 1850. Mother St. John, whose formal preparation was in the education of the deaf, had also been the first superior of the Philadelphia hospital staffed by the Sisters of St. Joseph from 1848-1851.

As is obvious from comments in her letter to Lyon, Mother St. John made up for her lack of formal preparation in nursing by her willingness to serve and lead others to do what they never thought themselves capable of doing. It was that attitude of readiness to learn and to respond to the unmet need which characterized the first Sisters of St. Joseph who served as teachers, nurses, childcare workers and administrators.[60] By the early 1850s, the community was gaining a far-flung reputation for apostolic freedom and willingness to serve their dear neighbor in any way they could. Thus it was not a surprise that Bishop Richard Whelan appealed to Mother Celestine at Carondelet for sisters to staff a hospital he was inaugurating in Wheeling, Virginia.

---

58 Sister Seraphine Coughlin was born in New York and received the habit of the Sisters of St. Joseph at Carondelet in 1846, having resided in St. Louis previous to entering the community. Before she went to St. Paul she had been novice director in St. Louis. Bishop John Ireland described her as "a woman whose intelligence, refinement, and saintliness of character stamped her in the memory of the diocese as an ideal daughter of Christ and an ideal servant of Holy Church." (Savage, 89).

59 This number is conservative and is based on Logue (321) which lists 22 sisters in ministry in the diocese and the Carondelet reception book which lists 80 members as of 1853, recognizing that some Carondelet sisters had gone to Philadelphia, two had returned to France and one sister who entered at Carondelet had died.

60 In the 1850s, nursing was far from being a developed profession in the U.S. The first hospital in Philadelphia was also the almshouse and jail and had untrained prisoners serving in the capacity of nurses. In 1832, Sisters of Charity of Emmitsburg went to Philadelphia to nurse during a cholera epidemic when the regular hospital attendants demanded increased wages only to spend the money on liquor and disrupt the hospital. The drunken attendants were reported for engaging in drunken brawls over the beds of patients while others "lay in a stupor beside the bodies of the dead." The Sisters came immediately upon receiving Bishop Kenrick's request and,

MISSION TO WHEELING

Bishop Richard Whelan (1809-1874) was born in Baltimore, studied at St. Mary's Seminary in Baltimore and then in Paris where he was ordained in 1831. In 1840, he was named Bishop of the Diocese of Richmond which included the entire State of Virginia. As a result of his persistence and the support of his fellow bishops, Rome created the Diocese of Wheeling out of Richmond, and Richard Whelan became its first bishop.[61] Carondelet has no record of Whelan's correspondence with Mother Celestine and therefore no information about how he knew the Sisters of St. Joseph or decided to ask them for help. He quite likely heard about the community from his brother bishops, most particularly from Archbishop Francis Kenrick whom he would have known particularly from the First Plenary Council of Baltimore in 1852, at which Archbishop Francis P. Kenrick presided. Bishop Whelan had been ordained in 1831 for the Diocese of Baltimore and taught at St. Mary's Seminary before he was named Bishop of Richmond in 1840.[62]

Mother Celestine accepted Bishop Whelan's request and sent four sisters to begin work in the hospital he was planning. The sisters she chose for the mission were Sisters Agatha Guthrie, Anastasia O'Brien, Sebastian Reis and Alexis Spellicy. Sister Agatha was a Pennsylvanian born in 1829, who made vows at Carondelet in 1852; Sister Anastasia (1820-1868) was born in Ireland and made vows at Carondelet in 1850; Sister Sebastian was born in Germany in 1829, and

---

"They took in hand the whole desperate situation, at once restored order and disseminated about them an atmosphere of tranquility and quiet energy." See: M. Adelaide Nutting and Lavinia L. Dock, A History of Nursing: The Evolution of Nursing Systems from Earliest Times To the Foundation of the first English and American Training Schools for Nurses, (N.Y.: G. Putnam's Sons, 1907-1912) Vol. 2, 329-335.

61 Whelan, ordained in 1831 for the Diocese of Baltimore, was reputed to be an austere missionary who qualified his request for priests from All Hallows Seminary in Ireland with the caveat that they should be priests with zeal and energy, devotion and piety. Talent was desirable, but good sense preferable to brilliance. Whelan's diocese eventually received more priests from All Hallows than any other U.S. diocese apart from California. (See Gerald P. Fogarty, S. J., *Commonwealth Catholicism* (Notre Dame Indiana, University of Notre Dame Press, 2001) 83-85.

62 The three Plenary Councils of Baltimore were so named because they were the first held after there was more than one Archdiocese in the United States. The First Plenary Council in 1852 brought together the bishops from six established U.S. archdioceses, California (not yet incorporated in the U.S. Church structure) and Canada. Among the decrees of the council the thirteenth stated that every parish should have a Catholic school and the fourteenth stated that every province should have a seminary. From his position in Baltimore, Archbishop Francis Kenrick was appointed the Apostolic Delegate and convener of the first of the three plenary councils; the other two were held in 1866 and 1884. Whelan had also tried to enlist Kenrick in a plan to encourage Catholics to colonize western Virginia. (Fogarty, 91.)

made vows in Wheeling in 1853. Sister Alexis (1834-1908) was born in County Cork, lived in Cincinnati before entering the congregation, made vows at Carondelet in 1854, and eventually became a member of Carondelet's Troy Province.[63]

On April 3, 1853, the four sisters arrived in Wheeling to be greeted by their new bishop with the news that the home he had arranged for them was suddenly unavailable. The problem was that the Protestant landlady felt that she had been misinformed. She had assumed that the "sisters" coming were members of a family, not Catholic women religious. Nuns were not welcome to rent from her. These unexpectedly homeless but flexible sisters simply took up residence in the attic of the small hospital building. About a month later, Mother Celestine Pommerel accompanied Agnes Spencer, the new superior, and Sister Liguori Leigh from Philadelphia to Wheeling. Their arrival brought the founding community of Wheeling to a total of six.

The new superior, Mother Agnes Spencer, had come from serving as superior of the orphanage in Philadelphia. She remained just over one year in Wheeling because in October, 1854, Mother Celestine called her to return to Carondelet in preparation for the opening of a mission in Canandaigua, New York.[64] Mother Agnes was followed, as superior for one year, by Sister St. Protais, next by Sister Agatha Guthrie, who served for two years and then by Sister Teresa Struckhoff who served as superior from 1858-1859. The quick succession of superiors suggests that Mother Celestine and the sisters in Wheeling had no idea that they were founding a new congregation that would need long-term stability and autonomous organization; more likely they simply intended to open another new, distant mission in which various sisters would serve as needed.

The hospital, the sisters' first home and ministry site in Wheeling, was a simple house that had been a private physician's office and infirmary. Between 1850 and 1852, Bishop Whelan had joined with area residents to arrange the legal incorporation of what would be called Wheeling Hospital with its first location in that building.[65] The small Wheeling Hospital was the only health care institution

---

63 The Wheeling documents and others spell her name "Alexis" while official records at Carondelet also spell her name Alexius and Alexious.

64 As will be seen, Sr. Agnes Spencer would open the mission in Buffalo in 1856, and in 1860, the mission that became the Congregation of the Sisters of St. Joseph of Erie.

65 Rose Anita Kelly *Song of the Hills, The Story of the Sisters of St. Joseph of Wheeling* (Mt. St. Joseph, Wheeling, W. Va., 1962) 33.

in the more than 400 miles between Cincinnati and Pittsburghh and the building accommodated a maximum of twelve patients with the sisters making creative multi-faceted use of the private quarters which consisted of two small rooms. With that amount of space, they still found a way to receive two Protestant orphan girls, Beth and Sue Saunders whose brother had been taken in by a local family. As was typical of the Sisters of St. Joseph, no matter the size of their home, there always seemed to be room for orphans.

Good will notwithstanding, the hospital space was cramped to the point that some patient beds occupied the hallways. Sister Rose Anita Kelly, one of the Wheeling community chroniclers, wrote a colorful narrative about the development of the sisters' ministry as well as the answer to their prayers for a more spacious ministry site. It all began with an incident that took place while Sister St. Protais was superior in 1854. Sister Rose Anita wrote:

> On the morning of April 23, as the sisters walked to…Mass, they decided God had answered their prayer in a very strange way…He had placed a small, pathetic-looking orphan boy in their path, a boy who needed a home.
>
> The little lad seemed to loom up out of the mist hovering over the Ohio River…a picture of distress and bewilderment…"A cherub in a beggar's disguise," thought Mother St. Protais…She asked, "What is your name, my child?" Lifting a pair of tearful gray eyes, he replied simply, "My name is Tommy Saunders. My two sisters live in the hospital with you ladies."…Tell me, Tommy, why you are here on the street all alone so early in the morning?"
>
> With trembling lips the child sought to explain, "She (meaning his foster mother) gave me money to buy coffee at the market. I lost it! I cannot find it! I'm afraid to go back! They will beat me again…I want Beth and Sue. Let me go to Beth and Sue."
>
> "Very well, my dear," promised Mother St. Protais, "you shall go to Beth and Sue as fast as your sturdy little legs will take you to the hospital…You will find Beth in the kitchen…Tell her Sister said to give you a good breakfast…."
>
> Mother St. Protais remarked to the sisters as they resumed their way to Mass, "Since God has sent us another little orphan to shelter, perhaps this is His way of telling us He is going to give us the additional space for which we are praying."

…Mother St. Protais was a good prophet when it came to speculating on God's infinite goodness. Her trust in Divine Providence knew no bounds. When the sisters returned to the hospital after Mass, Mother St. Protais…found Tommy…enjoying the first good meal he had had in a month…Love was taking care of little Tommy. Beth and Sue were loyally standing by their little brother… Mother St. Protais said reassuringly, "You need not return to the country, Tommy. You will stay here and go to school with your sisters." A pair of thin arms encircled Mother St. Protais' waist and in that moment Wheeling's first orphanage had grown from two to three.

Later in the morning Mother St. Protais brought the matter of Tommy's dilemma before Bishop Whelan…[who] willingly consented to the sisters' taking charge of rearing and educating the child. He said, "You are crowded for space now, Sisters, but it won't be long before the new hospital will be ready for occupancy. Then you'll have a whole wing to shelter your motherless children until we can erect a separate building for them." God had answered their prayer.[66]

Sister Agatha Guthrie
1829 – 1904
Born in Springfield PA.
Received: Carondelet, 1850
Vows: 1852
1852 - 3, Teacher, Carondelet
1853 to Wheeling
1855 -1858 – Superior, Wheeling
1858 - 59 – Director of Novices, Carondelet
1861- 66 First Provincial, Troy, N.Y.
1866 -72 Carondelet, Asst.Superior General
1872 - 1904 Superior General, Carondelet.

In 1856, Bishop Whelan arranged a charter for a new hospital/orphanage. That same year, when Sister St. Protais returned to Carondelet, twenty-seven year old Sister Agatha Guthrie who had made vows just four years earlier was appointed superior of the community and administrator of the community works in Wheeling. She took over that responsibility just as the sisters moved to their new home, a hospital with room for 100 patients with space for the orphans in an area well-separated from the sick.[67]

---

66 Kelly, 194-5.
67 Agatha Guthrie's parents had named her Minerva. As a young teacher in St. Louis she became a convert and took the name Philomena. She entered Carondelet in 1850 and after only three months postulate received the habit and the religious name Mary Agatha. (See Kelly, 199)

The community grew slowly with local vocations supplemented by sisters sent from Carondelet. The first woman from the area to enter the community was Mary Feeny (Sister Immaculate) whom Sister St. Protais sent to the novitiate at Carondelet. In 1856, Eliza Mathews entered the community and received the name Sister Mary Stanislaus. She was the first postulant received into the community at Wheeling. While Sister Agatha was superior, Sister Immaculate (Mary) Feeney returned from the novitiate at Carondelet to become the first Sister of St. Joseph to make vows in Wheeling. Sister Agatha Guthrie returned to Carondelet in late 1858, where she would remain for three years, before being named Provincial Superior of the Troy (New York) Province of Carondelet.

When Sister Agatha returned to Carondelet, Sister Theresa Struckhoff became superior in Wheeling.[68] Sister Theresa who had entered the congregation at Carondelet came to Wheeling in 1858, from Toronto, Canada, where she had been elected Superior General in 1856, after the death of Mother Delphine Fontbonne, the founder of the first Canadian mission.

When Sister Teresa Struckhoff returned to Carondelet, on June 7, 1859, Mother St. John Facemaz appointed Sister Stanislaus Mathews, who had been Wheeling's first novice, to succeed her. Sister Agatha Guthrie who had received her into the community and had recently returned to Carondelet to be director of novices must have been able to assure Mother St. John that even at the age of twenty-four and professed for only two years, Sister Stanislaus was ready to be superior. In the months that followed her appointment, Sister Stanislaus received three candidates into the community, one of whom was her own cousin.[69]

Shortly into her term as superior, Sister Stanislaus was called to represent the Wheeling community at a formal

First Superiors at Wheeling
Sister Agnes Spencer: 1853-1854
Sister St. Protais DeBoille, 1854-1855
Sister Agatha Guthrie, 1856-1858
Sister Teresa Struckhoff, 1858-1859
Sister Stanislaus Matthews, 1859-1860
Sister Immaculata Feeny, 1860-1864
Sister de Chantal Keating, 1864-1876

---

68 Caroline Struckhoff was born in Holdhof, Germany in 1822 and was received into the congregation at Carondelet in 1844. Before being missioned to Toronto in 1853, Sister M. Theresa had ministered in child care and taught in St. Vincent's German school in St. Louis. Her personnel record at Carondelet indicates that she was elected Superior General in Toronto on March 19, 1856. In 1858, she was missioned to Wheeling as superior. In 1859, she returned to Carondelet and later ministered in Illinois and then in St. Louis where she remained until her death in 1905, having lived 61 years as a Sister of St. Joseph.
69 Kelly, 203-4. Sister Rose Anita's book mistakenly indicates that Mother Celestine appointed Sister Stanislaus, but in 1859, Mother St. John Facemaz was superior at Carondelet. Mother Celestine had died in 1857.

meeting of superiors at Carondelet planned by Mother St. John Facemaz and Archbishop Kenrick to discuss plans for organizing the American houses of Sisters of St. Joseph into provinces of a unified congregation in the United States. It was Sister Stanislaus who had to communicate Bishop Whelan's decision that the Wheeling sisters would not be allowed to become part of that new congregation. When the superiors decided to form the Carondelet congregation, Bishop Whelan gave the sisters in Wheeling the opportunity to choose whether to remain as part of a new diocesan congregation or return to Carondelet. On May 4, 1860, Sisters Stanislaus Mathews and Immaculata Feeney, both natives of Virginia, and novices Sr. Vincent Smyth of Virginia and Sister Aloysius Sullivan, originally from Maryland, chose to remain in Wheeling along with postulant Sarah Breslin who would be known as Sister M. John Evangelist. These five comprised the Wheeling community while Sisters Anastasia O'Brien and Sebastian Reis who had come from Carondelet and Sister Mary Xavier Stillwagon, a Pennsylvania native who had made her novitiate at Carondelet, returned to St. Louis.

One wonders what Bishop Whelan thought as he assessed his new autonomous congregation of four professed sisters. Any concern he had at first surely increased as he saw that Sister Stanislaus was not recovering from a serious cold she had contracted in St. Louis. Hoping that a respite would speed her recuperation, the sisters convinced her to go to her family home. Unfortunately, all the care lavished on her was insufficient and Mother Stanislaus Mathews, the first superior of the Sisters of St. Joseph of Wheeling, died on October 19, 1860, a little more than five months after the congregation had separated from Carondelet. Her dying wish was to be buried in Wheeling and Bishop Whelan celebrated her funeral in the same hospital chapel where she had received the habit and professed vows.[70]

On December 1, 1860, Bishop Whelan appointed Sister Immaculata Feeny as the new superior of the Wheeling

Mother Francis de Chantal Keating
1833 - 1917
Born in Tipperary,
1857 entered SSJ's in Brooklyn
1862-64 Novice Director
1864-76 Superior, Wheeling
1874-1917 Superior, St. John's Home for Boys

70 Kelly, 205-209 and Ann Hoye, Seasons of Nature and Grace, 30.

community. This Carondelet-trained twenty-five year old who had entered the community just before Sister Stanislaus, assumed responsibility for the community and novitiate as well as the administration of the hospital and the orphanage. Mother Immaculata had a very small community with large responsibilities at a time of immense national and local turmoil. We know little about the pressures on her except for the fact that after a little more than three years, on February 26, 1864, she found it necessary to resign.

Bishop Whelan must have prepared for her resignation with some anticipation because he had a replacement on the scene when she left office. In order to do that, he had to have obtained the collaboration of Bishop Loughlin and Mother Austin Kean. On February 28, 1864, he formally installed Mother Francis de Chantal Keating, a Sister of St. Joseph of Brooklyn, as the seventh superior appointed to the Wheeling community in its eleven years of existence.

Mother de Chantal's leadership in Wheeling brought extraordinary results. When she came to Wheeling in 1864, there were eight sisters conducting two small schools and the hospital/orphanage. When she finished her term in 1876, there were fifty-seven sisters serving in the hospital/orphanage and five schools. Under her leadership, not only did the community grow but the number of sisters available for the ministries at hand had increased enough to allow them more time for the prayer and community life that complements ministry. In that period they also played a significant role among the sister-nurses who served the victims of the Civil War. That portion of their story belongs to the history of the Sisters of St. Joseph in the ministry of health care.

CANANDAIGUA – THE PIONEERS OF THE BUFFALO AND ROCHESTER CONGREGATIONS

In 1845, there were three Catholic churches in the northwestern New York city of Buffalo whose growing population had reached 40,000.[71] In 1847, at the strong insistence of the U.S. bishops, Rome created the dioceses of Albany and Buffalo from the territory of the Diocese of New York and named the Vincentian Visitor, John Timon, as the first bishop of Buffalo.[72] His long-standing relationship with

---

71 See Sister M. of the Sacred Heart Dunne, *The Congregation of the Sisters of St. Joseph of Buffalo, 1854-1933: A Brief Account of its Origin and Work* (Buffalo: Holling Press, 1934), 67. Buffalo's first Catholic church was built in 1831, by French Canadians and by 1837, an English speaking congregation had been founded. Steven Badin (1768-1853), the first priest ordained in the U.S. and St. John N. Neumann (1811-1860) were early missionaries in the Buffalo area. (See: Thomas Donohue. "Buffalo." The Catholic Encyclopedia. Vol. 3. New York: Robert Appleton Company, 1908, <http://www.newadvent.org/cathen/03037a.htm)
72 The role of the Visitor was comparable to the provincial in other congregations. John Timon, C.M. was born

the Sisters of St. Joseph made their superiors, Mother Celestine and Mother St. John, friends to whom he could turn when seeking help in his new diocese. When Father Edmund O'Connor sought sisters to staff St. Mary's School in Canandaigua, Bishop Timon referred him directly to Mother Celestine. In response to his request, in December, 1854, Sisters Agnes Spencer, Theodosia Hagemann, Francis Joseph Ivory and Petronilla Roscoe left St. Louis to travel by riverboat and train to Canandaigua.[73]

English-born Sister Agnes Spencer (1823-1882), then thirty-two years old, had been a Sister of St. Joseph for eight years. In 1851, she had been missioned to Philadelphia where she served as superior at St. John's Orphanage, in 1853, she was the founding superior in Wheeling. Sister Theodosia, a German-born immigrant, was received in 1852, and made vows at Carondelet in 1854. In 1856, she helped open the mission in Brooklyn. In 1857, she returned to Carondelet and received a dispensation from her vows. Although Sister Francis Joseph indicates that Sister Petronilla was a novice when she came to Canandaigua, there is no record of her reception in either the Carondelet or the Philadelphia congregation. The Buffalo congregation records her profession date as June 24, 1856 which indicates that she may have been a postulant when she went to Canandaigua.[74]

Nearly forty years later, Sister Francis Joseph could still recall details of their adventure. She wrote:

> Our trip was rather a fatiguing one – We left St. Louis Dec. 3, 1854, Feast of St. Francis Xavier. We traveled by boat to Alton, Ill…We then took seats in a rickety R.R. car, about midnight. The weather was extremely cold…our feet were almost frozen…We arrived in Chicago late the next day - we then took some kind of conveyance, rode up to the Cathedral…

February 12, 1797, the third of twelve children of Irish immigrant parents. His education included study at St. Mary's College in Baltimore where he may have been a school companion of Mother Seton's sons. In 1822, Timon was admitted to the Vincentian seminary in St. Louis and in 1823, he was accepted into the Vincentian community. Rosati eventually tried unsuccessfully to get Timon to accept being his coadjutor in St. Louis. In 1847, he did accept the nomination to become the first Bishop of Buffalo. Timon had known the Sisters of St. Joseph since their arrival in New Orleans in 1836, where he was with Bishop Rosati to greet them and travel with them to St. Louis. Sisters St. John Fournier and Celestine Pommerel, the two major superiors in 1854, did not arrive in the U.S. until 1837.

73 The small town of Canandaigua is located about 30 miles southeast of Rochester. In 1850, Canandaigua had a population of 3,200.

74 Further investigation suggests that Sister Petronilla's name may have been omitted from Carondelet's reception records because, by the time a formal record was made from the original notebooks, Sister had received a dispensation - sometime after 1863. (Information gathered through a collaboration with congregational archivists Kathy Urbanic of Rochester and Britt Call of Buffalo.)

Mother Agnes Spencer...wished to see the Bishop (O'Regan) who was a special friend of our Sisters.[75] He received us most cordially...gave us a good warm meal; -- our train left late in the evening. We had a long way to ride...

Finally we arrived at Buffalo on the evening of the 6th of Dec. We stopped at some place near the depot, refreshed with a warm drink, but suffered terribly from cold feet. Next morning, 7th, we started for Canandaigua. When as far as Rochester, 75 miles from our destination, the officials announced that we must stop until the track could be cleaned of snow...and poor dear Mother, whose kind heart felt for us more than herself -- she told us her money was all gone...

We proposed to look up some of the Churches and ask a loan from the pastor. So we started out. We had not to go far when the Christian Beacon (the Cross) stood up before us. It proved to be...a house of the Sisters of Charity...We were received most kindly by the good Sisters who made us quite comfortable, gave us a lovely cup of hot tea, and the Sister who waited on us proved to be an old friend of my youth. We enjoyed our meeting in our religious costumes.

The Lady Superior (whose name I have forgotten) supplied us with the required funds (which was returned in due time). We trudged back to the depot. The train was ready about 7 P.M. as the R.R. was cleared of snow. We got along better and arrived at our new home about 10 P.M.[76]

A detail that only comes out through anecdote is the fact that the sisters going to Canandaigua, unlike those who went to Wheeling a few years previously, wore their religious habit on the journey. The major factor deciding whether or not to travel or appear in public in the habit had to do with the prejudice the sisters could expect to encounter.

The author of the Rochester annals described the sisters' first days from the perspective of those who knew the pioneer sisters.

Arriving there on the 8th of December, 1854, that day forever glorious in the Annals of the Church, that day on which - to use bishop Timon's own expression "the Christian world crowned its Mother," they place under the glorious invocation of Mary Immaculate the Academy for young ladies which they then opened. The first building used as a convent and schools stood on Daltonstall Street. The convent was incorporated as an

---

75 Bishop O'Regan was an Irishman whom Archbishop P. R. Kenrick appointed as the first president of the theological seminary he established in Carondelet in 1849. He became the third Bishop of Chicago in September, 1854 and resigned the See in 1857.
76 Ivory "Letter."

Academy and orphan Asylum in 1855. The object of this association as set forth in the articles of incorporation was "the care, support and instruction of orphans and other children who need such care and instruction, and for no other object or end whatsoever." This occurred during the pastorship of Rev. Edmund O'Connor.[77]

The way the Annals record the founding story allows us to understand what the early sisters deemed most important about their experience. We learn from what follows that parishes which had Catholic schools preferred having sister teachers, even if they were begun with lay teachers. The preference probably had as much to do with their preparation and stability as with the reduced expense involved in maintaining a faculty of religious.

> The school formerly taught by Messrs. Moran, Donnelly and Hynes, in the basement of the church, now came under the control of the Sisters. This school had been organized by Rev. E. O'Connor in 1850.
>
> Mother Agnes Spencer as Superioress, with Sister Francis Joseph Ivory and two others were the first sisters sent to Canandaigua. The zealous, well-known Mother M. Julia [Littenecker] with two more sisters came to Canandaigua in April of the following year.
>
> Very thorough teachers were in charge of the Academy as is testified by old programmes [sic], manuscripts etc. still in existence. The teaching was based on thoroughly French methods, and the Sisters themselves were largely from France. Their pupils numbered the daughters of some of the best families in Western New York...

The annals go on to narrate the reception of the first novices in the community, an event which may have seemed a long time coming and was at least as important as the sisters' ministry.

> Three years after the Sisters came to Canandaigua, and during the administration of Mother Agnes Spencer, a young girl, scarcely sixteen years old, Miss Margaret Leary of Corning, N.Y. was admitted Oct. 15, 1856 and received the holy habit on the 14th of February 1857 with the name of Sister Mary Stanislaus.[78]

---

77 Book 1 of the Annals of the Community, pgs. 15-16. (Archives of the Sisters of St. Joseph of Rochester (ASSJR)

78 Annals (ASSJR). (The three year calculation is not quite precise.) Dunne (72-73) adds that Sr. Julia Littenecker "was a native of the Grand Duchy of Baden, a state Southwest of Germany that existed between 1806 and 1918. At the age of 23, she entered the Carondelet novitiate in 1853, a few months after coming to America with her parents. She was well educated, an accomplished musician, a woman of strong

The Annals continue with a first person narrative by Sister Anastasia who was Margaret Leary's companion. The two were the first to receive the habit of the Sisters of St. Joseph in the State of New York. Sister Anastasia describes their reception as a remarkable event, not only for the sisters, but for the people of the area who had never witnessed anything like it.

> It was in St. Mary's Church, Canandaigua, that the late Mother Stanislaus and myself were clothed in the garb of the Sisters of St. Joseph on Sunday, the fourteenth day of February 1857, by the saintly Bishop Timon. As he was instrumental in having us enter at Canandaigua, he made it a point to come on from Buffalo to invest us with the habit. A little incident in connection with our reception will amuse you. It is this: Good Father Lee, who was pastor of a little mission in a village nearby, announced to his flock that the Bishop would be in Canandaigua on the day above mentioned, for the purpose of giving the veil to two nuns. He told them he would be present, and added he would like them to be present also. "He said an early Mass for his people, and just imagine them wending their way to St. Mary's to see the sight. The consequence was a well crowded church at the 10:30 o'clock Mass on that memorable Sunday morning. The two prospective nuns, preceded by a procession, were a spectacle to Angels and to men as they marched around the aisles, whilst the sisters in the organ loft rendered sweetly a Litany of the Blessed Virgin.
>
> Our reception, as far as I know, was the first one held in the church. Sister Aloysius Hendrick received the habit two months later in the church from the hands of Rev. Edmund O'Connor. The following year, Sisters Nativity, Alphonsus and Nicholas received the habit in the Convent chapel. These were the last received in Canandaigua, as the Novitiate was removed to Buffalo.[79]

Sister Francis Joseph Ivory's memoir offers some details about the early days in western New York and the communities they opened in Canandaigua, Rochester and Buffalo. As she told it:

> We opened a Boarding School for young ladies, a day school, the Parochial School for boys and girls, --also opened a novitiate. The first in

---

faith, serious by nature but of sweet and affable manner, whose influence for good stamped itself on all who were fortunate enough to come under her teaching. As she was only a novice when sent to Canandaigua, she made her vows at the expiration of the time of novitiate, January 13, 1856, in St. Mary's Church....When the Sisters were recalled to St. Louis, Mother Julia returned to Carondelet where she spent a long life of faithful service in various posts of her Community."
79 Annals, Vol. 1, 16-18. (ASSJR)

the State of NY, in 1855 – two Sisters went to Rochester, opened a
Parochial School for boys and
girls – St. Bridget's Church.
The next year, 1856, we

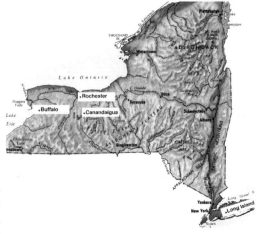

Early Foundations in New York
Distances from one to another

St. Louis - Canandaigua – 828 mi.
Canandaigua - Buffalo – 93 mi.
Buffalo to Rochester – 75 mi.
Canandaigua - Rochester – 29 mi.
Buffalo - Long Island – 377 mi.

opened a Parochial School in
Buffalo, also commenced the
Deaf Mute Institute for which
purpose a large grant of land
had been given. Mother Bernard [Dinan] of Toronto, Sister Philoméne
[Vilaine] and Sister Francis Joseph [Ivory] opened the mission. After that
Mother St. John Fournier came from Philadelphia, brought Sr. Veronica
[Chiers] and Sisters DeSales [Morrissey] and Camilla [Phelan?]. They
also commenced a novitiate, several new members were received – and
the Sisters took charge of the male orphan asylum on Limestone Hill,
which has developed into a very large Institution, Reformatory, etc. The
Sisters have fine Institutions in Buffalo and Dunkirk, Niagara, Black
Rock, and Cold Springs. Some good everywhere.[80]

Sister Francis Joseph's narrative illustrates a rapid succession of events; the sisters
opened schools, received community members from elsewhere as well as aspiring
vocations and opened houses in distant cities, all within the space of a few years.
For whatever reason, Sister Francis Joseph highlighted the fact that the founding
sisters came from different ethnic backgrounds: English, German and Irish.
They were an interesting group to offer what the annals author called a "French
education," something they had perhaps learned about through their formation at
Carondelet when some of them may have also been able to learn methods of
teaching the deaf. Another subtle piece of information Sister Francis Joseph's letter
reveals is how the established houses worked together; Mother St. John Fournier

---

80 Ivory, "Letter." Comments in brackets are in the document from the Carondelet archives, perhaps
clarifications by Sister Monica Corrigan for whom the memoir was written.

came with sisters from Philadelphia for Buffalo and Mother Celestine had sent sisters from Carondelet. This and other evidence about the relationships among the sisters in the early missions makes it clear that Mother Celestine at Carondelet was functioning like a superior general. She was founding missions that were interrelated through the Carondelet motherhouse even after they had established local novitiates as had Philadelphia and eventually St. Paul and Wheeling.[81] In addition, if Mother Celestine was unofficially the superior for the American houses, Mother St. John Fournier in Philadelphia was her second in sending sisters to open missions and, as will be seen later, in ongoing communication with bishops.

The same spirit of easy interchange among the American (U.S. and Canadian) communities is obvious in the choices the major superiors made regarding formation, vows and the naming of local superiors. Sister Julia Littenecker was a German immigrant who entered the congregation at Carondelet shortly after her family arrived in St. Louis. Before she had finished the novitiate, she was sent to Canandaigua and pronounced her vows there in St. Mary's Church. She was soon named superior of the Canandaigua house and then took Mother Agnes Spencer's place as superior and teacher of the deaf at Buffalo until she returned to St. Louis in 1861.[82] While the Carondelet and Philadelphia communities were sending sisters to New York, local women were also being attracted to join the community. Sister Francis Joseph alluded to the fact that Sisters Stanislaus and Anastasia were received in February and an Irish immigrant, Sister Aloysius Hendrick, was received on April 12, 1857. There followed the receptions of Sister Nativity Flood on September 13, 1857, and Sisters Alphonsa Durchordwi and Nicholas Bersinger on February 13, 1858, natives of Ireland, Buffalo and Alsace, France respectively. After Sisters Julia Littenecker and Petronilla Roscoe made vows in Canandaigua later receptions and vow ceremonies took place in Buffalo.

As Sister Francis Joseph mentioned, Father James Early asked the Sisters of St. Joseph to open a parish school in Buffalo in 1856. Sisters Francis Joseph Ivory and Bruno Nolan opened the school and were soon joined by Sisters Bernard Dinanand, and Philomena Sheridan, both sent from Toronto to help

---

81 In Philadelphia, Mother St. John received novices within months of her arrival; the St. Paul community established a novitiate in 1854, and the Wheeling community in 1855. See Dougherty, 142 and Ann Hoyle, *Seasons of Nature and Grace, History of the Sisters of Saint Joseph of Wheeling 1853-2003*, (Wheeling: Sisters of St. Joseph of Wheeling, 2003) 28.
82 Upon leaving Buffalo, Sister Julia was missioned in Illinois and then from 1863-69 she was novice director, from 1866-72 she was a general councilor, from 1872-96 assistant general superior. Beginning in 1896 she was in charge of the Mission Territories until nearly the time of her death in 1913. (Archives Carondelet)

with the new school which was temporarily housed in the parish church and sacristy.[83] The sisters first stayed in the pastor's house and then in cottages that had been vacated by Sisters of Charity until a convent was eventually prepared for them.[84]

The opening of classes for the deaf in 1856, marked the New York inauguration of what became a distinctive specialty of the Sisters of St. Joseph. Before sufficient funding for a full-fledged school for deaf children became available, a few students began their education in temporary classroom space. A school for the deaf had been one of Bishop Timon's hopes from his earliest days in Buffalo. In 1853, even before he approached Mother Celestine asking for the help of the Sisters of St. Joseph, he had formed the Le Couteulx St. Mary's Benevolent Society, named for the donor of land on which Bishop Timon hoped to realize his dream of a school for the deaf. One of the reasons for the delay in beginning the work was that the two sisters officially trained as educators of the deaf, Mother Celestine of Carondelet and Mother St. John Fournier of Philadelphia, were otherwise occupied. Nevertheless, within a short time, not only did the community provide prepared teachers, but the bishop and his associates successfully lobbied the local and state

governments to provide funding for approximately two-thirds of the student body, thus allowing the sisters to accept children whose families could not afford to pay for private education. Sisters Agnes Spencer and Rose Geghan, the first sister deaf-educators from the U.S., had received "some technical training." Then in 1861, Bishop Timon arranged for Sister Mary Anne Burke to go to Philadelphia to study the latest methods for deaf-education at Penn State University. Sister Mary Anne became the administrator and superior of the Le Couteulx Institute which continued to professionalize and prosper under her leadership from 1870 until her death in 1927.[85] The history of the congregation written in 1934 glosses over Mother Agnes' departure from Buffalo, saying only that she left in 1859.[86] Mother Julia Littenecker took her place as

Sister Mary Anne Burke
in 1863

---

83 This is yet another example of the frequent sharing of personnel among the various communities of Sisters of St. Joseph in the U.S. and Canada.
84 Dunne, 73-74.
85 Dunne, 78-80.
86 That is according to the census of 1850. See www.census.gov/population/www/documentation/twps0027/tab08.txt At that time Philadelphia ranked fourth with a population of 121,376; St. Louis, eighth with a population of 77,860; Albany, tenth with 50,763; Buffalo, sixteenth with 42,261; Rochester, twenty-first with

superior, but she too returned to Carondelet in 1861. With Mother Julia's departure, Bishop Timon turned to Mother St. John Fournier for help and she sent Mother Magdalen Weber to take over as superior and Sister Stephen Hesse as her assistant and director of novices.[87] Like Bishop Whelan in Wheeling, Bishop Timon was left without sufficient leaders to direct his newly established diocesan community when the Carondelet sisters returned to St. Louis rather than sever their ties with their original congregation. Sister Magdalen remained in Buffalo for only two years. The community elected Sister Anastasia Donavan to take her place and Mother Anastasia appointed Sister Mary Anne Burke as her assistant. When Mother Anastasia resigned in 1869, Bishop Ryan appointed Sister Mary Anne to fill out her term.[88]

Under Mother Mary Anne's leadership the community finally established itself as a diocesan community. They had been using Carondelet's 1847 translation of the French Constitutions and then Philadelphia's rule. When Philadelphia received approbation of their Constitutions in 1895 the Buffalo community had to choose between affiliating with Philadelphia or submitting their own Constitutions as a diocesan congregation. In 1899, Bishop Quigley, the third Bishop of Buffalo, authorized the community's Constitutions which were based on the 1847 translation. Those Constitutions became the rule for the 137 professed sisters and 85 women in formation who formed the community in 1900.

After her appointment in 1869, Mother Mary Anne Burke was continuously reelected as superior until she refused the office in 1913.[89] Like her French predecessors, this deaf-educator not only established one of the outstanding Catholic schools for the deaf, but she lived out her call in congregational service for the majority of her religious life.

THE SISTERS OF ST. JOSEPH OF ROCHESTER - BEGINNINGS

When the Diocese of Rochester was created in 1868, its territory included the 1854 mission in Canandaigua where Sisters of St. Joseph had their "select school," St. Mary's Academy, and St. Mary's Orphan Asylum. Their first mission in the city of Rochester began in 1864 when Sisters Stanislaus Leary, Xavier Delahunty, Clare O'Shea and Martina opened St. Mary's Boys' Home at the invitation

---

35,404; Wheeling, fifty-ninth with 11,435. Brooklyn was the first U.S. diocese erected which was exclusively urban, comprised only of Long Island.

87 Sister Magdalen Weber had gone to Philadelphia as one of the founders of that community with Mother St. John Fournier in 1847.

88 Dunne, 111-113.

89 Dunne, 148 and 158.

of Father James Early.[90] The sisters arrived on the Feast of All Saints, and on that same day received the first orphans into what would be called St. Mary's Boys' Home. The sisters made do with next to nothing as is clear from a report on the orphanage which stated:

> The managers...paid only $40 a year for each orphan boy they kept... this left no margin for any profit as the sum included a yearly's food and clothing. In fact, maintenance at this rate was only possible because of the economical organization of the Asylum...It will be evident to all that the low figure of $24 per annum for each orphan and their kind and pious guardians, the Sisters of St. Joseph, would not suffice were it not for the farm...and also that the low rate of $15 per annum for clothing would by no means suffice were it not for the care and needle work of the Sisters who receive no compensation but the low allowance of $50 per annum for their own clothing and all their expenses except food; the pay they expect is from God in a better world.[91]

The influence of such poverty was, if anything, a stimulus to vocations. The community of the Sisters of St. Joseph of Buffalo continued to grow and in the Rochester environs the Sisters were running St. Mary's Academy and Orphan Asylum in Canandaigua and St. Mary's orphanage in Rochester.

Shortly after his episcopal installation in July, 1868, Bishop McQuaid visited the Sisters of St. Joseph in Rochester with the plan to reform them into a diocesan community under his authority. He had considered the circumstances of all the communities serving in the area in the light of his plans. Among the largest of those communities were the Sisters of Mercy and Sisters of Charity from Emmitsburg, both of which, like the Sisters of St. Joseph, were related to motherhouses outside the new diocese but he found them less attractive than the Sisters of St. Joseph for carrying forth his ideas for the diocese. The Sisters of Charity were part of an international community and both they and the Sisters of Mercy followed rules which restricted their work with boys. In contrast, the Sisters of St. Joseph were open to any ministry that served the dear neighbor and when

---

90 This is how they are named in Garvin, 41. On the previous page, the author indicates that Sister Magdalen "Weaver" sent these sisters, but the name should be Weber; she is one of the sisters who accompanied Mother St. John Fournier to Philadelphia in 1847.

91 Life and Letters of Bishop McQuaid, (online source: https://archive.org/stream/MN5184ucmf_2/ MN5184ucmf_2_djvu.txt . Chapter: "Works of Mercy," pg. 231) The source calls the orphanage "St. Joseph's," but seems to refer to St. Mary's Home. If it was not correctly referring to the Sisters of St. Joseph, the source still gives a sense of the economy of the day.

Bishop McQuaid studied their 1847 *Constitutions* he was pleased to read that the bishop of the diocese in which the sisters resided was their first religious superior, to be obeyed as if he were Jesus Christ himself.[92] He couldn't have asked for more. The Rochester community history explains that the bishop went to the sisters with his project:

> His decision made, the Bishop visited the Sisters at St. Mary's Orphan Asylum…He unfolded his plans and explained that it would be necessary for the Sisters in Rochester to withdraw from the mother community in Buffalo and establish an independent diocesan community in Rochester. The Sisters recognized the Divine Will in the request of their Bishop and the change was effected in the autumn of 1868.[93]

Unfortunately, the letters and memoirs, the documentation that would tell us how the sisters really felt about the new plan have not been preserved. Surely the division of the community and separation of sisters was difficult for some of those who returned to Buffalo as well as for some who stayed in Rochester. Then again, if there were serious disagreements among the sisters, the separation of the Rochester community from Buffalo could have resolved those issues as sisters were free to belong to the community with which they were most comfortable. Thus, at the very least, we can suppose that the sisters who chose to form the new Rochester community wanted to be together in the new endeavor and expected a reasonable relationship with their new bishop.

In terms of the sisters and their relationships with the bishops, in 1868, the landscape was as yet uncharted. Bishop McQuaid, little known because he was newly arrived, would prove to be at least as authoritarian as Bishop Timon. The Buffalo sisters' predicament was more complicated. Bishop Timon had died on April 16, 1867, and his replacement, Bishop Stephen Ryan had been named in March, but was not consecrated bishop until November 8, 1868. By this time Bishop McQuaid had made his arrangements to found his Congregation of the Sisters of St. Joseph in Rochester.[94] Additionally, with Bishop Timon's death,

---

92 Sisters of St. Joseph *Constitutions*, 1847 translation, Section VI.
93 Garvin, 51.
94 Bishop Stephen Ryan, like his predecessor, was a Vincentian who had been the "Visitor" of the community since 1857, nine years after he had been ordained by Archbishop Francis Kenrick in St. Louis. There was apparently enough bad feeling between Ryan and McQuaid that McQuaid refused to attend the Silver Jubilee of Ryan's episcopate saying that past insults had not been accounted for…" (See Zwierlein, Vol II, 9.) Also, in 1876, Father James Early who had founded St. Mary's Asylum with Mother Stanislaus and had become rector of the Rochester Cathedral returned to Buffalo. From there he began a suit against McQuaid and the diocese to recuperate money he had loaned for the Cathedral. When McQuaid turned to Bishop Ryan for support

Mother Magdalen Weber who had eventually replaced Mother Agnes Spencer was recalled to Philadelphia, leaving the community in the hands of the Vicar General and a newly elected superior for whom leadership was so costly that she resigned within two years of being elected. Under those circumstances, even if they were not in agreement with the separation of the community, in 1868, the sisters in the Buffalo congregation were in no position to dispute Bishop McQuaid's plans.

As Bishop McQuaid began to create his diocesan community, twelve sisters chose to remain in the Rochester Diocese as part of the new foundation.[95] The bishop chose Sister Stanislaus Leary from among them to be superior of the new congregation.[96] With the installation of Bernard J. McQuaid as the first bishop of Rochester and his choice of Mother Stanislaus Leary as the first superior of the Rochester community, the Sisters of St. Joseph in the United States began a new chapter of their history conspicuously marked by the force of personalities and convictions of the first superior and the new bishop.

Mother Stanislaus Leary
1841 - 1900

MOTHER STANISLAUS LEARY AND BISHOP MCQUAID

Margaret Leary was born on August 15, 1841 and grew up in Corning, New York, one of a family of seven raised by a widowed mother. On February 14, 1857 at just less than sixteen years of age she received the religious name Sister Stanislaus when she and Sister Anastasia (Margaret Donavan) became the first women in the State of New York to receive the habit of the Sisters of St. Joseph.[97] According to Sister Anastasia, Mother Agnes Spencer sent Sister Stanislaus "for a change of air," to spend a good part of her novitiate under the care of Sister Baptista Hanson in the newly founded mission in Brooklyn.[98] Just two years after her reception, in

---

against Early's claims, Ryan refused to become involved in the dispute, seeing it as a personal argument between the two. (See Brennan, 77-78.)

95 There may have been as few as four sisters who chose to return to Buffalo. See Margaret Brennan, *Persistence of Vision: A Portrait of Mother Stanislaus Leary* (Rochester: Instantpublisher.com, 2005) 42.

96 In 1860, Rochester was a fast-growing city of nearly 50,000 residents; Buffalo had slightly more than 80,000. The first members of the Rochester Congregation were Sisters Stanislaus Leary, Xavier Delahunty, De Pazzi Bagley, Claver Hennessey, Lucy Gorman, Patrick Walsh, Clare O'Shea, Michael Brown, James O'Connell, Ambrose McKeegan, Camillus Payne, and Paul Geary. All but the last three were missioned in Rochester at the time of the formation of the diocese. Ibid. 51-52.

97 See Chapter 4 and Brennan, *Persistence of Vision: A Portrait of Mother Stanislaus Leary* (Rochester: InstantPublisher.com, 2005), 11-13.

what must have been her first assignment as a vowed member, Sister Stanislaus became a trustee and the secretary of the Orphanage and Academy in Canandaigua; her full-time ministry was not specified.[99]

In 1864, twenty-three year old Sister Stanislaus was named the founding superior of St. Mary's Asylum for Orphan Boys in Rochester and was also the only woman named to the Asylum's board of trustees.[100] Obviously a competent leader, she continued in that position when Bishop McQuaid arrived as the first bishop of Rochester.

Bernard J. McQuaid was born in 1823 to Irish immigrant parents both of whom died before he turned seven, leaving him to be raised by Sisters of Charity in their Manhattan orphanage after being taken from his unsympathetic step-mother.[101] That background forged in him "a firm, rigid and unyielding personality which both helped and hampered him in later years" and his childhood experience in the orphanage could not but have had an effect on his outlook and his relationship with women religious. [102] He attributed his success in life to Sister Elizabeth Boyle, the orphanage superior, who not only cared for him but probably brought him to the attention of Bishop Hughes who arranged for McQuaid to attend a minor seminary in Montreal and later St. John's Seminary at Fordham in New York.

Bishop Bernard McQuaid
1823 - 1909

---

hardly seems the most fitting place to find a healthful change of air. As mentioned earlier, Sister Baptista's mission to Brooklyn in 1856 was motivated as much by the decision to remove her from Buffalo as by the desire to send her to Brooklyn. Whatever the reasons, Sisters Baptista and Stanislaus developed a deep friendship that lasted over the years. ****

99 Information Kathleen Urbanic, archivist, SSJ archives, Rochester.

100 Thomas, Footprints, 84.

101 Mother Seton's sisters opened that New York orphanage in St. Patrick's Parish in 1817. In 1846, when the Emmitsburg community affiliated with the Daughters of Charity and the sisters could no longer care for boy orphans, thirty-three members of the community chose to accept Archbishop Hughes strong suggestion that they sever their affiliation with Emmitsburg to establish a new diocesan community.

102 Sister Norlene Mary Kunkel, ("Bishop Bernard McQuaid and Catholic Education" dissertation: Notre Dame University, 1974, Introduction).

103 Kunkel, 54, citing Sister Mary Agnes Sharkey, The New Jersey Sisters of Charity (3 volumes; New York: Longmans, Green and Co., 1933), I, p. 66. Kunkel (61) goes on to describe some of the ecclesiastical rivalry of the day in explaining that when Hughes, who became New York's first archbishop in 1844, invited the Jesuits to replace the Vincentians in the direction of the seminary in 1846, he sought the Kentucky Jesuits lest the Maryland Jesuits let Fordham be second in importance to Georgetown. Hughes wanted Fordham to be the top Catholic college in the United States.

As a young priest Bernard McQuaid was the protégé of James Roosevelt Bayley, the first bishop of Newark and nephew of Saint Elizabeth Ann Seton. While Rev. McQuaid served as rector of the cathedral and vicar-general of the Newark diocese and in 1856, he helped found Seton Hall College and became its first president – an office he held until his 1868 appointment as first bishop of Rochester.[104] During his Newark years Reverend McQuaid became ever more convinced that free Catholic schools were essential to the very survival of the faith in the United States. In conjunction with that he said that his "whole soul was wrapped up in the future success of the diocese" and that success could not happen "without a sisterhood for the diocese…independent of all outside superiors."[105] Therefore with Bishop Bayley he enlisted the help of the Sisters of Charity and Bishop Elder of Cincinnati to found a diocesan community in Newark. They sent aspiring novices to study with the Sisters of Charity of Cincinnati and when they returned to New Jersey, Sisters Xavier Mehegan and Mary Catharine Nevin came from New York's Sisters of Charity to help establish the congregation of the Sisters of Charity of St. Elizabeth to serve the Diocese of Newark. Reverend Bernard McQuaid was their first superior.[106]

Father McQuaid held a well-deserved reputation as being demanding. One biographer comments that as Vicar General in Newark he was unmerciful; quick to suspend priests and rarely pardoning an offense. Giving subtle testimony to his attitude about both the priests and his bishop he himself wrote to Bishop Bayley saying that when he returned from travels many priests "will rejoice at your return and I devoutly hope that they will be able to appreciate a gentle, kindhearted and unsuspecting Bishop when they are again under his management." He added "I am always sure to be right, and when I put my hands on a poor fellow, I take a firm hold until he yields."[107] With that as his background in Newark, it comes as no surprise to hear Bishop James E. Quigley recall: "I remember distinctly the Bishop's first greeting to the Catholics of Rochester, as in a clear and decided tone

---

104 Although Bishop Bayley was one of McQuaid's chief promoters, McQuaid seemingly felt that Bayley took too much credit for McQuaid's accomplishments in the College and other diocesan endeavors. This was supposedly the reason that as bishop, McQuaid refused to preach at Bayley's funeral in 1877, after Bayley had been given the prestigious position of Archbishop in Baltimore in 1872. (Kunkel, 76, citing Joseph M. Flynn, *The Catholic Church in New Jersey*, Morristown, NJ, 1904, 270.)
105 Kunkel, 134.
106 Kunkel, 135-136. Bishop Bayley was pleased with the arrangement because his aunt, Mother Seton, had close connections with the Cincinnati community. Sister Xavier who came from New York as the first superior was the first sister received into the New York community under Mother Elizabeth Boyle and the two of them were life-long friends of Bernard McQuaid.
107 McQuaid to Bayley, May 24, 1867. Cited in Kunkel, 86.

of voice he announced his purpose in accepting the bishopric: 'I come here without fear, knowing what is to be done. If God gives me health and strength and length of life, I shall do it."108 From the very beginning there was little room for doubt that Bishop McQuaid intended to run his diocese as he saw fit.

THE ROCHESTER SISTERS OF ST. JOSEPH, BISHOP MCQUAID AND CATHOLIC EDUCATION

The eleven sisters who chose to remain in Rochester to form a congregation with the newly named Mother Stanislaus were younger than she in religious life. Those sisters were:

> Sister M. Patrick Walsh: received 1859; professed 1860;
> Sister M. Francis Xavier Delahunty: received 1859; professed, 1861;
> Sister M. Magdalene de Pazzi Bagley: received, 1862; professed, 1864;
> Sister Claver Hennessy: received, July 22, 1865; professed, Oct. 15, 1867;
> Sister M. Camillus (or Camilla) Payne: received, 1866; professed, 1868;
> Sister Ambrose McKeegan: received, 1863; professed, 1866;
> Sister M. Michael Brown: received, 1865; professed, 1867;
> Sister M. Clare O'Shea: received 1865; professed, 1867;
> Sister M. James O'Connell: received, 1866; professed, 1868;
> Sister M. Paul Geary: received, 1866,); professed, March 19, 1869,
>   in Rochester;
> Sister M. Lucy Gorman: received 1867; professed, 1869, in Rochester.[109]

In 1868, the most experienced of those young women had been a Sister of St. Joseph for nine years and the majority of them for three years or less; two of them, Sisters Mary Xavier Delehunty and Clare O'Shea had founded the Rochester mission with Mother Stanislaus in 1864. Two orphanages and an academy were left in their hands when the other sisters returned to Buffalo.

The new community proved so attractive to young women that they inaugurated the year 1869 with a January 1 celebration of reception for the first two novices of the new congregation: Sisters Mary Bernard Pigot and Mary Josephine Leary. Those sisters were followed in August by Sisters Agnes Hines

---

108 Bishop James E. Quigley was born in Ontario in 1854 and raised in Rochester and Buffalo. In 1896 he became bishop of Buffalo and became Archbishop of Chicago in 1903. *History of the Sisters of St. Joseph of Rochester*, 50.
109 Archives, SSJR. Sister Mary Paul Geary was a novice at the time of the separation of communities and on March 19, 1869, became the first sister professed in the Rochester congregation. Her companion, Sister Lucy Gorman, made vows in August of that year. Brennan also lists Sister Ignatius Hanlon who was at one point superior in Canandaigua, and who "did not persevere." (Brennan, 49)
110 Garvin, 52.

and Mary Aloysia Lee. By the end of the year 1870, the community numbered twenty-eight.[110] The community's growth must have encouraged Bishop McQuaid who had decided that the Sisters of St. Joseph would be the foremost community in his diocese.[111] A step toward assuring their dominance took place when in 1870 a dispute led to the removal of the Daughters of Charity from St. Patrick's Girls' Asylum in Rochester where they had been for twenty-five years. The crux of the problem centered on the decision of the priest superior of the Sister of Charity to remove Sister Hieronymo O'Brien, a beloved founder-administrator, from St. Mary's Hospital in Rochester where she had served for thirteen years. In her years at the hospital Sister Hieronymo had become a legend in the city, an excellent fund-raiser and famous for being able to pacify inebriated soldiers and soothe raving mentally ill patients. Her transfer brought outspoken protests from both civic leaders and the bishop who had been out of town when the move was effected.[112] Bishop McQuaid began a combative correspondence with the ecclesiastical superior of the Daughters of Charity, Father Burlando.[113] Sister Hieronymo had been transferred in September and on October 14, the bishop wrote Father Burlando saying: "Having made other arrangements for the care of the orphan girls and the teaching of the Parochial school connected with the Cathedral, you will oblige me by withdrawing your Sisters from the Orphan Asylum at your earliest convenience." [114] After Father Burlando wrote asking for reconsideration, the bishop responded saying that he had considered the priest's reasoning, but found it wanting. Replying to Father Burlando's reminder of the sacrifices the sisters had made at the orphanage over the course of more than two decades, the bishop replied that he had visited the Asylum in 1843 and the sisters did not seem to have suffered the "gloomy" situation Father Burlando described.[115] Bishop McQuaid went on to explain that his demand that the sisters leave

---

111 Bishop McQuaid favored the Sisters of St. Joseph in giving them charge of every school possible, by encouraging priests to direct vocations to them and even refusing the Sisters of Mercy permission to admit new members except to replace those who died, thereby thwarting any growth of that community. (Kunkel, 148)

112 Bishop McQuaid apparently had known Sister Hieronymo and she was a nurse in New York.

113 Father Francis Burlando, C.M. had been superior of the U.S. Daughters of Charity since 1853. (See Ellen M. Kelly, *Numerous Choirs: A Chronicle of Elizabeth Bayley Seton and Her Spiritual Daughters*, (St. Meinrad, Indiana: Abbey Press, 1996) Vol. II, 177. Some documents do not distinguish between Sisters and Daughters of Charity.

114 Letter from Bishop Bernard McQuaid to Father Burlando, cited in Frederick J. Zwierlein, *The Life and ;Letters of Bishop John McQuaid*, vol. 2, 77-79, (Louvain, Librairie Universitaire, A. Uytspruyst, 1926).

115 The Daughters of Charity opened St. Patrick's in 1845, at which time they found terrified orphans and such poverty that the sisters had only borrowed beds – a problem of which they were not aware until the fall when the priests whose beds had been commandeered for them returned to the city and asked that they be returned. (Kelly, *Chronicle*, Vol. II, 129.)

was not motivated by Sister Hieronymo's transfer, but that:

> On my arrival I found your Sisters usefully at work in the Hospital
> and in the Asylum. In the Asylum they had charge of the Orphan girls,
> dependent for their support on the Bishop and the people; and in the
> parochial school, they were, on account of their rules and irresponsibility
> to the Bishop, except in a very general way, in my way...
>
> For the sake of the Hospital, I concluded to sacrifice my own interests
> and maintain the Sisters at the Asylum...[116]

Interestingly, although he wanted absolute authority in his own domain, Bishop
McQuaid felt free to inform the ecclesiastical superior of the Daughters of Charity:
"Your argument that you are in the habit of removing Sisters without advising
the Ordinary has no application in this case."[117] Bishop McQuaid consistently
opted to keep matters under his own control; his commitment to his priorities
overshadowed consideration of others' authority or the autonomy of a religious
congregation. He seemed intent that his role with the Sisters of St. Joseph would
prevent them from being, like the Daughters of Charity, "in his way."

In November, 1870, following the orders of the bishop, six Sisters of St.
Joseph took over what had been the ministries of the Daughters of Charity at the
Academy, Orphanage and parochial school at St. Patrick's. A letter from Father
Burlando to Archbishop McCloskey of New York explains that the transition was
less than peaceful:

> I feel confident that neither I nor the Sisters are responsible for the
> troubles which followed their removal. Much as the Sisters desired to
> go from the asylum as quietly as possible, the fact became known and
> the people naturally complained. The...sisters were notified two days
> after the Sunday of the dedication of the Cathedral of Rochester, and the
> Sisters left on the Friday following that establishment which cost them
> 28 years' toil and privation...[118]

One can only imagine how the newly assigned Sisters of St. Joseph felt as they

---

116 Zwierlein, 77-79.
117 Ibid.
118 Burlando to McCloskey, December 12, 1870, cited in Zwierlein, Vol. II, 81-82. Father Burlando went on in
that letter to describe the monetary investments the Daughters of Charity had made in the institution and the
fact that they had purchased contiguous property and left the deed with the Bishop which he told another sister
he would have had to purchase if the Daughters of Charity had remained at the Asylum.

presented themselves to the school children, the parents, and most especially the orphans who would have seen them as the strangers attempting to replace the women who had cared for them. One sign of the general consternation around the affair was the fact that before Bishop McQuaid preached at the Cathedral on November 27, 1870, he took time to denounce "certain false reports and slanders" which rumored that "Bishop McQuaid was about to drive away the Daughters of Charity also from the Hospital and the Christian Brothers form St. Patrick's Academy."[119]

Bishop McQuaid's resolution of the problem was finally quite simple. As a Daughter of Charity, Sister Hieronymo made annual vows; when her vows expired in March of 1871, she left the community and with Bishop McQuaid's encouragement joined the Rochester Sisters of St. Joseph, being received in April, 1871.[120] There is no record of the Sisters of St. Joseph's deliberations about the transfer: Bishop McQuaid was the superior. This incident, which came to its conclusion before Bishop McQuaid had completed three years as bishop indicated how he would maintain control in his diocese.

Without a doubt, free Catholic elementary education was the bishop's first priority and the Sisters of St. Joseph were his chosen leaders in establishing his system. In 1870, the community had grown from twelve to twenty members and as the novitiate needed more space it was transferred to St. Patrick's soon after the Daughters of Charity left the premises. But even that space proved insufficient and in 1871, Mother Stanislaus purchased a home in "what was then one of the finest residential parts of Rochester."[121] The new mother house was christened "Nazareth" and on August 15, 1871 Bishop McQuaid blessed it, using his homily to extol the ministry he planned for the sisters. Connecting their Nazareth motherhouse to their vocation and reminding the sisters of what he considered the incomparable importance of their work he said:

> Here you will also care for Jesus in His little children and the labor and the training and the love you will bestow on them will be given to Jesus...The life to which you are to devote yourselves is one of great responsibility...To those confided to your care you will give your best energy of mind and body. For this end you will improve all the best faculties which God has given you...

---

119 Zwierlein, Vol. II, 82. Given the above mentioned letter from Burlando, this was apparently at the celebration of the dedication of the Cathedral.
120 Garvin, 63.
121 Garvin, 53.

Let me remind you that there is not a charitable work in the country, whether in hospitals, asylums, or refuges of any sort, which for far-reaching, widespread and lasting charity, can for one moment be compared with the work of the parochial school.[122]

When the sisters settled in their new home Mother Stanislaus had already arranged for the legal incorporation of the institution under the name of "The Nazareth Convent and Academy," making the sisters official property owners and a legal entity in the State.[123]

The 1871 school year opened with the inauguration of two new parochial free schools. At the Cathedral school, the Sisters of St. Joseph taught the girls and younger boys and the Christian Brothers continued their work with the older boys. The Immaculate Conception Parish School opened with 500 students. With this, the bishop had begun his all-consuming fundamental project of building a Catholic School system.[124] In order to assure its success, he concentrated on the education of his teachers, giving weekly Saturday conferences to the sisters at Nazareth, finding lecturers to add to his offerings and eventually sending sisters to study in Europe as well as in U.S. colleges and universities.[125] The bishop even saw to it that the sisters were able to study during their summer vacations at property they rented from him on Lake Hemlock.

The sisters of St. Joseph opened Catholic schools at an astonishing pace. Having started with an orphan asylum and school in Canandaigua in 1854, and an orphan asylum in Rochester in 1864, they took over St. Patrick's Orphan Asylum in 1870. In 1871, they opened Nazareth Academy, and assumed the Cathedral (St. Patrick's) School and Immaculate Conception in Rochester. In 1873, under the leadership of Sister Hieronymo O'Brien, now a Sister of St. Joseph, they opened the Home of Industry, a career school for young women, and Excelsior Farm, a training school for young boys and St. Mary's School in Auburn. By 1882, the

---

122 Ibid. 54-55.
123 Garvin, 55.
124 While Bishop McQuaid made his impassioned efforts to build up the Catholic schools, little was said about the five already existing German Catholic schools in the diocese which were educating about 3,000 students in 1871. Their achievements surely played a dual role. They pleased the Bishop McQuaid, who unlike Bishop Ireland and his fellow assimilationists, wanted Catholic education and was not ideologically opposed to a German-language based education. On the other hand, the German dominance could have smacked of the old Trustee crisis and would not have set as comfortably with proud people of Irish descent.
125 In a summer entry in 1871, the Rochester community annals note: "The sisters during these months devoted all their time to preparation for school work. The Rt. Reverend Superior then imposed upon each Sister the obligation, in virtue of Holy Obedience, of spending at least one hour daily in Study. The expression "my hour" became a by-word of sacred import in the community and meant very much in regard to its intellectual prosperity." An entry in 1872

Sisters of St. Joseph of Rochester numbered 163 and were running nineteen institutions as well as their motherhouse and novitiate.Both the sisters and the bishop took education very seriously. It was not enough to have schools, their quality had to match if not exceed that of the public schools. [126]

THE SCHOOL QUESTION

The drive to establish a system of Catholic schools brought Rochester to the forefront in one of the thorniest controversies in the U.S. Catholic Church of the latter 19th century. The gist of the problem was the question of how to provide an education for Catholic children that was, at the very least, not detrimental to their faith, and at best formed them as well-educated Catholics and loyal citizens. One approach to the problem, represented by Bishop Ireland of St. Paul, put a high priority on assimilating the Catholic immigrants into the fabric of U.S. society. He was most willing to collaborate with the state in education and was a strong advocate of finding ways for the state to pay an equitable share of the cost of educating students in schools sponsored by religious denominations. He promoted an arrangement in which the public system would pay teachers and even rent Catholic owned facilities for the teaching of non-religious subjects. Varieties of that plan had been tried in multiple places, including the first school at Carondelet. The most famous examples of the plan were carried out in Poughkeepsie, New York and Stillwater Minnesota. In Minnesota, Bishop Ireland had arranged for sisters to be paid by the state for teaching students of any religious persuasion, with the agreement that religion would not enter the classroom during school hours. Bishop McQuaid, highly influenced by Archbishop Hughes of New York and early experiences like that of Bishop Kenrick in Philadelphia, saw the Ireland plan as a diabolical compromise with the godless state.[127] Convinced that the future of the Church in the U.S. depended on Catholic education, Bishop McQuaid's allies were dedicated to free Catholic schools, no matter the cost to the parishes. Theirs is the plan that eventually won the day even though if Bishop Ireland's strategy had been implemented, it would have assured professional salaries for teachers in shared Catholic/State schools in the U.S. as happened in Canada and some European countries. In the course of fifty years, the U.S. bishops made ever

---

adds the fact that on Saturdays the study requirement was three hours, at least one of which would be in class with other sisters. (Archives Annals, Vol. 1, Archives SSJR.)

127 The issue was more complex, but those are the broad lines. Eventually, Ireland's style of compromise was defeated and the Catholic school system became financed through church funding. Kunkel (73-74) points out that McQuaid opened the first Catholic school in New Jersey in the basement of his parish and taught there himself to alleviate the need for a teacher's salary.

stronger pronouncements about the need for a Catholic School System.[128] The fact that the bishops gradually and increasingly-strongly opted for the necessity of Catholic education created the need for the corps of scores of thousands of sister-teachers who would serve the Church for 100 years beginning after the U. S. Civil War.

THE SISTERS OF ST. JOSEPH IN ROCHESTER:
CRISIS, SUFFERING, CHANGE AND EXPANSION

In 1882, Mother Stanislaus had been a superior in Rochester for twenty-eight years and for half of that time had served as the General Superior of the Rochester community. When she was first appointed superior of the new Rochester community they were twelve in number; in 1882, there were at least 100 sisters. Something was going right. In the beginning, Mother Stanislaus' relationship with the bishop had been smooth, but over the years certain issues of contention arose, some of which were serious, at least when dealing with someone like Bishop McQuaid who so carefully protected his authority.[129] After fourteen years, Bishop McQuaid decided that the time had come for another to replace Mother Stanislaus as superior.

The real motives for Bishop McQuaid's dissatisfaction with Mother Stanislaus may never be known, and they probably varied in both nature and seriousness. One possibility is that Mother Stanislaus did not pass the bishop's test of loyalty when it came to his falling out with Father James Early, one of Mother Stanislaus' long-time friends. Father Early had known Mother Stanislaus from

---

128 The Fourth Provincial Council of Baltimore (1840) spoke of public education as a "grave risk" to the faith of Catholic children who were obliged to listen to the Protestant Bible, sing Protestant hymns and hear sermons against the Church. The Fifth Provincial Council of Baltimore spoke of the "methods used in the common schools to poison the minds of Catholic boys and girls" and admonished parents to uphold their rights By the time of the Sixth Provincial Council in 1846, the bishops were urging the clergy to begin at once a system of Catholic schools. The First Plenary Council of Baltimore in 1852 advanced the cause by exhorting the bishops per viscera misericordiae Dei (by the "tender mercy" of God, or more literally, "from the bowels of God's mercy) to begin parochial schools wherever possible. By 1866, the Second Plenary Council strengthened its call for parochial schools, a demand that would take on new dimensions as the Council also called the bishops to the imperative of providing a Christian education to the more than four million freed slaves. See Peter Guilday, A *History of the Councils of Baltimore (1791-1884)*, (New York, the MacMillan Company, 1932) 125, 141, 146, 179. Bishop McQuaid outdid the almost all his contemporaries in his insistence on Catholic education. He proudly explained to Bishop Bayley that once a school was available in a parish "I refuse absolution to all parents who send their children to public schools." (McQuaid to Bayley, June 29, 1874, Zwierlein, Vol. II, 96.)
129 The annals do not criticize or complain about Bishop McQuaid, often referring to him as wise. An entry in 1872 comments "Every Saturday the Bishop said Mass at Nazareth and...gave us a practical Conference on our duties as religious teachers...no one has equaled [him] in his words of fatherly kindness...[he] could point out the faults to be avoided and the virtues to be practiced in the school room. He particularly warned us against falling into ruts."

her Canandaigua days. He had been Vicar General of the Rochester diocese and lived with the bishop until 1872 when he resigned his office and rejoined the Diocese of Buffalo. After his resignation he and Bishop McQuaid sustained a long-term dispute over finances.[130] In spite of the bishop's disapproval, Mother Stanislaus maintained her friendship and corresponded with Father Early after his departure from the diocese.[131] Another possibility is that Mother Stanislaus had become too independent, among other things having decided without permission to put an addition to the Motherhouse – while the bishop was in Rome.[132] Mother Stanislaus and the bishop also disagreed about her reluctance to admit a "visionary" novice to vows and her travels to visit friends, particularly Sister Baptista Hanson in Brooklyn and Mother Agnes Spencer in Erie.[133]

A further bone of contention between them may well have centered on the bishop's vacation property at Hemlock Lake. When the Bishop arranged for the sisters to spend their summer vacations at the property he made a contract through which he rented the large residence to them for $1,000 per year for a period of ten years, beginning in 1876.[134] While it was a beautiful, healthful spot, the sisters there remained under the constant supervision of the bishop and were often expected to serve him and the guests to whom he wanted to show off "his sisters."[135]

---

130 Apparently, Father Early had used some of his own money for the construction of the Cathedral, a project that incurred serious debts. The acrimony of his departure from the diocese was obvious as he sued for those funds. The Rochester SSJ archives have copies of correspondence indicating that Fr. Early was willing to drop his claim for $8,000 and wished to make peace with the bishop before he died, but was not able to do so. (See Rev. Peter Colgan to Bishop McQuaid, Feb. 18, 1890: Archives SSJR)

131 See note 33 above. To exacerbate the situation, it seemed to be fairly common knowledge that when the Diocese of Rochester was created, Bishop Timon suggested Father Early as his first candidate to become the new bishop.

132 See Brennan, 86-87.

133 Ibid. 112. M. Stanislaus had known both sisters since she entered the congregation, S. Baptista being the sister with whom she spent part of her novitiate and Mother Agnes the superior under whom she was admitted to the Congregation. Both of them had also had their problems with clergy and/or bishops. While the bishop told the sisters that unnecessary travel was a waste of money, he was a frequent visitor to Europe, telling Bishop Corrigan in 1878 "My intention is to leave about the end of October, spend Christmas in Rome, ramble through Italy, after Easter gto Germany, Switzerland, France, Great Britain, home in the beginning of the Summer of 1879. Letter of McQuaid to Corrigan, March 15, 1878 (Zwierlein, Vol. II, 165).

134 See Sr. Evangeline Thomas, *Footprints on the Frontier, A History of the Sisters of St. Joseph of Concordia, Kansas*, (Westminster, Maryland: The Newman Press:, 1848) 89. As a point of comparison, the same manuscript indicates that in 1872, the Nazareth Motherhouse building and grounds were valued at $40,000, annual tuition had brought in $7,200 and the annual charge for a tuition was $150 for a 36 week school year. The summer house seems not to have been a bargain. There is another document in the SSJR archives which indicates that the bishop received $2,200 as payment for occupying the house at Hemlock for 10 years and having the benefit of the boats and boat house and milk from the farm.

135 Brennan relates that on one occasion "he had the Sisters service his dinner party. After dinner, he called one of the Sisters...and gave her 'a lecture about awkwardness and shyness...for not saluting in the proper way

Mother Stanislaus and her blood sisters had apparently received an inheritance; she and the bishop may have disagreed about her freedom to use it. Finally, there was the rumor that she had access to a vacation house that would offer an alternative to Hemlock, one where there would be no episcopal supervision.[136]

Whatever the cause of tensions, when it came to a serious problem all the power lay on one side of the equation. After returning from a trip to Rome, in May, 1882, Bishop McQuaid announced to the community that it was time to bring their governance into harmony with their Constitutions. He indicated that the problem was that Mother Stanislaus had been too long in office. He wrote a letter to each sister explaining that the "rules prescribe that superiors shall hold office for three years, although the same superior may be re-elected or re-appointed." More importantly, the Constitutions used by the Rochester congregation gave the bishop nearly unlimited power over the life of diocesan communities. In addition to being accorded "the place of Jesus Christ, and invested with his authority," the Constitutions go on to specify that:

> The bishops can visit the houses...demand an account of both the temporal and the spiritual state of their houses; they can examine, correct and even punish...
>   They can make regulations for their general good...
> They can also, if they deem it useful or necessary, change Superiors and Sisters from one house to another...
>   When any Superiors or other Sisters in office desire to renounce their charge, or when it is found necessary to depose them, the Bishops can do so and name others in their places. [137]

Thus, the bishop was entirely within his formal rights in calling for an election. In a letter dated on Monday May 15, 1882, Bishop McQuaid laid out his careful, six-step plan for holding an election on the Tuesday after Ascension Thursday: Tuesday, May 23. With precise instructions for prayer and a strict prohibition

---

ecclesiastical dignitaries." (Brennan, 107, citing *Jubilee Annals*, p. 419) The minutes of the Council Meeting of June 5, 1882, mention that some sisters do not want to go to Hemlock and the bishop wants the matter settled by the council. (Archives SSJR)

136 The annalists were careful to avoid scandal, therefore many details are left to be surmised. See Maureen T. Connaughton, "*Journeys Begun: A History of the Sisters of St. Joseph of La Grange*" (Manuscript: Archives CCSJ), 13. See also Brennan 127-128.

137 *Constitutions* of the Congregation of the Sisters of St. Joseph, English translation 1847, Chapter VI. This is the original *Constitutions* used in Buffalo and then in Rochester.

against speaking with one another about their preferences, he included with the letter slips of paper on which each sister was to write the names of the three sisters she would suggest as the new superior. The superior of the house was to collect the papers and forward them to the bishop.

Before the election, Mother Stanislaus wrote to the sisters encouraging them to do their duty and "submit in all humility and to show no opposition of any kind." She went on to ask them to write the three names as the bishop had asked, and if they could not think of three apt sisters, "then write the names of two or one." She went on to say,

> This change will not deprive me of watching over the Community and its interests, which are the dearest objects of my life. I would be a miserable religious, indeed, if I could not bear it with resignation and conformity to God's will...I have always tried to do my duty...None of us can do all things perfectly.
>
> Now, my dear Sisters, pray that God may direct your choice. I trust that as good religious you will try to be satisfied with the one the Bishop appoints.[138]

It was quite clear to any sister who read these letters that the bishop was inviting their vote, but that he would make the final choice. Many of the sisters, recognizing that the *Constitutions* allowed for re-election, wrote only one name on their ballots: Mother Stanislaus. Bishop McQuaid then named Mother Agnes Hines as the new superior of the community. She would hold that office for the next thirty-nine years.

From this point on, Mother Stanislaus would have a hard time finding peace in the Rochester diocese. The story of her deposition got out and after the secular press of Rochester printed the story the Catholic paper in Buffalo picked it up and repeated it with all the unpleasant if not absolutely verifiable details. It said:

> Mother Stanislaus, who for eighteen years past has had charge...is no longer the Mother Superior. At the recent election held, although all the members of the community of Nazareth voted for her reelection, Bishop McQuaid preferred that a change should be made and installed Sr. Agnes in her place...

---

138 Evangeline Thomas, 94, citing Annals of the Sisters of St. Joseph of Rochester, Vol. I, 197-198.

"We were all against her removal," said the sister who furnished the information, 'and quite a stir was caused in our little community by the Bishop's action...

It was learned that the deposed Mother Superior has left for St. Joseph's Convent in St. Louis, Mo.[139]

Even if Mother Stanislaus had nothing to do with it, such publicity did nothing to lessen the bishop's irritation with her. From then on she was persona non grata and the bishop forbad her to correspond with the sisters.[140] After she returned from Carondelet, she was assigned to St. Mary's Asylum and then went to visit her friend Sr. Baptista in Brooklyn. Apparently she had received the bishop's permission for that trip, but he later rescinded the permission and it is unclear if Mother Stanislaus received notice of the change before leaving for Brooklyn.[141] The bishop's reaction is clear from a letter Mother Stanislaus' wrote him dated June, 1882:

Right Reverend Bishop,
Sister Xavier told me that you sent word to her that I was not to receive Holy Communion for going to Brooklyn. I told you in my letter I did not understand that you had withdrawn such permission, but I however I will perform any reparation you desired. Will you please let me know when I am to receive Communion. It is the first time in my life I have been deprived of Holy Communion and I can assure you I have never had a greater trial...
Your Lordship's most humble servant,
Sister M. Stanislaus.[142]

The strife over her visit to Brooklyn continued when the bishop accused her of talking about him to others. This was a struggle between two strong personalities

---

139 Quoted in Brennan, 130, citing The Catholic Union and Times June 8, 1882, pg. 5 (Buffalo Diocesan Archives). This story from the Buffalo Catholic Press was underneath some the discord between Bishop McQuaid and Bishop Ryan of Buffalo.
140 The minutes of the council meeting of June 7, 1882 state that "because of some difficulties occasioned by the disagreement...in the election of a new general superior" and false rumors and disedification, "refractory members" would be forbidden to keep up correspondence with the former Superior. A year later, the council minutes of June 13, 1883, noted that a request by Sr. Armella to join Mother Stanislaus in Kansas led the counsellors to "infer that secret correspondence between Mother Stanislaus and discontented members is still going on." The council resolved to refer the matter to the Rt. Rev. Bishop and to act as he deems best. (Archives SSJR)
141 This detail is recorded in an interview of Sister Evangeline Thomas conducted by Sister Marcia Allen in 1989, (Archives CSJC), pg. 10.
142 Sister Stanislaus to Bishop McQuaid, June, 1882. (Archives SSJR)

with unequal power bases. Three months after the trip she wrote the following:

> Right Reverend Bishop,
> While in Brooklyn I never spoke of our trouble here to anyone but to my friend, Mother Baptista, and if you should care to hear what I said to her, I shall be very happy to oblige you. I will now return the compliment you gave me in my last letter from you. You hear too many lying stories and unfortunately receive the first one brought without an investigation…I do not think it very honorable in such a great man to carry on such a warfare with a poor weak little creature like me. I promise your Lordship I will never again mention your name wither for good or evil if you will just let me alone.
>
> Asking your lordship's pardon for anything I either have done or said that may have offended you,
> I remain with much respect,
> Your obedient servant in Christ,
> Sister M. Stanislaus[143]

Shortly after writing this letter Sister Stanislaus received the bishop's permission to visit the Sisters of St. Joseph in Florida and/or Georgia both of which were houses of the community that had come from Le Puy in 1866. Presumably, Bishop McQuaid lifted his imposition of interdict, allowing her to again participate in the sacraments.[144] Mother Stanislaus and Sister Ursula, her companion, left New York for Florida before the end of October, 1882.

Bishop McQuaid gave Mother Stanislaus permission to return to Rochester in May, 1883. She arrived in March. By April she had received the bishop's permission to go west to begin a new community in Arizona with a group that would eventually include Sisters Francis Joseph and Josephine Leary, her two blood sisters, along with Sisters Armella McGrath, Domitilla Gannon and

---

143 Sister Stanislaus to Bishop McQuaid, September 12, 1882. (Archives SSJR)
144 While the interdict was lifted, McQuaid maintained his order forbidding her to correspond with Rochester sisters. On May 25, 1884, Mother Stanislaus wrote McQuaid from Newton, Kansas asking him "Will you allow me to correspond at times with my dear Community of Rochester? I promise you Right Reverend Bishop that there will be nothing in this correspondence objectionable." She finished the letter inviting him to read her correspondence before it was delivered. The Rochester community annals of 1884 mention that His Lordship… forbids communication with those who have deserted our community. He feels that his former orders concerning this have not been obeyed in all communities. (Council Book, August 2, 1884: Archives SSJR) McQuaid had also forbidden M. Stanislaus to have any correspondence with Sister Baptista Hanson in Brooklyn. (Archives: SSJR) A copy of the May 25 letter is also kept in the Concordia Congregational Archives.

a novice, Sister Antoinette Cuff.[145]

Mother Stanislaus was not entirely alone as she moved through the ordeal of her deposition and the Bishop's restrictions on her communications with her sisters in Rochester. Even when her communications with the Rochester sisters were restricted she could turn to friends and especially to Sisters of St. Joseph in other dioceses. As mentioned, the Rochester annals indicate that after she was removed from office she visited the Sisters at Carondelet, Sister Baptista Hanson and the Sisters in Brooklyn, Sister Sidonie and others in St. Augustine, Florida and Sisters in Eire and Buffalo. In that wide-flung group she would have found very understanding companions. The Erie sisters knew that Mother Agnes had been deposed by Bishop Timon, Sister Baptista had been removed from Buffalo and sent to Brooklyn under questionable circumstances[146] and the superiors at Carondelet had experienced various bishops' concerted efforts opposing their endeavors to unify the Sisters of St. Joseph in America. The only sisters on Mother Stanislaus' visiting list who had not suffered something similar to what she was going through were the sisters in St. Augustine – and their time would come soon enough.

Under the leadership of Mother Agnes Hines, the community in Rochester continued to grow, opening additional schools, receiving new members and enlarging another signal institution in the diocese, the Home of Industry under the leadership of Sister Hieronymo O'Brien.[147] In 1894, when Mother Agnes Hines celebrated her 25th Jubilee, there were two hundred Sisters of St. Joseph of Rochester to celebrate with her. She would continue leading the community to open schools, including, in 1921, a Normal School. On May 31, 1921, Mother Agnes Hines died in Rochester. A Sister of St. Joseph of Rochester for fifty-two years, and superior of the Congregation for thirty-nine, having survived Bishop McQuaid by twelve years and Mother Stanislaus by twenty-one. At the time of her death there were 552 Sisters in the community with 77 novices and 18 postulants.[148]

---

145 See Thomas, 97. On July 31, 1883, the Rochester Council minutes state: "Sr. Armella, not having received the rquested obedience has on this day secretly left St. Patrick's Asylum during the absence of Sr. Eulalia, Superior." (Archives SSJR)

146 Father O'Connor of Buffalo wrote to Mother St. John Fournier on August 4, 1856, saying that Sister Baptista should be removed from Buffalo because her salvation was in danger there; on August 12, Bishop Timon gave her the letter missioning her to Brooklyn. (Archives: CSJB)

147 When Sister Hieronymo returned to Rochester she began to minister in St. Patrick's Girls' Asylum where she established a "House of Industry" which became a nearly self-sustaining home for orphan girls and young women boarders who came to the city to find work. See *The Life of Mother Hieronymo, Gerald Kelly* (Rochester, N.Y., Christopher Press, 1948).

148 The figures are from Sadliers Official Catholic Directory for 1921.

FOUNDATION IN THE DIOCESE OF BROOKLYN

When the Diocese of Brooklyn was created in 1853, Brooklyn was the seventh largest city in the U.S. with a population of 96,838, a little less than one-fifth that of neighboring New York whose population of 515,547 made it the largest city in the United States.[149] John Loughlin, Brooklyn's founding bishop, was a child of six when his parents immigrated from Ireland to New York in 1823. He studied for the priesthood at St. Mary's in Baltimore, was ordained in 1840 and was consecrated as a bishop in 1853 at the age of thirty-six.

In 1856, Bishop Loughlin asked Mother St. John Fournier in Philadelphia if she could send sisters to his diocese. His request came with an explanation of the circumstances that made him consider his need for help as a near emergency. His letter offers a window on how informal religious communities could proliferate in that era.

Brooklyn Jany 25, 1856 [sic]
Respected Mother [St. John Fournier],
I beg leave to submit a case to your charitable consideration.

Some time ago (about 9 months) without my knowledge, consent or approbation a number of girls under the direction of a clergyman here assembled together and, with the aid of one who said she belonged to the Third Order of St. Francis, formed them into a Community...a school was commenced which promised well, and I am satisfied would have succeeded; but as the whole proceeding was irregular, and as good order required that it should be established on a different basis I considered it my duty to intervene, and accordingly the community was broken up...I secured the services of two competent young ladies to continue the school, but they will leave in a few days for a Religious home.
So then we are trusting to Providence, and I hope we shall not be disappointed.

Yesterday morning I went to Philadelphia carrying with the hope that I could prevail on the good Sisters of St. Joseph to send a few of their members to Brooklyn. I did not make known to the good Sister whom I saw what I have stated to you as I did not think it necessary and as I was obliged to return home the same evening I had not time to see the Rt. Rev. Dr. Neumann. I learned from the Sister that if I wish to have some of the Sisters I should apply to you.

---

149 That is according to the census of 1850. See www.census.gov/population/www/documentation/twps0027/tab08.txt At that time Philadelphia ranked fourth with a population of 121,376; St. Louis, eighth with a population of 77,860; Albany, tenth with 50,763; Buffalo, sixteenth with 42,261; Rochester, twenty-first with 35,404; Wheeling, fifty-ninth with 11,435. Brooklyn was the first U.S. diocese erected which was exclusively urban, comprised only of Long Island.

This I now do, most humbly, respectfully, and confidently. I have endeavored to state briefly to you the circumstances of a case demanding immediate attention from me. I am satisfied that the good sisters would succeed admirably, that they are very much needed, that under their experienced and careful culture many a tender plant would be (?) that in a very short time they would see that they had done immense good and prevented much evil. There is here a wide field open for their labours.

On our part we will afford them every facility and encouragement and support. If you could send us at once even the smallest number necessary for a new foundation, their number should soon increase that their usefulness be extended and the glory of God promoted.

It is possible that you would be obliged to make a little sacrifice in order to meet my request. In the name of God, let it be made cheerfully for his glory and I hope He will reward you abundantly.

Don't refuse...Don't say "we cannot." We shall leave nothing undone on our part to make the poor Sisters happy.

Awaiting an answer at your earliest convenience,

I remain, Your humble servant in JC

+John Loughlin Bp. of Brooklyn[150]

Of course, Mother St. John consulted Bishop Neumann before responding to Bishop Loughlin's request. Within a week of the Mother St. John's receipt of Bishop Loughlin's letter, she received a letter from Bishop Neumann dealing with a number of topics. He apparently did not consider the request for sisters in Brooklyn a major decision because he commented on it almost as an afterthought. His major concern in the letter focused on how to garner the collaboration of the clergy who were not following through on their obligations to the sisters and apparently paid little heed to their bishop. He wrote:

Feb. 1, 1856

Dear Reverend Mother [St. John Fournier]

You have of course a perfect right to remind again those hesitating Pastors of their obligations, and to urge your claim the best you can. You can calculate on my cooperation, though it proves sometimes of no avail. Such like things must teach us to keep better our own promises and duties towards God – our tardiness must be very provoking to Him! I see no possibility to allow to the Rt. Rev. Bp. of Brooklyn any Sisters...[151]

While Mother St. John was experiencing difficulties with local pastors the bishop

---

150 Bishop Loughlin to Mother St. John Fournier, January 25, 1856 (Archives SSJ Philadelphia) Sister Magdalen Weber had gone to Phila delphia as one of the founders of that community with Mother St. JohnFournier in 1847.
151 Bishop Neumann to Mother St. John Fournier, February 1, 1856. (Archives SSJ Philadelphia)

claimed to share her problem rather than be able to resolve it. Did she hope that Brooklyn might offer better possibilities of collaboration with local priests? By 1856, there were more than 60 sisters in the Philadelphia community, with new vocations arriving steadily. Mother St. John could hardly afford to take on missions that could not support the sisters.[152] But if her concern was for self-sustaining ministries, Bishop Neumann's was apparently to assure sufficient sisters for Philadelphia's growing needs, and he thought they had none to spare.

Whether Bishop Loughlin was able to lobby Bishop Neumann or perhaps convince Mother St. John that Brooklyn was fertile ground for vocations as well as ministry, Mother St. John did not follow Bishop Neuman's advice and Bishop Loughlin got what he had requested. Taking Bishop Loughlin at his word, Mother St. John sent him "the smallest number necessary" from Philadelphia in the person of Mother Austin Kean. She also must have collaborated with Mother Celestine of Carondelet and Bishop Timon of Buffalo to arrange for Sisters Baptista Hanson and Theodosia Hagemann to go to Brooklyn from their mission in the diocese of Buffalo.[153]

MOTHER AUSTIN KEAN AND THE BROOKLYN FOUNDATION
SISTERS, SUPERIORS AND BISHOP

Mother Austin Kean

Mother Austin (Mary Elizabeth) Kean had entered the congregation at Philadelphia in 1849 from Loretto, Pennsylvania. The daughter of what was for Pennsylvania an old and prominent Catholic family, her roots went back to the McGuire clan who had settled in the area of Cambria County before the U.S. Revolution. One of her ancestors, Rachel McGuire, is credited as the person who brought the Russian prince, now "Servant of God," Augustine Gallitzin to become the first pastor in the region in 1795.[154] How

---

152 The Philadelphia archives indicate that at the end of 1853, there were 47 sisters, presumably including novices. That number grew so quickly that they counted 72 by 1856. (Statistics contributed by Sr. Patricia Annas, SSJ, Archives, SSJP.)

153 This is one of the most obvious cases in which more than one congregation/community was involved in the foundation of a mission. Mother Austin was sent from Philadelphia while Sisters Baptista and Theodosia came from Buffalo. Carondelet had opened the Buffalo mission and Sister Baptista had made her novitiate in McSherrystown, PA., which at one time was separate from Philadelphia. Sister Theodosia was received into the community at Carondelet. Clearly, the two largest communities were working in concert as they responded to needs beyond their immediate areas.

154 The Reverend Augustine Demetrius Gallitzin was a Russian prince and convert from the Russian Orthodox tradition. A friend of Bishop John Carroll, he was a missionary who accepted a plea to come from Conewago (near McSherrystown) to minister to a dying Protestant woman in "McGuire's Settlement," later known as

this young woman from western Pennsylvania learned of the Sisters of St. Joseph is uncertain. Quite possibly she had known Eliza (Sister Francis Joseph) Ivory, also from Loretto, who entered the congregation at Carondelet in 1847. But knowing of Carondelet does not explain how she encountered the sisters in Philadelphia, nearly 250 miles from her home.[155] Priests of the Diocese of Philadelphia, which then included most of the State of Pennsylvania may have been promoting the community to women who desired the ministerial breadth of the Sisters of St. Joseph.[156] However it happened that they learned of the community, between 1843 and 1861 ten of the 175 women who the entered the congregation at Carondelet hailed from various areas of Pennsylvania, not to mention all those who the congregation at Philadelphia.[157]

Mother Austin Kean (1825-1905) received the habit of the Sisters of St. Joseph on March 19, 1850. She made her novitiate under the tutelage of both Mother St. John Fournier and Sister Delphine Fontbonne. This made her one of the privileged few sisters in the U.S. who could claim to have been novices under sisters who had been formed by Mother St. John Fontbonne.[158] An old memoir, "Life of Mother Austin Kean, SSJ," describes Mother Austin and her abilities as follows:

> As a girl she was fond of athletics, rode horseback and indulged in all the pranks which any country girl knows well. However, there was in her an austerity and dignity, coupled with a keen sense of humor which continued throughout her long life...
>
> On August 25, 1856, only six years after her religious clothing, her Superiors deemed her competent to assume the responsibility of making a foundation requested by Bishop John Loughlin in Brooklyn...With two other Sisters, Mother Austin began the arduous task of building a

---

Loretto. From that time on he served the people in what became his "parish" which included the territory of what are now the dioceses of Pittsburgh and Erie and a large part of that of Harrisburg. Three Sisters of St. Joseph credit him for influence on their vocations: Sisters Austin Kean, Francis Joseph Ivory and St. George Bradley. See Logue, 12-13 and Thomas F. Meehan, "Two Pioneer Russian Missionaries" *Historical Records and Studies, United States Catholic Historical Society, Vol. xix (1929) 105-109* (New York: The United States Catholic Historical Society).97 See Chapter 4 and Brennan, Persistence of Vision: A Portrait of Mother Stanislaus Leary (Rochester: InstantPublisher.com, 2005), 11-13.

155 Loretto PA is almost 650 miles from St. Louis.

156 The Diocese of Pittsburgh was created from Philadelphia in 1843, and the Diocese of Erie came from that diocese in 1853. In 1868, the dioceses of Harrisburg, Scranton and Wilmington were created from Philadelphia's territory and Philadelphia became an archdiocese in 1875

157 That number is calculated from the official "Profession Book," (Carondelet Generalate Archives) and the total includes the French missionaries who founded or joined the congregation in the United States.

158 After Mother Delphine Fontbonne left Philadelphia in 1851, there was not another director of novices who had been formed by Mother St. John Fontbonne. Mother St. John Fournier's influence continued for years to come in both Philadelphia and St. Paul.

new Community...She governed the Community wisely and successfully from its inception...until...incapacitated by ill health, she resigned her charge as Superior General.[159]

Before going to Brooklyn, Mother Austin had served in hospital ministry in Philadelphia.

There are various accounts of the sisters' arrival in Brooklyn, but it is most probable that Sisters Theodosia and Baptista arrived shortly before Mother Austin. They traveled directly from Buffalo to Brooklyn as indicated by the following letter of permission from Bishop Timon:

> Buffalo, August 12, 1856
> To Sisters Baptista and Theodosia
> Of the Sisterhood of St. Joseph
> By these presents we appoint you to start on Monday, 18th August, to begin under the direction of the Sister Superior whom Mother St. John will send, a house of your order in the Diocese of Brooklyn and we beg that Holy St. Joseph protect you, and that God help you in this great and most important work.
> John, Bishop of Buffalo[160]

That short letter of obedience yields a few interesting facts and implications. While Bishop Neumann and Mother St. John Fournier had somehow agreed to send Mother Austin Kean from Philadelphia, Bishop Loughlin of Brooklyn also received help from his confrere in Buffalo, Bishop John Timon. Although Bishop Neumann of Philadelphia indicated that he could not spare sisters, Bishop Timon felt free to send two sisters from his diocese, one of whom, Sister Baptista, had entered the Congregation from Philadelphia and had been missioned to Buffalo by Mother St. John Fournier. The other, Sister Theodosia Hagemann, had been missioned to Buffalo by Mother Celestine at Carondelet.[161] Bishop Timon assumed the authority to send Sisters Baptista and Theodosia from his diocese to another while apparently assuming that Mother St. John had the authority to send and

---

159 "Life of Mother Austin Kean" (An anonymous document found in the CSJ archives, Brentwood, identified as a document from Chestnut Hill.)

160 "Letter of obedience" from Bishop Timon, August 12, 1856, giving Sisters Baptista and Theodosia permission to go to Brooklyn on August 18 to be "under the direction of the Superior Mother St. John will send." (ACSJBr)

161 As will be seen below, the timing may have been right for these two sisters to leave Buffalo. Also, Timon and Loughlin were in communication about the Sisters of St. Joseph as demonstrated by a letter from Timon to Mother St. John Fournier in which he said The Rt. Rev. Bishop of Brooklyn, an intimate friend, has often spoken to me of Institutions for his diocese. I have spoken to him much in favour of yours..." (Timon to Fournier, March 29, 1856: Archives SSJ Philadelphia)

appoint their superior in that new mission. We see here an interesting intermingling of authority, with bishops like John Timon assuming the authority to transfer sisters who had come from a different diocese. The Constitutions the Lyon sisters had brought from France gave each bishop ultimate authority over the sisters in his diocese, no matter from what motherhouse they had been sent. Given that, it is little wonder that Mother Celestine was beginning to work on organizing the dispersed communities of Sisters of St. Joseph into a multi-provincial congregational structure.[162]

The two sisters who opened the mission with Mother Austin came from different backgrounds. Sister Theodosia Hagemann, as mentioned above, was among the first sisters missioned to Canandaigua where she taught in the Academy before being missioned to Brooklyn at the age of twenty. She remained in Brooklyn for a few years and then returned to St. Louis where she obtained a dispensation from her vows. Her companion, Sister Baptista, had a longer and more varied history as a Sister of St. Joseph. Originally from Baltimore, Sister Baptista entered the congregation at Philadelphia; she received the habit in 1852 and served as director of St. Joseph's Academy for girls in Philadelphia and then in the Diocese of Buffalo before going to Brooklyn.[163]She would succeed Mother Austin in 1869 as Superior General of the Brooklyn Congregation in 1869.

BEGINNINGS IN BROOKLYN

Mother Austin recalled their first days in Brooklyn saying that she arrived in Brooklyn with Mother St. John Fournier and Mother Salome. The two sisters from Buffalo met them there. In Mother Austin's words,

> It would not take long to give here the inventory of the house as four beds, a few chairs, one table and a scarcity of utensils were all it contained... the only light they had was a candle placed on a bottle found in the cellar and their first meals were bought with the few coins left over from the traveling expenses...[164]

On September 1, 1856, the three founding sisters and the two superiors from Philadelphia inaugurated the mission in the Williamsburg area of Brooklyn.[165]

---

162 The two superiors who were sending sisters to distant missions at this time were the cousins, Mother Celestine Pommerel at Carondelet and Mother St. John Fournier at Philadelphia.
163 In 1856, Reverend Edmund O'Connor from Canandaigua wrote to Mother St. John in Philadelphia regarding the necessity for Sister Baptista to leave that mission because "her salvation is in danger by staying here." (E. O'Connor to Mother St. John Fournier, August 4, 1856: ACSJBr)
164 Community Annals Vol. V, 267-9. (Archives CSJ Brentwood)
165 Williamsburg began as a village, was incorporated as a town in 1840 and as a city in 1851. By the time the

The Philadelphia superiors soon left the three sisters in their modest setting where the newcomers began to scrape together all they needed for community living and ministry. The community annals explain:

> The three first members of St. Joseph's Convent, left in utter poverty, set to work, borrowing a few desks to start their little school and Academy which opened on September 8.[166]

It must have been quite a scramble for the sisters since the academy opened with sixty students.[1167]

Once the fledgling academy opened, the next event of moment was the acceptance of their first postulant. Miss Maria Tello came to the community on December 4, 1856, just three months after the sisters had arrived. Maria was an accomplished musician and linguist who, after five months teaching with the community in Brooklyn, was sent to the novitiate in McSherrystown. There, on April 14, 1857, she received the habit and name Sister Hortensia. She returned to Brentwood on April 6 of the following year and made vows in 1859.[168] The next women to enter the community were Sisters Mary de Sales McCudden, Mary John Boylan and Mary de Chantal Keating, all of whom received the habit in New York. Around the same time as they were received, Sister Theodosia Hagemann returned to St. Louis where she would receive a dispensation from her vows.

In September of 1857, under the leadership of Sister Mary Baptista, the community opened classes in Saints Peter and Paul church, their second mission in two years. That same year four women entered the community, each on a different date between October 5 and December 31. In 1858, the community received four more candidates and saw the reception and profession ceremonies of sisters who had already entered. The rapid growth of the community was more than matched by requests for their services. In 1859, they took charge of a parochial school connected with St. Mary's Parish.[169]

By 1860, the community had outgrown its original home. Mother Austin began negotiations with an Episcopalian minister to purchase property in Flushing which would serve as the motherhouse and novitiate for the next forty-three years. Father James O'Bierne of St. Michael's parish in Flushing encouraged the sisters to

---

sisters arrived in 1856 it had been subsumed into the City of Brooklyn.
166 Annals, Vol. 5, 267-9. (Archives CSJ Brentwood)
167 Sister Mary Ignatius Meany, notes. (Archives CSJ Brentwood).
168 Mary Ignatius Meany, *By Railway or Rainbow, A History of the Sisters of St. Joseph of Brentwood*, (Patterson, NJ, St. Anthony Guild Press, 1964) 39-40.
169 Meany, notes.

make the move to that spacious "country" area.

Soon thereafter he helped them take the steps to legally incorporate the community in the State of New York, a process which was completed on July 30, 1860. Mother Austin moved to the Flushing property on August 19, 1860 with seven sisters and three postulants. One month later they opened St. Joseph's Female Academy on the grounds.[170] Mother Austin would continue in her role as superior until 1865. The account of her resignation is preserved in the community annals which say that on Tuesday, August 29, 1865 after a community retreat the sisters came together for an election.

> In the afternoon the Bishop assembled the Sisters in the Chapel spoke to them on the sentiments which they should have after the Retreat and announced to them that he had acceded to the repeated petitions of Mother M. Augusta to resign her office and that an election would immediately take place. He spoke to them also of giving their votes to such only as they deemed worthy, and reminded them that though from necessity as it was almost the season for the schools to commence, no time could intervene between the resignation and election, they would nevertheless act in a conscientious manner according as the Holy Spirit would inspire them. The Veni Creator was then said and the votes having been duly examined the Rt. Rev. Bishop announced that Sister M. Baptista was elected Superioress who accordingly made her Profession of Faith and was confirmed in office by the Rt. Rev. Bishop.[171]

After her resignation, on September 12, 1865, Mother Austin visited the Sisters of St. Joseph in St. Paul, a trip the annals described as "for her health." She remained there for nearly a month. Although in 1865, Mother Austin felt she could no longer guide the community, she would recover well enough to continue the work of founding new communities, first in 1869 at Ebensburg, Pennsylvania, near her family home and then at Rutland Vermont in 1873.[172]

---

170 By Railway, 39-40, and Margaret Quinn, "Mother M. Austin Kean: Woman of Faith and Courage" (Manuscript, Archives, ACSJBr)
171 Erie Annals, page 21, (Archives, CSJ Brentwood). The Annals also note that Sr. "Augusta" went to St. Paul for the benefit of her health on Sept. 12, 1865 and that Sr. "Austin" returned on October 8. (She is more than once referred to as Sr. Augustine, perhaps because she was named for Rev. Augustine Gallitzin) Sister Mary Ignatius' notes indicate that while Sr. Austin was in St. Paul she wrote to Bishop Loughlin (September 27, 1865) apologizing for "the trouble I have given you during my stay in authority" and saying that although her health was not good, she would return to New York the following month. (Archives CSJ Brentwood)
172 The Ebensburg foundation was the origin of the Baden Congregation and Rutland was founded as an independent congregation that eventually joined the Springfield, Massachusetts congregation.

THE DEATH OF MOTHER CELESTINE
AND THE PASSING OF THE TORCH

Between the foundation of Brooklyn and that of the third New York mission in Oswego, Mother Celestine Pommerel, the heart of multiple foundations and unofficial general superior of the Sisters of St. Joseph in the United States died at Carondelet on June 7, 1857. Sister Lucida Savage describes Mother Celestine's missionary life as follows.

Mother Celestine
Pommerel
1813 – 1857

> Generous as her sacrifice had been in leaving home and country, Mother Celestine felt the parting with them keenly, and the trials of life in the New World often bore heavily on her…but the Sisters of her community knew only her cheery smile, the gracious manner and joyousness…She was not a woman of many words… but by daily acts of loving kindness, she taught great lessons…
>
> The last rites of the Church were administered by Father Feehan…and on the afternoon of Sunday, June 7, Mother Celestine died, surrounded by her sorrowing community. At the solemn Requiem Mass on June 9, Archbishop Kenrick, who had frequently visited and consoled the patient in her illness, assisted.

Sister Lucida goes on to quote the press of St. Louis which reported on Mother Celestine's funeral saying:

> The venerable and beloved Mother is gone…If a reward is promised to the cup of cold water given for the sake of Jesus, will not hers be exceedingly great?
> …The funeral on the ninth presented a scene that Catholics cannot easily forget…As the ceremonies concluded, the procession moved slowly toward the grave. The cross-bearer…the coffin borne by the Sisters, the long train of religious, the young ladies of the academy, nearly one hundred in all; and finally, crowds of citizens, each as if some dear friend were dead.[173]

Ten days after Mother Celestine was laid to rest the community gathered to choose her successor. There are varying accounts of what happened at that meeting. According to all reliable accounts, the gathered sisters' first choice was Sister

---

173 Savage, 109-110.

Seraphine Coughlin who was superior of the community in St. Paul.[174] She declined the office on the grounds of her inability and delicate health. What other concerns she may have had are open to conjecture based on various reports of the election.

According to the history of the Sisters of St. Joseph of Moutiers, the chapter of elections was plagued by dissension among sisters of different ethnic origins. Apparently based on evidence from letters written to France that account says:

> A few hours before leaving this earth she had called for Bishop Henrick [sic], the archbishop of Saint Louis to come see her and she designated Mother St. John [Facemaz] as the only sister capable of succeeding her in the governance of the congregation. The Archbishop thus named Mother St. John as provisional superior...
>
> Before the opening of the general chapter, the institute was troubled by hot-tempered and very human "cabals." The German sisters were plotting in favor of a superior of their nationality, the Irish and Americans agitated for the same. The French sisters, seven in number, felt like they were drowning in the midst of hundreds of religious and were so overwhelmed by what was going on that they were prepared to accept the invitation of a northern bishop who offered them an escape.[175]

While not reliably objective, the Moutiers understanding of the situation must have had some basis in evidence. By 1857, six members of the Moutiers community had come to the U.S. and four more would arrive in that year.

A letter written by Sister Febronie Boyer who received the habit in 1849 records a different story – perhaps no more objective than the previous. Sister Febronie said that when Mother Celestine became ill, Archbishop Kenrick had placed Sister St. John in full charge until Mother Celestine should recover or someone be appointed to take her place. She continued:

> The Archbishop came to the funeral and said that he would return in 8 days for the election and ordered prayers said every day. On the appointed day the election was held and Mother Seraphina [sic] of Saint Paul was chosen. While preparations were being made for her arrival, the Arch. sent word that he would meet the sisters in the chapel on

---

174 Born in New York in 1826, and later a resident of St. Louis, Sr. Mary Seraphine (Mary) was received into the congregation at Carondelet in 1846. She died in St. Paul on August 1, 1861.
175 J. Trésal, *Les Soeurs de Saint-Joseph de Moûtiers* (Savoie) En France Et Au Brésil, 1828-1928 (Paris: Librairie Lecoffre, 1929) 127-130. (Hereafter: Sisters of St. Joseph of Moutiers) That history also indicated that Mother Celestine had requested sisters from France because their help was badly needed to counter the lack of religious discipline found at Carondelet. Other evidence indicates that the Moutiers sisters came to the U.S. at the request of Bishop Miege of Kansas who was originally from the Moutiers area who hoped they would come to his diocese via Carondelet.

Thursday. He told us who were assembled there that Mother Seraphina had given good reasons for not accepting the office and he appointed Sister St. John to fill the vacancy. This announcement caused great excitement. The sisters screamed – threw themselves on the floor etc---- The Archbishop left immediately, even ran from the chapel and would not hear or see anyone.

Many of the Sisters were so dissatisfied that they went to other houses…All the Sisters excepting Sister Michael and I made the retreat given by Father Convers. He tried so hard to reason with them and "bring them to their senses." Finally he said that all those who rebelled against authority should leave. Many did so, but others who still were not in favor of Mother St. John stayed. After retreat, Mother Helena… was elected and Mother Angela and Mother Felicite as counsellors and Sister Clare was named Mistress of Novices.[176]

It is hard to be certain what Sister Febronie meant by saying that many sisters somehow left the community. The Carondelet profession record notes very few dispensations in the years around these events which leads one to believe that Sister Febronie Boyer's memory may not have been perfectly accurate. Whatever the precise details of the circumstances under which Mother St. John Facemaz began her term as superior at Carondelet, it is certain that she had enjoyed Mother Celestine's full confidence as Mother Celestine had named her novice director and councilor shortly after her arrival to Carondelet from Moutiers in 1854 and she remained in those positions until Mother Celestine's death.

When Mother St. John Facemaz began her term as superior, approximately 148 sisters had received the habit or arrived as missionaries at Carondelet. Of those, twenty-five had been born in France, twenty-seven in German lands, sixty in Ireland, nine in Missouri and the remainder in Canada, England, and the east or north of the United States. This number did not count those who had received the habit in Philadelphia, New York and Wheeling.

The French sisters who were part of Carondelet at the time of Mother Celestine's death included Sisters Felicite Bouté, Philoméne Vilaine, and St. Protais DeBoille who had arrived in 1836 from Lyon; Mother St. John Fournier who had arrived from Lyon in 1837, and was superior in Philadelphia; Sisters St. John Facemaz, Euphrasia Meiller, Gonzaga Grand and Leonie Martin who arrived in 1854 from Moutiers; Sisters Victorine (no last name available), and Cecelia Rosteing who arrived in 1856 from Moutiers. Sisters Ambrosia Arnichaud, Philoméne Billex, M. Agnes Facemaz and Hyacinth Blanc arrived from Moutiers in 1857, but there is no record that indicates they arrived before the death of Mother Celestine. (Archives, Carondelet and Dougherty,)

176 "Memoirs of Sister Febronie Boyer – Copied from handwritten notes" (Generalate Archives, Carondelet). The Carondelet profession book records three undated dispensations around that time, Sister Theodosia Hagemann, received in 1851 and Sisters M. Barbara Quinn and Chrysostom McCann, both of whom were received in 1852.

FOUNDATION IN OSWEGO - 1858

Soon after assuming responsibility for the community, Mother St. John Facemaz received a request for sister-teachers from Reverend Father Guerdet of Oswego in the Diocese of Albany, New York. The Albany diocese had been created in 1847 with John McCloskey (1810-1885), the first native New Yorker ordained to the diocesan

priesthood, as the founding bishop.[177] In 1852, Bishop McCloskey had attended the First Plenary Council of Baltimore at which the assembled bishops and major superiors of religious priests addressed the question of Catholic education and decided that every parish in the country should have a Catholic school whose teachers would be paid from parish funds. Church leaders, especially in the eastern states, were extremely concerned over the widespread and unjustifiable harassment to which Catholic children were subject in many public schools. One incident which took place in a New York school represented an all too common situation:

Corporal Punishment
in 19th Century School

On the 8th of August, 1853, William Callahan, a Catholic pupil in the district school…was, with the sanction of the trustees, severely punished with a ferule and expelled from the school…for declining to read and study the Protestant Testament…there was no safeguard of positive law, and Catholic children remained liable to similar treatment.[178]

Motivated by the desire to promote growth in the faith as well as to escape discrimination and maltreatment, bishops and parishioners alike sought the help of women religious in the service of education.

---

177 John Cardinal McCloskey was born in Brooklyn to Irish immigrant parents. After ordination he volunteered to work with cholera victims, but due to his poor health Bishop Dubois sent him instead to study in Rome. In 1843, on his 34th birthday he was ordained Auxiliary Bishop of New York where he was influential in the conversions of Isaac Hecker the founder of the Paulist priests and the then Episcopal priest, James Roosevelt Bayley, the nephew of Mother Seton who eventually became the Archbishop of Baltimore. As the founding bishop of Albany he gave the necessary permissions to invite the Sisters of St. Joseph to found their first communities in the diocese. In 1864 he was named Archbishop of New York and in 1875 he became the first U.S. Cardinal.

178 John Gilmary Shea, *History of the Catholic Church in the United States*, (New York: McBride 1886-1892) vol. 4, 479. Illustration from The Adventures of Tom Sawyer, by Mark Twain Illustrated by True Williams, (American Publishing Company, 1876.

When Mother St. John Facemaz received Father Guerdet's request in 1858, communities of Sisters of St. Joseph from Carondelet and Philadelphia were already serving in the areas Rochester, Buffalo and Brooklyn, New York. Nevertheless, Mother St. John saw the possibility of sending more sisters east. On April 15, 1858, Sisters Stanislaus Saul, Patricia Pyne, Hyacinth Blanc, Flavia Waldron, Eusebius Verdin and Chrysostom McCann arrived in Oswego to be welcomed by Father Guerdet who over the space of the past three years had already purchased land, a house and supplies for them.[179] The sisters immediately began their ministry of teaching and also welcomed orphans into the three-story building that served for classrooms, convent and an orphanage which had become home to thirty children by 1867.[180] Of those first six sisters to serve in Oswego, only Sister Mary Eusebius was born in the U.S., Sisters Patricia, Mary Flavia and Chrysostom were Irish by birth, Sister Stanislaus was born in Germany and Sister Hyacinth was from Bourg, Saint-Maurice, Mother St. John Facemaz's hometown.[181]

Somehow, either the great need or good relations with the bishop and his priests worked such an effect on Mother St. John and her council that for the next few years they continued to send communities to serve in the Albany diocese. In 1860, Sisters Philoméne Billex and Mary Flavia Waldron arrived at St. Bernard's Parish in Cohoes, a town some ten miles north of Albany and more than 165 miles east of Oswego. In 1861, the sisters opened four new missions in the parishes of The Cathedral, St. Joseph's and St. Peter's in Troy and St. John the Baptist in Salina which eventually would belong to the Syracuse diocese. In 1862, the community opened a school at St. Patrick's Parish in Binghamton.

By 1862, Mother St. John Facemaz had missioned thirty-one sisters to the Albany diocese where they were serving in six parishes. In 1863, the community opened a novitiate which also functioned as the provincial house for the newly erected Eastern Province of the Sisters of St. Joseph of Carondelet.

---

179 The list of the original sisters is found in Mary Aida Doyle, *History of the Sisters of St. Joseph of Carondelet in the Troy Province* (Albany: Argus Press, 1936), 46. Giving witness to his hope and early preparations to have sisters in the parish Fr. Guerdet's parish cashbook included the following entries: "1855, Purchase of the Sisters' House; 1856, $1,650, Second lot for Sisters' House, $500; 1857, Finishing and repairing Sisters' House, $207; 1858 Furnishing Sisters' House $197; 1858, First Addition to Sisters' House, $1,350." (Dougherty, 216)
180 Doyle, 48.
181 None of these sisters died as members of the Troy/Albany province. Sister Chrysostom eventually received a dispensation from her vows, Sister Hyacinth died in Tucson in 1904, and the others died in houses of the St. Louis Province. Sister Philoméne Billex, a missionary from Moutiers who opened the mission at Cohoes died there in 1860 at the age of 25, only months after arriving. Sr. Philoméne Billex was the first of the French missionaries to die in the United States, although Sister Delphine Fontbonne had died in Toronto in 1856. (Archives, Generalate, Carondelet)

꒰꓾

Chapter Five: Designing Evolutionary Structures And Relationships

Cast of Characters

Mother Celestine Pommerel 1813 - 1857
Superior At Carondelet 1839 - 1857
Mother St. John Fournier 1814 - 1875
Founder And Superior In Philadelphia 1847 - 1851, 1853 -1875
Mother St. John Facemaz 1821 - 1900
Missionary From Moutiers, Superior Of Carondelet 1858 - 1872
Mother Mary John Kiernan - 1825 - 1888
Second Superior General Philadelphia 1875 - 1888

Archbishop Peter Richard Kenrick 1806 - 1896
First Archbishop Of St. Louis, Bishop From 1841 - 1896
Bishop Francis Patrick Kenrick 1797- 1863
Bishop Of Philadelphia 1830 - 1851
St. John Neumann 1811 - 1860
Bishop Of Philadelphia 1852 - 1860
Bishop James Wood 1813 -1883
Bishop Of Philadelphia 1860 - 1883
Bishop John Timon 1797 - 1867
Vincentian Priest, First Bishop Of Buffalo, 1847 - 1867

RELATIONSHIPS BEFORE STRUCTURES

In their first ten or fifteen years in the U.S. the Sisters of St. Joseph seemed to be rather unconcerned about the formal status of their widespread communities. Sisters Celestine and St. John Fournier who arrived in 1837 were the last sisters Lyon sent to the U.S. Still the sisters in the U.S. maintained simple, strong connections with one another and with the congregation in Lyon.[1] The community in America rapidly expanded its geographical frontiers sending sisters east and north and back and forth.

Mother Celestine Pommerel, the much loved and respected superior at

---

1 We have but one extant letter from Mother St. John Fontbonne to the sisters in America. The 1858 fire at Carondelet most likely destroyed much of the correspondence of the early years.

at Carondelet died on  June 7, 1857.[2] During her time in leadership, the community had grown prodigiously. She had opened eight communities in the Archdiocese of St. Louis and had sent sisters to missions in the dioceses of Philadelphia (1847), St. Paul (1851), Toronto (1851), Wheeling (1853), Buffalo (1854) and Natchez (1855).[3] The foundations in Toronto and Brooklyn could be considered joint foundations from Carondelet and Philadelphia. Mother Delphine Fontbonne and Sister Martha von Bunning, both of whom had been sent from Carondelet to Philadelphia, founded the first mission in Toronto, Canada. In 1856, Mother St. John Fournier missioned Mother Austin Kean from Philadelphia to open a community in Brooklyn with the help of two sisters then missioned in Buffalo: Sister Baptista Hanson who had entered the community in Philadelphia and Sister Theodosia Hagemann who had entered at Carondelet. The two major superiors, the cousins who had studied deaf education together, were working in collaboration as they founded and staffed missions.

Mother Celestine
Pommerel
4/13/1813 – 6/13/1857

By 1857, the communities in the dioceses of Philadelphia, Toronto, St. Paul, Wheeling and Buffalo had established novitiates and while the younger communities had fewer members, the Philadelphia community numbered 54 professed sisters and Carondelet 107, fifteen of whom were professed that very year.[4] Although she suffered from ill health, Mother Celestine tried to visit all the communities. In 1853, she accompanied Mother Agnes Spencer from Philadelphia to open the mission in Wheeling just as Mother St. John Fournier would go with Mother Austin Kean when she founded the Brooklyn community in 1856. Although Mother Celestine's activity appeared tantamount to that of a general superior for the various communities, the juridical lines were blurry if not nonexistent. In the early years the sisters were more involved in carrying out the mission than in establishing governance structures. The friendships and shared roots among the sisters maintained a strong sense of mutual support and respect for Mothers

---

2 Mother Celestine had been superior at Carondelet since 1839 when Mother Delphine Fontbonne resigned.
3 The number of sisters is calculated from the Carondelet profession book. It includes all the sisters received by June, 1857, as well as the missionaries who had by then arrived from France. St. Louis became an Archdiocese in 1847. The community in Brooklyn was jointly founded by sisters from Carondelet and Philadelphia. When Mother Delphine and Sister Martha von Bunning opened the Toronto mission they left from Philadelphia where they had been missioned by Mother Celestine at Carondelet.
4 Profession Records, Archives Philadelphia, thanks to Archivist, Sister Patricia Annas and CSJ Profession Book, Carondelet.

Celestine and St. John's leadership seemingly supplied all the structure they needed, but the situation grew more and more complicated as the sisters found themselves working with a variety of diocesan bishops. As both their numbers and the distances that separated the sisters increased, Mother Celestine and Bishop Kenrick began to talk with others about formalizing their interrelationships and creating a congregational structure.

While very little correspondence has survived chronicling the original efforts to form a single American Congregation, a letter to Mother Celestine from Father August Paris, the priest Bishop Kenrick had appointed as ecclesiastical superior of the Carondelet community, refers to a plan they intended to carry out.[5] In the course of an 1856 trip to Europe, Father Paris had visited communities of St. Joseph in the east and was planning to represent Mother Celestine in visits to sisters in France as well. He wrote to Mother Celestine from Europe urging her to accomplish their plan for her to make a general visitation because he thought that her presence was much needed in communities in the U.S. and Canada. Unfortunately, her health did not permit such arduous travel. [6] Although she was not able to make a final visitation, after her death various sisters including Sister Seraphine Coughlin of St. Paul and Mothers Austin Kean of Brooklyn and St. John Fournier of Philadelphia visited Carondelet in the autumn of 1859. These visits seem to have been preliminary meetings to talk about forming a congregational structure among them.

Even though the canonical dependence of the U.S. community on Lyon proved too difficult for either side to maintain, the spirituality and *Constitutions* brought from France as well as the pattern of growth and development of the French Congregations of St. Joseph, provided models for the U.S. sisters. The original eight missionaries from Lyon and the sisters they introduced to religious life would have been greatly influenced by developments in the Congregation of Lyon. Before the French Revolution the Sisters of St. Joseph were generally organized as independent foundations, often with more than one autonomous community in the same diocese.[7] After the Revolution, Mother St. John Fontbonne

---

5 It was Father Paris who founded the school for "liberated Negroes" in St. Louis in which the Sisters of St. Joseph taught until it was forced to close.

6 Savage (107-110), refers to discussions between Mother Celestine and Bishop Kenrick. On May 11, 1856, Father Paris of St. Louis wrote to Mother Celestine from France saying that he would try to get sisters from Lyon and Savoie for the St. Louis community. As spiritual father and collaborator with the U.S. sisters, Fr. Paris would have been interested in the development of the community in France and would have brought news of them back to St. Louis. Father Paris' letter can be found in the Carondelet archives.

7 For an approximate list of communities founded between 1649 and 1789 see Vacher, Nuns Without Cloister, Appendix 5, 375 ff.

in Lyon and Mother Anne-Marie Grand in Le Puy were among the superiors who regrouped dispersed sisters and communities and began to organize them as Congregations with centralized governance.[8] The new French congregations grew almost as quickly as did the demands for their services at home and beyond. By the time the first eight missionary Sisters of St. Joseph had come to the United States, the Lyon sisters had experienced a congregational model of religious life and most recognized Mother St. John Fontbonne as the beloved and saintly superior whose efforts unified them as a Congregation strong enough to found other Congregations. When Lyon could no longer send missionaries to the U.S., it was Lyon's daughter congregation in Moutiers that took over. The inestimable contribution of the Moutiers congregation to the Sisters of St. Joseph in the United States has been all but forgotten until recent years.

THE MOUTIERS MISSIONARIES AND MOTHER ST. JOHN MARCOUX
The history of the Moutiers congregation illustrates the remarkable growth of the French Sisters of St. Joseph and their missionary spirit in post-revolutionary France.[9]

Mother St. John
Marcoux
1785 - 1855

---

8 The Le Puy and Lyon Congregations were not alone in their reorganization, but all the Sisters of St. Joseph in the U.S. trace their roots to one or both of these restructured congregations.

9 Sister Benedicte de Vaublanc of Chambéry describes the Sisters of St. Joseph's expansion in France with the following details: in 1843, at the death of Mother St. John Fontbonne, the Lyon congregation had 244 houses and three thousand sisters; in 1827, Le Puy brought together fifty-two houses. New congregations came into existence in Chambéry in 1812; Turin, Italy, in 1821; Saint-Jean-de-Maurienne in 1822; Bourg in 1823; Oulais in 1824; Moutiers in 1825; Novarra, Italy in 1826; Cuneo and Aosta in Italy in 1831; and Annecy, 1833. In 1836, Lyon sent missionaries to St. Louis and in 1855, Bourg sent missionaries to Louisiana. The Le Puy community sent fourteen missionaries to St. Augustine, Florida in 1866. (See Benedicte de Vaublanc: "Sisters of Saint Joseph Today: Their International Expansion and the Movement Toward Unity," Monograph from Barbara Baer Collection, Archives of the Federation of the Sisters of St. Joseph.)

The Moutiers history begins with Mother St. John Marcoux and the foundation of the Chambéry congregation. Mother St. John the Baptist Marcoux (1785-1855) had been one of Mother St. John Fontbonne's original "Black Daughters" in St. Etienne and was one of the elder's dearest and most respected junior sisters.[10] Mother St. John Fontbonne's decision in 1812 to send this great leader to open a community in Aix-les-Bains in the Diocese of Chambéry was as right as it was difficult. In 1815, as a result of diocesan reorganization, the Chambéry community became independent from Lyon.[11] As founding superior and eventually the General Superior in Chambéry, Mother St. John Marcoux established communities in Saint-Jean-de-Maurienne (1822) and Pignerol, Italy (1823), each of which became an independent congregation.[12] In 1825, at the invitation of Senator Bal, a wealthy government official appalled by the lack of education and formation available to young women from poor villages, Mother St. John Marcoux accompanied two sisters from Chambéry to Moutiers to open a new community. There Senator Bal had obtained a house and garden and added the sum of 10,000 francs to help the sisters found a community in Moutiers that eventually became independent from Chambéry.

Mother St. John Marcoux's administration and foundations mirrored what Mother St. John Fontbonne was doing from Lyon as she continued to send her sisters to new towns and dioceses. Active religious life was flourishing in France. The Napoleonic reforms promoted the social services offered by the sisters and called for the formation of centralized congregations with dependent houses as a more efficacious model for apostolic religious. Many French congregations became organized on the diocesan level while others, including some congregations of St. Joseph, followed the lead of the Daughters of Charity who by then had been an international apostolic community with centralized governance for over a hundred years.[13] The sisters who came to the U.S. from Lyon and Moutiers had experienced the congregational model of religious life in France. They realized

---

10 Mother St. John Marcoux's name is listed as Soeur Saint-Jean-Baptiste Marcoux in Bois, *Les Soeurs de Saint-Joseph, Les Filles du Petit Dessein de 1648 à 1949* (Lyon: Editions et imprimerie du Sud-Est, 1950), 235.
11 In 1815, the Congress of Vienna restored the French region of Savoie to the kingdom of Sardinia; because it was no longer in French territory, the Chambéry community became independent of Lyon. (Tarsal, 17.)
12 Saint-Jean-de-Maurienne is the community that founded the Sisters of St. Joseph of Buenos Aires, Argentina, in 1882.
13 By 1848 the Sisters of St. Joseph of Annecy had decided to open a community in India, thus extending the missionary reach of the French sisters from Europe to the Near East as well as the American continent. French and Italian communities of St. Joseph would extend their reach to include not only North America but various countries in Asia, Africa and South America.

that through shared resources and the flexibility to serve wherever they were needed, that model offered an advantageous complement to their openly defined ministries as Sisters of St. Joseph.

As the Sisters of St. Joseph grew and diversified in the United States, Lyon's inability to send additional missionaries and the difficulty of maintaining ongoing communication between Europe and America led the Carondelet community to become formally independent of Lyon's official authority. The separation did not affect the sisters' love of their French roots, their devotion to the French communities or their cherished two-hundred year shared history and spiritual legacy.[14] The separation did however affect two other dimensions of the sisters' life: it emphasized the need for missionaries from the other congregations and it highlighted the growing importance of the question of official organization of the sisters in America. Even as Lyon's influence waned in America, between 1854 and 1887, the Moutiers congregation sent thirty-nine missionaries to America, a tremendous contribution to the newly forming communities of St. Joseph in the U.S. and Canada. Of all those missionary sisters, the one who would become most influential, Sister St. John Facemaz, came in the first group.

MOTHER ST. JOHN FACEMAZ

There are varying accounts of how the first Moutiers Sisters were drawn to go to the United States. A history of the Moutiers congregation tells the story as follows:

> The Sisters of St. Joseph of Lyon founded an establishment in the diocese of Bishop Rosati in 1836. Within a few years the community had founded numerous houses, too many actually, because postulants did not have time to make a novitiate or be formed in the religious life which left everything in a state of decadence.
>
> In order to remedy this state of affairs, Mother Celestine...asked the superior general of Moutiers to send some fervent sisters who could serve as a model for her community. Bishop Miège...took the request to Moutiers.[15]

---

14 Carondelet has no official records documenting the discussions or the decision to separate from Lyon. It may have come about as a natural progression, particularly as Bishop Kenrick assumed a growing role in supporting and guiding the community. After Sisters Celestine and St. John Fournier left Lyon, the Carondelet archives have no correspondence between the sisters and Bishop Le Pins, the Apostolic Administrator of Lyon or Father Cholleton, Bishop Rosati's Vicar and emissary between the bishop and the Lyon community. The U.S. congregations have only one letter from Mother St. John Fontbonne to her daughters in America.
15 Trésal, 127-129.

There is ample reason to suspect that this account is less than objective and accurate. For one thing, while we know about disagreements involving the Reverends Fontbonne and Saulnier and the sisters during the early days at Carondelet, there is no evidence of "decadence" in the life of the Sisters of St. Joseph.[16] Additionally, the author's opinion could well have been influenced by the inevitable culture shock that French missionaries underwent in adjusting to life in a multi-cultural, multi-racial, religiously diverse society which valued democracy above every sort of hierarchy.[17]

Another version of the original motivation for the Moutiers mission to America explains that although in 1854, Carondelet celebrated the profession of twelve novices, Mother Celestine continued to receive more requests for sisters than she could grant. Then in 1854, Bishop Miège, a Jesuit newly assigned as Vicar Apostolic of the Indian Territory east of the Rocky Mountains, sought the aid of his brother, Abbé Miège of Savoy, a friend of the Sisters of St. Joseph of Moutiers.[18]

---

16 It is true that the demands for the sisters' services were so great that novices were quickly engaged in ministry. As Mother Celestine's necrology explains the situation:

> She was obliged to fulfill the office of Mistress of Novices during those years [as superior] not being able, through the necessities of the times, to refuse sending the Sisters whose experience might relieve her at the Novitiate to conduct the various establishments. She was obliged to undertake even more before she had time to have subjects properly trained to a religious life. (Archives: Carondelet)

17 The French Sisters of St. Joseph shared a common culture. The major diversity among them would have been a difference in social status manifested primarily in levels of education and taking concrete expression in the distinction between "choir" and "lay" sisters. The choir sisters served as superiors, administrators, teachers, etc. and the lay sisters took responsibility for domestic tasks, often including care of orphans and the sick. While the division seened natural for the French, it did not sit well with people in the United States who prided themselves on living in a supposedly classless democracy.

A letter Mother St. Theodora Guerin wrote from Indiana to her French sisters provides an enlightening sample of how the French could feel about the Americans. Mother Theodora saw cultural differences as exhibitions of pride and a strange value system, an assessment that the Americans surely returned in kind. Mother Theodora wrote:

> When dinner time came, there was my washerwoman sitting down at table with us. I was so indiscreet as to say it would be better for her not to take her dinner with the Community. I wish you could have seen the change in the countenance of our American postulants! ...The mere name of "servant" makes them revolt...

Mother Theodore added:

> Nothing is more odious in America than the office of superior, for from it flow dependence and submission, virtues which the Americans do not recognize.

(See Mary Ewens, *The Role of the Nun in Nineteenth-Century America, Variations on the International Theme* (Thiensville, Wisconsin: Caritas Communications, 2014, Kindle Edition, Loc. 1508-1523.)

18 Bishop Miège (1815-1884) studied in Moutiers before he joined the Jesuits in Milan. In 1849 he was missioned to the Indian missions, beginning in St. Charles, MO. In 1850 he was appointed Vicar Apostolic for the Indian Territory east of the Rocky Mountains, a domain comprising what is now Kansas and Nebraska, Wyoming, the Dakotas, Montana and half of Colorado. In 1855 he established his episcopal see in the prosperous town of Leavenworth (Kansas). Before making contact with the Sisters of St. Joseph he had obtained the help of the Sisters of Loretto for a school for Osage girls.

Bishop John Baptist Miège, in need of all the help he could get, began to correspond with Mother Celestine and Mother Marie Thérèsè of Moutiers who agreed that the Moutiers community would send missionaries to Carondelet who would then serve Native people in Kansas.[19] The first sisters chosen for the mission were Sisters St. John Facemaz, Gonzaga Grand, Leonie Martin and Euphrasia Meiller.[20] They left Moutiers on Sept. 3, 1854, and after sailing in the company of a bishop and four seminarians, they arrived in St. Louis on December 22, incorporating themselves into the Carondelet community.[21]

Mother St. John Facemaz
1821 – 1900
1845: Received the habit at Moutiers
December 1854: Arrived in St. Louis
with 3 companions
1855 – 1857: Mistress of Novices
1857 – 1872: Superior of Sisters of St. Joseph
of Carondelet
1860: Organized General Governance
1872 – 1898: General Councilor, Superior
at Nazareth Convent

The Carondelet archives preserve a document which quotes Sister St. John Facemaz as presenting herself saying,

> I learned at a young age to care for cattle in the pastures. This work suits my talents and is the only thing that makes me useful and able to render service to the mission.

Ross to the area where she founded the Sisters of Charity of Leavenworth.

19 Savage, 102-103.

20 According to the Moutiers history, a fifth sister had been named, but she died before the group left Moutiers, leaving one to think that life in France may have been nearly as precarious as in America.

21 Sister St. John Facemaz, born in Bourg-Saint-Maurice in 1821, made vows in the Moutiers community in 1847. Sister Gonzaga Grand born at Bourg, St. Maurice in 1834, was received into the Moutiers community in 1853, and made vows in 1854, just months before leaving for America. Almost immediately she became director of the Carondelet boarding school and later served in New York, Michigan, and Colorado before becoming Provincial Superior in Tucson in 1881. Sister Gonzaga served as Congregational Visitor, Assistant Superior General and interim General Superior after the death of Mother Agatha Guthrie in 1904. Retired in 1905, she died in 1916 at the age of 82. Sister Leonie Martin was born in Hauteluce of Savoie in 1835 and made vows in 1853. In her 36 years in the U.S. she was a teacher and local superior; she cared for orphans and served as assistant Superior General. Sister Euphrasia was born in 1812 in Aime, made vows at Moutiers in 1831 and spent only five years in Missouri before her death at the Carondelet Motherhouse on April 11, 1859.

By 1855, Mother Celestine, relying on her own judgment over Sister St. John's, had named her Director of Novices. Sister St. John Facemaz became Mother Celestine's trusted aide and would only too soon be in the position of taking over for her.

THE *CONSTITUTIONS* FROM 1729 TO 1858

The question of the *Constitutions* and the way they organized the life of the Sisters of St. Joseph in the United States and Canada became more and more important as the sisters served in a number of dioceses under bishops with very different ideas of their relationship to the communities. Until the 1850s, the sisters seemingly functioned as a quasi-congregation under the major leadership of Mother Celestine Pommerel and Mother St. John Fournier. No archives in America have documentation about a formal break with the Congregation in Lyon, but that break seemed inevitable given the difficulties of communication and the fact that the Lyon Congregation was unable to send additional sisters to America after 1837.

The edition of the *Constitutions* that Sisters of St. Joseph of Lyon brought to America in 1836 was published in Lyon in 1827 and translated into English in St. Louis in 1847.[22] According to the Lyon congregation, their 1827 edition was an exact reproduction of the *Constitutions* approved in 1730. In 1858, at the same time as the sisters in America were moving toward formalizing their structures, Lyon published a revised edition of their *Constitutions* updating the 1730 version to bring it into conformity with the practices instituted under the leadership of Mother St. John Fontbonne.[23]

All of those editions of the *Constitutions* begin with a brief history of the Sisters of St. Joseph. The 1858 version adds post French Revolutionary history and explains the changes that came about in that period. The preface to the revision introduces the changes showing great care to assure the sisters that the new *Constitutions* remain faithful to the community's tradition. It says:

In offering our dear Congregation this collection of their *Constitutions* and Rules, we should explain the reason and the nature of the changes

---

22 The translation and publication of *Constitutions* in English was a significant step in the community's recognition of diversity, signaling that the Sisters of St. Joseph would no longer be identified as French or even European. The French sisters would learn English and the American sisters would not be required to learn French.
23 The Lyon process is emphasized here because all of the French sisters in the U.S. at the time had roots in the Lyon congregation. That situation would change in 1854 with the first mission of Bourg Sisters in the New Orleans Archdiocese and then with the Le Puy congregation in 1866 in St. Augustine, Florida. But those sisters came as an ongoing mission of their motherhouses that developed into provinces before their separation from France.

that differentiate this from that which appeared for the first time in 1730 and was reprinted without modification in 1827...[24]

After an almost exact reproduction of the history published in previous editions, the Preface affirms that the new elements are nothing more than a faithful extension of the founding charism brought to new life following the Revolution:

By adding the words about the renaissance [rebirth] of the Sisters of St. Joseph after the French Revolution and about its erection as a General Congregation in the diocese of Lyon we can discover at a glance what those times add to the work of the first founders.

The preface explains how the hand of Providence worked through Mother St. John Fontebonne and Father Cholleton:

It is well known that the Revolution not only dispersed this humble institute, but also the greatest monasteries. God nevertheless permitted that some houses were respected by the storm...The ecclesiastical superiors of the diocese of Lyon searched and sought to discover the ruins...A first establishment was founded in Saint-Etienne...with Mother St. John, the former Superior of Monistrol, who courageously confessed the faith and who was saved from the scaffold by the fall of Robespierre...M. Cholleton later became the Vicar General and called this holy religious to Lyon where in 1816 she created the establishment of Chartreux... Thanks to Cardinal Fesch, the government gave them authorization...

Reminding the sisters that the congregation's development under Mother St. John Fontbonne necessarily included creative responses to the needs of the times, the Preface presents the history as a theological reflection on that charismatic moment in the life of the congregation:

These were blessed times in which fervor substituted for instruction and experience gave birth to prodigious events. As if by magic, a great number of communities were born where the religious, barely novices, entered quickly in the work and began to open schools...attending to the great establishments that were coming back to life, as the final

---

24 This and the citations from the *Constitutions* that follow are from the Preface to *Constitutions pour La Petite Congrégation des Soeurs de Saint-Joseph, Etablies Dans Le Diocèse de Lyon*, Deuxième Edition, Publiée par ordre de Son Eminence le Cardinal de Bonald, Archevêque de Lyon et Vienne, Primat des Gaules, etc. (Lyon: Maison-Mère des Soeurs de Saint-Joseph, 1858.)

crowning of the religious regeneration.

Then, having explained that times of such extraordinary flowering are more prone to exuberance than to prudent, long-term planning, the preface presents the reasons for establishing a "general congregation" with many houses under the leadership of one superior general:

> But we must admit that in the absence of traditions and single direction, there was much trial and error, inadequate and varied rules and discipline. The need was felt for all to be in union. To achieve this there was a need to imitate what was happening in a number of other institutes and we erected a General Congregation governed by a Superior General assisted by a Council...
>
> As Superior General, Mother St. John continued the work she began as founder with great faith and heroic simplicity. Under her leadership all the existing communities agreed to unity.

CONSTITUTIONS
de la
CONGRÉGATION
des
SŒURS DE SAINT JOSEPH
DU PUY-EN-VELAY

LE PUY-EN-VELAY
IMPRIMERIE "JEANNE D'ARC"
Place du Cloued
1900

Having recapped more than forty years of experimentation and resistance with that gracious summary, the preface gently introduces the topic of the changes God wrought among the sisters, indicating that the modifications were so wise and so obviously superior to previous ways, that they are hardly notable except for the fact that they made the Congregation as great as it had become:

> The implications of this new principle were gradually developed and applied in a wise and gradual way maintaining communication between the Motherhouse and the others. The necessary changes ensued in the former Rules. They passed imperceptibly into use in some areas and [in others] created new Rules. This gradual process inspired by the Holy Spirit at the very least allowed the Congregation to pass without tumult from its first state in which all the members were isolated to the organization it has today...that of a great, strong body [which] grew to twice its size and finally with a firm and active vigilance for management, there was reform in the individual establishments.

Then, having subtly acknowledged that major change had actually taken place in the life of the community, the editor of the *Constitutions* explained that the time had come to codify the practices and structures that had evolved by revising the *Constitutions*. The careful language of this section gives inadvertent witness to some sisters' reservations if not serious discontent or rejection of the new rule. Defending the new as the product of a generation and a half of experience, the editor insists over and again that nothing essential had changed and the core values remained intact:

> There is nothing new in spirit…the original thought has not changed, but is only modified to better achieve the end goal. Authority has been concentrated, but the life has remained essentially the same and we could say that above all we have conserved the spirit of recollection, simplicity, gentleness and the cordiality that were always part of this beloved Institute.
>
> The statutes have not added anything new in fundamental dispositions during their thirty years of existence. Their use continues out of necessity in some ancillary positions, in order to apply the principles that will be fruitful to a unified and general organization.

With all of that – and much more – in the preface, one might wonder what concrete changes had been made and what were the concerns of the sisters for whom that preface was so carefully crafted.

The changes the revised Constitutions formalized were precisely what Mother St. John Fontbonne had begun to implement from at least the time she went to Lyon: the organization of a Congregation with centralized governance, a common novitiate and the possibility for sisters to move from one house to another in response to community or ministerial needs. The French missionaries who established the Sisters of St. Joseph in the United States had been formed under this "new" model of religious life. All but Sister Febronie Fontbonne were born after Mother St. John went to Saint-Etienne and all of them entered the community after there were not only multiple houses under one governance, but after the Chambéry congregation had become independent of Lyon. That meant that the French missionary sisters' understanding of religious life had developed under a Congregational model in which communities enjoyed complex webs of interrelationships and created structures to facilitate the best possible response to the needs of the times and the possibilities open to them wherever they were called to serve.

THE MOVEMENT TO FORM AN AMERICAN CONGREGATION

Father Paris' 1856 letter indicated that he and Mother Celestine, surely in concert with Bishop Kenrick, recognized the need to establish a more formal union among the various communities of St. Joseph that had sprung from Carondelet. It would also seem natural that other sisters shared in the planning. Those would have included local superiors, the members of the council and especially Sister St. John Facemaz, the assistant superior in whom Mother Celestine had placed such great confidence.

Mother Celestine's death at the age of 44 not only caused great anguish but it inevitably changed the atmosphere of the community at both the local and the national level. Mother Celestine was the sort of woman who seemingly won the heart of everyone she met, and especially the sisters and students she taught. When asked to speak of her, Sister Aloysius Fitzsimmons recalled her lively, affable personality:

> Sister Celestine was very energetic and kind-hearted…She visited all the houses yearly, encouraging and consoling us as only she knew how to do. What truly happy days we spent together under the guiding hand of our venerated Mother Celestine, who was in every sense of the word a true and loving friend to all that had the happiness of knowing her, which was to love her.[25]

Sister Adelaide O'Brien wrote of her talent and humility:

> Mother Celestine was an accomplished scholar and very expert at all sorts of needlework but her humility guided her better genius in procuring a subsistence for herself and the other Sisters. When all other measures failed she did not disdain the making of shot bags.[26]

While Mother Celestine had great confidence in Sister St. John Facemaz, as often happens in a deep friendship or working relationship, they seem to have been very distinct personalities. Carondelet historian Sr. Lucida Savage described Mother St. John saying:

> The new Superior was cast in the heroic mold of martyrs and ascetics… In the exercise of authority she countenanced no half-measures, but expected of all a generous spirit of sacrificing everything, even as she herself had done. She had piercing dark eyes…and their quick glance detected every remissness; but she never failed to notice the least sign of weariness or suffering and such occasions revealed the deep tenderness

---

25 Sister Aloysius was received in the community in 1844. (Her testimony is from a file compiling commentaries regarding Mother Celestine at the request of Sister Monica Corrigan in the early 1890s. (Carondelet Archives)
26 Sister Adelaide was received in 1847. At one point, the Carondelet sisters made and sold shot bags to help increase their meagre income at Carondelet. (Carondelet Archives) The shot bags the sisters made from cloth were used by soldiers to carry lead balls for their guns.

of her nature. To these qualities were added a shrewd and practical business instinct, and a talent for organization that was soon felt in the Congregation.[27]

Sister Lucida leaves the impression that Mother St. John was more outwardly austere than Mother Celestine, yet a superior who was both extremely talented and easily moved to tenderness when she observed that a sister had spent herself in service. Moreover, when a beloved leader dies it often seems that no one is capable of filling her shoes. Mother St. John was not only faced with that challenge, but the additional difficulties of being a relatively newly-arrived French sister who was not the sisters' first choice as their superior – no matter that Mother Seraphine from St. Paul whom the sisters elected declined the office for very solid reasons.[28] If Mother St. John had wanted to advance the plan for general government quickly, a tragic fire at Carondelet in January, 1858, forced her to focus on local matters. Among other irreplaceable treasures, the fire destroyed the log cabin that had been the first permanent residence and motherhouse of the Sisters of St. Joseph in the United States.[29] Even in the process of recovering from that loss, the community sent sisters to open two new houses: five sisters took over an academy from the Kentucky Sisters of Loretto in Ste. Genevieve, MO., and the previously mentioned group of six sisters opened the Oswego mission in New York, the first community in what became Carondelet's Albany Province.[30] In the meantime, by 1860, eight additional missionaries had arrived from Moutiers and forty-two women had received the habit at Carondelet.[31]

---

27 Savage, 113. Sister Lucida Savage was received into the community in 1887 and thus, in addition to her research and the materials she inherited from Sister Monica Corrigan, the first Carondelet historian, Sister Lucida would have personally known Mother St. John (+1900) and her contemporaries.

28 Chapter 4 narrated Sister Seraphine Coughlin's decision to decline and Bishop Kenrick's subsequent decision to appoint Mother St. John as superior after Mother Celestine's death.

29 Savage (113-114) explains that when the fire started, Mother St. John and another sister were ill. The volunteer fire fighters were aided by local seminarians and the two ailing sisters were rescued through second-story windows. The fire was a financial disaster for the community and probably destroyed priceless communications between Mother St. John Fontbonne and her missionary daughters as well as other documents and letters from the period between 1836 and 1858.

30 The Sisters of St. Joseph apparently purchased the Academy from the Sisters of Loretto who had opened it in 1838. Interestingly, in 1847, the Sisters of Loretto took over the academy of the Religious of the Sacred Heart just outside of St. Louis in Florissant, MO because the RSCJs who had been there since 1819 left the school and moved their novitiate to McSherrystown, PA, a site which would eventually be taken over by the Sisters of St. Joseph from Philadelphia. See Anna C. Minogue *Loretto: Annals of the Century*, (NY: The America Press, 1912), 112 and 122.

31 Information from the Congregational Profession Book. Of the sisters who entered in those years only two were born in St. Louis. Sixteen were born in Ireland; seven in Germany; one in Canada and the rest in Ohio, Kentucky and Pennsylvania. In 1860, the Moutiers Sisters in the United States numbered fourteen; four had arrived in 1854, 2 in 1856, 4 in 1857, 1 in 1858 and 3 in 1859. (Dougherty, 421.)

There is almost no extant correspondence or other record of the conversations, discussions or debates that prepared the way for widely scattered local superiors to discuss how they wanted their communities to be related in the future. The Brentwood archives mention that Mother Austin Kean visited Carondelet in the autumn of 1859 and Sister Assissium of Philadelphia remembered that Mother St. John Fournier did the same. While there is no indication of their reason for the trips, one could safely surmise that those visits included discussion of Bishop Kenrick and Mother St. John Facemaz's ideas about organizing the Sisters of St. Joseph in America as a congregation.[32] Whatever the long and short-term, formal and informal preparations, early in 1860, Mother St. John wrote to all the superiors of Sisters of St. Joseph in the U.S. inviting each community to send a representative to a meeting to be held at Carondelet on May 2, 1860. There they would discuss the possibilities for organizing a single, unified Congregation of Sisters of St. Joseph in America. The invited communities presumably included the nine houses in the St. Louis archdiocese, one in the Diocese of Natchez, Mississippi, and those of the foundations made in the dioceses of Philadelphia, St. Paul, Buffalo and Brooklyn as well as the two Canadian foundations in Toronto and Hamilton. [33] All of these communities sent delegates with the exception of Buffalo, Brooklyn

St. John Neumann
1811-1860

and Philadelphia. There is no documentation to explain how the decision was made that those three communities would not participate; it is safe to assume that the bishops had a hand in making that decision.

PHILADELPHIA:
MOTHER ST. JOHN FOURNIER AND THE BISHOPS

In Philadelphia, Bishop John Neumann had died unexpectedly in January, 1860, and his coadjutor, Bishop James F. Wood, took over leadership of the diocese, becoming the third bishop with whom Mother St. John Fournier worked with

---

32 Mother Austin, the founder of the Brooklyn community, entered the Congregation in Philadelphia. Whatever her reason for visiting, she had no formal connection with Carondelet. (See Brentwood Archives "Expenditures and Receipts" October, 1859 "Expense to St. Louis, $154.29" and a letter of Emma Thursby, Nov. 3, 1859, documented by Margaret Quinn in May, 1982).

33 In 1855, the Sisters of St. Joseph opened Our Lady of Mount Carmel School in Sulphur Springs, in the Natchez diocese. Civil War tensions caused the sisters to withdraw in 1861. (Dougherty, 112)

in Philadelphia.[34] Bishops Neumann and Wood seem to have been quite different
in their style and in their relationship to the Sisters of St. Joseph. All the available
evidence indicates that Mother St. John and Bishop Neumann had enjoyed a
harmonious relationship of collaboration and mutual respect, one that was
strong enough that Mother St. John felt free to send sisters to Brooklyn in 1856
after Bishop Neumann expressed the opinion that they did not have enough
personnel to be able to do so.[35] Mother St. John, who seemed to have a knack for
befriending everyone, including bishops, retold an anecdote that demonstrated
her appreciation of Bishop Neumann's saintly counsel and solid help for sisters
in need:

> Once…he arrived at a convent, where the religious were in great poverty,
> and destitute, sometimes, of the very necessaries of life. "We find it very
> hard to get along, my Lord," said one of the Sisters "sometimes we have
> nothing to make a fire, and again when we have a fire, we have nothing
> to cook on it."
>
> He turned towards a picture of the Crucifixion, almost the only
> article of furniture in the apartment, and pointing to it, said "There is
> a book, my Sisters, which you must study and meditate on; that sight
> will make your trials easier, your crosses lighter." The tone of voice and
> manner in which the words were uttered, made a deep impression on all
> those present, and they felt consoled and encouraged to suffer patiently.
> Not satisfied, however, with mere words of consolation, he added acts,
> the touchstone of true charity. Pleasantly alluding to his custom of
> distributing little medals among the Sisters at his visits, he said "Now I
> am going to give you Yankee medals," and he handed to the Superior

---

34 James F. Wood was born in Philadelphia to a Unitarian family and converted to Catholicism at the age
of 25. A year later he went to Rome for seminary studies. Ordained in 1844 for the Diocese of Cincinnati,
in 1857, he was made coadjutor to Bishop Neumann who presided at his consecration together with Bishop
Whelan of Wheeling. Unlike his Redemptorist predecessor, Bishop Wood grew up Protestant. He was not a
member of a religious community making it probable that he had little contact with women religious before
serving in Cincinnati. While he was in Cincinnati, he would have been aware of the process through which
Archbishop Purcell arranged for the Sisters of Charity in Cincinnati to be separated from their founding group
in Emmetsburg. The Emmetsburg sisters had united with the Daughters of Charity in France, a move which
restricted the ministries they had become accustomed to doing in the United States. The Cincinnati community's
separation took place six years after Archbishop Hughes of New York had Sisters of Charity in his archdiocese
separate from Emmetsburg for similar reasons. Those incidents fit into a larger history of the relationships
between bishops and religious communities. The Sisters of Charity were not the only community who dealt with
bishops who sought to have at least some of the religious in their dioceses remain under their exclusive control.
35 As noted above, three sisters founded the Brooklyn mission: Mother Austin Kean who came directly from
Philadelphia, and Sisters Theodosia Hagemann and Baptista Hanson who went to Brooklyn from Buffalo. Sister
Theodosia had entered the community at Carondelet and Sister Baptista in Philadelphia.

fifty dollars in gold to supply the pressing wants of the house.[36]

Based on the stories they told, none of the sisters who knew Bishop Neumann would have been surprised at his 1977 canonization.

It is not as easy to discover the tone of the collaboration between Mother St. John and Bishop James F. Wood. Sister Maria Kostka Logue explains that Bishop Wood, apparently the power behind the painful decision to remove the Sisters of St. Joseph from Philadelphia's St. Joseph's Hospital, may have had good intentions, but "often seemed ruthless in his method of remedying finances."[37] While Bishop Wood served as coadjutor to Bishop Neumann, misunderstandings abounded between the two prelates in spite of their attempts to keep them in check.[38] Additionally, it was Bishop Wood who, in 1871, "against the inclination of Mother St. John," arranged for Sisters of St. Joseph to perform domestic service at the diocesan seminary.[39] While that ministry did not violate the rule, neither was it typical for the community whose domestic or lay sisters generally ministered only in institutions run by the sisters such as hospitals or orphanages or in their own convents. At the very least, we may surmise that Mother St. John's relationship with Bishop Wood lacked the friendly mutuality she had enjoyed with Bishop Neumann.

Mother St. John Fournier
1814 - 1875

---

36 Mother St. John Fournier, letter of Nov. 23, 1872. (Archives, SSJ, Philadelphia) The gift was quite generous; in 1860, a barrel (196 lbs.) of flour cost $7.62, a pound of roasting beef, $0.11, and a quart of milk $0.04. (See http://www.choosingvoluntarysimplicity.com/) According to the Philadelphia Council Book, Bishop Neumann had determined that the salary for sister teachers should be $50 per year. (See Council Book, page 5, entry for August 28, 1848)

In regard to her friendships, Mother St. John's correspondence with Bishop Cretin of St. Paul also gives witness to a relationship of great friendship and mutual understanding. (See Mother St. John correspondence: Archives SSJP)

37 Logue, 102. One of Bishop Wood's primary responsibilities as coadjutor was to remedy the financial situation of the diocese.

38 Neumann was known as a very holy, humble man and Wood as a hard-working, capable administrator. Wood had accepted the Coadjutorship in 1857 with the understanding that Neumann was about to retire or move to a smaller diocese; Neumann was most willing to accept a lesser position if the diocese were subdivided, but that did not happen and he therefore remained as Bishop until his death in 1860. See James F. Connelly, Ed. *The History of the Archdiocese of Philadelphia* (Philadelphia: The Archdiocese of Philadelphia, 1976), 237-250. Logue notes "The lack of understanding between the heads of the diocese created a strained atmosphere. Archbishop Kenrick of Baltimore...[said] that the new coadjutor was 'not strong in prudence and humility." (Logue, 51)

39 Logue, 142, explains that the sisters cooked and cleaned and nursed the sick at the seminary, earning the gratitude of Archbishop Wood who would bring visiting prelates to see the sisters.

While Mother St. John Fournier served as superior in Philadelphia, she seemed to maintain good communication with Carondelet and her beloved cousin, Mother Celestine. Between 1855 and 1860, the Philadelphia community and its 1856 foundation in Brooklyn had fewer exchanges of personnel with Carondelet than they did with communities in the eastern part of the country. By 1860, the growth, founding spirit and stability of the St. Louis and Philadelphia communities led to what could be understood as two incipient models of governance. The first grew from Carondelet with continual interchange among the missions in and beyond the Archdiocese of St. Louis. The Carondelet community was informally instituting a congregational model of governance in the sense that sisters moved freely among the missions, and when novitiates were established, they remained under the authority of a superior in St. Louis.

The alternative was the Philadelphia model which, with the help of at least twelve sisters who came and went from Carondelet, grew rapidly, gradually becoming functionally autonomous and then sending the founding superior to a mission in Brooklyn which in turn became autonomous.[40] When Bishop James Wood assumed leadership of the diocese after Bishop Neumann's unexpected death, the Philadelphia Sisters of St. Joseph were well established and had founded multiple missions in and beyond their home diocese. Philadelphia also continued to collaborate in staffing the missions in Buffalo and Erie which had been officially founded from Carondelet. In 1860, with the exception of the Sisters of St. Joseph of Bourg who had opened a mission in Bay St. Louis, Louisiana in 1856, all of the Sisters of St. Joseph in America were somehow connected to one another even though their structures lacked formal ecclesial definition.

SISTERS AND THE BISHOPS - THE MEETING IN MAY, 1860
CALLING THE MEETING

Obviously, movement toward founding an American congregation began before 1860. In addition to the 1856 letter in which Father Paris encouraged Mother Celestine to make a general visitation, we have the witness of Sister Assisium of Philadelphia, the secretary who compiled Philadelphia's "First Council Book." She notes that in 1859, "Mother St. John, dressed in secular attire, went to the

---

40 Between 1847 and 1860, Carondelet sent only twelve sisters to Philadelphia. These included Srs. M. Magdalen Weber, Mary Joseph Clark and M. Elizabeth Kinkaid who accompanied Mother St. John Fournier in 1847; Srs. Martha Bunning and Delphine Fontbonne in 1850; Sr. St. Joseph Daly in 1854; Sr. Adelaide O'Brien in 1851 and Sr. Agnes Spencer in 1851. Some of these sisters remained in Philadelphia, others returned to Carondelet and/or went to other missions. As previously mentioned, the foundation in Brooklyn included one sister, Theodosia, who formally belonged to Carondelet rather than Philadelphia.

Chapter at St. Louis."[41] She added:

> At the Chapter in St. Louis…separation from Lyons was brought up. M Celestine was dead. The question of what part this Comty would take must have been debated by the Senior Srs. and the Bishop Neumann or Wood.

She added:

> Philadelphia was opened under [Mother Celestine], and hence was subject to St. Louis until about 1860. I know only that there was conferring and meetings here and finally Bishop Wood held a meeting here in 1860, when several returned to St. Louis. . . . I was a novice and know the feeling there was. [42]

Although Mother St. John Fournier was able to visit Carondelet in 1859, she did not attend the 1860 meeting, perhaps because she was not allowed to do so. Sister Assisium makes it clear that the decision to be independent of Carondelet was made primarily by Bishop Wood and was not to the liking of all the sisters, forcing some to take sides in the separation by remaining in the autonomous Philadelphia community or returning to Carondelet. When their communities were separated from Carondelet, Sisters missioned in Buffalo and Wheeling were also forced to choose between their current mission and Carondelet. Many sisters chose to remain a part of the community nearest their place of birth.

Undoubtedly, Mother Celestine and Bishop Neumann's untimely deaths were significant factors in the way the communities formed. Mother Celestine might have commanded more loyalty for St. Louis than did Mother St. John Facemaz, especially with her special relationship with Mother St. John Fournier. Would Bishop Neumann have made the same decision as Bishop Wood about the future of the Sisters of St. Joseph in the United States? If, as Archbishop Kenrick was proposing, the Philadelphia community had become a province, would the other dioceses have separated? Those questions lead to larger questions. What were the bishops' priorities in 1860 and what were the sisters' desires?

---

41 From the time of their arrival in New Orleans in 1836, Sisters of St. Joseph quite often had to disguise their habits when outside the convent or place of ministry. They would wear bonnets and cloaks and sometimes use only secular clothes so that they would not draw unwanted attention from people who had no respect for Catholic nuns. See Savage 35, 70 and Ewens, loc. 1854.
42 "First Council Book" (Archives SSJP) Sister Assissium served as the congregational secretary and compiled the annals.

THE BISHOPS IN COMPETITION

One of the ways to discover the bishops' priorities is through an examination of their public statements delineating the ministries for which the sisters were needed. In 1852, the bishops meeting in the First Plenary Council of Baltimore decreed the necessity of establishing parochial schools wherever possible in their dioceses.[43] At the end of that national meeting the bishops wrote a pastoral letter to U.S. Catholics which stated that:

> We have to provide for the Catholic education of our youth. Not only have we to erect and maintain the Church, the Seminary and the Schoolhouse, but we have to found hospitals, establish orphanages and provide for every want of suffering humanity which Religion forbids us to neglect.

Speaking of the progress the Church had made in regard to those services, the bishops expressed their gratitude to God and their predecessors for all that had been accomplished in providing these services. They said:

> We thank the Giver of all good gifts for the extraordinary benediction which He has bestowed upon our efforts and those of the venerable men whose places we fill. [44]

From that statement, one might think that they and their episcopal predecessors had themselves built and staffed those much needed institutions! Somehow they failed to recognize or even mention the religious women without whom almost none of it would have been possible.

In succeeding councils, the bishops' determination to provide for Catholic education as well as other social services only grew stronger. They knew that they had to have the help of women and men religious to staff all of those institutions in a way the dioceses could afford, and each bishop seemed to make his own his first concern in the matter.[45]

In 1860, Archbishop Peter Richard Kenrick was the highest ranking prelate with Sisters of St. Joseph serving in his jurisdiction.[46] He had worked

---

43 Peter Guilday, *History of the Councils of Baltimore*, 1791-1884, (NY: The MacMillan Co., 1932) 179.
44 Guilday, 185.
45 One of the novelties of Vatican II was its insistence that bishops are ordained for the whole Church, not a diocese, and therefore are to serve the entire Church, with special care for the neediest parts of the world. See The Second Vatican Council's document Christus Dominus 6, 7.
46 St. Louis had been made an Archdiocese in 1847 and was the only archdiocese in which Sisters of St. Joseph served in 1860. The dioceses in which there were Sisters of St. Joseph included Natchez, Chicago, St. Paul, Philadelphia, Buffalo, Brooklyn and Wheeling.

with the Sisters of St. Joseph from the time he succeeded Bishop Rosati in 1841, and was, without a doubt, the primary episcopal advocate of the formation of an American congregation of Sisters of St. Joseph.[47] Beginning in 1847 when the Sisters of St. Joseph in St. Louis opened a mission in Philadelphia, Archbishop Kenrick gave the community his blessing as they sent sisters to other parts of the country. Very few other bishops were as generous as Peter R. Kenrick in encouraging Sisters of St. Joseph to serve in other dioceses.

Archbishop Peter Richard Kenrick
1806 - 1896

In St. Paul, after the death of Bishop Cretin in 1857, two years passed before the Dominican Friar, Thomas Grace, was named to succeed him. In 1860, the Sisters of St. Joseph in the diocese were still receiving personnel from Carondelet and at least seven local women had entered the congregation, some of them making their novitiate at Carondelet. When it came to the question of forming a Congregation of Sisters of St. Joseph, Bishop Grace was reluctant, apparently preferring that St. Paul be a province of Philadelphia with Mother St. John Fournier as their superior. When Bishop Wood decided that the Philadelphia sisters would be a diocesan community, Bishop Grace accepted the sisters' ongoing affiliation with Carondelet.[48]

In Albany, Bishop McCloskey apparently had no reservations about sending the superior from Oswego to the St. Louis meeting to affirm the congregational plan. One reason for that may be that in 1858 six Sisters of St. Joseph had come to his diocese and he was awaiting the fulfillment of a promise that a second group would arrive from Carondelet to open a second mission in his diocese in July, 1860.[49] Bishop McCloskey also had experience in working with an international

---

47 P. R. Kenrick had arrived in St. Louis on December 28, 1841 as the coadjutor while Rosati was in Haiti. Rosati returned to Rome and died there in 1843, never joining Kenrick in St. Louis and leaving him with a debt of $53,000 for all the building that had been started. According to the St. Louis archdiocesan website, upon Kenrick's arrival the diocese stretched from the lower Mississippi to Canada and included territory between the Missouri River and the Rocky Mountains. Forty-five dioceses would eventually be carved out of that vast area.
48 See Dougherty, 70. A manuscript by Sister Ignatius Cox of St. Paul explains that Mother Seraphine Coughlin, the superior in St. Paul, pleaded with Bishop Grace and he "withdrew his opposition and allowed the community to accept the modified rule that Mother St. John was making strenuous effort to have approved by the Holy Father." Also cited by Genevieve Shillo, CSJ, "Dynamics for Change: Papal Approval and General Government in the Sisters of St. Joseph of Carondelet: 1837 to 1877." (Archives Carondelet)
49 The sisters arrived in Cohoes on July 17, 1860, in the company of Mother St. John Facemaz who was on her way to Europe with the new rule.

congregation; the Sisters of Charity from Emmitsburg were already serving in the diocese.[50] Bishop Elder of Natchez, who had only a few Sisters of St. Joseph in what would be a short-lived Carondelet mission in Sulphur City, seemingly offered no objections to their sending a representative to the 1860 meeting.[51] As noted previously, Bishop Whelan of Wheeling allowed Sister Stanislaus Matthews to attend the meeting but she was commissioned to let the sisters know that Bishop Whelan had decided that the Wheeling community would not be part of the larger congregation.

Bishops Wood, Timon and Loughlin (Philadelphia, Buffalo and Brooklyn) did not allow the sisters in their dioceses to attend the May, 1860 meeting.[52] Correspondence preserved in the congregational archives at Philadelphia reveals that Bishop Timon of Buffalo was definitely not in favor of a new congregation and suggests that his opinion may have influenced his confreres in their opposition.

Archbishop Wood
1813 – 1883

---

50 Bishop McCloskey would have also been aware of the controversy of 1846 when Archbishop John Hughes had effected a painful separation of the Sisters of Charity in New York from their motherhouse at Emmitsburg because Emmitsburg's affiliation with France imposed restrictions on their ministries, particularly in work with boy orphans. According to Ewens (loc. 1983), a large part of the problem was financial; Hughes "did not have the funds to pay the salaries" of lay women.

51 The Sisters of St. Joseph of Bourg had also been in Bay St. Louis, MS, in the Natchez diocese since 1854. Beginning in 1858, there was some talk of their joining with the sisters in St. Louis, a topic that will be discussed in the section about the Bourg-Médaille history.

The Sisters of St. Joseph had to leave the diocese of Natchez due to Civil War tensions. Bishop Elder became quite famous as a short-term federal prisoner sentenced in 1864 for refusing to compel people of his Mississippi diocese to pray for the President of the United States. Bishop Elder was later made bishop of Cincinnati and was highly involved in various ecclesial debates of the era.

52 The only firm evidence we have that bishops decided against the sisters' attendance comes from the "Datebooks" from Erie where we find the following entry:

> May 2: Mother Saint John Facemaz, on the advice of Archbishop Kenrick of St. Louis invited representatives from each house of the Congregation of the Sisters of St. Joseph to an assembly at Carondelet for the purpose of considering the proposed measure for general government.
>
> Buffalo, Philadelphia, and Brooklyn sent no delegates; the Bishops of these dioceses had intervened, preferring autonomy for their respective communities.

(Archives: SSJE) This is the only contemporary statement we have found indicating that it was the bishops' decision that the sisters would not participate.

This is somewhat surprising as Bishop Timon had known the Sisters of St. Joseph since their arrival in New Orleans in 1836. Beginning in 1854, he had been a beneficiary of their freedom and willingness to serve beyond their original boundaries. One might think that because he himself was a religious who had served as the "visitor" (comparable to a provincial) for his congregation he would have understood the sisters' desire to form a united congregation with various provincial centers. On the other hand, his experience as superior had proven that a congregation of pontifical right could exercise some independence from individual bishops. Once his shoes were on episcopal feet, he opted to assure that he as bishop could exercise supreme power over the religious in his diocese.[53] Although it was Mother Celestine at Carondelet who had sent sisters to Bishop Timon's diocese, he maintained ongoing correspondence with Mother St. John Fournier in Philadelphia about the sisters and his opinions about Carondelet, including complaints about sisters sent to his diocese under Mother Celestine's and then Mother St. John Facemaz' authority.[54] Those letters detail his decisions to change sisters' missions, references to his problems with Mother Agnes Spencer and, in June of 1859, the telling statement:

> We will wait with hope for some good from St. Louis. Now, if we had the right person all would go on well.[55]

For whatever reason, Bishop Timon was not pleased with Mother St. John Facemaz. In regard to Bishop Timon's disapproval of the plans for forming a congregation, after the announcement of the May 1860 meeting, he wrote to persuade Mother St. John Fournier to resist encouragement to join with Carondelet, a project from which he expected little fruit:

---

53 Leonard R. Riforgiato, a Timon scholar, wrote that one of the reasons Timon accepted the appointment to Buffalo after he had refused coadjutorships in other dioceses was that being named the first bishop would allow him to "create a church in his image," something that suited his personality as "a one man show" who "ran his diocese singlehandedly." (Monograph: The Life and Times of John Timon, C.M., First Bishop of Buffalo," 79-81. Ewens (loc. 1918) states that, "Bishops resented the fact that motherhouse superiors in another diocese might have the power to limit the works...which sisters could staff within their dioceses."

54 His major complaints were about Mother Agnes Spencer. Mother Celestine had accompanied Mother Agnes from Philadelphia when she became superior in Canandaigua, indicating that Mother Agnes was missioned primarily by Carondelet and was superior of a group missioned from Carondelet, making one wonder why the bishop took his concerns to Mother St. John in Philadelphia.

55 Letters from Bishop Timon to Mother St. John Fournier, January 7, 1859, June 8, 1859, and others. Regarding St. Louis, May 26, 1859. (Archives SSJ Philadelphia)

The Sisters of St. Joseph were not the only community to become the objects of Bishop Timon's demanding authority. The First Council Book from Philadelphia includes a note from May 6, 1857: "Bishop Timon tells of his dismissal of the Bros. and Sisters of Holy Cross from Buffalo." Various entries in the Council Book mention visits from Bishop Timon indicating that he was well-known to the Philadelphia community.

God will protect his work. Time too will enable those who press upon you to see that the movement is wrong, and will scarcely be encouraged anywhere. But try d[ear] and respected Sister to be very kind, though firm in your answers. We will all pray that God would give you [strength], and surely He will, for you seek but to live up to your rules...[56]

Whatever his motivations, Bishop Timon was clearly against the Sisters of St. Joseph becoming one American congregation. His ongoing contact with Mother St. John Fournier and references to travel to Philadelphia indicate that he could have influenced Bishop Wood who had been coadjutor there since 1857 and became the ordinary in January, 1860. Bishop Timon also claimed Bishop Loughlin of Brooklyn as an "intimate friend" for whom he had lobbied to obtain Sisters of St. Joseph.[57] All told, Bishop John Timon could have exercised considerable influence among the bishops, uniting them in opposition to having the sisters in their diocese become part of a larger congregation.

Another dimension that may have affected the bishops in their resistance to the congregational movement was that Archbishop Kenrick was not universally popular among his confreres. Some believed that through his brother's influence he and his diocese had been promoted too quickly when St. Louis was elevated to the status of an archdiocese.[58] For some others he was one more example of the Irish who were hoarding the leadership of the Church in the U.S., a charge that could hardly have influenced Bishops Timon, Loughlin or Whelan. On the other hand there were bishops who recognized Peter Richard Kenrick as a leading theologian. All told, he enjoyed more favorable influence among bishops from the "western" side of the country where many of the newly formed dioceses, including St. Paul, had come from the territory of his immense archdiocese.[59]

When it came time to write recommendations to Rome, ten bishops wrote official letters in favor of the new Carondelet congregation. Some remained

---

56 Timon to Fournier, February 28, 1860. (Archives, SSJ Philadelphia)

57 In a letter of March 29, 1856, Bishop Timon said to Mother St. John, "The Rt. Rev. Bishop of Brooklyn, an intimate friend, has often spoken to me of Institutions for his diocese. I have spoken to him much in favor of yours. (Archives, SSJ, Philadelphia)

58 See Hugh J. Nolan, *Francis Patrick Kenrick, Bishop of Philadelphia 1830-1851*, (Philadelphia, American Catholic Historical Society of Philadelphia, 1948), 362. St. Louis became an archdiocese in 1847, New York which had been established as a diocese in 1789 became an archdiocese in 1850 and Philadelphia in 1875.

59 In all, at least 15 dioceses were formed from the original territory of St. Louis. The Archbishop found allies on behalf of the rule of the Congregation in those dioceses and when letters of support were needed the bishops of St. Paul, Dubuque, Alton, Chicago, Albany, St. Joseph, Marquette, Nashville, Natchez and Arizona wrote to the Vatican in favor of the new rule. It is notable that with the exception of Albany, all of those dioceses were from the middle or "western" part of the country. (Copies of all these letters are kept in the Carondelet Archives)

reluctant to support a Carondelet congregation because the proposed Constitutions stated:

> The religious of the whole Congregation, in whatever Diocese...shall also be subject to the Archbishop in whose diocese the Mother House [is found]...as to their first Ecclesiastical Superior and the common Father and Protector of the entire Congregation.[60]

When bishops jealously guarded their authority and were seeking all the sisters they could find to staff their institutions, the privileged role of the archbishop of St. Louis could not have pleased them. That statement was removed from the *Constitutions* before their approval in 1867.[61]

Both the desire to assure workers for their particular vineyards and rivalries among prelates probably played a part in motivating those bishops who opposed the formation of a unified Congregation of Sisters of St. Joseph in America. It is clear that some bishops were doing their best to thwart the movement for union and to promote autonomous diocesan communities. In June, 1862, Bishop Timon wrote to Mother St. John Fournier saying:

> As soon as I came to Rome, I called upon the Cardinal to obtain the approbation of your rules. He gave me great hope, and I called together the bishops of Philadelphia, of Toronto, Brooklyn, of Hamilton, and we five have been for some time preparing for the work.

The "work" to which he referred was the promotion of *Constitutions* for Philadelphia as a diocesan congregation.

Bishop Timon's letter also exposed some of the rivalry among the bishops. At one point, Bishop Timon made the process of seeking approval for *Constitutions* sound almost like a race among different congregations.

> I must tell you that the bishop of Albany says that he is commissioned by St. Louis to get their new rules approved. You must pray and get others to pray. I had made my petition for your approbation at least

---

60 *Constitutions* of the Sisters of St. Joseph of Carondelet, 1860: VI, 2. This was a significant addition to the 1847 *Constitutions* which recognized the bishops of the dioceses in which the sisters resided as their ecclesiastical superior.
61 In 1867, the Carondelet *Constitutions* were approved, but had to be put into practice for ten years before their definitive approval, granted July 31, 1877.

two weeks before Bishop McCloskey could have his.[62]

Two weeks later, Bishop Wood wrote to Mother St. John Fournier indicating that various bishops were collaborating for the approval of the Philadelphia rule because its approval would portend success for other diocesan congregations of St. Joseph. He said:

> The approbation of the Rule, I have already initiated. It has to pass through the usual formalities which I think in our case will be shortened. Rome is entirely in favor of the Rule as it stands, desires no Generalate, but that the Sisters should remain under the care and jurisdiction of their respective Bishops. I have obtained the Apostolic Benediction with Plenary Indulgence to be imparted to the members of the several communities by their respective Bishops of Philadelphia, Buffalo, Brooklyn, Toronto and Hamilton on their return and first visitation of the respective houses.[63]

The proposed Philadelphia rule of the 1860s was diocesan while the Carondelet model proposed a congregation of pontifical right. Some bishops seemed to see the process as a competition between models of governance or among themselves. Bishops Wood, Timon, Loughlin, from the U.S. and Bishops Lynch of Toronto and Farrell of Hamilton all exerted their influence to assure that the Sisters of St. Joseph in their dioceses would remain firmly under their authority.[64] The ten bishops who signed letters in favor of Carondelet's proposed *Constitutions* were open to an alternative that allowed the sisters greater independence and flexibility. Because there seemed to be a sense that Rome would eventually favor one model over the other, the stakes were high.

Bishops Timon and Wood maintained a strong alliance in the effort to win papal approval for the Philadelphia proposal. In June, 1862, Bishop Wood wrote from Rome, this time not to the superior but to the sisters serving as nurses during the Civil War. He said:

---

62 Bishop Timon to Mother St. John Fournier, June 6, 1862. (Archives SSJP) Bishop McCloskey of Albany was no insignificant foe. At the age of 34 he became coadjutor bishop in New York in 1844; in 1847 he became the first bishop of Albany; in 1864 he became the archbishop of New York and in 1875 was the first bishop from the United States to be named a cardinal.
63 Bishop Wood to Mother St. John Fournier, June 23, 1862. (Archives SSJP)
64 Bishop Lynch of Toronto, like Timon was a Vincentian. On April 26, 1860, Lynch succeeded Bishop Charbonnel who had brought the Sisters of St. Joseph to Toronto. Bishop Farrell, a strong advocate of Catholic schools, had been bishop of Hamilton since 1856, and would later exercise autocratic authority over the Sisters of St. Joseph, particularly in the case of Sister Martha Bunning whom he deposed and exiled from the diocese.

We have obtained for all the sisters Spiritual privileges and have initiated the process for the approval of the Rule as it is in the Book of *Constitutions* which you have in your hands and faithfully follow as your guide; and we have no doubt that Rome will regard our petition favorably and after the usual formalities give it full and favorable acceptance.[65]

Bishop Timon kept up his efforts on behalf of the Philadelphia rule. Writing to

Mother St. John Fournier in January, 1863, he assured her, "I will not lose sight of your great wish, the approbation of your order. What I can do for it, you may rest assured that I will do."[66]

Unfortunately, the matter did not proceed as quickly as hoped. Five years later during another visit to Europe, Bishop Wood wrote to Mother St. John Fournier saying:

Bishop John Timon, C.M. 1797 – 1867

I have neither forgotten nor neglected the principal interest of which they treat. We have got as far as the translation of the Rule into French, and I have already examined a portion of the translation. I am sorry for the way that the whole business has been neglected by the person in whose hands I placed it in 1862 at Rome. No matter…It is all, no doubt, for the best. We must do what we have often done before, wait a little longer![67]

By that time, Carondelet's Constitutions were well on the way to full approval.[68] The Philadelphia congregation's rule was not finally approved until 1895. In 1881, Father Pacificus Neno who became Superior General of the Augustinians, wrote to Mother Mary John Kieran, then General Superior in Philadelphia, explaining the difficulty:

I shall do all in my part to have your Rules approved when they will be sent…But I must warn you beforehand that the Holy See is very slow in such matters. Moreover….as I understand…your Congregation would pass from the jurisdiction of Bps to the immediate jurisdiction of the

---

65 Bishop Wood to Sisters of St. Joseph, June 24, 1862. (ASSJP) That edition of the *Constitutions* would have been the one translated in 1847 from the French of 1827.
66 Bishop Timon to Mother St. John Fournier, Jan. 8, 1863 (ASSJP).
67 Bishop Wood to Mother St. John Fournier, August 12, 1867 (ASSJP).
68 Mother St. John Fournier had begun the process of seeking papal approval in 1860. The Carondelet *Constitutions* received a commendation in 1863, were given a 10 year trial period in 1867, and received definitive approval in 1877. (Savage, 119-122)

Vatican. In such a case you would find the greater obstacle in the Bps themselves, who want to have you under their control exclusively. Hence I am of your opinion that it is only a loss of time.[69]

In the face of seemingly endless delays, Mother Mary John asked to go to Rome to present the petition herself, but Archbishop Wood refused her permission. She then wrote to her friend Fr. Neno about her frustration and said that she wished she were a priest and thus free to take the cause to Rome by herself. Fr. Neno replied "Although your wish, to be a Father, is a pretty queer one; still I wish too that you could be one."[70] He went on to explain the difficulty of gaining approval for an order with simple vows, saying that such were merely tolerated. Urging her to read between the lines of the signs of the times, he went on to encourage her about the future of the Congregation, no matter what its official status. As he did so, he spoke not just of the Philadelphia Congregation, but the ministry and presence of Sisters of St. Joseph throughout the world:

Were you spurious, or not aiming at great good, the Church would not allow your existence....Look in the Map of the World. There is no land, where your Sisters are not, and everywhere they keep the fervor of the first Founder, and do the greatest amount of good – in the Hospitals, in the School room, at the bed of the dying. God does not prosper in his Church parasite plants for a long time. If you exist in it for over 200 years that is the most evident sign, even for the blind, that your Order is not only recognized, but encouraged and cherished as a dear branch of the same Church.[71]

Encouragement notwithstanding, the situation seemed only to grow more complicated.[72] By 1888, Mother Mary John and Rev. Neno had both died and the cause was assumed by Mother Clement Lannen and Father Locke, O.S.A. In December, 1889, Rev. Locke wrote to Mother Clement explaining that the diocesan bishops' plan to have their own communities was losing favor in Rome.

---

69 Rev. Pacificus Neno to Mother Mary John, April 8, 1881. (Cited in Logue, 174) Mother Mary John Kieran was born in Ireland on August 15, 1825, she entered the Chestnut Hill congregation in 1853, receiving the habit from Bishop St. John Neumann. In 1859, Neumann appointed her as assistant to Mother St. John Fournier. When Mother St. John died in 1875, Mother Mary John became superior general, an office she held until 1888. (Logue, 171 ff.)
70 Logue, 174, citing correspondence in July, 1882.
71 Rev. Neno to Mother Mary John, July 10, 1882. (Cited in Logue, 175)
72 In 1888, Mother Mary John wrote to Archbishop Ryan suggesting that Philadelphia could "adopt...the Rule approved for...Carondelet...altered so as to suit our existing circumstances since our Sisters wish to remain subject to the Ordinary of the Diocese as their first Superior." (Logue, 179)

The Holy See does not at present wish to approve Institutes that are purely diocesan. It leaves such institutes solely to the care of the bishop....It seems that too many new institutes were springing up...and the Holy See would much prefer to see existing bodies spreading...
Mgr. Jacobini however told me that he is sure your body will find no difficulty in having your rules & *Constitutions* approved even as they stand, if the Archbishop of Phildela [sic] take the matter seriously in hand...[explaining] the reasons why this form of government is the most useful for the efficiency of the Institute...[73]

Cardinal Gibbons, Archbishop of Baltimore, the pre-eminent prelate of the United States, probably spoke for any number of his colleagues when he admitted that his objection to congregations being present in several dioceses was that they "would be entirely outside of his jurisdiction and that you would do what you please against his will."[74] Nevertheless, Archbishop Ryan of Philadelphia eventually supported the Congregation's petition to become a congregation of pontifical right and on July, 5, 1892, the *Constitutions* of the Sisters of St. Joseph in Philadelphia received temporary approval from Pope Leo XIII with final approval on February 29, 1896. The Congregation of the Sisters of St. Joseph of Philadelphia was thus approved as a Congregation of Pontifical Right with sisters serving in more than one diocese.[75]

WHICH *CONSTITUTIONS*?

As various Congregations of St. Joseph worked on their *Constitutions*, they adapted the Lyon models to their particular circumstances. One of the major differences among them came to be the role of authority in the congregations of pontifical right and the diocesan congregations. The first English version of the *Constitutions* was an 1847 translation of the Lyon *Constitutions* of 1827. That rule had been written for congregations serving in only one diocese. As practice changed, the *Constitutions* needed modification. One of the most striking adaptations in addition to the authority of a "Superior General" in later editions was a difference in the authority held by bishops. The 1847 translation and the French versions state:

The Sisters shall consider the bishops of the respective Dioceses in which

---

73 Rev. Joseph Locke, O.S.A. to Mother Clement, Dec. 11, 1889. (Cited in Logue, 196)
74 Letter from Rev. Aloyusius Sabetti, S.J., to Mother Clement, Sept. 14, 1890. (Cited in Logue, 197)
75 By the time the *Constitutions* were approved Sisters of St. Joseph from Philadelphia were serving in the Archdioceses of Baltimore, and Newark as well as the diocese of Camden. (McSherrystown was in the Harrisburg diocese. In 1899 the McSherrystown community formally reaffiliated with the Congregation of Chestnut Hill. See Logue, 212-213.)

they reside as their Superiors: they shall show them profound respect, submission and obedience in all things which they may prescribe considering them as holding the place of Jesus Christ and invested with his authority over them.[76]

Carondelet's 1860 Constitutions state:

> In accordance with the decrees of the holy Council of Trent and Apostolic *Constitutions*, the Sisters of the Congregation are subject to the authority of the bishop in whose Diocese they reside as to their Ordinary, in all things appertaining to his Episcopal Jurisdiction; and they shall render him the obedience and respect...which are due to the authority with which he is invested.[77]

The Carondelet *Constitutions* were approved as written above. By the time the Philadelphia Congregation obtained approval as a congregation of pontifical right in 1896, their *Constitutions* omitted any reference to the authority of the bishop over the sisters except to mention his role at the election of a superior general. In spite of that trend, some of the congregations which remained diocesan continued to use the older rule which recognized the ultimate authority of the bishop in governing the congregation. This included the 1880 Buffalo *Constitutions* and the 1884 *Constitutions* of Brooklyn.[78] Obviously, the Philadelphia sisters and their advisors had some concern about the amount of influence bishops could exercise in their life; some congregations were able to write *Constitutions* which protected the autonomous governance of the congregation while others were not.[79]

THE SISTERS AND THEIR *CONSTITUTIONS*

While it is clear that the bishops wielded significant influence over the development of the various communities of St. Joseph, the sisters were not powerless. In the first place it must be remembered that every woman who became a member did so of her own free will having chosen the vocation to the particular congregation for personal and religious reasons unconstrained by any authority. Although none of them probably read the *Constitutions* as part of their discernment process,

---

76 *Constitutions* of the Sisters of St. Joseph (St. Louis, 1847) Chapter VI.

77 *Constitutions* of the Sisters of St. Joseph (St. Louis, 1860), Chapter VII. As mentioned earlier, the privileged role of the bishop of St. Louis was dropped after the 1860 edition of the St. Louis *Constitutions*.

78 See the Buffalo *Constitutions*, Chapter VI, page 9, (printed in West Seneca, N.Y., 1880) and the Brooklyn *Constitutions* with the exact same chapter and page numbers (printed in New York, O'Shea and Co., 1884.)

79 One of the impediments to the sisters' autonomy was that the bishops of the dioceses in which the sisters served had to approve of the *Constitutions* before Rome would approve them. (Ewens loc. 1664, 1754)

something about the constitution of the community – the spirit or attitude or reputation of the sisters – attracted them, or at least appealed to the person who recommended the community to them.

Constitutions provide one sure source of information about the sisters' formal sense of their vocation. While much of what is found in the documents may seem generic or rule-oriented, the Preface to Constitutions of the Sisters of St. Joseph explains clearly why the Congregation was formed and remained in existence. All that follows the Preface may be interpreted in the light of its explanation of who chooses to be a member. The Preface states that Sisters of St. Joseph are:

> pious females, who have freely chosen to live in community, for the purpose of applying themselves to the attainment of Christian perfection, and the service of their neighbor, by observing the rules which are prescribed in the following Constitutions.[80]

The life of the Sisters of St. Joseph was characterized by an emphasis on service to the neighbor and the spirituality of Jean Pierre Médaille as expressed in the Maxims or in references to Father Médaille which appeared in every edition of the Constitutions. The Sisters of St. Joseph were called to a life of humble and broadly defined service carried out in the context of prayer and community. Their traditions taught them that communal life, including their life of prayer, enhanced their apostolic service. They strove to maintain a balance of community and ministry in which one dimension did not make sense without the other; prayer, community and apostolic service formed the life of the Congregation. That was the American sisters' heritage from the Le Puy foundation of 1650 and all the sisters who had preserved and developed the life since then.

The question of 1860 was how the American context affected and should orient the life of the Sisters of St. Joseph. First of all, unlike the French communities of previous centuries, the sisters in America (Canada and the U.S. and its territories), followed the example of their missionary pioneers and embraced great mission mobility. The original French missionaries were well emulated by women like Sister Agnes Spencer who ministered in the dioceses of St. Louis, Philadelphia and Buffalo before remaining with the community she founded in Erie. Another, Sister Martha Bunning, was born in Germany, entered Carondelet from Pennsylvania and then served in St. Louis, Philadelphia, Toronto, Hamilton and Erie before

---

80 Constitutions of the Congregation of the Sisters of St. Joseph, Part I, 1, pg. 3. (St. Louis, 1847) The various iterations of the Constitutions in the U.S. were similar in this section.

returning to Canada shortly before her death. Sister Francis Joseph Ivory entered at Carondelet from Pennsylvania and ministered in St. Louis, St. Paul, Canandaigua, Buffalo, Kansas City and finally in various cities in Carondelet's Troy province where she died after spending 55 years as a Sister of St. Joseph. Those sisters are but a few examples of how flexible Sisters of St. Joseph could be in service to the neighbor. The sisters' geographic mobility not only allowed them to found and support new communities and institute new ministries, it also kept alive the strong mutual bonds among all of them. Those who had been missioned in a variety of cities or dioceses would have shared their knowledge about the sisters and life of each place with the others with whom they shared community. With the likes of Sisters Frances Joseph Ivory and Martha Bunning moving hither and yon, in

1860, even sisters who never left their home dioceses could have had at least second-hand knowledge of every other sister of St. Joseph with roots in Carondelet or Philadelphia and their foundations. At that time the sisters numbered nearly 175 and may have made their novitiate anywhere from Lyon or Moutiers to St. Louis, Pennsylvania or Toronto. They resided in cities and towns as distant as Carondelet, Toronto, Sulphur Springs, St. Paul, and Brooklyn, New York. In spite of the overwhelming difficulties of communications and travel, their relationships were real because the sisters who ventured from place to place communicated their unique experiences of mission and their shared heritage. Such knowledge had positive and negative dimensions. A bad reputation would have been hard to overcome and

Sister Martha Bunning
1824 - 1868

opinions about policies or proposals may have been as influenced by the person giving the critique or approval as much as by the soundness of the idea itself.[81]

THE MOMENT OF DECISION

When the superiors met at Carondelet on May 2, 1860, Archbishop Kenrick had

---

81 Who knows how much some sisters' dissatisfaction with Mother St. John Facemaz influenced sisters who had never met her? What did the sisters think of a superior whom everyone knew had been deposed by a bishop? For these early sisters anonymity was an unattainable luxury. (The first two superiors deposed by their bishops, Mothers Agnes Spencer in Buffalo (Bishop Timon) and Martha Bunning in Hamilton (Bishop Farrell), had been in the novitiate together at Carondelet.)

prepared a "memorandum" with details for organizing a Congregation of Sisters of St. Joseph in America. He made it clear that the plan was based on how the Lyon community had reorganized itself beginning with the days of Mother St. John Fontbonne. His proposal included the establishment of three provinces: St. Louis, Canada, and "one for the Eastern states," a designation that suggests he was already aware that Philadelphia might not participate in the new organization.[82] Additional provinces could be erected with the approval of the superior general wherever there were three or more houses of the Congregation. All of the invited superiors attended the meeting with the exception of those from Hamilton, Philadelphia, Buffalo and Brooklyn. [83] Archbishop Kenrick made no public statement about the groups that did not attend, but it was commonly understood that their bishops refused to give them permission to participate.[84] Archbishop Kenrick was so convinced of the advantages of the congregational plan that he wrote to his Vicar General saying that the absence of the four communities

> may be taken as equivalent to a refusal to accept the proposition made to them. Still I deem it very likely that when the matter is represented to them as forming them into a distinct province, they will accede to the matter.

At the same time, he was realistically ready for an almost complete rejection of the plan and said he believed that such a rejection would eventually be overcome:

> Should none of the dioceses outside that of St. Louis be willing to adopt these regulations, but prefer to remain as they are, then I would advise the communities in the diocese of St. Louis to organize on the above plan, and I have every confidence that sooner or later, their example will be followed by others.[85]

---

82 Kenrick, "Memorandum," (Carondelet Archives). The fact that the Memorandum specified "Eastern States" rather than the obvious choice of Philadelphia may be evidence that Kenrick was already aware of the reservations Bishop Wood seemingly shared with Bishop Timon and perhaps also Bishop Loughlin. An unanswered question in the story is what Archbishop Peter R. Kenrick might have asked his brother, then Archbishop of Baltimore, to do in relation to the disagreements among bishops. (Bishop F. P. Kenrick was Archbishop of Baltimore from 1851 until his death in 1863.)

83 Dougherty (365) mentions that Toronto was represented at the meeting but says nothing of a superior from Hamilton. The first superior at Hamilton was Sister Martha Bunning, who served in that role from the foundation in 1852 until she was deposed in 1862 by Bishop John Farrell.

84 See Dougherty, 365 and Dunne 88. Dunne explains that when the sisters who decided to return to Carondelet left Buffalo, Bishop Timon was able to obtain two sisters from Philadelphia: Sisters Magdalen Weber and Stephen Hesse who became respectively the Superior General and the Director of Novices.

85 "Memorandum." It should not go unnoticed that Archbishop Kenrick speaks of "advising" the community about the course to take. To all appearances, he was not insisting that he had the authority to make the decisions about what the sisters would do.

In the end, the plan for an American Congregation with provinces was accepted only by the communities serving in the dioceses of St. Louis, St. Paul, Albany and Natchez. The representatives from Canada and Wheeling, following the instructions of their bishops, remained independent of the new Congregation. On May 4, 1860, the sisters elected Mother St. John Facemaz Superior General of the new Congregation of the Sisters of St. Joseph of Carondelet and provinces were eventually established in St. Louis, St. Paul and Albany.[86] Within six weeks of the meeting, Mother St. John Facemaz began a journey to Europe where she would visit communities of St. Joseph in France and begin the process of procuring approval for the Congregation in Rome. Mother St. John's first visit to Rome on behalf of the Congregation took place in March, 1861, when she presented Archbishop Kenrick's petition for the approbation of the new rule to Pope Pius IX. Judged by the standards of the day, the process of approbation went quickly and the Carondelet rule received temporary approbation in 1867 and final approbation in 1877.

Between 1860 and 1912, sisters founded multiple Congregations of St. Joseph, some as diocesan and others as congregations of pontifical right. All of them benefitted from the work of the sisters who translated, adapted and struggled to obtain approval for their Constitutions, slowly but surely assuring the stability of their congregations and those who would be founded from them. Unfortunately, conflicts with bishops over authority and autonomy had only just begun.

---

86 If there had been question of the sisters' support of Mother St. John Facemaz in 1857, her election in 1860 resolved the doubts. Given how quickly she traveled to Europe, it seems possible that the sisters had faith in her ability to accomplish quickly what they were hoping for, and perhaps they knew she had the right contacts to obtain additional personnel from Moutiers as well.

್ಞ

Chapter Six: The Design: From Erie to Cleveland, Watertown, Tipton and Nazareth-Kalamazoo

Cast of Characters

Mother Agnes Spencer: 1823 – 1882,
Founder Of The Erie Community – 1860
Mother St. John Facemaz
Superior General Carondelet, 1857-1872
Mother St. George Bradley –
Provincial Superior, St. Paul, Founder Of The Cleveland Community, 1872
Sister Mary Herman/Mother Margaret Mary Lacy:
Founder Watertown 1880, Nazareth, Michigan, 1889
Mother De Chantal Keating:
(Brooklyn) Friend and Promotor Of Mother Margaret Mary
Mother Agatha Guthrie:
First Carondelet Provincial In Albany,
Superior General Of Carondelet 1872-1904
Mother Josephine Donnelly,
Superior General Of Watertown, 1889 – 1926, 1929 – 1935
Mother Gertrude Moffitt:
Founder Of Tipton, 1880

Bishop John Timon: Bishop Of Buffalo, 1847 - 1867
Bishop Richard Gilmour: Bishop Of Cleveland, 1872 - 1891
Bishop John Hogan: Bishop In St. Joseph and Kansas City MO 1868 -1893
Bishop John J. Conroy, Bishop Of Albany, 1865 – 1877
Bishop Francis McNeirny, Auxiliary/Bishop Of Albany 1871 - 1894
Bishop Edgar P.P. Wadhams, Vicar General In Albany,
First Bishop Of Ogdensburg, NY 1872 - 1891
Bishop Joseph Dwenger, Bishop Of Fort Wayne, In, 1872 – 1893
Monsignor Frank O'Brien, 1821 -1921,
Brought the Sisters Of St. Joseph To Kalamazoo, MI

THE FOUNDATION IN CORSICA/ERIE PENNSYLVANIA – 1860

Less than three weeks after the meeting to discuss the foundation of what became the Carondelet Congregation, Sister Agnes Spencer left St. Louis for Pennsylvania. Responding to the invitation of Erie's Bishop Josiah Young to open a school, she and three companions set off on the 700 mile journey to the town of Corsica.

This mission would mark the last of Mother Agnes Spencer's series of foundations.

Mother Agnes, baptized as Mary Spencer, was one of the most influential and accomplished Sisters of St. Joseph of the late 19th Century. While her brief résumé outlines the responsibilities others were quick to give her, additional details fill out a more ample portrait of this remarkable woman. There is no clear indication of why her family emigrated from England when she was only eight years old, although, unlike the Irish immigrants of the day, the Spencers were landowners in England, suggesting that they may have been fleeing religious persecution rather than seeking an escape from

Mother Agnes Spencer - 1823-1882
1823 Born: August 15, Brindle, Lancashire, England
1831 Immigrated to Utica, N.Y.
1836 Family relocates to St. Louis
1846 Received the Habit of the Sisters of St. Joseph, Nov. 11
1848 Pronounced vows, November 15 at Carondelet
1851 Superior St. John's Orphanage, Philadelphia
1853 Founding Superior and opened hospital at Wheeling
1856 Superior and Founder of School for the Deaf, Buffalo
1858 Superior St. Mary Orphanage, Dunkirk, N.Y. (Buffalo)
1860 Founder Superior St. Ann's Academy, Corsica, Diocese of Erie
1860-1882 Superior, Sisters of St. Joseph of Erie

poverty.[1] After living for a few years in New York, the family moved to St. Louis where Mary and her sister Martha enrolled in St. Joseph's Academy at Carondelet which had been established in 1840. Although there are no records of Mary's activities between graduation from high school and her entrance into the Congregation of St. Joseph at the age of 22, she was reputed to be a good musician and later activities amply demonstrated her good business sense.

After two years of novitiate, Sister Agnes Spencer made vows on November 15, 1848. On that same day that her sister Martha was received into the Carondelet community and given the name Sister Augustine. Carondelet did not keep a record of the early sisters' every assignment, but it is likely that between

---

1 Although the discriminatory British laws were being repealed gradually, it was not until 1829 that Catholics could be admitted to Parliament and it was only in 1871 that they could be admitted to the universities. Sister Helene Garvin, SSJ, (*The Sisters of St. Joseph of Rochester* [Rochester: Sisters of St. Joseph of Rochester, 1950] 37), says that Mother Agnes was a convert who entered the Congregation at the age of nineteen, but Carondelet has no record indicating that Sr. Agnes or her sister, Sr. Augustine, were converts. (The book lists the author as "A Sister of St. Joseph," but it is known that Sister Helene Garvin, S.S.J. was the author.)

1846 and 1851, Sister Agnes taught and quite possibly cared for orphans. In 1851, three years after she had made vows, Mother Celestine Pommerel missioned her to Philadelphia to replace Mother Delphine Fontbonne as director and local superior in St. John's Orphanage.

After only two years in Philadelphia, Mother Celestine accompanied Sister Agnes from Philadelphia to Wheeling. There they met four sisters from Carondelet who were to open that mission with Sister Agnes as the superior. Three years later, in 1854, Mother Celestine called her back to Carondelet where preparations were being made to open the mission in Canandaigua of the Diocese of Buffalo. By the time she went to Erie in 1860, Mother Agnes had served as founding superior in two missions outside St. Louis and she had opened the school for the deaf in Buffalo and then St. Mary's Orphanage in Dunkirk, New York.

While many of Mother Agnes' moves seem to have been dictated by the need for a strong superior/leader in newly forming communities, there was more underneath the departure from Buffalo which led her to Erie. Letters Bishop Timon sent to Mother St. John Fournier in Philadelphia indicated that he and Mother Agnes had found themselves in serious conflict. In June of 1859, Bishop Timon wrote to Mother St. John saying:

> Dr. Sr. Superior
> I wrote the other day to you stating that I had deposed Sr. Agnes and named Sister Julia in her place and that Sr. Agnes would start for St. Louis two days after…[2] She seemed to feel her error; expressed her sorrow, promised to obey in everything and in any position. I told her that it was now too late to restore her to her former position; but that in her State of a good Sister, she would find me a kind father. I permitted her to go to St. Louis on a visit; she declared that she will return and obey…
> + John[3]

The bishop then explained other changes he had made in local communities in the diocese making it obvious that he considered himself the major superior and was simply informing Mother St. John Fournier of his decisions. Four days after writing the letter cited above, Bishop Timon wrote again to Mother St. John in Philadelphia saying:

---

2 "Sister Julia" is Sister Julia Littenecker who has already been mentioned in the section on Canandaigua/Buffalo.
3 Timon to Fournier, June 10, 1859, (Archives SSJP).

D. Sister,
I thank you for your kind and prompt answer yesterday. I received my
answer from Carondelet. I send it to you, read it and send it back with
your first letter of answer...Sr. Agnes...wants to go to her Brother in St.
Louis; if she does not return to go elsewhere...I hope she will not.

In this ambiguous letter Bishop Timon seemed to be playing one superior off the
other. He wrote to Mother St. John Fournier in Philadelphia about a Sister who by
all rights was responsible to Carondelet, by then under the leadership of Mother
St. John Facemaz.

Mother Agnes apparently did make the trip to St. Louis in 1859 and then
returned briefly to the Buffalo diocese. The situation appears not to have improved
significantly. Eight months after the correspondence found above, Bishop Timon
wrote to Mother St. John Fournier explaining the problems he saw. On March 8,
1860, he said:

Sr. Cesarine seems to be intriguing and urging Sister Agnes to evil acts.
They have written to various bishops without knowledge of Sister Julia
or me to obtain a place. Of course I know not what day they may silently
depart. The priest gave Sister Agnes [cash]...she kept some in the
house...and has deposited [the greater quantity] in Bank in the name of
Agnes Spencer.
Her sister, Sr. Augustine, was made superior in Canandaigua, she
there keeps up the old spirit.[4]

Bishop Timon avoided any clear statement about the reasons for his discontent
with Mother Agnes, but not long after he wrote the above letter Mother Agnes
Spencer left the Diocese of Buffalo.

FOUNDING IN THE DIOCESE OF ERIE

Mother Agnes returned to Carondelet and two weeks after the close of the meeting
about forming a congregation, she left for Corsica accompanied by Sisters St.
Protais Deboille, Cesarine Mulvey and Augustine Spencer. The sisters arrived

---

4 Timon to Fournier, March 8, 1860, (Archives, CSJP). The date of this letter contradicts the Buffalo history's
assertion that Mother Agnes left Buffalo definitively in 1859. The letter also makes one wonder what source the
bishop had for his information since he states that neither he nor Sister Julia had knowledge of Mother Agnes'
correspondence with other bishops.
Sister Cesarine Mulvey was Irish-born and entered the congregation at Carondelet, being received in 1849 and
making vows in 1851. She was first missioned to the Long Prairie Indian Mission in Minnesota. According to the
Carondelet archives, she left the congregation in Minnesota to found the Community of the Love of God. After
that community failed she was in Buffalo with Mother Agnes in 1858 and later went with her to found the mission
in Corsica. Her time and place of death are not recorded. Carondelet's records simply state that she

in Corsica on May 24, 1860, to take charge of St. Ann's Academy, a school which had been opened four years previously by an enterprising pastor.[5] Of the sisters who accompanied Mother Agnes in the Erie foundation, Sister St. Protais was the only one who had not been missioned in Buffalo with Mother Agnes.[6] Sister St. Protais' presence refutes suspicions that the Corsica group left Carondelet in protest over the new congregational plan. Sister St. Protais remained a member of the Carondelet community through her time in Pennsylvania and in 1864 accepted a mission to St. Paul.

Sister Cesarine, whose interesting history included having been excommunicated by Bishop Cretin for temporarily abandoning the community in Minnesota, was later missioned to Buffalo where she was one of the sisters who opened St. Louis School with Sister Julia Littenecker.[7] Sister Victorine who joined the group in Pennsylvania was originally from Minnesota, made her novitiate in Canandaigua and Buffalo and pronounced her vows in Buffalo in January, 1860. Apparently a protégé of Sisters Augustine and Cesarine whom she would have first known in Long Prairie, Minnesota, Sister Victorine came to Corsica in January, 1861, and died there of consumption on May 8, 1861.[8]

Previous to opening the mission in Corsica, Sister Augustine Spencer, Sister Agnes' blood sister, had been missioned in Minneapolis, St. Paul, and Long Prairie, Minnesota. She remained in Pennsylvania until 1863, when she was missioned to Peoria, Illinois, part of the St. Louis Province of Carondelet.[9]

---

received a dispensation.

5 The brief annals of the Sisters of St. Joseph of Erie indicate that it was Bishop Young who invited the sisters to Corsica. According to material in the archives, the pastor who built the Academy was Father Ledwith whose plans for the school were more hopeful than circumstances warranted. The next pastor, Father Mollinger, probably more realistic than his predecessor, did not support the school. See: R.G. Barcio *Shepherds and Sheep – A History of the Diocese of Erie*, Vol. 3 (Erie: Meridian Creative Group, 2002) and Archives, SSJE. Hereafter the Erie annals will be referred to as Annals E, implying that they are housed at the Archives SSJE.

6 At this point, Sister St. Protais, one of the original six French missionaries, had been in the United States for 24 years and had served at Carondelet and Cahokia as well as other missions in St. Louis and then also in Wheeling and St. Paul. After leaving Erie in 1864, she returned to St. Paul, and was missioned in St. Louis and Chicago before spending the last twenty years of her life at St. Francis Xavier Mission in Assinins, Michigan, among Native American people who revered her such that they insisted that she be buried in their territory rather than have her body returned to St. Louis.

7 See Hurley 55-63 and Letter from Sister Mary Angela of St. Paul to Sister Clemenza Mazzei of Erie, April 11, 1951, copied to Sister Grace Aurelia in the Carondelet Generalate. (Archives, Carondelet)

8 Hurley letter. St. Paul historian, Sister Helen Angela Hurley, suggests that Sister Victorine Lequier may have been from Long Prairie, MN as her surname is common on the rolls of families from the Long Prairie and Blue Earth reservations. She would thus have been the first Native American sister in the Congregation.

9 Sister Augustine Spencer apparently returned to the St. Louis Province definitively in 1863, although there is some record of her having been in Canandaigua again before her final assignment to St. Bridget's half-orphan asylum in St. Louis where she died in 1881. (Carondelet Archives) Sister Augustine's mission to Peoria is

The Sisters of St. Joseph began their ministry in the Erie diocese with a short-lived attempt to make a success of St. Ann's School in Corsica. Mother Agnes put forth great efforts to assure the success of the school as evidenced in the advertisement she published in the Pittsburgh Catholic after their first year.[10]

St. Ann's Academy
For Young Ladies
Corsica Jefferson County, PA.
Under the charge of the Sisters of St. Joseph
This institution is situated in one of the most delightful
and healthy locations in Western Pennsylvania.

Being on the turnpike between Brookville and Clarion,
it is of easy access by stage.
The system of education embraces every useful and ornamental
branch suitable for young ladies.

The scholastic year commences on the first of September
and ends on the 15th of July.
Terms:
Tuition, board, washing, bed and bedding per annum $80.00
Music (extra charge) $10.00
French (extra charge) $10.00
For further particulars address the Superioress of the Academy
Sister Agnes Spencer - Superioress

Advertising and determination were not enough to overcome the factors militating against the school's success. In spite of the advertisement's optimistic description, other sources indicate that the Academy was situated a considerable distance from main roads. Not only was there a new pastor who did not support the school, but community records succinctly describe the situation as follows:

Finding the people too poor to sustain a boarding school, [Mother

---

evidently the reason that the Erie Annals have the following entry from April of 1863, "Father Abram Ryan, pastor of St. Mary's Church Peoria, Illinois, brought Sisters of St. Joseph to his parish." This entry may have referred to the separation between the Erie and Carondelet communities at that time.

10 Advertisement cited in Leonie Shanley & Mary Francis Becker, *Come to the Waters* (Sisters of St. Joseph of Northwestern Pennsylvania, 2010) 41.

Agnes] closed it and went to Frenchtown in Crawford County…The conditions there were not much better and there were no provisions for the regular reception of the sacraments. In 1864, the little band moved to Meadville. It was here that she purchased the site upon which stood St. Joseph's Hospital.[11]

Mother Agnes had left Sister Augustine in charge of St. Ann's in Corsica while she pursued a better opportunity by opening St. Hippolyte's Academy at Frenchtown, nearly 70 miles northwest of Corsica. Judging from the community annals, the two most significant events during the sisters' short time in Corsica counterbalanced one another: two months after Sister Victorine's untimely death on July 2, Sister Mary Hoagg, the community's first postulant, received the habit.

MEADVILLE

While Mother Agnes was in Frenchtown in 1863, she began to confer with Bishop Young about the future of the community.[12] In the summer of 1864, with his permission, the sisters left both Corsica and Frenchtown. According to the Erie community annals,

When Mother Agnes moved from Frenchtown to Meadville, the convents in Corsica and Frenchtown were vacated and the whole Community settled in Meadville during the summer months, residing in temporary quarters until the Meadville Convent was ready for occupancy.[13]

The sisters' new residence in Meadville served as both convent and orphanage. Although the community did not keep detailed annals and left no correspondence

In 1860, Corsica, between Brookville and Clarion, had a population of 250. Meadville's population was 3,700. Frenchtown, 8 miles southeast of Meadville is much smaller. Erie had a population of 9,420.

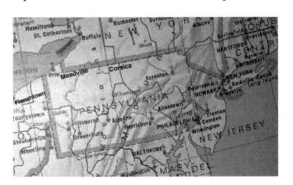

---

11 Notebook "Mother Agnes Spencer," (Archives SSJE.)
12 The entry in the annals for May 26, 1863, notes that the Bishop made a pastoral visit to Meadville.
13 Annals E.

to tell us of their everyday hopes and challenges, some inference is possible on the basis of general knowledge of the times and the area. One of the social undercurrents of the era was an ongoing subtle, sometimes blatant, anti-Catholicism. The Sisters of St. Joseph in Erie may have gotten their first taste of that – and seen Mother Agnes' creative response – when she encountered a problem with some bankers.

Mother Agnes had decided to purchase property so that the sisters would have both a secure motherhouse and a patrimony in the area. When local bankers refused to give the necessary loan to a woman religious, Mother Agnes went home and put on secular garb. Then, using identification papers with no reference to her status as a woman religious, she obtained her loan on April 11, 1865, and with the help of her family inheritance acquired the land the sisters needed.[14] The land she purchased served for a motherhouse and orphanage and also became the original site of Spencer Hospital in Meadville.[15] Using her patrimony for the purchase seemed to indicate that Mother Agnes was putting down roots and signaled her independence from Carondelet. Refusing to let chauvinistic prejudice thwart her plans she taught her sisters and future generations to pursue their hopes and to face obstacles with creativity.

Catholics, and sisters in particular, remained the object of Protestant prejudice through the 19th and well into the 20th century.[16] With their unique dress and lifestyle, women religious stood out not only as representatives of the Church but also as women who defied the acceptable and restricted role of women in U.S. Protestant society. An incident which took place in 1869 demonstrates how dangerous anti-Catholic prejudice could be. It also reveals something about the community's rule at that time. The Erie annals record the problems of the Sisters of St. Brigid, in a neighboring town:

> St. Brigid's Academy at Titusville, conducted by the Brigidine Sisters, was destroyed by fire. Seventeen orphans, besides other boarders were made homeless…

The sisters presumed that the fire was the work of anti-Catholic thugs:

---

14 Annals E entry, April 11, 1865. Another source from the archives, a presentation titled, "Health Care Social Services," records the date as May 8, 1864. It would seem possible that Mother Agnes' family assets may have helped the unmarried "Agnes Spencer" obtain her loan. (SSJE)

15 See Centenary of the Sisters of St. Joseph of Northwestern Pennsylvania in the Diocese of Erie, 1860-1960. (Archives, SSJE)

16 Andrew Greeley has called anti-Catholicism one of the most acceptable and perduring prejudices in the U.S. See: Andrew Greeley: An Ugly Little Secret: Anti-Catholicism in North America (Kansas City: Sheed, 1977).

The temporary shelter of the Sisters of St. Brigid in Titusville, together with all their possessions, was burned – probably the work of an incendiary.

Six months later the Erie annals make an interesting note about the community's rule:

> At the suggestion of Bishop Mullen, the two Brigidines, the Eardly [sic] sisters entered the Benedictine Convent in Erie, the Sisters of St. Joseph, according to their rule not being able to receive them into their community. The other professed Sisters went to Rochester and Troy, N.Y. Father Mignault took the novices to the Grey Nuns in Ottawa, Canada.[17]

The description of this incident indicates that in the course of less than a decade, the Erie community was using a rule that was more restrictive than that of their founding congregation at Carondelet whose Troy province, like the Rochester community, was able to receive the displaced Brigidine sisters.[18]

It can be said literally that the Erie Sisters' healthcare ministry began accidentally. When a train crash occurred in Meadville, the sisters caring for orphans responded with their typical compassion and flexibility, bringing the injured to the orphanage, thus inadvertently instituting the ministry of Catholic Health Care in the town and diocese. That apostolate would soon demand more than makeshift treatment space in the sisters' home. The unanticipated addition of caring for the sick or injured to the ministries they were already carrying out was in keeping with the sisters' well-established mode of operation. Wherever Sisters of St. Joseph went, they were free to allow local needs to call forth their services. Especially in the time before canon law would legislate uniformity among congregations, the Sisters of St. Joseph's dedication to the "Dear Neighbor" implied that their ministries would be determined by the circumstances in which they found themselves as much as by advanced planning or even their professional preparation or lack thereof. The flexibility of their tradition typically allowed Sisters of St. Joseph to serve in ways that many other communities could not. St. Joseph's Hospital in Meadville, eventually named Spencer Hospital,

---

17 Annals E entries for January 14, April 18 and June 20, 1869. The Erie Sisters were using a different *Constitutions* or Rule than the Sisters of St. Joseph in Rochester and Troy who, although they had distinct *Constitutions*, were apparently both free to receive the displaced sisters.

18 The congregation's official incorporation did not take place until 1874, but this entry makes it clear that in 1869 the Erie sisters were not living under the Carondelet *Constitution* which had been in the process of formal approbation since 1863. (See Shanley, 43)

was the first hospital in Northwestern Pennsylvania.[19] Although Mother Agnes had secured some of the necessary funding for the work, in May, 1865, the sisters asked the people of the area to contribute to the cause. In June, Bishop Young made the interesting announcement that the funds collected for the jubilee year that were not used in other charities would be for the Meadville Orphanage – somehow underlining the importance of the orphanage while still granting priority to other causes.[20]

Soon after that announcement, believing that she could safely leave the Meadville projects in the care of Sister Mary Hoagg, the indomitable Mother Agnes accepted another request from Bishop Young. [21] On August 15, 1865 she moved to Erie with two orphan girls to open St. Vincent Hospital. This institution, the sisters' first home in the city, soon became the congregational center for the Sisters of St. Joseph of Erie. In the beginning, St. Vincent's Hospital on Fourth Street in Erie also housed an orphanage and a Select School (academy). Growth in the number of sisters and the needs of the people gradually led the sisters to make several moves to larger quarters.

TEMPORARY MEMBERS FROM OTHER COMMUNITIES

During these early years the original pioneer sisters added new members to their ranks and also received the help of a few Sisters of St. Joseph who arrived from other places under unusual circumstances. One of the latter was Sister Martha Bunning who joined Mother Agnes in Erie at St. Vincent Hospital. Sister Martha was born in 1824, in Hanover, Germany and entered the congregation at Carondelet, making vows in 1848.[22] After teaching with Sister Delphine Fontbonne in St. Louis, the two of them went to Philadelphia in 1850 and then founded the Toronto mission in 1851. In 1852, Sister Martha opened a mission in Hamilton, Canada. When Hamilton became a diocese she ran into troubles with Bishop John Farrell, the first bishop of the area.[23]

---

19 The name change happened because anti-Catholic prejudice made it difficult to collect donations for "St. Joseph's Hospital." With Bishop Mullen's permission the name was changed in 1877 to "Spencer Hospital." (Document: "Health Care Services" Archives SSJE.)

20 Annals E entry, June 24, 1865.

21 Sister Mary Hoagg was the first postulant accepted into the Erie community. A timeline of Mother Agnes' life and activities indicates that in 1865 Sister Mary Hoagg was in charge of the hospital and orphanage while "Mother Agnes was working in Erie and other Community Business. ("Mother Agnes Spencer 1860-1877," Archives: SSJE)

22 Sister Martha's last name is sometimes recorded as Von Bunning, which may indicate that her family came from the nobility in her native Bohemia.

23 Bishop John Farrell was born in Ireland in 1820 and moved to Canada with his family in 1832. Consecrated on May 11, 1856, he became known for building up Catholic education in the diocese.

The community had grown well under Mother Martha, receiving 23 novices in their first decade. But in 1862, while Mother Martha was meeting with the sisters, some of the boarding school students went to the chapel to play at Mass and confessions. When the bishop got word of their pranks, he deposed Mother Martha and exiled her from the diocese, forbidding her sisters to allow her to stay in the convent. She returned to Philadelphia for a time and then went to Erie where Mother Agnes put her in charge of the orphanage. Sister Doreen Kaminski of Hamilton explains what happened after that.

> In 1868, [Mother Martha] had a dream in which she met Mother Delphine [who] said to her: "If you only knew the value of one act of humility, you would go to the ends of the earth to perform it." Fearing that there be any lingering trace of bitterness in her heart, she went to beg pardon from the bishop. Bishop Farrell refused to see her or even admit her into his house. The Hamilton Sisters were even forbidden by the bishop to allow her into any of their houses. Martha made her sad way back to Toronto where the Sisters lovingly cared for her and where she died...nine days later, June 13, 1868. ...Just before she died, she was asked if she was afraid to die. Her response was, "O no, the first thing I'll do will be to throw myself at His feet and He'll not send me away!"[24]

The tradition is that Mother Martha died of a broken heart.[25]

Another of the sisters who found refuge with Mother Agnes is Mother St. George Bradley. Mother St. George turned to Mother Agnes when she left her mission in Peoria, Illinois under atypical circumstances. Mother St. George had been the provincial of the Sisters of St. Joseph in the Diocese of St. Paul and was assigned to Peoria in 1868. Apparently because of her disagreements with the Carondelet rule, she left the Carondelet community from Peoria and Mother Agnes gave her a place to minister, providing a step along Mother St. George's road to becoming the founder of the Cleveland congregation in 1872, the foundation story of which follows below.

ECONOMIC STRUGGLES

Mother Agnes had spent her inheritance to stabilize the community and still the funds were never enough to meet all the needs. The community annals frequently noted fund-raising efforts and large and small donations including the following:

---

24 Information from correspondence with Sister Doreen Kaminski, November 16, 2015.
25 Letter from Sr. M. Carmela of Hamilton to Sister Clemenza Mazzei of Erie, Sept. 2, 1946. (Archives SSJE)

❖ March 17, 1866, a supper given at Farrar Hall for the benefit of the orphans;

❖ September 10, 1866, Sister Martha received a donation of $193.25 from the employees of the Pittsburgh docks;

❖ October 28, 1867, Orphans' Fair in Erie, net profit of $1,850;

❖ June 8, 1871, the State appropriated $2,000 to St. Joseph's Orphan Asylum;

❖ February 20, 1874, in a letter to the clergy Bishop Mullen instructed all the people to make a generous donation for the orphans on Easter Sunday [April 5].

On December 19, 1874, the Sisters published a "card of thanks" in the local paper which read:

> We return our sincere thanks to John Casey, Esq., for a donation of fifty dollars (50) on the morning of the eighth. This is not the first time this benevolent gentleman has sent liberal offerings to the little orphans. Also to Mr. Bernard Donnally, $5.00, Mr. Smith for seven boys' winter caps, Mrs. Matthews 29 pounds of pork, Mrs Valentine Schultz, 2 gallon crocks of butter. May God bless the cheerful giver.
> Sisters of St. Joseph, Orphan Asylum[26]

The following year a similar card of thanks was published in the city papers which again demonstrated the sisters' need and the revealed something of financial situation of their benefactors:

> On behalf of the orphans, who, by gracious dispensation of Divine Providence have been made so, and placed under our care to be provided for during the winter which is now upon us, we return our most heartfelt thanks to those who have in any way contributed to their comfort and alleviation of their many wants. Chief among these is a generous supply of coal, sufficient for the winter for the Hospital and Asylum, which has been delivered to us at little expense. Donors: Curtis and Boyce, Sharon, Pa. 43 tons free...Others whose names we are not free to publish, furnished the delivery of the same at the Hospital and Asylum. To all our benefactors, we offer our grateful thanks, and in conjunction with the "little ones" will daily employ the Throne of Grace to grant them blessings in this life and eternal happiness in the next.[27]

---

26 The list and the Card of Thanks are found in Annals E entries for 1874. (Archives, SSJ Erie)
27 Annals E, December 8, 1875.

What becomes clear from reading these snippets is that the sisters relied on small donors as much as on the major contributions they received from the State or through their annual fairs. The large contributions were vital, but they did not provide for all the food and clothing the orphans needed, nor even the coal to heat the buildings. The published thanks for a gift of $5.00 makes it clear that such a gift was as indispensable to the sisters as to the benefactor who sacrificed to give it. In this first decade after the Civil War, the community was living hand-to-mouth as they tried to respond to the needs of their neighbors in Erie and the surrounding area.

Although in the early days the sisters may have borne the brunt of anti-Catholic prejudice, they eventually won widespread esteem. In 1877, the Erie Dispatch carried an article about St. Joseph's Orphan Asylum that said in part:

> The asylum is managed by fourteen Sisters of whom Mother Agnes has been the moving spirit. Five of these teach in parish schools and contribute all they earn outside of their expenses to the wants of the Asylum; two teach in the Asylum, two do the sewing and the remainder attend to the household duties. The cost of running the institution during the last fiscal year was $3,500, all of which came from collections from different churches in the diocese, receipts from entertainments, picnics, gifts and the earnings of the Sisters in the parish schools. In time of sickness, the inmates are administered to by Dr. Freeman, whose services like those of the Sisters, are gratis and for his faithfulness he should be publicly commended.[28]

A week after that article was published, the community annals recorded the following:

> Mother Agnes left Erie for the oil regions, where she solicited donations for the orphans. The Asylum was in so great need at this time that the city papers carried pleas for food, bedding and clothing.[29]

Mother Agnes left for that trip on September 10 and returned on October 13. Afterwards she published another card of thanks for the $130 she realized from the people of Oil City, including those "whose circumstances would scarcely permit" their contribution for the orphans.

Mother Agnes continued as superior of the congregation until 1877, when Sister Ambrose Powers was elected to succeed her as general superior of the

---

28 Newspaper article quoted in the Erie Annals, entry for September 3, 1877.
29 Annals E entry for September 10, 1877.

Congregation. In her time as superior, Mother Agnes Spencer founded orphanages and the first hospitals in the area and provided teachers for the parochial schools. She received 44 women into the community along with welcoming the aid of various sisters of other St. Joseph congregations who joined her for different amounts of time, particularly from Carondelet and Buffalo.[30] Seemingly always on the move, she was quick to share her authority, beginning good works and then allowing others to complete them as she moved forward to respond to the next need. She was generous with her inheritance and unafraid to beg on behalf of her orphans or to dress however it might be necessary to obtain a loan. Mother Agnes attracted others to join her endeavors, a fact made obvious by the number of women who entered the community, the professed sisters who came with her to found the community and Mothers Martha Bunning and George Bradley to whom she was a friend in need when they found themselves in difficult circumstances.

After the election of her successor in 1877, Mother Agnes continued her fund-raising efforts and served as superintendent of St. Vincent Hospital. On March 22, 1882, Mother Agnes Spencer, then a patient at St. Vincent Hospital, died of cancer of the stomach. She was fifty-nine years old and had been a Sister of St. Joseph for over thirty-five years. She had been a member of communities that eventually became five distinct congregations of Sisters of St. Joseph and was founder of three of them.[31] In addition, Mother Agnes' influence was surely felt by congregations to be founded after her death as she had been the superior who gave the habit to Sisters Stanislaus Leary and Bernard Sheridan, the foundresses of the Concordia, La Grange and Wichita congregations. By the time Mother Agnes died, there were fifty-five professed sisters in the Erie community serving 150 orphan children, running two hospitals, teaching in four select schools and eight parochial schools with a combined total of over 2,300 students. Beyond any shadow of a doubt, Mother Agnes Spencer was one of the great leaders and organizers of the Sisters of St. Joseph in the mid-nineteenth century. When Bishop John Timon decided to remove her from office in Buffalo he could have had no idea that he was giving her the impulse to begin good works that are still being carried out in Erie.

---

30 That number from the Erie archives includes the sisters who came with Mother Agnes but not those who later came from other foundations to help her.
31 In chronological order those communities are Carondelet, Philadelphia, Wheeling, Canandaigua/Buffalo and Erie.

THE CLEVELAND CONGREGATION:
FROM ST. PAUL, THROUGH ERIE TO OHIO
MOTHER ST. GEORGE BRADLEY AND THE "NEW RULE"

Mother St. George (Mary) Bradley was four years old when her family emigrated from Ireland to the area of Loretto, Pennsylvania in 1828.[32] The scant information available about her childhood indicates she was born in the same year and grew up around the same place as Sister Francis Joseph Ivory who entered Carondelet in 1847 and Sister Austin Keane who entered the Sisters of St. Joseph at Philadelphia in 1849. All three of them would have known Reverend Demetrius Gallitzin as their pastor and spiritual mentor.[33] Mary Bradley came to Carondelet on September 1, 1847, received the habit on June 6, 1848, and made vows on April 20, 1850 at the age of twenty-six. The time of her postulate would have coincided with Sister Agnes Spencer's novitiate.[34]

There is no precise record of Mother St. George's ministry before 1855 when she taught in St. Paul, MN, but some documents from Cleveland indicate that she had been in Wheeling where Mother Agnes Spencer founded a community and hospital in 1853. According to Carondelet records, Mother St. George taught in St. Paul from 1855 to 1865, serving as the administrator of the Cathedral School for the latter five of those years. In 1865, Mother St. George was named provincial superior in St. Paul.[35] By the time her three year term was ending, the Carondelet Congregation had received temporary approval of their *Constitutions* and every

---

32 Mother St. George Bradley's name had a number of variations. In some Carondelet records she is referred to as Sister Georgiana, more often as Sister George or Mary George. She had the title "Mother" in St. Paul as well as in Cleveland where she was consistently referred to as Mother St. George Bradley. Here we will refer to her as Mother St. George as that was her final and most likely preferred appellation.

33 Demetrius Gallitzin died in May, 1840, when each of these future sisters were young women, but his influence in the area was legendary. He had established Loretto, PA as the first English-speaking Catholic settlement in the United States west of the Allegheny Front. (At that time the Catholic populations of the West and Southwest were not part of the United States.)

34 Among the pioneering sisters at Carondelet in the late 1840s, Sister Francis Joseph (Eliza Ellen) Ivory came to Carondelet on June 12, 1847 and received the habit on October 30, 1847. Mother St. George entered on September 1, 1847 and received the habit on June 6, 1848. There was not a set date for reception of the habit at the time and records indicate that some sisters had a longer postulate that others.

Sister Agnes Spencer received the habit on November 16, 1846 and made vows made vows on October 15, 1848. Sister Scholastica Vasques, the first CSJ missioner to Native Americans in Minnesota, made vows on November 15, 1849. While their times in formation coincide, novices were often sent to teach, so there is no guarantee that Mother St. George and Mother Agnes actually lived together in the years of their initial formation, but since Mother St. George was just the 31st sister to become a member of Carondelet they would have known one another.

35 The Carondelet records are scanty in regard to Mother St. George's term as provincial. According to Sister Helen Angela Hurley, "The six provincials who administered the young province before Mother Seraphine Ireland...are now shadowy traditions." (Dougherty, 151)

sister had to renew her vows under the new *Constitutions* or choose a different path.[36] A total of eight sisters chose to join other communities rather than affiliate with Carondelet under the revised *Constitutions*. Mother St. George was not among them.

Even as provincial superior, Mother St. George was dissatisfied with Carondelet's new *Constitutions*. In September of 1866 she wrote to the Cardinal Prefect of the Congregation of Bishops and Regulars in Rome expressing her discontent. She explained that she and other sisters had made their vows under the "old rule" approved by Henri de Maupas in 1651. She claimed that the majority of the sisters in St. Paul had been against adoption of the "new rule" even though they eventually voted for it. She maintained that she and others found themselves "in a religious order, essentially and totally different from that to which we did primitively bind ourselves," and that they were subjected to rules "which we never vowed to observe." She requested permission to be able to "separate from Carondelet, to resume the "Old Rule" and live under it in the diocese, subject to the Ordinary." Her letter was signed by six sisters who said many others agreed with them, although the others did not add their signatures to the letter. Mother St. George also asked the Cardinal that Carondelet not be informed about their request.[37]

Mother St. George's letter to the Prefect spoke of the sisters' great consternation about the new rule without delineating the precise changes that so disturbed them. The last phrase quoted above underlines the key difference between the "old" and the "new" rule. The only significant divergence of the 1860 rule from the Constitutions brought from France in 1836 was the congregational model which designated a sister Superior General as the major superior of sisters serving in various dioceses with Provincial Superiors governing the provinces which could also be multi-diocesan. The "old" rule had specified that the local bishop would be each community's major superior with nearly unlimited authority. Although no one apparently publicized the fact, the change adopted by Carondelet copied most of its essential elements from the Lyon *Constitutions* of 1858 which may have been based on that of Le Puy which was approved in 1852. Like Lyon, Carondelet explained the changes as modifications designed to "increase the mutual support and dependence of the various Houses among

---

36 Carondelet's "new" 1860 *Constitutions* received a Decree of Commendation in 1863, a decree of temporary approval in 1867 and final approbation on May 16, 1877. (Dougherty, 367)
37 The six signers were Sisters M. George Bradley, Mother Provincial, M. Victorine Shoultz, Assistant, St. Protasia Deboille [sic], Instructress of Novices, Agnes Veronica Williams, Counselor, Aurelia Bracken, Directoress of Schools and Ignatius Cox. (Archives, Carondelet)

themselves…[and] give greater stability and uniformity to the whole congregation."[38] One can only surmise that the discontented sisters preferred a clerical superior or were perhaps unaccepting of the actual Carondelet superior, Mother St. John Facemaz.[39]

There is no record that Mother St. George received a reply to her letter to the Prefect and she remained in office through 1868. After completing her term as provincial, Mother St. George was assigned to the Academy of Our Lady in Peoria, Illinois. In the summer of 1868, without informing superiors at Carondelet, she left Peoria for Erie where Mother Agnes Spencer received her. The two sisters had surely maintained contact over the years and would have enjoyed some mutual understanding. By the time Mother St. George arrived in Erie, that Congregation had been established for eight years and was apparently operating as a diocesan congregation under the authority of the local ordinary.[41]

Mother St. George
Bradley
1824 - 1901

Mother St. George arrived in Erie in the company of Sisters Emilena Ellis, Aurelia Bracken and Madeline Hipples.[42] Upon receiving them, Mother Agnes asked Mother St. George to take charge of the hospital in Meadville.[43]

The precise circumstances of Mother St. George's withdrawal from Peoria are somewhat unclear. Undoubtedly there was some ill feeling on all sides as the Carondelet community struggled with the implications of congregational governance. In addition, Mother St. George's assignment to Peoria seems to have

---

39 As noted earlier, Mother St. John Facemaz was one of four missionaries who came from Moutiers in 1854. Mother St. John assisted Mother Celestine until her death in 1857. As part of the first group of missionary Sisters of St. Joseph to come to the congregation after 20 years, she may have been considered an outsider from France in a community made up of primarily of native-born sisters and immigrants from other countries. Under Mother St. John's influence an 35 additional sisters eventually joined Carondelet from Moutiers.

41 Sister Leonie Shanley, (Come to the Waters, 54) states that the original Constitutions guided the community through the greater part of the 20th century.

42 A letter from Sister Helen A. Hurley of St. Paul to Sister Grace Aurelia at the Carondelet Generalate states that "Sister Aurelia Bracken and Sister Madeline 'ran away the night before renewal of vows under Carondelet rule to join Mother George." (Hurley to Grace Aurelia Flanagan, June 10, 1950. Archives: Carondelet)

43 The coming of the sisters from Peoria/St. Paul must have been a godsend as Mother Martha Bunning had returned to Canada in May, 1868, after having had charge of the orphanage in Erie. When Mother Martha left, Mother Agnes took charge of the Erie orphanage and brought the novitiate and orphanage to that site. The Meadville site was designated as a hospital and Mother St. George and her three companions were there by January, 1869. The portrait of Mother St. George is the work of Sister Magdalen Prochaska, taken from Sister Margaret Quinlan, Sisters of St. Joseph of Cleveland, illustrated by Sister Magdalen Prochaska (mimeograph publication: St. Joseph Convent, Cleveland, Ohio, 1963).

been an unfortunate choice of mission for a sister who was not happy with the current state of affairs in community. Sister Assissium Shockley of Carondelet spoke of grave problems in Peoria when she wrote her memoirs. She said that after completing a term as superior in a difficult mission in New York, she returned to Carondelet and was "enjoying sweet repose" until:

> I was appointed to replace Mother George who had left Peoria to open a mission in the state of Ohio, independent of Carondelet.
> I supposed that the Peoria mission would close considering the circumstances under which it was left, "But man proposed but God disposes." I found the mission in a bad condition in more ways than one. I had little courage to attempt a new work but I felt that I was not there to complete the destruction which had already begun…[44]

Sister Assissium explained that the major reason she thought the mission was headed for demise was a $7,000 debt.[45]

Sister Assissium's account offers two interesting bits of information that add context to Mother St. George's departure from the Carondelet congregation. First, upon leaving her role as provincial, Mother St. George was sent to a mission in serious trouble. Secondly, the circumstances and motive for Mother St. George's departure from Peoria were not clear to the members of the Carondelet community. While Sister Assissium believed that Mother St. George left to found a community in Ohio, Mother St. George went from Peoria to Mother Agnes Spencer in Erie and spent some time under her leadership before going to Ohio. Clearly, at least for some time, there was little communication between the sisters who left from Peoria and the Carondelet community. As Mother Seraphine Ireland of St. Paul later related her understanding of the story,

> On July 1, 1868, she [Mother St. George] left her mission in Peoria, Ill. without the knowledge or permission of her superiors. This false and unfortunate step was soon repented of and through the mediation of Bishop Grace of St. Paul she was granted full release from all obligations to the Congregation of the Sisters of St. Joseph of Carondelet, thus leaving her at perfect liberty to establish herself elsewhere.[46]

---

44 Memoir of Sister Assissium Shockley. (Archives: Carondelet)
45 Sister Assissium learned of the debt from parish trustees who were willing to lend her the money to salvage the situation. The Peoria Academy continued to function well into the second half of the twentieth century.
46 Letter of Sister Seraphine Ireland to Mother Theresa of Cleveland, June 1, 1922. (Archives: Carondelet) Mother Seraphine Ireland was Provincial Superior in St. Paul from 1882 to 1921. She wrote this just after she left office. Mother Seraphine gives no explanation of what Bishop Grace of St. Paul had to do with the case as Sister M. George left from Peoria, which was then in the Diocese of Chicago and under the St. Louis Province

Obviously, there were tensions among the sisters that were not documented beyond the evidence gleaned from Mother St. George's letter to the Prefect, Sister Assissium's memoires and Mother Seraphine's letter. Mother Seraphine gives the impression that it was Bishop Grace who helped Mother St. George when she was at odds with her Carondelet superiors. At the same time, demonstrating her ability to interpret everything in the most favorable sense Mother Seraphine continued her letter, sharing her own sense of Mother St. George, her assessment of the happenings and the eventual outcome. Writing to Mother Teresa, the second superior at Cleveland, she said:

> I knew Sister Mary George intimately both as a teacher and fellow religious, and can therefore speak of her with authority. While with us, she was at all times most edifying and was highly esteemed by all who came in contact with her....In 1867, when we received from Rome the Decree of Commendation of our *Constitutions* – the last step toward final approval, Sister Mary George along with a number of other sisters, became dissatisfied with the new form of government....Thus it seems that Almighty God in his wisdom and goodness draws good out of all things. He has drawn great glory to Himself and great good to souls by the zealous works of the excellent and edifying community of the Sisters of St. Joseph of Cleveland, founded by Mother St. George Bradley.[47]

Looking back on the events of her early days in community Mother Seraphine clearly had no rancor about the divisions of the 1860s.

THE SISTERS OF ST. JOSEPH IN OHIO
In 1871, within three years of Mother St. George's arrival in Erie, Mother Agnes sent sisters to staff a school in Painesville, Ohio. After they had been there little more than a year, Bishop Mullen, the successor to Bishop Young in Erie, decided that he wanted the members of the Congregation to serve exclusively in his diocese.[48] When the Erie sisters had to withdraw from Painesville, Mother Agnes saw it as a perfect opportunity for Mother St. George to relocate from Meadville to the school

---

of the Sisters of St. Joseph. Mother Seraphine's letter is the only source of information about this.
47 (Archives, Carondelet) The letter is also quoted in Sister Margaret Quinlan, Sisters of St. Joseph of Cleveland, 70-71. Mother Seraphine had entered the St. Paul Province of Carondelet in 1858 and had been one of Mother St. George's students as well as a younger member of her province community and a colleague.
48 Bishop Tobias Mullen, an Irish immigrant, became the third Bishop of Erie in 1868, two years after the death of Bishop Joshua Young who had invited the Sisters of St. Joseph to Erie in 1860. Mullen remained in office until 1899, when he resigned due to ill health and died in April, 1900. It seems that Bishop Mullen may have exerted more control over the sisters than did his predecessor, or at least he thought that the Erie diocese needed their exclusive service.

in the Cleveland Diocese. By turning the mission over to her, Mother Agnes was able to conform to Bishop Mullen's directive while not leaving the mission untended.[49] The Erie "Datebook" entry for August 16, 1872 noted:

> Mother M. George Bradley, accompanied by Sister M. Aurelia Bracken and Sister M. Madeline Hipples, left the Erie Diocese to take charge of St. Mary's School, Painesville, Ohio, which our Sisters had relinquished... This was the initial step in the foundation of the Sisters of St. Joseph in the Diocese of Cleveland.[50]

Two events solidified the status of the Ohio mission as a new foundation. On February 8, 1873, Bishop Mullen wrote a transfer of obedience for the three sisters, saying:

> To whoever may read this letter we make known and testify that the obedience, given to us, of Sisters George, Aurelia and Magdalen of the Sisters of St. Joseph, now residing in the town of Painesville in the State of Ohio, is transferred to the Most Reverend and Illustrious Richard Gilmour, Bishop of Cleveland.
> + T. Mullen, bishop of Erie[51]

That document gave the sisters official canonical status in their new mission. The second occurrence, equally important in terms of their future, was noted quite simply in the Erie datebook. Under the date of March 19, 1873, it said: "The first investiture of Mother St. George's foundation in the Cleveland Diocese took place with Bishop Gilmour officiating." The women who received the habit that day were Theresa Sullivan (Sister Josephine) and Mary Herlihy (Sister Seraphine) who had come from Meadville to Painesville with Mother St. George

---

49 Painesville was not the only mission of the Erie Sisters in Ohio. The "Datebook" (annals) for November 1, 1870, states: "Reception at the Mission House, Akron" for Sisters Mary Teresa and Elizabeth and notes that Sister Teresa Killian after making one year and nine months of novitiate in Akron transferred to Erie where she completed her novitiate. An entry dated "August" adds "The Akron mission of the Buffalo Sisters...having closed, Sisters Teresa Killian, Celestine Donnally, and Josephine Donnally, came to Erie to assist the Sisters of St. Joseph there." Apparently there was some collaboration between Buffalo and Erie in those years, an interesting fact given that Mother Agnes Spencer had left Buffalo because of serious disagreements with Bishop Timon. Bishop Timon died in 1867, ironically in the same year that Carondelet obtained temporary papal approval of their Constitutions.

50 "Datebook," (Archives SSJE).

51 Quinlan, 2. Except for the reference made by Mother Seraphine to Bishop Grace's releasing Mother St. George of obligations to the Carondelet congregation, there is no official record of the sisters' transfer from Carondelet. The Carondelet profession book notes imprecisely that Mother St. George "left to found another community in Cleveland 1869."

and companions.[52]

FROM PAINESVILLE TO CLEVELAND

The Sisters of St. Joseph's beginnings in the Diocese of Cleveland is best understood in light of the history of Catholicism in that area. Until 1835 the city of Cleveland had no resident priest and its first permanent church building was dedicated in 1840. Surprisingly, given that background, Cleveland was made a diocese in 1847 and Catholic immigration was such that by 1880 nearly one-third of the 261,353 people in the city were Catholic and thousands of students were attending Catholic schools staffed by the Ursulines, Sisters of Charity, Sisters of the Immaculate Heart of Mary, Sisters of the Humility of Mary, the School Sisters of Notre Dame and the Sisters of St. Joseph.[53]

When Mother St. George and her companions began their ministry in the Diocese of Cleveland in 1872 they would have been more conscious than almost any previous founding group that they were beginning a venture destined to become an autonomous Congregation of St. Joseph. Mother St. George had left the Carondelet community because she disagreed with the multi-diocesan congregational/provincial model instituted in 1860. After finding a temporary home with the Erie Sisters, a need in the Diocese of Cleveland that the Erie congregation could not continue must have appeared as a gift and call of the Holy Spirit. Not surprisingly, the Cleveland Community adopted the 1836 *Constitutions* brought from France which designated the local bishop as the major superior of the Congregation. Bishop Gilmore seemed to have a solid rapport with Mother St. George and her growing community. It was under his direction that the sisters opened their schools and his was the final and perhaps also the the first word when it came to decisions about moving the motherhouse, purchasing property, etc. Although the community was ultimately under his control, his correspondence with Mother St. George seemed to be cordial and non-authoritarian as evident in a letter of July 1888. Bishop Gilmour wrote:

---

52 Quinlan, 3. Sister Josephine, born in Ireland, was twenty when she was received and Sister Seraphine of New York was sixteen.

53 See The Encyclopedia of Cleveland History: Parochial Education, http://ech.case.edu/cgi/article.pl?id=PE Bishop Gilmour promoted Catholic education and successfully fought a movement to tax the Catholic schools and eventually take over their buildings. After a 6-year court battle, Bishop Gilmore won his case and became widely known for his promotion of quality Catholic education and his legal expertise in matters of church property. The population count is from the U.S. Census.

July 12, 1888
Mother George,
Dear Child,
I would be much pleased could you arrange to send Sisters to Ashtabula for the coming scholastic year. That would be acceptable to Rev. Fr. Smyth. To withdraw your sisters from there as proposed would seriously interfere with the good of the schools & would greatly inconvenience Rev. Fr. S.
Please let me know your answer at earliest convenience. If you call here Sat. this week between 9 & 10 you can see me.
Yours truly in Christ,
+ R.G.[54]

Some other bishops would have simply told Mother St. George where the sisters should be; that was his right under the "old" Constitutions. Bishop Gilmour was clearly asking her to take his reasoning into consideration – and he gave her a little time to do so as July 12 of that year was a Thursday.

One feature which distinguished the Cleveland Sisters of St. Joseph from other diocesan communities in the early days was that they were a small group in a diocese already served by a number of religious communities. Bishop Gilmore apparently had a freer relationship with Mother St. George and her small community than did bishops in dioceses in which the Sisters of St. Joseph were the principal diocesan community upon whom the bishop depended to staff his works.

As in almost every foundation, the Cleveland sisters struggled financially at the beginning. They augmented their income with creative endeavors, possible in part because Sister Madeline was talented as both a seamstress and portrait artist. By November, the community was able to make a down payment on a $150 piano which they planned to pay off monthly with their earnings of $10 to $12 per month for music lessons. At the end of 1873, the community had excess funds of exactly $6.41 and had received two

Ledger
Sisters of St. Joseph in Painesville
Expenses as of August 28, 1872
❖ Groceries $20.60
❖ Delivery of Trunks 4.40
❖ Wood for cooking 5.00
❖ Bedding 40.50
First Salary Payment:
October: $100

---

54 Archives CSJoseph, copied from Archives of the Diocese of Cleveland.

novices from the local area. The community had grown to a total number of seven sisters.[55]

After the sisters had been in Painesville for three years, Bishop Gilmore invited them to open a mission at Annunciation Parish in the city of Cleveland. There, three sisters established a small boarding school and offered private instruction in music, French and art. Within a year of opening the Cleveland house, the community experienced its first death. Sister Josephine Sullivan, the first local woman to enter the community, died on March 19, 1876, exactly one year after she had received the habit.[56]

With the new mission and twelve sisters in the community, finances were improving and in June 1877, they were able to purchase a two-story "motherhouse" on Fulton Street in Cleveland.[57] At that time the community members were:

Mother St. George	Bradley Sister Celestia Giblin
Sister Madeline	Hipples Sister Eugenia Bowan
Sister Seraphine	Herlihy Sister Angela Kennedy
Sister St. John Murphy	Sister Vincentia Dillon
Sister Augustine Spencer	Sister Josephine Powers
Sister Evangelista O'Brien	Sister St. Joseph Walsh.[58]

A sign of the harshness of life in that era is the fact that this list includes the second young sister the community would lose to death in their first five years. Sister St. John Murphy died on November 5, 1877.

---

55 Quinlan, 5-6. Quinlan adds that they bought a second piano in 1873 and that the sisters' accounts were checked annually by the bishop or his representative.
56 Quinlan, 9.
57 This house had been the diocesan seminary and, according to some of the sisters, it was haunted. (Quinlan, 11.)
58 Quinlan, 11. Notable in the list is the absence of Sister Aurelia Bracken and the presence of Sister Augustine Spencer, Mother Agnes' blood sister. Sister Aurelia would later appear among the Sisters of St. Joseph in Watertown and Idaho. Sister Augustine's biographical record at Carondelet indicates that she was missioned in the St. Paul area from 1853 to 1855 and then at Long Prairie, Minnesota from 1855-60, thus she was there at the same time as Mother St. George. Sister Augustine was listed as beginning at the Peoria mission in 1863 and her time of leaving there is not noted, but Erie records show her in Erie in 1864. By 1879, Sister Augustine was with the Carondelet community, ministering at St. Bridget Half Orphan Asylum where she died in 1881. It seems that some sisters' understanding of membership in a particular congregation could be rather fluid.The illustration is from Quinlan.

The sisters opened a select school on the Fulton Street property and in September 1877, they purchased a horse and carriage for $217.50. By 1880, they needed additional space to accommodate the school and the community which now had nineteen members. With helpful friends who loaned them the necessary funds they purchased a house with five acres on Starkweather Ave. where they moved the Motherhouse and Select School in July 1880. In 1890, they purchased more land and built a three-story building. [59] The addition was needed as thirty-three women had entered the community since 1875.[60]

The sisters were served by priests from a Franciscan community nearly an hour's walk from the Starkweather motherhouse, a trudge frequently alleviated by sending a hired man or some sisters in the carriage to bring the chaplain to the house.

In 1885, Mother St. George completed the process of securing the legal incorporation of the community in the State of Ohio under the title "Sisters of St. Joseph." The community continued to grow and to take on teaching missions in the area, including for a time a school in Muncie, Indiana. In the mid-1880s Mother St. George considered founding an independent Indiana community in Muncie or Tipton but conversations with Bishop Gilmour led

"New Starkweather"

the community to abandon the plan and the sisters in Muncie were recalled to Cleveland in 1886.[61]

In 1889, Mother St. George was 65 years old and had been a Sister of St. Joseph for 42 years. She had ministered in St. Louis, St. Paul, Peoria, Meadville, Painesville and Cleveland and had established the Cleveland community on solid footing. In August of that year Bishop Gilmour, concerned about the amount of responsibility she carried, wrote her the following letter.

---

59 Quinlan, 11, 12. The account book cited above lists loans from the Bishop, two pastors and the father of one of the sisters totaling $3.463.95, a sum which included the odd amount of $1163.95 from Rev. E. O'Callaghan.
60 Quinlan, 14.
61 Quinlan, 14. For additional information about disagreements in regard to the mission see the section on the foundation of Tipton.

August 3, 1889
Mother George,
D. Child,
I think it will be well for you to have some assistance in the increasing work connected with the management of your community. And as I do not think it in order just yet to have an election for officers, I hereby appoint Sister Teresa [Fitzmaurice] your assistant. This appointment is to take effect on receipt of this letter.
Yours truly,
+R Gilmour
Bishop of Cleveland[62]

The letter sounds somewhat curt and there is no record of conversations the bishop may have had with Mother St. George before sending it. For a variety of reasons the bishop's directive had little effect on the community.

Bishop Gilmour, born the same year as Mother St. George, was in failing health by 1889, but he continued as ordinary of the diocese until his death in April, 1891.[63] His successor, Bishop Ignatius F. Horstmann, was consecrated nearly a year later, on February 25, 1892. Bishop Horstmann came to Cleveland from Philadelphia where he had served both as a pastor and as Chancellor which would have made him familiar with the Sisters of St. Joseph in Philadelphia. In October 1892, clearly concerned about the state of the Cleveland community, he appointed Reverends W. Moes and H. Knappmayor, S.J., to conduct a canonical visitation of the congregation. The priests' report to the bishop underlined a number of concerns. The first was Mother St. George's age and inability to govern the community adequately. Connected to that they

Mother St. George
in her later years

---

62 Archives: CSJoseph, copied from the Archives of the Diocese of Cleveland. Quinlan writes that Mother St. George was in her 80s at this time, but if her birth year is 1924, she was 65, a venerable age in those years when the average life expectancy was under 50 years. Sister Theresa Fitzmaurice, Mother St. George's newly named assistant, had received the habit in 1879.
63 See Michael J. Hynes, *History of the Diocese of Cleveland: Origin and Growth* (1847-1952), (Cleveland: Diocese of Cleveland, 1953), 195-197. Bishop Gilmour's ability to maintain calm and befriend all sides in the shoals of controversy is well attested to by the fact that Archbishops Elder of Cincinnati and Ireland of St. Paul and twelve other bishops attended his funeral at which Bishop McQuaid of Rochester preached. Some of those bishops had been in open and public disagreement with one another for years, particularly around issues of Catholic education.

perceived a dedication to the apostolate that overrode the need for a solid program of religious formation.[64] The priest visitors concluded that the sisters had taken on responsibility for too many schools, that a change of leadership was necessary and that a novice director should be brought in from another community until such time as a Cleveland sister would be adequately prepared to fill that role. They also suggested that an election for a new superior take place as soon as feasible and that the bishop himself name the director of novices and assistant.

The community's rationale for sending novices to teach had been that they needed to know if they were suited for the apostolate of the Congregation. The priest-visitors suggested that rather than diminish the novitiate program, sisters should make temporary vows, thereby giving them time to experience the apostolate before being accepted for perpetual vows. Finally, the visitors said that the *Constitutions* then being used were "vague on various points" and suggested that the community adopt the *Constitutions* of either Buffalo or Philadelphia, both of which were in the process of receiving Vatican approval.[65]

As a result of the visitation Mother St. George resigned her office in 1892 and Sister Madeline Hipples took her place until December 29 of that year when the sisters held their first congregational election, presided over by Bishop Horstmann.[66] Thirty-four sisters voted and elected Mother Evangelista O'Brien as superior and Sister Angela as her assistant. Mother St. George, Sister Presentation Carey and Sister St. John Quilty were named as councilors.[67] In addition to the election and appointment of the council, Bishop Horstmann arranged for Sister Teresa Fitzmaurice to go to Philadelphia for six months to be trained as novice mistress. Mother Evangelista served her three year term as Superior General and then asked to be relieved of the responsibility. When Sister Teresa Fitzmaurice

---

64 See "Report on Canonical Visitation, 1892" copied from Chancery Archives, November 14, 1950 (Archives CSJoseph). 65 The major difference between the two would have been that Buffalo was approved as a diocesan congregation and Philadelphia as a congregation of papal right. The Buffalo Constitutions seem to be those published in 1880 in West Seneca, NY. (This edition seems to have been used by various congregations in New York) It is a reproduction of the 1847 translation of the French Constitutions brought by the first missionary sisters from Lyon. The major difference between the papal and diocesan congregations of St. Joseph is that in the diocesan, the bishop holds ultimate and somewhat detailed authority over the congregation.

66 Quinlan, 15, states that Mother St. George resigned her office at the end of the 1892 August retreat, but the visitation happened in October and indicated that she was still superior and wanted to resign.

67 Quinlan, 15-17. Mother Evangelista was about thirty-six at the time she was elected and some twenty years previous had been the first woman from the Cleveland diocese to enter the Congregation. Quinlan notes that in January, 1894, Mother Clement of Philadelphia, the same who offered a home to Mother Bernard Sheridan and her poverty-stricken Kansas community, wrote that Sister Theresa had acquired the knowledge and skills necessary to run the Cleveland novitiate. In 1892, when Sister Theresa went to Philadelphia, the community had seven novices and six postulants.

returned to Cleveland she served as novice director for only two years before being elected to replace Mother Evangelista as superior General. Mother Teresa was first

elected in 1895. Between 1895 and 1943, she served for two non-consecutive twelve-year periods and one additional six year period, giving her a full thirty years in office.[68] It was during Mother Teresa's first term as Superior General that Bishop Horstmann approved the use of the *Constitutions* of the Sisters of St. Joseph of Philadelphia by the Cleveland community.

Mother St. George died on July 12, 1901 at the age of 76. Her last days were spent in the sisters' new home on Rocky River Drive, the property that would serve as the motherhouse for the Sisters of St. Joseph of Cleveland for more than a century. During her 53 years as a Sister of St. Joseph, Mother St. George had known her share of contention and risk. She

Mother Teresa
Fitzmaurice

had left one congregation, stayed with a second and founded a third. She lived to see one of her own sisters repeat her pattern when Sister Gertrude Moffitt and companions went to Watertown and eventually founded the Congregation of the Sisters of St. Joseph of Tipton, Indiana. Undoubtedly strong of will, Mother St. George Bradley forged her own path and brought others along on adventures that Mother Seraphine Ireland recognized as works that flowed from God's wisdom and goodness and brought great good. Nearly eighty-five Sisters of St. Joseph of Cleveland, the entire congregation, gathered to celebrate her life and to lay her to rest with the fourteen Cleveland sisters who had preceded her in death.

MULTIPLE CONGREGATIONS, ONE SPIRIT

After the Sisters of St. Joseph of Carondelet initiated their congregational union in 1860, other independent congregations continued to be founded in response to local needs, often by unconventional leaders or small groups who would have never guessed where the Spirit and circumstances would lead them. The connections, and sometimes the dissensions, among these intrepid women led to the establishment of Congregations of St. Joseph from the east to west of the United States. Each congregation gave its own particular expression to the

---

68 Mother Theresa Fitzmaurice served from 1895–1907, 1913-1925 and 1937–1943.

charism of living and and spreading the Great Love of God.[69]

As communities of Sisters of St. Joseph were formed in different parts of the country not only were there myriad friendships connecting the groups with one another, but many sisters, like Mother St. George Bradley, served in a variety of local communities that only later became defined as distinct congregations. It seems that in some cases these women identified themselves generically as sisters. Because of the habit they wore they quite likely thought of themselves as Sisters of St. Joseph, but clear congregational identities were only in process in the years between 1836 and the turn of the twentieth century. Talk of charism was at least 75 years away even as Sisters of St. Joseph were distinguishable by the unusual breadth of their ministries. The sisters' sense of congregational identity may have been analogous to that of diocesan priests whose identity and ordination as priests took some precedence over their sense of belonging to the diocese for which they had been ordained. This is particularly striking for the Sisters of St. Joseph of Watertown whose founders came from Carondelet, Erie and Buffalo and many of whose members joined other congregations after having been in Watertown.

THE "CHECKERED CAREER" OF MARGARET MARY LACY AND THE FOUNDATION OF THE SISTERS OF ST. JOSEPH OF THE DIOCESE OF OGDENSBURG

Margaret Mary Lacy entered the Carondelet Congregation on November 2, 1860 a few days before her twenty-first birthday and six months after Carondelet had decided to organize as a Congregation with multiple provinces.[70] The daughter of Peter and Catherine (Toole) Lacy, she was born in Cohoes, New York, and would have known the congregation through the sisters in the diocese of Albany. On March 19, 1861, Margaret Mary received the habit and was given the name Sister Mary Herman. While she was beginning her formation at Carondelet, Sister Agatha Guthrie was appointed the first Provincial Superior of the Troy Province and in 1862, Sister Mary Herman, although still a novice, was sent as one of the founders of the new province's mission in Saratoga. She made her vows on July 30,

---

69 Although they all knew Father Médaille's Maxims, when Sisters of St. Joseph of the 19th century articulated their charism, they generally referred to being founded in the spirit of St. Francis de Sales, saying that they should endeavor "to emulate the spirit of the Sisters of the Visitation." (Chapter 1, *Constitutions* 1884, New York.)

70 According to the Carondelet records, Margaret Mary Lacy was born 12/04/1839 in Cohoes, New York. Some sources cite her baptismal name as Mary Helen, but the records from the congregation she first entered indicate that she was named Margaret Mary. That adds to her reasons for taking that name after she left the Carondelet congregation in 1876.

1863 in St. Joseph's Church in Troy under the auspices of Mother Agatha Guthrie.[71] From 1863-1865 Sister Mary Herman taught at St. Joseph Seminary in Troy and in 1865 she was both the director and a teacher at the Cathedral Grade School in Albany.[72]

Between 1863 and 1875, Sister Mary Herman was missioned in a variety of locales, almost always in a position of leadership. Her assignment record for that time reads as follows:

1863 - 1865: St. Joseph Seminary, Troy: Teacher
1865 - 1871: Cathedral Grade School, Albany: Directress and Teacher
1871(March) - 1872 (January): St. Bridget Grade School, St. Louis:
   Founding Directress and teacher
1872 - 1873: St. Joseph's Academy, Chillicothe, MO: Founding Superior
   opened the school
1873 - 1874 (November): St. Bridget Grade School, Chicago: Teacher
   and Superior
1874 - 1876 (April): Cathedral Grade School, Albany: Superior.

Hidden in that résumé are two periods of great distress involving conflict with local bishops.

THE KANSAS CITY INCIDENT

After her first years in Albany, in 1872, Sister Mary Herman opened the school and was superior in Chillicothe, a small western Missouri town about 90 miles northeast of Kansas City. It was there that she encountered the wrath of Bishop John Hogan.[73] According to Sister Winifred Mahoney, Bishop Hogan of Kansas City unjustly deposed Sister Herman from the position of local superior.[74] Sister Winifred narrated the details of a series of incidents that took place in 1872 while

---

71 Mother Agatha served as provincial superior until 1866 when she became Assistant Superior General and then 1872 when she was elected as Superior General and would continue to be elected to that office until her last term ended with her death in 1904. According to the profession book, Sister Herman was the first Sister of St. Joseph to make vows in the province of Albany.
72 The "seminary" was a school, not an ecclesiastical seminary.
73 Bishop Hogan, born in Ireland, was ordained in St. Louis and served as a missionary in rural western Missouri for many years before being named Bishop of the new diocese of St. Joseph (1868) and later of Kansas City (1880). As a missionary, he worked extensively in the areas of Chillicothe and Brookfield where Sisters of St. Joseph would open communities under his episcopal jurisdiction.
74 Sister Winifred's story was transcribed in 1951 and preserved by Sister Wanda Swantec. (ACSJ) Sister Winifred had known Sister Herman slightly and had lived with some of her closest friends from whom she heard the stories she shared.

Sister Herman was superior of the community at Chillicothe.[75]

In the days before automobiles, superiors, for the sake of economy and sociability, would go at stated times during the year from their little country or small-town missions to the nearest large city to do the community shopping. Thus it was that Mother Mary Herman made regular trips to Kansas City…where she was welcomed and assisted by her dear friend, a superior at one of the Kansas City houses.

On one such visit, a few of the sisters confided to her that their superior was too friendly with a priest. Mother M. Herman weighed the matter and spoke to the Superior who passed it off lightly. Mother Herman then took the reports to be the result of jealousy. Confidence in her friend remained unshaken. She did not feel obligated to do more than to listen and offer advice. After all, she was merely a visitor. [76]

Criticisms reached Bishop John J. Hogan. He took the affair seriously and sent for Mother Agatha [superior general at Carondelet]. He questioned her and called her to account for not changing the Superior. Knowing nothing about the affair, Mother Agatha was chagrined at his accusations. She inquired among the Sisters and chided them for not informing her. They told her they had spoken of the matter to Mother Herman on several occasions, and therefore, they considered their duty performed.

Reverend Mother sent for Mother Herman…she obeyed. Shockingly surprised at all that had been made of what she considered unimportant, in an interview with the Bishop, with the accused friend present, Mother Herman became indignant. She defended her friend, quoting canon law (of which she was a scholar) to prove her points. When the interview was over, she, not her friend, nor Reverend Mother, the clergyman in question…but Mother Herman was deposed from her office as superior and ordered to St. Louis. She obeyed, although the injustice of it all must have weighed upon her.

Thus far the incident paints Sister Herman as a well-educated and articulate

---

75 As Sister Herman Lacy was a local superior in some Carondelet communities, but never in provincial or general leadership, we will refer to her as Sister Herman, unless a quoted text reads otherwise. She will be called Mother Margaret Mary when referring to her role in the Watertown and Nazareth congregations.
76 At that time St. Teresa's Academy was the only local convent in Kansas City. In the surrounding area there were only two others: Chillicothe and Brookfield which was about 30 miles east of Chillicothe. The indication that Sr. Herman was a "visitor" intimates that the sister in question was Sister M. de Pazzi O'Connor, the superior at St. Teresa's Academy from 1871-1877. Sister De Pazzi entered the congregation a few months after Sr. Herman and was missioned in Binghamton, NY, from 1861-1869. She made vows at Troy less than a month after Sr. Herman made vows there. Thus the two would have been novices together and then were both in western Missouri in 1871.

woman who could believe in her own prudential judgment. The fact that the bishop found no fault with the priest or the sister about whom complaints had been made actually supported her original conclusion about the triviality of the matter and points to the idea that the bishop took action because he was upset because of her response to him. Sister Winifred plainly said that Sister Herman became indignant, defended her friend and quoted canon law as an expert; apparently either her attitude or her aptitude moved the bishop to have her deposed. Mother Agatha's later actions showed her support for Sister Herman. Sister Winifred continued her narrative saying:

> Reverend Mother Agatha sympathized and realized what all this meant to Mother Herman. It was a crisis in her life. Her stay at Carondelet was short. Reverend Mother sent her to Troy, New York for a visit and rest. In those days a home visit was a rarity, but Reverend Mother wanted to soften the sorrow for Sister and the time thus gained would help people to forget.[77]

According to Carondelet records, in 1873, Sister Mary Herman went to Chicago as a superior and then returned to Albany in 1874, again as a local superior.

SISTER MARY HERMAN: FROM CARONDELET TO SACRED HEART TO WATERTOWN

When Bishop McCloskey became Archbishop of New York in 1865, Bishop John J. Conroy was named second bishop of Albany and Sister Mary Herman was made Directress of the Cathedral grade school in Albany, a position which would have brought her into close working contact with the new bishop and his vicar general, Rev. E. P. P. Wadhams.[78] According to reports, she had a very good relationship with the bishop. When Bishop McNierney was named coadjutor and expected to take over the administration of the diocese great divisions ensued and Sister Herman supported Bishop Conroy.

Sister Winifred Mahoney's plain-spoken narrative explained the situation succinctly:

---

77 Sister Winifred's narrative is titled "Sister Mary Herman, Carondelet Archives: Story by Sr. Winifred, C.S.J., 1951." The interview notes are found in the Archives of the Congregation of St. Joseph and were used by Sister Wanda Swantec in writing Sisters of St. Joseph, Nazareth, Michigan, 1889-1929 (Nazareth, MI, Printed by Borgess Hospital, 1983).
78 In 1872, Wadhams would be named the first bishop of Ogdensburg, where he and Sister Herman would again be in contact.

Bishop McCloskey…was the first Bishop of Albany (1847-1864). Bishop
Conroy was appointed his successor in 1865. He became an alcoholic.
Bishop McNierney was made his coadjutor bishop in 1872 and Bishop
Conroy was asked to surrender the See. He refused. In 1874, Bishop
McNierney was made administrator of the diocese of Albany. Factions
arose among the priests of the diocese and Monsignor Walsh headed
those in favor of Bishop Conroy…

Sister Emily Joseph Daly adds the following details to this part of the story:

During the closing years of his [Bishop Conroy's] episcopacy, the
nature of his illness…enlisted the sympathies of his friends among the
clergy and religious, many of whom resented Bishop McNierney's role.
Among these latter was Mother Herman. As a consequence, she fell into
disfavor not only with Bishop McNierney, who requested that she be
removed from office, but also with her religious superiors in St. Louis.

Recapping the details, Sister Herman had been in Albany until the year the
coadjutor came. Then came her ill-fated year in western Missouri followed by
a mission to Chicago. She returned to the Cathedral school in Albany until the
events of 1876 changed the course of her life.

The problems in Albany led to Sister Herman's return to Carondelet
and in December, 1876. Rather than receive a different assignment, she arranged
to transfer from the Sisters of St. Joseph to the Religious of the Sacred Heart in
Kenwood, New York.[79] According to some sources, she had always had a love for
that community and thought that her current circumstances indicated that she
should transfer to it. She did not seek a dispensation from her vows, but rather
received permission and $100 from the Carondelet community with the promise
of an additional $100 to bring to the community in Kenwood. She traveled from
Carondelet to New York in the habit of the Sisters of St. Joseph and was received
by the Religious of the Sacred Heart.[80]

Unfortunately, Sister Herman's problems followed her to her new locale.
Sister Wanda Swantec explains what happened next.

She was there but a few months when the superior announced one day

---

79 Sister Winifred's narrative indicates that neither the Troy provincial nor the Superior General of Carondelet
would see Sister Herman at this point, but that Monsignor Walsh of Albany gave her the train fare to reach
Kenwood. The documentation from Carondelet contradicts that perception.
80 This information comes from files on Sister Mary Herman in the Carondelet Archives.

that there would be a community Mass said by a visiting prelate, Bishop Hogan...At the Mass the bishop apparently recognized Sister Herman. After breakfast he asked to see the postulants and novices. Sister Herman, dreading the encounter with Bishop Hogan, begged leave to be excused. The superior acceded to her request and Sister Mary Herman did not appear. The Bishop remarked that not all the postulants had come to the parlor. The superior explained that Sister Mary was indisposed. The Bishop insisted on seeing the missing postulant. They met, but both pretended this to be their first meeting.

After leaving the convent, Bishop Hogan wrote the Brooklyn prelate of his encounter with Sister Mary Herman in Missouri. The next day the Religious of the Sacred Heart received an order from their bishop to dismiss Sister Herman immediately[81]

What happened between her leaving the Religious of the Sacred Heart in 1876 or 1877 and December of 1880 is unclear. There are some indications that Sister Herman visited her friend Sister Jane De Chantal Keating at St. John's Home in Flushing, New York. Other accounts say that she spent her time with the Sisters of St. Joseph in Rochester where Mother Stanislaus Leary had been Superior for eight years. Another report said that she stayed some time with the Carondelet Sisters outside of Albany. No matter which stories conform to fact, they each indicate that she sought refuge with Sisters of St. Joseph and continued to identify with them, even if not with one particular congregation.

In 1880, Sister Herman, now identifying herself as Sister Margaret Mary, became aware that a priest friend who had been Vicar General in Albany, Rev. E. P.P. Wadhams, had been named Bishop of Ogdensburg, New York and was looking for sisters to serve in the new diocese.[82] This was the opening for which she had been waiting – another chance to live out her vocation to serve the Dear Neighbor from the context of community.

THE FOUNDATION IN WATERTOWN

The Diocese of Ogdensburg in which Watertown is located was founded in 1872 and was comprised of over 12,000 square miles separated out of the northern part of the Diocese of Albany. The first bishop, Edgar P.P. Wadhams, was one of a

---

81 Swantec, 4.
82 Swantec indicates that the news may have come through Sister De Chantal, or from Mother Margaret Mary's old friend, Monsignor Walsh or that the Rochester sisters may have informed her, all of which are reasonable possibilities.

number of convert-bishops of the era.[83] He was born in Essex County, New York, near Burlington, Vermont. Ordained an Episcopalian deacon in 1843, he became a Catholic in 1846, and was ordained to the Catholic priesthood in 1850. He became Rector of the cathedral and Vicar-General of Albany before being named to Ogdensburg in 1872, the same year that Bishop McNierney was named as Coadjutor to Bishop Conroy of Albany.[84]

The newly formed Ogdensburg Diocese experienced the tensions typical of the Catholic Church in the 19th century, beginning with discord among immigrants from different nations. When Father Joseph Durin, a French Missionary of the Sacred Heart, took over Sacred Heart Parish in Watertown, the primary clashes were between the Irish and the French Canadian immigrants, the former anxious to assimilate and the latter wanting to preserve their culture and language. That tension lead to the establishment of separate parishes to accommodate their conflicting interests. Father Durin and the Sacred Heart Missionaries had charge of Sacred Heart Parish where French was the primary language. Perhaps because of his European background, he did not take the divisions as seriously as did his people. When he proposed to establish a Catholic school he decided that the planning committee should include the pastors of the two parishes and laymen from each parish. As it turned out, people of the two nationalities had little interest in a collaborative venture; Father Durin decided to open his school at Sacred Heart, the French-Canadian parish.[85]

When Father Durin began his search for a religious community to teach in his school he informed Bishop Wadhams that Sisters of St. Joseph "like Sisters of Cohoes, Troy, Flushing, etc. are ready to come," but that was more of a hope than a reality.[86] It appears that when Father Durin appealed to those communities the best help he got was from Sister de Chantal Keating of Brooklyn who may have referred him to Sister Margaret Mary who was apparently in Buffalo at that time. Somehow, Father Durin contacted Sister Margaret Mary in Buffalo and the two of them began arrangements for the opening of a mission in Watertown, including

---

83 Among others, Archbishop James F. Wood of Philadelphia was raised as a Unitarian and Archbishop J. R. Bayley of Baltimore (Mother Seton's nephew) was raised as an Episcopalian.

84 Wadhams was ordained to the episcopacy on May 5, 1872 by Archbishop McCloskey of NY, assisted by Bishop Louis de Goesbriand of Burlington and Bishop John Williams of Boston. For whatever reason, neither Bishop Conroy nor Bishop McNierney (ordained as a bishop on April 21, 1872) took part in the ceremony.

85 See Sally Witt, CSJ, Sisters of the North Country, *The History of the Sisters of Saint Joseph of the Diocese of Ogdensburg, Watertown, New York*, (Watertown, NY: Sisters of St. Joseph), 2005, 2-4.

86 Again we see the identification of generic Sisters of St. Joseph, regardless of their congregational affiliation: Cohoes and Troy were Carondelet; Flushing was Brooklyn.

the tricky task of obtaining Bishop Wadham's approval.[87]

While some felt that the parish lacked the funds for a school, Father Durin's attitude was that they could not afford to do without it. In a letter dated December 7, 1880, he used his best persuasive arguments and even the occasion of the Feast of the Immaculate Conception to sway the bishop to his position:

> Monseigneur,
> I dare again to solicit permission to have a parish school conducted by two Sisters of St. Joseph...More and more I understand that it is only with school [sic] that I can save this people. Two-thirds of them never go to the Church. Parents do not send their children to the Catechism. I know that the good education of children will draw their parents to the practice of religious duties.
> Therefore on the Eve of the great feast of the Immaculate Conception – in the name of our Heavenly Mother on a day in which you grant so great a favor to the Missionaries of the Sacred Heart in conferring the priesthood to my confrere...I come to implore the permission to open a parish school under the direction of two Sisters of St. Joseph. It will be open not far from our Church.
> The French congregation is poor indeed...and unable to support Sisters but Sisters who will come are not penniless and they are ready to help my mission. I will receive help from some friends outside of the diocese...I have a remainder of my patrimony which I am ready to give if necessary.
> Before all, I want to save souls confided to my care and I know that out of primary good education our works are vain.[88]

A week later Father Durin pressed his case to the limit by telling the bishop:

> The necessity of a parish school is so pressing that I prefer to abandon the attendance of this French congregation rather to keep it without school. I keep the hope that your Lordship will not impose a longer delay to my petition. Sisters promised for Watertown desire a definite answer before Christmas, since they must be sent to another place at that time if they cannot come to Watertown.[89]

---

87 Sisters de Chantal and Mother Margaret Mary were said to be friends and in 1889, Sister de Chantal acted as the intermediary between Mother Margaret Mary and Father O'Brien of Kalamazoo as they began to make arrangements for Mother Margaret Mary to open a community there. (See the section on the foundation at Nazareth, Michigan.)
88 Rev. Joseph Durin to Bishop Wadhams, December 7, 1880. (ASSJWa)
89 Durin to Wadhams, December 15, 1880 (ASSJWa).

When Father Durin wanted to invite Sister Margaret Mary to his parish in
Watertown, Bishop Wadhams was less than enthusiastic about the idea of receiving
sisters who might form a diocesan community.[90] It is safe to assume that Bishop
Wadhams had known the Sisters of St. Joseph and Sister Mary Herman herself
when she served as director of the Cathedral School in Albany from 1865-1871,
and he expressed a favorable opinion of religious communities led by their own
superior. He replied to Father Durin:

> The want of Sisters for the French Canadian Catholics…is not only
> apparent but is great and the demand of a Parochial School is so
> imperative that I am constrained to grant your application for the three
> Sisters of St. Joseph to come from the Diocese of Buffalo….although I am
> compelled to say that I would very much prefer sisters who were subject
> to a Woman Superior, in a large and well-regulated Community. – Really,
> I have no confidence at all in these small isolated and independent
> community [sic] of Women.[91]

Two days later the bishop reiterated his opinion and placed firm restrictions on the
upcoming foundation:

> The conditions I make in granting this permission for these three (3)
> Sisters to come to Watertown, for the French Canadian Catholic children
> are these: First, that in the event of your Community leaving, then the
> Sisters are to go also. The 2d condition is that on no condition are the
> Sisters to open a novitiate or boarding school.[92]

In the long run, those conditions were abrogated and the community would soon
come under the auspices of the Diocese.

Just as interesting as the bishop's conditions are the assumptions under
which Mother Margaret Mary and her companions came to Watertown. When
Bishop Wadhams requested more information about the sisters planning to come,
Father Durin explained that they were coming from Buffalo where they had their
motherhouse. It is true that Sisters Thomas Ryan and Teresa Cusick, both Irish by
birth, had been received and made vows in the Buffalo Congregation but Mother
Margaret Mary's status was less clear. She left the Carondelet congregation in good

---

90 Although they would have known each other through the Albany controversies, the bishop's hesitation had
nothing to do with that affair, and he may not have even realized that Mother Margaret Mary of Buffalo had also
been known as Sister Mary Herman of Albany.
91 Wadhams to Durin, Dec. 15, 1880, cited in Witt, 4.
92 Wadhams to Durin, Dec. 18, 1880, cited in Witt, 5.

standing without seeking a dispensation. There is no indication that after leaving the Sacred Heart novitiate Mother Margaret Mary formally joined any other congregation before opening the mission in Watertown. In 1880, she was ostensibly a Sister of St. Joseph without formal membership in a particular congregation, a fact neither the bishops nor the clergy involved seem to have investigated with vigor.[93] Until they met in person, Bishop Wadhams may have had no idea that Mother Margaret Mary had been known as Sister Mary Herman and had worked for him at the Cathedral School in Albany.

1880 – 1889: MOTHER MARGARET MARY'S DECADE

By the time Sister Mary Herman began her journey to Watertown in December

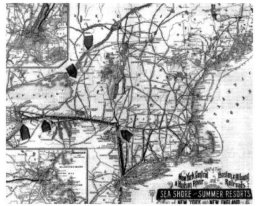

of 1880, she had been through intra-ecclesial drama and life-altering events that seemingly only strengthened her commitment to mission as a Sister of St. Joseph. She was removed from the Diocese of Albany in 1876 for her loyalty to Bishop Conroy and had been deposed as local superior in Chillicothe and later dismissed from the Sacred Heart community at the behest of Bishop Hogan for defending another friend.[94] Now, as Mother Margaret Mary, she was ready for a new beginning.

Map of New York railroad routes in the 1880s. Arrows from left to right: Buffalo, Rochester, Watertown, Ogdensburg, Albany.

Mother Margaret Mary arrived in Watertown with Sisters Thomas Ryan and Teresa Cusick on Tuesday, December 27, 1880.[95] That indicated that they

---

93 According to Father Durin, the sisters had the permission of Bishop Ryan to go from Buffalo to Watertown. We have no indication that Mother Margaret Mary and Bishop Wadhams were in contact at this time. Mother Margaret Mary's status was analogous to that of Mother St. George Bradley in the time between her leaving the Carondelet community and her establishment as founding superior in the Diocese of Cleveland. Mother Agnes Spencer had welcomed her but Mother St. George was apparently not bound to the Erie community because when the bishop recalled the sisters from Ohio, Mother St. George was free to take over their mission.

94 This comes from memories recorded by individual sisters whose details were far from consistent with one another. Sister Herman's assignment record from Carondelet is the only official document testifying to her story from entrance in the community until her death, but that includes a gap in the details about the fourteen years she spent outside the Carondelet Congregation.

95 Witt, 1.

celebrated Christmas in Buffalo and then made the 200 mile trip to Watertown.[96] With all the hurried arrangements, they had to wait five days after their arrival before the harried Father Durin was able to purchase a house for them. On January 13, the local newspaper announced that the sisters had between fifty and sixty pupils, a very promising start.[97] Before the sisters had been in Watertown a month, they received their first novice, Mary Manning (Sister Agnes Gertrude) from Ashtabula, Pennsylvania. Miss Manning arrived as postulant in the company of Sister Aurelia Bracken and received the habit on January 21, 1881. The fact that she came as a postulant ready for the habit indicates that at the same time that the bishop was laying down restrictions, Mother Margaret Mary was preparing for a foundation including a novitiate; she was doing much more than simply opening a mission of an existing community.[98] She solidified her intentions within five months of their arrival by committing to the purchase of the property Father Durin had obtained for the convent and school. On June 30, 1882, Mother Margaret Mary arranged the legal incorporation of the community in the as "The Sisters of St. Joseph of Watertown, N.Y." The trustees of the new corporation included Mother Margaret Mary and the novice, Sister Agnes Gertrude. Another signatory to the document was Sister Josephine Donnelly who had come to Watertown from the Erie Congregation in 1881. Sister Josephine had brought two postulants Margaret Kane and Martha Carey, but they were subsequently dismissed from the community.[99] The community's early days were far from easy.

With the purchase of additional property in July, 1882, Mother Margaret Mary was able to begin construction of a building for boarding students, making education available to the children of dairy farmers from the region and providing the sisters with necessary income. Mother Margaret Mary's next important task

---

96 The map gives a sense of the distances that separated the communities and also demonstrates that while there was no easy communication between Ogdensburg/Watertown and Albany, train service made Watertown relatively close to Rochester, Buffalo and presumably to Erie and other points south and west.

97 See Witt, 12. Except as noted, the information about this decade at Watertown is based on S. Sally Witt's *Sisters of the North Country*.

98 Sister Aurelia (Ellen) Bracken was born in Maine and lived in St. Paul before entering the Carondelet Congregation in 1861. She made vows on January 6, 1864 in the Carondelet Congregation and although Cleveland history indicates that she "ran away before renewal of vows" that apparently refers to the 1868 renewal of vows under the Carondelet Rule first approved in 1867. In 1861, there were no temporary vows for Sisters of St. Joseph. (See Hurley, On Good Ground, 139) Sister Aurelia accompanied Mother George Bradley to Erie and founded the Congregation in Cleveland with her. Sometime after this visit to Watertown she became a founder of the Sisters of St. Joseph of Lewiston, Idaho. After that she seems to have left that community, leaving no indication of where she went. (See below on Lewiston)

99 Witt, 14, notes that neither of Mother Margaret's original companions from Buffalo seemed to have remained in Watertown long enough to participate in the legal incorporation.

was to find a music teacher as music lessons were a vital source of supplementary income to teaching communities; the schools, even the academies and boarding schools, brought in a bare minimum income. Once again, Brooklyn's Mother de Chantal Keating came to the rescue.[100] Mother de Chantal recommended a young woman from Wheeling who not only taught music but eventually entered the Congregation along with three other women linked to Mother de Chantal and Wheeling and one from Piermont, New York.

Of the sisters who joined the community in the early years, the one to wield the greatest influence was Sr. Josephine Donnelly. Born in Ireland and raised in Massachusetts, she came to the Sisters of St. Joseph almost by accident. When she was on her way to enter the Congregation of the Sisters of Charity in Cincinnati, she visited her cousin who was a Sister of St. Joseph of Buffalo ministering in Akron, Ohio. Miss Donnelly decided to stay with that group, eventually transferring her loyalty to the Sisters of St. Joseph in Erie. When she heard of the need in Watertown she reportedly volunteered to be among the founders but had to wait nine months for Bishop Whelan to give her permission to go.[101] She arrived in Watertown in 1881.

By 1885, the community had opened a mission in Carthage, a village about 15 miles from Watertown where the sisters' school was soon serving a student body of 235 children. In 1887 the community counted three missions with a total of twenty sisters and four postulants, plus mortgages for additional properties outside of Watertown.

In spite of positive appearances, all was not well with the little community. Their financial condition was a concern. The worst moment had come at the end of 1884 when Mother Margaret Mary's accounting journal listed her only resource as "The Kind Providence of God," but even after that the community continued to have far more debt than prospects. Additionally, relationships with the clergy in Watertown left something to be desired and there was apparently a growing tension in the community that centered on Mother Margaret Mary and Sister Josephine Donnelly.

Once again getting support from Mother de Chantal Keating in Brooklyn,

---

100 Although Sister de Chantal Keating was not a major superior after leaving Wheeling, people continued to address her as Mother. A supportive friend to any number of sisters and congregations, beginning with her years as visiting superior in Wheeling, her relationships and creativity helped resolve many a problem.
101 There is no record of her reception or profession, leading to the assumption that she was received in Akron where the community maintained a mission for only two years. See Witt, 18-19 for more information about the connections between Wheeling, Buffalo and Watertown and Sister Josephine's probable role in it all.

Mother Margaret Mary began to look for an alternative.[102] Her next opportunity came through Father Francis O'Brien of Kalamazoo, Michigan, who had a well-endowed hospital just waiting for sisters to take charge of it. On July 4, 1889, Mother Margaret Mary departed for Kalamazoo with more than half of the community. Just seven sisters remained with Mother Josephine Donnelly, the newly appointed superior.

THE COMMUNITY UNDER MOTHER JOSEPHINE

Mother Josephine was left with a small, rather diverse community which included one sister professed at Watertown, two or three sisters who had entered the Buffalo Congregation, one who had entered at Knoxville, one postulant, and three others who eventually left the community. The letters the sisters who left the community wrote to Bishop Gabriels, successor to Bishop Wadhams, indicated that life with Mother Josephine was less than easy for at least some of them.[103] Other women entered the Congregation, some only for a short time, and the community survived.

At the time that Mother Margaret Mary left Watertown, the community was running a school in Watertown and another in Carthage and their music teacher was offering lessons in both places. Their income depended primarily on music lessons and an annual fair. That situation was greatly exacerbated by the fact that Mother Margaret Mary had not only taken furniture and household items to Michigan, but had reputedly made purchases for the new mission, running up a debt of $10,000 for Sister Josephine to repay.[104] Five weeks before leaving, Mother Margaret Mary even mortgaged the Watertown property leaving an additional debt of $3,500 to be paid within the year, a maneuver Mother Josephine successfully fought in court.[105] It is hard to imagine what precipitated Mother Margaret Mary's behavior at this juncture but the Watertown community could have been very justifiably angry at being left in such straits.

After taking over the community, Mother Josephine received new

---

102 The full extent of Mother de Chantal's influence on Mother Margaret Mary and the various ways she helped her find ministries remains a mystery except for the fact that her advice and connections seem to come into play at some important turning points in Mother Margaret Mary's life.

103 See Witt, 27-28. Henry Gabriels, a Belgian who had been teaching at St. Joseph's Seminary in Troy, was consecrated Bishop of Ogdensburg on May 5, 1892. He served in that capacity until 1921.

104 This information comes from an extensive letter about Mother Margaret Mary by Sister Celeste Williamson, archivist in Watertown, to Sister Mary Murphy of Albany on September 30, 1980. (Carondelet Archives) Hereafter referred to as Williamson.

105 See Witt, 30-31. Mother Margaret Mary made some other shady financial moves before leaving, including deeding community property to her brother-in-law, which led to another court fight won by Mother Josephine. She tried, unsuccessfully, to sell other community properties as well.

members and undertook their formation in Carthage, effectively making that convent the motherhouse. Although the community was receiving new members, sisters continued to leave and others complained to the bishop or, in at least one case, to the apostolic delegate. While a small diocesan community could seem helpless under the authority of a bishop and the superior he appointed, some sisters did not hesitate to take their cause to a higher level, even though that rarely brought about significant change.[106]

In spite of a series of problems, the sisters continued to teach in the schools they had opened. When Father Cornelius O'Mahoney became superior of the Sacred Heart Fathers in Watertown, he lacked his predecessors' enthusiasm for the parochial school and the sisters. He actually demonstrated more interest in the property than in the ministry being carried out on it. Seeing his waning support, Mother Josephine reminded the bishop that the school was the property of the Sisters of St. Joseph, and although she said "I would rather give it to them than quarrel over it," she also made plans to convert it into a pay school, "making the tuition low enough for the poor; say twenty-five cents per week." She concluded that although the priests would not be a help to her, "God is rich and will do His own work and will take care of us."[107]

Trusting that God would indeed finance necessary good works, the sisters took on an orphanage in St. Patrick's Parish in Watertown. The arrangement gave the sisters and orphans the use and responsibility for three stories of the building where the sisters cared for up to one hundred children.[108] In return they had the right to hold two fairs per year and they could receive elderly women into the home for the price of $2 per week. Sister Gertrude Welsh became the first superintendent of the orphanage in 1897. This spirited woman who did not waver when given the task of caring for numerous orphans and senior citizens, knew how to confront the authorities, and when necessary she let them know with whom they were dealing. She explained how she began to get the institution under her control saying:

They gave me a few dollars and told me to go ahead and do the work. They put us in the upper part of the building and downstairs they would

---

106 Witt, 34, explains that sisters in Watertown wrote to the Apostolic Delegate complaining that they were living "under a depraved superioress." When the Delegate asked about the situation, Bishop Gabriels' response was sufficient for the Delegate and the sisters heard no more about their complaint.

107 The letters O'Mahoney and Mother Josephine sent to the bishop attest to their mutual animosity in this matter. See Witt, 38-40.

108 In a rather odd arrangement for the use of the building, the first floor was apparently first rented from the parish by an undertaker, leaving space for a dance floor on the same level.

run dances all night and expect me to take care of the children while they were kept awake by music. I told them they would have to stop the dances or I would leave the Home. They did not think that I meant it so they ran another dance and I walked out the next day.

The parish authorities got the message: Sister Gertrude ran the orphanage for the next thirty years – apparently on her own terms.[109]

Sister Gertrude had the necessary strength of personality to find and maintain her place among Mother Josephine's sisters. It seems that Mother Josephine could be rigid and stubborn, picking up on the perfectionism that could be extracted from the community's spirit and missing the impulse to temper excellence with gentleness. In that she reflected the Jansenist spirituality of her day. Perhaps for that reason an unusual number of women left the community, beginning with Mother Margaret Mary's band and continuing with others, some of whom sought and sometimes received permission to transfer to other communities.[110] Nevertheless, the community did grow under Mother Josephine's strong direction.

By 1908, when the sisters held their regular Chapter of Elections, the community numbered 30 members eligible to vote. By then, Mother Josephine had been the superior for nearly twenty years. The community was governed by almost exactly the same Constitutions that the first French missionary sisters had brought from Lyon. The Constitutions recognized the local bishop as the major superior of the community and allowed for election of a superior every three years, subject to the bishop's approval. The official record of that election, signed by Bishop Gabriels says:

> At the election held August 22, 1908 at the Mother House of the Sisters of St. Joseph of the Diocese of Ogdensburg located at Watertown N.Y., Rev. Mother Josephine was unanimously re-elected Superior. At the urgent request of the thirty Sisters present Rt. Rev. Bishop Gabriels confirmed Mother Josephine in office for life.[111]

Mother Josephine accepted that decision and served as superior and as director of novices until the 1920s when she named Sister Ursula Sewell to the latter position. By then the community had become well established in the area with about

---

109 Witt, 41.
110 Witt has documented the stories of sisters who joined the New Orleans (Bourg) community and others who applied to Carondelet. (28-29)
111 Witt, 56.

seventy sisters teaching in a variety of institutions. The community had also acquired land in different areas and had even established a Conservatory of Music in Watertown.

Through the years, Mother Josephine had striven to be sure that her sisters were well prepared for their teaching ministries. She was just as ardent about seeing that they fulfilled all that was implied in their vocation as religious. In 1924, she obtained permission to open a normal school for the sisters, a first in the state of New York. That arrangement endured well until 1934, when New York's laws demanded that sisters complete a residency before obtaining a bachelor's degree. That meant that they would have to attend a state institution for at least one year, a demand Mother Josephine would not accept. In essence, although the sisters were adequately prepared, a conflict between state requirements and community regulations prevented them from having the official documentation.[112]

Although Mother Josephine had been legitimately named superior for life, not everyone was content with the situation. Over the years sisters had communicated their grievances to the bishop who would talk to Mother Josephine and accept her perception of the situation. But there were some concerns that came up again and again: adequate care of the sick, a prayer schedule that was overly demanding for a community of teachers and serious questions about the spiritual formation of the sisters. By the early 1920s, those complaints had been addressed to three different bishops. That list included Bishop Joseph H. Conroy, a native of Watertown who had been Vicar General of the Diocese since 1901, was made the auxiliary bishop in 1912 and who became the third bishop of Ogdensburg in 1921.[113]

At the behest of Bishop Conroy, the Vicar General of the diocese began consultations about the community's situation. He bluntly asked one canon lawyer "What are we to conclude as regards the legality of Mother Josephine's appointment for life? The superior is getting to be old and notional, and a change might be a great benefit to her community."[114] The community's situation did not conform to the 1917 Code of Canon Law and Bishop Conroy determined that it was time to do something about it. After he and his representative conducted a formal visitation in which they interviewed each sister, Mother Josephine gave

---

112 Witt, 70-73.
113 When Mother Josephine came to Watertown, Bishop Wadhams led the diocese. Bishop Henry Gabriels came in 1891, less than two years after Mother Josephine had assumed leadership of the community. Although there is no record that Mother Josephine had served in a parish with him, since he had been a priest of the diocese since 1881, Bishop Conroy would have known her well by reputation if not in person.
114 Witt, 75.

Bishop Conroy a report on the Congregation. That report included the information that as of March 12, 1926, there were sixty-six sisters with perpetual vows, "thirteen novices with annual vows," another eighteen novices without vows and seven postulants.[115] After numerous consultations about what to do with a sister named superior for life, Bishop Conroy called for a community election. According to his advisors, he could have named the superior, but he preferred an election. Although he had consulted her, the bishop obviously had not anticipated Mother Josephine's response. Mother Josephine mailed ballots to the sisters in April, 1926, with the following explanatory note:

> ...In order to give our voting Sisters their legal right of official and secret expression of their wishes...all the members of the present chapter, with one exception, have graciously resigned their respective offices and their resignations are accepted...The one exception is the Rev. M. who was appointed for life by Rt. Rev. Henry Gabriels on August 22, 1908... You are therefore respectfully invited to register in type or script...your vote...[116]

Midst mounting speculation, the bishop decided to announce the results of the election at the end of the school year, on July 6, two months after he had received the ballots. By that time the community was in turmoil; some sisters were talking about transferring to another diocese or establishing a separate congregation; others were declaring regret that some had given the impression of disunity; still others felt that they were under pressure from the superior to support her position. With the hope of healing internal strife, the bishop decided to exercise his power over the community. On July 6, 1926, he told the assembled Chapter of Elections:

> Your Mother General and her Assistants...very graciously placed their resignations in my hands...I have decided to name for you a Mother General and two Assistants – to hold office until such time as may seem opportune for a general election. In no case shall their present term of office extend beyond three years from this date...
> I am guided by the secret written vote...indicating your preferences...[117]

---

115 See Witt, 76. The "novices with temporary vows" seems to have been Mother Josephine's invention, together with a rule that classified sisters with perpetual vows as non-voting companions of the novices until they had completed five years of perpetual profession. (Witt, 75)

116 Witt, 76-77, citing Mother M. Josephine, letter to Reverend dear Sister, 30 Apr., 1926.

117 Witt, 77, citing "Memoranda of Election – Mother General Sisters of St. Joseph Watertown, N.Y., July 6, 1929" (Archives of the Diocese of Ogdensburg).

The bishop named Sister Rose-Marie Bennett as superior general with Sisters Ursula Sewell and Gabriels Giblin as her assistants. He gave them the freedom to name additional councilors and a novice director. A week later he learned that the new leaders had chosen Mother Josephine as one of the counselors. He immediately wrote both Mother Rose-Marie and Mother Josephine explaining that in accord with canon law and to give the new administration full freedom, it was not advisable for a superior whose term had expired to continue to participate in the governance of the congregation. With as much tact as possible, he suggested that Mother Josephine immediately take up residence in Port Henry, some 175 miles distant from Watertown, and that if she should later decide to return to Watertown, she live at the Music Conservatory or the orphanage.

As could be anticipated, when it came time for elections in 1929, Mother Josephine was reelected. Although Bishop Conroy was investigating the possibility that the Congregation might eventually join the Carondelet Congregation, the sisters, most likely under Mother Josephine's influence, chose not to pursue that possibility.[118] Mother Josephine continued in office until July 5, 1935. On that day, the last of her final term of office, she died at the age of 87, having spent all but three of the years from 1889 – 1935 as Superior General of the Sisters of St. Joseph of Watertown. At the time of her death the community had approximately 100 members, clear title to various properties and served in the dioceses of Ogdensburg and Pittsburgh. It would fall to her successor, Sister Rose Marie Bennett to begin to heal divisions and fill in the gaps of what Mother Josephine had not been able to accomplish in her forty-three years as Superior General.

MOTHER GERTRUDE MOFFITT: FROM CLEVELAND TO TIPTON – VIA WATERTOWN

The Sisters of St. Joseph had begun their ministry in the Cleveland Diocese in 1872 under the leadership of Mother St. George Bradley. By 1880 they had acquired the motherhouse property on Starkweather Avenue and the community numbered 19 members. It was on March 21 of that year that the twenty-nine year old Miss Mary Margaret Moffitt of Piqua, Ohio, was received into the community and given the name Sister Gertrude. Mary Margaret Moffitt came from a wealthy family and according to tradition, from the time she

"Starkweather"

entered the congregation she dreamed of going "out West." By that she apparently meant at least as far as Indiana. Her hope was to use her father's fortune to found a new community.[119] Thus begins the pre-history of the Sisters of St. Joseph in Tipton, Indiana.

Before she would embark on her westward adventure, Sister Gertrude Moffitt taught in the Cleveland community's missions in Leetonia and Freemont, Ohio, and had been able to contribute an average of $50 per month to the community coffers by giving music lessons. [120] As a young sister she would most likely have been aware of tensions in the community around the far-flung mission in the Diocese of Fort Wayne.

Although the precise details are hard to ascertain, around 1884, the Cleveland sisters opened a mission in Muncie, Indiana. Sisters Genevieve Forestall and Seraphine Herlihy were among the sisters who taught there at St. Lawrence School where the Rev. W. Schmidt was pastor.[121] In 1886, the community authorities in Cleveland decided that the mission should close, much to the dismay of the pastor and the sisters themselves. Some of the discord about the mission seems to have come from hopes that the sisters could establish themselves permanently in the Fort Wayne diocese. Those in favor of the idea included Sisters Genevieve and Seraphine, Father Schmidt and the local bishop, Joseph G. Dwenger.

The first documentation we have of the situation comes from a letter Bishop Dwenger of Fort Wayne sent to Bishop Gilmour of Cleveland.[122] On July 9,

---

119 The History of the Sisters of St. Joseph, Tipton, Indiana, compiled by Sister Ruth Whalen, S.S.J., from Sister M. Gerard Maher, S.S.J. and Sister M. Caroline Daele, S.S.J. *A Modest Violet Grew: Historical Sketch of the Sisters of St. Joseph Tipton, Indiana, and Sister Agneta: "Moving On" and "On the Move"* (Tipton, 1986), 13. Hereafter, Tipton History. Unless otherwise noted, the information in this section is based on Tipton History. An enigmatic note in Sister Ruth Whalen's files says "There is no information...about Mary Margaret Moffit's marriage and tragic accident (groom killed on the way to station to pick up tickets)...Mother Xavier...had a newspaper clipping which Tipton community learned about in 1988 from Mother Xavier's niece." Mary Margaret's hometown, Piqua, was the site of an 1846 settlement of nearly 400 freed slaves whose owner's will had provided for both their freedom and relocation to Ohio, including the finances necessary to purchase land and establish a settlement. (See: http://www.shelbycountyhistory.org/schs/blackhistory/randolphsohio.htm)

120 Leetonia was a town of about 2,550 inhabitants about 90 miles southeast of Cleveland; Fremont, 85 miles west of Cleveland had a population of nearly 8,500.

121 This school is mentioned only in passing in Quinlan (History of the Sisters of St. Joseph of Cleveland) 14. According to the Catholic Directory for 1887 (data from 1886), the Sisters of St. Joseph of Cleveland numbered 19, with five novices and three postulants, and they were serving in six schools in the diocese plus one in Indiana.

122 The two dioceses were under the Metropolitan Archdiocese of Cincinnati, so the two would have had a working relationship. The two bishops were appointed to their dioceses in the same year, 1872. Bishop Dwenger was a member of the Missionaries of the Precious Blood (C.PP.S.) by whom he was educated after being orphaned.

1886, Bishop Dwenger wrote to remind his episcopal colleague of the collaboration they should be able to expect from one another as fellow bishops.[123] The motivation for the letter was what he inferred was an "unlikely rumor" that the Sisters of St. Joseph would be withdrawn from Muncie. He also hinted about the possibility that the sisters from Cleveland working in his diocese could establish their community in his diocese as well. Might he have been thinking of a province as would have been allowed under the Carondelet *Constitutions*?[124] Tucking multiple possibilities safely between the lines and putting his most diplomatic foot forward Bishop Dwenger wrote:

> Rt. Rev. and Dear Friend:
> Rev. Wm. Schmidt of Muncie was here last night and left me no rest till I promised to write to you. For the last two or three years the Sisters of St. Joseph from your city are established in Muncie…doing very well. There was also some talk about these Sisters establishing a regular convent in my diocese, either in Muncie or Tipton. I answered that I would be glad if the sisters could do this and ledged my consent. Father Schmidt now understands and fears that you intend to break up the already established Muncie school and order the entire withdrawal of the sisters.
>
> I told him that I was confident that he was mistaken. You might for very good reasons feel unable to allow more of these sisters to leave your diocese so as to establish a regular Convent and Academy, but that I felt sure that you would not destroy an already established mission and school without consulting the ordinary of the place: that we Bishops could withhold our consent when a new establishment was spoken of – but when an establishment was once made, the Ordinary of said new mission had acquired certain rights that could and would not be ignored by the Ordinary of the parent house. I told Father Schmidt that I was sure you had no idea of breaking up his school.

---

123 Catholic Dioceses are formally organized in "provinces" under the authority of a "metropolitan" archbishop who holds limited authority over his "suffragans" or the bishops of the dioceses in the province. In 1886, both Cleveland and Fort Wayne belonged to the province of Cincinnati where Archbishop John Purcell was the Metropolitan. The bishop of a diocese can be referred to as the "ordinary" and he may have "auxiliary" bishops or a "coadjutor" who would be an auxiliary with the right to succeed the bishop upon his retirement or demise.

124 In 1888, Carondelet was the only U.S. congregation of Sisters of St. Joseph with provinces. The Philadelphia *Constitutions* approved in 1895 also allowed for the establishment of provinces although the congregation never used the privilege. While the Cleveland congregation eventually adopted the Philadelphia *Constitutions*, that did not happen until after the events in question. In 1886, Bishop Gilmour was considered the congregation's major superior and he could decide if the sisters could serve outside his diocese. The Sisters of St. Joseph of Bourg/ Médaille eventually also had three provinces in the United States: New Orleans, Crookston, MN, and Cincinnati.

The 21st inst., Deo volente, we will meet in Cin. With sincere regard I
remain your humble servant in Christ.
Joseph Dwenger
Bishop of Ft. W.[125]

Bishop Dwenger's letter did not have the intended effect. Bishop Gilmour seemed
as unpersuaded as Mother St. George; neither of them supported the possibility
that a separate community could be established in Indiana. Less than two weeks
later, Father Schmidt of Muncie wrote informing Bishop Gilmour about a rather
contentious interview he had had with Mother St. George regarding the sisters in
Muncie.

Father Schmidt was obviously unprepared for his encounter with Mother
St. George. He may have believed that clerical authority would suffice to get her to
acquiesce to his desire to have the sisters remain in his parish. How sorely he had
misjudged his debate partner is palpable in what he wrote to the bishop:

I said to Mother George that the Bishop has promised me sisters...for the
coming year.
She replied, you shall not have them.
I said I would.
She then raised up her hand and shook her finger at me...and said, "I
will write the Bishop tomorrow morning and I will tell him all."
The manner in which this was said...showed me there was an ugly
charge to be made against me...There was a sister teaching there who
never had a kindly feeling towards me. When she went home those
rumors started...
Until last year I was always praised for my kindness. Now I am
condemned. My school is broken up – the hard work of 5 years is in
ruins and I feel sick at heart.[126]

There was obviously more to the story. On the same day that Father Schmidt wrote
to Bishop Gilmour complaining about his altercation with Mother St. George, he
wrote to Sister Seraphine Herlihy who had been in his parish. This letter indicates
that the possibility of a foundation in Indiana had already reached the stage of
plotting if not yet solid planning. They were working out a proposal with the
pastor at Tipton. Father Schmidt wrote:

---

125 Letter of Bishop Dwenger to Bishop Gilmour, July 9, 1886, (ACSJoseph).
126 Schmidt to Gilmour, July 21, 1886. The letter is considerably longer than the section quoted here.
(ACSJoseph, copied from Diocesan Archive)

July 21, 1886
Kind and Dear Sister,
Your welcome favor arrived on the 3:12 p.m. train today and I hasten to
reply. I received a postal from Rev. F. G. Lentz to come to Tipton Monday
and he…wished to speak to me about establishing in Tipton, but I had
only 10 minutes…You know our bishop is more in favor of establishing
at Tipton than Muncie…[127]

As the situation stood, two or more Cleveland sisters had been missioned to
Father Schmidt's parish in Muncie and Sisters Seraphine and Genevieve who had
been there most recently were the ones investigating the possibility of establishing
a permanent foundation in Indiana. Mother St. George apparently would hear
nothing of it, and seemingly had her own source of negative information about
Father Schmidt.

THE WATERTOWN CONNECTION AND
MOTHER MARGARET MARY LACY

When Mother St. George Bradley recalled the sisters from Indiana in July of
1886, they apparently refused to go to Cleveland but were willing to meet her
in Ashtabula, Ohio, a growing city about 60 miles up the coast of Lake Erie. The
Cleveland congregation had a mission there. Although there is no record of that
meeting, by the time it ended the two sisters in question found themselves at odds
with Bishop Gilmour as well as with Mother St. George. They wrote to Bishop
Gilmour in August, 1886 to explain their perception of the situation:

Dear Bishop,
It grieved us to the heart that you would not give us a hearing when we
called at your house yesterday. However, since it is your wish…we shall
explain…
    We left Muncie because Mother St. George commanded us home. The
reason we did not come to Cleveland was that we were in dread lest the
Sisters here knew all about the affair and we felt that we could never be
happy in this community again with that hanging over us. So we went
to Ashtabula where we met Mother George, who by great persuasion
gave us permission to go to Watertown and see if we would be received
into a community of our sisters there.
    We…stopped overnight with our Sisters at Erie…and went to
Titusville…From there we went to Watertown. After arriving there I told

---

the Mother Superior my business. She kindly invited us to rest a few days and advised us to return to Cleveland and speak to our Bishop before we determined on anything…We had not the least idea that Mother George would ask you for our obedience to leave your diocese before you had given us a hearing, for we understood that you wanted to see us when we returned home…

Please forgive us for the trouble and anxiety we have given you. We did not wish to be independent dear bishop without your hearty approval and blessing. Begging you once more to pardon us and give a hearing very, very soon or we will be frantic. Asking you to pray for your children, we are your humble servants.
Sister Genevieve,
Sister Seraphine[128]

In writing this letter, the sisters did not deny that they had hoped to establish a community in Indiana. They simply said that they hoped to do it with Bishop Gilmour's approval and neglected to mention that they already had Bishop Dwenger's support. When their relationships with the Cleveland community became unmanageably strained, they turned to the Sisters of St. Joseph in Erie and Watertown for hospitality and succor.[129] After staying a short while in Erie, the sisters went on to Watertown.

Mother Margaret Mary Lacy of Watertown, while not rejecting the sisters, enjoined them to obtain the necessary permissions. As their letter to Bishop Gilmour indicates, they understood that Mother St. George had already arranged that without their knowledge. The two sisters stayed at Watertown for some time, apparently under the impression that they had received Bishop Gilmour's permission to do so.

In the meantime, Mother Margaret Mary and Sister Gertrude Moffitt were making plans. When and where Sister Gertrude first crossed paths with Mother

---

128 Sisters Genevieve and Seraphine to Bishop Gilmour, August, 25, 1886. (ACSJoseph) There is no explanation of the "affair" to which they referred, but Father Schmidt's correspondence indicates that he had a serious conflict with one of the Cleveland sisters in Indiana and that there may have been conflicts among the sisters as well. That situation exacerbated his problems with Mother St. George.
129 According to some quips of the late 1800s, Erie was referred to as the "Vatican" or sanctuary of the Sisters of St. Joseph. Under Mother Agnes Spencer (+1882), Erie had received various sisters seeking temporary refuge. She had taken in Sister Martha Von Bunning of Hamilton, Canada, and later Mother St. George and her companions. Mother Stanislaus Leary visited her as well. By 1886, Mother Eugenia Quirk had become the superior in Erie, an office she would hold until 1917. In 1886, Mother Eugenia released Sister Bernard Sheridan to join Mother Stanislaus in Kansas.
In addition to having served as a sanctuary to Sisters of St. Joseph seeking refuge, Erie was a natural stopping place along the way north from Cleveland or Indiana. Ashtabula is about half-way between Cleveland and Erie.

Mary Lacy is a matter for speculation, but by 1887, they were in correspondence about a joint venture for which Mother Margaret Mary anxiously awaited Sister Gertrude in Watertown.[130] Mother Margaret Mary was ill and sought Sister Gertrude's help with the novitiate. In return she was promoting the growth of a new community in Indiana and even had news that its first potential candidate was being prepared to come. She wrote to Sister Gertrude replying to a letter that has not been found in the sisters' records. Mother Margaret Mary said:

> I too wish you were here at my side. You could be great assistance to me, and be assured, dear Gertrude, any help given me now in helping to form and encourage our dear novices would be gratefully and eternally remembered. Come soon and help me and later you will find me anxious and determined to help you. I wrote our friend and bade him send a postulant he has for the proposed Mission.[131]

Sister Gertrude
Moffitt

While the letter includes other details about Mother Margaret Mary's delicate health and dedication to work, the last line indicates that Sister Gertrude was also already in contact with clergy in Indiana about a mission there even though her name does not figure in the correspondence involving Father Schmidt, the bishops and Mother St. George. Bishop Gilmour knew of Sister Gertrude's plans to leave Cleveland and apparently thought she was doing so as a result of conflict in the community. He wrote her in August, 1877, chiding her for pride and self-sufficiency, and accusing her of wanting to run away from problems by seeking support from another community.[132] Bishop Gilmour's scolding did not sway Sister Gertrude from her plan. Two weeks after writing to her, Bishop Gilmour wrote to Bishop Wadhams of Watertown saying that two very foolish Sisters of St. Joseph had attempted to run away from their community in Cleveland and that he would be happy if Bishop Wadhams would give them no acceptance.[133]

---

130 Letter of Mother Margaret Mary Lacy to Sister Gertrude, July 6, 1887. (ACSJoseph) With this letter and the fact that Sisters Genevieve and Seraphine turned to Mother Margaret Mary in Watertown, we might speculate that Mother Margaret Mary may have spent some of the time she is unaccounted for in Cleveland, thereby getting to know some of the sisters well enough that they would turn to her in time of need.
131 Quoted in Tipton History, 15.
132 Gilmour to Gertrude, August 15, 1887, copy from ACSJoseph.
133 Letter from Gilmour to Wadhams, September 2, 1887.

Bishop Richard Gilmour
1824 – 1891

When Bishop Gilmour's communications with Bishop Wadhams and Sister Gertrude brought no results he took more drastic action. On September 29, 1887 he absolved Sisters Gertrude and Seraphine from their vows. Although his letter said that the dispensation came at their request, he stipulated that upon receipt of his letter they were directed to "put on a secular dress and return to a fitting and Christian secular life." In May of the following year he wrote a similar dispensation for Sister Genevieve and sent it with a note to Mother St. George asking her to forward it to her address. The stipulations and the request that someone find one of the recipients to deliver the letter lead one to suspect that the sisters' "request" may have been implied from their non-submission to the bishop rather than being a genuine and formal petition for dispensation. With that, one might wonder if those sisters ever received the letters and the order to discontinue wearing the habit and if they ever accepted the dispensation.[134] The possibility that they did not accept those letters is reinforced by the fact that none of the three ceased to identify themselves as Sisters of St. Joseph. Within six months of Bishop Gilmour's communications with her, Sister Gertrude founded a community in Tipton. Sister Genevieve remained at Watertown for a time, then joined Mother Margaret Mary at Kalamazoo before returning to Cleveland where she lived out the rest of her religious life. Sister Seraphine joined the Tipton group after they had become established.

FROM WATERTOWN TO TIPTON

On March 10, 1888, Sisters Theresa Thistlewaith and Josephine Hynes, both of whom had come to Watertown to enter the community under Mother Gertrude, received the habit of the Sisters of St. Joseph at Watertown with the intention of going immediately to Indiana. Bishop Dwenger had already given them permission to found in his diocese.[135] The sisters began their trip from Watertown to Tipton

---

134 Copies of the bishop's letters of dispensation are found in ACSJoseph, but there is no evidence of the sisters' requests for them.

135 The key letter is dated Feb. 15, 1888, from Father Lang, Bishop Dwenger's secretary. Addressed to Sister Margaret Mary he says that the bishop has notified Father Lenz of Tipton that he may receive the sisters as soon as all the details can be arranged. *(Tipton History*, 16.) In the absence of any official permission from either Mother St. George or Bishop Gilmour, Mother Margaret Mary seems to have assumed the authority to receive the postulants and to send the sisters, not unlike what she had apparently asked the Buffalo community to do for her before she herself went to Watertown.

the day after their reception ceremony, traveling for three days via a uniquely circuitous route determined solely by the itinerary of the trains on which religious could receive reduced-rate tickets.[136]

One might wonder why Bishop Dwenger chose Tipton as the site for the sisters' foundation. The Cleveland Sisters had been in Muncie, a town with 11,345 inhabitants, Tipton's population of 2,700 made it seem more like a village.[137] In the words of the community chronicle,

> This sparsely populated country was a western wilderness, where education was but little encouraged and parochial schools were unknown. True, some Sisters had at various times passed through the town, but never had they been tempted to stop, still less to remain.[138]

One source suggests that the reason for the choice of Tipton was that Mother Gertrude had agreed with Bishop Dwenger that her community would "have a special care for the poorer and smaller schools of the diocese."[139]

Whatever the clergy's reasoning, the three sisters, a thirty-seven year old superior and her two young charges, arrived at Tipton in March, 1888. The house designated for their use was not quite ready, so for two weeks they received the hospitality of the McAvoy family who lived in the parish.[140] Although the sisters did not take over the school until the fall of 1888, they had enough to keep them occupied as they were asked to make the altar linens, train the choir and visit the sick of the parish, all while two of them were novices and the other their superior and novice director.[141] The school they opened was a high school for girls which

---

136 The need for free/reduced passage may have been the reason to wait to travel until after the postulants had received the habit and could take advantage of the concessions offered to religious. (See *Tipton History*, 17.)

137 Today, Tipton forms part of the metropolitan district of Kokomo, some 20 miles to the north. In 1890, Kokomo had 8,261 residents, so that even combined with Tipton, it did not match Muncie. In 1888, there was one Catholic parish in each of these places, a sign of the low percentage of Catholics in the populations.

138 *Tipton History*, 18.

139 See: "A Copy of a Letter Concerning Information of Mother Gertrude," (ACSJoseph). This copy seems to have been filed by Sister Ruth Whelan, former archivist in Tipton.

140 *Tipton History* (23) identifies the two Mrs. McAvoys as sisters, Mary being the one who received them into her home while Nora provided the meals. Nora later became the mother of Rev. Thomas McAvoy, C.S.C., a renowned historian and the organizer of the Notre Dame Archives. For more information about Thomas McAvoy and the Sisters of St. Joseph of Tipton see: http://www.catholicauthors.com/mcavoy.html

141 *Tipton History*, 19. The school is called an elementary and high school and according to Sadlier's Catholic Directory for 1889, St. John's School had 75 pupils, an increase of 25 from the previous year. At the same time the Muncie Catholic school had 90 pupils taught by 2 secular teachers, and Kokomo had 60 students with one secular teacher.

graduated its first three students four
years later.[142] The sisters held classes in
their cottage, using the one room that
had plastered walls as classroom and
parlor during the day, refectory in the
morning and evening and dormitory
at night, each setting demanding
the appropriate change of furniture.
The community soon received its
first new members with Sister Agnes
Carr receiving the habit in February
of 1889 and Sister Xavier Donahue in
1891.[143] In between their receptions, in
the summer of 1889, Sister Seraphine
Herlihy who had been missioned in
Muncie joined the new community.

Sister Theresa Thistlewaith
and Mother Gertrude

In 1889, the little group opened a second school, St. Francis Academy in
Kokomo. They then purchased land in Tipton where, with loans and a generous
donation from Mother Gertrude's father, they built a $10,000 convent that was
dedicated in August, 1891. That building would serve as motherhouse and
academy until 1904 when the community built on land outside the city. The major
investment they made in land and buildings made clear the sisters' commitment
to sink their roots in Tipton, little as it was.[144]

As more women entered the community the sisters were able to open
missions in Logansport (1894) and Elwood (1895). By 1900, there were 32 sisters
in the community and four of their members had already died. The first of those,
Sister Seraphine Herlihy died on October 15, 1893. She had lived in communities
in Cleveland, Muncie, Watertown and finally in Tipton.[145]

---

142 St. Joseph's Academy in Tipton remained open until 1972 when its last class graduated.

143 According to "A Saga of the Tipton Hills," an informal history written in the 1960s, Mary Donahue was a
public school teacher who met the sisters when they opened the Kokomo Academy. (Archives CSJoseph)

144 *Tipton History* (27) copies correspondence from Bishop Dwenger encouraging Mother Gertrude to remain
in Tipton as it was "as good as Kokomo, if not better" and because "Your Community especially devotes itself
to poor parochial schools."

145 After Sister Seraphine's death, Sister Agnes Carr died on May 4, 1894. She had been the first to receive the
habit in Tipton. In 1895, Sisters Veronica Thomkins and Alacoque Buck died within two months of one another.

In 1900, with the help of Father Anthony Kroeger, their ecclesiastical superior, the sisters were able to obtain two-hundred acres of land they called "St. Anthony's Farm."[146] After Father Kroeger purchased the land, the sisters assumed responsibility for raising funds by selling art and needlework, and putting on fairs, all augmented by the inheritances of a few of their members who came from well-to-do families.[147] Their hard work inspired donors and by 1904 they were able to dedicate a "commodious" building that had cost $60,000 and would serve as the inaugural construction on a campus that would grow for decades to come.[148] In spite of the considerable sum invested in it, the building was more utilitarian than luxurious. A contemporary description explained:

> The Convent is a very unpretentious edifice of red brick and stone, four stories high. The south wing on the second floor was called "Kroeger Hall," in honor of Father A. J. Kroeger...The Chapel, occupying two floors, is Roman in architecture, very simple in design.[149]

Before the motherhouse was built, Mother Gertrude had extended the community's reach to the Pacific Northwest. In 1903, she sent Sisters Magdalene Thomas, Angelica Heenan and Borgia Tourscher to help a group of Sisters of St. Joseph in Lewiston, Idaho who were working with a Jesuit mission. Sister Xavier Donahue accompanied them because she needed the Idaho climate for reasons of health. Except for Sister Borgia who was an exceptionally well-trained nurse and greatly needed in Idaho, the sisters only stayed about a year before returning to Tipton.[150] In 1904, the community opened a boys' boarding school, St. Joseph's Seminary, in Tipton. Like other congregations, the community continued to grow steadily, opening and closing schools according to local needs and the sisters' possibilities. Mother Gertrude's vision could not be confined to limits of the Fort Wayne Diocese. In addition to their short-term ministry of health care in Idaho, the Tipton community went to the southwest in 1913 to teach in public schools in San Miguel and Ribera, New Mexico.

---

146 The sisters showed their devotion to Father Kroeger not only with the name of the farm but also by creating the "Kroeger Medal" for elocution at St. Joseph's School in Elwood, a tribute to his eloquence and solid counsel. (*Tipton History*, 79.) 147Among the sisters whose inheritances came to their aid were Sisters Theresa Thistlewaith, Xavier Donahue, and De Sales Burns. (Tipton History, 35)
148 *Tipton History*, 34-39.
149 *Tipton History*, 37.
150 Sister Borgia had graduated as a nurse from the Philadelphia Hospital Training School before entering the congregation.

In 1908, with the hope of increasing the number of sisters in the community Mother Gertrude and Sister DeSales Burns traveled to Europe and returned with a group of Irish postulants. That venture was successful enough that they repeated it immediately in 1909, with more visits in the future. Additional members were not the only novelty that came from those trips.

THE MINISTRY OF HEALTH CARE

Tipton Motherhouse in the late 20th century

It was on the ship returning from one of her trips to Ireland that Mother Gertrude met Father Luke Sheehan, a Capuchin Friar bound for Bend, Oregon. The enthusiastic Irish missionary began recruiting help for his mission even before he arrived in the United States.[151] He dreamed of a Catholic hospital and although he and Mother Gertrude shared their dreams about future possibilities, the Tipton Sisters were not involved in health care and she did not have the sisters to give to the venture. But Father Sheehan would not give up on getting the Sisters of St. Joseph to Bend.[152]

The community's first venture into hospital ministry began much closer to home in Kokomo, Indiana. The city of around 17,000 residents was about thirty miles north of Tipton and had one small clinic in lieu of a hospital. In 1912, Dr. Cox, the town physician, helped the sisters establish a 12-bed hospital in a house in which twelve sisters, ten nurses and two cooks shared the attic as their living quarters. As one of the sisters commented later, "Everything in it bespoke poverty...Even the best was poor."[153]

---

151 Mother Gertrude must have met Father Sheehan in 1909 because he himself did not arrive in Bend until 1910 when he was 37 years old and had already served in the missions in the Middle East. See: http://www.crystalballroompdx.com/blog/2016/6/7/284-Father-Luke-s-Legacy

152 Bend's first U.S. census (1910) registered a population of 536. It grew immensely in the next ten years, registering a population of 5,415 in 1920, and 8,848 in 1930.

153 The information on Kokomo comes from *Tipton History*, 45-46 and the The Catholic Moment website: http://www.thecatholicmoment.org/archive/2013/04-28/kokomo-hospital-100-years.html.

As it turned out, poverty may have been a small problem compared to the anti-Catholic prejudice the sisters faced. Did they know they were moving to a stronghold of the Ku Klux Klan? In Kokomo they found themselves in the odd position of serving people who professed to hate them. But that was the problem of the intolerant. Klan or Catholic, it made no difference to the sisters, most especially in 1918 when the flu epidemic called them to make so many house visits that only a few sisters could remain on site to staff the hospital. But even the reputation for service they gained early on made little difference when, in 1923, one of the largest Klan rallies in history took place in Kokomo. The ceremonies included a collection that supposedly garnered $50,000 to build a "Klan hospital" so that Klansmen and their families would not have to use the Catholic hospital. The Klan's new 50-bed hospital failed after five years and the sisters purchased it and its 17 acres of land for $20,000.[154]

The most telling anecdote of that affair came from the day of the Klan rally, July 4, 1923. With 200,000 Klansmen meeting in a town with a population of about 30,000, they started a night-time parade in full regalia. Then, as one of the sisters later told the story:

> As they neared the hospital, strangely enough, one of the leaders fell from his horse with an attack of appendicitis. He was rushed into the hospital, robes and all. The sisters were in the operating room, dressed for the surgery.
>
> As they uncovered the victim, Sister Louis said to him in a surprised voice, "John, what in the world are you doing in that robe dressed like that?" They operated. He recovered and went out of the hospital, one of the best friends the sisters ever had.[155]

Those first sister nurses had little formal training. To remedy that, the community opened a school of nursing that received its accreditation in 1917.

Only three years after the Tipton sisters' first venture into health care, Father Sheehan, the Irish priest Mother Gertrude had met on the ship, was again asking for sisters for Bend, Oregon.

---

154 The Catholic Moment, "History." Additional information and citations can be found at: https://en.wikipedia.org/wiki/Kokomo,_Indiana#Ku_Klux_Klan.
155 The Catholic Moment, "History."

In November, 1915, the general council sent him word that
they would not come. In 1916, Bishop Charles O'Reilly,
the first bishop of the Diocese of Baker City, Oregon, took
it upon himself to find sisters for Bend.[156] Although the
Apostolic Delegate seemingly guaranteed the bishop that
the Sisters of Charity of Nazareth would help, that promise
remained unfulfilled. Then, unwilling to abandon hope,
Father Sheehan traveled to Tipton to appeal to Mother
Gertrude in person. She finally agreed to send him five
nurses but she died on April 28, 1916, before having been
able to carry out the plan.

Fr. Luke Sheehan

Mother Gertrude's successor, Mother Xavier, felt
bound by her predecessor's promise and on Christmas Day, 1917, five sisters
departed from Good Samaritan Hospital in Kokomo on their way to Bend,
Oregon. In 1918, the Sisters of St. Joseph of Tipton took over an existing hospital in
Bend and by 1922, they built St. Charles Hospital which remained under their care
until 1972 when its assets were transferred to the St. Charles Memorial Hospital
Corporation.[157] Although Mother Gertrude was a teacher, as were her first sisters,
it was the ministry of health care that would take the community over 2,000 miles
and almost to the shores of the Pacific Ocean. That more than fulfilled Mother
Gertrude Moffitt's youthful dream of establishing a community "out west."

NAZARETH FOUNDING - A CONVERGENCE OF INTERESTS AND CONFLICTS
MOTHER MARGARET MARY LACY AND FATHER FRANK O'BRIEN

The convergence of circumstances that brought the Sisters of St. Joseph to
Kalamazoo began unpredictably when a diocesan priest was called to give the last
rites to a man dying at the city jail. Father Frank O'Brien, the priest in question,
tells the story as follows:

> In the 1880's the County Poor House was the hospital…the jail was
> used for emergency cases…a "plain drunk" was carried to the jail and
> afforded there the time to sober up amid squalid surroundings…
>
> On one of the State Fair Days a visitor was found in a stupor and
> escorted to the jail and reported as "dead drunk." A few hours afterwards

---

156 Baker City was made a diocese in 1903, with territory removed from the Archdiocese of Oregon City (later
Portland) which was the second archdiocese in the United States, established in 1846. Canadian-born Bishop
O'Reilly served there until being named bishop of Lincoln, Nebraska in 1918. He died in 1923 at the age of 63.
157 In 1943 the military built an annex to the hospital, raising the bed capacity to 60.

the turnkey told the sheriff that he imagined something greater than drunkenness affected the last caller. A physician...pronounced him dangerously ill...a rosary in his pocket proclaimed him a Catholic and a priest was sent for.

The patient was removed from the cell to the corridor. Amid the filth...mingled with curses and coarse jests...the last rites of the Church were administered.

The patient died within an hour. Then and there that priest resolved, God willing, Kalamazoo should have a hospital.[158]

Once Father O'Brien made up his mind, nothing was going to stop him. His first major supporter was the recently retired bishop, Rt. Reverend Casper Borgess who gave $5,000 to support Father O'Brien's dream.[159] Even before having the money in hand, Father O'Brien had been actively trying to recruit sisters to staff his hoped-for hospital. Between 1884 and 1888, Father O'Brien turned to various communities and priests in search of the help he needed. His list of prospective communities included Sisters of St. Joseph from two congregations of St. Joseph in Canada, as well as from Rochester, Brooklyn and Carondelet in St. Louis.[160]

Bishop Caspar Borgess

His petitions ranged from a simple request for sisters to a plan in which he promised to provide postulants for a congregation who would either train them for him or send him a certain number of sisters in return. Time and again superiors turned him down. Then Mother de Chantal Keating arranged an invitation for him to visit the sisters in Brooklyn to plead his cause. [161]

---

158 Wanda Swantek, SSJ, *The Sisters of St. Joseph of Nazareth: 1889-1929, A Chronicle* (Nazareth, Michigan, 1983) 113-14. Except as otherwise noted, Swantek is the major source for material in the Nazareth founding story.

159 Bishop Borgess was the second bishop of Detroit. He succeeded Bishop Frederick Rese who had been consecrated by bishop Rosati in 1833 and was the first German born bishop in the United States. After only four years he "became demented" and returned to Europe where he was institutionalized but did not resign his see. The Detroit diocese was therefore under the leadership of an administrator for 30 years until Borgess assumed the title in 1871. Borgess resigned in 1888 and died at Kalamazoo two years later at the age of 65. He was succeeded by Bishop John S. Foley.

160 Included in O'Brien's correspondence are letters from Mother Agatha Guthrie of St. Louis who said they did not have sufficient sisters to meet their existing commitments and one from the Chancellor of the Diocese of Rochester who spoke for the Rochester Congregation with the same message adding that they were a diocesan congregation. (Swantek, 15-16)

161 Sister de Chantal Keating of Brooklyn seemingly maintained contacts throughout the Congregations of St. Joseph in the eastern part of the U.S. beginning with the years she spent as "superior on loan" in Wheeling. She seemed to have the pulse of the Church and knew how to make fruitful connections for people even when she and her congregation couldn't respond to a given need. In a letter to Father O'Brien she admitted that the

He was allowed to speak to the community, but the superior general would not release any sisters to go to Michigan. Father O'Brien and his SSJ agent were disappointed but far from defeated. Sister de Chantal helped him get in touch with Mother Margaret Mary Lacy in Watertown, the contact that would finally bear fruit.

Although the extant letters between Sister de Chantal, Father O'Brien and Mother Margaret Mary date from early January, 1889, Sister Elizabeth Vary, a member of the founding group in Michigan, remembers that arrangements were being made a few months before that. She wrote:

Sister Mary Herman
Mother Margaret Mary Lacy

> On November 21, 1888, I received the Holy Habit. The same afternoon Reverend Mother Margaret asked me if I could keep a secret. I said, "Yes." "Well, sister, I have been asked to go and start a Community in the diocese of Detroit. If I go, will you come with me?" I said, "Yes," and I meant it....I heard nothing more till April.[162]

In January, 1889, the letters that passed between Mother de Chantal, Father O'Brien and Mother Margaret Mary discussed everything from names of the sisters to be sent to salary arrangements. They even conferred about the possibility of adopting the Carondelet rule in Watertown so that the Detroit bishop might see it favorably.[163] Eventually, Sister de Chantal stepped back and the correspondence

---

for Brooklyn sisters "to satisfy our Houses in this diocese we would want about fifty more Sisters." She went on to suggest that "Dean O'Brien" might send three or four promising subjects to them so that he "might have a claim to a like number of Sisters for a foundation." She added that the Brooklyn community was in the habit of sending a few sisters to found new communities that would quickly become independent. (Keating to O'Brien, November 19, 1888, ACSJBr)

162 Quoted in Swantek, 18.

163 According to Swantek (19), O'Brien, uncertain that the Detroit bishop would want the Carondelet rule, asked Sister de Chantal to persuade the bishop of Ogdensburg to adopt it, thereby giving it greater credibility for Bishop Foley of Detroit. That raises interesting questions about her potential influence with Bishop Wadhams with whom she had never worked. It adds to the evidence that Sister de Chantal may have been influential in making the first connections between Mother Margaret Mary and the Ogdensburg diocese.

As noted in the section on the Watertown foundation, Bishop Wadhams would likely have been happy for a rule similar to Carondelet's as he, unlike many of his contemporaries, avoided becoming involved in the internal affairs of the community and seemingly had far more reticence than desire to have a religious community under his jurisdiction.

continued directly between Mother Margaret Mary and Father O'Brien.[164] That correspondence covered such topics as expected income, a house for a novitiate, the conditions for nursing, sisters' responsibility for an orphanage, etc. At times the exchanges were somewhat contentious with Father O'Brien concerned that nobody involved be "grasping" and Mother Margaret Mary speaking from the experience of previous mistakes and wanting to be as clear as possible about details.

One of the issues that demonstrated the balance in the relationship was Father O'Brien's announcement that he had named his assistant, Father Ryan, as spiritual director for the community. Mother Margaret Mary immediately replied that she thought the sisters should have some say in who would be appointed. Although she herself liked Father Ryan, she insisted that the sisters should all be in Kalamazoo for some time to have the opportunity to know him and give their opinion on the matter before he would be named their director. Father O'Brien acquiesced.

BEGINNINGS – BORGESS HOSPITAL

If Mother Margaret Mary's process of leaving Watertown was marked by conflict, the situation in Kalamazoo promised more of the same, only this time it would involve the civic community rather than the sisters themselves. The Protestants of Kalamazoo who made up the vast majority of the population had great reservations about the establishment of a Catholic hospital in their hometown. A letter to the editor of the Kalamazoo Gazette explained the objections as follows:

> Kalamazoo certainly needs a hospital…but why in the name of all that is reasonable should the Protestants, who are possessed of ninety-nine percent of the wealth, intellect and influence in the city, so quietly yield it into the hands of the Romanists? Once given, it cannot be recalled. The Roman Church is gaining a wonderful power in this country, and as every reader of history knows, it is exactly opposed to all free institutions. Not one cent of public money should go to swell Rome's wealth and power…[165]

The protest and venom was enough that the debate was popularly called "The Hospital War," but that had little effect on Father O'Brien and his supporters. In

---

164 Swantek notes that Sister de Chantal asked that her name not even be mentioned in conversations with Bishop Wadhams. (21)
165 *Kalamazoo Gazette*, January 10, 1889, cited in Swantek, 41-42.

fact, Bishop Borgess, an early proponent of the advertising adage that any publicity is better than none told Father O'Brien,

> The "Hospital War" I am sure will prove a great blessing because it will bring the question before the public in a manner which otherwise would take years to accomplish – and that is all that's necessary for success.[166]

Father O'Brien completed the purchase and remodeling of the property for the hospital in the first six months of 1889. To the chagrin of his adversaries, the complex was blessed by Bishop Foley on June 30, 1889, in the presence of 2,000 onlookers who were led in prayer by a fifty-member choir vested in surplices. The Reverend Thomas Walsh, the President of the University of Notre Dame, presided over the ceremony.[167] The hospital was duly blessed, but the construction was not quite finished.

The sisters who would staff the hospital did not arrive from Watertown until July 6, after a two-day journey that took them through Syracuse, Rochester and Buffalo.[168] The group of ten founders included Mother Margaret Mary and Sisters Angela Kane, Eulalia Ward, Jane Frances de Chantal Cox, Catherine McGuire, Philomena Demers, Elizabeth Vary, Scholastica McHugh, Gertrude Keenan and one postulant, Libbie Nicholson. Sister Genevieve Forestal from the Cleveland congregation joined the group later.[169] The group was to have included one more sister, but in one of her manifestations of volatile decision-making, on the evening of their departure, Mother Margaret Mary summarily dismissed Sister Thecla from the founding group. She simply told her, "I do not want you." With no further explanation she instructed the sisters not to put her trunk with the

---

166 Burgess to O'Brien, February 26, 1889, cited in Swantek, 43.

167 The cornerstone was sealed with a document in Latin that recorded the event as having happened in 1889, while Pope Leo XIII reigned as sovereign Pontiff, John S. Foley being Bishop...Frank A O'Brien being in charge of the Catholics of Kalamazoo County...Benjamin Harrison being president of this glorious republic, etc. One could hardly look for a stronger expression of the Catholic identity of the new enterprise! (See Swantek, 44-45) In 1888, Bishop Foley was consecrated as the third bishop of Detroit by Cardinal Gibbons, assisted by Bishops John Loughlin and Edgar Wadhams. Born in Baltimore in 1833, he attended the Third Plenary Council of Baltimore in 1884 and was a co-author of the Baltimore Catechism. In 1911, he established the first parish for African American Catholics, St. Peter Claver. He died in office in 1918 at the age of 85.

168 The group stayed in a hotel in Syracuse on the night of July 4, probably because they arrived at 2 a.m. and either the hour or Mother Margaret Mary's leadership made it inopportune to seek hospitality with the Carondelet sisters living there. On July 5, they did stay with Rochester Sisters of St. Joseph in Seneca Falls before making the last leg of their journey to Kalamazoo. (Swantek, 46-48)

169 Swantek 46-47. Sister Genevieve was called a "borrowed sister," and needed permission from Bishop Horstman of Cleveland to join the group. He gave her permission only to help the group become established and then to return to Cleveland. She left Kalamazoo on October 20, 1889.

others and they left without her.[170]

The sisters' arrival in Kalamazoo was hardly what they expected. Sister Eulalia Ward recalled the details of that day saying:

> Mother Margaret Mary, a woman of noble mien, frail stature, with intelligence written on every line of her face, stood with her little band of devoted religious in the Kalamazoo depot, satchels in hand, somewhat dazed, as no one, priest or layman, showed signs of recognition. The Sister inquired from strangers about the location of St. Augustine's. Each one carrying her heavy satchel, the band trudged the two blocks to find the school and convent deserted. The doors were locked. We all knew that a telegram had been sent. It seemed a rather cool reception, but we were taught that lasting foundations such as our greatest orders, were built on the cross.[171]

St. Francis Home For Boys, Monroe

Mother Margaret Mary wasted no time before going to the rectory to inform Father O'Brien that they had arrived. He opened the convent for them and invited them to lunch at the rectory where both his mother and his sister Mary had a meal prepared to welcome the group. He then settled the sisters temporarily with the Sisters of the Immaculate Heart of Mary.

On August 15, after spending a little more than a month in the Immaculate Heart convent, the Sisters of St. Joseph moved into the nearly completed hospital. On that same day they received their first two postulants – five more would join them in the coming months. In the evening of August 15, the sisters met with Father O'Brien to make plans to take over St. Francis orphanage in Monroe, 140 miles southeast of Kalamazoo. Six sisters assumed charge of the orphanage on August 19. The hospital was officially dedicated on October 13, 1889. According to the local newspaper, it boasted thirty-of Kalamazoo. Six sisters assumed charge of the orphanage on August 19. The

---

170 Sister Elizabeth assumed that Sr. Thecla was left behind because she had not kept the secret about the new mission, but her last minute dismissal only added to the list of Mother Margaret Mary's inexplicable behavior at this time. Given the tension and divisions in the community, it must have been difficult for Sister Tecla to remain with the group she had planned to leave.

171 Sister Eulalia Ward, "History of the Founding of the Sisters of St. Joseph in Kalamazoo," from Swantek, 48-49.

hospital was officially dedicated on October 13, 1889. According to the local newspaper, it boasted thirty-four rooms for which patients would be charged $3.00 per day. Each room was equipped with a heating grate, a washstand, two chairs and an iron bedstead with two mattresses. In addition there were two wards with six beds each. The report went on to say:

> Mother Margaret who is in charge of the hospital is a pleasant and agreeable person. She has opened two hospitals in the East before coming here and is an experienced and capable nurse.[172]

The newspaper article did not indicate the source of that information.

Sister Gertrude Keenan, one of the founders of the Kalamazoo congregation unabashedly admits the sisters' original inexperience and naiveté. Speaking to the assembled community in 1929, she told them of the early days:

> It was in the month of April, 1889, that Mother Margaret, of loving memory… assembled us in our little Convent in Watertown…to tell us of the new adventure and to ask for volunteers; stating that our immediate work in the West would be the care of the sick in Hospitals, and later on… the work of education.
>   Not having the slightest idea of what a Hospital was like, I formed my own conception – that of the care of the wounded and dying soldiers, as was suggested to me by that well-known picture of the Sister of Charity caring for the wounded soldier…after due consideration, I decided that what that Sister could do, I too, with God's help could do, so I willingly volunteered…

Sister Gertrude's reminiscence provided a delightfully detailed description of the sisters' paucity of preparation:

> Then came our first operation, a wonderful day for us, the preparations made are indescribable, we did not know what the name of the operation meant, but we knew it was an operation and every instrument from the saws to the finest needles were laid on trays, ready for use. We did not

---

172 Swantek, 59-60, citing the Kalamazoo Evening Telegraph, October 14, 1889. One is hard pressed to find information about her nursing/hospital experience in Mother Margaret Mary's assignment records.

know what the doctors thought, but we thought it a grand success, that the Mayo Brothers had nothing on us...

One day a new born baby was brought in to us. Not knowing what to do, we asked an old lady, Mrs. McGH, to take care of it...but the next morning she did not come near us, so we had to do it ourselves. We had just finished caring for it when the Doctor came in. He looked at the baby, then at us and said, "Sisters, that is just fine, and you have grease enough on it to fry it. Of course, we accepted that as a compliment![173]

What Sister Gertrude did not mention were small details like the fact that the operating table was also the sisters' dining table or that the "trays" were the meat trays they used at meals.

On December 9, 1889, the community celebrated the reception of its first five novices: Sisters Mary of the Immaculate Heart Hastings, Bernadette Lamb, Winifred Rooney, Agnes of the Sacred Heart Murphy and Anthony Nolan. This first religious reception in the area garnered extraordinary public attention. Bishop Foley officiated with the assistance of four priests and the 2,000 people in attendance had to produce admission tickets that specified if they had a place in the pews, on stools or only as standing observers.[174] The hope and enthusiasm of this auspicious beginning would be dampened considerably in the next year as Mother Margaret Mary and Father O'Brien came at loggerheads, a situation that would not be resolved peacefully.

THE END OF MOTHER MARGARET MARY'S TERM OF OFFICE

In early 1890, Mother Margaret Mary and Father O'Brien began to disagree on

various details of the sisters' lives. He took his authority as the ecclesiastical superior appointed by the bishop quite seriously and, far from Father Médaille's ideal, he intervened and exercised

Rev. Frank O'Brien
1851-1921

---

173 "Account given by Sr. Gertrude Keenan" @1929," (Archives CSJoseph) Some punctuation has been changed for easier reading. The picture comes from Suzy Farren, A Call to Care: The Women Who Built Catholic Health Care in America (St. Louis: The Catholic Health Care Association of the United States, 1996), 19. (their photos are without attribution)
174 Swantek, 68-69 reproduces a newspaper account of the event with those details.

significant authority in the internal affairs of the community.[175] According to Sister Scholastica McHugh, in spite of what he had promised before the sisters' arrival, Father O'Brien appointed his assistant, Father Ryan as the sisters' confessor and instructor in Kalamazoo. Father Ryan assumed the role also made him the sisters' superior. Mother Margaret Mary not only rejected that usurpation of authority, but also challenged Father O'Brien's decision to alter the community horarium. The conflict grew and Sister Scholastica, the superior at the orphanage in Monroe, got involved and reported to Father O'Brien that Mother Margaret Mary had insulted her and told her she should return to Watertown. The three of them began to exchange argumentative and sometimes insulting correspondence; eventually Bishop Foley stepped in. Following Father O'Brien's advice, the bishop moved sisters from one mission to another and hinted that Mother Margaret Mary's resignation from office would be readily acceptable.

Bishop John Foley

By Holy Week at the end of March, 1890, even though the sisters themselves had come to agreements, Mother Margaret Mary and Father O'Brien had reached an impasse; she seemed to be as stubborn as he was authoritarian. Mother Margaret Mary wrote various letters to Father O'Brien asking that he meet with her, but there is no indication of whether he did so. The situation began to affect Mother Margaret Mary's delicate health and on June 27, 1890, Bishop Foley met with her and gave her permission to take time away from the area to recuperate. One of Sister Margaret Mary's friends described the next events as follows:

> In order to relieve the tenseness of the situation, Father O'Brien had recourse to a ruse. He suggested that Mother Margaret Mary and his sister take a trip…. Mother Margaret protested that she was not inclined…and that she had not time to give away from her present duties. Father insisted that the trip would be beneficial to both of them

---

175 The role of an ecclesiastical superior in the *Constitutions* Father Médaille gave the sisters had only the terse statement: "Their superior will be the bishop or any one he chooses to appoint for them." The sister superior's role was described at much greater length, beginning with the statement that she "should be firmly convinced that she is the representative of God, appointed by the Sovereign Goodness to lead the whole community." (*Primitive Constitutions*, First Part and Fourth Part) Later editions of the *Constitutions*, including that which came to the United States in 1836, described the bishop, not the sister superior, as the representative of God for the sisters. (See discussion in Chapter 5.) The conflict that led Mother Margaret Mary to leave the Kalamazoo community is told in detail in Swantek, 69-107.)

and that he would defray all expenses. As she remarked, "If I had refused him so many things and gone against things he had wanted – this being a thing of minor importance, if it pleased him, why should I not acquiesce?" He insisted there was no time limit…Accordingly Mother Margaret bade her dear Community an affectionate goodbye, promising to write them all the details of the trip. They in turn promised to keep her informed about themselves…

No sooner was she out of the house, according to Sister Eulalia, Mistress of novices, than Father O'Brien came in and said, "Now she is gone and not coming back." He had called them together to elect a new superior. The Sisters were stunned. They said they wanted no election. They cried and argued and in the end he appointed a new Superior.[176]

The bishop stepped in and named Sister Scholastica as the new Superior General under obedience. He also named other officers of the community and ended his communication of the decisions saying:

My principal object in the change of superior is that peace and concord may reign in the Community. I therefore earnestly beseech the members thereof to render strict obedience to the newly constituted Mother and I sincerely trust that the late Superioress will give an example to all.[177]

When Father O'Brien read the bishop's decision to the community he made great efforts to explain his own position. He told the sisters that Mother Margaret Mary had upset the resolution of their problems, that she was "double dealing." He told them that in the year they had been in Kalamazoo, they had made very little spiritual advancement and that "the crisis has arrived." He went on to say:

This Bishop's delegate is more than his vicar-general…And therefore you owe me the same obedience you owe him. I have all along been loath to exercise this power…
Hereafter my actions will be in accordance with my appointment and my authority will be exercised. There cannot be two heads in this Community. The Bishop is the only head. He uses me as his tool, and the Mother must be my tool…The Bishop alone is responsible for the success or failure of this community. Not Mother or any Sister, and while Mother's queer way of acting may have been prompted by feeling that the responsibility rested with her, she was in error. I find it impossible for me, her community Superior, to get along with Mother…I am

---

176 Sister Winifred Maloney "The Story of Sister Mary Herman," quoted in Swantek, 80-81.
177 Bishop Foley to O'Brien, July 1, 1890. Quoted in Swantek, 81-82.

convinced unity cannot exist between us. Hence I have requested the
bishop for the good of the Community to depose the present Superior.
This he has done.[178]

As might be expected, Father O'Brien's explanations did not relieve the tension in
the community. The sisters accused him of withholding the letters Mother Margaret
Mary wrote them as well as those they wrote to her. When Mother Margaret Mary
wrote complaining that the sisters had neglected her, he read that letter to the
community to show them her lack of care for them.

Mother Margaret Mary did return to the community around the middle
of October but the conflicts raged on. Father O'Brien counseled the community to
not pay her travel expenses. They refused her permission to copy the new custom
book, presuming she wanted to submit it for inspection outside the community.
Mother Margaret Mary's letters to Father O'Brien became so angry that he accused
her of using vile language and lacking all respect for authority.[179] He actually
suggested that she might be insane and arranged to have her examined by the
Chief of Staff at Borgess Hospital. The physician reported that he found her in
a condition of physical and mental prostration due to continual impaired health
and mental anxiety and unrest resulting from inharmonious relations with the
superior at Borgess Hospital. But he did not find her insane.

Very soon after her return to Kalamazoo, Bishop Foley began a process
of dispensing Mother Margaret Mary from her obligations to the Kalamazoo
community. On October 30, 1890, she and Mother Scholastica signed a written
agreement in which the community provided Mother Margaret Mary with
$200 and she absolved them of any claims she might have brought against the
community "from the beginning of the world to the present." She neither asked
for nor received a dispensation from her vows, simply a release from mutual
obligations between herself and the Kalamazoo community. Where she went at
that point is uncertain, perhaps she visited other Sisters of St. Joseph or family.

---

178 Reverend O'Brien "Address to the Community," July 2, 1890 (Swantek 81-84)
179 Swantec (89-90) copies letters airing a particularly heated argument in which Mother Margaret Mary refused
to apologize to O'Brien. On October 15, 1890 she wrote to him that she could easily ask pardon for an offense, in
fact, "I would ask pardon of a Negro had I deliberately wronged him." She went on to say that she had asked his
pardon when she felt there had been no offense and asked him to explain his reason for demanding an apology
at this time. His reply turned her words around saying "you state you would ask pardon of a Negro as soon as
you would of the spiritual father of the community." He went on to reiterate his belief that she was insane. He
concluded with the statement that "The vile language of your letters must be atoned for...When you express a
desire to do this in the proper language of a lady, not to say religious, I will then, and only then, consent to an
interview." Once again Mother Margaret Mary would suffer the consequences of being ecclesially powerless
when involved in a dispute with clergy.

She was, for the second time in her life, a sister without a congregation. Before the end of the year she approached the Carondelet community where her first superior in New York, Mother Agatha Guthrie, was now superior general. Mother Agatha, who was also the superior under whom Mother Margaret Mary's problems with Bishop Hogan had begun, readmitted her to the congregation. She re-assumed the religious name Sister Mary Herman and as a sister on probation took her place with the lowest rank in the entire community. In December of 1891, on the day of the anniversary of her return to the community, Mother Agatha Guthrie stood up from her place at the head table in the dining hall, went to Sister Mary Herman and asked her to accompany her back to the table of the professed sisters where she was seated in the place and with the rank she would have occupied had she never left the community.

After spending some years in St. Louis, Sister Mary Herman was missioned to Kansas City where she renewed her relationship with Sister Monica Corrigan, a friend who was her intellectual match and with whom she enjoyed discussions and debates on a variety of topics ranging from philosophy to current events. In 1908, Sister Mary Herman was missioned to Los Angeles where she lived at St. Mary's Academy until her death in 1926.

Margaret Mary Lacy, Sister Mary Herman, Mother Margaret Mary, lived an unusual, difficult and surprisingly fruitful life as a Sister of St. Joseph. A woman of great intelligence and spirit, she followed her own lights and was also plagued by weak physical health and emotional unpredictability. Her early problems with Bishop Hogan and the dissension in the Albany diocese seem to have been rooted in her strength of character and fidelity to friends. Between the years of 1888 and 1890, she exhibited irascible and erratic behavior that cannot be explained solely by the tensions of the situations in which she found herself. The conflicts she had with Sister Josephine of Watertown and Father O'Brien were surely not the sole fault of either side, but her explosive temper and occasional vindictiveness showed the marks not only of her strength of character but also hint that she may have had another serious problem that led at times to unbecoming conduct and even seriously unjust treatment of others. Whatever that problem, she seemed to overcome it at the time she returned to Carondelet at the age of sixty-one. If her life story was a mystery to most of the sisters she lived with in her later years, her kindness and prayerfulness, and even her playfulness brought her into their hearts.[180]

---

180 Sister Winifred Riecker of Los Angeles recalled that one summer day she was in the hall when "All at once a

THE COMMUNITY UNDER FATHER O'BRIEN

With the bishop's help, Father O'Brien had rid himself of Mother Margaret Mary and thought he had the superior he wanted in charge of the community. He made it known that Mother Scholastica was to seek his approval for almost every decision she made and he was quite willing to rule in the smallest of matters. At the same time, he did what he could to assure the future of the community, including removing the Sisters of the Immaculate Heart from his parish so that the Sisters of St. Joseph could staff it and receive its income.[181]

Mother Mary Scholastica
Mc Hugh
1890-1891

Before long, Mother Scholastica was finding herself in conflict with Father O'Brien. Just about a year after she had been appointed, on the profession day of five novices at the end of the year 1891, the bishop called for a meeting of the community at which he "gave them a sermon on pride and removed Rev. Mother Scholastica from office" and also dismissed one of the sisters from the community.[182] He appointed the new community officers, naming Sister Philomena Demers as Superior General. In response to discontent in the community, Father O'Brien told Sister Mary Hastings that she must accept appointment as novice director and told another sister to cease her murmurings against the new arrangements "under the pain of mortal sin."[183] Father O'Brien continued to issue directives regulating minute details of the sisters' lives, and his major complaint against sisters centered on their lack of respect for authority.[184]

As the community grew they were able to open new missions, but the

---

very slight little nun...an octogenarian, came up to me and, with a smile in her sparkling eyes as well as on her thin lips, said: "I'll bet I can beat you running up the stairs." I took up the challenge and surely enough, she reached the top before I did. Then we both laughed and became engaged in conversation." (Swantek, 102) Sister Winifred was born in 1881, Sister Mary Herman, the octogenarian in 1839.

181 Swantek, 111.

182 Swantek, 113.

183 Swantek, 115-116. Sister Scholastica apparently appealed to both Carondelet and Watertown to receive her as a transfer from Kalamazoo, but she remained with the community until her death.

184 Swantek (120) notes that O'Brien edited a customs book which spent 13 pages explaining "obscure" passages in the Holy Rule and went on to every aspect of the sisters' lives including how to walk, talk, play, study, teach, and what was to occupy their time at each interval from 5 a.m. to 9:15 p.m., all intended to "promote uniformity of manners among the members of our little congregation."

center of their concern was Borgess Hospital. Due to financial straits the hospital was on the verge of being sold at the end of 1891, but the people of the city rallied to give it moral support while Father O'Brien used his personal funds to make up deficit even as he looked for donors. For their part, the sisters not only begged but also used their income from schools to underwrite their healthcare ministry until it became self-supporting.

In 1896, the community purchased a farm as the site of the motherhouse they needed. The 120 acre site would not only serve as novitiate and motherhouse, but also house an academy. Although only two of the sisters invited to name the new property suggested the name Nazareth, the community invited Father O'Brien to choose a name for it, and after asking the consent of Bishop McQuaid of Rochester where the Sisters of St. Joseph's motherhouse bore that name, he named the property Nazareth.

Mother Philomena, first appointed by Bishop Foley in 1891, was the first superior to serve a full term of office; the bishop then appointed her to a second term which came to an end in 1897. On August 12, 1897, the Sisters of St. Joseph of Kalamazoo held their first election and the forty-nine professed sisters who voted elected Sister Anthony Nolan as their new superior general. Under her leadership the new motherhouse opened and the community quickly began receiving students into their Academy. At the beginning of the school year they had eight students and they ended the school year in June, 1898 with twenty-four young women enrolled. Although a sister was named as directress, Mother Anthony was the de-facto administrator under Father O'Brien's supervision. Father O'Brien took it upon himself to oversee the girls' writing classes.[185] He also did all he could to make the Academy known. He wrote articles for newspapers and was able to arrange for famous people to make public appearances there. His list of visitors ranged from the President Benjamin Harrison to senators and church dignitaries including bishops and apostolic delegates. Father O'Brien's dreams were as large as his guest lists and included the exploration of the possibility of opening a medical college for women religious. Undoubtedly some of his enthusiasm for the idea came from the fact that his own sister, a physician, entered the congregation after completing her medical education. He submitted his idea to the apostolic delegate but apparently did not get the support he would have needed to begin the endeavor. He was, however, able to override Mother Anthony's reservations

---

185 O'Brien was an author who published a history of the diocese, *The Diocese of Detroit. What it was. What it is.* (1866) and several historical articles in Michigan journals.

and allow the sisters who worked in the operating room to wear white instead of black.

In 1902, the community opened a boys' section of Nazareth Academy that soon became independent and outgrew its original quarters. By 1911, they had an enrollment of 136. In 1901, Borgess Hospital needed to expand and the cornerstone was laid for a new building on June 10. The modern building included an equipped operating room, something which Sister Gertrude surely appreciated, as well as a bed elevator, clothes chute, electricity, bath facilities and more. Sister Agatha Ganley was elected in 1903 to succeed Mother Anthony as superior general and she presided over the chapter following her election which considered a variety of issues including whether newly professed sisters could join the sisters in the community room, if sisters could wear black aprons and sleeves in the classroom and whether the community should open a Normal School. After discussion, most decisions were postponed until Father O'Brien could be present.[186]

In 1905, the community finished the construction of a new building to serve as convent and academy. It opened in September with 42 pupils. They opened additional schools of which perhaps the most unusual was Villa St. Anthony, opened in 1899 for girls with intellectual disabilities. By 1912, the community had opened Nazareth College as the collegiate department of Nazareth Academy; it was chartered in 1924 as a four-year liberal arts college.[187]

The Catholic Directory of 1912 indicates that the community of The Sisters of St. Joseph of the Diocese of Detroit numbered 176 sisters, 15 novices and 7 postulants. By 1922, the Directory listed 219 sisters, 31 novices and 12 postulants. The community was growing steadily.

Until his death in 1921, Father O'Brien remained involved in community affairs making his influence felt in everything from Chapters to schools, the campus grounds and the lives of the sisters. In the last year of his life he arranged for Mother Evangelista, the Superior General, to continue in her term for an extra year because "he felt that because of his failing health it would be too difficult for him to direct the affairs of the community through a new superior general."[188]

During that year the bishop directed the community to prepare any improvements they thought necessary in the community rule so that the General Chapter of 1922 could approve it. The bishop also authorized the community

---

186 Swantek, 171.
187 Information compiled by the Archivist at Nazareth, Winter, 2107. (Author's files)
188 Swantec, 253.

to obtain their official incorporation as the Sisters of St. Joseph of the Diocese of Detroit. As they neared their Silver Jubilee as a community, in spite of the myriad of troubles they had been through, the community was on solid ground.

ଚ

Chapter Seven:
The Design Spreads: Brooklyn to Baden, Rutland, Boston and Springfield

Cast of Characters

Mother Teresa Mullen – Superior General, Brooklyn, 1868-1892
Mother Austan Keane – Founder: Brooklyn (1856), Baden (1869), Rutland (1883)
Mother Hortense Tello – Second Superior General – Ebensburg/Baden
Mother Mary Regis Casserly – Founder: Boston – 1873
Mother Cecilia Bowen – Founder: Springfield - 1883
Mother Albina Murphy – Second Superior General, Springfield

Father R. C. Christy – Pastor in Ebensburg
Bishop Domenec – Pittsburgh
Father Charles Boylan – Pastor in Rutland
Bishop Goesbriand – Burlington
Father Thomas Magennis – Pastor Jamaica Plain
Bishop Thomas O'Reilly & **Bishop Beaven** – Springfield

MOTHER TERESA MULLEN

As Superior General of the Sisters of St. Joseph of Brooklyn, Mother Teresa Mullen sent her sisters to open the missions that became the Congregations of the Sisters of St. Joseph of Baden (1869), Rutland (1873), Boston (1873) and Springfield (1883). In 1868, she became the third general superior and the first elected superior of the Brooklyn congregation. Succeeding Mother Baptista Hanson, she served eight terms in office, a total of 24 years.[1] When she came into office the Congregation had a debt of $41,000 on their properties. At the end of her last term, all debts had been paid, leaving the community in full, free ownership of their properties. In addition to her acumen as a businesswoman, her piety and friendliness made for a legendary combination. As one of her sisters explained,

> Mother Teresa had great devotion to the Rosary and the Psalter and a Sister who perhaps wanted to make but a brief visit to the Chapel would prefer to go two or three pews ahead than within reach of the Superior who was likely to call on the one beside her to join in one of the favored devotions.

---

1 Mary T. Mullen was received into the Congregation of the Sisters of St. Joseph of Brentwood on March 19, 1859 and received the name Sister Teresa.

Mother Teresa's kindness and thoughtfulness in regard to the Sisters and their relatives, especially a good old father and mother, endeared her to the Community. She was also particularly interested in the students of the Academy and on leaving home, even for a short trip to the City, her last words would generally be "Take good care of the children."[2]

In sum, she was "a woman of warmth, vision and great good sense."[3] It was to Mother Teresa Mullen, holy, practical, kindly and competent, that Bishops and priests turned with frequency, seeking the aid of the Sisters of St. Joseph in their dioceses.

THE DIOCESE OF PITTSBURGH

The Diocese of Pittsburgh was separated out of the Diocese of Philadelphia in 1843 after Bishop Francis P. Kenrick had insisted for seven years that such a division was necessary.[4] The first bishop, Michael O'Connor, a native of Ireland had studied in France before being recruited as a missionary to the U.S. Bishop O'Connor would serve the diocese until his resignation in 1860.[5] Aware that his new diocese had 33 churches and fourteen priests to serve a population of approximately 45,000 Catholics, Bishop O'Connor quickly recruited seminarians and men and women religious to his territory. The first sisters to serve in the diocese were Irish Sisters of Mercy who opened a hospital in 1847.[6] They were soon followed by Irish Franciscan Sisters in Loretto, and Sisters of Notre Dame and Sisters of Charity who

---

2 These quotations and general information are found in the Barbara Baer collection of documents copied from the Brentwood archives under the title "Mother Mary Teresa." (Archives CSJBr)

3 Sister Consuelo Maria Aherne, SSJ, Joyous Service: *The History of the Sisters of St. Joseph of Springfield* (Holyoke, MA, Sisters of St. Joseph, 1983), 28. (Hereafter, Aherne)

4 In 1835, Bishop Francis P. Kenrick proposed the division of Philadelphia and offered to take Pittsburgh, leaving Philadelphia to Rev. John Hughes who later became bishop of New York. Rome accepted the idea but "some obstacle intervened and the appointments were recalled." It was not until the Fifth Council of Baltimore in 1843 that the U.S. bishops attained success in their request for the diocese. At that time, Rev. Michael O'Connor of Philadelphia was in Rome petitioning permission to join the Society of Jesus. Instead of granting that permission, while he was kneeling before Pope Gregory XVI, "he was forbidden to rise till he promised to accept the see of Pittsburgh." (See: John G. Shea, *History of the Catholic Church in the United States*, Vol. IV, (NY: D.H. McBride & Co., 1892) 67.

5 In 1853, Bishop O'Connor was named founding Bishop of the newly formed Diocese of Erie, but when Father Joshua Young who was to succeed him in Pittsburgh declined the nomination to Pittsburgh, Bishop O'Connor returned to Pittsburgh and Joshua Young became the first bishop of Erie. Although he was only 50 years old, O'Connor resigned in 1860 for reasons of health. He then went to Europe where he entered the Society of Jesus and was later assigned to Boston where he ministered almost until his death in 1872 at the age of sixty-two.

6 Shea, 74.

opened convents in Pittsburgh.[7]

The most significant number of religious brothers and priests were the Benedictines under Dom Boniface Wimmer; the Redemptorists, the Franciscans and Oblates of Mary Immaculate also added to the number of religious men serving in the diocese.[8] In 1860, Bishop O'Connor was succeeded by the Spanish born Michael Domenec, C.M., who became Bishop of Pittsburgh at the age of forty-four. By the time the Sisters of St. Joseph came to the diocese, the Diocese of Erie had been detached from Pittsburgh and Bishop Domenec had been in Pittsburgh for nearly a decade.[9] According to the Catholic Directory of 1871, the Sisters of Mercy were the largest community of women religious in the diocese with 126 members, including novices and postulants. There were 15 Sisters of Charity, and 4 Ursulines, one fewer than the recently established 5 Sisters of St. Joseph.[10]

MOTHER AUSTIN KEAN AND THE BADEN FOUNDATION - 1869

Mother Austin Kean began her religious life surrounded by courageous, creative women who could not but have had a significant influence on one another. Sister Austin had entered the Sisters of St. Joseph in Philadelphia at the age of age of twenty-five and made her vows in 1852 in the presence of Mother Celestine Pommerel of St. Louis and under the ecclesial authority of Bishop (Saint) John Neumann. During her formation Mother St. John Fournier was her first superior and Sr. Delphine Fontbonne who arrived in Philadelphia in June, 1850, was her novicedirector and superior of the orphanage.[11] Before she founded the mission in

---

7 Canevin, Regis. "Pittsburgh." *The Catholic Encyclopedia.* Vol. 12. New York: Robert Appleton Company, 1911. 27 Jul. 2016 http://www.newadvent.org/cathen/12121a.htm (The article's author was the Bishop of Pittsburgh in 1911, the time of its publication.)

8 Ibid. 72-73. Shea mentions that a group of Irish Presentation Brothers who came to take over Catholic education stayed only a short time; their decision to return home came after two of their brothers were killed by lightning. (Ibid. 71)

9 Bishop Domenec, C.M., was born in Spain and educated in France. He was recruited to the U.S. by Bishop John Timon, C.M., and named Bishop of Pittsburgh in 1860 when Bishop O'Connor's resignation was accepted allowing him to fulfill his earlier desire to become a Jesuit (Shea, 419-421).

10 The preface to Sadliers Catholic Directory for 1870 indicates that the statistics it contains are up to date, except for the data from Diocese of Pittsburgh which was reprinted from the previous year. Therefore, 1871 is the first year in which Sisters of St. Joseph would be found in Pittsburgh.

11 The dates for Mother St. John and Mother Delphine's departures and Mother Celestine's visit to Philadelphia come from citations of document in 1886 correspondence between Sister Assissium of Philadelphia and Sr. Adalaide of Carondelet who were collaborating in archival research for their congregations. (Archives, Carondelet)

Brooklyn in 1856, Sister Austin had seen various members of her community depart to found new missions far from their Philadelphia motherhouse. That list began in 1851 when Mother John Fournier went to St. Louis and then to St. Paul and Sister Delphine accepted the call to found a community in Toronto. After them, Sister Agnes Spencer left Philadelphia to found the mission in Wheeling in 1853 and then in Canandaigua in 1854. In addition to knowing these sisters and their comings and goings, Sister Austin would have been among the sisters who happily received Mother St. John Fournier on her return to Philadelphia from St. Paul in 1854.[12] In Sister Austin's early years in the community, the Sisters of St. Joseph were attracting exceptional women. Bishops were seeking them out, in no small part because their rule and community culture encouraged this community to disregard unnecessary limitations and overcome apparent obstacles in order to respond to the needs of their dear neighbor. The bishops knew that they needed, and thought they wanted, strong women religious who could initiate new ministries with the creativity that could make up for minimal resources and little or no professional training. Time and again those bishops got just what they asked for; more than once, it turned out to be more than they had bargained for.

As noted in the account of the foundation in Brooklyn, Mother Austin's withdrawal from office in 1865 came about under ambiguous conditions. While the official documentation indicated that the bishop had acceded to her repeated requests to be relieved of her leadership responsibility for reasons of health, other correspondence indicates that there may have been more to the story. On August 29, 1865, Bishop Loughlin had called the Brooklyn community together to elect a successor to Mother Austin whom he said had repeatedly asked to be allowed to resign. In spite of the bishop's explanation, the election seemed to be hastily arranged. The community annals state that just about two weeks after that election, Mother Austin traveled to St. Paul.[13] The archives retain a copy of a letter she wrote to Bishop Loughlin on September 27, apologizing for the troubles she had caused him and saying that in spite of her health problems, she would return to New York

---

12 Because Mother St. John Fournier had been the superior who received her into the community and a friend to whom she would later turn for support, it is easy to postulate that it was through her connections with St. Paul that Mother Austin turned to that community when she needed to be away from Brooklyn in 1865.

13 The date of her trip was September 12. When Mother Austin went to St. Paul, Mother George Bradley was provincial. The two of them grew up around the same time in the same area in Pennsylvania. Within a few years of their visit, Mother George was expressing her dissatisfaction with Carondelet's "new rule" and was seeking an alternative to being part of a province of Carondelet.

in October. She also asked him not to mention her letter to anyone as she had not communicated with the sisters about the matter. The community annals simply say that she returned to New York on October 8, 1865. The Brentwood archives indicate that in 1868, Mother Austin was serving as superior at St. Joseph's Parish in Brooklyn.[14]

THE MISSION IN EBENSBURG

In 1869, with the approval of Bishop Domenec of Pittsburgh, Father Richard Callixtus Christy from Mother Austin's hometown of Loretto, Pennsylvania, asked the Sisters of St. Joseph of Brooklyn for sisters to serve in his parish, mentioning Mother Austin by name in the request. In September of 1869,when she was almost 45 years old, Mother Teresa Mullen sent Mother Austin as the founding

The Ebensburg Motherhouse

superior of the mission in Ebensburg Pennsylvania. Opening the mission with her were Sisters Hortense Tello and Xavier Phelan. Sister Hortense had been the first woman to enter the Congregation in Brooklyn and had made her novitiate in McSherrystown, under the auspices of the Philadelphia community. The twenty-year-old Sister Xavier had been one of Sr. Hortense's students before entering the congregation.[15] This small founding group could have seen themselves as representing three generations from founder to first postulant to younger member of a then-thriving congregation. Within the space of a few days, the three sisters opened Mount Gallitzin Seminary for boys – an unusual beginning for the community which had generally focused on the education of girls or coeducational classes in parochial schools. According to the local parish history, the sisters counted on the school to serve as their means of support and lived in the "McGuire Property," a house adjacent to the Church.[16] That school, remained open until 2009.

---

14 St. Joseph's on Pacific St. was the eighth parish founded in Brooklyn. The church was dedicated in 1853 to be replaced by a new building begun in 1861.

15 Community records list Sister Xavier as Sister Francis Xavier Phelan, born in 1842 and received in 1863. After returning to Flushing in December, 1869, she was missioned in the Brooklyn Diocese and in the Springfield Congregation. She died in 1903.

16 This detail is from Sister Genevieve Ryan's essay, "The Sisters of St. Joseph of the Diocese of Pittsburgh," (Archives CSJBa).

Within months of their arrival, Miss Kate Beiter of Pittsburgh, a woman who had been helping the sisters with the cooking, asked to join the community. She was sent to Philadelphia for initial formation and on April 21, 1870, she was received into the community, apparently as a lay sister, and given the name Sister Mary Daria.[17] Her act of profession provides an interesting testimony to the fact that the Sisters of St. Joseph in different dioceses collaborated among themselves and seemed unconcerned about strictly defining boundaries, Sister Mary Daria received her religious formation in the Philadelphia community as well as in Ebensburg:

> I, Sister Mary Daria, lawful daughter of Joseph Beiter and Philomena Failar, born in the parish of St. Philomena, county of Allegheny, State of Pennsylvania, aged Eighteen Years, Six Months and Nineteen days, declare and certify, that by the grace of God I have received the habit of the Congregation of the Sisters of St. Joseph, in our house of Mt. St. Joseph Chestnut Hill, and afterwards I made my noviciate [sic] in our house of Mt. Gallitzin Ebensburg, Cambria Co, Pennsylvania, during the space of Two Years and Two Days; in which time having practiced the exercises and observed the rules of the said Congregation, I have on this the twenty-third day of the month of April, in the year Eighteen Hundred and Seventy-two voluntarily and freely made my profession in the hands of Rt. Rev. Michael Domenec, in the Chapel of St. Joseph, taking the simple vows of perpetual poverty, chastity and obedience in the said Congregation according to its Rules and *Constitutions*.[18]

The bishops often seemed to consider the sisters in their diocese as quite distinct from other communities of St. Joseph because such separations assured their control over the sisters and the availability of the sisters they needed for their diocese. In contrast, during much of the 19th century, the sisters demonstrated a more inclusive sense of their identification. They maintained contact with one another and could allow postulants to receive the habit and novices to go through formation in communities other than the one where they entered and to which they would return. It was as if there were a general preparation for religious life among Sisters of St. Joseph rather than formation for a particular congregation.

---

17 See Ryan.

18 "Community Register," Archives of the Sisters of St. Joseph of Baden (ACSJBa). Italics added. The record of Sister Daria's reception record in the Chestnut Hill reception book is signed by Mother St. John and Sister Hortense. Sister Hortense must have accompanied her to Philadelphia for the reception ceremony and entry into the novitiate.

An unexplained detail in this story is that Sister Daria was sent to Philadelphia for part of her formation rather than to Brooklyn, the community which founded Ebensburg. Without any documentation to explain the motive, a few possible explanations suggest themselves. The decision could have been influenced by discord between Mother Austin and sisters in Flushing. Another possibility is that Mother Austin felt closer to Mother St. John Fournier who had been her first superior and remained as General Superior in Philadelphia. Another motive may have been that Sister Hortense Tello, one of the Ebensburg founders, had also gone to Philadelphia for part of her initial formation, giving two of the three founders roots in that Congregation. Whatever the reasoning, Sister Daria was apparently the only sister of the Congregation sent to Philadelphia for formation.

MOTHER AUSTIN'S SHORT, TROUBLED AND PRODUCTIVE STAY IN EBENSBURG

Within a year of her arrival in Ebensburg Mother Austin found herself in what she saw as an untenable situation. The core conflict had to do with Father Christy, the priest who had invited the sisters to the area. Worse yet, her problems with him were compounded by unspecified conflicts with Mother Teresa in Flushing.

At a problematic time in her relationship with Mother Teresa Mullen in Flushing, Mother Austin sought counsel from Mother St. John Fournier, her first religious superior, who was now ageing and infirm, but still the major superior of the Philadelphia congregation.[19] Her rather extensive letter tells parts of her story and illustrates the kinds of struggles the sisters could encounter as they founded missions far from their communities of origin. The opening of the letter indicates that the two had already been in correspondence regarding Mother Austin's troubles:

My dear Mother,
I received yours of August 13th. I delayed answering until Father C. returned from N.Y.[20]

The next lines refer to Mother Austin's desire to leave the Ebensburg mission and

---

19 Mother St. John Fournier spent her latter years plagued with illness that prevented her from traveling to visit the community's missions but did not halt her work as superior and translator of literature, ministries she continued until the time of her death. She died on October 15, 1875, a little more than a month before her 61st birthday and 43 years after she had entered the Sisters of St. Joseph in Lyon.
20 The quotations in this section are all from Mother Austin's undated letter to Mother St. John Fournier, presumably written in August, 1870. (Archives SSJP.)

Father Christy's assumption that he and the Erie diocese had an irrevocable claim on her:

> I told him I was advised to be directed by him and I would do whatever he thought best. He said, "I will not then tell you to go, you belong to the Diocese and I will hold on to those I got."

As Mother Austin continued, she revealed that the problems she faced included Father Christy's drinking and erratic behavior combined with his own poor health. Her letter also indicates that Father Christy had visited the Sisters of St. Joseph in the East, intimating that he had made an appeal to higher authorities in the Brooklyn community. Mother Austin explains that after he had spent an hour with Sister Hortense,

> He came back to the house, asked for me and when I went into the Parlor I found him very much intoxicated. He told me to put the postulants in retreat that evening, that he would be back from Loretto…and give them the Habit on Monday…He raved and talked a great deal about his visit to you and to Flushing…He went to Loretto but did not return until Saturday when he came home sick and was not able to say Mass on Sunday. He continued to get worse…and he kept to his bed for ten days.

She then explains that a Passionist priest gave them a retreat, a short reprieve from the turmoil

> We had a good time of it while it lasted. But scarcely had we finished our thanksgiving after Communion when Father C. sent me a note and such a one as I did not expect. I trembled from head to foot when I read it. Mother Dear, I will lose my soul if I have to stay here unless some things take a change.

While Mother Austin makes her anguish clear, except for specifying Father Christy's drinking and frighteningly tyrannical ways, she does not explain the specifics of their conflict. Indicating that she feels confident in the justice of her cause, toward the end of the letter she says:

> I hear our Bishop is on his way home. May he hasten his steps is my fervent prayer.

The rest of the letter deals with her distress and anger at the lack of support and communication from Mother Teresa Mullen in Flushing.[21] Obviously at her wits end, Mother Austin tells Mother St. John:

> I wrote to Mother Teresa telling her I had been advised to return to Flushing, she did not answer my letter. I wrote again after receiving your last letter. I told her that you thought it would be better for me to return to Flushing if she would receive me – never answered. I presume I may infer from her silence I am not wanted.

In the next paragraph she pours out her sad and angry heart:

> Is it not hard, Mother, to have to return to the World after being so many years toiling for a Religious Comty [sic]. I would do it, Mother, before I would return to a Comty. who have so little feeling for God or Religion, as to leave a good Mission as this is in the condition Mother T. knows this one to be in.
>
> I have prayed fervently that I may do God's will. But I feel rather uncharitable sometimes. If this Mission and work were my own individual work I would not think so hard. But is it not for God's honor and glory, for the cause of Religion, for the salvation of souls?[22]
>
> I feel that what they in Brooklyn have done against this Mission they have done against the very Vocation they profess to embrace. I thus have naturally come to the conclusion their vocation is a humbug and the Holy Habit they wear a mere cloak for their humbug dispositions. Pardon me dear Mother for speaking so plain. I think your opinion of such work would be very much the same as my own. I believe in generosity in the service of God.

She ends the letter by explaining that Sister Hortense is "worse than ever since Retreat" and says that she fears for the soul of their youngest member, Sister Daria, who is "a good child," but "only a child." Giving vent to her desperation she signs off, calling herself "Sister," and adding a puzzling description that reveals her distraught state of mind and heart:

---

21 With so many unspecified difficulties, it is hard to know what the problem was with the superior, but it is at least possible that Mother Teresa was not at Flushing. Her name did not figure on the 1870 U.S. Census list for the Flushing motherhouse and no community records indicate where she might have been. (Information from the 1870 census thanks to Brentwood Archivist, Virginia Dowd.)

22 Mother Austin apparently has no need to explain the details to Mother St. John. It seems possible that, since Sister Xavier returned to Flushing in December, 1869, Mother Austin felt the need for additional sisters whom Mother Teresa did not, perhaps could not, send.

Very Dearest Mother pray for, I dare not say your child, as I hear you do
not consider me such.
Well, for the poor Imaginary, Visionary Individual.
Sister M. Austin

Unfortunately, we do not have Mother St. John Fournier's reply. Mother Austin
remained in Ebensburg for another eight months, that she then returned to the
community at Flushing. Bishop Domenec appointed Mother Hortensia Tello
superior in Ebensburg, a community which had already begun accepting its own
members.

Although Mother Austin's letter provides no more than a snapshot of her
feelings on one particular day, it contains hints about the context of the life of the
community in their early days. Except for mentioning
that Father Christy drank too much and implying that
he dealt with the sisters in an autocratic manner, Mother
Austin did not explain the problems between them.
Nevertheless, the context of their time and place suggest
various possibilities as to what may have been at the
root of their problems. Father Richard Callixtus Christy
came from Loretto, Mother Austin's hometown, and
was five years her junior. Like her, he was baptized by
Father Gallitzin. His father was the village postmaster
and the family lived in the village post office. One could

A Catholic
Civil War Chaplain
in Action

surmise that the Christy family's means were modest in comparison with the
Kean-McGuire clan for whom the town of Loretto was originally named.[23] Father
Christy's greatest fame came from his service as a chaplain in the Civil War. One of
the few Catholic chaplains to be elected and lauded by Protestants and Catholics
alike, Father Christy was known as "The Fighting Chaplain" and was recognized
for his extraordinary bravery and willingness to sacrifice for the wounded of every
stripe regardless of the danger to himself.[24]

In Ebensburg, Mother Austin was working with someone whose family

---

23 For more about Father Christy see Ferdinand Kittell, *Souvenir of Loretto Centenary* (Cresson, PA.: Swope
Bros., Printers, 1889), a book that is also available online. Mother Austin's family roots in the area went back to
pre-revolutionary times. Her McGuire ancestors were responsible for having attracted Demetrius Gallitzin to the
area originally known as McGuire's settlement. (Meany, 11-14)
24 Another account of Father Christy's war record can be found in Robert C. Brown, *History of Butler County,
Pennsylvania* (Chicago: R.C. Brown, 1895) chapter 18. (The book has been available on the internet.) Thephoto
is in the public domain and can be found at ttp://www.acton.org/pub/religion-liberty/volume-21-number-4/
onward-catholic-soldiers-catholic-church-during-am

she had known for decades, a priest who was not far removed from the trauma of the Civil War. No matter what elements of their backgrounds, experience or personalities may have been behind the tensions, because he was the cleric and probably the sisters' ecclesiastical superior, Father Christy had the upper hand in any dispute. That was made clear by the fact that he could call for Sister Daria to return to Ebensburg from the Philadelphia novitiate without consulting or even informing Mother Austin.

Without giving any hint as to why, Mother Austin's letter indicates that there was a serious lack of understanding between herself and Mother Teresa Mullen, the superior in Flushing. Whatever was in the background, when Mother Austin wrote to Mother St. John in Philadelphia, she was uncomfortable with the community she had founded in Brooklyn and at odds with the pastor in the one she founded in Pennsylvania. She had also made a cryptic comment that indicated all was not well with Sister Hortense, but she did not specify whether the problem was between the two sisters or Sister Hortense and the pastor. At that moment, it seemed as though Mother Austin felt she had nowhere to turn except to Mother St. John Fournier, her first superior.

To say the least, this does not sound like a letter from the strong, responsible foundress who had the charisma and acumen to set the Brooklyn community on a solid path during its first decade. The problems she encountered in what had promised to be a happy foundation in her home territory were overwhelming her. Surely, the sisters and the pastor shared responsibility for the problems at Ebensburg but the only solution Mother Austin could find was to leave the mission. She returned to Flushing on March 14, 1871.[25] Sister Hortense Tello became the General Superior in Ebensburg and served in that capacity until August 18. 1880, when she too returned to Flushing as a member of the Brooklyn congregation.[26] From 1880 on, the community was in the hands of sisters who had entered to be a part of the Ebensburg congregation.

In Mother Austin's short time in Ebensburg she accomplished a good deal. Not only did she found Mount Gallitzin Academy but she procured the official incorporation of the community in the State of Pennsylvania. Under the simple

---

25 See Margaret Quinn, "Mother M. Austin, Woman of Faith and Courage" (Archives, CSJBa).
26 Margaret Quinn's biographical essay on Sister Hortense explains that sister's mother, Mrs. Jane Tello, lived with the sisters in Ebensburg until her death in 1874 and that she is buried at the end of a row of the sisters' graves. After Sister Hortense returned to Flushing she was named principal and superior at St. Mary's School and Convent where she died at the age of 51 on July 8, 1889, preceding Mother Austin in death by 16 years.

title "The Sisters of St. Joseph," from which come the congregational initials, S.S.J., the community described its purpose in terms that could have come from 1650 Le Puy. They explained that their mission was to:

- Perform in general the duties of charity and mercy,
- To visit the sick poor in hospitals and prisons,
- To take charge of destitute orphans and
- To keep schools for the education of youth.

The document went on to say that the "management" of the association "shall be vested in 'The Mother Superior' duly elected or appointed according to such rules or by-laws as they may from time to time establish," and the official signatories were Sister Mary Austin Kean, Sister Mary Hortense Tello and Sister Mary Joseph Burke.[27] While the civil document recognized the authority of the sister superior, the *Constitutions* adopted by the community were the same as that of Brooklyn's, the translation of the French version from the 1700s brought by the first missionaries which gave the local bishop ultimate authority over the community in most aspects of its life.[28] From its foundation until 1948, the community would remain under diocesan auspices with the bishop of Pittsburgh as their ultimate ecclesial authority.

The signatures on Articles of Incorporation indicate a change in the membership of the local community. Although nothing documents the reason, Sister Xavier Phelan had returned to Flushing in December, 1869.[29] Sister Mary Joseph Burke, the third signatory of the document, had received the habit on December 8, 1870 and, was the first woman to complete her postulate and novitiate in Ebensburg.[30]

---

27 Articles of Incorporation copy from Archives CSJBa.

28 That edition of the *Constitutions* was printed in New York in 1884. The history recounted in the preface includes the U.S. foundations at Carondelet, Philadelphia, Toronto, Brooklyn and St. Augustine. Bishop J.F. Wood of Philadelphia authorized the printing in 1862, two years after the Carondelet community had begun the process to approve a revised *Constitutions* and more than 30 years before the Sisters of St. Joseph of Philadelphia would receive final approbation of their *Constitutions*.

29 Without citing any sources, Sr. Genevieve Ryan says that she "could not endure the mountain climate and hardships incident to pioneer work." In the same essay Sr. Genevieve explains that "During the interval of two years, many aspirants came and went discouraged by the inclemency of the weather and the poor prospects of the dreary location."

30 Sister Daria's date of reception was April 21, 1870. but she made her noviciate in Philadelphia. Sister Daria made vows on April 23, 1872, 8 months before Sister Mary Joseph's profession on December 12, 1872. Sister Mary Joseph was 27 years old at the time of her profession and Mary Daria only 18. Sister Mary Joseph would

MOTHER HORTENSE TELLO AND
COMMUNITY GROWTH IN EBENSBURG

When Mother Austin returned to Flushing in 1871, Sister Hortense Tello was appointed General Superior.[31] Sister Hortense had made vows in 1859 in the Brooklyn community and her first assignment was as director of the music programs at the St. Joseph's Academy. By 1864, was named novice director and in 1868 she returned to St. Joseph's Academy as director until she accompanied Mother Austin to Ebensburg. In 1871, at the age of 32, she was named Superior in Ebensburg held that office until 1880, when she returned to Brooklyn.[32]

Under Mother Hortense's leadership the community opened Holy Name school in Father Christy's parish in Ebensburg and St. Mary's in Hollidaysburg, a town about 20 miles southeast of Ebensburg. Among the women to enter the community while Mother Hortense was superior, Miss Catherine Dunlevy became one of the most influential and one who left some of the most descriptive records of life during the community's early decades. She recorded her own vocation story as follows:

> Orphaned at an early age, Catherine [Dunlevy] was cared for by the Sisters of St. Joseph in Philadelphia. At the age of eighteen years she wished to dedicate her life to God in religion but was troubled as to where she should enter, Philadelphia or Ebensburg...Sister Monica of... Philadelphia had been as a 'mother' to her during her early years. In the designs of God her place was with the Ebensburg community...
>
> A few days before Christmas of 1872, Miss Catherine Dunlevy of Pottsville...braved the snow and ice of the Allegheny Mountains to join the chosen few in Ebensburg. She left Pottsville on the morning of December 22nd in care of a friend...At Cresson [100 miles southwest of Baden] she had to go by sleigh to Ebensburg as the snow had drifted so high...At 2 a.m. the sleigh stopped at the motherhouse.
>
> In response to Catherine's knocking, Mother Hortense inquired from a window above who was there. Following the instructions given her by the Sisters when she was leaving, Catherine answered "It's the girl from Pottsville."

Sister Mary Dunlevy said no more except, "It was the design of God," to explain

---

31 See: "Sister M. Hortense Tello: Our First Postulant" (author not identified), Archives Sisters of St. Joseph of Brentwood (ACSJBr) According to research from the Archives of the Brentwood Congregation, Sister Hortense (Hortensia) was baptized in Portugal on Feb. 2, 1839, indicating that she was born near that time in that country.
32 Information from "Our First Postulant" and Archive biographical file (ACSJBr). Sister Hortense died on July 8, 1889 at the age of 50.

why she entered the community at Ebensburg instead of Philadelphia where she had been raised by the sisters.

Although the sisters kept no records to document their poverty, Sister Mary Dunlevy's diary gives an intimation of their struggles, their piety and Mother Hortense's practical personality. Speaking of the year 1872, she wrote:

> The Sisters now had three schools under their charge besides those in Ebensburg. Sister Mary [Dunlevy] was in charge of the Boys' Seminary. As the needs of the Community increased with its members, Mother Hortense...suggested to the Sisters that they pray to St. Joseph for a horse and wagon. A few mornings later, as Sister Mary, the sacristan, left the chapel and stepped out the door to shake the duster, she saw coming down the road a gentleman and a fine horse.
>
> Stepping inside she said to Mother Hortense, who was writing nearby, "Here comes St. Joseph and the horse." "Rather early," replied Mother Hortense, and kept on writing.
>
> In a few minutes the man and the horse stopped at the convent gate and asked for the superior. Mother Hortense went down to him and heard these words, "I have the honor of presenting this horse to the Sisters of St. Joseph."
>
> Mother, lost for a moment...Thinking it too good to be true, she astonished the man by asking him to give her a receipt for the donation. She was afraid the owner might return before nightfall and demand his beautiful horse.
>
> Turning to the sacristan she asked, "Did you know the horse was coming?" Sister Mary answered, "No, not at all. But when I saw the horse I knew it was only St. Joseph who would send it so soon.

Sister Mary Dunlevy went on to explain,

> The gentleman through whom St. Joseph sent the gift was Mr. Corbett. This was not the only instant [sic] of his generosity. Many times he sent them food as well as money...[33]
>
> Mother Hortense's motto was "freely ask when freely given."... The horse, of itself, was not likely to be of such benefit. Therefore, to give St. Joseph another opportunity to show his power, she asked him for a wagon. In those days of advanced progress some might wonder what use the Sisters could make of a horse and wagon. One must recall that Ebensburg is surrounded by farming towns and having a way of reaching these farms, the Sisters could procure garden produce for very little money and by means of the wagon they could bring home

---

33 Mr. Corbett's daughter eventually entered the community and received the name Sr. Mary Paul.

vegetables and fruits to be put away for the winter. Two months passed when a new spring wagon was presented to the Sisters by Mr. Mulvehill. It was not long before Mother Hortense found a new use for the horse and wagon. It was used as an EXPRESS CONVEYANCE [sic]. Instead of spending car fare for their trips to Hollidaysburg and elsewhere, they would travel in this handsome conveyor.[34]

The pragmatic Mother Hortense returned to the Brooklyn Congregation in 1880, having spent eleven years in Ebensburg, nine of them as superior. By the time she returned to Flushing the Ebensburg community counted sixteen professed sisters and six novices. The community was teaching at Mt. Gallitzin Academy and parishes in Ebensburg and Hollisdaysburg. In addition, the sisters from Ebensburg and Brooklyn had accepted responsibility for a foundation in the Diocese of Columbus, OH, where some sisters had hoped to establish a new congregation. When that community did not flourish, the founders returned to their original congregations and the women in formation were received into the congregation at Ebensburg and three sisters were sent from Ebensburg to take over the school in Columbus.[35]

THE COMMUNITY COMES INTO ITS OWN

The first superior to be elected in Ebensburg was Sister Mary Joseph Burke who had been the first sister to complete her formation in Ebensburg and made vows in 1872. Sister Mary Joseph was something of a transition superior between the community in Brooklyn and the independent Ebensburg community. Although she entered the community and completed her formation in Ebensburg, she was an Irish-born resident of Brooklyn before entering the community. Her coming to Ebensburg only months after the foundation indicates that she very likely knew the foundingsisters and chose to join them in their new venture rather than enter at Flushing. Just three years later she became the founding superior at St. Mary's

---

34 Mother Mary Dunlevy's Diary (Archives CSJBa)

35 The background information on this foundation is unclear. A letter Mother Mary Grace of Baden wrote in 1950 indicates that the foundation began in 1879, at the invitation of Bishop Rosecrans, the first bishop of Columbus. A document ascribed to Mother Genevieve, "St. Lawrence School, Ironton, Ohio," indicates that in 1875, three unnamed Sisters of St. Joseph, "obtained permission from...Bishop Rosecrans to establish a Novitiate in the Columbus Diocese, and he assigned them to the City of Ironton as a suitable location to lay the foundation of their work." The document goes on to say that they received two candidates, Sisters Genevieve and Angela, but realized that the community would not flourish and the Ebensburg sisters took over the school. The document also states that in 1879, "Mother Mary Charles returned to her own community in Flushing and Sisters Margaret Mary and Mary Joseph went to Carondelet where they had been received." The Brentwood archives cannot identify Mother Mary Charles and the Carondelet archives have no Sister Margaret Mary from that era.

Parish in New Castle, the community's first mission outside of Ebensburg.[36]

Among the many missions Mother Mary Joseph opened during her four terms in office, the most memorable would be St. Patrick's School in Gallitzin, PA. The chronicler who recorded highlights of Mother Mary Joseph's life explains the situation as follows:

> By 1880, the pastor, Father John Boyle, brought the need for Catholic education to the townspeople. The public school board - all Catholic - saw no problem in asking the Sisters of St. Joseph to teach in their schools. The requirements were that each teacher be certified and that these examinations be administered by the board. Children from all denominations were admitted to the classroom. The first sisters to be assigned were: Sisters Clare Berry, Stanislaus McGinniss, Angela Bryan, and Regina Gunning. Little did they foresee that within a few years, Church and State would conflict thereby causing the Sisters of St. Joseph to make history.[37]

This was just one of a number of public schools in this and other dioceses in which the Sisters of St. Joseph would receive state funded salaries until legal challenges put an end to the practice.[38]

One would have thought that teaching in the public schools would have brought the sisters sufficient income, but that does not seem to have been the case. A history of the school explains that because no religion classes could be taught during the official school day, Catholic pupils remained with the sisters for an extra half-hour to complete their religious instruction and the sisters still had to teach music to augment their income:

> It was nearly five o'clock when the Sisters reached home, and there, found the teaching of piano awaiting them. Sisters Stanislaus, Genevieve and Angela gave the lessons...[In the house] There were neither water, bath or toilet to minister to our wants, and the furnace was fired by the Sisters during the winter.[39]

---

36 Newcastle is 100 miles northwest of Ebensburg and 55 miles north of Pittsburgh. The information about Mother Mary Joseph is based on "Mother Mary Joseph Burke, 1880, First Elected Mother Superior" (no author cited). (Archives CSJBa) Hereafter, "Mother Mary Joseph.")
37 "Mother Mary Joseph."
38 The Church-State conflicts over Catholic education will be covered more fully in Volume II of Anything of Which a Woman is Capable.
39 "St. Patrick's School, Gallitzin, PA" (Archives CSJBa)

The sisters worked hard and the difficult conditions took their first victim on October 26, 1876, when one of the novices died of consumption. Sister Mary Dunlevy described the scene of the funeral as follows:

> After going in procession to the Chapel with the remains of their loved little novice, Mother Hortense took the members of the choir and went to the gallery. Mother herself was the organist and chief singer. We got through the singing of the Mass fairly well, but at the absolution of the corpse, there was no response from the choir. The Bishop waiting a moment, then raised his eyes to the gallery where the organist and the singers were sobbing aloud. He and the assisting priests finished the ceremonies, and also sang the De Profundis and the Miserere while going to the cemetery. This shows the love and union that existed among us from the very beginning.[40]

After Mother Hortense Tello had been superior in Ebensburg for more than 8 years, the community held its first election, choosing Sister Mary Joseph Burke as the superior general of the congregation. She would hold that office for 12 years, serving three consecutive three-year terms from 1880 – 1889 and one more from 1898-1901. In her first year in office she opened an additional mission in Ohio, this time in the town of Delaware.[41] The availability and reputation of the sisters opened unexpected venues as they accept accepted the responsibility for public schools in 1881, in St. Patrick Parish in Gallitzin and in 1887, St. Brigid Parish in Lilly. The Lilly parish had a mission in Beaver Falls where the sisters held classes in a Salvation Army barracks. In 1888, the community accepted a request to teach in Cumberland, Maryland at a parish from which the Sisters of Mercy had withdrawn.

ELIMINATING THE DISTINCTIONS: NO MORE LAY SISTERS
Toward the end of Mother Mary Joseph's third term of office, the community dealt with the question of whether or not to maintain the distinction between lay and choir sisters. The practice of having two classes of religious had come from France where it seemed normal that lay sisters would serve in domestic roles and pray a

---

40 Dunlevy Diary.
41 The chronicle, "Mother Mary Joseph Burke," (Archives CSJBa) explains "We have no record of the name of the school. However, it may be stated here that the pioneer sisters were too busy making history to keep records." The information about Mother Mary Joseph's term comes from this essay unless otherwise noted.

different office than the choir sisters who served in the classroom. The lay sisters' habit was distinct from that of the choir sisters; the lay sisters held rank below the youngest of the choir sisters and did not exercise either active or passive voice in the affairs of the community.[42] To the mind of many, the lay/choir distinction was not in keeping with the democratic culture and egalitarian ideals of the United States. In 1898, Mother Mary Joseph brought the matter to a community vote. Sixty-eight sisters had the right to vote and 60 of them voted to give the lay sisters the choir habit; 54 voted to admit the lay sisters to rank according to their profession; 43 sisters voted in favor of giving the lay sisters active voice in the affairs of the community. The community's ecclesiastical superior almost immediately assured the sisters that they could put the changes into practice. At the same time, the sisters voted (42-20) to limit the term of office of the "Mother Superior" to two consecutive terms, which explains why Mother Mary Joseph left office the following year.[43]

THE MOVE TO BADEN

As the community grew, the existing buildings at Ebensburg were proving insufficient for their needs: the Catholic Directory for 1900 listed the community as having 110 sisters and 30 novices. Additionally, Ebensburg's distance from major population centers was effectively limiting the school's enrollment; the town was about 75 miles east of Pittsburgh and Altoona, the nearest town of significant size had a population of 30,337 and only one Catholic parish, indicating that the Catholic population was a minority.[44]

In 1894, the congregation purchased a 32 acre plot of land in the area of Grafton, PA. Before they began plans for building, Father Canevin, the local pastor, advised them to hold off. The local water company needed that property and the community nearly doubled their $34,000 investment by selling the land. In April of 1899, they purchased a farm near Baden. There they built the motherhouse they were able to occupy on December 28, 1901. They called the property Mount

---

42 The question of rank was as symbolic as real. Sisters would be seated in the dining area, process and participate in some other activities according to rank which was determined by the order in which they entered or were received into the congregation. Active voice refers to the right to vote and passive voice refers to the right to be elected.

43 The changes required a change in the *Constitutions*, and the community's ecclesial superior, Father J. Boyle, carried the question to Rome and told the sisters to make the changes, assuring them that they would be approved.

Gallitzin and held the official blessing ceremonies on January 1, 1902. By the time of the move, Mother Genevieve Ryan was the Superior General. Unusual for her time, she only served one term in that office. She also went on to be the first administrator of St. Joseph's Hospital, supervisor of schools, and assistant superior general, all before serving in the community's missions in China. Sister Mary Dunlevy, "the girl from Pottsville," served as Superior General for a total of 21 years. She had three consecutive terms from 1889-1898 and after a 6 year hiatus she served four more terms from 1904-1922. During Mother Mary's time, Bishop Regis Canevin of Pittsburgh decided that all the sisters serving in other dioceses should return to the Diocese of Pittsburgh as befitting a diocesan congregation. That decision brought 42 sisters back from Ohio and Maryland.[45] By 1922, the community numbered 226 professed members with 48 novices and 6 postulants. Although they were all concentrated in the Diocese of Pittsburgh, in 1925 they would send sisters to China to work with the Passionist Fathers who worked in the Diocese. In retrospect, as difficult as Mother Austin's return to her home territory may have been for her, the community she founded there would have a long and fruitful future in the area and far beyond that territory.

THE DIOCESE OF BURLINGTON AND FATHER CHARLES BOYLAN

In 1843, the Diocese of Burlington, Vermont was created from the over-extended territory of the Diocese of Boston, a diocese that had itself been created from Baltimore, the first diocese in the United States. Previous to 1843, the Diocese of Quebec had taken responsibility for the French-speaking Catholics of Vermont. The first resident priest in the area was Father Jeremiah O'Callaghan who settled in Burlington around 1830. For the next twenty-five years he ministered to the Catholic population residing between Rutland and the Canadian border, a significant territory in which many of the Irishman's parishioners were French-Canadians who probably spoke more French than English.[46] After 1843, new immigrants, especially Irish, would come to populate the area.

The first bishop of the Burlington diocese, Most Reverend Louis de Goesbriand, a Frenchman who was ordained by Bishop Rosati in 1840, had served

---

45 Before becoming a bishop, Cannevin was the one who advised the sisters not to build, but to sell their property. The information about the recall of the sisters is found in the anonymous essay, "Mother Mary Joseph Burke." (Archives CSJBa)
46 In 1860, almost half of Vermont's 16,580 inhabitants were French Canadian, by 1880, that number had gone down to 5,360 of the 33,500 inhabitants of the state. (See Damien-Claude Bélanger, "French Canadian Emigration to the United States 1840 – 1930." (http://faculty.marianopolis.edu/c.belanger/quebechistory/readings/leaving.htm)

as the Vicar General of the Diocese of Cleveland before being named to Burlington in 1853. When he became bishop, the diocese had five priests and eight churches to serve 20,000 Catholics.[47] Like his confreres facing such a situation, Bishop Goesbriand traveled to Ireland and France in search of missionary priests. His success in attracting priests to the diocese was such that twenty years later the Catholic Directory listed the diocese as having 52 churches with 26 priests to serve a Catholic population that had grown to 34,000. There were also nine parochial schools, two of which were under the direction of the Sisters of Providence, one each under the Sisters of Mercy and the Sisters of Notre Dame from Montreal, and the remaining five were staffed by lay teachers.

The sisters of St. Joseph from Brooklyn went to Vermont at the behest of Reverend Charles Boylan of Rutland. Although the sisters recorded little about Father Boylan's background, he was renowned as a successful builder and fund raiser. In 1859 he took part in a "clerical exchange" through which he spent some years in ministry in Brandon, Connecticut, during which time he remodeled the parish church to increase its capacity and purchased land on which to build a new parish complex.[48] After that, he found himself in Wallingford, VT where he

Irish Immigrants in Rutland in the 1880s

organized the people to build St. Patrick's Church which was blessed on September 2, 1866.[49] In Rutland, Father Boylan got his parishioners behind a 4-year construction project to build St. Peter's Church. Faced with the need for a parish church and parishioners whose monetary resources left them with nothing to spare, Father Boylan organized the men into a rotating workforce. Each Sunday he would announce from the pulpit which days of the coming week would be dedicated to construction work. After

---

47 Information from Bishop Goesbriand's obituary notice in the New York Times, November 4, 1899.

48 See Wm. Byrne, *History of the Catholic Church in the New England States*, (Boston: The Hurd & Everts Co., 1899), 500.

49 See, Ronald Chase Murphy, Janice Church Murphy, *Irish Famine Immigrants in the State of Vermont: Gravestone Inscriptions* (Baltimore: Clearfield, 2000) 33. The U.S. Census of 1880 lists Charles J. Boylan as the son of Irish parents and the immigration records for 1830 list Charles as one of five children of an Irish born, U.S. citizen mother who arrived in the U.S. on May 10, 1930. He died in 1886 in Rutland at the age of about 56.

the community had dug the foundation, they laid the cornerstone on July 4, 1869 and dedicated the church on July 29, 1873.[50]

Father Boylan knew how to organize his people to build, but getting the French-Canadians and the Irish-Catholics in the town to collaborate in the cause of Catholic education was a different matter.[51] In 1873 there were four Catholic Churches in Rutland and three priests. In East Rutland, St. Peter's was English-speaking and Sacred Heart of Mary was French-Canadian. In West Rutland, the parishioners of St. Bridget's spoke English and had their own pastor while Sacred Heart of Jesus Parish was attended by the French-speaking pastor of Sacred Heart of Mary. There was a Catholic school on each side of the city where a few lay teachers struggled with overcrowded, ungraded classes. In 1870 the Sisters of the Holy Names of Jesus and Mary had opened a school but found it financially impossible to continue. Father Boylan's dream was to create one Catholic school in East Rutland. When he failed to convince the French-Canadians to join his efforts he continued on his own in St. Peter's Parish.[52]

As the Catholic population burgeoned with the waves of immigrants, parishes throughout the country sought the sister-teachers they needed to create a Catholic school system. Because Father Boylan had two cousins who were Sisters of St. Joseph in Brooklyn, he knew the congregation and may have hoped that family ties could work to his advantage in obtaining sisters for his parish.[53] He wrote to Mother Teresa Mullen asking her for sisters for his school. She wrote back "informing him that she could not see her way clear to send him any at this time."[54] Undaunted, Father Boylan decided to present his case in person and traveled to New York where he met with Mother Teresa. Hearing him out, she allowed him to present his case to the assembled sisters. His powers of persuasion proved more effective than his correspondence; Mother Austin Keane along with Sisters

---

50 Unless otherwise noted the material in this section specific to the Rutland SSJ Congregation is based on Sister Mary Cephas, S.S.J. "Educational Work of the Sisters of St. Joseph in the Diocese of Burlington" (A thesis Submitted for the Degree of Master of Arts at St. Michaels College, August 10, 1945), Archives Sisters of St. Joseph of Springfield, hereafter Archives SSJS.

51 The picture is from *The Rutland Historical Quarterly*, Vol. XIV, No. 1, Winter, 1984. http://www.rutlandhistory.com/documents/rhsqvol.xivno.11984.pdf

52 The Catholic Directory for 1873 lists St. Bridget Parish (French-Canadian) in West Rutland and St. Peter's (English speaking) in East Rutland as having schools with lay teachers. Given the French Canadian desire to maintain their own culture, it is no great surprise that they didn't join with St. Peter's in a school project.

53 Father Boylan's cousins were Sisters Borgia and Mary John Boylan. Sister Mary John died in 1871, before Father Boylan began pleading his cause with the community.

54 Sister Mary Clementine, "Notes on Mount Saint Joseph Convent Centenary," April, 1973. (Archives SSJsp)

Irene, Patricia, Anastasia and Paul volunteered to move 250 miles to the north and take over St. Peter's school in Rutland.[61] The five volunteers left Flushing on Friday, September 5, 1873, arrived the next day and on Tuesday, September 16, they opened their school in the old church building.

RUTLAND: HARDEST START OF ALL

This was the third mission Mother Austin had founded. In 1856, when she was 32 years old, six years after she received the habit, she was the founding superior of the congregation in the Diocese of Brooklyn where she served as superior for nine years. In 1869, she returned to the area of her birth to found the Sisters of St. Joseph of Baden at Ebensburg, PA. In March, 1871, she returned to Flushing and remained active in that community until, at the age of 49, she took on the task of founding another mission. The sisters who made the foundation at Rutland were Mother Austin and Sisters Irene Branagan, Patricia Lorrigan, Anastasia Brown and Paul McGuire.[55]

Although Mother Austin had seen her share of problems in both Brooklyn and Ebensburg, no founding community of Sisters of St. Joseph went through the heartbreak and difficulties that came to the founders at Rutland. Within four years of going to Vermont, Sisters Anastasia, Irene and Patricia had died, two of them within 18 months of one another. [56] Mother Austin herself did not remain long in Rutland; she had returned to New York by September, 1874, and then was missioned from Flushing to open a day nursery at St. James Parish in Boston.[57] Sister Mary Paul Maguire who received the habit on August 22, 1863, left the congregation from Flushing, probably in 1880.

During their first year in Rutland in addition to the cultural adjustment required for women from Brooklyn to settle among the small town folk of Vermont, the sisters went through the trauma of losing their youngest sister to death. Then, in the depth of winter, the convent caught fire. Sister Mary Clementine, one of the early historians of the community, tells the story as follows:

---

55 Sister Ignatius Meany adds the details that Sister Irene returned to flushing after six months, went back to Vermont in September, 1876, returned to Flushing in june, 1877 and died in Flushing on August 15, 1877. Sister Patricia died March 12, 1875. Sister Anastasia returned to Flushing in September of 1873 and died on November 28 of that year (Meany, *By Railway or Rainbow*, 93-96, 279.)

56 Mother Austin took Sister Anastasia back to Flushing within two weeks of the founding; she died on November 8, 1873. Sister Patricia remained in Rutland and died there on March 12, 1875. Sister Irene returned to Flushing in December of 1873 and died on August 15, 1877.

57 "History Boston" entry for September 4, 1874.

For almost a year and a half, the old rectory served as the Convent. But on January 21, 1875, while the Sisters were teaching school, the building caught on fire…About 11:00 a.m. the fire department was called and within a few minutes the horsedrawn engines and the hook and ladder were on the scene. Going directly to East Creek, a few rods west of the house, the firemen quickly cut holes in the ice and soon had a stream of water on the fire. The flames were confined to the roof, and, owing to the amount of snow on it, it burned slowly.

Neighbors quickly removed the furniture and all movable goods before the house was deluged with water. Mrs. James Donahue… suffered a broken wrist while helping with the removal of the furniture. The roof was entirely burned off and…the chimney fell in. This, with a portion of the upper floor, was all the damage that was done, except by water.

Father Boylan invited the sisters to occupy the parochial residence until after arrangements could be made. For himself he found other quarters.[58]

Then, less than two months after the fire, on March 12, 1875, Sister Patricia died in Rutland at the age of 27. It is hard to imagine how the small group of sisters dealt with such loss without losing heart. It is nearly as hard to imagine how the superiors in Flushing continued to send sisters so that the little group in Rutland would not be depleted or defeated.

THE SCHOOL WAR AT BATTLEBORO

Mother Teresa continued to mission sisters from Brooklyn to Vermont and the new community soon received requests to send teachers to parishes in the nearby towns of Brattleboro and Bennington. Shortly before the sisters came, the town of Brattleboro had achieved widespread fame for a school controversy that was, at root, an expression of long-held anti-Catholicism. Even before the controversy, Catholics had been less than welcome in the town. The situation was exacerbated when newly arrived Catholics began to establish themselves in the area. Sister Mary Cephas explains how the anti-Catholic atmosphere that characterized the town began to erupt when a Catholic purchased land for on which to build the first Catholic church.

Between seventy-five and eighty Irish Catholics assisted at the first Mass offered here in the open air under a tree on a Sunday in September,

---

58 Sister Mary Clementine, "Notes."

1848. Both Fathers O'Callahan and Daly said Mass in a hall of…a private home…and in a small brick building…the first permanent place of worship was an old paint shop, fitted up as a Chapel by Father Druon…

Father Charles O'Reilly (1855-1869) was the first pastor. Although he had much to endure because of the anti-Catholic bias of many of the people of Battleboro…in 1863 Father began the erection of a brick Church. Stephen O'Hara, coachman for the Honorable George Folsom, a rich lawyer of New York, was able to purchase the property for $450. Influential men went to Mr. Folsom asking him to discharge O'Hara. The former replied, "I wouldn't discharge O'Hara for all the ministers and churches in Brattleboro."[59]

The need to purchase land via subterfuge was only the beginning of the community's prejudicial response to the Catholic presence. When Father Henry Lane was pastor in 1874, the conflicts came to a head over the treatment of Catholic children in the public school. According to Sister Mary Cephas, the conflict erupted when Father Lane, a "man of giant stature and of strong convictions" who had "a stormy seven years' pastorate," responded to mistreatment of Catholic children in the public school.

The conflicts came to a head in 1874 because the Catholic students in the public school did not attend classes on Thursday, June 4, the feast of Christ the King which was a holy day of obligation for them. The next day, those children were refused readmission to the school unless they promised to abide by the school calendar. The Catholic families decided to take the school committee to court, suing for the right to practice their religion. Father Lane defended the Catholics' case in a letter to the editor in the local newspaper, The Vermont Phoenix. His letter explained:

> The real difficulty consists in this, that the school committee have made rules, interfering with the religious rights and duties of Catholic children in the free public school of Brattleboro; and the priest and Catholic

59 Mary Cephas, 56.

(as in duty bound) protest against the enforcement of such rules.

Now it will not do for the committee to say that they claim equal rights for all that they have no desire to "hamper the consciences or prevent the devotions"...they have acted in opposition to such assertions...by expelling...the Catholic children who in the practice of their religion attended services on the feast of Corpus Christi...

Was it not tampering with our rights to demand of our children under threat of expulsion to procure Protestant Bibles?...was it not endeavoring to bring odium on our religion to tell...that it was the Catholics that banished the Puritans out of England, when the person that made such an assertion must have known it to be historically false...or must have been scarcely capable of holding the position of teacher...[60]

When the court ruled in favor of the school committee, Father Lane forbade his parishioners to send their children to the public schools. Those who did not comply with the pastor's request came to their next showdown on December 8, the Feast of the Immaculate Conception, when the public school refused the Catholic children permission to be absent during the time of their Mass. The children who attended Mass were expelled. With that, Bishop Goesbriand got involved in the case and visited the town. His diary entry for December 13, 1874 said:

Battleboro was visited – the school committee having expelled from their schools 125 children of Catholic Parents, because they attended Mass...on the 8th December...I directed the Catholic Parents not to send their children to those schools. Steps were taken in the evening to procure the establishing of Catholic schools. $900 being subscribed by the Congregation.[61]

By this time, public opinion had turned against the school committee. On December 18, 1874, the Vermont Phoenix published an editorial criticizing the school committee for "engendering bitter feelings and jealousies between the Catholics and Protestants." The more serious charge was that they had provoked "the establishment of a separate Catholic School," a prospect that offered "an incentive for extending and adding to the power of the Romish Church in this community."[62]

As in Philadelphia in the 1840s, the Catholics understood that the public

---

60 Father Lane to the *Vermont Phoenix*, published July 17, 1874. (Cited by Sister Mary Cephas.) *The Vermont Phoenix* was a weekly that covered local, regional and national news, published from 1834-1955 and available online at http://chroniclingamerica.loc.gov/lccn/sn98060050/. (Paragraph breaks added)
61 Bishop Goesbriand, "Diary" quoted in Sister Mary Cephas, 60.
62 Sister Mary Cephas, 60.

school program was designed to undermine the Catholic faith and its institutions. The editorial all but admitted that openly when it protested that the disadvantage of having Catholic schools was that they strengthened the influence of the Catholic Church, including over her own members. Perhaps because of that, the school committee relented and published a notice that, "for the welfare of the schools" they would allow the children to "be absent [for religious services] not later than half past ten o'clock in the morning."[63] The capitulation was too late in coming. The men of the parish worked to complete their school building and the pastor went on a speaking tour seeking funds and teachers. The Catholics had made their decision.

In March, 1875, the people of the parish were informed that Sisters of Charity from Manchester, NH, would staff the school, but those sisters never arrived and the classes were taken over by two lay women. The school was still under construction when Father Lane appealed to Flushing for sisters. In September, 1874, Mother Teresa Mullen sent five sisters, including one postulant, for the school at Brattleboro. Father Lane gave them his rectory for a home and they opened the classes soon after their arrival.

In 1937, Sister Teresa Joseph O'Brien, the postulant in the original group, wrote her memories of her short time among the sisters who opened the school. Her story illustrates otherwise unmentioned details about the harshness of the sisters' life and some of the prejudices with which they had to contend. She said:

> As near as I can remember the Yankees of Brattleboro were very hostile against the Irish, as they called the Catholics…In September, 1874, five of us were sent to Brattleboro. We were Sr. M. Catherine, Superior and teacher of the highest class; Sister M. Gregory, teacher of the next class; Sr. M. Athanatius [sic], teacher of the third class; and myself….I taught the small children to sing hymns…Sr. M Zita was the housekeeper. Her people lived there and really fed us that first year.
>
> We lived in Father Lane's house while he lived…in the school. The house had no locks on the doors or windows so we spent many sleepless nights at first.
>
> In the kitchen there was a small stove…All our fire and heat was from this stove. When it was very cold we used to heat bricks and put them in our beds to keep us warm. We chopped our own wood. There were only two real beds in the house but with the help of Pat Fleming and Mike Baker we soon had two more. Dishes too were pretty scarce.

---

63 Announcement printed in the local paper, December 21, 1874 , quoted by Sister Mary Cephas, 60-61.

The people were very good to us…Mrs. Moran used to bake every week and bring it to us. The people used to send us fresh eggs, potatoes and chickens. We never went hungry.[64]

Sister Teresa Joseph inadvertently explains what made life so difficult for the New York sisters who went to Vermont. In January, the average temperature fluctuates between 8 and 29 degrees Fahrenheit, significantly colder than New York's January averages of 26 and 38 degrees, especially when the house has no source of heat except the kitchen stove. The fact that 60 years later, Sister Teresa Joseph could remember the names of people who came to their aid indicates just how important they were to the sisters. It is notable that all of them had Irish surnames.[65]

The community's third school in Vermont was St. Francis de Sales in

Bennington. With that, the three convents were situated in a long triangle: Rutland was 55 miles northeast of Bennington and 70 miles northwest of Brattleboro with 40 miles separating Bennington from Brattleboro on an almost straight east-west line.[66] The distances notwithstanding, the conditions in each of the small towns were similar. Sister Teresa Mullen sent sisters to St. Francis de Sales in 1876 even though the Vermont community had become independent of Brooklyn. The Brooklyn community would continue to send sisters until the Vermont community achieved the stability and numbers they needed to manage on their own.

The school and convent at Bennington were, if anything, poorer than their counterparts. Sister Mary Cephas describes the conditions saying,

The house was a mere framework, so slightly covered that one could see out through the crevices. However, it was fairly well furnished… Each sister took her turn in pumping water from the cellar to the tank in the attic…[which] would last several days. Rain water and snow were saved for washing…kerosene lamps served as the source of light…

---

64 Letter of Sister Teresa Joseph O'Brien to Sister Mary Ambrose, September 24, 1937, quoted in Sister Mary Cephas, 63-64.
65 Both Fleming and Moran are common Irish names; Baker could be English as well as Irish.
66 See Google Maps: https://www.google.com/maps/@43.1999097,-73.2056386,9z.

When a wind storm would sweep down, the Sisters would sit huddled together on the stairs. As the convent rocked back and forth, they expected every moment that it would be swept away. The fatherly hand of Providence certainly protected them.

If conditions were bad in the convent, they were worse in the school.

Sisters served as janitors…[going] at six o'clock in the morning to light the fires…the roof leaked…Many a time…the children held umbrellas over the Sisters.
These young people manifested their strong faith by the fact that they had to pass by a beautifully located and equipped public school building to go up to the little shack at the foot of Town Hill.[67]

Just as Rutland had lost some of their pioneer sisters, Sister Mary Gregory, the first superior in Bennington died in May, 1877, becoming the third of the sisters who had been missioned to Vermont to die within the space of four years.[68]

THE SISTERS OF ST. JOSEPH OF RUTLAND SEPARATE FROM BROOKLYN
In spite of what might have seemed like overwhelming hardships, Brooklyn sisters continued to be willing to go to Vermont. As sisters left, Mother Teresa could find others to come in their place. Nevertheless, Bishop Goesbriand decided that the Vermont sisters should be formed into a separate congregation. He may have believed that Vermonters could better withstand the climate and knew the challenges of the culture. He was probably also in agreement with many of his episcopal confreres who believed in the advantage of having local sisters in the diocese who were not dependent on a distant superior who could remove them at her will. A year before the Boston community opened their own novitiate, Bishop Goesbriand made an entry in his diary that read:

August 17, 1875
Today I informed Mother Theresa [sic] superioress of the house of the Sisters of St. Joseph, Flushing, Long Island, that I desired a separation and a Novitiate for our Sisters of East Rutland.[69]

There is no doubt that the bishop understood that the decision was his to make.

---

67 Sister Mary Cephas, 74-75.
68 As noted above, on August 15, 1877, Sister Irene Branagan, became the fourth of the early Vermont sisters to die.
69 Cited in Sister Mary Cephas, 28.

His diary entry does not mention either a request to Mother Teresa or a conversation with Bishop Loughlin. He simply announced his decision.

It is one thing to declare the opening of a novitiate, but until candidates come, it has little meaning. The first woman to enter the community was Miss Mary Sheridan who became a postulant on October 15, 1876 and later received the name Sister St. Joseph. She was joined by Miss Mary Grace O'Connell of New York City and Miss Lizzie Theresa Dixon of Brooklyn. When these three women received the habit on March 19, 1877, they were joined by three novices, Sisters Mary Anastasia, Miriam and Mary Antoinette, who had entered the congregation in Flushing but completed their novitiate in Rutland. Clearly, even though the bishop had declared the separation of the communities, they were still collaborating among themselves, sharing vocations and formation programs.

The first reception and vow ceremony in Rutland was open to the public and so impressive that the local press covered it at length. Included among the details was an explanation that the Bishop had officiated together with 14 priests from Vermont, New York and Maine. This was the first reception or vow ceremony of a community that belonged to the Diocese of Burlington, implying that it was the first in the State of Vermont. [70] By the time that the first Vermont native was received into the congregation, the sisters had survived the worst of the birthing pangs of the Congregation. The sisters celebrated their next reception ceremony in December, 1877, followed by one in 1879 and another in 1881. The community was growing at a steady pace.

Boylan's Folly - St. Joseph Convent in Rutland

Father Boylan had continued his vigilance for the needs of the sisters. After their first home burned, he began plans for a new convent that would be adequate to the sort of future he dreamed of for them. He sold the old property, raised funds and then enlisted his parishioners with their horses and wagons to begin the work of building the motherhouse he believed the sisters deserved. The bishop and numerous priests and guests arrived for the blessing of the cornerstone on July 4, 1879. As the people watched the construction of the four-story building

---

70 Sister Mary Clement's "Notes" have extensive citations from the local press about this and subsequent reception ceremonies.

going up for the four sisters resident in the town, "St. Joseph's Convent" acquired the nickname "Boylan's Folly;" no one could understand why he wanted so much space for them. The sisters moved into their not-quite-finished convent on February 2, 1882 and later that spring they opened the doors of Mt. St. Joseph Academy in the same building. On August 2, 1882, everything was ready and, with Bishop Goesbriand and other clergy in attendance, Father Boylan blessed the new convent and Chapel of the Immaculate Conception. By 1886, there were twenty Sisters of St. Joseph of Vermont who called "Boylan's Folly" their home. That number would more than double in the next twenty years.

In 1896 the community completed the process of formal incorporation in the State of Vermont as the Association of the Sisters of St. Joseph Society. Everything had been prepared to send them into the next century of service of the Dear Neighbor. They would continue as a diocesan community until they united with the Sisters of St. Joseph of Springfield, Massachusetts in 2001.

Life would never be easy for the small community in Vermont. The sisters would continue to share their neighbors' struggles with poverty and geography. Because of that they would always be an integral part of the life of the people in each institution in which they served and in the Diocese of Burlington as a whole.

FOUNDATION IN BOSTON

In 1873, the diocese of Boston included 275,000 Catholics, 87 parish churches and another 7 churches under construction. In the decade from 1865 to 1875 the Boston diocese had seen a significant influx of religious men and women; those communities included the Gray Nuns of Montreal (1866), the Oblates of Mary Immaculate (1868), Third Order Franciscan Sisters (1868), the Sisters of the Good Shepherd (1869), the Little Sisters of the Poor (1870) and the Sisters of St. Joseph (1873).[71]

The Sisters of St. Joseph from Brooklyn came to to Boston at the invitation of Father Thomas Magennis, the pastor of St. Thomas Parish in Jamaica Plain and Roxbury.[72] He had only recently completed the construction of a parish church, having used the town hall for the celebration of the Eucharist during his first

---

71 Robert H. Lord, John E. Sexton, Edward T. Harrington, *History of the Archdiocese of Boston In the Various Stages of its Development, 1604 to 1943*, Volume III (NY: Sheed and Ward, 1944) 19. The authors go on to say that the growth of charitable institutions in the diocese had seldom been equaled in the history of the Church in the U.S.

72 By the time of these events, the Sisters of St. Joseph of Brooklyn had their motherhouse at Flushing. Even when they moved to Brentwood, they remained part of the Brooklyn Diocese until 1957 when the Diocese of Rockville Center was created and its territory included the Brentwood Motherhouse.

year in the area.[73] The large, gothic church Father Magennis built in Jamaica Plain was dedicated on August 17, 1873. Even before it was finished he began his search for religious who would start a school situated in the basement of the church, the only building the parish had at the time.

According to one account kept in the Boston community archives,

> Father Magennis talked with Archbishop Williams about securing Sisters to teach the children of his parish. The Archbishop opened the Catholic Directory, ran his finger on a page saying, 'Sisters of St. Joseph…in charge of many Parochial Schools.'

That was enough information to send Father Magennis to visit the motherhouse at Flushing to see the sisters in action. He was so impressed by their work that after he reported back to the diocese, Archbishop Williams asked the Motherhouse at Flushing for Sisters.[74] A slightly different account in the Brooklyn congregational annals states that on June 7, 1873, Father Magennis wrote to Mother Teresa Mullen asking for sisters. Both accounts may be true.

In 1873, Sisters of St. Joseph in the Diocese of Brooklyn listed a total of 94 professed sisters, 27 novices and 15 postulants, a number which had grown by 24 in the two years.[75] Mother Teresa Mullen must have felt that they were rich enough in personnel to be able to share with another diocese, and they may even have been looking for additional missions so that they could place all their sisters.

However the variety of precipitating events and motivations worked together, Mother Teresa Mullen and a companion visited Jamaica Plain in the summer of 1873 to see the place where Father Magennis hoped their sisters would open a coeducational school and teach liturgical music. Apparently, the two visiting sisters arrived without advanced preparations. As the annals tell the story:

---

73 Father Magennis was born in Lowell, MA in 1843 and ordained in 1866. His father emigrated from Ireland and married the widow Mary Murphy in Lowell MA. The Catholic Directory for 1864 lists 19 Catholic schools in the diocese, nine of which were under the auspices of the Sisters of Notre Dame; others had listed a priest director and some indicated that the teachers were "seculars," but although the Sisters of Charity ran a girls' orphanage, no other women's religious community was teaching in the diocese.

74 From a manuscript kept in the Magennis files, (Archives, CSJBo).

75 Figures from Sadliers Catholic Directories, 1872 and 1874. The statistics listed in each edition are those reported at the end of the previous year. In 1880, the community counted 168 members, nearly doubling their numbers in less than a decade. The Sisters of St. Joseph began their ministry in Brooklyn in 1856 and moved the motherhouse to Flushing in 1860 where they remained until 1903 when they went to Brentwood. At the time of the moves, all of those locations were in the Diocese of Brooklyn. For this time period the community will be referred to as the Sisters of St. Joseph of Brooklyn.

As they wished to remain overnight, they made inquiries at two convents for hospitality. They were refused. They then made inquiries at St. Thomas Rectory, Jamaica Plain, and they were cordially invited to accept the hospitality of the rectory which they accepted gratefully.[76]

Mother Teresa must have been very favorably impressed with Father Magennis and his plans. The annals explain that they lost no time before agreeing that the community would work with Father Magennis.

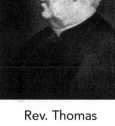

Rev. Thomas
Magennis
1843 – 1912

In the morning arrangements were made for the Sisters to come as soon as possible to take charge of the school which would open in the basement of the church. The Sisters went with Father in the morning to see the projected classrooms and to talk over the business of beginning in the Fall.[77]

Following their agreement, four sisters left Brooklyn for Boston on Thursday, October 2, 1873. They were Sisters M. Regis Casserly, the superior, Clare Corcoran, Felix Cannon and Dolores Brown. The first three of those sisters planned to teach while Sister Dolores would care for the house, a five room "cozy little cottage just big enough for the small community." Father Magennis had moved this house to the parish site from another part of the city.[78] The annals' description of the opening day of school explains that girls who had not been able to continue to study in public schools helped fill the "classrooms" which consisted of spaces partitioned off in the church basement.

The following Monday, October 6th, we opened the School with two hundred girls. A number of large girls who had left the public school

---

76 This is from the Boston congregational annals, found in Boston CSJ History Book I, 1873-1907, (Archives CSJBo). This book is a compilation of sources,distinguished from one another by typeface. Hereafter, "History Boston," 1. Mother Mary Regis was the one of the original authors as deducible from times she writes in the first person.
77 "History, Boston," 1.
78 The quotes are from "History of the Sisters of St. Joseph, Boston, Mass." written anonymously but almost certainly by Sister Mary John (Annie) McLaughlin, one of the first women to enter the congregation. (Archives, CSJBo.) Hereafter, "McLaughlin."

some time before came because it was the Sisters' school.[79]

Within a week of the school opening, Mother Teresa of Brooklyn arrived to visit accompanied by Sisters Helena and Marcella. Once she had seen all the arrangements, Mother Teresa returned to Flushing the following Tuesday and the two other sisters remained with the new community. Mother Teresa obviously had no worries about leaving Sister Mary Regis Casserly in charge of the new venture.

In 1892, the Sacred Heart Review described the area of Jamaica Plain as:

> One of the most beautiful suburbs our city possesses. Bounded on one side by acres of hill and meadow-land in the magnificent Franklin Park, adorned with miles of shade trees....you have a wealth of landscape and scenery that...could scarce be duplicated in all New England...and right in the heart of all this natural beauty stands the magnificent church property of St. Thomas.[80]

The fledgling community led by Mother Regis seemed very well situated. Sister Mary Regis, like so many of the people she would serve in Boston, was an Irish immigrant. Born in Roscommon in 1843, her family came to Long Island in 1852. She enrolled in St. Joseph's Academy in Flushing in 1861, at the age of seventeen. Shortly after graduating, she entered the Sisters of St. Joseph of Brooklyn, received the habit in 1863 and made vows in March, 1866.[81] She taught in Brooklyn before volunteering for the mission to Boston. Through her years of leadership of the Boston Sisters of St. Joseph, Sister Mary Regis would prove to be a woman with a keen grasp of what needed to be done and the ability to accomplish it.

Mother Teresa's confidence in leaving the 30 year old superior in charge in Jamaica Plain did not indicate that the sisters were free from problems. The ideal of the parish school at that time was that it would provide a free and high quality education to Catholic children. That left the question of how to pay the sisters in the hands of the pastors. Before long, Father Magennis was unable to come up

---

79 "History," Boston, 1. We might assume that by saying "large girls" the author meant "older girls." They may have been too old for the public school, or their parents may not have wanted them in a public school.
According to Mary J. Oates, CSJ, the 200 children who came to the school comprised 15% of the enrollment of the school district. See Mary J. Oates, "Mother Mary Regis Casserly," in Maxine Schwartz Seller, Ed., *Women Educators in the United States, 1820-1993: A Bio-Bibliographical Sourcebook* (Westport, Connecticut: Greenwood Press, 1994), 96.
80 *The Sacred Heart Review*, Vol. 7, # 25, 14 May, 1892. http://newspapers.bc.edu/cgi-binbostonsh?a=d&d=BOSTONSH18920514-01.2.2
81 Oates, 95-96.

with the stipends he had promised and his prospects were so precarious that he thought he might have to send them back to New York. Mother Mary Regis was not so easily stymied. The sisters earned additional income by doing piece work, sewing everything from liturgical vestments to beanbags and baseballs, with shrouds being one of the items for which there was an unfortunately large demand.[82]

With all that Mother Mary Regis did, keeping detailed annals did not figure anywhere near the top of her priority list. She passed months without making an entry, often recording only such simple details as the March celebration of the feast of St. Thomas with songs in honor of the pastor, followed by an entry in May to note the children's first coronation of the Blessed Virgin and the preparations that went into it.[83]

When the second school year opened in 1874, Mother Mary Regis summarized the entire first semester's events into one entry:

Mother Mary Regis
Casserly
1843 – 1917

> September 7:
> Opened school. All the children returned except those who went to work. No complaints were heard after the vacation, only one left because she was not promoted. We had Forty Hours Devotion at the end of the month. I [Sister Regis] took charge of the Blessed Virgin Sodality. Father wanted us to take it last year but I asked him to wait until we would be acquainted. I also took charge of the Married Women's Sodality. Received at Christmas a present of Fifty Dollars from them. No excitement until Saint Thomas Day.[84]

Mother Mary Regis subtly packed a great deal of information into that 92 word entry, obviously written long after the first day of school. From what she said, we know that the school was doing well and the sisters felt secure enough in their relationship with the pastor that they could refuse or at least postpone one of his requests for their service. The sisters were involved in that favorite ministry of Father Médaille, a sodality, allowing them to share their spirituality with the laity. Sister Mary Regis

---

82 Oates, 96. Disease, accidents and complications of childbirth and the occasional outburst of contagious disease (flu, cholera, etc.) were factors that caused early death and a steady population of orphans.
83 In spite of all the feast days they noted the first mention of St. Joseph's Day came in 1878 when the notation was that none of the sisters went to communion because they had not had confessions for two weeks.
84 "History Boston" entry for September 7, 1874.

also noted that the women of the sodality were quite generous. Another detail that opens a window onto life in that period is that some of the girls could not return to school because they had to work. The "children" in the sisters' school were of an age that the guidance they needed went beyond the three R's to a preparation for dealing with the working world and the particular challenges it offered young women.

The entry immediately preceding that quoted above indicates that the Brooklyn community had accepted a second invitation in the Boston diocese:

> September 4
> Mother Austin, Srs. M. Clare and Helena came. Mother A. remained here until her house was ready.[85]

Sister Mary John McLaughlin's memoir fills out the details:

> The Pastor of St. James church, Boston, applied to Flushing for sisters to take charge of a Day Nursery, which he was about to open for the benefit of mothers who were obliged to go out working where they could leave their little ones and feel that they were safe with the Sisters. Mother Austin was sent to take charge of this work. Two novices were sent with her. One of the novices was a candidate that Mother Regis had sent from Jamaica Plain to Flushing, Miss Deneif, now Sister M. Thomasine.
>
> The mission did not prove a success, so the Sisters returned to Flushing. The failure of this undertaking was a handicap on Jamaica Plain mission for a while, but St. Thomas School prospered and the Sisters proved themselves efficient teachers and devoted religious.[86]

As often happens, the annals bring up issues and answer questions the author was not necessarily intending to address. What remains unanswered from the above entry is why the school was not a success. It reveals is that shortly after her return from Rutland, Mother Austin was again venturing into new territory. In addition to what Sr. Mary John wrote, the the Brooklyn annals note that Rev. James A. Healy, the pastor at St. James, had written to Mother Teresa in Flushing asking her to recall the sisters.[87]

An entry for April 27, 1875 says: "Return of Mother Austin,

---

85 "History Boston" entry for September 4, 1874. "Mother Austin" was Mother Austin Keane who had opened the mission in Vermont in 1873 and had returned to Brooklyn in time to be a part of this mission in Boston.
86 McLaughlin. (See note # 8)
87 Letter from Father Healy to Mother Teresa, April 2, 1874. (Annals, Vol. II, 1874-1885, p. 11. Archives CSJBr.) Father James Augustine Healy was born in 1830 in Macon, Georgia, the eldest son of Michael M. Healy, an Irish

Srs. Dolorosa and Thomasine from Boston. St. James Mission broken up."[88] The next day's entry says "Visited St. James – saw Bishop."[89] Beyond those bits of information, no letters, memoirs or annals entries document the reasons for the sisters' apparently abrupt departure from St. James. But the mission at St. James was the last that the Boston sisters would receive for a number of years.

In 1879, Father Magennis, still the sisters' ecclesiastical superior/spiritual director, was concerned about the lack of invitations for the sisters to teach in local Catholic schools. Looking for an endorsement that would override any negative information or lack of knowledge, he wrote to Bishop McQuaid, the famed Catholic school champion in Rochester, asking him for an endorsement of the Sisters of St. Joseph as educators.[90] Sister Mary Oates sees Bishop McQuaid's commendation of the Sisters of St. Joseph as the key to resolving the problem. As she noted, an annals entry dated June 26, 1879 proclaims:

> Wonderful announcement today. Father Higgins [South Boston] has the approbation of the Archbishop to get us to teach in his school and no less than ten sisters are required to take charge. Poor Jamaica Plain will get a dreadful clearout.[91]

The need for ten sisters would indeed have meant a "clearout." According to The Catholic Directory for 1879, at the end of 1878, the Sisters of St. Joseph in Jamaica Plain had 13 professed sisters and 7 novices. One half of that number was needed for Father Higgins' school.

A NOVITIATE IN BOSTON – A BOSTON CONGREGATION

Before the sisters accepted a second mission, the community had been gradually

---

immigrant and Eliza Smith, a slave woman who was Michael Healy's common law wife. (Interracial marriage was illegal at that time and remained so in some parts of the U.S. until 1967.) James Augustine Healy was not allowed to study in the Jesuit novitiate in Maryland because it was a slave state. He went to Sulpician seminary in Montreal and later to Saint Sulpice in Paris. In 1854, he became the first ordained African American, but most people assumed he was Irish by background. When he returned to the U.S., he was incardinated in the Diocese of Boston and in 1866 became the pastor of St. James Parish, the largest parish in the diocese at that time. In 1875 he was named as the second bishop of Portland, Maine. An entry in the annals for May 30, 1875 says "Father Magennis went to Portland." Undoubtedly that was to attend the June 2 consecration of Bishop James Healy.

88 Annals, Sisters of St. Joseph of Brooklyn, Vol. II, pg. 12. (Archives, CSJBr.)

89 Annals, Sisters of St. Joseph of Brooklyn, Vol. II, pg. 12. (Archives, CSJBr.)

90 Oates, 97, citing letter from Maginnis to McQuaid of May 2, 1879 (Archives, Diocese of Rochester). This is another bit of evidence of how Sisters of St. Joseph were understood as a collective even though they belonged to a variety of independent congregations. Bishop McQuaid had arranged for the Sisters of St. Joseph of Rochester to break from the Buffalo congregation in 1864 when he became the first bishop of the diocese.

91 "History Buston," entry for June 26, 1879.

formalizing structures and was moving forward in the process of becoming independent from Flushing. The first institutional step in that process was the establishment of a local novitiate. In her own inimitable way, Sister Mary John explained the events as follows.

The Sisters were not very long in Jamaica Plain when young ladies came to the convent asking permission to join the community. Sister Mary Regis sent their names to Flushing and afterwards sent the young ladies themselves. Some of them were received and returned occasionally to visit their relatives and friends in Jamaica Plain and the suburbs.

About this time someone conceived the idea, "Why not open a novitiate in Jamaica Plain?" Father Magennis spoke to the Archbishop and he approved of the undertaking. Straightaway the work of opening a novitiate began. This made a little disturbance in the community, for if Jamaica Plain was to become a novitiate, then the community would belong to the diocese of Boston.[92]

The Novitiate in Jamaica Plain

The community annals are rarely as detailed and not much more precise than Sister Mary John's account of the community's history. The annals do note that on October 24, 1876, "Our novitiate opened. Miss Bannon entered." Simple entries followed that, mentioning a new kitchen and dining room (November 5) and Forty Hours Devotion and First Communions, (November 9). Then on December 5, with less ado than about the kitchen, the annalist noted "Miss Annie McLaughlin entered." In the same simple tone, the record for December 6 says, "Miss Katie Cassidy entered" and on December 18, "Miss Kate Gregory entered." Another source added, "Mother Helena appointed to take charge of novices and postulants. Mother Teresa visits from Flushing, New York."[93] Obviously, the writer of the annals did not feel the need to emphasize the arrival of new community members or to elaborate on the establishment of the novitiate.

If the Archbishop was not actually the moving force behind establishing

---

92 McLaughlin.
93 "History, Boston."

the novitiate, he was surely happy that it was happening. In 1849, Bishop Fitzpatrick of Boston had arranged for the Sisters of Notre Dame de Namur in Cincinnati to send sisters for his diocese. Before long he was trying to get them to make an independent Boston foundation, an idea that their Superior General quickly put to rest. The bishop accepted the Notre Dame superior's conditions and the community continued to send sister-teachers to Boston.[94] Bishop Williams of Boston succeeded where his predecessor failed when he approved the establishment of a diocesan congregation of Sisters of St. Joseph.[95]

The opening of the novitiate seemingly did not imply a definitive break between Boston and Brooklyn. The sisters continued to travel back and forth, the Boston-based sisters were often listed as going "home" to Flushing and Mother Teresa "visited" on various occasions, some of which appear to have been official visitations.[96] Mother Teresa's attendance at the community's first reception ceremony may have been in an official capacity. Recording that event with the effusiveness of a prime participant, the author of the annals wrote:

> Celebration of the great day – St. Thomas'. Blessing of the Chapel and Katie and Annie received the Habit. The Archbishop in the best of humor assisted by twelve priests. Father said the low Mass...Father Donnelly did all the honors of the day. Everything passed off nicely and orderly. The ceremony was very impressive. First of the kind ever took place in Boston. Just about twenty years since the first reception in Brooklyn.[97]

Another source added:

> Mother Teresa and Sister Clotilda came from Flushing to be at this first ceremony. There were in the community at this time 3 professed members, 3 novices and 3 postulants...Mother Teresa and Sister Clotilda

---

94 See Robert Howard Lord, John E. Sexton, Edward T. Harrington, *History of the archdiocese of Boston: in the various stages of its development, 1604 – 1943* (NY: Sheed & Ward, 1944) 614-619. [caps done as in the title]
95 John Joseph Williams became Bishop of Boston in 1866 and archbishop in 1875. A Bostonian whose parents were Irish immigrants, he studied for the priesthood in Montreal and Paris and was ordained by Archbishop Affre of Paris who was later killed in the French Revolution of 1848. +
96 The annals did not use the term "visitation" of a sister superior until 1905; previous to that it was used once in regard to Archbishop Williams formal visitation on January 1, 1881.
97 "History, Boston" under the date of March 8, 1877. It is interesting that there was no set day for postulants to come to the community and that the first reception happened on the Feast of St. Thomas, just 11 days before St. Joseph's Day. The community was serving in St. Thomas Parish and the pastor was Rev. Thomas Magennis.

returned to Flushing a few days later, taking with them Sister Theodore and Sister Helena.[98]

Sister Helena's departure signaled the loss of the Brooklyn sister who had been novice director for the Boston community, a further sign of Boston's independence.

In 1878, the annals entry for June 16, notes that Mothers Teresa and de Chantal came for Mother Regis' silver jubilee. After 1879, such visits become less frequent and references to Mother Teresa all but disappear. Whatever her reasons for early visits to Boston, she stopped the practice – or the annals stopped mentioning it; no one recorded official visits from Mother Teresa after 1879.

At the end of 1879, Mother Mary Regis wrote the following letter to Bishop Loughlin of Brooklyn.

Rt. Rev. Father,

I find myself obliged to ask you for my obedience, not that I wish for one instance to be cut off from Brooklyn, but I feel myself virtually separated in having to receive subjects, answer for the vows of the Sisters and open missions.

Believe me, I have still and shall always have the interest of Flushing at heart, and sincerely trust that her mission in Boston may do credit to the diocese from which I came and to which my heart is still attached. For the last few months we have had Professor Dunbar, master of the training school in the city to give the sisters instructions in the method of teaching.

The Archbishop heartily sanctioned this movement, he thinks it is just the right thing for us. We are looking for a visit from his Grace during the Holidays. He made his visitation this time last year and appointed Father Magennis our Spiritual Father.

Wishing you a very Happy New Year,
I remain yours in Christ,
Sr. M. Regis

---

98 "History, Boston" under the date of March 8, 1877, but with a typeface that indicates the information is not from the annals themselves.

Mother Regis' letter, in which she refers to herself simply as "Sister M. Regis," revealed the complicated but friendly state of the relationship between the communities. There is no reason to doubt about the sincerity of her explanation that she felt an obligation rather than a desire to ask for release from obedience in the Diocese of Brooklyn. The responsibilities she had assumed as a major superior had brought about a virtual separation from Brooklyn's authority and she saw the necessity to formalize what had evolved over the course of the six years she had been superior in Boston. She assured the bishop that she would remain loyal to Flushing and wanted to do credit to the place of her origin and to which her heart remained attached. Up to this point, Mother Mary Regis was expressing her deep feelings of loyalty and responsibility, explaining that the conflict between those feelings provided the only rationale for the letter she was writing.

As the letter continued, it was almost as if Mother Mary Regis wanted to change the subject as quickly as possible, moving from a formal request for a transfer of obedience to a report on the progress and plans of the community. But reality set in again as she ended her letter with news that reminded her and Bishop Loughlin that the Boston sisters were now answerable to a different authority: they were looking forward to the official visitation of Archbishop Williams who had already appointed their ecclesiastical superior. At this point, Boston's break from Brooklyn seemed to be formalized only through Mother Mary Regis' from obligations to Brooklyn. She said nothing about *Constitutions*.

Most of the communities founded after 1836 maintained the "old rule," the French *Constitutions* which came with the first missionaries from Lyon and were translated into English in 1847. These *Constitutions* generally remained in force until they were revised in accord with the Canon Law of 1917. This edition of the *Constitutions* put each community formally under the authority of the bishop of the diocese in which they lived and ministered. Informally, at least in the case of Brooklyn and Boston, the bishops invited the sisters into their dioceses but there is no indication that they controlled the assignments of sisters from one diocese to another.[99] The sisters seemed rather fluid in their sense of belonging; they would go from Brooklyn to Boston or Rutland and back, with Boston sending sisters to Brooklyn for formation before they opened their own novitiate.[100] Although the

---

99 Mother Teresa was the Brooklyn superior behind the foundation of communities in Baden, Boston, Rutland (Vermont), and Springfield, MA, each of which eventually became independent of Brooklyn.

100 One of the more extreme examples of the fluidity of membership happened when Mother Teresa of Brooklyn sent Mary Ellen O'Brien as a postulant to Bourg, France. She received the habit from Bishop Marchal of Belley, made her novitiate in Bourg and returned to Brooklyn ready to teach French as Sister Therese Joseph. (See Meany, *By Railway or Rainbow*, 98-105 and 280.)

records make no mention of the formality, the evidence from Mother Mary Regis' request to be freed from obligation to Brooklyn and the end of Mother Teresa's visits indicate that the Boston community became formally independent of Brooklyn at the end of 1879 or in early 1880. By 1880, the Boston community had accepted 31 postulants; 24 women had received the habit, all of whom made vows.[101]

SOLIDIFYING STRUCTURES

On March 25, 1880, Mother Mary Regis, now the single major superior of the Sisters of St. Joseph in Boston, received the legal charter establishing the community as a legal corporation in the State of Massachusetts.[102] The community had finally opened a second school and women were steadily coming to join the community.

Even before the sisters opened their second school, St. Thomas became co-educational, making the school "the first of its kind in New England, offering to boys and girls alike, opportunity for a Catholic Education through all the grades."[103] Once the community had accepted the invitation to teach at St. Agnes School in South Boston, they had broken though the barriers to their acceptance as a teaching community and would receive as many invitations as they could accept. In 1883 they opened St. Mary in Stoughton followed by three more schools before the end of 1889.[104]

The Fresh Pond Hotel
Mount St. Joseph Academy

Although all the sources downplay the drama, one of the major challenges during Mother Mary Regis' time as superior and one that extended beyond her days in leadership had to do with the purchase of "Fresh Pond" a property the sisters planned to use as Motherhouse and Academy. Fresh Pond in Cambridge was a tourist resort that had gone bankrupt. The sisters purchased it in 1885 to house a novitiate and motherhouse as well as Mount St.

---

101 The first in the list of receptions and vows is Sister Mary John (Annie) McLaughlin. All but two of the women received, Eliza Pourbeau and Sarah Perley, had Irish surnames.
102 "Boston, History" under the date of March 25, 1880, exactly 44 years after the first French Sisters of St. Joseph had arrived in St. Louis.
103 A Sister of St. Joseph of Boston, *Just Passing Through, 1873-1943* (Boston: The Sisters of St. Joseph of Boston, 1943) 30.
104 *Just Passing Through*, 22.

Joseph Academy. The community made a major investment in the site which included twelve acres, the hotel and two additional buildings. The hotel became the Academy and the other buildings served as motherhouse and novitiate.[105] Again, we turn to Sister Mary John for the ordinary sister's view of the affair.

> When the Sisters went to Fresh Pond the entire estate was in a dilapidated condition. Mother had many drawbacks. Water was not to be had, notwithstanding that the great body of Fresh Pond extended on two sides of the convent property. Drinking water was hard to get. However, when the windmill started, the water supply for drinking and cooking was salvaged – and enough to last till the windmill started again.[106]

The sisters rehabilitated the property at great sacrifice and the Academy became successful. But for a variety of reasons, Fresh Pond was a short-lived experience. Again, as Sister Mary John explained the situation:

> After the Sisters had been living in Fresh Pond and beautifying it for five years, the city of Cambridge decided they needed the property. They thought they had made a mistake in allowing a Catholic Institution on the premises. So in 1891 the community purchased the present place on Cambridge Street, Brighton, Mass.[107]

Sister Mary John's opinions are corroborated in *Just Passing Through*, a brief history of the community's life between 1873 and 1943. The author states:

> …perhaps there seemed too much progress to jaundiced eyes in the situation as it developed during the four years…since the Sisters had taken over the property…
>
> Aggrieved from the start that the sisters had obtained possession of the estate against their wishes, the authorities of Cambridge sought to get it back, to devote it to the use of a park. Finally, after much debate about the matter, a settlement was made for a transfer to their hands. They enforced the claim, by right of eminent domain, May 31, 1891. God's plan with this little community would seem to be to test mightily its spirit of endurance and submission.

---

105 See Lord et al., 348. The picture is public domain: https://commons.wikimedia.org/w/index. php?curid=9471416 and the building has been moved from the original site to 234 Lakeview Ave., Cambridge, MA and is on the National Register of Historic Places.
106 McLaughlin.
107 McLaughlin.

The Academy was removed immediately to Cambridge…Later, about October 29, 1891, the Novitiate and Mother House were removed thither, and the Day School was formally opened.[108]

Mother Mary Regis remained as Superior General until 1890. After 17 years as the leader of the community, she resigned and the community elected Mother Mary Theresa Donnelly as her successor. Mother Mary Theresa remained in office only three years. The end of the drama of Fresh Pond came during her term, giving her the final responsibility for the settlement, the purchase of property in Brighton and overseeing the move. She refused reelection, but when she left office the community was situated on the land that would be their motherhouse for decades to come.

After finishing her terms as Superior General, Mother Mary Regis served as a local superior in Amesbury. In 1898, when the community was celebrating its 25th anniversary, she returned to Jamaica Plain at Pope Leo XIII School from where she helped to establish a school for the deaf in 1899. When Mother Mary Regis died in 1917, the community she had begun with three companions had grown to number 400 sisters. The group that had spent its first half-decade wondering if pastors were going to make use of their services was then teaching in 24 schools. Her first collaborator, Father Thomas Magennis, born in the same year as she, had preceded her in death by five years. Between them they left the Sisters of St. Joseph of Boston with more sisters, more missions and more stability than either of them would have ever dreamed possible in 1873 when they first met as two thirty-year old descendants of Irish immigrants who hoped to serve the Church and their own people in Boston.

THE SISTERS OF ST. JOSEPH OF SPRINGFIELD
THE DIOCESE OF SPRINGFIELD

The Diocese of Springfield was formed in 1870 from territory that had belonged to the Diocese of Boston. Patrick Thomas O'Reilly, Springfield's first bishop, had come to the U.S. at the age of nine with his immigrant parents and was ordained for Boston in 1857.[109] He was serving as pastor of St. John's Parish in Worcester, MA, when he was named as bishop and, given that St. John's was a large and

---

108 *Just Passing Through*, 75-76.
109 Before his consecration as Bishop of Springfield, O'Reilly had served in only two parishes: St. John's of Worcester and St. Joseph's in Boston. He had been an assistant at St. John's before going to St. Joseph's and then was appointed pastor of St. John's. When the Worcester Diocese was created in 1950, St. John's was given the distinction of being named the mother-church of the Diocese.

beautiful church in a diocese that had no cathedral, he remained at that parish while making plans for building his cathedral in Springfield, some 50 miles away. When the Cathedral was completed, the bishop began construction of St. Michael's School which he dedicated on November 26, 1882, announcing that it was the largest parochial school in Western Massachusetts. All he then needed were teachers and students.

Priests from the Springfield area had been making requests of the Brooklyn congregation since at least 1876, but as often happens, it was a providentially timed, personal and insistent visit, not incidentally fortified by a letter from a bishop, which bought the desired results. In November, 1879, Father Patrick Stone traveled to Flushing to convince Mother Teresa Mullen to send sisters to his parish school, St. Patrick's, in Chicopee Falls. His discussions with her took place a little more than a month before Mother Regis Casserly of Boston formally asked Bishop Loughlin of Brooklyn for her "obedience," beginning the formal process through which the Boston community became juridically independent from Brooklyn. Although Mother Teresa turned down his request, Father Stone was persistent enough to ask again in April of 1880. After being turned down a second time, he appeared again at Flushing in May of that same year accompanied by Bishop O'Reilly to reinforce the request.[110] By then, both the Rutland and the Boston communities had separated from Brooklyn and Mother Teresa saw the possibility of promising Father Stone that she would send sisters in September.

Mother Cecilia Bowen
1840 – 1890

Mother Teresa chose Sister Mary Cecilia Bowen as the superior to open the new mission. Sister Cecilia a native of Elizabethtown, NJ, had entered the Brooklyn congregation and on August 26, 1860, she was a member of the first group of sisters to receive the habit in the sisters' new home at Flushing. After teaching for a number of years, Sister Cecilia served as director of novices in Flushing from 1874-1880.[111] On September 2, 1880, Mother Cecilia and ten companions arrived

---

110 Part of Fr. Stone's insistence came from the fact that the Sisters of Notre Dame who had many sisters serving in the diocese could only teach girls. (Aherne, 254)

111 This information is from an anonymous essay, "Mother Cecilia Bowen, A Short Biography," (Archives SSJS)

at St. Patrick's Parish to staff Father Stone's parish school.[112] The original group of Sisters of St. Joseph in the diocese was soon augmented by sisters who would teach in the Catholic schools in the towns of Webster and North Adams, spreading the communities over a span of 100 miles in Western Massachusetts.

In 1883, after the Cathedral and St. Michael's School were completed, Bishop O'Reilly and Father Stone turned again to Mother Teresa Mullen of Brooklyn, this time asking not only for sisters for the Cathedral School but that the community open a novitiate in Springfield, effectively establishing another independent congregation. The bishop, who had visited the sisters in Chicopee with some frequency, stipulated that he wanted Mother Cecilia Bowen to be the superior in Springfield.[113] When the sisters arrived at St. Michael's on August 22, 1883, "Bishop O'Reilly stood at the door of the beautiful convent to greet Mother Cecilia and her three sisters," a sign of his understanding of the importance of their presence and plans for their future in the city.[114] The secular press, not usually given to praise of things Catholic, covered the event saying:

> The new convent adjacent to St. Michael's School…is a three story French roof structure; it is a substantial building…the cost of erection being about $25,000.
> The Sisters of St. Joseph, whose home it will be, at first will number about twelve. Their duties, though primarily those of education, will embrace a much wider field…They will visit the friendless, and assist in other parish works, besides giving lessons in music and needlework…
> The convent being intended for the Motherhouse in the Springfield Diocese, novices will be admitted to this House…The senior establishment of the Community is at Flushing, L.I., the only other branches of the Order in this State at present are at Jamaica Plain, near Boston, at Webster and Chicopee Falls.

Then, shifting from its positive, friendly tone, the newspaper article finishes with the warning:

---

112 The above mentioned essay names the others as Sisters Gonzaga, St. Cyril, Leocadia, Ursula, Victorine, Pelagia, Domitilla, Macarius, Callista and Dora. Ten of them would work in the school while Sister Dora "presided over the domestic arrangements." Aherne says that the original group was comprised of only seven sisters whom she does not name. The practice of designating some sisters as lay or domestic sisters was discontinued by different congregations at different times.
113 "Annals, Sisters of St. Joseph of Springfield, Mass. 1880-1909," (Archives SSJS), 2. This is a typed copy of the annals which were written almost like a history some years after the original events. Hereafter, "Annals, 1880."
114 Aherne, 29.

The new parochial school will probably effect [sic] more or less the attendance of the other schools of the city.[115]

The reporter who wrote that the school might affect public school attendance could scarcely have guessed that a few days after the sisters' arrival they would receive 800 students – a number that certainly had an impact on the local public schools.[116]

Before St. Michael's School had been open for a year, Father Gagnier, the pastor of St. Joseph's Parish asked Mother Cecilia for sisters to teach in a French-language school he wanted to open in his parish. Believing they could manage to accept it, she went with Sisters St. Hilary and St. Genevieve, the two she had chosen as the teachers, to ask the bishop's blessing on their venture. He blessed them, but added,

"God help you. I hope you will succeed, but I doubt it."[117]

With that unenthusiastic support to back them up, they went to the school. The pastor had planned a memorable opening day, celebrating a High Mass for the students before leading them and their teachers in procession to the two classrooms "situated in the low, dark basement of the church" where neither the light nor ventilation were sufficient and for which the children were expected to pay for all of their textbooks and a tuition of twenty-five cents a month.[118]

Amazingly, the school succeeded as the sisters switched classrooms so that each class had the French-speaking sister for half of each school day. The student population grew to 275, some of whom came from the Cathedral school, requiring the assistance of a lay teacher and giving some respite to the overcrowded St. Michael's.

As success bred success, the sisters opened a high school in the following year, housing it in rooms above the side altars of the Cathedral. At the end of the year it boasted its first two graduates, young women who both then passed the examinations to receive public school teaching certificates.[119] The school continued

---

115 The article is quoted in "Annals, 1880" and referenced in Aherne, 29.
116 Aherne, 30. The Springfield population saw an immense increase in the decades between 1860 and 1890, beginning with a population of 15,199 in 1860, the next decade saw a 75% increase, then slowing but significant growth until the population of 1890 was measured at 44,179. Much of that growth would have been due to increased immigration of Catholics from Europe and Ireland in particular.
117 "Annals, 1880," 6.
118 "Annals, 1880," 6.
119 Aherne, 33.

to graduate students but their classes were small because many young people, especially the boys, had to work rather than finish their education. The sisters, like their fellow Catholics who at least had the advantage of being less visible on the streets, had to endure anti-Catholic prejudices in as they adjusted to New England. The harassment the sisters had to put up with was frequent enough to mention in the annals. The story which best illustrates the situation featured the sisters, impertinent teenagers, a Good Samaritan and a parish priest who acted like the sisters' big brother:

> Several times in 1884 and 1885 the Sisters were ridiculed and jeered at by young Americans, as they were silently wending their way to the bedside of some poor sick or dying person. Several times, however, the taunting words were followed by well-directed snowballs. One Friday after school...Sister Gertrude and Sister Teresa, while on their way to visit a very sick man...were hooted at by a crowd of youths, who after the Sisters had passed struck them with several well-packed and well-aimed snowballs. Some unknown bystander wrote an indignant article to the Union, saying that this was not the first time he had seen this...and appealing to the better feelings of the Community in behalf of the unoffending religious, and demanding protection from such molestation. Father Goggin read the article...and came to the Convent to inquire into the affair. The two "victims" somewhat amused, related the experience of which they thought lightly, but Father Goggin regarded it differently...at all the Masses in the Cathedral on Sunday, he mentioned it; declaring that another such offence would not be allowed to pass unnoticed. Henceforth, the Sisters were never annoyed on the Streets of Springfield.[120]

EARLY GROWTH

The community had moved into their motherhouse at St. Michael's in August, 1883 and in spite of the amazing amount of work the sisters had taken on, the community seemed marked by real Salesian joy. Their life was attractive enough that the annals report that "the teaching corps was increased within a few weeks by the arrival of the first three postulants...who were capable of giving much needed assistance in the overcrowded classrooms." In December, the three, later known as Sisters Mary Magdalen, Mary Gertrude and Mary Mechtilde, were sent to Rutland where they received the habit from Father Boylan. The Rutland sisters' willingness to receive these sisters in their novitiate was a great relief to the new

---

120 "Annals, 1880," 9.

community in Springfield who, while happy to have the vocations, would have been very hard pressed to offer them an adequate formation program. Nevertheless, as other women joined the community, Mother Cecilia took on the responsibility of being hometown novice director while accepting help for formation from both the Brooklyn and the Rutland communities.

Little by little, Flushing's ability to shore up the new community lessened and Brooklyn sisters were gradually withdrawn. In 1885, the first to go was Sister Dora, the cook and homemaker. Until the sisters found a replacement, Mother Cecilia tried to take over her duties, a task for which she was more willing than able. The annalist explains:

> Several times when the sisters came home from school, tired and hungry, the dinner was not ready; and a few times they found no fire in the grate. Laughingly the Sisters hustled about, one preparing the potatoes, another attending to the fire…and when the hurriedly prepared dinner was served, Mother Cecilia would give "Benedicamus" and gaily ask the Sister if they were not enjoying the dinner she had cooked for them. After a few such experiences, the three young Religious recently received, dismissed their classes by turns a few minutes earlier than the others and hurried to the convent to attend to the dinner.[121]

In August, 1885, the community ended its first annual retreat with the celebration of the religious profession of their first five members, Sisters Mary Albina, Mary Rosalia, Mary Bertille, St. Hilary and Mary Valerian. Describing the ceremony, the annals say,

> They joyfully made their profession to their beloved Bishop, and requested under his direction to teach and labor in the schools of the Diocese.[122]

That final statement, makes it sound as if the request to teach were part of the profession ceremony itself. It gives the impression not only that the community saw itself integrally involved in the diocese, but also as specialists in teaching. But Mother Cecilia would see to it that their apostolate never narrowed.

MOTHER CECILIA LEADING THE WAY FROM NOVITIATE
TO ALMSHOUSE TO HOSPITAL TO JAIL

The original five sisters to join the Springfield community were joined by a steady

---

121 "Annals, 1880," 5. According to their customs, the sisters would often eat in contemplative silence. When the superior said, "Benedicamus," it signaled permission for conversation at the table.
122 "Annals, 1880," 7.

flow of companions such that by the end of the year 1888, the community numbered 38.[123] As more women joined the community, they were able to take on additional schools, but Mother Cecilia's vision and sense of mission went far beyond the classroom and even the parish. Sharing the inspiration of the original sisters in Le Puy, she seemed to have an innate drive to divide the city and uncover the needs of the neighbor. Even if she didn't have time to be a full-time novice director, she knew how to lead her sisters to understand the implications of wearing the habit of a Sister of St. Joseph. An incident preserved in the annals for 1887 illustrates Mother Cecilia's character:

> On St. Joseph's Day, 1887, the three postulants who had entered the previous autumn received the Holy Habit from Bishop O'Reilly...On the same day, after dinner, the newly received were told that they were to accompany Mother Cecilia to the almshouse to visit the poor inmates, and to bring there a trunk containing the altarstone, linens vestments, etc. to prepare for the first Mass to be celebrated in that Institute the following day. The trunk was one belonging to a Sister of the morning's Reception Party, and was used as a receptacle for the altar belongings for many years.
>
> Mr. Ivers came with the roomy carriage and in it were stowed, besides Mother Cecilia and her three new children, a large basket of oranges, bags of candy, etc., with which to gladden the poor...These good things however were shared by many a ragged urchin on the way. At the sight of any neglected looking child on the way, Mother's hand tossed an orange...
>
> After visiting the old people and making bright that short afternoon for many of them, and preparing the altar for the Mass of the morrow, the party returned to their convent home. The next Sunday, March 20, 1887, the good Bishop O'Reilly drove to the almshouse and offered the Holy Sacrifice within its walls for the first time. It was through the zealous efforts and prayers of Mother Cecilia that permission had been granted to have Holy Mass celebrated in this institution.[124]

It must have made quite an impression on the first-day novices that their superior

---

123 "Annals, 1880," 16.
124 "Annals, 1880," 12-13. Almshouses in the 1880s housed the indigent elderly and ill, some mentally ill persons and a smaller number of families or children. They were under the control of city or town governments which would typically spend between $1.50 and $2.50 per week on the care of each inmate. Many of the buildings were old and dilapidated. See: "Management of Almshouses in New England" (The Social Welfare History Project: socialwelfare.library.vcu.edu)

would immediately lead them to serve the people at the almshouse. Added to that was the symbolic yet practical gesture of using the trunk in which one of them had put all her possessions as the container in which they would transport everything necessary to outfit a temporary altar.

Mother Cecilia made a weekly practice of visiting the almshouse – and no doubt, she never went alone or empty-handed.[125] In her wake, both her sisters and the people of the area learned what the habit of the Sisters of St. Joseph was intended to symbolize.

After her determination brought her success in obtaining permission to visit and arrange for the celebration of the Eucharist at the almshouse, Mother Cecilia took on more challenging projects. First, she won the freedom to visit patients in the public hospital, a cause in which she demonstrated that the overwhelming strength of her gentle persistence. As in the sisters' educational endeavors, one success led to another and Mother Cecilia was not easily deterred. The annals explain how she won the right to visit patients in the hospital:

> Shortly before the coming of the sisters to Springfield, Father McDermott had gone to the old hospital to see one of his parishioners who was being cared for there and who wished to receive the Sacraments. But at the door he was refused admittance. He demanded to enter and said if he were again refused he would enter by force. The door was then opened for him.

Mother Cecilia heard of this and decided she would break down the barrier of prejudice and bigotry. Going to the hospital one day, she too was denied admittance, but she insisted, stating that one of her special works was to visit the sick.

> [Then,] saying, "Come, Sister," she brushed by the doorkeeper and, once in, requested to be taken through the hospital. After this, either she or the Sisters went there every week for years; reading to the patients and bringing them fruit and flowers.
>
> Then, certain that if she could bring a Catholic presence to the hospital, the little ones at the Children's Home deserved the same, she took on her next challenge. Hearing that at the Buckingham Street Home many Catholic children were being brought up in ignorance of their Faith, Mother Cecilia visited that institution and a most unwelcome visitor she was in the beginning. Her genial, kindly manner and words, and her generous offerings of clothing to the children, together with the many

---

125 Aherne, 37.

many little pleasures she gave them by bringing toys, fruits and candy, soon gained a welcome for her.

There she began her work of instructing these waifs, teaching them their prayers, and striving to keep alive in them the Faith they were in such danger of losing. She provided beads, catechisms, prayer-books and gave many a generous gift to the good old woman, a Catholic, who waited on the door, begging her to hear their prayers and to speak to them as often as possible of the Faith of their fathers. This was before the present just laws were framed, granting that Catholic children could be cared for by the Church. If they were then first given to Protestant homes or institutions, they were lost to us.[126]

As she had tried to gain popular support and lessen public suspicion about the sisters and their schools, Mother Cecilia had made it a point to get to know the leading politicians and businessmen of the city, but she relied as much on prayer as on influence. Thus, when it came to securing entrance to the most closed of all the city institutions, the jail, the annals explain how she accomplished her goal against all odds and expectations. At the same time as she was winning her way into the almshouse,

> Mother Cecilia was trying to gain a like privilege at the York Street Jail, although Bishop O'Reilly felt this could not be obtained. Some of the means used by Mother Cecilia in order to obtain this request were journeys to meet people of influence, generous offerings to cloistered religious for prayers, promises made to donate statues to poor churches…Above all, she believed God would grant her this request if her own children were models of exact observance of the Rule…

When she was convinced of a cause, Mother Cecilia Bowen literally stormed heaven and earth to win her desired outcome. The story continues:

> Mother Cecilia had called on every person of prominence and influence who could aid her in this good work, and the final decision rested with County Commissioner Root, whose home was in Westfield [10 miles from Springfield]. During the time of her absence when she went to his home to present her petition, prayers were continued in the little home chapel.
>
> Arriving in Westfield, Mother Cecilia entered a carriage and requested the driver to take her to the church where, kneeling before the she

---

126 "Annals, 1880," 19.

pleaded fervently for the success of her interview with Mr. Root. Rising from her knees, she noticed the diminutive statues brought from the former old church and unsuitable for present use in their abode. The promise was made to furnish new ones should Mr. Root give a favorable decision, which, through the goodness of God was all she desired…
To the surprise of all except herself, the great favor was at length granted late in the fall and the first Mass was offered in the prison on the Feast of St. Stanislaus, Nov. 13, 1887…We know of two churches in this vicinity to which Mother Cecilia gave statues in thanksgiving for this favor…[127]

Unfortunately, no record exists recording Commissioner Root's impression of the whole affair and what brought him to make his decision. It must have been quite a surprise to have Mother Cecilia visit him at his home where he surely had never before received Catholic woman religious. Mother Cecilia had no doubt about why she attained her outcome. Everyone around her could see that she used the faith that moves mountains as the key to open doors traditionally barred to Catholics who desired to serve their brothers and sisters in the faith – no matter where they were or why.

Once she had a foot in the door at the jail, Mother Cecilia instituted her own brand of prison ministry. The priests offered Mass every two weeks, but Mother Cecilia was there every Sunday in the company of her sisters. She would send two sisters to visit the cells with gifts of holy cards books, etc., while she taught the Catechism to the women prisoners. Her combination of strength of character and humorous self-deprecation came to the fore when she confessed to her sisters that some of the women had come to her class for the primary motive of exacting revenge against another prisoner. She found the way to calm the waters and reprimanded them and later laugh with her sisters about what a captivating teacher she was turning out to be.[128]

Dismayed at the intellectual destitution of the jail, Mother Cecilia obtained permission to establish a prison library. She then wrote to Catholic publishers, personal friends and anyone she could think of asking for the donation of two books from each. Her modest request brought such generous results that she was able to bring over 300 books to the prison library.[129]

---

127 "Annals, 1880," 13-14. She also conspired with a Protestant physician, Dr. Catherine Kennedy, to prevent Catholic children who had been removed from their homes from being placed with Protestant families who would not respect their religion. (19)
128 "Annals, 1880," 17.
129 "Annals, 1880," 17. By way of comparison, the 1871 Sadliers Catholic Directory recorded that St. Xavier's Academy near Latrobe, Pennsylvania boasted a library of 700 volumes. The annals interchange the words "prison" and "jail," all referring to the same local institution.

The archives of the Sisters of St. Joseph of Springfield preserve a letter of thanks in which the prisoners express their gratitude for the "large amount of time, labor and money the sisters expended in order to introduce such a magnificent library as you have into this prison."[130]

Into the Second Generation: Sister Educators, Mother Albina and Bishop Beavan

Mother Cecilia served the community as Superior General for nine years.

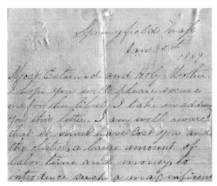

Letter from
Mother Cecilia's inmates

During that time the sisters who belonged to the Brooklyn Congregation gradually withdrew and only those who entered in Springfield or had chosen to be permanent members of the new congregation remained. But new members continued to come such that the community frequently held more than one ceremony of reception of the habit per year. In 1890, the sisters were serving in eight missions, including two in Newport, Rhode Island and one in Winterlocks, Connecticut.[131] At the close of 1889, there were 28 professed members of the community and 20 novices with six postulants ready to receive the habit in March of 1890.

In August, 1890, Mother Cecilia traveled to Flushing for a short retreat and last visit with her dear friend, Sister de Sales.[132] She returned to Springfield only to find herself growing weaker. On September 8, her birthday and a favorite feast-day, she was too ill to attend the Eucharist, but Bishop O'Reilly visited and heard her confession and brought her communion. She was anointed in the presence of all the sisters present in the motherhouse. On September 10, 1890, Mother Cecilia Bowen died while one of her friends was celebrating the Eucharist for her in the

---

130 "Annals, 1880," 17.

131 The statistical information is found in "Annals, 1880," 22, where it notes that Sacred Heart in Pawtucket, Rhode Island was the last mission opened by Mother Cecilia who, in spite of increasing weakness and illness, insisted on accompanying the sisters as they opened their new mission which was only 90 miles to the southeast of Springfield but in a different state and diocese.

132 Sister de Sales seemed in fine health when they were together but died suddenly just after bidding Mother Cecilia goodbye. When Mother Cecilia arrived at Flushing, the community was amazed to see her because Mother Teresa had received the message the mixed-up message she, not Sr. de Sales, had died. Mother Cecilia remained in Flushing for the funeral and then returned home. ("Annals, 1880," 23.)

convent chapel and other priests were gathered with her sisters around her bed. At her funeral, Bishop O'Reilly summarized his eulogy saying "She had the courage to lead a battalion and for the last ten years the only fault I have found with her was that her heart was so big she could never refuse a call for help."[133] In witness to the breadth of her influence, the priests, sisters and laity who thronged to her funeral were joined by Sheriff Brooks in representation of the prison officials. Among the letters of condolence there was, of course, one from the inmates.

After her funeral, Bishop O'Reilly met with the sisters before they returned to their various missions and asked them to write him after they returned home, giving him a preferential list of the names of three sisters they would recommend to become the acting superior until the normal time for elections. Following their suggestions, the bishop named Sister Mary Albina. The following summer, in August of 1891, the community assembled in a chapter of elections and voted unanimously, electing Sister Albina as the second Superior General of the Sisters of St. Joseph of Springfield.

MOTHER ALBINA AND BISHOP BEAVEN
SET THEIR MARK ON THE COMMUNITY

In 1885, at the age of 25, Sister Albina had been one of the first five sisters to make vows as a Sister of St. Joseph of Springfield. She was from Chicopee Falls and would have known Mother Cecilia from the time of the community's arrival in western Massachusetts. The thirty-year old superior immediately received support and then ongoing counsel from Brooklyn's Mother Teresa Mullen who remained close to and concerned about the community. As Sister Consuelo Maria Aherne, the community historian comments, Mother Teresa's questions and suggestions served as a handbook for a new superior and Mother Teresa not only kept in touch but also visited the community in person.[134]

When Bishop O'Reilly died in May, 1892, Mother Albina told Mother Teresa of her contentment with the choice of Bishop Thomas D. Beaven as his successor. With that, the elder sister gave the young Mother Albina her advice regarding relationships with the clergy, telling her, When you have God on your side and the Bishop and priests you are all right. God

---

133 "Annals, 1880," 26.
134 Aherne, 45. Aherne explains succinctly, "Mother Teresa felt very close to the Springfield Community which she was guiding so tactfully and discreetly from afar." (45)

keep them so…they are very dangerous if they ever take a turn to be otherwise.[135]

Although it didn't seem that Bishop Beaven was dangerous, neither did he permit the community to exercise as much independence as they had known in the days of Bishop O'Reilly. Seemingly closer in style to Bishop McQuaid of Rochester, Bishop Beaven took an active part in the leadership of the community, not only in financial affairs, but particularly in the religious and intellectual formation of the sisters. The annals explain,

> Desirous of the promotion and advancement of the Sisters in every way beneficial to their work of teaching, Bishop began in December 1893 to give them subjects for composition; the papers to be sent to him. This was kept up for about thirteen years…
> During the first Visitation made by Bishop in 1893, he required of Reverend Mother Albina, that she write out her meditations and submit them to him. This was continued for several months when it was changed to the more pleasant and less laborious task of writing in a book – specially kept for that purpose, a daily thought, original or selected…[136]

One wonders if the annalist had tongue in cheek as she wrote,

> During the following September, "Thought Books" were required of all the Sisters at the Motherhouse who, apart from the pleasure of seeking literary gems, were spurred on by the thought that their books were to be collected for the bishop's perusal several times a year. Rewards were given for excellence of thought selected, neatness, good writing, etc.…[137]

As the community moved into its second generation, much had changed. Their beloved Mother Albina was ten years younger than the new Bishop and had fewer

---

135 Aherne 46.
136 "Annals, 1880," 36. The bishop's commitment to the "thought books" was such that in 1908 he was not home more than two hours from a trip to Rome when he called for the books to be brought to him for inspection. That evening, says the annalist, he sent over the beautiful medals, pictures, gloves and side beads which he had brought back with him that the Sisters might see them." Later she explains that the bishop returned the thought books and gave sisters prizes according to the quality and completeness of their work in them. (76, 78)
137 "Annals, 1880," 36-38. On occasion the annalist included wry commentary in her record. In one example she recounted the sisters' reaction to the Jesuit who directed the sisters' 1895 retreat: "Some very holy and eloquent men have given our Retreats, but their holiness and eloquence are no so vividly remembered as Father Cassidy's remarkable custody of the eyes. This was somewhat of a distraction to several, who began at length to watch to see if he ever opened his eyes; but not once during his instructions were they opened for a moment." ("Annals, 1880," 41.)

than ten years' experience of vowed life when she came into office. Hardly anyone else in the Congregation had sufficient experience for her to turn to them for advice. Mother Teresa of Flushing was a strong leader, but far away and not officially of the same congregation. The bishop expressed real affection for Mother Albina and the sisters exercised a consistently strong influence on the daily life of the community.

Under the bishop's influence, intellectual advancement became a priority, even to the point that Mother Albina assigned the sisters specific times to practice their handwriting: a half an hour on Saturdays and one hour on Sundays so that they could be awarded with a Palmer Method Certificate "which the Bishop graciously distributed."[138] The community historian concluded:

> Mother Albina was an outstanding and visionary educator because, through her policies, she enabled sisters to develop their native abilities and to become more effective teachers. In a period when few men or women had a high school education, she steadfastly struggled for higher standards and used whatever gifts came to hand...[139]

At the end of her administration, Mother Albina summed up her sense of the importance of education in the life of the community by telling her sisters

> It is only through our work as teachers that we can give our Community that repute and prestige which we all so ardently desire; it is only through our life as religious teachers that we can merit the respect of the Catholic world; it is only by a constant zeal for greater efficiency, that we can be worthy spouses of our Lord and Master-Teacher.[140]

One of the major developments in the sisters' ministry of education was the establishment of The Elms Academy, a school that Bishop Beavan had sanctioned in Pittsfield 1897, but which was moved to Chicopee when its success proved improbable in that remote area. Bishop Beavan purchased an estate to house the school which held its open house and inauguration on August 20, 1899. Under the auspices of the Sisters of St. Joseph, the school offered a normal school certificate and came to be known as the "College." Little by little it grew, evolving into Our Lady of the Elms College, an institution prized because it gave the sisters of St. Joseph the opportunity not just to teach but to inculcate their philosophy of

---

138 Aherne, 75.
139 Aherne, 79.
140 Aherne, 79, citing a letter of Mother Albina to SSJ, Springfield, Mass. Annals, p. 74.

education in others, thereby amplifying their influence on Catholic education and educators in general.[141]

Mother Albina served the congregation as Superior General for 20 years, from 1891-1911. During Mother Albina's term the sisters served in 16 elementary schools, 8 parochial high schools and their academy/college. The sisters taught in mill towns and the Berkshires, from Springfield to Rhode Island and Connecticut, in well-equipped schools and basement classrooms partitioned by temporary walls or curtains, always and everywhere striving to live out Father Médaille's maxim, "be content to have much, to have little or to have nothing, for our little design requires perfect detachment."[142]

While Mother Albina was in office, Bishop Beavan purchased "Mont Marie" in the sisters' name. The property was a summer vacation spot where they eventually added buildings to serve as a retirement home and a novitiate. The beloved motherhouse on the Cathedral grounds, beautiful as it was in 1883, began to show its age and was not adequate to meet all the needs of the growing community.

Bishop Beavan expected to be the decision-maker on every matter of consequence. He made the purchases of land and solicited and approved building plans. He handed out the sisters' annual assignments and approved their travel plans. In the days before the invention of antibiotics, the population was vulnerable a variety of potentially fatal diseases. The Springfield sisters, like sisters from Rochester and other communities, and other groups in the north found respite and a healing climate by spending time with sisters in Florida, Georgia and even Los Angeles. The annals make frequent mention of Mother Albina accompanying sisters to visit Sisters of St. Joseph in one of those places and even needing the respite herself. In 1911, Mother Albina decided to travel south with a companion at a time when the bishop was not available to give her the necessary permission. As a result of that unauthorized trip, he removed her from office on September 1, 1911, appointing Sister John Berchmans Somers as her replacement until the time for a chapter of elections.[143] When that chapter was celebrated in June, 1912, "Mother John Berchmans was elected Superior General, Mother Albina, assistant."

---

141 Aherne 83.
142 Quoted by Aherne, 89.
143 Aherne, 90. The exact motive for her removal is not openly discussed or recorded. It is possible that other undisclosed reasons or disagreements played their part in the bishop's decision. The implication that it was for reasons of health overlooks her rather consistent struggles with health through the time of her leadership; he health problems were not new or apparently exceptional in 1911.

Indicating that Mother Albina held no grudge against the bishop, the community history goes on to explain, that Mother Albina "continued to see Bishop Beaven, to attend his Masses in the Motherhouse chapel, to breakfast with him often where he was a guest."[144]

Mother Albina remained on the council until 1924. In 1925, her diabetes and other health problems became aggravated and on February 20, 1925, she died at the motherhouse where almost 40 years previously she had made vows as one the "five foundation stones" of Mother Cecilia's new Congregation of the Sisters of St. Joseph of Springfield, Massachusetts. Her successor, Mother John Berchmans served as Superior General from 1912 until 1948.

The Sisters of St. Joseph of Springfield received a diverse legacy from their first two superiors general. From Mother Cecilia, they learned the implications of living Father Médaille's Maxim 7: "Embrace at least in desire the salvation and perfection of the whole world and apply yourself seriously and totally to do with perfection the present will of God." To that spirit, Mother Albina added the impetus of Maxim 90: "Accomplish with great diligence and perfection everyday actions and extraordinary ones."

Springfield was the last congregation that would be founded out of Brooklyn. It is highly unlikely that Mother Teresa Mullen had any idea of how much would result from her willingness to send sisters to missions outside the Diocese of Brooklyn. She seemed to do what she did simply because there was a need and she was able to respond. She exhibited a rare, graced ability to maintain ties, offer support and allow groups to establish their independence even as the door remained open to those who wished to return. She gave generously and her own Congregation would remain one of the largest and strongest in the country.

---

144 Aherne, 91.

∞

Chapter Eight: The Design Goes West and North: Arizona, Concordia, Wichita, La Grange

CAST OF CHARACTERS

Sister Monica Corrigan, Diarist: Recorded the trek to Arizona with Sisters Mary Emerentia Bonnefoy, Mary Ambrosia Archinaud, Euphrasia Suchet, Hyacinth Blanc, Maximus Croissat, and Martha Peters

Mother Stanislaus Leary: Foundress Rochester (1868), Concordia (1885), La Grange (1899)
Mother Bernard Sheridan: Foundress Wichita
Mother Alexine Gosselin: Entered at Concordia in 1866, Foundress La Grange
Mother Bernard Gosselin: Entered at Concordia, went to La Grange after first vows in 1900, Founded Orange (1912)

Bishop Jean Baptiste Salpointe, 1825 – 1898, First Bishop of Arizona
Bishop Jean Baptiste Miège, 1815-1884, Vicar Apostolic of the Indian Territory, Kansas
Archbishop Patrick Feehan: Archbishop of Chicago, 1880 – 1902
Bishop Richard Scannell, Bishop of Concordia, 1887 – 1891
Bishop John J. Hennessy, Bishop of Wichita, 1888 -1920

Bishop Peter Muldoon: Auxiliary Bishop of Chicago, 1900 – 1908, First bishop of Rockford, IL, 1908 – 1927
Archbishop James E. Quigley, Bishop of Buffalo, 1897 – 1903, Archbishop of Chicago, 1903 -1915
Archbishop George Mundelein, Auxiliary Bishop of Brooklyn, 1909 -1915, Archbishop of Chicago, 1915 -1939.

THE SISTERS OF ST. JOSEPH IN THE ARIZONA TERRITORY

On December 8, 1869, Sister Mary Emiliana (Elizabeth) Kinsley became the 400th woman received into the Congregation of the Sisters of St. Joseph of Carondelet.[1] In 1867, the Congregation had received temporary Vatican approval of the Constitution and the community had opened forty-one missions in the provinces of St. Louis, St. Paul and Troy / Albany. In 1868 the Congregation received a record

---

1 The number comes from the Carondelet Congregational Profession Record data base. Sister Emiliana, from Wyoming County, PA, had come to Carondelet August 28, 1869, and was received after a postulate of slightly more than three months. She served in Hannibal and Kansas City, Missouri before going to Tucson in 1883 where she remained until her death in 1888 at the age of forty-one. The map is public domain and may be found at: https://upload.wikimedia.org/wikipedia/commons/2/29/UnitedStatesExpansion.png

number of forty-two women into the provincial novitiates.[2] Carondelet sisters were active in the states of Missouri, Illinois, Minnesota, Wisconsin, Michigan, and New York in ministries that included primary and secondary education, child-care, ministry to Native Americans and health care. The Congregation had grown significantly in 33 years.

In the time since the first missionary sisters had come from Lyon to Missouri, the U.S. had extended its Southwestern border to the Pacific Ocean. The 1845 annexation of Texas was quickly followed by the Mexican-American War with the result that what now comprises the states of California, Nevada, Utah, much of Arizona, New Mexico, Colorado and part of Wyoming were added to U.S. territory. That immense increase in territory demanded rapid reorganization of the Catholic Church in the west at the same time that immigration was bringing

National expansion: The light colored southwestern area represents Mexican territory lost to the U.S.

millions of Catholic immigrants to the east of the country. The first bishop of Arizona, Jean Baptiste Salpointe,[3] left a picture of the early missionaries' challenges in the southwest when he described the 1850 selection of Bishop Jean Baptiste Lamy as first bishop of the new Vicariate Apostolic of New Mexico.

> The young priest, full of zeal…labored…in several missions of Ohio and Kentucky until, to his great surprise and amazement, he was notified of his appointment as Bishop of the recently created Vicariate Apostolic of New Mexico. The limits of the Vicariate were those of the territory conceded in 1848 by the Mexican government to the United States by the treaty of Guadalupe Hidalgo…[4]

---

2 Forty-two was an unusual number of new novices: in 1867 there were 31 receptions and in 1869, 18. Of the forty-two women received in 1868, seven belonged to the Troy/Albany Province, five to the St. Paul Province, one came from Moutiers, France and the remaining twenty-nine belonged to the St. Louis Province.

3 French missionaries continued to offer themselves to the Church in the U.S. and among those were three from the area of Clermont-Ferrand who ministered together and would have a significant impact on the history of the Church in the West: Jean-Baptiste Lamy, first Archbishop of Santa Fe, Jean-Baptiste Salpointe, first bishop of Arizona, and Joseph Machebeuf who became the first bishop of Colorado.

4 The other part of Colorado and territory east was part of the Vicariate Apostolic for the Indian Territory east of the Rocky Mountains for which Jean-Baptiste Miège from the area of Moutiers, France, was named as bishop in 1850.

The young Bishop…was anxious to start for the field of his labors, but the Far West was yet very little known to most of the inhabitants of Cincinnati and still less did they know what route would safely lead to New Mexico. What was called "the traders' trail," started from St. Louis by steamboat to Independence and from that place, by wagon to Santa Fe, about 900 miles…through prairies without any settlements. This was the most direct route for New Mexico…it was rather dangerous…on account of the roving Comanche Indians and during the winter season on account of the snow.[5]

In 1867, Bishop Lamy of Santa Fe started petitioning Carondelet for sisters to serve in New Mexico. He began by sending a priest to the motherhouse with his request and followed the visit of his emissary with a letter, adding a request for sisters to go to Arizona as well as New Mexico. The response Mother St. John Facemaz sent the bishop exhibited French diplomacy spiced with straightforward American candor. On April 20, 1868, she wrote:

Right Rev. Bishop,
In reply…allow me to say that I regret having been absent when the Rev. Father from Las Vegas called here. It would have spared me the additional regret of having to refuse your Lordship a request which is certainly very flattering to our Community; although we appreciate the honor of the preference shown to us before others more worthy, we cannot possibly arrange matters to accept your proffered kindness.

Explaining that the resources of the Congregation were stretched as far as possible and admitting that someone else may have made an impulsive promise she went on to explain:

Our Constitution does not allow us to employ the novices in the works of our Institute until after their profession, and we have as many establishments open at present as we have professed members to undertake the work of them for the next two or three years.

---

5 Salpointe, Jean Baptiste, *Soldiers of the Cross. Notes on the ecclesiastical history of New Mexico, Arizona, and Colorado*, (Banning, CA: St Boniface's Industrial School, 1989), 194-5. What Lamy called the traders' trail is more widely known as the Santa Fe Trail. Arduous travel was but one problem. When Bishop Lamy arrived in Santa Fe he discovered that neither the few priests of the territory nor even the Bishop of Durango to which it had belonged had received notification of the change in jurisdiction. Lamy immediately left for Durango, Mexico, an 850 mile trip on horseback, to resolve the situation, leaving his companion, Rev. Joseph Machebeuf, in Santa Fe. Because Machebeuf spoke no Spanish, the local people were slow to believe that he was a Catholic. (Ibid. 196 - 199)

In regard to the promise of sending Sisters…allow me to inform your
Lordship it was only an anticipated conjecture; the Sisters did not know
that the Holy See, before approving our Rule, would require us to keep
the novices confined to the novitiate; and very reasonably thought
we could spare some professed members who could be replaced by
novices, but having to call home the novices employed in teaching in
St. Louis and other places, we find our numbers very much diminished
and cannot spare any for opening any more houses at present.
Requesting Your Lordship will have the kindness to excuse us…I remain,
Your Lordship's humble Svt. In J.C.
Mother St. John, Surpss. Gen.[6]

Bishop Lamy acknowledged her letter without allowing it to divert him from his
goal. On June 25, 1868, he wrote again, explaining the significance of the place and
the people's readiness to accept the sisters.

Mother Superior,
I was asking sisters of your community for two places, Las Vegas in New
Mexico and Tucson in Arizona. Both places are becoming important;
more so Tucson being the capital of Arizona with a population of about
three thousand people, more than half of it Catholics and the others
well disposed for the establishment of our school there.[7] The house has
been built large enough for boarders and day scholars, and has ample
grounds.[8] We have there in Tucson three priests…There is a great deal of
good to be done there, and as you have many sisters, I hope we will not
be disappointed in having applied to you.

Almost as an afterthought he added:

The English and Spanish will have to be taught. The Spanish is a very
easy language, especially for one who knows French.

---

6 Mother St. John Facemaz to Bishop Jean-Baptiste Lamy (Carondelet Archives). Bishop Lamy was a native
of the Auvergne region of France which included Le Puy. He could well have known Sisters of St. Joseph in his
homeland before becoming a missionary to the U.S. Mother St. John's reference to the rule was timely as in
1867 the community had received a 10-year probationary approval of the *Constitutions*.
7 For a comparison, St. Louis had a population of 310,864 in 1870 and it would grow to 350,510 during the next
decade.
8 The bishop neglected to narrate the details of the construction. The building was made of adobes, and the
timber for the roof had been brought from the mountains 65 miles from Tucson at a cost of $300 – an immense
sum for a poor western town in the 1860s. (See Very Rev. James J. Defouri *Historical Sketch of the Catholic
Church in New Mexico* (San Francisco: McCormick Bros. Printers, 1887), 63.)

Hoping to have a favorable answer I remain
Your humble Servt.
John B. Lamy[9]

Although Mother St. John was obliged to refuse Bishop Lamy's request, the western clergy remained in hopeful contact with her. One of the priests mentioned by Bishop Lamy was another Frenchman also from the area of Clermont-Ferrand, Jean-Baptiste Salpointe whom Bishop Lamy had named as his vicar and pastor of the parish in Tucson in 1866.[10] In 1868, the Territory of Arizona was made a Vicariate Apostolic and when Jean-Baptiste Salpointe was named its first bishop, he went home to Clermont-Ferrand for his episcopal consecration and to search for missionaries to help him and the other priest in the area care for the needs of the people. While he was visiting the Society of the Propagation of the Faith in Lyon, Bishop Salpointe wrote to Mother St. John Facemaz at Carondelet:

Lyon, June 5th 1869
Dear Sister in Christ,

You will remember that last year you promised to Rt. Rev. Bishop Lamy of Sta. Fe some Sisters for the Territory of Arizona. I was then the priest of Tucson and it was for me that the Bishop wrote to you. Since that time, I have been elected Bishop of Arizona...

Now I have received notice that the said [convent for Sisters of St. Joseph] will be prepared by the middle of next month and that our people is [sic] very anxious to receive the Sisters announced to him a long time since...

I hope your determination has not changed and the Sisters will be ready to start when I will go for them, in August, I think. Now Dear Sister, how many Sisters can you let me have? If it was possible, I would like to have a sufficient number for two houses; one in Tucson and another in Las Cruces...It is not necessary to tell you how advantageous it would be for the Sisters to have two houses of the same order in the territory.

---

9 Lamy to Facemaz, June 25, 1868 (Archives, Carondelet)
10 Jean-Baptiste Salpointe had been in New Mexico since 1859. In 1864, the Jesuits withdrew from Arizona and the territory was left without priests until 1866 when Salpointe and two companions accepted Lamy's request to serve the area. The mission was far from easy with frequent news of settlers killed by Indians, frequent illnesses from brackish water and little in the way of beds beyond a blanket on a dirt floor.

Please let me know what you think about that.
Your respectful and obedient Servant in Christ,
J.B., Salpointe[11]

Even though he was writing from France, Bishop Salpointe was thinking from the perspective of an intrepid missionary in a vast territory: the second location he suggested for the sisters was a mere 275 miles from Tucson.[12]

Six months after writing from Lyon, Bishop Salpointe visited Mother St. John in St. Louis and she assured him that she would send sisters for his mission. On January 6, 1870, he wrote again saying that he was raising the funds for the sisters' travel and seeking advice about the route they should take. He

1870 U.S. Rail System

wrote from Tucson to let Mother St. John know of the arrangements he had made:

> Good Mother...
> On my arrival in Tucson I had the pleasure of finding the house of the Sisters of St. Joseph (this is the name we are giving it) entirely furnished and all my people almost in anger against me because the sisters had not arrived...we have been in quest of the money which is sufficient for their journey which I will have reach you in a few days. I will send herein a plan...of the establishment...To assure the Sisters the right to the property, an arrangement has been made...Be kind enough to tell me if it should be made in your name or in that of the superior you are going to send us....Beyond that I can make a deed of gift to the Sisters of a kitchen garden to an extent of 200 square yards...[13]

The bishop went on to apologize for the fact that the house was "not as good as

---

11 Salpointe to Mother St. John Facemaz, June 5, 1869 (Archives, Carondelet)
12 The bishop did not specify where Las Cruces of which he spoke was located, but New Mexico seems the obvious place. When Bishop Lamy had applied for sisters his suggestion was that they come for Tucson in Arizona and Las Vegas in New Mexico, cities more than 550 miles apart, all separated by desert and mountainous terrain. To put the request in perspective, at its widest point, France is 572 miles wide, a little more than twice the distance from Tucson to Las Cruces.
13 Salpointe to Mother St. John, Feb. 17, 1870.
The rail map is from http://users.humboldt.edu/ogayle/Hist%20111%20Images/RR1870.jpg

that of Carondelet," but that it was in good condition. He also said that it would be best for the sisters to travel by way of San Francisco and San Diego as that would be less dangerous than crossing the plains, mountains and desert from the east.

THE TREK OF THE SEVEN SISTERS

On April 20, 1870, seven Sisters of St. Joseph left Carondelet, headed for Tucson, Arizona. The superior of the group, thirty-seven year old Sister Mary Emerentia Bonnefoy, had made vows in 1856 and came to Carondelet as a missionary from Moutiers in 1858. She had served as a teacher in Sulphur Springs, Mississippi and Oswego, New York, before being chosen for the Arizona mission.[14] Sister Mary Ambrosia Archinaud entered the Sisters of St. Joseph of Moutiers at the age of 17 in 1833. She came to the U.S. in 1857 and served as a superior in St. Louis and Illinois before going to Tucson.[15] Sister Euphrasia Suchet, another missionary from Moutiers, came to the United States in 1867 and served as Director of Novices in St. Paul before going to Arizona where her ministry would include teaching in the mission school at San Xavier del Bac.[16] Thirty-seven year old Sister Hyacinth Blanc had entered the congregation at Moutiers and arrived in St. Louis in 1857 within two months of her vows. She had been missioned in Oswego and Troy, New York and was a superior in St. Louis and Hannibal, Missouri, before joining the pioneer group to Arizona.[17] Sister Maximus Croissat came from Moutiers in 1861, shortly after making vows in Moutiers. As a founder of a mission among Native Americans in Assinins, Michigan in 1866, she was prepared to open the San Xavier del Bac Indian School in Arizona in 1873.[18] Sister Martha Peters, a native of Ireland, made vows as a lay sister in St. Louis in 1861. She served in Arizona from 1870 until 1891, when she returned to St. Louis where she died in 1894 at the age of 56. The chronicler for the group was Sister Monica Corrigan, a convert born in Quebec who entered Carondelet from Kansas City and made vows in 1869 at the age of 23. In addition to writing a diary of the sisters' journey, in the 1890s Sister Monica began the work of collecting the history of the Carondelet Congregation.[19]

---

14 Sister Mary Emerentia died in Arizona on August 1, 1874.

15 When Sister Emerentia died, Sister M. Ambrosia became superior for one year. She died as a member of the California Province in 1888.

16 Sister Euphrasia was also a provincial counselor from 1876 to 1882. She died in Tucson on April 10, in 1904 at the age of 66.

17 Sister Hyacinth taught in Tucson, Fort Yuma, and Florence and was also a local superior. She died in Tucson on July, 15, 1904 at the age of 71.

18 Sister Maximus also served at Fort Yuma and St. Joseph Academy in Tucson and was both assistant provincial and mistress of novices. Her name is variously spelled as Maxime and Maximus.

19 The information about each of the sisters is from their personal files in the Carondelet Archives.

Mother St. John Facemaz asked Sister Monica to keep a journal of the sisters' journey to Arizona. Although she did not include an entry for each of their thirty-seven travel days, her diary verifies that there was little that could be considered mundane about their adventure. From the beginning their missionary spirituality is clear. Sister Monica openly admitted the cost of leaving friends, family and the known. Describing their train ride to Kansas City, a journey normally familiar to many sisters, she recalled the group's melancholy compared to others who had traveled the same route:

> It is certainly true that none of them ever went over it with the sad hearts we experienced on that ever memorable night… It is quite probable we may never again meet here below; and it is only when this thought occurs to me, that I know how deeply I love them. Oh! The incomprehensible beauty of our Holy Faith! How consoling to know with an infallible certainty that we are accomplishing the will of God with an assured hope of being reunited in our heavenly country to those beloved ones we have left here below, for the love of Jesus and the salvation of souls. With these, and similar reflections, we passed the first night. We were then in Kansas City.[20]

The cost of leaving loved ones is the only negative sentiment Sister Monica expresses. She never dwelt on the very realistic fears the sisters might have had; she wrote a simple chronicle of the difficulties that more dramatic writers might have dwelt on, if not embellished. The group's ability to tackle adversity with straightforward determination may have been influenced by the fact that six of the seven had already left home and hearth and crossed the Atlantic in the desire to live out their missionary zeal. As evidenced in the diary, the group also made use of a good measure of humor to supplement their missionary fervor.

The trip brought the sisters into contact with a variety of experiences and people that would never have been part of their normal circle. When they reached the Rockies, of all of the group, Sister Monica seemed to be the least enamored with the grandeur of the scenery while the dizzying heights riveted her attention. In her entry for April 24, she wrote:

> This afternoon we entered in the Rocky Range…at an elevation of 8,242 feet…It is a frightful and desolate region; nothing to be seen but snow-

---

20 This and all the diary quotes which follow are from "*The Trek of the Seven Sisters, Diary of Sister Monica Corrigan*," (Archives, Carondelet). An Online copy can be found at http://cssjfed.org/about-us/history.

clad mountains of rock, whose summits appear to touch the clouds. The cars pass over frightful chasms; the rails are laid on logs resting only pillars, whose only support are the craggy rocks beneath. Some of these chasms seem to extend about the length of three city blocks; going over these places every person appeared to hold his breath; and it was only when safe on firm ground that conversation was resumed and commendations made on the terrors and perils of the place.

I chanced to be sleeping when crossing one of these places. Sister Martha awoke me, telling me to "Wakeup and take notes of this beautiful scenery." When I saw where we were, sleep forsook me immediately. I was really terrified.

The Sisters enjoyed the scenery very much.

In addition to the scenery, the sisters had little choice but to interact with the different characters who shared their train car. Making it clear that they had not left behind the geography of religious prejudice, the entry for April 24 also recounted:

In one car were four Protestant ministers and their ladies who were on their way to China, to convert those benighted idolaters. There were almost as many religious denominations represented as there were persons in the car. Whether owing to our presence, or not, we do not know; but, however, religion was the principal topic of conversation throughout the entire journey. Everyone maintained his own opinion and proved it from the Bible, agreeing only in one point that "Catholicity is intolerable."

In spite of the prejudice, the sisters were able to cultivate good relationships among their fellow travelers.

As difficult as their leave-taking had been and as harrowing as the train ride through the Rockies proved, those experiences were but a mild introduction to what would await them in the later stages of their adventure. After arriving in San Francisco and enjoying the hospitality of the Sisters of Mercy, the sisters boarded a steamship for a four day journey to San Diego. With little ado, Sister Monica then explained the beginning of the next and most extraordinary leg of their journey: travel by wagon from San Diego to Tucson. Now, for the first time, the sisters traveled without the protection of train or boat. Sister Monica described both their conveyance and the experience of being on the trail.

Saturday, May 7, 1870, Leaving San Diego
The carriage was too small for all to ride inside, consequently one was obliged to ride outside with the driver. Sister Ambrosia volunteered to make the great act of mortification and humility. It is beyond description

what she suffered in riding two hundred miles in a country like this, without protection from the rays of a tropical sun... We camped, about sunset, at the foot of a mountain; made some tea, and took our supper off a rock. All were cheerful. We wished Reverend Mother could see us at supper. After offering thanks to the Giver of all good, we retired to rest – Mother, Sisters Euphrasia and Martha under the wagon, others inside where there was room for only two to lie down.

Sister Euphrasia and I sat in a corner and tried to sleep. We had scarcely closed our eyes when the wolves began to howl about us. We were terribly frightened and recommended ourselves to the safe-keeping of Him who guides the weary traveler on his way. We feared they would consume our little store of provisions and thus let us perish in the wilderness, but the driver told us not to fear. During the night Sister Euphrasia was startled from her sleep by one of the horses licking her face. She screamed fearfully, and we concluded she was a prey of the wolves.

The next day, May 8, which the sisters celebrated as the Feast of the Patronage of St. Joseph, their adventures with Mother Nature were supplemented by their first interactions with cowboys.

At noon we came to a cool, shady place in which we rested. The ranch man, (a person who keeps refreshments, stable feed, etc. on the western plains), invited us to dinner. He offered us a good meal of all we could desire. There were several ranch-men there from the neighboring stations, but no women. There are few women in this country. After dinner they became very sociable. We retired to the stable, where our driver and only protector was, and they followed. Some of them proposed marriage to us, saying we would do better by accepting the offer than by going to Tucson, for we would all be massacred by the Indians. The simplicity and earnestness with which they spoke put indignation out of the question, as it was evident they meant no insult, but our good. They were all native American.[21] For that afternoon we had amusement enough.

On May 13, after crossing 40 miles of desert, the group reached Fort Yuma where the Vicar General of Arizona awaited them. He had arranged for a few days' stay with a Mexican family which gave the sisters their first taste of an Arizona life-

---

21 At that time "native American" implied that they were Anglo-American's rather than of Hispanic or African background or very recent immigrants.

Fort Yuma Arizona, 1875

style in which Spanish was the primary language. The sisters thought that the worst was well behind them as Father Francisco provided not only a carriage, but also a cook and a well-stocked larder to carry them through the remainder of the journey. Their confidence was premature. Sister Monica narrated the next tale with the humor born after the fact:

> When we were about to resume our journey, Mother started in advance of us for a walk. On coming to a place where the roads crossed, she took the wrong direction. After a short interval, not perceiving any traces of her, we became alarmed for her safety. Father and Sister Ambrosia immediately started in pursuit. When the driver descried her in the distance, he ran as fast as possible in order to overtake her; and she on perceiving a man running after her and not recognizing him, ran too, with all her might.

Once captured and then assured that she was in no danger, Sister Emerentia contented herself with riding inside the carriage.

About a week after leaving Yuma, as they took their mid-day rest, the sisters got a new perspective on the Native Americans among whom they would minister. With obvious delight and fascination Sister Monica explained:

> When we stopped at noon, there was no room for us in the inn, so that we had not even a tree to shelter us from the burning rays of a tropical sun. The ruins of some old buildings were near; Mother went there to rest, and fell asleep. A troop of nude Indians came in the meantime, who were peaceable. They had the consideration to be quiet and let her sleep. Sister Martha was resting on an old cowhide. A noble warrior perceiving her, stole softly up and sat down beside her as her Guardian Angel. The

in washing our stockings and handkerchiefs, and amused myself by taking notes for my "Journal."

Although that encounter had been more than peaceable, the group knew that they were crossing through the most dangerous portion of their journey. Then, for inexplicable reasons, when they had stopped for the night, a group of soldiers appeared saying that they had been sent as an escort for an unidentified group of travelers. When the sisters realized just how dangerous the last 75 miles of the journey would be, they deduced that St. Joseph had sent the necessary guard to ward off the unfriendly Apaches who were known to attack travelers on the route. On Ascension Thursday, May 26, 1870, after the sisters had journeyed for nearly forty days, a procession of priests and people came to accompany the sisters for the last few miles of their trek to the city of Tucson. By the time they arrived, the accompanying crowd had swelled to three-thousand and they were welcomed with a tumultuous reception that included the discharge of guns, fireworks, the ringing of church bells and the city lit up as for a great fiesta. Sister Monica ended the journal saying:

> On reaching the convent we found our good Bishop in company of several ladies and gentlemen, awaiting our arrival. The crowd then fired a salute and dispersed...The Bishop conducted us to our dormitory; one of the priests brought us some water and...the ladies ushered us into the refectory where a nice supper was prepared for us...
> When we had finished our repast, they departed, leaving us in quiet possession of our new home: "St. Joseph's Convent, Tucson, Arizona." Our first act was to return thanks to our merciful Lord, to our dear Mother, Mary, and likewise to our glorious Patriarch, St. Joseph, for preserving us from the many and great dangers to which we were exposed for the love of Jesus and the salvation of souls.

Ten days after their arrival, on June 6, 1870, the sisters opened what the townspeople called "The French School." The popular name indicates that one of the sisters' first urgent tasks would be to learn Spanish, the language spoken by the majority of the population of that area since before Father Kino established the mission San Xavier del Bac in 1692 until 1848, when the territory became part of the United States. In spite of the sisters' struggles with the language, the school succeeded in providing a desperately needed service as the only school in the Territory.[22]

---

22 According to an early history of Arizona, "The first regular educational establishment was opened by the sisters [sic] of St. Joseph in Tucson. For years this was the only school in the Territory and from many isolated

A little more than two years after the sisters arrived, Bishop Salpointe asked them to open a school at San Xavier del Bac, a Papago mission 16 miles south of Tucson. Sisters Maximus and Euphrasia staffed the school which remained open only for three years because the U.S. government rearranged the tribal living situations, removing the native people from their homes in the area.[23] The original seven sisters would not be joined by others for three and a half years.  In 1873, Bishop Salpointe stopped at Carondelet on his return from Rome and met with Mother Agatha Guthrie, Carondelet's second superior general, to arrange for additional sisters for the Arizona mission. The second group, Sisters Lucretia Burns, Francesca Kelly and Martha Dunn, left Kansas City together with Bishop Salpointe going by rail as far as the town of Kit Carson in southeastern Colorado, and from there by wagon, a trip that took almost two full months.[24]

Sister Basil Morris

Before a third group of sisters arrived from the east, the Congregation had received permission to make the Arizona mission a province of the Congregation. In 1876 Mother Irene Facemaz was named as the first provincial superior.[25]

---

towns...parents sent their children to the Academy of St. Joseph. Although...the instruction given partook somewhat of a religious character, yet no discrimination was shown by the good sisters. The children of poor people of all denominations...were received and taught gratis...the legislature of 1877 voted it $300 out of the Territorial treasury. It was not until the year 1878 that public schools were established." See: Patrick Hamilton, *The Resources of Arizona* (San Francisco, 1884) 248. At the behest of Bishop Lamy, the Sisters of Loretto from Kentucky had come to the New Mexico in 1852 and had ventured as far as Denver by 1864, but there were no other sisters in the entire Arizona Territory in 1870.

23 The sisters would open a school at San Xavier again in 1888. See Mary Williams, CSJ, *All Things New, The story of the Sisters of St. Joseph of Carondelet in the Los Angeles Province*, (St. Paul: Good Ground Press, 2104), 20.

24 They left on December 1 and arrived in Tuscon on January 27. (Williams, 21) Sister Lucretia from Troy NY was received at Carondelet in 1867; Sister Francesca was Irish born and entered from Kansas City, being received in 1868; Sister Mary Martha of Jesus Dunn was born in Canada and lived in Chicago before being received at Carondelet in 1868. These three sisters had been in the novitiate together and while they diminished the French character of the mission, two of the next four sisters sent (1876) were Moutiers missionaries. Along the way, the troupe stopped in Denver where they met French-born Bishop Joseph Machebeuf who gave them advice based on his experience in the territory.

25 Mother Irene Facemaz was Mother St. John's younger sister. Received in Moutiers in 1854, the same year that Mother St. John arrived in the U.S., she came to the U.S. in 1867 with seven other missionary sisters. Before being named provincial in Arizona, she had been director of novices in Troy, N.Y. She returned to St. Louis from Arizona in 1883. A third Facemaz sibling, Sister Mary Agnes, came from Moutiers in 1857 at the age of 25 and served as director of novices and a local superior before being assigned to Troy where she died in 1882 at the age of 50. The Facemaz sisters also had two nieces, Sisters Mary Daniel and Mary Joseph who were missioned from Moutiers to the U.S.

After one year, Mother Basil Morris, who had come from Moutiers in 1861, replaced Mother Irene as provincial superior and served in that role for three years.[26]

In 1878, the Santa Fe Railroad asked the sisters to open a hospital in Prescott, the Territorial capitol of Arizona, a week's stage coach journey from Tucson. The small institution, at which payments came as often in produce as in cash, remained open only seven years as circumstances indicated that the need was not great. Two years later Bishop Salpointe opened a 12 bed hospital in Tucson and asked the sisters to take charge of it, implying that they would take on the nursing, maintenance, cleaning and cooking. In 1882, Mother Gonzaga Grand, a Moutiers missionary who became the third provincial, arranged to buy St. Mary's Hospital from the diocese and purchased additional land where she built a new academy which also served as the provincial house and novitiate.[27]

When Mother Gonzaga Grand became provincial superior in 1881, the Arizona province included five communities with a total of 25 sisters serving in three select schools, three parochial schools, and two hospitals.[28] In spite of the growth of ministries and the influx of missionaries from Carondelet, only six women from Tucson entered the Congregation between 1870 and 1889.[29] Because of that, the province was temporarily suppressed and the membership came under the aegis of the St. Louis Province.

By 1899, the sisters had opened schools in Tucson, Florence and Yuma in Arizona, and in Oakland, California, as well as Academies in Prescott and Tucson Arizona, and in San Diego, Oakland and Los Angeles. They were also serving on Indian missions in Yuma, San Diego and Banning, California and had an orphanage in Tucson and a Home for the Deaf in Oakland. It was little wonder then that the Carondelet General Chapter of 1899 voted to reopen the province and settled on making its province center in the booming city of Los Angeles.[30]

---

26 Sister Basil had served as director of novices and Assistant Provincial in Troy and was a local superior in Hancock, MI, before going to Arizona. In 1881, she was named superior of the newly founded hospital in Georgetown, CO, from where she went to Oconto and Keshena, WI, the latter being a mission among the Menominee people. She died in St. Louis in 1918 at the age of 80.

27 In 2016, St. Mary's claimed the fame of being the oldest continually operating hospital in the State of Arizona,

28 See Williams, 24, which includes the data reported to the 1881 General Chapter that the sisters were teaching a total of 490 students and that 650 patients had been treated in the previous year.

29 Those were Sisters Mary Agnes Orosco, Amelia Leon, Teresa Ortiz, Clara Otero, Mary Joseph Franco and Mary Juan Noli. After the latter three sisters were received in 1879, there would not be another vocation from Tucson until Mary Josefa Elias entered in 1889; the next to enter was Mary Alfrida (Mary) Doyle who was received in 1901.

30 In 1870, Tucson had a population of 3,215 and Los Angeles 5,728. Between 1890 and 1900, Los Angeles more than doubled its population from 50,395 to 102,479 while in 1900, Tucson's population was 7,531.

By then, over 1650 women had become Sisters of St. Joseph of Carondelet and the congregation's provincial structure would continue with four provinces until the 1920s when the Sisters of St. Joseph of Georgia, a foundation originally from Le Puy, would become the congregation's fifth province.

As they grew and spread, one area the Carondelet Congregation seemingly skipped over was the vast state of Kansas which lay between their Missouri and Colorado missions. Although the missionaries who had come from Moutiers had originally planned to minister there, the Sisters of St. Joseph would not be established in Kansas until 1883 when Mother Stanislaus Leary and companions accepted the invitation of Bishop Louis Mary Fink, the first Bishop of Leavenworth, whose diocese included the entire state of Kansas.

THE EARLIEST WESTWARD EXPANSION

GEOGRAPHY OF THE CONGREGATIONAL SPREAD

St. Louis to Philadelphia 1847, 900 Miles
St. Louis to St. Paul 1851, 530 Miles
Philadelphia to Toronto 1851, 475 Miles
St. Louis to Wheeling 1853, 545 Miles
St. Louis to Canandaigua 1854, 830 Miles
Philadelphia to Canandaigua 1854, 300 Miles
Philadelphia to Brooklyn 1856, 300 Miles
St. Louis to Oswego 1858, 895 Miles
St, Louis to Erie, PA. 1860, 660 Miles
St. Louis to Tucson 1870, 1,500 Miles
Erie to Cleveland 1872, 100 Miles
Brooklyn to Rutland VT 1873, 475 Miles
Brooklyn to Boston 1873, 220 Miles
Rochester to Newton, KS 1883, 1,230 Miles

The sisters of St. Joseph had been in the United States for twenty years before they founded a mission west of Missouri or Minnesota. In distinction to the national westward trend, they had founded missions in the dioceses of Philadelphia, St. Paul, Toronto, Wheeling, Buffalo, Natchez, and Brooklyn. Much of that movement seemed to result from long-standing relationships between sisters and bishops. They went from St. Louis to Philadelphia at the behest of the brother-bishops Kenrick, to Toronto due to the Fontbonne family connection with Bishop Charbonnel, to St. Paul and Buffalo in response to requests by Bishops Cretin and Timon, long-time friends of the community. Bishop Loughlin of Brooklyn had relied on his friend, Bishop Timon, to encourage Mother St. John Fournier to send sisters to his diocese. After that the connections become less clear as the community accepted missions in the dioceses of Wheeling, Albany and Erie, apparently in response to bishops' requests, but not with the long-standing relationships that had marked the earliest foundations. The Carondelet and

Philadelphia archives have ample evidence that bishops and priests continually wrote to ask the superiors to send sisters to help them and it seems quite possible that bishops who did not know the sisters learned of them from their brother-bishops, especially when they attended the Baltimore Councils which brought the bishops in the U.S. together almost every three years between 1829 and 1884.[31]

The Sisters of St. Joseph went west for the first time in 1856, venturing nearly 300 miles from St. Louis to Weston in northwestern Missouri. A decade later, marking the real beginning of westward expansion, they opened missions in the Missouri towns of Hannibal (1865) and Kansas City (1866). By 1883, when Mother Stanislaus Leary traveled from Rochester to Kansas, Carondelet Sisters were serving in Kansas City, Chillicothe, and Sedalia, Missouri, in Central City and Denver, Colorado and had established a province in Tucson, Arizona.[32]

MOTHER STANISLAUS EXPLORES WESTERN POSSIBILITIES

In 1882, after Bishop McQuaid removed her from office, Mother Stanislaus Leary and Sister Ursula Murphy, visited the Sisters of St. Joseph of Le Puy in Florida for rest and regrouping.[33] During that time Mother Stanislaus reopened correspondence with bishops in the West who had previously asked her for help. One of those bishops was Jean Baptiste Salpointe, Arizona.[34] Suggesting that her delicate health would benefit from a change of atmosphere and that her sisters would do quite well in his diocese, Bishop Salpointe wrote to Mother Stanislaus:

You have not to be afraid of the climate, it is rather warm for a few

---

31 The 10 Provincial Councils of Baltimore were held regularly between 1829 and 1869. After 1852, the bishops also held three Plenary Councils of Bishops: 1852, 1866, and 1884. The U.S. bishops did not again have any effective organization to unify their work until 1917, when they founded the National Catholic War Council to coordinate response to World War I, and then the National Catholic Welfare Council founded in 1919, precursor to today's United States Council of Catholic Bishops. (See Jay Dolan, The American Catholic Experience (NY: Doubleday, 1986), 353, passim.

32 The first Carondelet mission to the west was to Weston MO in 1855, to a parish school so small that it closed in 1859. The trip would have been arduous as Weston is north-west of Kansas City, nearly 300 miles from St. Louis. Next, the sisters opened St. Teresa Academy in 1866, followed by various missions including St. Joseph's Hospital in Kansas City in 1874, and in Georgetown, Colorado, a school in 1877 and a hospital there 1880 (900 miles from St. Louis).

33 Sister Ursula's last name is not mentioned in her letter but Brennan gives it in Persistence of Vision (128). Sr. Ursula entered the Rochester congregation in 1871. The Le Puy sisters were known in Rochester because Sister Sidonie had visited Rochester from Florida and later invited Mother Stanislaus to accompany her on a trip to Europe to seek German candidates for the community. (Undated letter from Mother Stanislaus to Bishop McQuaid asking permission to travel. Archives: SSJR)

34 Bishop Salpointe had been working with Sisters of St. Joseph of Carondelet since 1870, and by 1882, they had opened six missions in the Arizona territory. (See Dougherty, 436.)

months during the summer season, but it is healthy... If you could come and see for yourself, it would be the best. The Sisters being here can get more help from the people in a few days than the priest in the same number of years.
Hoping to hear soon about what you determine, I remain,
Your most devoted in Xt,
J.B. Salpointe, Vic. Ap. Of Arizona[35]

Perhaps because her recent experience in Rochester cautioned her to keep her options open, Mother Stanislaus also arranged for correspondence with Bishop Fink, the successor to Bishop Miège in Kansas. The following letter to Bishop Fink was signed with Sister Ursula's name:

Rt. Rev. L.M. Fink,
I trust your Lordship will pardon the liberty I take in addressing you. Could you give a little corner of your vineyard to a few of the Diocesan Sisters of St. Joseph? I promise you good religious and competent well trained teachers.
I brought an invalid to this place and will wait here for your answer.
I ask this in honor of the Sacred Heart of Jesus.
Your Lordship's unworthy servant,
Sister M. Ursula
St. Joseph's Convent
Jacksonville, Florida[36]

Thus, before Mother Stanislaus returned to Rochester from Florida, she had renewed contacts with two western bishops who had sought the help of the Sisters of St. Joseph.

THE SISTERS OF ST. JOSEPH AND THE BISHOPS OF KANSAS

The first Sisters of St. Joseph invited to Kansas were the Moutiers sisters in France.

---

35 Bishop Salpointe to Mother Stanislaus Leary, Feb. 7, 1883. Quoted in Evangeline Thomas, Footprints on the Frontier: *A History of the Sisters of St. Joseph of Concordia Kansas* (Westminster, Md: Newman Press, 1948) 96.
36 Undated letter signed with the name of Sister Ursula, in the fall or winter of 1883-4, presumably at the behest of Mother Stanislaus. The penmanship closely resembles Mother Stanislaus' style. (Archives CSJC and Thomas, 97.) Most sources say that Sister Ursula wrote the letter quoted on behalf of Mother Stanislaus, but her letter does not specify that. Additionally, the handwriting in Sister Ursula's letter closely resembles Mother Stanislaus' own writing.

Bishop Miège who had a priest brother in France had made contact with the Moutiers congregation in the early 1850s, and the community decided accept his request for missionary sisters, apparently with the idea that they would be in contact with the Lyon sisters at Carondelet. As it turned out, the sisters who came from Moutiers never went to the Indian Missions in Kansas.[37] After arriving in America they made their home at Carondelet, but almost all of them soon left St. Louis to serve in mission territory.[38]

By 1883, when Mother Stanislaus and Sister Ursula were looking at Kansas, Bishop Miège had died and Bishop Louis M. Fink, O.S.B., had taken over the diocese.[39] It was with him that the sisters corresponded regarding the possibility of opening a mission. As it turned out, Mother Stanislaus and her companions chose the vineyard of Kansas as the place of their new foundation.

THE SISTERS OF ST. JOSEPH AND THE CHURCH IN KANSAS

Years after the events took place, Mother Stanislaus wrote a brief account of the foundation and how the sisters decided to settle in Kansas. She explained that she recorded her story, "so as to let our sisters see how much the foundation suffered." She told them:

---

37 Sr. Evangeline Thomas explains that before Miège became Vicar Apostolic of Kansas, he sought bishops who would receive missionary sisters from Moutiers but eventually wrote to the superior saying that although the bishops would be happy to receive sisters, their means were too limited to assist them (Thomas, 125-6). According to Sr. Lucida Savage, Bishop Miège did not send to St. Louis for them because after their arrival from France he found another group to help him. When he came to St. Louis in 1857, "the Superior of a colony of Sisters of Charity from Nashville, looking for a home in another diocese, appealed to him on the advice of the Jesuit, Father De Smet; and with the permission of Archbishop Kenrick, was received with her community under his jurisdiction" (Savage, 103). That "colony," led by Mother Xavier Ross, founded the Sisters of Charity of Leavenworth.

38 In addition to Mother St. John Facemaz, the first Moutiers missionaries were: Sister Euphrasia Mieller who went to Weston, MO, in 1858, and returned to St. Louis where she died on March 11, 1859; Sister Gonzaga Grand who served in Missouri, New York, Upper Michigan, Ste. Genevieve, MO, Colorado, and Arizona before becoming assistant superior general at Carondelet in 1902; and Sister Leonie Martin who served in Sulphur Springs, MS; Troy, NY; St. Louis, Ste. Genevieve, and Memphis, TN, before she died at Carondelet in 1880 at the age of 45. Mother St. John Facemaz seems to be the only one of the original Moutiers group who did not serve in a distant mission after arriving in St. Louis.

39 Bishop Fink was ordained in 1857 by Bishop Young of Erie and ministered in Newark during the time Father Bernard McQuaid was in the diocese. In 1868, Fink was named Prior of St. Benedict's Abbey in Atchison, Kansas, and in 1871 he was made Coadjutor to Bishop Miège of the Vicariate of Kansas and became the bishop when Miège retired in 1874 . In 1877, the Vicariate became the Diocese of Leavenworth. In 1887, the dioceses of Concordia and Wichita were created from its territory and in 1891, the Diocese of Leavenworth was renamed the Diocese of Kansas City.

We, Sisters Stanislaus, Josephine and Francis Joseph and Joseph Teresa arrived at Newton Kansas, June, 1883.

When we received our obedience from Bishop McQuaid from the Diocese of Rochester we had offered our services to Rt. Rev. Salpointe, Bishop of Arizona and were on our way to Florence, Arizona to open a school.[40] We had purchased our tickets at Chicago for that place but when we arrived at Kansas City, learning of the Indian troubles there we were afraid to continue our journey. We then offered our services to the Bishop of Leavenworth, Kansas and he kindly accepted us and appointed us to Newton, Harvey Co…

We opened the school on October 2, 1883…We suffered much from poverty till our school opened. The necessities of life we often needed. Our beds were poor thin straw mallets and our pillows shavings and straw…

We often became discouraged enough to break up the mission but when we considered the wants of the poor children and how much they would lose we cheered up and continued the good work.[41]

It was not only the physical conditions that made the early days difficult. As Mother Stanislaus would make quite clear, the missionary priest with whom the sisters worked in Newton seemed to be at a loss in terms of how to deal with his new assistants. As Mother Stanislaus explained the troubles the sisters experienced she showed admirable restraint in her criticism of the pastor:

The Jesuit Rev. Father Swemberg had shown marked unkindness towards us, we were not even allowed to arrange our house to our own liking…One act of kindness from him we have never received. Still he is a good pious man…but has been so long used to roughing it and among the Indians no doubt but he has lost all feeling of kindness. In our isolated and unprotected position we feel this very much.[42]

---

40 Florence was a town of around 900 inhabitants about 90 miles north of Tucson.
41 Mother Stanislaus Leary, "A Book of Records of our Community of Newton, Harvey County Kansas." (Manuscript, Archives CSJC) Newton is about 185 miles southwest of Leavenworth and 115 miles south of Concordia. In 1880, Newton had a population of approximately 2,600. Even with train travel, those were significant distances in the 1880s.
42 Book of Records The use of verb tenses in this selection suggests that Mother Stanislaus may have copied something she wrote earlier when she composed this story for the sisters.

In addition to setting up a situation in which the sisters felt so "unprotected," Bishop Fink seemed to expect the sisters to drift along the tides of his changing plans. Early on he arranged for them to visit the town of Hanover with the possibility of establishing themselves there. Mother Stanislaus scraped together the $18 train fare for two of them to go there and the day after their visit, the Hanover pastor wrote to the bishop saying:

> They came last night and like the place so well on account of the new schoolhouse (which is a daisy) and the church that they at once made up their minds this would be their headquarters.[43]

No sooner had Father Pichler posted that letter than he received notice from the bishop that the Benedictine Sisters from Atchison would staff his school.[44]

Disappointed but not defeated, the Sisters of St. Joseph continued with their plan and opened their school in Newton. Within a year they had two schoolhouses with about 100 students, half of whom were Protestants.[45] More important than either the number of students or their disillusionments with local clergy, two additional sisters had come from Rochester to join the original group of three sisters. By September 28, 1883 the community was made up of:

Sister Stanislaus Leary: received in Canandaigua, 1856;
Sister Josephine Leary: received in Rochester, January, 1869;
Sister Francis Joseph Leary: received in Rochester, December, 1869;
Sister Domitilla Gannon, received in Rochester, July, 1874;
Sister Armella McGrath: received in Rochester, 1877;
Sister Antoinette Cuff, received in Rochester, October, 1880.[46]

Perhaps the best omen during the early days was that on September 15, 1883, the community received the addition of Miss Agnes Groser, a novice from a Notre Dame community in Rochester. Miss Groser was an immigrant and with her help

---

43 Fr. J. Pichler to Bishop Fink, July 13, 1883. (Quoted in Thomas, 134.)
44 In her Book of Records, Mother Stanislaus mentions the cost of the trip which Father Pichler offered to pay but never did. One would be tempted to think that the bishop may have given preference to the Benedictines because he too was a Benedictine. There is no other extant explanation for why he changed the plan so abruptly.
45 Book of Records.
46 Thomas, 131-132. Sister Joseph Theresa had been part of the original group. According to Mother Stanislaus' records she "lost her mind" on August 17, 1883 and was taken to an asylum run by the Sisters of Charity in St. Louis from where, after being released, she did not return to the Kansas community.

the sisters could offer German language classes in their school.[47] The opening of the school alleviated the crushing poverty of the sisters' first Kansas summer.

In April, 1884, Bishop Fink appointed Rev. Dominic Meier, O.S.F., as the ecclesiastical superior of the community.[48] Concerned about the community's difficulties with Father Swemberg in Newton, Father Meier wrote to Bishop McQuaid to ask if the sisters who had come from Rochester had left there in good standing.[49] Although there is no record of the bishop's response, the fact that the sisters remained in the diocese indicates that Father Meier did not receive any information that would discredit Mother Stanislaus or the other sisters.

One of the best glimpses we have of the spirit of zeal and adventure that marked sisters' beginnings can be gleaned from a letter Father James Leary, an old friend from New York, wrote to Mother Stanislaus in February, 1884, less than a year after the foundation. He congratulated her saying:

> I am very pleased that you have established a religious community of the Sisters of St. Joseph in the State of Kansas…Undoubtedly, as the pioneer of your community in a young and rapidly growing State, you will have many…trials to bear. But…there is no reason why, with God's blessing, your undertaking should not succeed, for with your experience and zeal, you will leave no stone unturned in laying the foundation in a substantial and durable manner. You will probably meet with many obstacles but you have met such before and were not discouraged by them, but bravely overcame them as many lasting monuments of your energy and zeal proclaim in the city of Rochester. I shall pray God to

---

47 Mother Stanislaus Leary "Book of Records" and Thomas, 135. It seems likely that Miss Groser soon left the community as neither source mentions her again.

48 Father Meier's parish was in Emporia, Kansas, about 75 miles from Newton, far enough away that he could not be involved in their day to day affairs although he probably could have made a good portion of the trip by train.

49 Father Meier's letter revealed that he had suspicions about the sisters. It is interesting that he wrote to Bishop McQuaid without mentioning Bishop Fink, whether to say that the bishop had asked him to seek that information or to admit that he questioned the bishop's judgment in accepting the sisters. His letter said: "Shortly after their arrival they got into trouble with their Pastor…& this has continued until the present day…Please let me know whether they left the Mother House with the required faculties & permissions? I have been warned that they were persons who could not agree with the Ven. Mother Agnes and therefore they left with the intentions of establishing a house of their own. Any information your Lordship will give me will be accepted with the greatest thanks!" (Rev. Dominic Meier, O.S.F. to Bishop McQuaid, April 26, 1884. Archives CSJC) There is no record of Bishop McQuaid's response but that the problems most likely originated with the pastor becomes clear from the fact that Bishop Fink later wrote to Bishop McQuaid saying , "In case Reverend Swemberg should call on you,

bless you and aid you.[50]

Downtown Concordia in the 1880s

Father Leary's letter points to the idea that the sisters likely understood themselves as pioneers among pioneers and as missionaries to the settlers. While it was hardly new for Mother Stanislaus to forge an uncharted path, this time she and her companions had embarked on an adventure neither they nor their New York friends could have easily imagined. Writing from Rochester, then a city of nearly 90,000, it would have been nearly impossible for a New Yorker like Father Leary to picture Newton or the sisters' next hometown of Concordia. The two places were 100 miles distant from each other and had populations of 4,000 and fewer than 1,900 respectively.[51]

In reality, Kansas was quite a new adventure for everyone concerned. Occupying a territory of nearly 82,000 square miles (nearly twice as large as Pennsylvania and almost 1½ times larger than New York), Kansas became a state in 1861. The short, bloody process leading to Kansas' statehood was most intense at the time of the 1854 Kansas-Nebraska Act which decreed that the populace could determine whether each of the two states would be slave or free at the time of their admission to the Union. The desire to influence the balance of slave and free states and generous opportunities for homesteading spurred immigration campaigns by both abolitionists and slave-staters who rushed to populate the area, creating a

---

he is suspended...In case he present papers as if from me, they must be forgeries." (Fink to McQuaid, June 1, 1886, Barbara Baer Collection, Avila U. Archives) Fr. Meier's letter also leads to the question of who had informed him that the sisters "could not agree" with Mother Agnes Hines.

50 James J. Leary to Mother Stanislaus Leary, Feb. 11, 1884. (Cited in Thomas, 138.) 51 According to the U.S. census bureau in 1880, Newton had a population of 4,199 and Concordia 1,853. According to Fr. Richard Bollig, "There had been almost no white population in Kansas prior to 1853, and there seemed to be no special desire to create one." See: Richard J. Bollig, O.F.M. Cap., "History of Catholic Education in Kansas 1836-1932" (A Dissertation submitted to the faculty of The Catholic University of America, Washington D.C., 1933) 2. A Kansas State Historical Society map of the railroad system indicates that to travel by rail from Newton to Concordia, one had to go 180 miles east to Kansas City, then return northwest about 170 miles to Concordia. The direct trip north by such roads as there were probably would have taken as long as the circuitous train route. The above picture of Concordia can be accessed at http://www.kansasmemory.org/item/213612.

population designed to be at odds with one another.[52]

The vast territory's relatively few Catholics were concentrated in particular areas and there had been very few religious women serving in the area. The Religious of the Sacred Heart had ministered in Kansas from 1841 to 1879 with St. Philippine Duchesne spending a year among them from June 1841 to June 1842.[53] When Bishop Miège invited Mother Xavier Ross and the Sisters of Charity to Leavenworth in 1858, Kansas was "a territory scarcely considered within the pale of civilization."[54] Theirs was the first motherhouse established in Kansas. In 1877, the Atchison Benedictine Sisters had opened a motherhouse and by the late 1880s there were twenty-four Catholic schools serving a Catholic population of 80,000 in the State of Kansas.[55]

FROM NEWTON TO CONCORDIA: 1884

Before Mother Stanislaus and her sisters had been in Newton a year, a French missionary, Father Perrier, was asking Mother Stanislaus to send sisters for his parish in the town of Concordia.[56] Not only did she accept the invitation, but she helped fund the building which would become their new school and convent.[57] Her readiness to invest indicated that she must have seen a future for the community in Concordia. Her attitude reflected the exceptionally optimistic spirit of the town itself; Concordia had been named the County Seat of Cloud County before the town had actually come into existence.[58]

---

52 An article in a Chicago newspaper in 1887, after the Civil War tensions had subsided in the area, described Kansas as the garden of the world, "redolent with the fragrance of the orchard...teeming with the homes of thrifty people, pulsating with the vim and vigor of progress." Quoted in Eileen Quinlan, CSJ, *Planted on the Plains, A History of the Sisters of St. Joseph of Wichita, Kansas*, (Wichita: Greg D. Jones and Associates, 1984), 76.
53 Information thanks to Sister Carolyn Osiek, RSCJ, archivist for the Religious of the Sacred Heart in St. Louis.
54 Bollig, 45. 55 See: Joseph Shorter, The Catholic Encyclopedia ("Kansas." The Catholic Encyclopedia. Vol. 8. New York: Robert Appleton Company, 1910. 2016 http://www.newadvent.org/cathen/08597a.htm).
56 Father Joseph Perrier was educated in Chambéry, arrived in Kansas in 1866 and ministered there until 1913, when he retired to La Grange, Illinois. He died in Los Angeles, California, in 1917. (Thomas, 140)
57 Thomas (144) records that Mother Stanislaus sent a total of $1,409 in two installments in the summer of 1884. Some of the necessary financing must have come from fund-raising activities as a letter from Mother Stanislaus to Bishop Fink asks him for the permissions for "Sisters Francis and Antoinette to collect in the East." (Mother Stanislaus to Bishop Fink, June 24, 1884. Archives CSJC) Another letter makes it clear that family as well as old friends were willing to help the new mission: on June 10, 1884 Mother Stanislaus had informed the Bishop that her mother would soon be sending her $1,600, half the purchase price, as a free donation, and the rest "we will be obliged to collect from friends in the East." (Archives CSJC)
58 According to W.G. Cutler, "When Concordia was made the county-seat, by vote of the people, in the fall of 1869, there was not one solitary building upon the town site, and the only houses subsequently embraced within its limits, then in existence, were two small structures owned, respectively, by G. W. Andrews and J. M. Hagaman." See William G. Cutler, *History of the State of Kansas, Cloud County, Part Two* (http://www.kancoll.org/books/ cutler/cloud/cloud-co-p2.html#CONCORDIA).

While Father Meier, the sisters' ecclesiastical superior in Newton, was reluctant to see Mother Stanislaus move to Concordia, some of the sisters took it upon themselves to write to the bishop asking him to encourage her to make the move because Concordia had a better, warmer convent. It seems Father Meier's concern was to keep the motherhouse in Newton while the sisters' concern stemmed from Mother Stanislaus' generally delicate health.[59] Mother Stanislaus left no record of her motivation for accepting the Concordia mission or for going there herself, but the invitation to "the more" seemed to beckon her ever onward and she was ready to make an investment in Concordia and its people at the invitation of Father Perrier.

When Kansas became the destiny for thousands of farming settlers, the area around Concordia was a center for a significant movement of French Canadian immigration. As a result, the French-Canadian Catholics in Cloud County gradually outnumbered the Protestants and the towns of Concordia and St. Joseph were populated by a substantial number of Catholics with Canadian roots.[60] Bishop Fink encouraged Mother Stanislaus to help these communities. In 1885, she followed the Concordia foundation with a school in St. Joseph, some 18 miles southeast of Concordia. Already in 1884, Mother Stanislaus had begun the process of procuring legal incorporation for the community in Concordia, thus stabilizing their civil status in the state and solidifying her choice of Concordia as the locale for their motherhouse.

Starred key cities for early Sisters of St. Joseph in Kansas: Top to bottom: Concordia, Abilene, Newton, Wichita, Parsons.

---

59 The sisters said: "Our Reverend Mother's health at best is poor. Last winter she suffered extremely from colds...The sisters feel bound in conscience to do something for her if she won't do it for herself." They went on to explain that the Concordia house was very warm and had a chapel in it. They finished the letter saying "Reverend Mother knows nothing of our writing this letter...Nothing but the tenderest regard for her welfare has prompted the sentiments expressed. (Thomas, 145, citing a letter signed Sisters of St. Joseph, Newton, Kans. to Louis M. Fink, August 23, 1884.) Mother Stanislaus' delicate health was a motivating factor for some of the most significant changes in her life; those included her respite in Florida after being deposed, the choice to move the motherhouse to Concordia and her eventual migration to Chicago after her term as superior in Concordia.

60 See Norma Meier, "Once Upon A Time...French Canadians Sought Their Fortunes in Kansas" (The Clifton, Illinois Advocate, November 13, 1980).

The sisters in Kansas were able to take on these missions because they were receiving an influx of new members and because some additional sisters were coming to the community from Canada and the eastern U.S. Julia Perry, the first woman to enter the Kansas community, had known Mother Stanislaus in Rochester and followed her to Newton where she was received into the community on August 15, 1884, and was given the name Sister Madeline de Pazzi.[61] A little more than a month later, three young women from Montreal became postulants, bringing much needed expertise in French to the teaching community. On March 19, 1885, six women received the habit of the Sisters of St. Joseph in Concordia where Mother Stanislaus had established the novitiate. This diverse group hailed from France, Ohio, Pennsylvania, Illinois and St. Mary's, Kansas. The following July, two more novices, Sister Mary Ann Picard of St. Paul, Canada, and Sister Mary Louise Cuff of Carbondale, Pennsylvania, were received into the congregation. Such growth in membership gave witness to the appeal of the life of the Sisters of St. Joseph and the successful recruitment trips made by the sisters from Concordia.[62] The breadth of background of the first new members of the community was a sign of the breadth that would characterize the mentality of the congregation in the decades to follow. Of the vowed sisters who came to join Mother Stanislaus, the one whose role would be surprisingly important was Sister Bernard Sheridan who came to Concordia from Erie in June of 1886.

MOTHER BERNARD SHERIDAN AND THE
SISTERS OF ST. JOSEPH IN SOUTHWESTERN KANSAS

By 1886, the Sisters of St. Joseph of Erie numbered 35 and were teaching a total of 2,295 students in eight parochial schools, with an additional five academies, two hospitals, one orphan asylum and one home for the elderly under their care.[63] The various congregations of Sisters of St. Joseph in the country continued to maintain contacts with one another, with some of them sharing personnel as well as the bonds of friendship and shared history and spirituality. Mother Eugenia Quirk, the third Superior General, must have felt that the community was strong enough to release a sister to join Mother Stanislaus in her western mission. Mother Eugenia

---

61 Thomas, 139.
62 Thomas, 149, 151.
63 Shanley, *Come to the Waters*, 53, The Catholic Directory, 1886 (203-206) and Archives SSJE. Between 1860 and 1890, an average of four women were received into the congregation each year. In some years there were no candidates while the largest single number was 10 in 1888, indicating that there were at least 10 postulants in the year that Mother Eugenia released Sister Bernard to go to Kansas.

also may have been moved by the great needs Mother Stanislaus described and her talk of the young Kansas community which then numbered fifteen sisters serving in three dispersed towns.⁶⁴ When Mother Eugenia sent young Sister Bernard Sheridan to Kansas, she had no idea of what would result from her gesture of solidarity.

Sister Bernard (Jennie) Sheridan was born in County Roscommon, Ireland, and had a story sadly typical of many immigrants. Before she was two years old, her father had to flee Ireland for having struck an officer of the law who was evicting a poor, aged widow from her cottage. Although his plan was to go to the U.S. and send for his family, he purportedly ended up on a famous Confederate ship, the *Alabama*, which was sunk by Union forces off the coast of France in 1864. In 1866, assuming that she was a widow, Mrs. Elizabeth Sheridan immigrated to Lockport, New York, with six of her children. When she arrived, she found it necessary to place her three younger daughters, including Jeanne, the youngest, in the care of the Sisters of Notre Dame

Mother Bernard
Sheridan
1860 - 1924

de Namur. By 1870, Mrs. Sheridan was able to purchase a home, but within five years, failing health demanded that she move with her younger children to be near her older daughters in Erie. Elizabeth Sheridan died on September 24, 1875, nine years after the shipwreck that presumably killed her husband. Two years after her mother's death, on October 20, 1877, the seventeen-year-old Jeanne received the habit of the Congregation of St. Joseph at Erie being given the name Sister Bernard. For the next nine years, Sister Bernard Sheridan taught in the towns of Corry and Meadville and also ministered in St. Vincent's Hospital and the orphanage. A quick learner, she acquired knowledge of the art of anesthesiology and became the first recognized nurse anesthetist in the United States.⁶⁵

During the years she spent in Erie, Sister Bernard would have had various opportunities to meet Mother Stanislaus, the superior of the new mission in

---

64 In diocesan communities of that time the bishop's permission was necessary to allow a sister to transfer from one community to another. The bishop of her home community would have to free her from obligation to that diocese, and then she would follow the regulations and deal with the bishop and superiors of the community she joined. The number of sisters is found in the 1886 Catholic Directory.
65 See Marianne Bankert, *Watchful Care: A History of America's Nurse Anesthetists* (NY: Continuum, 1989) 25. In 2003, a Pennsylvania Historical Marker at St. Vincent Hospital in Erie was dedicated to Mother Bernard as the first Nurse Anesthetist.

Kansas. Mother Stanislaus had visited Mother Agnes Spencer from Rochester, she also attended Mother Agnes' funeral in 1882 and returned to Erie in 1885 seeking help for her Kansas mission.[66] Mother Eugenia Quirk, the superior in Erie in 1886, let Sister Bernard know of Mother Stanislaus' needs, and one year later, with Bishop Mullen's permission, she gave the young sister permission to join with the Kansas community.[67]

One of Sister Bernard's early protégés, Sister Gregory (Catherine) Finucane, shared recollections of her mentor, not only portraying Sister Bernard but also divulging interesting details about the life and ministry of the Erie sisters in the 1880s. Sister Gregory wrote in the third person saying:

> Sister Bernard had been assigned to teach mathematics to private pupils; and in her spare time was to make comforters for the Sisters's [sic] beds. The superior of the little mission was Sister Celestine Donnelly of the Sisters of St. Joseph of Buffalo, who had been borrowed from the sisters in Buffalo to serve in this capacity at Corry until the motherhouse in Erie would be able to supply a Sister from their own ranks. This procedure was common among the early communities of the sisters of St. Joseph.
>
> Among the private pupils who came to Sister Bernard were Catherine Finucane, then in her 17th year and Miss Donnelly of Buffalo, who was a niece of Sister Celestine…With the associations of the summer, there was more than mathematics and convent comforters; for there was impressed upon the two young girls a spirit of devotion to a religious vocation.
>
> This devotion was enhanced the following year when Sister M. Bernard, who long ere was the ideal of the young girls…announced to her community and her friends that her mind and her heart had turned to a new field of missionary work. She was answering a call for volunteers in Kansas. A community that owed its beginning to one of the oldest religious friends of the Sisters of St. Joseph in Erie, Mother M. Stanislaus, former superior of the Rochester community…

---

66 Additional information about Mother Bernard can be found in Quinlin, 88 ff. Mother Stanislaus' attendance at Mother Agnes Spencer's funeral is recorded in the Rochester annals for the year 1882, others of her rather frequent travels are documented in the annals as well as in letters from and about her.

67 Quinlan (91) explains that the Rochester Superior, Mother Eugenia Quirk, let Sister Bernard know of the need. This may be another instance of a lack of concern for juridical distinctions, with Mother Eugenia giving permission without a mention of a formal "obedience" from the local bishop.

The departure of the young religious was of no small concern to her young friends. Well they knew that she had decided upon a move that called for self-sacrifice and self-forgetfulness to an heroic degree…She was a young religious leaving a community of which she had been a member for ten years…And there were her many relatives…and there were her many friends, for she was that type who could count her friends by the people that she met, everyone was honored to be on her friendship list.[68]

Sister Gregory obviously admired Sister Bernard, explaining that her attractive personality encouraged others to share her spirit and spirituality. The young women around her were also amply impressed by her willingness to sacrifice for the sake of the mission. From Sister Gregory's description we learn how a teaching sister could be occupied with additional domestic tasks as well. She also reveals the ease with which sisters from one congregation could spend time with another, even taking on a role of authority. Finally, Sister Gregory's memoir indicated that Mother Stanislaus had a long-standing relationship with the Erie Congregation, a fact that is not surprising when one remembers that Mother Stanislaus had known Mother Agnes Spencer since her first days in the Congregation.[69]

Sister Gregory added that those two young women who knew Sister Bernard "could not go with her…But the aspirations lived on, garnered up and treasured amid all the chops and changes which great friendships are destined to go." Eventually she was able to join Mother Bernard in Kansas.[70] Adding to Sister Gregory's portrait of Sister Bernard, Sister Euphemia, the sister of the Erie congregation who accompanied her to the train on the day of her departure, described her on that day as, "joyous, fun-loving, and cheerful as well as zealous

---

68 The document, "Sister Gregory," from which this is excerpted was kept in Sister Evangeline Thomas' files in Wichita as part of her file on Sister Gregory Finucane. Now: Archives: CSJoseph.

69 As has been noted in earlier chapters, Mother Agnes Spencer was a founder of the mission in Canandaigua where Mother Stanislaus was received into the congregation.

70 See "Sister Gregory." Sister Gregory herself became a well-known and accomplished innovator. Apparently imitating Sister Bernard's willingness to learn anything necessary, her necrology describes her as: "A versatile educator among the pioneer religious of the dioceses. " It goes on to say, "this gifted religious adapted herself not only to the academic program of education, but also to the field of nursing education…By unstinted energy and with relentless courage, Sister Gregory, often forging alone, prepared herself to be a teacher, and few persons ever achieved the rank of instructor in such a diversified realm of knowledge. There was nothing too difficult for her to undertake; there was nothing she would not attempt. …she took up the study of medical technology and radiological technique…and became director of nursing education…and was appointed to the State Board of Nurse Examiners by the Governor of Oklahoma." (Archives, CSJoseph)

described her on that day as, "joyous, fun-loving, and cheerful as well as zealous to go to the missions of Kansas."[71]

NEW DIOCESES SPLIT THE CONGREGATION

Bishop Fink, knowing all too well that Kansas was too large to be cared for as one diocese, petitioned Rome for a division of the territory. While he was prepared and even anxious to let go of more than half of his diocese, he did not want to lose the Sisters of St. Joseph whose community had seen steady growth during their first few years. In 1886, Bishop Fink was already contemplating the division of his diocese and knew that Concordia was a likely site for a future diocesan see. In light of that he arranged for the Sisters of St. Joseph to open a mission in Abilene, counting on the fact that the city would remain a part of the Leavenworth diocese.[72] His plan was for Mother Stanislaus to move from Concordia and establish the motherhouse and novitiate there. To further the plan he encouraged the pastor and people of St. Andrew's Parish to support a project which would bring the Sisters of St. Joseph to Abilene and provide them with everything necessary for a new motherhouse and novitiate. With Bishop Fink's promise to cover half the expenses, the parish procured land two miles outside the town and started a building project, dedicating the cornerstone on July 31, 1887, over a month before the sisters arrived.

By the time the sisters opened their Abilene mission, the new dioceses had been erected, dividing the state into three roughly equal parts. The dioceses of Concordia and Wichita split the northern and southern two-thirds of western Kansas and the Leavenworth Diocese occupied the eastern third. The new mission of the Sisters of St. Joseph in Abilene was entrusted to Sisters Bernard Sheridan, Angela Costello, Amelia Fitzgibbon, Domitilla Gannon, Armella McGrath and Sebastian Collins. These sisters arrived in Abilene on September 12, 1887, and opened their school at St. Andrew's Parish just seven days later. Because the house on the new property was uninhabitable, the sisters stayed with a family until better arrangements could be made. While Sisters Bernard and Angela taught, Sisters Amelia and Domitilla applied their domestic and carpentry skills to the task of turning the farmhouse into a livable home.[73]

Meanwhile, Bishop Fink was making his plans for the future. In the spring

---

71 Quinlan, 91-92.
72 Thomas, 161-162.
73 Sister Angela Costello returned to Concordia.

of 1888, he wrote to Mother Stanislaus in Concordia to let her know of the progress being made in Abilene and his hopes for the future. He said:

> Rev. dear Mother Stanislaus,
> I send you these few lines to inform you about matters at Abilene. Poor Father Leary has accomplished a great deal...we got a loan of $5,000 at 6% at St. Louis...The sisters will get the deed for the thirty acres...and the new building....they will have to assume a mortgage of about $7,000 – besides the $7,000 mentioned above...
> For certain reasons of my own, I would like for you to be the superior there yourself, ...However if good Bp. Scannell would not wish you to go—some other good sister would be appointed...
> Bishop Scannell seems to object to the two houses having but one novitiate for 4 or 5 years...if the Bp. has any objection and desires a separation his wish must be respected. It will come out all right at the latter end, although it may be a little more difficult for some time.[74]

Bishop Fink, perhaps thinking he had the advantage of seniority, expected to house the sisters' single novitiate in Abilene. Bishop Scannell of Concordia, recently arrived from Nashville, a city with a population of over 43,000, had bigger plans for his new diocese and did not accede to Bishop Fink's proposal. Nor did Mother Stanislaus take up Bishop Fink's offer. Rather than become the superior in Abilene, she remained in Concordia where she had moved in 1884.[75]

When it became clear that Bishop Scannell was not going to let go of the Concordia motherhouse and that Mother Stanislaus had apparently decided to remain there, Bishop Fink advised the sisters in Abilene to form their own legal corporation, separate from Concordia. In March, 1888, he gave his vicar, Father John Cunningham, the responsibility of helping the small community organize

---

74 Bishop Fink to Mother Stanislaus, cited in Quinlan, 80-81.
75 It seems plausible that Mother Stanislaus remained in Concordia knowing that she had made significant investments there and perhaps believing that her sisters were better positioned as the only sisters in Bishop Scannell's diocese instead of being one among many communities in Bishop Fink's territory. The other sisters in the Leavenworth dioceses included the Sisters of Charity of Leavenworth and the bishop's fellow Benedictine Sisters in Atchison. In addition, Bishop Fink had not always proven to promote the best interests of the Sisters of St. Joseph as might be judged from his choice to send them to Fr. Swemberg and the incident with the possible mission in Hanover.

themselves as a civil and ecclesial entity.[76] As the division of the community became more certain, Sisters Amelia and Angela returned to Concordia and Sisters Armella McGrath and Sebastian Collins remained in Abilene. How the sisters chose which community they wished to remain with is a mystery, but the separation of the pioneers must have cost them pain and worry, not to mention the fact that it demanded a division of property which included furniture and a piano recently purchased by Concordia for the Abilene house.[77] The fact that the memory of the difficulties regarding the property was kept alive in the congregations, even if in jest, gives witness to the undocumented struggles that accompanied their separation.[78]

Community histories imply that the bishops bore the major responsibility for the formation of the two separate congregations of the Sisters of St. Joseph, but one must wonder what part Mother Stanislaus and Mother Bernard played. This was Mother Stanislaus' second experience of a diocesan division that would radically change circumstances for her congregation. This time she was the superior of the founding community from which the other community was to be cut off. Bishop Fink was surely behind the foundation in Abilene, but he did not get his wish of having Mother Stanislaus take over there.

When he was made the first Bishop of Concordia in 1887, Richard Scannell was a highly accomplished 42 year old Irishman who had spent the 16 years of his priestly career in Nashville and had become rector of the Cathedral eight years after his arrival in the country. When Bishop Feehan of Nashville was named the first Archbishop of Chicago in 1880, Father Scannell administered the diocese until a new bishop was named in 1883.[79] It seems possible that Mother Stanislaus and Bishop Scannell had much in common. She was his senior by only four years, both were bright and accomplished, and, although he had a reputation for being more introverted than she, he obviously supported the community and wanted

---

76 The legal process of incorporation was completed in 1894 with the purposes of the institute listed as "the reception and care of Novices, the education of young females...the performance of all works of mercy." In 1908 the charter was amended to include the building and administration of hospitals. (Quinlan, 81, 86-87)

77 A ledger found in the Wichita archives has as its first entry: "Furniture for Abilene, $155, piano $342." Those were no small sums and the piano's greatest value came from the income that would be derived from using it to teach music, a key source of supplementary income for the teaching sisters.

78 There was a long history of discussion over ownership of the piano between the two congregations. In 2015, when the Wichita Sisters were making major renovations to their property, they returned the piano to Condordia.

79 In 1886, Bishop Scannell was named Vicar General in Nashville, and shortly after was named to Concordia. See: John Gilmary Shea, *Defenders of Our Faith, The Church in the United States and Canada* (NY, Office of Catholic Publications, 1891), 414-415.

the sisters in his diocese. It is not surprising that Mother Stanislaus chose to remain in Concordia. What was not expected was that Bishop Scannell would spend only three years in that diocese before being named to the much larger diocese of Omaha, an unforeseeable circumstance which may have increased Mother Stanislaus' independence. From 1891 to 1898 Concordia fell under the administration of Bishop John J. Hennessy of Wichita.[80]

Abilene Beginnings

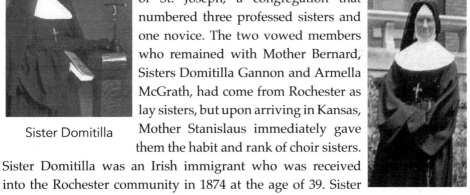

With the incorporation of the community in Abilene, the twenty-eight year old Sister Bernard Sheridan became the founding superior of a new congregation of Sisters of St. Joseph, a congregation that numbered three professed sisters and one novice. The two vowed members who remained with Mother Bernard, Sisters Domitilla Gannon and Armella McGrath, had come from Rochester as lay sisters, but upon arriving in Kansas, Mother Stanislaus immediately gave them the habit and rank of choir sisters. Sister Domitilla was an Irish immigrant who was received into the Rochester community in 1874 at the age of 39. Sister Armella, a New Yorker by birth, received the habit in Rochester in 1878.[81] The final member of the group, Sister Sebastian Collins, a native of Sacawana County in eastern Pennsylvania, had entered the congregation at Concordia in 1886 and was missioned to Abilene in May, 1888,

Sister Domitilla

Sister Armella

---

80 In 1890, the city of Omaha alone had a population of 140,000. According to the Catholic Directory, 1889, the diocesan Catholic school population was over 3,000 and there had been nearly 2,500 baptisms administered in the year before Scannell was named there. When Bishop Scannell left, Concordia came under the administration of Bishop John F. Hennessy of Wichita until 1898 when Father John Francis Cunningham of Leavenworth was named to the diocese where he would serve until his death in 1919.

81 It is rumored that the sisters leaving Rochester investigated the possibility of joining the Sisters of St. Joseph in St. Louis before they came to Kansas. Sister Eileen Quinlin's notes in the Wichita archives recorded an interview with Sister Imelda of La Grange who knew the pioneer sisters and explained that Sister Armella had been part of an altercation with Bishop McQuaid when he came to the Rochester motherhouse demanding to know the name of a priest who had defaced his portrait. Both Sister Armella and Mother Stanislaus refused to give him the information he sought. As mentioned above, the Rochester congregation's Council Book notes that when she did not receive permission to join Mother Stansislaus, Sister Armella secretly left the community. The sisters' pictures above are from the Barbara Baer collection.

where she died only two years after her religious profession.[82]

The early years in Abilene were, if anything, even more financially challenging than the founding at Newton. Although the pastor, Father Leary, had been unable to prepare the sisters' farmhouse for habitation in time for their arrival, he supported them as best he could, even to the point of giving them his retired racehorse, Charley, to help them make the daily two-mile journey between their rustic home and the parish. That help was essential during their first winter which turned out to be unusually severe.

The Abilene community began with significant debts: a $7,200 mortgage on their land. The mortgages were to be paid in annual installments at 6 or 7 percent interest rate – all financed by music lessons and the $20 monthly income of the two teaching sisters.[83]   Financial difficulties were plaguing the town and the workers were left with no alternative but to abandon the construction project. Countering that disappointment, the sisters found one of their greatest sources of non-financial help through their friendship with Father Patrick Henneberry, a Missionary of the Precious Blood, who recruited six young women to join the community during the sisters' first year in Abilene.

As soon as their first school year came to an end in June, 1888, Sister Bernard journeyed east with Sister Sebastian seeking financial aid.[84]   Their good news of success was reciprocated as the home sisters introduced them to "Snow," the cow that friendly neighbors had donated to the community. With all the support they had garnered, the sisters had acquired funds which, when added to their persistent hope, allowed them to reinitiate construction on their building. They were also receiving new members, the first being Miss Mary Shinners, an Irish immigrant who had been teaching in public schools in Junction City, Kansas. Joining her, the first group of postulants to come to the community through the influence of Father Henneberry included four young women, of whom the eldest, Mary Shinners, was twenty-six and the youngest, Nora McMillan, was seventeen. With special permission, after less than two months as postulants, the five received the habit during the same ceremony in which Sister Sebastian made vows. Within weeks, a second group of postulants began to arrive. The community had made

---

82 Quinlan, 94.
83 Quinlan, 87.
84 Quinlan, 95.
85 Quinlan, 97-99.

its start and the majority of the new members came from the local area with all but perhaps one being of Irish heritage.[86]

    With their first year of school behind them, a successful fund-raising trip and a growing community, the new congregation seemed to be off to a good start. Bishop Fink had encouraged them to hold a fair. Already in March of 1888, he had written to Mother Stanislaus saying:

> By next Fall the Sisters must hold a fair, if times turn out as we expect they will – God willing – I have not the least doubt, but that the proceeds of the fair will be sufficient to pay the installment of the amount payable next October...
>
> As good Bishop Scannell seems to have been under the impression that Concordia would be involved – I told him that Concordia was not expected to burden itself with the Abilene business; please tell him so again... [87]

The sisters held their first fair in October, 1888, and brought in the incredible sum of $1,217.15, with expenses of only about $200.[89] As much as the people of the area wanted to support the new community, poverty would be the sisters' companion for years to come. At Christmas, 1888, Mother Bernard wrote a letter describing the state of the community. Beginning by expressing Christmas sentiments typical of the epoch she went on to acknowledge their poverty. As if inspired by Father Médaille's Eucharistic Letter, she expressed contentment with the very little they had. Also, careful to convey grateful recognition of the labor of the sister who probably had the least formal education of them all, she said:

> In this year of beginning we ask ourselves where are we going? What does it mean? It was so casual in its happening, so unlooked for, so unexpected. Because of this we recognize the indication of God's ruling hand, and pray to be guided faithfully by it.

---

86 The next postulant to arrive, Annie Burke, came from Carbondale, PA, and in October of 1888, the two candidates who arrived hailed from Toronto, Canada, and Albuquerque, New Mexico. See Quinlan, 97-99, 102.
87 Letter from Bishop Fink to Mother Stanislaus, March 8, 1888. The other is cited above. (See Thomas, 164.)
88 Quinlan, 101.
89 See the Eucharistic Letter, #14. "In our poverty...we will always be perfectly content, whether we have much, little, or nothing at all."

We feel that we are called by Our Blessed Lord to prepare for the coming of others...Each one whom God has designed to be a part of this institute will be brought from far or near...The story of each vocation will be a story of spiritual life; of a choice, an election, a consent; then adventure, vicissitudes, of perils; even risks at times...

Finally, she looked to the coming years, and encouraged her sisters to continue to move toward God's future with an orientation toward excellence and a spirit of humility:

There may be long waiting, crises, or abrupt turning points; but, in the end, accomplishments and realization of plans...We pray that with a quiet mind and firmness of will all shall meet the challenge, as year follows year. Being buffeted they must learn to laugh, being unappreciated or misunderstood, they shall give thanks, or if fearful of failure, they shall determine to succeed.

We pray on this first visit of the Divine Infant to our Community that all of our Sisters, those of today and those of tomorrow, may enter anew into the spirit of lowliness of Bethlehem, to follow it more closely and more generously, by making less of self, and more and more of His service and glory.

Affectionately, Mother Bernard[90]

Although we are not certain to whom she addressed the letter, whether to the sisters of her own community or others who were a part of her life, it was a sharing of her heart, of her own prayerful discernment. Inviting others to comprehend the situation through her eyes, it offered a loving look at their actual circumstances, an interpretation of what brought them there and a projection of what the future was calling forth from them. Mother Bernard's letter is unique in the history of Sisters of St. Joseph as she reflects on how her little community unexpectedly took its place in the proliferation of congregations born from Le Puy and Lyon's first mission to the United States. The Congregation in Abilene, founded in 1888, was

---

90 The letter is replicated in Quinlan, 103 ff., which indicates that the original has not been found, but a copy was kept in the Wichita archives, now the Archives CSJoseph. To whom was it written? It seems strange that Mother Bernard would write this letter to the nine sisters with whom she shared the farmhouse. Could it have been to her friends from Erie? Concordia?

the sixteenth to spring from Lyon's original 1836 mission.[91] While some of those were planned from the beginning to be independent foundations, others seemingly evolved either into union or autonomy as they grew and, influenced by the decision-making authority of their local bishops, created the structures that would determine their future shape.

When Mother Bernard said "It was all so casual in its happening," she likely spoke for many of those who had preceded her. She surely had not anticipated a separation from Concordia. All the sisters likely assumed that Bishop Fink was correct with his prediction that it would "all come out all right at the latter end," implying that divisions would be short-lived.[92] But when the bishops apparently did not see eye-to-eye, Bishop Fink let Bishop Scannell know that he need not concern himself with Abilene and a painful separation process was underway.

THE KANSAS COMMUNITIES GROW INDEPENDENTLY
CONCORDIA: 1888-1899

After the Abilene community was separated from Concordia, in spite of what could have been a competitive situation, the Academies of both groups prospered. In 1890, a local historical publication spoke of the Concordia establishment saying:

> The convent and Academy of Nazareth, although only five years old, have taken a place in the rank of our institutions of learning. The Lady Superior, Sister Stanislaus, is one of the cultured ladies the State of New York sends us. She presides over the "Motherhouse," the Convent of Nazareth. She has the assistance of twenty-four sisters. One of the finest musicians in the West gives instructions in that department. All higher branches are taught.[93]

The description went on to point out that the Academy had fifty boarders and

---

91 The other congregations were Carondelet with its four provinces, Philadelphia, Toronto, Hamilton, Wheeling, Buffalo, Rochester, Brentwood, Erie, Baden, Cleveland, Rutland, Boston, Tipton, Watertown and Concordia. In addition, the Sisters of St. Joseph of Bourg and the Sisters of St. Joseph of Chambéry, both French foundations from Lyon, had by then established missions in America: Bourg in Natchez in 1854 and Chambéry of West Hartford in 1885. The Le Puy Congregation, the mother congregation of them all, opened their first U.S. mission in St. Augustine in 1866.

92 The idea that Bishop Fink hoped for an eventual reunion without making concrete plans for it or forging clear agreements with Bishop Scannell and Mother Bernard is evidenced in the fact that he sent Mother Stanislaus two letters on the same day as he apparently continued to think through the situation. (See Thomas, 163-164.)

93 John Letyham, *Historical and Descriptive Review of Kansas*, 2 vols., (Topeka, 1890), vol. 1, 188-189. Cited in Thomas, 166.

about forty day pupils while a second school had up to 200 students. In 1888, Mother Stanislaus received seven women into the congregation, followed by eight in March of 1889, and six more before that year was through. These women came from Illinois, New York, Kentucky, Missouri, Canada, Italy, Germany, and France.[94]

As postulants continued to arrive, Mother Stanislaus opened new missions. In 1889, those included five schools in Kansas and one in St. George, Illinois. In 1890 she added a mission in Danville, located in the new Diocese of Wichita.[95] In 1891, most likely due to the close friendship between Bishop Scannell, the first bishop of Concordia, and Archbishop Feehan of Chicago, the community ventured as far as Brighton Park, a French-Canadian suburb of Chicago. Continuing their northward expansion, in that same year the sisters opened schools at Somerset, Wisconsin, and Escanaba, in the Upper Peninsula of Michigan as well as in North Platte, Nebraska.[96] With all of those new missions, the most unprecedented came through the community's collaboration with Mother Katherine Drexel at whose request and with whose financial help, they opened a mission for Native Americans at St. Stephens, Wyoming in 1891.[97]

Such mission growth suggests that Mother Bernard believed her personnel resources could develop to become as vast and generous as her imagination. Confirming that faith, new members continued to come, more Kansans eventually joined them but women from outside the area still came as well. Except for the Carondelet Congregation which had established its far-flung provinces from New York to California, no other U.S. congregation of Sisters of St. Joseph had ventured so far from their home base, and such a humble home base it was.[98] In the sixteen years of Mother Stanislaus' administration (1883-1899), the community opened thirty-two missions located in Kansas, Illinois, Wisconsin, Michigan, Nebraska,

---

94 See Thomas 166-167. While those diverse places may have been the birthplaces, not the most recent residence of the women, it was not until 1892 that a Kansas woman entered the congregation: Isable Stenger (Sister Alcantara) from the town of Cuba.

95 See Thomas, 169-176. 96 Interestingly, the Carondelet St. Louis Province had opened its first missions in Chicago and the Upper Peninsula (Marquette) in 1871, but it was a rare bishop who did not seek any sisters he could obtain, whether or not a similar congregation was already in his diocese. Somerset, WI, was a French Canadian town in the Diocese of La Crosse. (See Thomas, 180-184.)

97 Thomas (185-188) notes that the Sisters of Charity of Leavenworth had staffed the Wyoming mission between 1889 and 1890. Mother Katherine Drexel visited Concordia in 1891, to make arrangements to underwrite the Sisters of St. Joseph at the mission. They stayed for only a few years.

98 According to the U.S. Census Bureau, the population of Concordia had its greatest growth between 1880 and 1890, from a population of 1,853 to 3,184. In 1900, it numbered 3,401 and a decade later, 4,415. In 2010, the population was 5,311.

Wyoming, Missouri, and Texas.[99]

CONNECTIONS AMONG COMMUNITIES OF ST. JOSEPH

Mother Stanislaus' breadth of vision was not confined to the missions she founded. She also attempted to establish lasting connections with larger congregations of St. Joseph. As early as 1886, she began a correspondence with the superior general in Lyon. In a letter which must have been an immense surprise to a superior general who probably had hardly a vague notion of where Kansas might be, Mother Stanislaus said:

> Nov. 26, 1886, from Concordia, Cloud County, Ks.
> Reverend Mother,
> Confident that you will be so good as to accept this letter, and since I have the happiness of being a member of the Congregation of St. Joseph, I respectfully take the liberty of introducing myself. I am writing to ask a favor which will be invaluable for us.
> Reverend Mother, would you be so kind as to send me the records which you have of your deceased Sisters. You could enclose a note of the mailing expenses which I shall gladly pay. If you grant this request I shall be much obliged, and, further, you will have the happiness of contributing to the spiritual growth of our young Community.
> Although we are not under the same sky, yet we are united to you in heart and souls, and our prayers ascend with yours right to the foot of the Throne of the Most High; also, our one wish is that our new establishment may be stamped with the same spirit of piety and fervor which reigns among our dear Sisters who live where our Congregation was born. Consequently, reading about the virtues practiced by our dear deceased Sisters will help a great deal to bring alive here the same spirit which prevails among you, a beacon light which will guide us in the way of perfection, and will also serve as wings to lift us from earth to our true fatherland.[100]

This letter reveals something of Mother Stanislaus' understanding of what it

---

99 Thomas, 364 shows the chart of missions. Of those thirty-two missions, Abilene became a part of the Wichita Congregation and eleven others were closed before the turn of the century.
100 "Mother Stanislaus, Correspondence with Lyon," ACSJC.

meant to be a Sister of St. Joseph. Hers was not an insular community isolated on the plains of Kansas, but part of an international movement of the Spirit. As superior, she wanted her sisters to have such a breadth of vision that, whatever their familial heritage, they would remember how their congregational ancestors had struggled and even undergone martyrdom. The Lyon superior responded quickly. In a little over six weeks Mother Stanislaus replied to her, promising the prayerful support of the Concordia sisters for the Lyon Congregation as they faced harassment due to the political situation in France. Commenting on the great number of vocations Lyon was receiving, Mother Stanislaus also expressed her personal willingness to travel to France to return to Kansas with any who wished to be missionaries.[101] Although the missionaries never materialized, the Lyon motherhouse did send Concordia copies of their necrologies and custom books, giving the sisters a vital spiritual link with their French heritage.

By 1899, Mother Stanislaus' fragile health had grown worse. Transition was in the air. Seven years after Bishop Scannell had left the diocese, Reverend John Cunningham, the Vicar General in Leavenworth, was named to be the second bishop of the Diocese of Concordia. In consultation with Bishop Hennessy of Wichita who had administered the Concordia diocese during that period, Bishop Cunningham convinced Mother Stanislaus to resign from office. He named Sister Antionette Cuff as her successor.[102] As the era of the founder closed, Mother Stanislaus traveled to Chicago for medical consultations and the last of her unique and unexpected contributions to the extension of the mission of the Sisters of St. Joseph in the United States.

ABILENE TO PARSONS TO WICHITA

As her little community settled in Abilene, Mother Bernard Sheridan continued to travel seeking donations, loans and vocations. Complementing her efforts in the local area, Sisters Domitilla and Armella would take a wagon through the countryside begging funds. In August, 1889, the community which now numbered fourteen was able to move into the Academy building and the Academy received its academic accreditation by the State of Kansas the following year.[103] Women continued to enter the congregation so that by the summer of 1890 it numbered 20. Then tragedy struck. Sister Sebastian Collins, the first postulant to come to the

---

101 Ibid., Letter of January 7, 1887
102 Mother Stanislaus' resignation is treated very briefly in Thomas, 197.
103 Quinlan, 105-106.

community and Mother Bernard's frequent traveling companion, succumbed to typhoid and on June 18, 1890, became the first member of the community to die. But in spite of the hardships, women continued to join the congregation.

The community's process of legal incorporation was finalized in April, 1894, under the formal title "The Convent of the Sisters of St. Joseph, Mount St. Joseph's Academy, Abilene, Kansas." By 1896, twenty-eight women had entered the community.[104] But even as the sisters enjoyed growth and success, they remained prey to the anti-Catholicism of the era. The most intrusive incident happened one day when the sisters were surprised by the arrival of fourteen members of the American Protective Association[105] who came to inspect the convent and environs to discover "how much ammunition was stored in the big convent on the hill." According to the sisters' recollections, Mother Bernard found humor in the incident and allowed the men access to every corner of the establishment, assuring them that the sisters had no intentions of taking over Abilene.[106]

In reality, the sisters were struggling just to survive. They had a beautiful building, but it lacked sufficient water for the needs of the sisters much less their animals and orchards. As Sister Clement Doyle explained:

We were very poor; so much so that many times we would be cold and hungry...Mount St. Joseph's did not have one drop of running water; there were three heating stoves in the whole building – two in the girls' department and one in the chapel...

But, she added:

There was a wonderful spirit in those days. No one ever grumbled about what she had to do...If we were hungry or thirsty, we said nothing about it.[107]

Between their teaching and trips to meet and ask the help of neighbors, the sisters

---

104 Of the twenty-eight women who became novices, three left the community and two died very young. (Quinlan 109)

105 The A.P.A. was an openly anti-Catholic organization founded in Iowa in 1887. Eventually in league with the Junior Order of United American Mechanics and like groups, it remained strong, particularly in the political realm, until around 1914. At one point it claimed to have more than two million members but a rival said that they numbered only around 120,000. They far outstripped the number of women religious in the country who numbered approximately 50,000 in 1900.

106 Quinlan, 106-107, citing notes by Sister Veronica Lake found in the Mount St. Mary Convent archives.

107 Quinlan, 111, citing Sister Clementine Doyle's notes.

had become an integral part of the life of the surrounding community. Sister Angelita Howe, recalling her childhood, told of Mother Bernard's visits to their home: "She would sit at the kitchen table with us for a little lunch of tea, homemade bread and wild grape jelly, of which she was very fond."[108] True to Father Médaille's plans for the community, the sisters mixed with their neighbors as well as bringing them into their own home for education.

The Abilene community had hardly become established when Bishop Fink asked them to move. The diocesan lines were being redrawn and, certain that Abilene would no longer belong to Leavenworth, he arranged for the sisters to move to Parsons in the southeastern part of the state.[109] While some sisters remained in Abilene, Mother Bernard and Sisters Gregory Finucane, Ursula Dixon, Assisium Hessnan and two postulants moved to Parsons, arriving in that railroad town in the spring of 1896. Although the pastor was willing to loan the community $300, Mother Bernard was faced with the challenge of building a new motherhouse when she had not paid off the one in Abilene. Their situation was exacerbated by the fact that pastors were unable to pay the sisters their promised salaries. Then, to Bishop Fink's great disappointment, new diocesan lines were drawn and Parsons became part of the Wichita Diocese while Abilene, as he had expected, went to Concordia.

No matter which diocese they were in, their financial situation was dire. All Bishop Fink was able to offer the sisters was the encouragement to pray that parish fairs would be successful enough for the pastors to be able to pay the sisters their back pay. At this point Mother Bernard was at her wit's end. There were forty-nine sisters in her community and the pastors were not able to pay their salaries. Sister Clementine Doyle recalled the options Mother Bernard presented to the community one day in their Parsons home. Sister Clementine said:

> I can see that room—a board broken in the floor where someone had stepped on it; a cellar door, from which the smell of the cellar came up. Mother could hardly keep the tears back. Her face was flushed and she could hardly speak. She said, "Sisters, I want to tell you something, and I want you to make a decision and be perfectly frank! We are poor; we have no money; we have large debts, no future.

---

108 Quinlan, 111-112.
109 In 1890, Abilene had a population of approximately 3,500, in 1896, Parsons had a population of almost 12,000, a number which would decline to 7,700 by the time of the 1900 census. (Quinlan, 115)

I have given you the habit and I am responsible for you. I have a friend in the East, Mother Clement [of Philadelphia], and Mother Clement has written to me that she will help me out of this difficulty. She has offered me, and any one of you who wants, to come to her, a home and will put you where you belong in her community.

Now, I want you to be perfectly sincere...if you want to go, we will furnish a way out there and you will be taken care of and you will be secure and have everything you need...

We are destitute. We are poor, as our Blessed Mother and St. Joseph were on their way to Bethlehem. If you want to stay with me and take what I have to take, all right. If you want to go to Mother Clement and a good home, all right.

She began with Sister Ursula, and she said, "Mother, I want to stay with you. Everyone said, "I want to stay." Mother was quiet for a while and then heaved a big sigh and said, "Well, we will see what we can do. We will have to pray harder and see what we can do."[110]

Having made the decision to stay, the community continued to grow. In 1898, Bishop Hennessy of Wichita began to place more schools under the auspices of the Sisters of St. Joseph, the only diocesan community in his territory. In 1899, after three years in Parsons, Mother Bernard moved to St. Paul, Kansas, a town less than 20 miles away which had been served by the Sisters of Loretto for over 50 years. That summer the community held its first election and asked Mother Bernard to continue in the role to which Bishop Fink had appointed her in 1888 in Abilene. The election was attended by Bishops Hennessy and Cunningham and after it was completed, Bishop Hennessy appointed the sisters who would serve as councilors. Poverty was not the community's only problem.They were put in an uncomfortable position by the fact that the bishop wanted to replace other teaching communities with the Sisters of St. Joseph.[111] In December, 1899, Bishop Hennessy asked the Sisters of St. Joseph to take charge of the orphans of the

---

110 Quinlan, 120-121. Mother Bernard's reference to her as "a friend" suggests that perhaps her travels east had brought her to Philadelphia. Mother Clement also helped the Cleveland community when they needed to train a novice director.
111 Quinlan mentions that the people of Parsons wished for a return of the Sisters of Loretto and when the bishop gave the Sisters of St. Joseph charge of the pro-cathedral school, taking it from the Sisters of Charity of the Blessed Virgin, the people of the parish were not happy with the loss of the sisters they had known and loved. Quinlan, 118,

diocese and he arranged for the purchase of an abandoned institution in Wichita to serve as the orphanage. He deeded that building to the Sisters of St. Joseph on March 19, 1900, giving them the $8,000 mortgage as well.[112] This site, named Mount St. Mary's would become the motherhouse of the Sisters of St. Joseph of Wichita. The novitiate moved to Wichita in May, 1900, and the convent, even though it lacked a steady water supply, boasted the modern conveniences of gas for lighting and a telephone.[113] By the end of the year the sisters had thirty-three children under their care. At that time the sisters had opened twenty-three schools, fifteen of which continued to function and all but one of which was in Kansas.[114] With the motherhouse firmly situated in Wichita, the community had established a stable home from which to grow for the next 110 years.

FROM CONCORDIA TO LA GRANGE: MOTHER STANISLAUS AND MOTHER ALEXINE GOSSELIN

Mother Stanislaus Leary's term as Superior of the Sisters of St. Joseph of Concordia came to an end in the summer of 1899 at the behest of Bishop John Cunningham.[115] Her departure was preceded by her own ill health and community problems serious enough that in 1897, she had investigated the possibility of having the Concordia community join the Sisters of St. Joseph of Philadelphia.[116]

Mother Stanislaus Leary
Aug. 15, 1841- Feb. 14, 1900

---

112 Quinlan, 126-128.

113 Quinlan, 133.

114 See Quinlan, 137. The one outside school was Sts. Peter and Paul, opened in 1895, in Atlanta, a town in southwestern Iowa. In 1900, Atlanta had a population of 5,046 inhabitants.

115 Born in Ireland in 1842, John F. Cunningham immigrated to the United States in 1860 and studied with the Benedictines in Atchison and then at St. Francis Seminary in Milwaukee. He was ordained by Bishop Miège in 1865 and became Vicar General to Miège's successor, Bishop Louis Fink, in 1881. Bishop Cunningham had first known Mother Stanislaus in the late 1880s.

116 In 1897, Mother Stanislaus wrote to Mother Clement of Philadelphia asking what conditions needed to be met for Concordia sisters to join Philadelphia. *See Journeys Begun: A History of the Sisters of St. Joseph of La Grange Park, Illinios, 1889-2007*, by Maureen T. Connaughton, Mary Ellen Rosemeyer, CSJ and Agnes Springer, CSJ, ed. Mary Lou Plietner, CSJ (Brookfield, IL: Priority Print, 2016), 20. Hereafter La Grange History. By the time Mother Stanislaus wrote that letter, the Philadelphia *Constitutions* had been approved for two years and the community was a congregation of papal right. It was not long before this that Mother Bernard Sheridan had told her sisters that Mother Clement of Philadelphia was willing to take in any of them who wished to leave Kansas.

Mother Stanislaus suffered from chronically delicate health which seemingly had gotten worse around this time. She had spent most of the year before her removal dealing with illness and strangely out of communication with the community in Concordia.[117] Accompanied by the former novice director, Sister Alexine Gosselin, she spent some months at the end of 1898 in Excelsior Springs Missouri. When treatment there brought her no relief she returned to Concordia for a time. In May, 1899, health problems led her to St. Joseph's Hospital in Chicago, then to Lake Geneva, Wisconsin, and back to the Chicago hospital. During her long absence, Bishop Cunningham decided to appoint Sister Antoinette Cuff as her replacement in Concordia.[118]

When the bishop decided on his course of action, Sister Antoinette was on vacation in Michigan and received a cable instructing her to return to Concordia without telling her why.[119] Sister Antoinette seemed as surprised as the rest of the community by her sudden appointment. In her autobiography she explained that on July 26, 1899,

> ...after Holy Mass, Right Reverend John Francis Cunningham, Bishop of Concordia, announced that Sister Antoinette was to be the Superior of the Community. She received this news with surprise and sorrow...
>
> It was a trying time for Sister Antoinette, more so than anyone knew, but since she was chosen, she had to make the best of it and she did. At the time the Community was composed of about eighty Sisters and the resources were anything but good. The foundation of the new Motherhouse had been started, but Mother Stanislaus Leary had been forced to abandon it for lack of funds. The old Motherhouse was badly in need of repairs. All in all, things were not the brightest for the young Superior, but Sister Antoinette, although new at such things, started with a good will to do her best.[120]

---

117 *La Grange History* (22) points out that during that year Mother Stanislaus and the Concordia sisters did not communicate, even to the point of exchanging holiday greetings.
118 Mother Stanislaus' departure from office was hardly unforeseeable. Thomas (197) refers to a letter from Wichita's Bishop Hennessy who had been acting administrator of the Concordia Diocese telling Bishop-elect Cunningham that it was necessary that the Sisters of St. Joseph have a change of administration. In 1883, when Sister Antoinette Cuff joined Mother Stanislaus she was a novice, the youngest of the founding group. (Thomas, 130)
119 *Journeys Begun*, 22.
120 From Mother Antoinette's autobiography, quoted in Thomas, 202.

Mother Stanislaus was in Chicago when these events took place.

MOTHER STANISLAUS IN CHICAGO

There is little doubt that Mother Stanislaus had left Concordia wounded in spirit as well as fragile in health.[121] But even if she had no control over her physical condition, her indomitable personality led her once again to transform disappointment into regeneration. Agreeing with the physicians who, with more than one shade of meaning, said that "the Kansas climate had much to do with her declining condition," Mother Stanislaus decided to remain in Chicago.[122]

The annals lack details regarding how the sisters began to arrange their foundation in Chicago. Although there is no evidence that Mother Stanislaus knew Archbishop Feehan before she went to Chicago, her friend Bishop Scannell who had gone from Concordia to Omaha in 1891 was his friend and protégé. It seems likely that if Bishop Scannell did not actually send Mother Stanislaus to Archbishop Feehan, he would have at least vouched for her based on their experience together while he was bishop in Concordia.[123] By the end of June, 1899, it had been worked out that Mother Stanislaus and Sister Alexine,

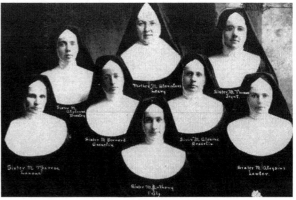

La Grange Pioneers:
Srs. M Theresa, M. Alphonse, M. Bernard, Stanislaus, M. Anthony, M. Alexine, M. Thomas, M. Aloysius

---

121 *Journeys Begun* (23) quotes Sister Evelyn Frazer, as saying that Mother Stanislaus' parting words were "I shake the dust of this place off my shoes."

122 Quoted from "The Annals of The Sisters of St. Joseph, Part First," Nazareth, La Grange, Illinios," (Archives CSJoseph) 7. Hereafter, "La Grange Annals." The text of the Annals seems to have come largely from Mother Alexine's hand but in some cases the way Mother Alexine or an event is described, it is obviously the work of a secretary or other annalist who may even had editorialized the text or dictation.

123 While the future bishop, John Cunningham, was Vicar General in Leavenworth, Mother Stanislaus had chosen to keep the motherhouse in Concordia under Bishop Scannell's jurisdiction rather than move to Abilene or other sites where the community would have remained with Bishop Fink. It was Bishop Cunningham who arranged for Mother Stanislaus' demission in 1899.

together with Sisters Francis Joseph Leary, Josephine Leary and Sister Madeline de Pazzi would settle into the home of Reverend Ulric Martell, pastor of St. John the Baptist Parish in Chicago. They were joined there by Sisters Constance Ryan and Berchmans Gray, all of whom seemingly joined Mother Stanislaus in Chicago rather than return to Concordia as the sisters usually did at the end of the school year.[124] Mother Stanislaus' health needs were the ostensible reason for opening the house in Chicago but with all the sisters who came there, it would seem there was more to the story.

Following the appointment of Sister Antoinette Cuff as superior in Concordia, the unspecified dissensions leading toward the separation of the small Chicago community from Concordia were coming to a head. It appeared that the sisters with Mother Stanislaus at St. John the Baptist Parish were in the process of establishing an independent foundation without Concordia's approval. The annals explain the next events as follows.

> While preparations were being made for the opening of the school... Rev. Mother Stanislaus decided to go to Concordia to interview the bishop of that place regarding this recent undertaking and at the same time to settle certain important matters of the Community. Sister M. F. Joseph [Leary] accompanied Rev. Mother on this short trip...
>
> The journey...seemed almost too much of an exertion for our Rev. Mother, who, upon her return to Chicago, felt quite oppressed for some time. By this time our new abode had been converted into a veritable Convent home...
>
> One morning while Sister M. Alexine had gone to the Drug Store to have prescription filled for her sick Mother, a knock was heard at the Convent door, and three Sisters from Concordia entering the peaceful little abode, stated that they had been sent by the Bishop of Concordia to take charge of the school.
>
> This was an unexpected blow which almost prostrated our dear Mother, and rather than cause any trouble or scandal, she at once notified her household to prepare for departure and leave the place to the intruders...
>
> Having notified Sister M. Alexine who was still at the Drug Store... she lost no time in ordering a conveyance to take the sisters and their

---

124 Diverse sources have slight differences in the lists of sisters. See Thomas, 198

belongings from St. John's and in the course of a few hours Mother Stanislaus and her faithful daughters were winding their way through the great city, not knowing where to go.[125]

Sister Evangeline Thomas in her history of the Concordia Congregation diplomatically reworks that breathless account, indicating that the problem was indeed Mother Stanislaus' intention to establish a separate congregation. She says

> When the authorities at Concordia realized that there was an undercurrent operating at Saint John the Baptist...Sister Mary Anne Picard was sent there by Bishop Cunningham and Mother Antoinette to assume charge as local superior. After some disagreeable misunderstandings, some of the Sisters went to La Grange to establish a separate community.[126]

Sister Evangeline's version passes very quickly from the departure from St. John the Baptist to the La Grange resettlement, skipping details that are an unforgettable part of the La Grange lore. The La Grange annals, largely written or dictated by Sister Alexine Gosselin, continue with their first hand witness.

> Putting themselves under the special protection of Divine Providence and after a few moments' deliberation over the situation, it was decided... that owing to the delicate condition of Rev. Mother, she should return to the hospital, taking Sister C. with her; that others seek hospitality with the Sisters of the Good Shepherd who were conducting an Industrial School for girls on Prairie Avenue and that Sister M. Alexine should take her cousin, Miss A.M. --- to the Loretta [sic] Academy at Niagara Falls, N.Y.[127]

The irony of finding refuge with the Good Shepherd Sisters whose charism was to care for women in dire straits was surely not lost on the little group who found

---

125 La Grange Annals, pg. 8.
126 Thomas, 198.
127 La Grange Annals, pg. 8. The text goes on to comment that the Concordia sisters who took over at St. John the Baptist were unsuccessful and gave up before the end of the school year. There are various expressions in the annals that indicate that Mother Alexine wrote them, while at times the hand of another author, perhaps a secretary or editor, is obvious.

themselves suddenly without a place to lay their heads.[128]

Meanwhile, Sister Alexine's journey with her would-be-postulant cousin was reported to the young woman's family by "desperate intermeddlers" who suggested that she had been kidnapped. The escapade later became more intense when one of the "intermeddlers," a total stranger, called on Sister Alexine after she returned to Chicago and demanded to know where the postulant had gone. The man warned Sister Alexine that she was subject to excommunication if she refused to abandon her new community and Mother Stanislaus. She succumbed to his threats to the point of revealing the whereabouts of the postulant but disregarded his intimidating attempts to disband the "new promising foundation in its infancy."[129]

After some time in the hospital, Mother Stanislaus joined the group at the Good Shepherd Home. While there she took up the task of regularizing the group's prospects via negotiations with Bishops Feehan and Cunningham and Rev. James Hagan who was pastor of St. Francis Xavier Parish in La Grange. The annals state that Mother Stanislaus had been in communication with Father Hagan for "some years" about the possibility of opening a girls' academy in "that very exclusive suburb."[130] The account goes on to describe the results of Father Hagan's meeting with Mother Stanislaus:

> As a result of this interview, everything having been satisfactorily arranged with the Archbishop, it was decided that Mother Stanislaus should found a diocesan house of the Sisters of St. Joseph in La Grange, Illinois. And on the feast of the Holy Angels, October 2nd, 1899, Rev. Mother Stanislaus, with her two natural sisters, Sister M. Josephine Leary, Sr. Francis J. Leary, Sr. Berchmans Gray and Sister Constance Ryan and the present Mother Alexine...having obtained their obedience

---

128 The Sisters of the Good Shepherd, an offshoot of the Order of Our Lady of the Refuge, were founded in France in 1831 by Saint Mary Euphrasia Pelletier who, like the Sisters of St. Joseph of Lyon and Le Puy, saw the advantage of a Congregation with a centralized governance. Approved as a papal congregation in 1835, the Good Shepherd Sisters specialized in providing a safe place and holistic education for women whose circumstances made them vulnerable to abuse or prone to illegal activities.

129 La Grange Annals, 10-11. This incident actually took place on the feast of St. Stanislaus when the sisters were celebrating their first day in what was at least their fourth home in the Chicago area. According to research done by Sister Sally Witt, "Miss A.M." was Agnes Martin of Hanover, KS. In January, 1900, she entered the Sisters of Mercy in Chicago and received the name Sister Mary Valeria. (Martin was the maiden name of Mother Alexine's mother.)

130 La Grange Annals, 9. Mother Stanislaus had overseen such a wide-ranging extension of the Concordia

from Concordia, they came to La Grange , where they rented a furnished residence…They remained there only a few weeks, a smaller residence near St. Francis Xavier's Church having been found, not as more suitable for their work, but less demanding upon their purse…They moved into this house on the eve of the feast of St. Stanislaus.[131]

Neither the hospital stays nor the eventual settling down in La Grange were sufficient to help Mother Stanislaus recover her health. Mother Stanislaus Leary died on February 14, 1900, exactly forty-three years after she had received the habit in Canandaigua, New York. She was buried from St. Francis Xavier Church in La Grange and her obituary described her as a woman revered by "numerous bishops and priests," adding that her crowded funeral was attended by "the wealthy and the cultured, and the poor and the lowly." High praise indeed since she had been such a short time in the Chicago area.[132] Her friend and inadvertent successor, Mother Antoinette Cuff described her as "a woman of strong character and great suavity of manner, whose confidence in God and filial reliance on the paternal care of St. Joseph…was an inspiration."[133]

MOTHER ALEXINE BEGINS

The annals explain that just before her death, Mother Stanislaus called for Mother Alexine and handed over her life's work to her young nurse/protégé who felt no shame in admitting that she felt incapable of taking on that burden. Mother Alexine wrote:

> The grief Mother Alexine experienced…may be better imagined than described as she had always held her in the highest esteem and respect… after her dear Mother had been laid to rest, Sister Mary Alexine's thought was to return to her Convent home at Concordia. This however, was not to be…
>
> Sister Alexine was taken ill…when she recovered, the Rev. Pastor, Father Hagan, informed her that the Archbishop wished to see her.[134]

Congregation that it is entirely possible that she had received requests from him. *The La Grange History* (26) indicates that the contact came through a Thomas McGrath of New York, a mutual friend who "encouraged Fr. Hagan to open his door to Mother Stanislaus."
131 La Grange Annals, 10.
132 *Journeys Begun*, 27-28.
133 *Journeys Begun*, 29.
134 La Grange Annals, 12.

In a fortuitous happenstance, Bishop Scannell of Omaha was visiting Archbishop Feehan around the time all this was occurring. The annals refer to Bishop Scannell as "a personal friend of the Gosselin family" and one of the clergy who set his eyes on Sister Alexine as Mother Stanislaus' successor. The annals describe the scene that took place when Sister Alexine arrived at the Archbishop's office and he told her his plan for her to take over the fledgling community.

> She simply laid before His Grace the many difficulties which she must encounter in such an undertaking – her inexperience, her youth, besides being destitute of means of existence. But His Grace was not to be discouraged by these words. He therefore endowed our good Sister M. Alexine with the faculty of Mother Superior of the Sisters of St. Joseph in the Archdiocese of Chicago, June 21st, 1900, and with a fervent blessing and many good wishes sent her forth to do the Master's will.

Fervent as the bishop's blessing may have been, Mother Alexine was about to take on more than her fair share of challenges. Previous to assuming the role of companion and nurse to Mother Stanislaus, Sister Alexine probably had never served outside Concordia where she had been director of novices.[135] While that had led her to develop a deep spirituality, nothing had prepared her for administration, a fact that was not lost on some of her companions. According to the annals:

> Mother Alexine was not welcome upon her return to the little Community in La Grange with perfect harmony by all its members. A few who were older, more experienced and who had many reasons to consider that they should have taken the place so lately filled by

Mother Bernard and Mother Alexine Gosselin

> Mother Stanislaus were slow to recognize the authority of so young a member of their body, she being then merely thirty-three years of age.[136]

---

135 It is possible but not certain that while she was novice director Sister Alexine was sent to Philadelphia to learn about that congregation and its formation. See *Journeys Begun*, 20.
136 La Grange Annals, 13.

Under the old French *Constitutions*, the dissenting sisters knew that the bishop had the final word about the life of the community. Rather than acquiesce, Sisters Josephine Leary, Francis Leary, Constance Ryan and Berchmans Gray left La Grange for Belvidere, Illinois where they intended to establish another community. The group left in October, 1900, and under Sister Josephine Leary's leadership they opened a hospital in March of the following year. Although they received several candidates, they eventually concluded that they could not sustain themselves and appealed for readmission and were accepted by the Concordia Congregation which maintained the hospital ministry for decades to come. The Belvidere group also had a role in establishing a community of Sisters of St. Joseph in Lewiston and Slickpoo, Idaho.[137]

The departure of the sisters to Belvidere left only three in La Grange: Mother Alexine, Sister M. Ligouri McDonald and Francis Smith, a forty-one year old widowed music teacher who had become a postulant under Mother Stanislaus. [138] The annals explain that their prospects were dim:

> One evening, when the remaining members of the Community.... assembled in the refectory to partake of a scanty meal, Rev. Mother related to them the wishes of the Archbishop in regard to their future prospects, and placing the contents of her purse upon the table, amounting to the gallant sum of thirty-three cents,...She told them that was all the capital she possessed on which to establish the community[139]

Miss Smith received the habit on July 2, 1900, and became known as Sister Mary James. Around the time she was received, Sisters Bernard Gosselin, Gertrude Green and Ernestine Le Pitre came from Concordia to throw their lot in with Mother Alexine. Now at least they were six and the five professed sisters had the necessary permissions to leave the Concordia congregation.[140]

---

137 La Grange Annals, 13. See also Thomas, 198, 213-214. *Journeys Begun* (31) mentions that after Archbishop Feehan's death in 1902, Archbishop Quigley, his successor, hoped that the La Grange and Belvedere communities might reunite. Mother Alexine replied that the La Grange sisters did not wish the union and asked that the Archbishop get to know them before making a decision. Finally, letting him know that he would be responsible for whatever decision he made she said, "Should any difficulty arise, it would necessitate us to ask you to remedy the evil."
138 *Journeys Begun*, 36-37.
139 La Grange Annals, 13.
140 That number did not remain stable, while other women entered, Sisters Liguori and James left La Grange for Wichita. Sister James made final vows under Mother Bernard Sheridan in 1902. (*Journeys Begun*, 37.)

The sisters survived some precarious months without any source of income. Unwilling to allow their hunger to be public knowledge, they secretly received baskets of food from the pastor, and as one of the sisters quipped, "They ate like little tramps in the basement."[141] They came up with a project for issuing "brick cards," soliciting donations for the school and convent they wished to open. In October, 1900, they were able to open a boarding school, requiring them to crowd their home with the initial six resident and eight day pupils from whom they earned the sum of $64 per month.[142] The school enrollment grew and fluctuated, amounting to a total of twenty students during the first year.

Just as the school was opening, Mother Alexine found a benefactor in Mr. J. R. Walsh, the President of the Chicago National Bank. They first met when Mother Alexine went to him for a loan and advice for building an Academy. In answer to his inquiry about the capital she had on hand, she said she had $35. Having no way of knowing that only months before she had less than 1% of that amount, he advised her to accumulate additional funds before thinking of building. She returned a week later and when he asked about her capital she was pleased to inform him that she now had $75. As the annals tell it,

> Mr. Walsh laughed and said, "That is fine," telling her to keep on increasing the sum and that she would have sufficient in a few years to build. But she insisted that she wanted to start as soon as possible even if she had to beg from door to door to procure the necessary funds. This heroic determination Mr. Walsh could not resist, and he told her to proceed with the work and send the contractors to him...He gave her a note of twenty-thousand dollars and she had good reasons to believe that the note never would be presented for payment. So engrossed was her benefactor in the success of the new Academy that every bit of architecture carried on was looked after by him personally.[143]

Obviously, Mother Alexine had received a portion of her deceased mentor's invincible spirit. Mother Alexine's new bravado also included a flair for advertising. In 1900 she published an article promoting the new Nazareth Academy which said:

---

141 La Grange Annals, 18.
142 The tuition was $10 per month for the boarders and 50 cents per month for the day students. (La Grange Annals, 17.)
143 La Grange Annals, 19.

This Boarding School for the practical education of young ladies…is directed by the Sisters of the Congregation of Saint Joseph, an order approved by the Holy See, whose members devote their lives in a special manner to the education of youth and whose establishments have, we firmly believe, justly earned the reputation of being numbered among the most successful schools in the United States.[144]

Just as she audaciously sought financial help from friends near and far, she apparently felt free to claim for her new community the papal approbation of previously established Congregations of St. Joseph.

Mother Alexine's advertisement went on to explain that the school's large, capable staff of instructors taught all branches of music, with "the same principles that have formed the basis of instruction in all the great art schools of Europe for the past four hundred years." The Academy she described was quite an endeavor to be carried by the six sisters at La Grange, but at least they had a professional music teacher among them.

The community struggled and sacrificed. At one point, when they lacked sufficient room for sisters and boarders to be able to sleep, they rented leaky attic space in a nearby house. They described it with good humor saying:

It has been the ambition of our sisters…to get as near heaven as possible. In this…the more fervent, who were anxious not to have even the roof to obscure the nearness, had ample opportunity. But their fervor usually cooled when the friendly rain persisted.

Another quip described the situation saying:

We had to use umbrellas to keep off the rain from our beds, but some of the sisters said, "We had such fine views of the stars that anyone who had a leaning toward…astronomy ought to study it while circumstances favored."[145]

At another point, overcrowded by 20 boarders and 19 sisters, they rented sleeping space across the street from the Academy under construction. Long-range planning being a luxury they could not afford, the annals recall that the sisters had to make

---

144 *Journeys Begun*, 40.
145 La Grange Annals, 21, 23.

the move after the evening meal:

> On the first night...after dusk as the Sisters were repairing to sleep in their new apartments, equipped with the necessary outfit such as bed-clothes, wash-stands, basins, and toilet articles, they were met on the way by our good chaplain. You may imagine his astonishment when confronted with this parade. He was unable to speak...not being aware of the fact that the Sisters had discovered new regions wherein they could rest their weary heads. However, he hastened to the Rev. Mother and asked her "if she knew her sisters were running away."[146]

Sisters were not abandoning ship, but the percentage of entrants who remained in the community seemed disturbingly small. On March 19, 1901, there was one profession and two women received the habit. August of 1901, saw the promising occasion of the reception of 13 women into the community. Unfortunately, only four of them remained to make vows. As the annalist explained:

> There was little to commend to their future prospects for they were too obscure and uninviting for some of the more timorous...These undecided souls felt incapacitated and thought it would be better to enter into a field where the harvest was more promising...In the face of this filing out it required no small courage on the part of [those] remaining...to hold fast. But trusting to the goodness of an All Wise Providence that called them, they persevered...They were young; their hearts were ever hopeful and they did not invite trouble to meet them half way.[147]

On July 14, 1901, the sisters laid the cornerstone of a new motherhouse and academy. The Chicago diocesan paper, *The New World*, explained that the Romanesque structure would be 110 feet wide and three stories high, including a "lofty story or attic," a detail which must have caused some knowing raised eyebrows among the sisters.

The sisters continued to seek funding near and far, advertising in the diocesan newspaper and calling on local and outside friends. On July 17, 1900,

---

146 La Grange Annals, 20.
147 La Grange Annals, 28.

Mother Alexine's feast day, the workers went on strike because they had not received their salaries. The annalist explained:

> They abandoned their work...determined not to resume it until they were paid. Placing themselves at ease under the trees, some smoking, others sleeping, they prepared to make a successful siege.
> The Sisters unhesitatingly took up the work of carrying mortar, laying bricks, nailing floor boards and all other work necessary. When the men saw that the Sisters were determined to go on with the work they became ashamed and one by one came back to work. The Sisters... worked several hours and when the Angelus rang...a collection was taken up among the men amounting to seven dollars and fifty cents, which they gave to the sisters in payment for the work the sisters did that morning.[148]

The Sisters moved into the new building just in time for the first celebration of the Mass in their new chapel on Christmas Day, 1901.

New members continued to come to the community and their welcome presence also increased the need for income. One of the first commercial ventures the sisters initiated, a portent of what would develop over the next 100 years, was the purchase of a printing press. There were two major drawbacks to the plan. First, none of the sisters had any experience in printing. Secondly, La Grange's electricity functioned only at night. Thus the amateur compositor and her assistants rearranged their horarium and worked with their "literary litter" through the night for the first two years of the project. Eventually Mother Alexine sent the chief of the press room to learn from printing houses in the area. The summary of their learning period reads:

> Nothing radically wrong happened, (at least nobody died)...To the printing department we may credit the decrease of expenditure and also the great aid that it has been in paying off our debts.[149]

The press, difficult as it had been to master, was more successful than the laundry service the sisters instituted in 1905. It was not lack of expertise that caused the demise of this business, but fear of contagion. After the community had installed

---

148 La Grange Annals, 28.
149 La Grange Annals, 38.

the industrial equipment necessary and sisters had successfully solicited patrons, there was an outbreak of measles in the school and the customers were afraid of coming near anything that had been exposed to the Academy environs.

The year 1907 brought the worst blow the sisters had to absorb as they struggled with poverty. John R. Walsh, the financier who had been so amused and helpful to Mother Alexine, fell into bankruptcy and disgrace. In addition to seeing the downfall of a loyal and trusted friend, the community was forced to deal with the fact that the $20,000 "loan" they thought they would never have to repay was now in the hands of debt-collectors and the community was on the brink of losing the little they had. Although the sisters' luck was poor, they had a wealth of connections. With Bishop Quigley's permission and a letter of introduction to Thomas F. Ryan, one of the wealthiest Catholics in the country, Mother Alexine and a companion headed to New York to find help.[150] Although Ryan's philanthropy seemed concentrated in the areas of New York, Washington and Virginia, Mother Alexine was at least able to meet him. As the annals explain:

> At first they received no encouragement, but upon leaving the house, Rev. Mother gave him an envelope containing scapulars, holy cards, and a medal of St. Joseph. This seemed to soften the good man's heart. He then asked for her New York address. She gave him her brother's address...In the afternoon of the next day, February thirteenth...Rev. Mother's brother, A. J. Gosselin, received a visitor...who holding a large envelope...stated that Hon. T.F.R. wished that the envelope be personally delivered to Rev. Mother Alexine. No time was lost...and upon opening...there was enclosed besides a check for one thousand dollars, a very kind letter , with a promise of twenty-four thousand more if the Sisters would pray so that he obtained a very special favor.[151]

The sisters persisted in prayer and Mr. Ryan continued to support them even though he apparently did not receive the sought-after favor.

In 1910, Mr. Ryan provided the necessary funds to purchase the land known as the Babcock Estate, a 77 acre expanse of land just three blocks from the Academy. It was to be the site of a boys' school named St. Joseph's Institute. There,

---

150 Ryan then lived in New York, having amassed a fortune in tobacco, insurance and transportation. Among Ryan's most conspicuous donations, he contributed the entire cost for the building of the Cathedral of the Sacred Heart in Richmond.
151 La Grange Annals, 47-48.

with the help of their advisor and friend, Brother Paul, C.S.C., the sisters began the work of clearing the land of "three to four hundred wagon loads" of manure, plus wood, stones and one recalcitrant tenant. Some of the most creative community members learned enough carpentry skills to fashion the trimmed wood into "new models in chairs" tables and "articles to be designed" from the wood they grubbed.[152] In October, 1910, the sisters held a fair that brought them $6,000, much to the credit of the two major donors who supplied a piano and a calf as the most "elaborate prizes."[153] The community struggled to eke a crop from their land, they opened paths and roadways and, with occasionally hazardous results, some of the sisters even took over janitorial duties including furnace maintenance.[154] The ground-breaking for the new Institute on the property took place on March 19, 1912. At the insistence of some of the boys, Mother Alexine was present although she had been hospitalized for forty-three days after the opening of the 1911 school year.[155] Immediately after the ground-breaking she followed doctors' orders and went to Hot Springs, Arkansas to seek a cure. She remained there until May 23, 1912. It was during her absence that her sister and assistant, Mother Bernard Gosselin, began correspondence with a pastor in Eureka, California, who invited her to establish a house of the community in that area. As soon as Mother Alexine returned, Mother Bernard traveled to California, a trip which would result in the foundation of the Congregation of the Sisters of St. Joseph of Orange.

FROM LA GRANGE TO LADYSMITH:
FOUNDING A NEW CONGREGATION IN A NEW TRADITION

Mother Bernard and her group left La Grange in June of 1912. Before they were fully settled, another group of sisters in La Grange decided to found a new Congregation. In the Spring of 1912, Father Boniface Efferenn, a Servite Friar, gave the community at La Grange a retreat.[156] He took note of the fact that La Grange

---

152 *Journeys Begun*, 57 and La Grange Annals, 67.

153 La Grange Annals, 71.

154 The La Grange Annals (49) tell of the explosion of a steam valve when the sisters fired up the boiler. Without any apparent irony, the paragraph that follows the story of the boiler explosion explains that each year "Mother Alexine has engaged competent instructors for the sisters....Nothing was spared for each one's accomplishment according to her talent and ability."

155 La Grange Annals, 73.

156 The Servites, or Friar Servants of Mary, were founded in 1233 near Florence, Italy by a group of cloth merchants who became known as the "Seven Holy Founders." They were established in the United States in 1870 at the invitation of Bishop Joseph Melcher of Green Bay who met them in Italy during the First Vatican Council. From Green Bay they spread to Menasha, WI and by 1874, they were also serving in Chicago. (See: http://www.servite.org/History/History-Origins.aspx)

had more sisters than active ministries while his community was building a school that had no prospects of having a faculty. That convergence of factors led six of the La Grange community to seek a dispensation from their vows so that they could participate in founding a new group, The Servants of Mary (Servites) of Ladysmith, Wisconsin. In September, 1912, the women who became known as Servite Sisters Mary Alphonse Bradley, Mary Rose Smith, Mary Evangelist Corcoran, Mary Irene Drummand, Boniface (Bernadino) Hayes and Mary Charles Kolmesh had received their dispensations and went to St. Mary's Parish in Ladysmith, Wisconsin, dressed "in a habit that resembled that of the Sisters of St. Joseph."[157] After formation in the Augustinian tradition they made vows as Servite Sisters. In 1919 their community received approval as a diocesan community and later affiliated with the worldwide Servite Order.[158] That was the third community to be founded by sisters from La Grange.

The departure of the sisters was a sign of problems in the community. When the Servite Provincial, Father Benetius Heil, contacted archdiocesan authorities in Chicago to inquire about the sisters coming from La Grange, he reported to Bishop Schinner that he had learned that their reason for leaving the community.

> [It is] dissatisfaction...there are something like eighty sisters in the community without anything to do but conduct a boarding and day school at La Grange. Up to now they have not been allowed to take schools.

Father Heil added some details that point to the sisters' sense of religious life and congregations. He said:

> Two of these sisters were here to see me this evening and left their dispensations with me. They are more than anxious to go to Ladysmith but want to go soon; two of them, I understand, are thinking seriously of joining the B.V.M.'s who are willing to take them. If nothing can be arranged in the near future we may not get them. I told them that they would have to wait until next week at least...

---

157 The list of the sisters' names in the website of the Servite Sisters differs slightly from that in *Journeys Begun.* (*Journeys Begun*, 66, see also 69.)

158 See https://servitesisters.org/ and https://servitesisters.org/images/newsandevents/SST_Newsltr_2012. pdf. The five founders ranged in age from 29 to 37 years old. With two Irish immigrants, two sisters from Iowa and one from Michigan, none of them shared the French-Canadian heritage of the Gosselins. The five sisters did not leave the community all at once, but did arrive in Wisconsin together.

...they are willing to go to Ladysmith to teach, even in secular dress if there be no other way...it is practically necessary for them to wear some kind of a habit, if they go to Ladysmith to teach, I would suggest that your Lordship permit them to wear a sort of habit so as to pass for Sisters, keep them that way for sometime, [sic] and if their conduct and ability prove satisfactory to you and to the Fathers, then either allow them to start a new congregation or permit me either to send one of them to one of our Third Order sister Novitiates in Europe or have one of those Sisters come to them in Ladysmith for their novitiate.[159]

Father Heil also mentioned that the women might join the Ursulines, but they were not interested in that congregation because, according to Father Heil, the sisters thought the same dissatisfaction existed among that group and they also disliked the class system still extant among them. So the Ursulines were out and the authorities allowed the group to dress as sisters while they adapted and eventually adopted a new rule as Servites. This letter not only explains some of the problems in the La Grange community, but also suggests that the women who were dissatisfied or ready to leave their community had more interest in their ministry than in the unique spirituality of a given community. They wanted to serve God's people as women religious; the fact that they did it as Sisters of St. Joseph, Servites or Sisters of Charity of the Blessed Virgin was a secondary consideration, perhaps a matter that seemed no more significant than changing the style of their religious habit and less important than the character of the superior.

THE TURN-AROUND OF 1912

The leave-taking of nearly a quarter of the community in the space of a few months did anything but incapacitate the community. On October 13, 1912, just weeks after the departure of the Ladysmith group, the community celebrated the laying of the cornerstone for St. Joseph's Institute for Boys. The ceremony was attended by a crowd of 3,000 including clergy from the Cathedral College, DePaul University and the Knights of Columbus. The building was dedicated some ten months later at a ceremony presided over by Archbishop Quigley and a crowd which included the Mayor of Chicago and other prominent politicians.[160] The next important

---

159 Letter from Fr. Heil to Bishop Schinner, Superior, Wisconsin, September 12, 1912, cited in *Journeys Begun*, 69-70. In the end, Sisters Charles and Irene did eventually leave the Servite community to join the B.V.M. community.
160 *Journeys Begun*, 69-70.

construction project was a grotto modeled on that at Lourdes.

For whatever reason, until 1912, the Sisters of St. Joseph in La Grange had not been invited to staff Chicago area parish schools and for that reason they had the most unusual problem of too many sisters with too few ministries to keep them gainfully employed. That problem began to wane in November, 1912, when the sisters were asked to staff Mount Carmel School in Chicago Heights. The poverty of the parish is evident in the fact that the Archbishop himself paid each sister's salary of $20 per month and the tuition of the children.[161] Under those circumstances the lack of a convent was not a surprise, but the sisters soon balked at sleeping in the auditorium. Instead they took over a classroom which served as an all-purpose space: dorm, kitchen, dining room, community room and bathroom. A kindly parishioner sent her son over each evening with lanterns so that the sisters would not have to do everything in the dark.[162]

The sisters opened their school shortly after arriving.[163] Following the pastor's orders to "get the children off the streets, they began with ninety-seven first graders on opening day and a total of one hundred prospective students had been turned away for lack of space. Just as challenging as the numbers, was the fact that in that Italian immigrant community none of the children spoke English. Within a year the sisters had opened the school at night for adults who wanted to learn English. The cultural adjustment had to be great on both sides as the sisters ministered to an ethnic group with whom they had no experience and who suffered from significant discrimination. In 1914, nine sisters were asked to staff another parish school for the Italian community in Kensington.[164]

In 1912 Archbishop Quigley approved the Constitutions of the Sisters of St. Joseph of La Grange, thus regularizing their status as a diocesan congregation. Then, nearly thirteen years from the time they arrived in La Grange, the community held an election and chose Mother Alexine Gosselin as their first official superior with Sister Mary Anthony Fritz as her assistant.

During Mother Alexine's terms in leadership, finances continued to be a significant problem. She had been building and purchasing land even though the community had little ability to generate its own income. Although she received help from family and friends both local and from as far away as New York, Mr.

---

161 *Journeys Begun*, 72.
162 *Journeys Begun*, 73.
163 *Journeys Begun* mentions two dates: December 8, 1912 (pg. 74) and January, 1913 (pg. 76).
164 *Journeys Begun*, 79. Kensington, home to Irish and German immigrants was nicknamed "Bumtown."
See: http://www.encyclopedia.chicagohistory.org/pages/688.html.

John Walsh's misfortune had seriously destabilized the precarious structure upon which she had constructed her projects. But before finances became an insurmountable problem, she faced a most unusual challenge in community life.

SISTER M. DE CHANTAL GOSSELIN

Mother Alexine came from a large Catholic family in Concordia, Kansas. Her parents and grandparents were born in Canada. Alexis Gosselin, the patriarch of the family, was fourteen years older than his wife Apolline and between 1862 and 1879, they had six sons and four daughters, two of whom became Sisters of St. Joseph of Concordia.[165] When Mr. Gosselin was 85 years old, he became seriously ill and all the children were called to his bedside before he died on December 7, 1913. Notified of her father's sickness, Mother Alexine and her cousin, Sister M. Raphael traveled from La Grange to Concordia to be with the family. Mother Alexine explains that after the funeral, although her brothers made arrangements for their mother, the 71 year-old widow had made her own plans. As she told the story:

> After the funeral...the boys asked that the immediate family assemble in mother's bedroom...having closed all the doors...brother Edward presented mother with the receipted bills, giving her the bankbook... and told her that the children, now that father was gone, desired to make her happy the rest of her days. If she wished to live with any of them they would be most happy to have her or if she preferred to keep the home, they would make provisions for someone to stay with her.
>
> When all the propositions were mentioned and the children anxious to hear her wishes, all waited for her to talk. After a pause, Mother said, " I wish to thank you all, my dear children for what you have done, for your thoughtfulness...but there is only one thing that will make me happy and that is to go to La Grange and to be a sister in Mother Alexine's community.

Mother Alexine explained that all of the children were astounded by the

----

165 The U.S. Census for 1880 listed the following family members: Alexis, 52 years old, Apolline (wife), 38; Edward (son) 18; Ida (daughter) 17; Medoild (son) 15; Agnes (daughter) 13; Arthur (son) 11; Augustine (son) 8; Anna (daughter) 6; Charles (son) 4; Isabelle (daughter) 2; Francis (son) 1. Apolline's occupation was "keeping house" and Edward and Medoild's occupations as "helps on farm." Both parents were born in Canada and all the children except Francis were born in Illinois, indicating that the family had moved to Kansas around 1879.

announcement, that even she had no hint of her mother's plan. She added,

> When Mother saw that they would blame me, she told us that she and
> Father had it all arranged before he died, and that no one knew of it, and
> that all the blame was hers.
>   She said that she wanted to act upon this decision immediately.[166]

Mother Alexine went on to describe how her mother traveled to La Grange within
a month of her husband's death. Once there, she asked to become a candidate and
while Mother Alexine "tried to divert her mind from the idea," Monsignor Joseph
Perrier, their former pastor from Concordia, supported the mother and went to
Bishop Quigley with a petition signed by the sisters asking that Mrs. Gosselin be
admitted. The bishop asked Mother Alexine to visit him and when he saw that she
was not in favor of the plan and had no idea that others had gone to him behind
her back, the bishop told her to allow her mother to stay as a secular, but to avoid
the problems that could be entailed by admitting her to the community.

Some months later, Mrs. Gosselin returned to visit her children in Kansas.
In July, 1915, one of her sons entered the house with the breaking news that Bishop
Quigley had died. As Mother Alexine told it:

> Mother stopped eating and told my brother to pack her trunk at once.
> She wished to come to La Grange, telling the folks that she knew that
> the next archbishop would give her permission to be received into the
> community. I was astonished upon receiving a telegram that Mother
> was on her way to La Grange so soon and was very much amused when
> she told me the reason as the Church is slow in appointing successions
> to Church authorities.[167]

Nearly six months later, Bishop George Mundelein, the Auxiliary Bishop of
Brooklyn, was named Archbishop of Chicago on December 9, 1915 and installed
on February 9, 1916.[168] Mother Alexine explains that in the summer of 1916,

---

166 "History of Sister M. de Chantal, CSJ, Martin Gosselin," a manuscript written by Mother Alexine Gosselin
which she introduced saying: "Mother Alexine Gosselin having been requested to write up the events which led
her mother, Sister M. de Chantal, to enter the community of the sisters of St. Joseph at La Grange, Illinois will
attempt to give as brief a history as possible." (Archives CSJoseph)
167"History of Sister M. de Chantal."
168 Coming from Brooklyn, Archbishop Mundelein would have known the Sisters of St. Joseph of Brentwood
who, according to the Catholic Directory of 1916, then numbered over 700. See: *The Official Catholic Directory
for the Year of Our Lord 1916*, (NY: P. J. Kennedy and Sons), 290

Father Jerome…was chosen to give our retreat previous to the feast of the Visitation, July 2. During the retreat, mother asked me if the retreat master could speak French as she wished to go to confession to him. Upon being told he spoke French, she prepared to go to confession, was in the confessional for about one hour…She retired about 10 p.m. and told me she was anxious for the dawn of the next day as she had hopes.

The next morning, July second while we were at breakfast the doorkeeper informed me that Msgr. Rempe had just come in for the reception. He was earlier than usual that day. When I came into the room, I was astonished to find Mother talking to Msgr. Rempe and the retreat master…They apparently had everything arranged by the time I appeared on the scene, as Msgr. Rempe greeted me as follows: "Yes, we have your Mother here and everything is settled. You must say no more to discourage her. We shall take care of her, and you keep out of it. I shall go to see the archbishop tomorrow and take up the matter with him. I know he will consent after I talk to him.

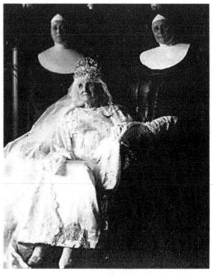

Mother Bernard, Mrs. G. and Mother Alexine on reception day

Then Mother left the room and both Monsignor and the retreat master told me that if there was ever a real, good vocation in our community, Mother had the most excellent disposition, that her sentiments were truly marvelous, that God's hand was there. Of that they were sure.

The following day I received word to call at the chancery office on Monday. The archbishop desired to see me on some business. When I was leaving for the city the following morning, Mother met me in the hall and said, "Put in a favorable word for me when you see the archbishop."

His eminence wished to speak to me regarding a new mission. When business was over, I started to leave. As I was closing the door, the Archbishop called me back and said, "By the way, Msgr. Rempe informed me that your mother desired to join your community, that he had interviewed the retreat master as well as your mother who seemed to be well disposed and most anxious to become a religious in your convent. I think it a noble idea and that she should be given some consideration.

He then said that he was going to New York...he would return to Chicago on August 20th and that he would come to Nazareth on August 21st to give Mother the Holy Habit.

This was more than I expected, and must have shown my surprise, for he added, "You will have nothing to do with it. The Church gives such privileges at times when there are weighty reasons for good."[169]

Mother Alexine goes on to explain that the Archbishop came as promised. When he asked her what name she wanted to give Mrs. Gosselin, Mother Alexine replied that she "was supposed to have nothing to do regarding her reception that I would prefer of him to give her the name." He asked the name of the saint of the day and hearing that it was St. Jane Frances de Chantal, he decided on that name. The reception ceremony was attended by sisters of the community, family, relatives and old friends as well as an impressive list of clergy. The Archbishop had made it clear who held the final authority in the community.

"THE CRISIS"

At the time of Sister M. De Chantal's reception into the community, all appeared to be well among the sisters and in the archdiocesan authorities' perception of the community. The Congregation had been given additional missions so that in 1916, the 73 Sisters of St. Joseph of La Grange were serving in the Nazareth Motherhouse and Academy, Novitiate and Scholasticate as well as at St. Joseph's Institute for Boys, St. Bonaventure, St. Rocco and Our Lady of Mount Carmel schools. In that year the community reported having 63 novices and 9 postulants.[170]

---

169 "History of Sister M. de Chantal."

170 The Catholic Directory, 1916, 51-72. The imbalance between numbers of novices and postulants may have to do with the date of reporting and the dates of entrance into the community. If a reception had recently taken place, there may have been few postulants who would be joined later in the year by others.

In 1916, Monsignor F. Rempe had been named Vicar for Religious of the Archdiocese and had visited the community on July 2. In addition to his encouragement of Mrs. Gosselin's aspirations, he expressed great satisfaction with what he found among the sisters. In spite of that, a year later Monsignor Rempe was asking Mother Alexine to resign from office, just one year before her elected term would come to an end.

In January of 1917, Archbishop Mundelein had written a letter which surely sounded the alarm for any with ears to hear. He said:

> For some time the financial condition of your community has caused your ecclesiastical superiors considerable anxiety, not because the situation is entirely hopeless, but because we realize that extraordinary efforts are necessary to establish the property of the community on a secure basis. We look for a more ready and intelligent cooperation on the part of all the members if they will thoroughly understand and conscientiously apply the principles of the religious life regarding the vow of poverty.[171]

It would have been no surprise at all to the sisters that they were in financial straits. But that had been true of their life together beginning with their first day when Mother Alexine had accounted for the thirty-three cents the community had as a patrimony. The Archbishop's letter made it sound as if some members of the community were holding back, perhaps retaining significant gifts or even inheritances instead of contributing everything to the common fund. Mother Alexine published the letter to the whole community.

More than six months later, on the feast of St. Alexis, Mother Alexine's feast day, the chancellor of the archdiocese phoned to say that the Archbishop wanted to speak to Mother Alexine that day. When she arrived, the Archbishop lamented the "disagreeable task" he had to perform, but announced,

> I must ask you to resign your office as Superior....I shall give you an indefinite leave of absence. Take your mother and go to your family, your brothers for instance.[172]

---

171 Letter from Archbishop Mundelein to the Sisters of St. Joseph, January 5, 1917, quoted in *Journeys Begun*, 84.
172 *Journeys Begun*, 85, apparently quoting Mother Alexine's diary.

The Archbishop's suggestion that she visit family is rather surprising in light of the fact that his January admonishment had insisted on a more communal attitude among the sisters. His directives seem even more curious when Mother Alexine states that he refused her permission to visit the Sisters of St. Joseph at Chestnut Hill. A convent visit would have been normal enough to have raised no eyebrows whereas an unexpected extended visit to family would have appeared most unusual.[173]

Although the Archbishop bade her leave immediately and to tell no one about it, that was an utter impossibility for a superior. Nevertheless, under his direct order she submitted her resignation which read,

My Dear Archbishop,
For the greater honor and glory of God, the edification of the community and the sake of our holy religion, I humbly resign my office as superior of the sisters of St. Joseph of La Grange, Illinois, and beg you to please grant Mother and I a leave of absence for at least six months or one year. Your obedient and humble servant in our Lord,
Sr. M. Alexine, CSJ, July 17, 1917

When she copied that letter in her diary she added the comment "dictated by his Eminence."[174]

The commentary in her diary went on to say:

To me, to resign in order to avoid annoyance or trouble, is a cowardly act, but I had to put all my principles aside and submit. I have ever since wondered what crime or disedification I could have been guilty of that I should, without warning, be deposed and not given a chance to finish my term of superiorship which expires one year from this August. Even the worst of criminals has a right to a trial by civil authorities. He knows for what he is being punished, yet is given a chance to vindicate himself.[175]

---

173 At that time Mother Mary James Rogers was superior general of the Philadelphia Congregation. She had been Assistant to Mother Clement who had been in touch with the Concordia and the Wichita Sisters and so would have known of Mother Alexine if they were not personally acquainted. As noted earlier, it is possible that Mother Alexine had visited Philadelphia before 1900 to learn of their formation program.
174 Mother Alexine's Diary, cited in Sister M. Aquinas Caffrey, "The Sisters of St. Joseph and their Foundations in America: A Brief Account of their Origin and Ideals of the Congregation and of Its Work in the Middle West, 1650-1930" (Master's Thesis: copies in Archives CSJoseph), 142.
175 Cited in *Journeys Begun*, 86.

Within a few days, Mother Alexine and her mother, Sister de Chantal, left La Grange for Eureka, California, to meet Mother Bernard. The Gosselin family rallied round Mother Alexine while Mother Bernard received the two exiles in California. The family solicited the help of Bishop Muldoon of Rockford who paid for Mother Bernard to come to Illinois to work on the problem. When she arrived, she was greeted by the news that nine sisters of French background from La Grange were about to leave the community on the head of all that had happened.[176] Mother Bernard in Eureka was ready to receive not only her sister and mother but also the others who wished to join her. The Bishop of San Francisco wrote official letters saying he would accept other sisters, but those letters were never given to the sisters in question.[177] On August 22, 1917, Archbishop Mundelein informed Monsignor Rempe,

> It looks like an organized effort to desert the community. I shall take good care that there be no nonsense of that kind.[178]

While the details are rather unclear and not well-documented, the overall situation of the community was one of disunion, mistrust, apparent nationalistic tensions between sisters of French and Irish descent and, perhaps exacerbating all those frictions, overwhelming debt. Between extensive building projects and too little rigor in collecting tuition, by 1916, the sisters' total debt had reached the sum of $195,000 with an anticipated deficit of $2,309.[179]

When the divided community was unable to elect a successor to Mother Alexine, the Archbishop appointed Sister Mary Daniel Whalen as her successor. She remained in office until July, 2, 1918, when the community elected Mother Patricia D'Arcy as superior to be assisted by Sisters Michael McCullagh, Daniel Whalen, Sacred Heart Murphy and Austin Brady.[180] The Irish faction had gained the upper hand.

---

176 Bishop Peter Muldoon had been the auxiliary bishop to Bishops Feehan and Quigley during a time of immense nationalistic tension with the Irish-born clergy in conflict with the Germans and those born in the U.S. Muldoon, born in California, became a target in the conflicts. When the Rockford diocese was created from the Archdiocese of Chicago, Muldoon was named as its first bishop and his name was suggested as Archbishop of Chicago after Quigley's death, but Mundelein was chosen instead. See: "Peter J. Muldoon, First bishop of Rockford, 1862-1927," (*Catholic Historical Review*, Vol. 48, No. 3, Oct., 1962) 365-378.
177 See *Journeys Begun*, 86-95.
178 Archbishop Mundelein to Monsignor Rempe, August 22, 1917, cited in *Journeys Begun*, 87.
179 Report from the archdiocesan auditors, cited in *Journeys Begun*, 94.
180 *Journeys Begun*, 99.

Mother Patricia may have been both a symbol and harbinger of the community's hopes for the future. She emigrated from Ireland at the age of 27, and entered the community three years later. She professed her final vows on July 2, 1912, just weeks after the departure of the sisters bound for California. She was 41 years old when elected.

By the time Mother Patricia was elected, Mother Alexine and Sister De Chantal had returned to Chicago. Sister De Chantal's health suffered in California and she was hospitalized immediately upon her return. On January 22, 1918, while Mother Daniel was serving as superior, Archbishop Mundelein had written a letter ordering Mother Alexine to reside at St. Roch's Convent until further notice, informing her that her status was simply that of a former superior. In the letter he admitted that he had not consulted the superior about the arrangement. In the same letter the Archbishop admonished Mother Alexine to avoid encouraging any dissatisfaction or criticism of the new leadership of the community and stated that:

> You will appreciate the fact that this is not dictated because of any past action on your part, but simply in the nature of an admonition and precaution...You have now an opportunity such as is not often given in the spiritual life, of showing...that you have that quality so necessary in a good religious, not only the capacity to rule, but also the knowledge and ability to obey.[181]

When Mother Patricia D'Arcy was elected she asked Mother Alexine to return home to the motherhouse at Nazareth.[182]

Mother Patricia's time in leadership lasted for twelve years, from 1918 to 1930, a historical period that saw the move from post-war prosperity to the beginning of the worst economic downturn known to the industrialized world. For the Sisters of St. Joseph of La Grange who had known serious poverty and indebtedness since their foundation, this was a period of progress. Mother Patricia increased educational opportunities, arranging for sisters who needed it to earn their high school diplomas and opening a summer school in 1919 which allowed others to begin their college education. During her years as superior, the sisters not only added to their own educational institutions, but were invited to staff more

---

181 Letter from Archbishop Mundelein to Mother Alexine, January 22, 1918, cited in *Journeys Begun*, 100.
182 *Journeys Begun*, 98.

parochial schools in the archdiocese. After the archdiocese consolidated some of their debts, Mother Patricia instituted economic practices that required each local community to submit a budget and send financial support to the motherhouse. By 1924, the community's debt had been reduced from $193,000 to $93,000, and in 1926, Mother Patricia felt that she could continue to build.[183]

THE LA GRANGE CONGREGATION AT 25

When the Congregation of The Sisters of St. Joseph of La Grange completed their first twenty-five years, they could look back on beginnings as difficult as almost any known to a Congregation of St. Joseph. A Congregation that seemed to begin in fits and starts and had progressed through times of individual and group departures was finally settling on a home turf that would be theirs for decades to come. They had ministered and grown under the administrations of Archbishops Feehan, Quigley and Mundelein and had benefitted from the supportive friendships of Bishops Scannell and Muldoon. At the ceremony of laying the cornerstone of their new motherhouse, Archbishop Mundelein praised the community saying "The Sisters of St. Joseph are peculiarly our own, because their work is largely concentrated here and their ranks chiefly from among our girls." Whether new immigrants or the descendants of long-settled French Canadians, whether they started their religious life in Kansas or Illinois, the sisters gathered for that ceremony on October 3, 1926, had good reason to hope. They had weathered the worst of storms and were indeed building on a well-honed foundation.[184]

---

183 *Journeys Begun*, 123
184 *Journeys Begun* (128) describes that day saying: "October 3, 1926 dawned, and the rain came down in torrents...The sisters were urged to change their plans and move the ceremony indoors but they insisted the sun would come out. Their confidence was rewarded and the Mass was begun at noon with a blazing sun overhead."

80

Chapter Nine: The Design In Lewiston, Superior, Muskogee, Orange

CAST OF CHARACTERS

Lewiston, Idaho

Sister Josephine Leary, Superior at Belvedere, IL.
Sister Aurelia Braken, Founder of the Sisters of St. Joseph in Idaho, 1902
Mother Gertrude Moffitt, Founder and Superior General, Sisters of St. Joseph of Tipton, Indiana
Sister Angelica Heenan, First official novice director and superior of the Sisters of St. Joseph in Lewiston

Slickpoo, Idaho

Father Joseph Cataldo, S.J., Missionary in Slickpoo, Idaho
Father Hubert Post, S.J., Missionary in Lewiston, Idaho

Superior, Wisconsin

Mother Evangela (Mary Agnes) Sheehan, Founder of the Sisters of St. Joseph of Superior, WI
Father Francis X. O'Neil, S.J., Mother Evangela's confessor and promoter in Cincinnati
Bishop Augustine Schinner, Founding Bishop, Diocese of Superior, WI

Muskogee, Oklahoma

Bishop Theophile Meerschaert, Bishop of Oklahoma Indian Territory
Father William Ketcham, Missionary who brought the Sisters of St. Joseph to Oklahoma
Mother Virginia Joyce, Foundress of the Sisters of St. Joseph in Oklahoma

Orange, California

Mother Bernard Gosselin, Founder of the Sisters of St. Joseph of Orange, 1912
Sister Mary Joseph (Fabiola Torison) Mother Bernard's niece, member of founding group
Father Charles Maddox, C.Ss.R., Retreat Master, Contact in California
Monsignor Francis C. Kelley, friend of the Sisters of St. Joseph, Founder of The Catholic Church Extension Society

Monsignor F. A. Purcell, Rector of the Quigley Seminary,
friend and benefactor of the Sisters of St. Joseph
Monsignor Lawrence Kennedy, Vicar General of Sacramento,
Pastor of St. Bernard Parish, Eureka
Bishop Thomas Grace,
Bishop of Sacramento, 1896-1921
Archbishop James E. Quigley,
Archbishop of Chicago, 1903-1915
Bishop John J. Cantwell,
Bishop of Los Angeles 1917-1947

THE SISTERS OF ST. JOSEPH OF LEWISTON: 1902 - 1925

In 1900, after the death of Mother Stanislaus Leary in La Grange, Illinois, her companion, Sister Alexine Gosselin reluctantly accepted responsibility for the mission. Eventually, four of Sister Alexine's companions in La Grange, Sisters Josephine Leary, Francis Joseph Leary, Constance Ryan and Berchmans Gray decided to establish a separate motherhouse in Belvidere, Illinois, about 80 miles northwest of Chicago where they had been invited to open a hospital.[1] The hospital was built and the sisters chose to make it their sole mission in the area. The project was not a financial success and within three years the sisters in Belvidere returned to Concordia together with six sisters who had joined the group since their separation from La Grange. Before their return, on May 12, 1901, the Belvidere community had received Sister Dominica (Mary) Ryan into the community and on the following December 26, she accompanied Sister Francis Joseph Leary to Lewiston, Idaho. There she became part of a small, diverse community of Sisters of St. Joseph who had accepted the invitation of Rev. Hubert Post, S.J., to provide health care in the Northwest.[2]

---

1 Evangeline Thomas, *Footprints on the Frontier*, 198.
2 The sources for the Lewiston/Slickpoo history include a manuscript, "The Origin of the Sisters of St. Joseph in Idaho," written anonymously around 1937 and held in the Carondelet archives; the research and writing of Sister Mary Ellen Sprouffske (Carondelet archives); and scattered references in the written histories of the Tipton, Concordia and Carondelet congregations. The sources are often mutually contradictory. Mary Ellen Sprouffske's research which contains copies of a significant collection of correspondence is the most comprehensive source and was completed with great professionalism due to her access to resources. Unless otherwise noted, the Sprouffske collection is the source of letters and newspaper articles quoted.

The Jesuit Fathers had been serving the people of the Pacific Northwest since Fr. Peter de Smet had first accepted an invitation from the Salish Flathead Nation in 1840. In 1900, two particular Jesuits were especially active in the area around Lewiston, Idaho. The first, Father Joseph Cataldo began work in the Idaho Territory in 1865 and in 1874, he founded a mission among the Nez Perce Nation for whom he desperately wanted the help of sisters who could run a school. The other Jesuit, Father Hubert Post, became pastor of St. Stanislaus Parish in Lewiston around 1900. Father Post's great hope was to have a hospital staffed by sisters because the closest hospital was in Spokane, Washington, 100 miles north of the growing city of Lewiston.[3] Both priests did all they could to entice communities of religious women to come to their aid. Their efforts were to little avail until Father Post came in contact with Sister Aurelia Bracken who apparently visited Lewiston in 1900 as one of a number of sisters the Jesuits invited to learn more about the proposed hospital and missions in the area.

Sister Aurelia Bracken figures among the small number of independent and itinerant Sisters of St. Joseph who participated in the life of various congregations of St. Joseph between 1860 and 1910. She had entered the Carondelet congregation's St. Paul Province in 1861. In 1868, she joined Mother St. George Bradley who, after serving as provincial superior in St. Paul, left a mission at Peoria to join Mother Agnes Spencer in Erie. Sister Aurelia was missioned with Mother St. George at the hospital in Meadville, PA, and then in Ohio where she became part of the new congregation at Cleveland in 1873. Sister Aurelia served in the congregation's schools in Ohio until 1878, then the Cleveland records simply state: "She left voluntarily, destination unknown." In 1881, Sister Aurelia's name appeared in the vow book of the Watertown sisters as a visitor and witness to the vows of one of the sisters.

Sister Aurelia seems to have stayed with the Sisters of St. Joseph in Belvidere, Illinois, in 1901 when they were among the communities to whom Father Hubert Post turned looking for sisters to staff his hospital in Lewiston. In November, 1901, Father Post informed Father George de la Motte, his Jesuit superior, and Bishop Alphonse Joseph Glorieux of Boise, that he had secured the

---

3 Lewiston was supposedly named for Meriwether Lewis who explored the area around 1805. The town grew during a short gold rush and again around the turn of the 20th century. In 1890, it had a population of 850; in 1900, 2,435; in 1910, 6,043. Lewiston is 100 miles south of Spokane, 320 miles north of Boise and 343 miles east of Portland. In 1900, Spokane's population had nearly doubled to 36,848 and it would nearly triple in the next decade.

help of Sister Aurelia Bracken of the Sisters of St. Joseph of Peace for Lewiston.[4] Even though the bishop had some questions because he could not find official information about that community, Father Post invited Sister Aurelia to Idaho and between November, 1901, and January 1, 1902, Sisters Aurelia, Francis Leary and Dominica Ryan, and perhaps some others, arrived in Lewiston. Sister Aurelia presented herself as the superior of the group.[5]

The sisters immediately began the search for a suitable site for the hospital, first settling on the idea of purchasing the Visitation Academy in the city, but later deciding to build rather than refurbish. The Lewiston *Morning Tribune* edition of February 5, 1902, published an explanation of their plans for the hospital saying:

> An important change in plans...It was originally intended to utilize the Sisters' Academy building, but upon the arrival here...[of] Sister Aurelia... the place was changed. Sister Aurelia is a trained nurse of many years' experience and upon her advice Father Post... consented to a change in the plans...It was then decided to immediately take steps for the erection of a fine hospital... The expenditures will reach about $10,000. The building will be a brick and planned in every detail to meet the full convenience of a modern hospital...Sister Aurelia expresses herself as highly pleased with the location of Lewiston for the site of a large hospital.[6]

The surprising details in this newspaper account include more than the change of building plans. Sister Aurelia's reputed nursing expertise would have surely have amazed any who had long known her. The only sure time during which she ministered in health care came from her three years with Mother St. George Bradley at the hospital in Meadville between 1869 and 1872. If she spent time with the sisters in Belvidere, she could have done service in their hospital as well, but there is no record that she had formal training as a nurse.

Under Mother Aurelia's direction, plans were made for a hospital unlike anything known in the region. The following April, the Morning Tribune

---

4 The origin of this name is a mystery. The Lewiston group had no known relationship with the Sisters of St. Joseph of Peace founded in England in 1884 and who came to the United States in that same year. The Sisters of St. Joseph of Peace have no connection with the Sisters of St. Joseph whose origins are from Le Puy.

5 The records are contradictory. Father Post's indicate that Sister Aurelia arrived with others in November, the 1937 manuscript, "Origin," says that Sisters Francis and Dominica arrived January 1, 1902. Sr. Aurelia's self-designation as superior would apparently have been acceptable to Belvidere as they avoided being seen as responsible for the Idaho mission and considered any of their sisters who went to Idaho as "on loan."

6 *The Lewiston Morning Tribune*, February 5, 1902.

continued its supportive publicity for the promised hospital writing:

> The hospital to be erected under the personal supervision of the Mother
> Superior [will include]...four stories...On the first floor, offices, parlors,
> guests" dining room, dispensary sterilizing, etherizing preparation
> and operating rooms. The operating room will have marble floors...
> Easy access, abundance of light...smoking room in the basement...
> building heated throughout by steam, wired for electric power and
> light...plumbing will be done on strictly scientific principles...electric
> bell system.[7]

By September the plans had grown more definite and elaborate. The Tribune's
story made the hospital sound almost like a hotel or club.

> "Sisters' hospital" Present capacity 78 beds
> Club Rooms, Guests' Restaurant, Medical Board, Nurses' Training and
> other Features
> The patient pays what he can...The handsome structure on the hill
> when completed and equipped will without any reservation be the
> finest institution of its kind in the northwest.
> Club rooms will be the most delightful innovation of the hospital
> work...fitted up with a billiard table, cards, chess, checkers and cribbage
> boards, a library and smoking room and, in fact, a little club where not
> only the convalescents, but the people of the city may go and enjoy
> themselves without cost.
> In connection with this will be a guest dining room...where those
> who are hungry and tired of Chinese cooking can procure a handsome
> meal at a nominal cost, where you can spend an evening, read and sip
> your coffee, tea or chocolate...It seems almost too good to be true.
> Operating rooms, the floor and wainscoting being of pure white Italian
> marble, the floor sloping to the center where there is a bell trap...steam
> thoroughly disinfects...[8]

On the date of December 12, 1902, Mother Aurelia signed articles of incorporation
legalizing the community as a "branch house" of the Sisters of the Order of

---

7 *The Lewiston Morning Tribune*, April 2, 1902.
8 *The Lewiston Morning Tribune*, September 6, 1902.

St. Joseph. The signatories to the document were Mother Aurelia and Sisters Catherine, Angelica, Dominica and Anetta.[9]

The hospital opened on February 9, 1903, having cost $40,000 and was able to be completed because the sisters had been able to secure loan of $25,000 the previous December.[10] By April the contractors and hardware suppliers had placed liens on the hospital for unpaid bills totaling nearly $7,000.[11]

The newspaper article about the hospital's inauguration included more praise for Mother Aurelia with her "many years of experience in hospital work," and explained that "At present she has two assistants but will leave shortly...to secure a corps of perhaps eight experienced hospital workers."[12] That expectation would be met in Mother Aurelia's unique style.

The best account of Mother Aurelia's trip east comes from one of her recruits, Frances Dillon of Worcester, Massachusetts, who wrote to Father Post in 1909. Miss Dillon explained that while she was working as a teacher, Sister Franklin in Boston let her know that Mother Aurelia was out from the West looking for help. She said that she went to Boston to see Mother Aurelia and,

> After having a long talk with her, she asked me if I could go at once with her as she was very short of subjects. I did not intend going off with her at that time, but as she insisted and telling me the need she had of subjects, I agreed to go.
>
> Mother told me she was going to let me travel in the holy habit as she wanted to get half fare. We left Sr. Franklin's place with the habit on Aug. 9th, 1903. After we were there an hour or so, Mother called me and told me she was going to let me keep the holy habit on as I could go

---

9 Very little accurate information exists about these sisters. Sister Dominica had arrived in Lewiston from Belvidere on January 1, 1902 as a novice. Sister Catherine was said to have temporarily been a transfer member of the Chestnut Hill community and to have used more than one last name at different times of her life, but there is no record of her arrival at Lewiston. The Tipton history lists indicates that Sister Angelica was appointed novice director in 1904, and made her final vows in 1906. There is no other information about Sister Anetta, but a Sister Loretta Powers is described as a teacher at Slickpoo in the unsigned memoir written around 1937. In a letter of July 8, 1903, Bishop Glorieux gave Father Post permission to receive the vows of Sisters Catherine, Angelica and Dominica. Either some dates or names were mistaken or sisters with the same name served in Lewiston at different times in the first few years.
10 Father Post's journal (December 30, 1902) notes that a Mr. James Monahan from Spokane provided the loan at 8% interest to be paid quarterly.
11 Post journal, April 9, 1903.
12 Lewiston Morning Tribune, February 8, 1903. The Tipton history indicates that in March, 1903, "Sisters went to Lewiston to Help Mother Aurelia of St. Paul, Minn. in the hospital she built" (Tipton History, 79-80)

through my postulantship [sic] just the same as in worldly dress. I guess the other seven that were with me were told the same thing. This, dear Father, is the way I happened to get to Lewiston.[13]

Miss Dillon's impression that her companions got to Lewiston in more or less the same way as she had is borne out by Sister M. B. Franklin in Boston who explained to Father Post what she knew of Mother Aurelia's recruits and methods, leaving the distinct impression that she would prefer to avoid further involvement with the question. She wrote:

I will say that Mother Aurelia from Lewiston spent some days here in Boston and on her return took with her six young women who volunteered for the distant mission in Idaho. As far as I know four of these...were former members of Religious Congregations. To these four she gave the habit of her community just at departure to travel, in order to get lower rates. ...She was recommended to me by Father Gasson, a saintly Jesuit of Boston College...any further information can be obtained from him.[14]

Sister Mary B. Franklin of Boston was but one of the first to distance herself from Mother Aurelia.

Before long things began to unravel around Mother Aurelia. The debt on the hospital was unpayable and the bishop was suspicious about Mother Aurelia's credentials. In July, 1903, Bishop Glorieux was carefully scrutinizing the Lewiston financial situation. By September he told the pastor that he believed that "the poor woman's mind is unbalanced" and that "the actual state of affairs cannot last much longer."[15] Around this same time Father Post discovered that he had been deceived about the "sisters" Mother Aurelia had recruited. With that Bishop Glorieux

---

13 Letter from F[rances] Dillon to Father Post, June 14, 1909. She goes on to say that she was sent to Slickpoo, then sent as a companion to Portland, only to return to Lewiston where she learned that her uncle had died and her presence was required in New York to arrange his affairs. As her saga went on, she said she traveled to New York with a sister who apparently sent her to Brookline "before returning to Lewiston." While Miss Dillon was away, her sister companion left New York, taking with her the contents of Miss Dillon's trunk. It would seem plausible that the sister in question may have been one of the spurious sisters recruited by Sr. Aurelia. Miss Dillon's long letter ended with a plea to be able to return to Lewiston and take up the life she had left nearly 6 years previous. There was no further mention of her name in the community files. (Sprouffske files.)
14 Sister M. B. Franklin, to Father Post, September 25, 1903.
15 Bishop Glorieux to father Post, September 6, 1903.

decided that "She has gone just far enough to be deposed and even dismissed." But he added, "Be very prudent and slow."[16]

Father Post took the bishop at his word in terms of going slowly, surely due in part to the public perception of the situation. On October 4, the bishop advised Father Post that "Mother Aurelia should not have general control," and authorized him to appoint a new superior. Whether she knew that, or it happened by simple coincidence, two days later the Lewiston Morning Tribune ran an article under the headline "FOR THE HOSPITAL, An Effort to Be Made to Lift Debt of $10,000." The article explained:

> The sisters in charge of the St. Joseph hospital have decided to make an energetic endeavor to secure a fund of $10,000 to clear the debt on the hospital and will shortly petition the assistance of the Lewiston businessmen toward this end…The great importance of such a hospital is thoroughly understood by all and that the splendid work anticipated is being accomplished can be fully appreciated when a visit to the hospital…is made…the institution is now receiving patronage from all sections of the surrounding country…it has been necessary to increase the force of assistants and the Mother Superior is definitely carrying out the plan of making the hospital the best in the inland empire country.[17]

The article makes it clear that the populace had no idea of the extent of the hospital's problems and exposure of elements of fraud would hardly have resolved anything. Although extant correspondence does not say so explicitly, it is easy to imagine that Mother Aurelia's charms and self-assurance allowed her to keep the confidence of the general public – or at least of those to whom she was not in debt.

Father Post expressed his assessment of the situation quite clearly in letters to superiors of various congregations of St. Joseph to whom he turned in near desperation. He opened his letter of appeal saying:

> Perhaps never before have you received a letter demanding your immediate attention more than the present one, and I hope that no one will ever be obliged to write under these or such like circumstances.

---

15 Bishop Glorieux to father Post, September 6, 1903.
16 Bishop Glorieux to Father Post, September 15, 1903.
17 Lewiston Morning Tribune, October 6, 1903

We appeal to your charity in a case where the honor of God, the welfare of the Church and the reputation of the Sisters of St. Joseph is at stake... The Sisters of St. Joseph have built a beautiful hospital here, but overstepped their means...Hence materially as well as spiritually, a collapse may be expected at any time. We have reached the decision that the Sister presently in charge must be removed and several others changed.

Now we do not <u>beg</u> for <u>money</u> nor do we beg for Sisters to stay out West. We only ask in your charity to grant us the loan of 3 or 4 sisters for the space of 2 or 3 years...one good well trained Sister to act as Superior, one good head nurse, and one to be fit for the training of Postulants and Novices...

Remembering that we must prevent the great collapse, which would cause scandal, I beg – again and again – to lay this matter before your Sisters...

Hoping to hear from you in a few days that you will be able to tell us that the Sisters are ready for further summons...I remain...[18]

Father Post received kind but negative replies from Sister Mary Clement of Chestnut Hill, Sister Seraphine Ireland of St. Paul, and Sister Josephine Leary of Belvidere.[19] Mother Gertrude of the Sisters of St. Joseph of Tipton was the only one to offer him hope. She asked clear-minded questions about the circumstances and suggested that he write her bishop saying that her council was in favor of helping him. In a letter of March 2, 1904, she said:

I fully realize the gravity of our undertaking. I would much rather form a new mission...but after the good people there know my Sisters I have no fears but they will have confidence in them.

The call is sudden and unexpected – my community is young and

---

18 Letter from Father Post to Sister Mary Clement, of Chestnut Hill, February 12, 1904. Because there is a record of a number of replies, it seems likely that he sent a similar letter to other communities.

19 In replies dated February 10 and 12, Sister Mary Clement wrote at length, and explained among other reasons that her sisters were not prepared to do health care. Sister Seraphine Ireland of St. Paul said that she had not enough sisters and, "to be candid...even if I could spare the Sisters, I would hesitate long before imperiling the good name of our Province by connecting it in any way with a work inaugurated by...Sister Aurelia." In turning him down, Mother Josephine Leary made it as clear as possible that the Belvidere community had no responsibility for the Lewiston foundation, but had only loaned Sister Aurelia a novice about whom they had received no further news.

small. All I could do now is to send a good nurse – a graduate of the Philadelphia Training School and another Sister. The Sister nurse is not strong nor rugged, has been local Superior…truly a good religious.

My Sisters are well trained in the school of poverty, and I believe you will not be disappointed in the management of this Institution.

Now if you wish to give us a trial – and I think it prudent…All we can do is arrange for a stay of a year or such time for the Sisters…[20]

In an undated entry between the dates of February 12 and March 8, Father Post's mission diary said:

Sister Aurelia Bracken and the other "bad element" left Lewiston "under cover of night." Two inexperienced sisters were left in charge of the hospital…kept Veronica…[21]

In mid-March Sisters Magdalene Thomas, Angelica Heenan and Borgia Tourscher arrived from Tipton to take over the work of the hospital.[22] On March 22, 1904 the sisters made the first entry in a new hospital record book, signaling that a new administration was in place. Their notation indicated that the hospital census was 36, with patients ranging in age from three to eighty-seven years.

While Father Post was struggling with the problems in Lewiston, his elder confrere, Father Joseph Cataldo had been conducting his own search for sisters to manage the school on his mission at Slickpoo. His quest took him to Philadelphia where, because no congregation could help him with missionaries, Bishop Ryan of Philadelphia suggested that he seek women to join a congregation of St. Joseph in Idaho.[23] Bishop Ryan's only condition on allowing him to seek vocations from Philadelphia was a promise that Father Cataldo would remain with the community

---

20 This was Mother Gertrude's second letter to Father Post, written on March 2, 1904.
21 Mission diary copied in Sprouffske research.
22 See Dougherty, 352-3. Sister Borgia, a graduate of the Pennsylvania Hospital Training School, was probably the only professionally trained nurse on the staff. The Philadelphia Hospital Training School, founded in 1875, was one of the first nursing education programs in the nation. Sister Borgia most likely entered the community after completing her training.
23 Born in Ireland, Patrick J. Ryan had come to St. Louis as a seminarian and was ordained in 1853 by Archbishop Peter R. Kenrick. After teaching in the seminary at Carondelet and serving as Vicar General, he was named co-adjutor bishop in St. Louis in 1872. The year after Archbishop Wood died in 1883, Bishop Ryan became the second archbishop of Philadelphia where he would serve until 1911. He would have been well acquainted with Sisters of St. Joseph in both St. Louis and Philadelphia.

until it was well established.[24] Father Cataldo succeeded in recruiting 12 women for Idaho and they arrived in Slickpoo on November 13, 1904. Sister Angelica became their novice director and the women received the habit on the Feast of the Epiphany, 1905, in a ceremony in which they "approached the altar, arrayed in spotless white, accompanied each one by their little Indian maids of honor." Nine of that original group remained in the community and others joined them, mostly from Idaho but a few additional intrepid Philadelphians followed the lead of the first twelve, all under the tutelage of Sister Angelica as director of postulants and novices.

Composed of sisters who had come from a variety of communities and working in two distinct missions, the Sisters of St. Joseph in Idaho evolved under the unofficial jurisdiction of Mother Gertrude Moffitt of Tipton, the one superior who had been willing to accept any kind of responsibility for the fledgling community. Although the Idaho community had their own novitiate, the Tipton congregation provided the experienced sisters and institutional stability the community so desperately needed in the early years. In 1912, Mother Gertrude traveled to Idaho to formalize the relationship between Idaho and Tipton. Then Bishop Glorieux called all the Idaho Sisters of St. Joseph to a formal vote on whether or not to become a part of the Tipton. When the sisters voted to become an independent congregation, those who wished to return to Tipton did so and the remaining sisters elected Sister Angelica Heenan as their first general superior. At that time, Sister Magdalen Thomas chose against either remaining in Lewiston or returning to Tipton, deciding instead to open a community in Oregon.[25] Sister Magdalen would later open a mission in Silver City, New Mexico which eventually became part of the Concordia congregation.[26]

The Congregation of the Sisters of St. Joseph of Idaho continued to

---

24 Except where otherwise noted the information in this section is from "Origin."

25 The author of "Origin" indicates that Sister Magdalen left Lewiston in 1912, while her biographical record from Concordia has 1908 as the date. "Origin" is more likely correct as the Sprouffske research has a letter to Father Rockliff, the Jesuit Provincial, from Mother Gertrude dated July 21, 1912, explaining reasons for removing Sister Magdalen as superior in Slickpoo, among other reasons because she was agitating to separate the community from the motherhouse. Mother Gertrude indicated that she had received various complaints about Sister Magdalen and about the pastor, Father Boll S.J., who had been too involved in internal community affairs. One of the complaints about Sister Magdalen was that she had separated the white boys from the Indians in the dormitories at Slickpoo. (Mother Gertrude to Father Rockliff, July 21, 1912.)

26 These are two examples of communities that sisters intended to found as independent congregations. Some of them joined established congregations and some went out of existence. It may be assumed that some remain unknown.

struggle with debt and misfortune. Although they received new members from the area as well as from the east, more was asked of them than they could continue to accomplish. Their first great tragedy struck on August 27, 1915 when a fire broke out at Slickpoo and destroyed the school and orphanage. As a result of the fire, the financially precarious situation of the community became desperate and the sisters found themselves forced to go begging on behalf of the children who had lost absolutely everything except the clothes they were wearing. "Temporary" buildings were hastily constructed and then used until the 1920s.

As the Lewiston Hospital was growing, another priest in the northwest asked the community to open a hospital, this time in Pasco, Washington. In 1816, six sisters went, leased a hotel building and found the local support needed to furnish hospital rooms and equipment. Sixteen days after their arrival, Our Lady of Lourdes Hospital opened its doors and received over 600 patients during the first year of its existence.

The sisters' next severe challenge came with the flu epidemic of 1918. Schools were closed from October, 1918, to January, 1919, and the sisters at the orphanage tried to protect the children by having them play outdoors as much as possible. Sister Aloysius, a seamstress and caretaker who went from Slickpoo to Lewiston to help in the hospital wrote back to the orphanage explaining the situation. She described for her friend Sister Dolores how the sisters were coping, standing in for one another and trying to hide the worst news from the sickest sisters.

> There are twenty-five Sisters in bed. Sister Cataldo and Sister Marie Therese and myself are on night duty...Sister Regis was in bed with a temperature of 103 degrees. The doctor went to ask her about surgery. She was getting dressed to come to the operating room [but I got there before her]...I asked about where everything was and went in to help the doctor. He said "I didn't know you were a nurse." Everything went on fine...
>
> Sister Clement died yesterday. Mother Angelica does not know she is dead and we do not intend to tell her.
>
> Sister Borgia is not allowed to be around...She has Miss Reilly take our temperatures...when we see her coming we get ice water and keep it in our mouths so we will have subnormal temperatures.[27]

---

27 Sister Aloysia Ames, With You I Shall Always Be, Memoirs of Sisters of St. Joseph in Idaho and Eastern Washington (Los Angeles: Sisters of St. Joseph of Carondelet, 1980) 20-21.

The community lost at least eight sisters in the epidemic, including their superior, Mother Angelica Heenan.

The First World War proved the need for highly professional nurses' training. Sister Xavier went to study under the Sisters of St. Joseph at St. Mary's Hospital in Minneapolis and in 1919, the community opened a nursing school in collaboration with the Lewiston State Normal school where the nurses could study chemistry, child care and dietetics. The first professionally trained sister-nurses graduated in 1922.

In 1922, Mother Borgia Tourscher, one of the original Tipton volunteers to Lewiston, was elected superior general. She realized that the community could no longer stand alone. In 1916, the sisters had rejected the proposal of merging with Carondelet, but she brought up the idea again and carried on conversations with Mother Agnes Rossiter in St. Louis. Mother Agnes visited Lewiston in 1925, and the Idaho sisters then voted nearly unanimously to affiliate with Carondelet. Mother Agnes wrote to Bishop Gorman of Boise saying:

> We were most favorably impressed by our visit to the Northwest, and by the great work that has been accomplished there for God and souls. There is a wonderful future for the Church in your beautiful state, and I consider it a privilege to cooperate with you, through our dear Sisters in Lewiston, in the development of that future.[28]

In November, 1925, Mother Mary Margaret Brady, the Provincial Superior of the Los Angeles Province of the Sisters of St. Joseph of Carondelet received the fifty-two Sisters of St. Joseph of Idaho and one novice into the Congregation. Sister Mary Madeline Lyons from the St. Paul Province was assigned to be the first Carondelet superior in Lewiston with the responsibility to help the sisters adjust to the change of congregation. Mother Borgia Tourscher who had done so much to accomplish the affiliation took the lead in integrating the Idaho and Carondelet communities by going to St. Mary's Hospital in Tucson, Arizona. She lived there for the three remaining years of her life and is buried in Holy Hope Cemetery in Tucson.

THE SISTERS OF ST. JOSEPH OF SUPERIOR, WISCONSIN

Communities of St. Joseph have been established through a wide variety of

---

28 Mother Agnes Rossiter to Bishop Gorman, March, 1925, (Archives, Carondelet) cited in Mary Williams, CSJ, All Things New, *The Story of The Sisters of St. Joseph of Carondelet in the Los Angeles Province*, (St. Paul: Good Ground Press, 2014) 73.

circumstances, perhaps none with more obscurities and contradictory stories than the Sisters of St. Joseph of Superior, Wisconsin. The story begins with the enigmatic Sister Evangela Sheehan, the founder of the Congregation.[29]

No researcher has discovered her birth certificate, but Mary Agnes Sheehan's baptismal record is dated November 25, 1856.[30] She is registered in the census of 1865 in Albany, NY, as the seven-year-old daughter of Irish immigrants, Jeremiah and Margaret Sheehan, NY. At that time she had two siblings, Catherine, aged 4, and Joseph, aged 2. According to recollections of the sisters who knew her, she was educated by the Religious of the Sacred Heart and the Sisters of St. Joseph in Albany. At the age of 19, she entered the Franciscan Sisters of Peekskill, NY, and received the name Sister Mary Anselma of Our Lady of Good Counsel. She made first vows on June 21, 1887.[31] Sister Mary Anselma Sheehan left the Franciscan community on April 6, 1897, and there is only one clear record of her whereabouts or activities between then and 1905. In 1902, Mary Agnes Sheehan signed a financial agreement in regard to her plan to enter the congregation of the Sisters of St. Joseph of Tipton. Although the agreement was kept in Tipton's files, there is no record that she became a member of the community.[32]

Sisters from the Superior congregation who knew her as Mother Evangela had been told that she had made her novitiate in St. Louis and was then sent to Troy. That account says that because she angered a superior in Troy by defending a fellow sister, she was punished by being sent to the laundry at Carondelet. The story continues, saying that the work assigned to her was too hard so she left the community but retained the habit. The Carondelet community has no record that she was ever a member.[33] By 1905, Sister Mary Evangela Sheehan was with the

---

29 The resources for the history of the Superior Congregation are very sparse and often contradictory. The major source is Sister Ursula Schwalen, CSJ, *Called...and Re-Called to Serve: The Story of the Sisters of St. Joseph of Nazareth on the Lake, Superior, Wisconsin, 1907-1987*, (private publication). Schwalen depends on a variety of sources, some written, some the memories of sisters who were present for the events under consideration.

30 The records of her baptism in 1856 and confirmation (1872) as well as her official history in the Franciscan Congregation were provided by the Sisters of St. Francis in Peekskill. (Letter from Sr. M. Laurenza Hickey, O.S.F., Assistant Provincial of the Peekskill Franciscans, to Sister Susan O'Connor, CSJ, of Albany, May 8, 1978. Archives: Carondelet, SP)

31 Schwalen, 3-4.

32 Schwalen, 7. Schwalen mentions that some sisters were sent to Idaho for reasons of health.

33 Schwalen, 5. Schwalen suggests that a fire at Carondelet destroyed records and that could be the reason for the lack of information about Mary Agnes Sheehan in that community. There was a fire at Carondelet, but it was in 1858 and the congregation's profession records were not lost in it. The Carondelet congregation has maintained its profession book since the beginning and it is assumed to be accurate with the exception of

Sisters of St. Joseph of Bourg as a visiting resident at Sacred Heart Home in Cincinnati. In Cincinnati, she seems to have presented herself to the Bourg as a Sister of St. Joseph from Idaho who wished to join their congregation.[34] Mother Maria, the local superior at Sacred Heart, was said to have "welcomed Sister Evangela and let her wear her habit and sit next to her at the table, but the General Council at their Motherhouse at Bourg, France, refused to accept Sister Evangela unless she began as a postulant and made her novitiate in their Congregation."[35]

In 1905, Father J. J. Cahalan of New Straitsville, Ohio wrote to Mother Maria at the Sacred Heart Home in Cincinnati asking her to allow Sister Evangela and her companion, Sister Athanasia, to return to his parish school where they had done much good in the previous year.[36] The letter raises interesting questions but offers few concrete details beyond establishing the fact that the two sisters had taught at St. Augustine School. Father Cahalan said:

> Rev. Mother Superior;
> I had the St. Joseph Community for teaching in my school last year. An attempt of a foundation also failed of success for want of a proper head. There are two sisters of the Community whom I would wish to have returned here; as the Congregation has experienced the great good done by the St. Joseph Sisters. I do not know in what terms of high appreciation to speak of St. Evangeline and St. Athanasia. All the virtues of true religious are found eminently in them.
> A true conception of a religious life and a strict adherence to the rule mark them as most valuable Members of the Community, and their conscience rebels against their continuance with one whom the Ordinary of the Diocese dismissed.

---

some duplicate numbering. (Information about the profession book is from Sister Rita Louise Huebner, former Congregational Archivist.)

34 This idea is repeated in various letters in the file on Mother Evangela Sheehan in the Archives of the Sisters of St. Joseph of Carondelet, Saint Paul. The Sisters of St. Joseph of Tipton were in Idaho beginning in 1904, and some of the women who joined the Sisters of St. Joseph of Idaho did so under irregular circumstances.

35 Schwalen, 6-7. Again, some sisters recalled that Sister Evangela did not have the St. Joseph habit, but that Mother Maria allowed her to wear it, a decision that caused some dissension in the local community. Father Cahalan's letter referred to below, indicates that she must have been using the habit in 1904. Although the Superior General in Bourg did not admit Sister Evangela to the congregation, she did give Mother Maria permission to allow her to reside at Sacred Heart when school was not in session. (Schwalen, 9)

36 Rev. J. J. Cahalan of St. Augustine's Parish, Straitsville, OH, to "Rev. Mother Superior" (Sacred Heart Home), Aug. 9, 1905.

The school term is soon to open, and the people look for these two
Sisters to be in their places in the class room, and will be at a loss to
understand why they are absent. The continued success of my school
rests altogether upon their return; and I confidently look for them. Do
not disappoint me and my people by withholding them.

The blessings they will bring to the school again this year will no
doubt increase one-hundred fold, and the 130 children are calling for
them...

Sincerely in Xto,

J. J. Cahalan[37]

The two sisters did return to Straitsville for the 1905-1906 school year. There is no
further information about the failed foundation or the sister Father Cahalan said
had been dismissed by the bishop.

There are various versions of the story about how Sister Evangela got to
Superior. One says that at the end of that school year, Mother Maria of Sacred Heart
Home told Sister Evangela that a bishop from the North wanted to interview her
about coming to his diocese.[38] That would have been Bishop Augustine Schinner,
who had been named the first bishop of the Diocese of Superior, Wisconsin in 1905.[39]
Bishop Schinner was a friend of Father Francis X. O'Neil, S.J., Sister Evangela's
confessor, and of Father Albert Dierkes, S.J., the president of St. Xavier College
in Cincinnati. Both priests recommended Sister Evangela to Bishop Schinner. The
interview went well and Sister Evangela accepted the bishop's invitation to open
a community in Somerset, Wisconsin, a very small town about 150 miles south of

---

37 The copy of the letter is from the Carondelet archives, SP.

38 According to Schwalen, Bishop Moeller of Cincinnati and Father Albert Dierkes, S.J., the rector of Xavier
College in Cincinnati, recommended Sister Evangela to Bishop Schinner. Sacred Heart Home was under the
auspices of the Sisters of St. Joseph of Bourg. See Chapter 10.

39 Bishop Schinner was a native of Milwaukee and served as Vicar General of Milwaukee before being named
to Superior where he was bishop from 1905 to 1913. In 1914, he was appointed as the first bishop of the new
diocese of Spokane, WA where he served until 1925. After his resignation, at that age of 62, he served for three
years in the missions in Bolivia. When he returned to Milwaukee in 1928, he became chaplain for the Sisters
of the Divine Savior in Milwaukee until his death in 1936. The website of the Diocese of Superior suggests
that Bishop Schinner's resignation from the see of Superior had to do with a combination of difficulties with
the climate and boredom, he told his priests that "the air of Lake Superior exercised a deleterious action not
in undermining my health but in impeding the efficiency of my work." See "Bishop Schinner, (1905-1913)" at:
https://catholicdos.org/bishop-schinner#early-life.

Superior and about 40 miles northeast of St Paul, MN.[40]

A variation on this story indicates that Sister Evangela took the initiative to found a community and that some of the Bourg sisters had serious doubts about whether she was the most appropriate person to do so. On January 3, 1907, Sister Martina, the superior in Argyle, MN, wrote to her Superior General in Bourg and commented that she had been in conversation with Father Le Guillou, the Vicar General of Superior, WI, about possibilities for their sisters in that diocese. She explained that in addition to the Bourg sisters, the bishop wanted his own community in the diocese. Her letter then adds another intriguing note to Sister Evangela's story. She said:

> We spoke of Somerset...The bishop's intention would be to set up a Mother House there so as to have a diocesan Congregation....In Cincinnati there is a religious of St. Joseph, an American, who says she is of Le Puy. She is there awaiting the time when she can found a Mother House. She has in mind a few postulants and novices. She asked the bishop to receive her in his diocese. His Excellency asked for reference about this religious. They are fairly good...If he is satisfied, he will permit her to get settled in Somerset.
>
> After Father Le Guillou had left, Sr. Assistant asked Sister Ste. Anne whether she had ever heard of a Sister of St. Joseph who was supposed to be a boarder with our Sisters in Cincinnati. Affirmative reply: and that this Sister Evangeline would have wanted to be received by our Sisters; that Mother Maria had requested that of you...and that you refused to accept her. It is, therefore, this sister who is attempting to found a Mother House. It would be very surprising if she succeeds, for she is not the appropriate person...[41]

---

40 The 1910 U.S. census listed the population of Somerset town as 1,484, (https://www.census.gov/prod/www/decennial.html), but Wikipedia listed the population of "Somerset" as 406 as counted in the U.S. census of 1920. The sources are unclear about the distinction between Somerset and Somerset Town. Sadliers Catholic Directory for 1905 listed one parish in Somerset with Sr. Mary Flavian as the superior of the Sisters of St. Joseph in charge of the school. The sisters in question belonged to the Concordia congregation and they left the town in 1905. (See Evangeline Thomas, *Footprints on the Frontier*, 182. The Catholic Directory refers to statistics of 1904, the year before the Superior Diocese was created, while the town still belonged to the La Crosse diocese. The Concordia sisters withdrew in the same year as the Diocese of Superior was created.

41 "Letters – Sr. Martina – 1/3/1907" from Argyle, MN. to Reverend Mother. (Archives Carondelet SP)

Sister Martina's reservations seem to have been born out in some of the conflicts that marked the community's early years in Superior.

Sister Evangela arrived at Somerset on March 25, 1907, accompanied by two postulants from Cincinnati. It was Tuesday of Holy Week. The next day, Bishop Schinner arrived and presided over the ceremony at which the two novices, Sisters Xavier Graney and Edna Joseph Haggerty, received the habit and their religious names.[42] The community's earliest days in Somerset were marred by tensions over the fact that the people of the parish had expected the sisters who would come to speak French. In addition, Mother Evangela and the pastor were quickly at loggerheads and he used the power of the confessional to discourage the postulants and to prevent Mother Evangela from being able to receive communion. By September, 1907, the bishop had assigned a new pastor to the town and the school opened with over 100 students. But the new pastor and people still wanted French speaking sisters. They did little to make the sisters comfortable, leaving them with a school and motherhouse that had no heat or stove, "no sleeping apartment for the sisters, no bathroom or toilet…no provision whatever…not even anything worthy of the name of refectory."[43] The pastor made it known that he was actively looking for another community to serve the parish and some of the leaders in the parish actively tried to undermine the success of the community. Although Mother Evangela asked the bishop more than once to remove the community from Somerset, he asked her to stay through the school year, promising her a mission in Superior and another in Hayward in 1908. Eventually the turmoil calmed down, a decent school building was completed and the sisters were given a reasonable living space for the remainder of their year in Somerset.

Due to the vocational promotion carried on by Father O'Neill, Mother Evangela's promoter in Cincinnati, additional women continued to join the community. By the end of December, 1907, Mother Evangela wrote to him saying that she had "eleven happy children" in the community. One of them, Sister St. Charles Shorthall, apparently joined them from the Sisters of St. Joseph of Wheeling and the rest entered as postulants.[44] Because that number of sisters stretched both

---

42 Schwalen 13. In this section Schwalen states that the sisters arrived on Good Friday, but as Easter, 1907, was on March 31, March 25 was Tuesday of Holy Week. She cites "a note in the archives files" as the source of the information about their reception of the habit.

43 Schwalen, 17, quoting Mother Evangela's September 30, 1907 letter to Bishop Schinner. (Archives: Carondelet SP)

44 Schwalen, 14, adds that the eleven were those who remained in the community, but that there were many others who "not possessing the spirit of the religious life nor the courage to endure the hardships…did not tarry long."

the available space and the budget, in September, 1907, Mother Evangela had accepted charge of St. Mary's School in Hurley, WI, about 180 miles northeast of Somerset and 100 miles east of the diocesan center in Superior. Unfortunately, within the year, Mother Evangela found herself in conflict with Sister Edna Joseph, one of the first novices in the community and the local superior in Hurley. She accused the younger sister of colluding with the Hurley pastor in an attempt to undermine the community's success. Shortly after the community moved to Superior in August, 1908, Sister Edna Joseph left the community.[45]

Almost immediately upon their arrival in Superior, Mother Evangela began the process of securing the legal incorporation of the community and sought a loan to buy a house. She found a real estate agent who had grown up in her home parish of the Cathedral in Albany and with that connection was able to secure a loan from the Knights of Columbus.[46] Before the end of August 1908, the sisters had moved into their new motherhouse and had become incorporated as the Sisters of St. Joseph of Superior, Wisconsin.

The first mission from the new motherhouse was to people of the Chippewa Nation in the area of Stone Lake, about 80 miles south of Superior. A school that should have provided a good source of income for the sisters did not live up to its promise as the U.S. government was often in arrears in paying the sisters' salaries. In spite of the poverty and difficult conditions, the community remained on the mission until 1920.[47] Their schools in the towns of Hayward and Hurley were also short-lived as the parishioners could not afford to support them.

The community's problems were not all external. Bishop Schinner came to believe that there were such divisive factions in the community that they might not survive the factionalism that had formed around Mother Evangela and Sister St. Charles, the sister who had come from Wheeling. The bishop thought that a new superior from Cincinnati might be able to resolve the problem, but Father O'Neil in Cincinnati contended that it was not necessary and could even be harmful to bring in a sister from the Bourg community. In the meantime, Father O'Neil suggested that Mother Evangela might do well to seek ministry in another diocese, advice that she did not take.[48]

---

45 Schwalen, 20-21. Schwalen says it is possible that Sister Edna Joseph joined the Rochester congregation of St. Joseph, but the Superior congregation had no evidence to verify that.
46 The Knights of Columbus, formed as a Catholic fraternal organization in 1881, boasted 230,000 members by 1909. Their insurance program provided the financial base out of which they could give loans.
47 Schwalen, 29.
48 Father O'Neil seemed to think that the priests of the Superior Diocese had something against the community. See Schwalen 21 and 30.

By 1911, Mother Evangela wrote to Bishop Schinner, offering to resign as superior, but the bishop, claiming that the sisters had decided in her favor, refused her resignation.[49] Around that same time, Sister St. Charles returned to Wheeling and the community archives note that there was an "exodus" that left only seven sisters in the community and after which some of the sisters who left the group wrote to the families of the sisters in formation disparaging the community and suggesting that it was not officially approved. The latter rumor was squelched with Father O'Neil's help.[50]

In 1914, the sisters opened St. Joseph's Academy in the Billings Park neighborhood where they already had their motherhouse. While the name "academy" may conjure up grand images, the reality was that something else:

> Because of lack of funds, the sisters made desks out of orange crates. They nailed boards to them, and covered them with wall paper on front and sides. These served the purpose well for the first twenty-six pupils who came on January 24, 1914.[51]

That academy merged with another in 1915 and eventually added a coeducational elementary school to the venture. The school became an annex of the Cathedral school in 1955, and continued to function until 1964.[52]

In 1917, the sisters opened a hospital in Frederic, Wisconsin, a small town about 100 miles south of Superior in which the majority of the population was of Danish background. Although the town needed a hospital, the population had so few Catholics that a priest visited the area only about once a month, leaving the sisters with very little sustenance for their spiritual life. By 1919, the community withdrew from the town and opened a hospital in Superior on land that had been purchased originally for Sisters of the Good Shepherd. A local newspaper reporting the plan for the hospital also describes how the sisters were perceived in 1919. It read:

> The Sisters of St. Joseph, who are establishing this hospital, are experienced in conducting hospitals and caring for the sick. They have

---

49 Schwalen, 32.
50 Schwalen, 32-33.
51 Schwalen, 34.
52 Schwalen, 35-36.

lately operated a hospital at Frederic, Wisconsin, where they were successful, but compelled to quit...The order is well established in this city, where it conducts a motherhouse on Iowa Avenue in Billings Park and an Academy for girls at John Avenue...With hospital facilities inadequate in the city, as they are at present, it is expected that the services of the St. Joseph's Hospital as the new hospice will be known, will be taxed to capacity.[53]

The only hitch in their plan was that the proposed site for the hospital was too close to two already existing hospitals run by the Sisters of the Poor Handmaids of Jesus. When that community protested, Mother Evangela decided that the Sisters of St. Joseph could convert their motherhouse into a hospital and use the other property for a new motherhouse. The move required not simply displacement, but immense work. The newly acquired building, beautiful as it had once been, had been so poorly maintained that the fireplaces were overflowing with ash and "it was evident that the last people living in the house raised chickens and kept them in a room on the second floor."[54] When the work was completed, the former motherhouse, now Good Samaritan Hospital, opened with an operating/delivery room on the first floor and 12 patient beds on the second. The new motherhouse, named Nazareth on the Lake, would be refurbished and, with later additions, it would serve the community for decades to come.

Speaking of the community's organization in their early days, Sister Ursula Schwalen, the community's historian, wrote, "Our original Rule was based on the Rule of the Sisters of St. Joseph."[55] That rather vague description leaves the impression that the sisters may well have brought the *Constitutions* from Cincinnati or found an English translation from one of the other communities in the U.S. Sister Ursula goes on to explain that the original rule was typed and hand-bound because the sisters lacked the funds to have it printed. There is no evidence of official approval of the rule before 1919 when the community asked the bishop to grant his approval to the hand-bound copy and to allow Father O'Neil who had helped the sisters adapt it to give the Nihil Obstat. The community revised that version of the Rule or *Constitutions* and finally printed a fully approved version in 1946.[56]

---

53 Schwalen, 38.
54 Schwalen, 39.
55 Schwalen, 49.
56 Schwalen (49-50) notes that the sisters recall hearing daily readings of chapters from the hand-bound copy until the time when the community printed the rule.

Mother Evangela Sheehan served as the superior of the community from March 25, 1907, the day of her arrival in Somerset, until the day of her death, January 24, 1927. She was the third member of the community to die, being preceded by Sister Agnes Rietz in 1921 and Sister Miriam Merkel in 1923. Nearly nine months after Mother Evangela's death, the community elected her assistant, Sister Augustin Bower, as her successor. The records leave no explanation for why the election did not take place earlier.[57]

The Sisters of St. Joseph of Superior would never grow to be a large congregation. They remained a diocesan congregation until 1987 when, seeing that they had too few sisters to continue as an independent congregation, they decided to become part of the St. Paul Province of the Sisters of St. Joseph of Carondelet.[58]

THE SISTERS OF ST. JOSEPH IN MUSKOGEE

In 1891, the Reverend Theophile Meerschaert, a Belgian missionary to the United States, was appointed as the Vicar Apostolic of the Indian Territory (IT) of Oklahoma. At that time the territory was served by 3 diocesan priests and 23 Benedictine monks[59] On March 13, 1892, Father William Ketcham became the first priest Bishop Meerschaert ordained and the first to be ordained in the Oklahoma Indian Territory.[60] Bishop Meerschaert sent Father Ketcham directly to the Indian Territory in Muskogee where his first accomplishment was the construction of a church. As soon as that was accomplished he wanted to establish a Catholic school for the people of his territory.

Sister Mary Aloysius Hurley, a Sister of St. Joseph of Carondelet, recalled the early history of the community in Oklahoma in a 1953 document she titled, "A Few Thoughts from Memory's Hall.". Just before she said:

---

57 Schwalen, 47. As she was dying, Mother Evangela asked one of her first companions, Sister Xavier Graney, "Take me home." Because the sisters thought she meant Albany, they celebrated her funeral in Superior and then had her buried in her home parish cemetery in Albany. It wasn't until the 1960s, that the community arranged to have her remains brought back to Superior so that she could be buried among the sisters of her community in Calvary Cemetery in Superior.

58 The story of that decision and process will be more fully explored in Volume II.

59 Theophile Meerschaert was born in Flanders in 1847, and came to the United States in 1872, shortly after his ordination. He went almost immediately to the diocese of Natchez, Mississippi where he served in rural areas, including Bay St. Louis until he was made Vicar General to Bishop Janssens in 1887. In 1891, he was named the third Vicar Apostolic of the Indian Territory. When the territory was made a diocese in 1905, he became the first bishop of Oklahoma. He was succeeded by Bishop Francis Kelly who been the friend of the Sisters of St. Joseph of La Grange and founded the Catholic Church Extension Society.

60 See Kevin Abing, "Directors of the Bureau of Catholic Indian Missions," Marquette University Archives: http://www.marquette.edu/library/archives/Mss/BCIM/BCIM-SC1-directors3.pdf.

Father Ketcham was sent to Muskogee Indian Territory and realized that a school was necessary...Mother Katherine Drexel gave him some financial help...so one day he started out on a sister hunt...to Brooklyn, New York. There he found a kindred soul...Mother Mary Virginia Joyce.[61]

According to one version of the story, in 1892, Father Ketcham, like others before him, asked Mother Teresa Mullen, the Brooklyn superior, if he could talk to the sisters about his mission in Oklahoma. She allowed him to talk to them but did not say she would send any sisters. However it happened, Sister Virginia Joyce of the Brooklyn Sisters of St. Joseph joined Father Ketcham in Oklahoma. Sister Mary Aloysius' story cannot be verified by records from the Brooklyn community archives, but she recounted it as follows.[62]

Mother Virginia Joyce...and two companions volunteered to go and do their best out in that unknown wilderness but where there were souls to save. Muskogee was their goal. They were determined to work for the salvation of the Red Man and his posterity.

On her way she stopped at Concordia, Kansas, there she secured another volunteer, Sister Evangelista, a novice. When they reached Muskogee there were two professed and two novices, also a few young women who wished to be sisters and work in the Indian Mission. They were from Canada. Among them were Sisters Francis Xavier, M. Fidelia, M Agnes, M. Victorine and St. Anne. Mother Catherine Drexel again came to their aid and helped build a convent and school.

Mother Virginia must have gotten more subjects because she opened a school at Quapaw Indian Territory and one in Antlers.

In time the new young bishop had looked over his field, he felt that to take on the responsibility of a struggling little diocesan community was more than he could carry. He gave the subjects who were there the choice of any community they wished to enter and he recommended them to the community of their choice. He had a preference for the

---

61 Sister Aloysius Hurley, CSJ, "A Few Thoughts From Memory's Hall" (Archives Carondelet) Sister Virginia Joyce was a native of Philadelphia and a convert. Unproven legends say that she was a niece of Henry Ward Beecher. She entered the Sisters of St. Joseph of Brooklyn in 1867 and was an educator and administrator.
62 According to Virginia Dowd, archivist for the Sisters of St. Joseph of Brentwood, the volume of the annals that would give details about this period has been lost.

Carondelet congregation.[63]

Sister Aloysius' memory is borne out in large part by the scant extant records from the Muskogee community. The community's growth is documented by the profession book which lists the sisters who were novices in Muskogee. These records give evidence that Mother Virginia did not follow a set formation plan, but apparently gave women the habit and then decided when they were ready for profession, with the shortest novitiate recorded being one and one half years and the longest a cumulative four and one half. Sister Marie Ann Brunet's record says in part:

> I made my novitiate in the said house [Nazareth Institute] during the space of four years, twenty days, two terms of which I spend in Antlers, Indian Territory...I have on March 25, 1900 made my profession in the hands of Rev. F. Yserman in the chapel of the novitiate of Nazareth Institute, Muskogee, I.T...

Sister Mary Xavier Duval's act of profession says:

> I, Sister Mary Xavier...born in Quebec, aged 17 years, received the habit of the Sisters of St. Joseph in our house of Nazareth Institute on 2, December, 1897 and made my novitiate for the space of two years, three months, six months of which I spent in Quapaw...and made vows on March 25, 1900.

Sister Mary Evangelist Sughruse wrote that she was born in Ireland and, received the habit at the age of 29 on December 27, 1891. After making a novitiate of one year and six months she was sent by Rev. Mother Stanislaus to Muskogee "when I made a novitiate of three years under Mother Virginia" and made profession on September 4, 1896. Sister Mary Joseph Kempt of Eau Claire, Wisconsin wrote that she had received the habit on December 8, 1893, made a novitiate of two years and ten months and professed vows on September 4, 1896.[64]

---

63 Hurley, "Memory's Hall."
64 All the profession information is found in the Muskogee Profession Record kept in the Carondelet Archives. "I.T." refers to the Oklahoma Indian Territory.

At the height of the community's activity, Mother Virginia Joyce was overseeing sisters in three Oklahoma missions: Muskogee, Antlers and the Quapaw territory. Father Ketcham described the sisters in one of his letters to Mother Katherine Drexel saying:

> Two Sisters of St. Joseph have gone to the Quapaws and opened a day school. They have commenced with 15 pupils which is good considering their miserable circumstances. They expect a greater number shortly. The lonely life of sacrifice of these Two Sisters should be an inspiration to anyone. More than one night in the week they are kept awake by the indescribable noise of the Indian Ghost Dancers just below them in the Valley which skirts the convent grounds.[65]

Father Ketcham knew well the mission difficulties that challenged the sisters in Oklahoma. Anonymous notes in the Carondelet archives hint at the sisters' sense of the mission saying:

> [There is] no extant record describing the hardships, the insecurity and loneliness of these first sisters. This poverty, the strange, primitive setting of the school, the lack of congenial associates all contributed to a constant, uneasy feeling of fear."[66]

Except for their description of the length of their formation program, the sisters left scant evidence about their life together. By 1900, the community had numbered at least 13 sisters, at least three of whom apparently came from the Concordia Congregation,. There may have been a second sister from Brooklyn; the rest received the habit in Oklahoma. None of these sisters were from Oklahoma. The Kansans were the closest, the majority of the others being from Canada and Wisconsin, with one Irish immigrant. With no one to teach them about culture or the language of the Native Americans, they must have felt like utter strangers, exiled far from anyone and anything they knew.

According to Sister Aloysius, sometime near the year 1900, Mother Virginia and Bishop Meerscheart came to a point of irreconcilable disagreement.

---

65 Father Ketcham to Mother Katherine Drexel, September 15 1894, cited in a doctoral dissertation by Sister Ursula Thomas, O.S.B., "The Catholic Church on the Oklahoma Frontier" St. Louis University, 1938. For additional information see http://www.okhistory.org/publications/enc/entry.php?entry=ST007.
66 File on Muskogee in the Carondelet Archives.

Without explaining the particulars of the problem, Sister Aloysius includes the detail that a Sister of St. Joseph of Bourg became involved with the struggling community. She says:

> When difficulties came up between her and the Vicar apostolic, the Rt. Rev. Theophile Meerchaert [sic] she [Mother Virginia] left and the community was taken care of by Sister Sacred Heart, a Sister of St. Joseph of New Orleans. She encouraged them to join Carondelet instead of New Orleans, due to the fact that they should go to an American, not a French foundation.[67]

Knowing that Bishop Meerschaert had spent years in the Diocese of Natchez, it seems logical that he would have asked the Sisters of St. Joseph of New Orleans for help when he thought the community was floundering. Although some of the sisters in Oklahoma were from a French-Canadian background, Sister Sacred Heart apparently thought that they fit better in the U.S. culture than the French. One wonders why she suggested that they join with Carondelet as none of them had any contact with that community and Concordia, from which at least some of them had come, was slightly closer to Muskogee than was St. Louis.[68] For whatever reason, at the instigation of the bishop, the majority of the sisters asked for admittance and were received into the Carondelet Congregation in 1900. Carondelet's St. Louis Province would continue to serve in Oklahoma for almost 100 years.[69]

STRETCHING THE VISION: FROM LA GRANGE TO CALIFORNIA

From January 2 to 6, 1907, Rev. Charles J. Maddox, C.Ss.R., preached a retreat for the Sisters of St. Joseph in La Grange.[70] His role as retreat master made him privy

---

67 Hurley, "Memory's Hall."

68 It is approximately 360 miles from Muskogee to Concordia and 400 to St. Louis. Another factor may have been the relative stability of the two congregations at the turn of the century. Mother Stanislaus Leary had left office and the Concordia community in 1898 and in 1900, the La Grange community was getting established and some Concordia sisters were leaving that community to join the new group in Illinois.

69 The Carondelet sisters ministered in Oklahoma until the year 2,000. In 1921, the Sisters of St. Joseph of Wichita began a ministry of health care in Poncha City, OK.

70 Charles Maddox, born in New York City in 1865, became a member of the Redemptorists in 1894, and was ordained in 1900. An impressive preacher, he spent the years from 1902 to 1922 giving missions and retreats throughout the western half of the United States. He died December 27, 1935 at Borgess Hospital in Kalamazoo, attended by the Sisters of St. Joseph of Nazareth, Michigan. ("Résumé" of Father Maddox' activities, Redemptorist Archives, Denver Colorado.)

to considerable information about the sisters and his experience as a religious gave him a context for understanding the dynamics of the community and the immense challenges they were facing.[71] From the day that Mother Alexine Gosselin had been named superior, lack of finances had been their most pressing problem.[72] Exacerbating that, they had a growing number of sisters but only two schools and a farm to keep them occupied.[73] Father Maddox heard about all of this during the retreat. He did not forget either their problems or the fact that he had promised to help them if he could.[74]

Five years later, the same problems still plagued the community and Mother Alexine's health had deteriorated. Whenever Mother Alexine sought healthcare away from the motherhouse, Mother Bernard Gosselin, her sister and the novice director, acted as de facto superior. While Mother Alexine was overwhelmed at La Grange, Mother Bernard focused on a larger world. In that, she had a soulmate in Monsignor Francis Kelley, the founder of the Catholic Church Extension Society.

THE CHURCH IN THE U.S. AND THE SISTERS IN LA GRANGE
LOOK BEYOND THEIR BORDERS

When Mother Alexine celebrated her Silver Jubilee in 1911, Archbishop Quigley honored her by presiding at the liturgy and inviting Monsignor Francis Kelley to preach the homily. In 1905, with Archbishop Quigley's support, Monsignor Kelley had founded The Catholic Church Extension Society, a home-mission association designed to support the growth of Catholic Church in rural areas.[75] Monsignor Kelley had established the first children's group of the Extension Society, the Child Apostles, at Nazareth Academy, the school founded by the Sisters of St. Joseph in La Grange. The Child Apostles, under the patronage of St. Joan of Arc, paid annual

---

71 One of the details the Redemptorists recorded about their preaching missions was the number of confessions they heard. Father Maddox recorded having heard 68 confessions during the retreat, implying that every one of the sisters could have seen him as confessor at that time.

72 The community began with a balance of thirty-three cents, and from the day she received her first loan through the rest of Mother Alexine's term as superior they would be in debt.

73 See *Journeys Begun*, 62.

74 At the time Maddox gave the La Grange retreat, he was stationed in Kansas City (1905-1911) and assigned as a preacher of missions. In 1911, he was missioned to California and based in Fresno. ("Rassely Maddox research" Redemptorist Archives, Denver.) On June 2, 1912, Maddox wrote to a priest friend about the La Grange community, telling him, "Strange to say, some few years ago his Grace, Archbishop Quigley of Chicago, told me to do all I could to help these sisters. I feel I could help…in no better way than to bring them to a veritable promised land in the Diocese of Sacramento." (Maddox to "V. Rev. dear Father," June 2, 1912. Redemptorist Archives, Denver.)

75 The idea of the Catholic Church Extension Society grew from an article Kelley published in the American

dues of 25 cents and promised to offer their Holy Communion once a month for the Church Extension Society.[76]

The Extension Society exemplified a new, dynamic mission spirit rising among U.S. Catholics. In 1908, Pope Pius X declared that the Church in the United States was self-sustaining and should no longer be considered mission territory.[77] In that same year, Monsignor Kelley organized the first American Catholic Mission Congress, a meeting held in Chicago which boasted an attendance of "tens and scores of thousands of men and women and hundreds of clergymen of all degrees."[78] Just over two years later, in 1911, the bishops of the United States approved the plan of Fathers James Walsh and Thomas Price to form The Catholic Foreign Mission Society of America, better known as Maryknoll and one year after that, Mary Josephine Rogers and seven companions founded the Maryknoll Sisters. The Church in the United States was moving into full scale missionary activity.

With the end of the Spanish American War in August of 1898, the United States gained political control over Cuba, Puerto Rico, Guam and the Philippine Islands, all of which had significant Catholic populations in need of the ministry of missionaries. Mission fervor was in the air and the La Grange Sisters were breathing it in. Mother Bernard consulted Monsignor Kelley about founding a mission in Puerto Rico but he suggested she consider California over "such a distant place."[79] Whether as a result of those conversations, or of Mother Bernard's active investigations or simple coincidence, in May, 1912, the community's old friend, Father Maddox, wrote to La Grange with a proposal that the community open a mission in California.

Ecclesiastical Review (Vol XXXII, 1905, pp. 573-585) and later reproduced as a pamphlet entitled "Little Shanty Story." Presenting the pitiful plight of a destitute country priest in Ellsworth, Kansas, the story launched Kelley's project to promote home missions. (See http://www.crisismagazine.com/2013/how-to-be-an-american-catholic-bishop-francis-kelley)

76 La Grange Annals, 52. (Archives CSJoseph)

77 The encyclical Sapienti Consilio removed the Church in the U.S. from the jurisdiction of Propaganda Fidei, recognizing it as a mature Church, on an equal footing with the Churches in Europe, self-sustaining both financially and in the vocations necessary to continue to build up the Church. (See Angelyn Dries, O.S.F., The Missionary Movement in American Catholic History (NY: Orbis, 1998) 62-85.

78 The number is reported by Father Francis C. Kelley, ed. The First American Catholic Missionary Congress (Chicago: T.S. Hyland & Company. 1909) 11.

79 Journeys Begun, 62. Msgr. Kelley's suggestion to choose California may have been tinged by his commitment to national missions. In the question of geographical distance, Sacramento is 2044 miles from Chicago while it is 2,049 miles from Chicago to Puerto Rico, away, a full 5 miles further.

MOTHER BERNARD, FATHER MADDOX AND CALIFORNIA

In March 1912, Mother Alexine Gosselin went to Hot Springs, Arkansas for reasons of health and remained away until late May. In May, 1912, Father Charles Maddox addressed the following enthusiastic letter to her:

> May 1, 1912
> Dear Mother Alexine,
> May Day Greetings to one and all the Sisters. You may observe that I am still taking a lively interest in your zealous community... I have an important letter to send you. It is its object to agreeably surprise you for I send you an urgent invitation to come and locate in California. Just think of it! It is certainly worthy of your serious attention to have a home where the roses and lilies bloom all year long.
>
> Yesterday I made a long talk on "Catholic schools – Methods—and Maintenance."...I paid your sisters very many compliments for efficient work, etc. Accordingly the Bishop told me to open correspondence with you and in his name to invite you to establish a foundation in his diocese – Sacramento. I therefore, by these presents send you a most cordial invitation to come to the Pacific Coast. I hope you will consider my favors graciously and arrange to commence your good work here next September...
>
> Hence I do hope that you will take up this subject directly with the Ordinary, Rt. Rev. Bishop Grace himself. He will expect to hear from you, I fancy, for...[this letter] is in his name.
> Praying for your progress and sending you the fervent, pious blessing of the Rt. Rev. Bishop, believe me to remain,
> Yours sincerely in J.M.J.
> Father C.J. Maddox C.Ss.R.[80]

Because Mother Alexine was away, Mother Bernard received the letter and responded quickly:

> May 10, 1912
> My Dear Father Maddox,
> Your letter was a very pleasant surprise. Your friends at Nazareth have often wondered what had become of you...we see that you have kept us in mind... Reverend Mother is not home and we do not expect her

---

80 Copy of letter from Maddox to Alexine Gosselin, May 1, 1912 (Archives CSJoseph).

for another two weeks, hence I take the liberty to answer your letter…I hope Mother will consider the contents favorably. I am sure she would find at least a dozen volunteers to take up the work in California if she would be assured that the Sisters would find enough work for support. Our Sisters are all young, healthy, and not afraid of hard work…

Mother and myself started here twelve years ago…now we have a community of ninety members…I am sending by today's mail a catalogue and little history which will give you an idea of the work we have accomplished…I also took the liberty of sending one to the Rt. Rev. Bishop Grace…Do you feel that we could do as well in California?…Rev. Mother could not take the work herself, as she could not be spared from this Community, but some of our Sisters might avail themselves of the opportunity to exercise their zeal in a western field, with the approval and good will of His Grace, Archbishop Quigley.

Reverend Mother knows nothing of this letter, as I shall wait till she returns to communicate this important matter to her…Rt. Rev. Bishop Grace may expect to hear from Mother in this regard as soon as she returns.

Words are inadequate to express our gratitude to you for your kindly interest…

Your Sister in the Sacred Heart,

Sr. St. Bernard, S.S.J.[81]

Father Maddox wrote back immediately with additional enticements:

May 15, 1912

My Dear Sr. Bernard,

I received your answer…The Bishop received those you sent him. He expressed himself as much pleased. He is patiently awaiting what you will do. When he hears from you he will turn the matter over to the Vicar General, Very Rev. Fr. Kennedy of Eureka.

This is the place he may first establish you.…I have heard several priests speak very laudably of this place. It is said that $20,000 remain in

---

81 Mother Bernard Gosselin to Rev. C. J. A. Maddox, May 10, 1912, Archives, CSJoseph)

the bank as a school fund. Besides the people are the best disposed Catholics anywhere. Some are immensely wealthy and are desirous of giving any assistance. While the Rt. Rev. Bishop would be pleased to have you come, he intimated that first a few would come to visit and make some definite settlement...Who knows but this foundation will have your big sister fix the trimmings for the realization of Nazareth complete for her golden, or, better, your silver jubilee? The future lies smiling before you...

Well, let me hear from you though so far away and let your Archbishop know how I am trying to help you in locating a summer home for the restful, peaceful, vacation time on the banks of the deep blue sea.

A prayerful blessing for one and all from

Yours sincerely in Christ

C. J. Maddox, C.Ss.R.[82]

If Mother Bernard had not been fully convinced after receiving Father Maddox's first letter, the intimation that a California could resolve the community's major problems offered an irresistible inducement. Without exploring the details, the initial correspondence between Father Maddox and Mother Bernard seemed to assume that a mission in California would not necessarily require a separation from La Grange.

MOTHER BERNARD'S FIRST EXPLORATIONS IN CALIFORNIA

On the day that Mother Alexine arrived home from her sick leave, Mother Bernard told her about her western project. In Mother Alexine's absence Mother Bernard had begun preparations to visit and then move to California. Surprised as Mother Alexine may have been, the annals record no dissension:

She [Mother Bernard] pleaded for permission to go at once "to explore", and Mother Alexine, who knew how to appreciate what her assistance had meant to her...acquiesced at once, saying that she was only too happy for an opportunity of granting her a rest and a trip so much to her liking, for it had ever been an ardent desire of Mother Assistant that someday she might visit California. Accordingly, preparations were

---

82 Letter from Maddox to Mother Bernard, May 15, 1912 (Archives CSJoseph)

made for her departure on the same evening.[83]

On Thursday, May 23, only hours after Mother Alexine had returned to La Grange, Father Purcell, the community's good friend, took Mother Bernard and Sister Ursula Hatting to embark on the 11 p.m. train, remaining with them until departure and handing them some much needed cash just as they boarded the train.[84] The sisters broke their trip at Denver, finding hospitality with the Sisters of Charity at St. Joseph's Hospital and doing what sight-seeing they could arrange.[85] They arrived in Sacramento on Tuesday, May 28, and Father Maddox immediately took them to the Cathedral.

Although Mother Bernard preferred a mission in the capital, Father Maddox cajoled her into investigating Eureka, saying "At least, it won't hurt to try."[86] Bishop Grace was also emphatic about Eureka, surely in part because Reverend Lawrence Kennedy, his friend and the Vicar General, served as pastor there.[87]

The sisters took an overnight boat from Sacramento to San Francisco, then embarked on a steamship headed to Eureka.[88] In Eureka they met parishioners along with Monsignor Kennedy and Father Cronan, of St. Bernard's Parish. As they were shown around, they cautioned the pastor that if some sisters came, they would arrive without any capital. Mother Bernard said that "all she asked on arriving would be a roof for a shelter and food to sustain the community until they would be placed in a position to care for themselves."[89] Delighted by the

---

83 La Grange Annals, 74.
84 La Grange Annals, 74.
85 La Grange Annals, 75. The Sisters of Charity of Leavenworth had established St. Joseph's Hospital in Denver. Mother Bernard quite likely knew the community from Kansas. In 1912, the Carondelet sisters also had two communities in Denver and two in nearby Colorado mountain towns.
86 La Grange Annals 76. Even though it is written in the third person, the section of the Annals describing the exploration of the California mission contains details that make it appear to be a first-hand account.
87 Kennedy, born in Ireland and educated there and at St. Sulpice in Paris, had a reputation as a brilliant theologian. Although he was slated to become a seminary professor in Ireland, he chose instead to join Father Thomas Grace and other classmates who were bound for the California missions. Bishop Thomas Grace (1841-1921), also an Irishman, was ordained in 1876 for the U.S. missions. He served as pastor in various parishes in California and Nevada, all in the Sacramento diocese, before being appointed bishop in 1896. For biographical sketches of Kennedy and Grace see: http://www.diocese-sacramento.org/diocese/archives.html.
88 The sisters' financial straits had by now reached the point that they did not have the price of the steamship ticket, but were able to engage the sympathy of the agent who gave them a discount and let them sail with the promise of payment on their return. (La Grange Annals, 77) The need to ask the priests for travel funds would have reinforced their description of the community's poverty.
89 La Grange Annals, 80.

"leniency" of Mother Bernard's demands, Monsignor Kennedy told her his only worry was that if he allowed her out of his sight, she and her sisters would never return. The Eureka priests and people proudly showed off the land destined for their future school and the temporary quarters the sisters could use until all was duly built. Upon their return to Sacramento, Father Maddox gave Mother Bernard the Bishop's formal invitation to the community to make a foundation in his diocese.

Mother Bernard had seen enough. By then, if not long before, the California foundation was a foregone conclusion in her mind. When she wrote a report to Mother Alexine in La Grange, she lightheartedly signed her letter "The Sisters of the Sacramento Diocese."[90]

According to the La Grange community annals, when Mother Bernard returned to La Grange,

> Mother Assistant [Bernard] told the whole story and succeeded in making Mother Alexine as enthusiastic as she herself over the prospects of such a glorious mission. She said she could not help her by giving her any money but that she could have her choice of a band of members of the Novitiate subjects whom she herself had trained.[91]

The day after Mother Bernard's return from California, Mother Alexine went to speak with Archbishop Quigley about the plan.[92]

> He reluctantly granted permission for Mother Assistant's leaving his diocese…[He] saw that her papers of acceptance in the Diocese of Sacramento made any disapproval worthless. He said, "She may go then, and take a few whom she can get to go along with her…[93]

---

90 La Grange Annals, 80.
91 La Grange Annals, 83-84.
92 Since Archbishop Feehan's death in 1902, Archbishop James E. Quigley had taken over the Archdiocese of Chicago. Quigley was born in Canada and raised in Buffalo where he also served as bishop before being named to Chicago. Famed as a champion of social justice, Quigley had worked on behalf of union members in Buffalo, gaining notoriety for mediating a strike settlement and, in the process, putting a halt to the practice of forcing workers to receive their pay in saloons where the saloon-keeper often had control over hiring. Quigley also wrote a pastoral letter in German defending union members' right to vote for union governance and condemning socialism.
93 La Grange Annals, 84.

Bishop Quigley quickly regretted his decision and wrote a letter rescinding his permission for the sisters to leave. Monsignor Purcell informed Mother Bernard that the bishop's letter was on its way and the sisters made plans for a departure before the bishop's letter could be delivered.[94]

On Sunday evening, June 16, sisters had gathered at La Grange for a scene the annals describe as follows.

> What a surprise to all this sad news would be! The secret, kept to the last minute, must now be revealed…All the Novices and Junior Professed Sisters were told to assemble…to enjoy an evening with Mother Bernard, this being the greatest privilege ever granted the – a social hour with their former Mistress…
>
> At eight o'clock, Mother Assistant entered, and as her visit was to be an intentionally brief one, she immediately opened the conversation by speaking of her plans for the future. What news could be more unwelcome? Weeping, lamentations…All reluctantly bade their dear Mistress a fond farewell, but were at a loss to know who her companions would be.
>
> Mother Assistant then said, "Let those who are to come with me, be quick to say goodbye to all for only a few minutes remain until we leave. So the fortunate young missionaries approached those remaining to say farewell, but were thus addressed, "You aren't going, are you?" "You're only trying to play a joke…I don't believe it…Oh, Florinda, trying to tell me that Mother Assistant would take a postulant with her…
>
> The farewell to the novices was followed by that of dear Rev. Mother Alexine and the Community sisters…The time being short, they hastily said good-bye to all and started for the depot…Their dear friend, Doctor Purcell, met them at the Union Station, Chicago, to see that they departed safely and comfortably….in his usual generous manner, Doctor gave Rev. Mother Bernard ten dollars…[95]

The day after their departure, Mother Alexine wrote to Archbishop Quigley saying

---

94 Mary Therese Sweeney, CSJ and Eileen McNerney, CSJ, *A Bold and Humble Love, Journey of Grace, Sisters of St. Joseph of Orange, 1912-2010*, (Sisters of St. Joseph of Orange, 2012), 24. (Hereafter, "Sweeney & McNerney.") The background information about the Orange foundation comes from Sweeney and McNerney unless otherwise noted.
95 La Grange Annals, 80-84.

not one word more than necessary:

> June 17, 1912,
> My Dear Archbishop,
> I wish to inform you that Sister Mary Bernard left here last night with
> a few sisters not under vows who would not remain here without her.
> Hoping to have you with us July second,
> I am,
> Your devoted child in our Lord,
> Mother Alexine[96]

The group of sisters who went to California comprised nearly ten percent of the congregation at that time.[97] Whether by coincidence or spurred by departures from the La Grange community, the Archbishop began to find additional missions for the community, beginning the following October, 1912, with St. Rocco's parish in Chicago Heights.[98]

EUREKA

Mother Bernard was the only one of the original ten sisters going to California who had been there before. She may have been the only one who had ever been further from Chicago than Kansas. Among the nine companions she chose for the California mission she included her eighteen-year-old niece, novice Sister Mary Joseph. More than sixty years later, Fabiola Torrison, the former Sister Mary Joseph, recorded the story of their departure and early days in Eureka.[99]

Mrs. Fabiola Torrison explained that Mother Bernard's preparations to move to California began before she ever saw the territory. On May 16, 1912, before Mother Alexine had returned to the motherhouse, Mother Bernard resigned from some of her leadership roles.[100] Her companions' preparation time would be

---

96 Mother Alexine to Archbishop Quigley, June 17, 1912 (Archives, CSJoseph)

97 *Journeys Begun*, 60, 64.

98 The Annals mention the departure and the mission to St. Rocco's in the same paragraph, suggesting a close connection in the mind of the sisters. (La Grange Annals, Chapter Thirteen, pages unnumbered.)

99 The quoted material which follows comes from the transcript of Sister Mary Therese Sweeney's (CSJ Orange) interview with that niece, Mrs. Fabiola Gosselin Torrison (baptized Albina Gosselin, also known as Sister Mary Joseph) in 1985. Mrs. Torrison left the Sisters of St. Joseph in 1923.

100 Sweeney & McNerney, 22. In *A Compassionate Presence*, (Orange: Sisters of St. Joseph of Orange, 1987, 56) Brad Geagley indicates that Mother Bernard resigned from the board of trustees of Nazareth Academy on May 16, 1912.

considerably shorter. Mrs. Torrison recalled,

> Some of us were not told [that we were going] until the last thing. I
> knew...just two or three days before...
> Mother Bernard...told us what we were coming here for and what
> would be expected of us. It would mean hard work and would be just
> like a mission, and of course, mission work interested us because we
> were going to meet different people.[101]

In addition to the promise of a mission that included ample work and new people,
there was the adventure of going somewhere entirely unknown and doing so
with little more than a vague notion of what would be entailed. Remembering
her eagerness, Fabiola said, "Every one of us [were excited]. I'd never seen a
mountain!"[102]

Mother Bernard's correspondence with Father Maddox had been honest
enough to indicate that the sisters would be bringing more willingness than
expertise, but she explained that for them this was nothing new:

> Our experience here may help out some, as none of us had any experience
> when we started here [La Grange]. Mother had never been on a mission
> and I was just out of the Novitiate a few days.

She explained exactly what he could expect from the Sisters of St. Joseph if they
came to California:

> Our Sisters are all healthy and not afraid of hard work. They have all
> been well tested. The Community here could not give them very much
> to start with...but some of our Sisters might avail themselves of the
> opportunity to exercise their zeal in a western field.[103]

The people of St. Bernard's Parish in Eureka hoped to open a school. Mother
Bernard wanted a place where the sisters could do at least as well as they had in La
Grange. Both sides were hiding high hopes behind those measured expectations

---

101 Fabiola Interview, 34, 16.
102 Fabiola Interview, 16.
103 Bernard to Maddox, May 10, 1912.

When Mother Bernard set out she was thirty-eight years old and had been in La Grange for the twelve years since she had first made vows. The sisters who accompanied her had all been her novices and were considerably younger.[104]

 The original group of eight included: Sisters Immaculata Hoyt, Isabelle Aubin, Angela Hutter, Mother Bernard, Sisters Winifred Lambert, Mary Joseph Gosselin and one postulant, Florinda Ferron. Within a few months they were joined by Sisters Ursula Hatting, Francis Lirette, Ella Kelly and Elizabeth MeKeon. In the same month that the last two of those sisters arrived from La Grange, the community received their first local postulant, Elizabeth MeKeon, a twenty-one year old graduate of the San José Normal School.

The first group arrived on June 22, 1912. Although they were not scheduled to open the school until the Fall, they immediately began religious education classes to prepare a hundred students for confirmation and younger children for First Communion – all of this with young women who had not yet finished their initial formation in the religious life.

It seemed as if everything had to be done at once. According to Fabiola Torrison,

> Well, we started awfully fast...I think we needed the money. Mother Bernard needed the money to feed the crowd. We did a lot...trying to acquaint ourselves...and getting things organized. And naturally with ten, brand new [sisters], like brand new kids...

Mother Bernard did what she could as novice director:

> We were instructed by Mother Bernard, we had conferences...more or less teaching us how to act and how to carry ourselves, how to live... There was never an organization where there was a specific time of day...We had a tremendous number of prayers...I liked that.[105]

On August 1, 1912, the sisters opened Nazareth Academy, later called St. Bernard's

---

104 Of the original twelve sisters, only Mother Bernard and Sisters Ursula and Angela were more than twenty years old. (Sweeney & McNerney, 25) Photo courtesy of the Sisters of St. Joseph of Orange.
105 Fabiola Interview 43-44.

Academy in the Knights of Columbus' YMI Hall.[106] By December, the student population had grown from 60 to 150. Just one year after Mother Bernard and Father Maddox began their correspondence, Mother Bernard procured a loan and on May 2, 1913, the community celebrated the groundbreaking for a proper school and motherhouse. They moved into their new building in January, 1914.

Unlike their sisters in La Grange, the California community quickly received not only candidates but invitations to open new missions. In 1915, the sisters opened a boys' boarding school in Ferndale, a town 20 miles from Eureka where they had already been active in religious education.[107] By October, 1915, Mother Alexine visited California and she and Mother Bernard explored the possibility of opening a mission in Brawley, a growing town in California's Imperial Valley, in the Diocese of Monterey-Los Angeles.[108] That first mission in Southern California took the Sisters of St. Joseph over 800 miles south of their first foundation, settling them only 20 miles north of the Mexican border. While the distance seemed formidable, taking that mission established the community in more than one diocese, preventing them from being under the control of only one bishop at a time when they had not formalized their *Constitutions*. Additionally, the contacts the sisters made by going south brought them invitations to open as many additional schools as they were able to staff. After opening Sacred Heart School in Brawley they added schools in Ontario and Santa Ana in southern California, all while maintaining the motherhouse and more in Eureka.[109] The schools were enough to keep the sisters busy, but they were sharing the poverty of the families they served with tuition sometimes paid in poultry and produce rather than cash.

THE MINISTRY OF HEALTH CARE

When Mother Bernard Gosselin got an idea for something she often took it well down the road toward completion before others recognized it as anything but a vague possibility. Although the town of Eureka might not have had a great need

---

106 The "YMI" is the Catholic Young Men's Institute, a fraternal organization founded in San Francisco in 1883 for the moral, social and intellectual improvement of its members. Membership offered benefits for sickness and funeral expenses. By 1900, 20,000 young men had joined the institute. Founded around the same time as the Knights of Columbus, it remained a simpler and smaller organization. For information about St. Bernard's Academy see http://saintbernards.us/about/history/.

107 Sweeney & McNerney (25), mention that Ferndale was a flourishing town with a port, roads, "and even a bridge."

108 This was one of a number of times that Mother Alexine visited California. In 1910, the U.S. Census listed 881 inhabitants in Brawley, the 1920 census listed 5,389.

109 See Sweeney & McNerney, 29-30.

for a hospital, the Sisters of St. Joseph did. By 1917, Mother Bernard was making remote preparations to add health care to the community's ministries. Without having a definite plan in hand, she secured Bishop Grace's approval for the potential venture.[110] In that same year, she turned to her brothers in New York for financial assistance.

In 1917, Eureka had at least two functioning hospitals and one that had

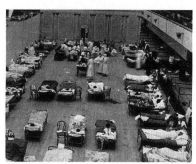

The Oakland Municipal Auditorium as a temporary ward for flu patients, 1918.

closed because the physician owner had gone into service in World War I.[111] When the owner of the temporarily closed facility returned from the war, he was unable to make a financial success of the venture because of the high cost of personnel. The Sisters of St. Joseph were poor but they had personnel in abundance. Mother Bernard knew that her sisters could offer hospital services at a fraction of what it cost to hire outside employees and the income would all belong to the community. She was still in the remote stages of planning when the influenza outbreak of 1918 made it necessary for the sisters to begin nursing before they had a hospital.[112]

The 1918 influenza pandemic affected 500 million people worldwide and killed up to five percent of the world's population, most of them apparently healthy young adults. Sister Mary Joseph explained that when the epidemic hit Eureka,

> We turned the academy into a hospital just to take care of the people who were coming in and out...I went into the homes; one farmer, for instance, had a large family. I had to use the table in order to take care

---

110 See Geagley, 105.
111 Hospitals at this time were often little more than private residences with the room layout adjusted to care for patients and treatment. As a means of comparison, when Mother Bernard visited the Sisters of Charity at St. Joseph's Hospital in Denver, she would have probably been in the third of their expanded buildings, a three-story, 30 bed hospital. They had begun in a six room house in 1873. For comparison, Denver's population in 1910 was 213,381, considerably more than Eureka's 11,845. See http://coloradohealthcarehistory.com/hospitals-st-joseph-denver.html
112 The picture is of the Oakland municipal auditorium as a makeshift ward. It is in the public domain, available through: https://en.wikipedia.org/wiki/1918_flu_pandemic#/media/File:1918_flu_in_Oakland.jpg.

of them because they didn't have enough beds...They were dying right and left. In the amount of about 175 in the town...Many of the sisters were stricken...
During the epidemic there were a lot of converts...a lot of people realized why we were there...I think that the sisters made an impression...they saw that we were really serious.[113]

As happened in other places, the sisters' selfless service in an emergency transformed previously prejudiced people's opinions and brought the sisters general acceptance and newfound respect.

Sincere as they may have been, the sisters' self-sacrificing service did not qualify them as nurses. Mother Bernard understood the need for professional education and sent six sisters to San Francisco for clinical education. She sent Sister Mary Joseph to the Mayo Clinic for training so that when the sisters opened a hospital she could set up both the lab and x-ray services.[114] Once she had provided for professionally trained sister-nurses, Mother Bernard's next challenge was the cash with which to purchase the hospital. Happily, the community had received a donation of timberland valued at $40,000 and on March 19, 1920, Mother Bernard closed the deal, trading the stand of timber for Dr. Falk's former Northern California Hospital. It took the community nine months of cleaning, clearing, sewing, painting and even digging out the basement to get the 28-bed hospital ready for its grand opening on November 1.[115]

As planned, the sisters provided all the labor, to the point that Sister Mary Joseph explains how she stood in as physician in an emergency:

The doctors all left town on weekends and I did the surgery. I sewed the busted, or knocked-off thumb. I had to put the patient to sleep...I even operated and removed a foot...There was just no emergency that I didn't take care of. Even a woman busted open after surgery, she was in the hospital...and by golly, the thing is this, after midnight they called me and I came over and set up for surgery...and just took care of her, put her bowels back in her abdomen, sewed her up, and the doctor came

---

113 Fabiola interview, 56-59.
114 Fabiola Interview, 3, 53.
115 Geagley (110) mentions that the spectacle of the sisters doing their own digging brought townsfolk to gawk, but that their only help came from two elderly gentlemen, Messrs. Kelly and Duffy.

the next day and said, "I couldn't have done any better."[116]

In its first full year of operation the hospital served 725 regular patients and attended the births of 100 babies. The success was everything Mother Bernard could have hoped for and the income from the hospital freed her to contemplate new vistas.[117]

MOVING THE MOTHERHOUSE TO ORANGE

Mother Bernard enjoyed a good relationship with each of the three California bishops she knew. Bishop Grace of Sacramento had been the first to invite the Sisters of St. Joseph to the state and remained supportive of their endeavors while not trying to limit them to ministry in his diocese. Bishop Hanna of San Francisco visited the community in Eureka and in 1921, he encouraged the Paulist Fathers in San Francisco to invite the Sisters of St. Joseph to staff their Chinese Mission School.[118] When Mother Bernard met Bishop Cantwell of Los Angeles, he expressed his pleasure that she had come to his diocese and, perhaps to his later chagrin, he gave Mother Bernard what she considered an open invitation to his diocese.[119]

Bishop Grace of Sacramento died in December, 1921, and while everyone assumed that his auxiliary bishop, Patrick J. Keane, would succeed him, an official appointment was held up by the death of Pope Benedict XV in January, 1922.[120] The delay gave the Sisters of St. Joseph time to consider their alternatives for the future. When Mother Bernard and her assistant, Mother Francis Lirette, visited Bishop Keane, the experience convinced Mother Bernard that the community's best future did not lie with the Sacramento Diocese. The community history explains that Mother Bernard believed that Bishop Keane's vision was not enough to allow for all that she dreamed of for the community.

---

116 Fabiola Interview, 4. She added: I used to deliver babies…I saved a baby that was only almost three pounds, I built an incubator myself to keep her alive because we didn't have the money to get her an incubator, so I made one out of an orange box and it worked out beautifully.
117 Sweeney and McNerney, 33-34.
118 Sweeney and McNerney (35) mention that Father Charles Bradley of the Chinese mission "wanted all the Sisters from Eureka but would settle for 24." Mother Bernard was able to send six.
119Irish born Bishop Cantwell had been Vicar General in San Francisco prior to being named Bishop of Monterey-Los Angeles. During his tenure the diocese became the Diocese of Los Angeles-San Diego (1922-1936) and then the Archdiocese of Los Angeles.
120 Pope Benedict XV died on January 22, 1922, after a long bout with pneumonia. He was succeeded by Pope Pius XI whose papacy ended in February of 1939.

It was clear to Mother Bernard and Mother Francis that they needed to complete a move out of the Sacramento diocese before Bishop Keane's investiture. In less than three months, the sisters needed to find and finance a new Motherhouse, secure the agreement of the congregation, move the novitiate and acquire ecclesial approval.[121]

In typical fashion, Mother Bernard went about the tasks in just about that order. Ecclesial approval was not her first concern.

Mother Bernard explained her move as follows:

Monsignor Kennedy, the Vicar General, was getting quite old and he didn't think that the diocese was doing enough for us...He said to me one day..."if you want to go...to San Francisco or to Sacramento or to Los Angeles...you will do much better there because you will be right in line for success, progress."

I had given them a school and a hospital and they didn't want any more than that...we wouldn't have progressed there...Monsignor Kennedy knew that and he said...this is no place for a progressive community...there is not enough...they can't keep up with you, with your community. It's progressive."

...I went down to Los Angeles, to our missions there and when I went in to see Bishop Cantwell he said to me, "You're down here now, you stay." "Oh," I says, "I can't do that..." There had to be more arrangements than that.

He said, "If you stay here you can work any place in my diocese and select the spot you want...I'll approve it."

...So when I left I went...to San Francisco and I spoke to Archbishop Hanna about it because I didn't want Archbishop Hanna to be hurt if I passed him by....he said, "Good. He will be good to you, he's my boy, I raised him, you know."[122]

Mother Bernard went on to explain how she found the money and the property to establish the motherhouse at Orange.

---

121 Sweeney and McNerney, 34.
122 Interview with Mother Bernard, pg. 19-22. Mother Bernard mentions in the course of this story that Bishop Cantwell had just turned down a request from Mother Cabrini to found in the diocese.

So when I went back, I went to the bank…and I borrowed, I think it was $90,000…the bank let me have it right away…Archbishop Hanna had spoken to them…

So I went out and Monsignor Henry Eummelen who was the pastor of Santa Ana took us all around and the last place he took us to was the Burnham Estate because he said he know that I would anchor that [sic]. So he said, you stay in the machine now and I'll go in and see those people and I'll get them to reduce it. The property was for sale for seven years for $200,000, they couldn't sell it.…[the owners] had bought it at a more reasonable price…they couldn't handle it…they were going under…they said "nobody will ever take it off our hands" and they were getting older.

So Monsignor Eummelen knew this and he went to them and talked to them…and he came out and said, "The property's yours, Mother. I paid the first payment, $500." He put down to bind the contract because he says, "They'll change their mind tomorrow."

So that's how we got that property…and we got it for $60,000…I had the money you see, that I had borrowed from the bank…
It took me three weeks to go up north and tell Monsignor Kennedy and to speak to Archbishop Hanna.

So I came in to see Bishop Cantwell. "Well," he said, "you finished your business, when are you coming down?" "Well," I said, "Your Lordship…will you look at this?" That was the deed – paid for. He just ran and touched the button for Monsignor Cawley[123] to come in… Monsignor Cawley came in… "What do you think?" he says, "that little sisters went to work and bought a piece of property here and I didn't know anything about it."

"Oh," I said, "Archbishop, you told me two weeks ago that I could borrow, I could go any place in your diocese and select a spot and you'd approve of it." "That's right," he says, "That's right," he tells Monsignor Cawley, "but it's a good thing she doesn't know much about the canon law…So, that's settled."[124]

Mother Bernard did not make a unilateral decision about the purchase. In February,

---

123 The manuscript does not have the name, but Msgr. John Cawley was listed by the Catholic Directory of 1921 as Chancellor in the Diocese of Los Angeles.
124 Mother Bernard Interview, pgs. 20-24.

1922, with sufficient time before bishop Keane would be installed as Sacramento's third bishop, Mother Bernard and the council decided that they would move their motherhouse to Orange in the Diocese of Monterey-Los Angeles. By March 21, just four days after Bishop Keane assumed care of the Sacramento diocese, the Sisters of St. Joseph were in Orange remodeling and repairing, transforming the dilapidated Burnham Estate into the motherhouse they named Nazareth. By June 23 of that year, they had pruned the trees and vines and learned to care for the pigs and other animals.[125] They were ready for Bishop Cantwell's first official visit, the house blessing and a ceremony of receptions and professions.

FIFTEEN YEARS WITH MOTHER BERNARD GOSSELIN

Mother Bernard Gosselin said that she arrived in California in 1912, with sixty cents and nine sisters. That was altogether just about twice what Mother Alexine had when she started in La Grange in 1899. When Father Cronin, the assistant pastor, visited the sisters on the day of their arrival in Eureka, he gave them sixty dollars. Mother Bernard spent $30 for food and held on to the remainder. Whether one would call it luck or blessing, from their first day, the Eureka foundation's trajectory would be vastly different from the community from which it sprang.

The sisters quickly had all the work they could take on. The income they received from schools, music lessons and most of all, from the hospital, allowed them the freedom to expand their horizons.[126] After establishing the motherhouse in Orange, Mother Bernard opened a hospital in the northern California town of Arcata.[127] Along with more schools, the sisters' ministries soon included catechetical work with farmworkers, the school for Chinese students in San Francisco and one for Mexican children in Los Angeles.

The California community received its first new member just five months after they arrived in Eureka. Although the number of women from the Eureka area who came to the congregation was small, Mother Bernard kept up recruitment efforts in the East and a steady number of women continued to enter so that in the 1920s, the community could say that at least 90 women had joined them in their first decade and a half in California. Many of the new members shared the

---

125 The produce of the orange groves would make a significant addition to the sisters' income.
126 Fabiola Torrison (Sister Mary Joseph) explained that sisters on special duty could earn seven dollars a day and "so many people needed special nurses and we gave the special work to the sisters…so we could make money and pay off the indebtedness." (Fabiola Interview, 32)
127 Arcata is about 8 miles north of Eureka. In 1920 the U.S. census registered 1,486 residents in the town.

Gosselin's French heritage and there were a number of families who had blood sisters and various cousins who entered.

In the midst of such prodigious expansion of personnel, properties and ministries, Mother Bernard also recognized the importance of securing the community's ecclesial status. The sisters who left La Grange went to California with the necessary official permissions – even if they accomplished that by leaving just before Bishop Quigley's letter retracting his permission could be delivered. Once in California, Bishop Grace's acceptance of the community and then Bishop Cantwell's support may have seemed enough to guarantee their status. When the Church promulgated the Code of Canon Law in 1917, the Sisters of St. Joseph of Orange, like all other communities, had to adjust the *Constitutions* they had been using to the requirements of the new code. Under the influence of the new canon law, the Sisters of St. Joseph of Orange wrote their *Constitutions* and on January 29, 1925, they sent the manuscript to Rome with Bishop Cantwell's approval.[128]

In 1927, Mother Bernard completed her time as superior general of the Sisters of St. Joseph of Orange. In the course of 15 years, she had brought the pioneer sisters from the Midwest to the California coast; she had established schools and hospitals, built and moved the motherhouse and received over 90 sisters into the new congregation. Among the women who entered the community under her leadership were Sisters Francis and Elizabeth Lirette, who were elected as the superior general and assistant to follow Mother Bernard. The founder expressed her delight with their election in a letter to Mother Alexine:

> Now, my dear Mother, is it possible for you to imagine the joy that filled my heart on that day? There is such a thing as a legitimate pride when it is for the good. I felt I had reached the limits of Mount Tabor, to see the day when two of my little girls whom I...received...and who have never left my side through all the care and worries of the responsibilities which were mine for so many years – and now to see them take the burden and carry it for the next six years – is another one of God's designs on this, His Community.[129]

In 1958, just a year and a half before her death, Mother Bernard gave an interview to Sister Miriam Rose of La Grange. Looking back on her life, Mother Bernard said:

---

128 The date is recorded in the document, "List of Significant Dates" (Archives CSJO).
129 Sweeney and McNerny, 40.

Sister, I saw three foundations. I was at Concordia when only five sisters were there...When I came as a boarder, only five sisters. I saw the beginning of that place. and I helped with all the hard work...[130]

As it turned out, Mother Bernard had seen and participated in the hard work of the beginnings of all three congregations. When she died on January 30, 1960, the Orange community numbered over 500 members and they had served not only in California, but also in Texas, Arizona and Papua New Guinea. That was surely more than even she could have dreamed of in 1912, when she and her companions rushed to board the night train from Chicago in order to be away from the city before Archbishop Quigley's letter could arrive to demand that she remain where she was.

---

130 Mother Bernard interview, pg. 25.

ଽଠ

Chapter Ten: The French Communities Continue To Bring the Little Design to the U.S.

CAST OF CHARACTERS

Mother Claude Monnet – Superior General – Sisters of St. Joseph of Bourg
Mother Eulalie Thomet – First Superior at Bay St. Louis (Bourg)
Mother Albina Thollot – Superior in Baton Rouge – Opened mission in Cincinnati (Bourg)
Mother Marie-Angele Morgera – Superior General, Bourg in 1897
Mother Leocadie Broc – Superior General of Le Puy in 1866
M. Sidonie Rascle – First Superior in St. Augustine (Le Puy)
Mother Lazare-Lazarus L'Hostel – Superior in St. Augustine 1899 and later in Fall River (Le Puy)
Mother Clemence Freycenon – First Superior of the Sisters of St. Joseph of Georgia (Le Puy)
M. Pélagie Boyer – Superior General of Le Puy in 1902
M. St. John Kennedy – Superior General in Georgia, 1877 -1899 (GA)

Mother St. John Marcoux – Founder, Sisters of St. Joseph of Chambéry
Jane Sedgwick – Brought Chambéry Sisters to the United States, 1885
M. Josephine O'Connor – First Provincial Superior of Chambéry Sisters in the U.S.
S. Marie Benedicte Nigay – Lyon sister who instigated the 20th century mission to America
Mother Henri-Xavier – Superior General of Lyon 1904
Mother Mary Philippine – First Superior In Maine (Lyon)

Bishop J. O. Van de Velde – Bishop of Natchez in 1854
Rev. Stanislaus Buteux – Missonary who invited Bourg Sisters to Natchez
Bishop Chalandon – Bishop of Belley (France)
Bishop William Henry Elder – Bishop of Natchez and then Cincinnati
Bishop Augustine Verot – Bishop of Savannah – then St. Augustine
Bishop William Gross – Bishop of Savannah in 1874
Bishop John Moore – Bishop of St. Augustine, 1877 – 1901
Father Giguère – Pastor who asked for Sisters in Fall River – 1902
Bishop Patrick T. O'Reilly – First Bishop of Springfield, MA 1870
Bishop Thomas D. Beaven – Bishop of Springfield MA, 1892 - 1920

THE SISTERS OF ST. JOSEPH OF BOURG'S MISSION TO MISSISSIPPI

The first Sisters of St. Joseph from France to come to America were sent from Lyon in 1836 and 1837 to Carondelet, Missouri. Until the turn of the 20th century, Lyon would send no more sisters to the United States, but Carondelet would continue to receive missionaries from the Moutiers community who sent a total of 39 sisters between 1854 and 1887. The next congregation which came to the U.S., the Sisters of St, Joseph of Bourg, eventually established three provinces in the U.S. which remained in union with France for over 100 years.

In 1854, the Sisters of St. Joseph of Bourg accepted the invitation of Bishop James Oliver Van de Velde of Natchez, Mississippi, to minister in Bay St. Louis, a small town on the Gulf coast of Mississippi about 60 miles northeast of New Orleans. The roots of the Bourg foundation reach back to St. Etienne and Lyon, to Mother St. John Fontbonne and the proliferation of French communities of Sisters of St. Joseph in the early nineteenth century. In 1823, Bishop Alexandre-Raymond Devie reestablished the Diocese of Belley some twenty years after it had been suppressed. [1] The Belley diocese was about 60 miles northeast of Lyon and Bishop Devie wanted to unite the twenty-seven local communities of Sisters of St. Joseph in his territory under one general superior. [2] He negotiated with Mother St. John Fontbonne and Bishop Jean-Paul Gaston de Pins of Lyon and won their consent to establish a Congregation of St. Joseph in the Diocese of Belley with a motherhouse in Bourg.[3]

Mother St. Benoit, the first superior general of the Bourg congregation

---

1 The Diocese of Belley, now known as Belley-Ars, was under the leadership of a Constitutional bishop from 1791 to 1793 and was suppressed by the Concordat of 1801. In 1822, Bishop Devie was named to reestablish the diocese. Bishop Devie was born in 1867 and ordained in 1891, just two years after the Revolution had begun. Named Bishop of Belley in 1823, he remained in that diocese until his death in 1852. In addition to the Bourg Congregation, the Society of Mary (Marists) began under Bishop Devie and struggled with him to be allowed to become more than a diocesan congregation.

2 Presumably, some of those communities had been founded by Mother St. John Fontbonne and others existed before the Revolution. Mother St. John had established more than 20 communities in the area before Bishop Devie was named.

Information in this section comes from papers Sister Jane Aucoin published in 2000 for the Sisters of St. Joseph of Médaille. These papers first appeared in the congregational publication *Journey*. (Archives CSJoseph, accessed from CSJ library at Baton Rouge.)

3 Cardinal Fesch had been banished from France in 1815; Bishop Le Pins was apostolic administrator of the Diocese of *Lyon from 1823 – 1850. See, Anonymous, Historical Notes of The Congregation of Saint Joseph of Bourg*, (51-52). (Hereafter, *Bourg*.) The book does not cite its publication date nor the pricise dare of the foundation of the Bourg Congregation.

received the habit of the Sisters of St. Joseph from Mother St. John Fontbonne at St. Etienne in 1809. Three years later, she was made superior of the community at Brou, just outside the city of Bourg en Bresse, about 50 miles northwest of Belley. In Brou the sisters operated an almshouse and cared for the physically and mentally ill of the area. When the sisters gathered for their first chapter in October, 1824, "the one hundred twenty-seven members of the new congregation elected Mother St. Benoit with a unanimous vote." [4] The bishop then decided that the asylum run by the sisters should also become the diocesan seminary. The motherhouse thus served as seminary, novitiate and asylum for the mentally ill until 1825 when the sisters acquired a separate motherhouse in Bourg.

Bishop Devie believed that Catholic education offered an indispensable key to the moral renewal of the Church in the aftermath of the French Revolution. Therefore he encouraged the community to make a priority of the intellectual preparation of the sisters. Sister Claude Monnet, who would later become Superior General, was the first of them to be sent to Lyon to be trained by the Christian Brothers, the experts in Catholic education at that time. Sister Claude not only returned to train her sisters but also published a textbook on teaching methodology that became a widely-used classic in its own day. For their part, the sisters who ministered in health care received the typical on-the-job training of the day, particularly from a group of Augustinian sister nurses who joined the community.[5]

The sisters' ministries increased rapidly as did their membership. In addition to schools and health care, their asylum for mentally ill women eventually served 1,000 patients. In 1828, the community obtained its legal approval as an Institute. By 1837, the community had the necessary personnel to found another congregation and Mother St. Joseph Chanay, the assistant superior general at Belley, reestablished the Congregation of the Sisters of St. Joseph of Gap. Three years later, she founded the Sisters of St. Joseph of Bordeaux.[6] By the time Mother St. Benoit, the first superior general, completed twenty years as superior she had seen the establishment of 122 houses and two new congregations.

---

4 *Bourg*, 60.

5 *Bourg*, 62-65. The Augustinians, suffering a dearth of vocations, joined the Sisters of St. Joseph in 1824 as did a community of Notre Dame from Ain in 1830.

6 *Bourg* 66-67. Gap is about 200 kl. south of Belley; Bordeaux is 650 kl. to the west, near the coast. The Bourg sisters in the U.S. formed a separate congregation in 1977. The French Congregation of Sisters of St. Joseph of Bourg and the Bordeaux Congregation reunited with the Lyon Congregation in 1996. The Sisters of St. Joseph of Gap had reunited with Lyon in 1954.

This was representative of how the post-Revolutionary era saw a tremendous surge of vocations to the various congregations of St. Joseph in southeastern France. Mother St. Benoit died on November 10, 1843, at the age of 59, just twelve days before the death of her first superior and mentor, Mother St. John Fontbonne. Her successor was thirty-nine year old Sister St. Claude Monnet who had entered the Bourg community in 1824. Under Mother Claude the sisters continued to teach, to open schools and care for the sick and orphaned. They also established a school for the deaf. Most surprisingly, given the anti-clerical tenor of the times, the General Council of Ain invited the sisters to open a state-financed normal school, staffed and hosted by the sisters.[7] That school functioned from 1854 until 1887 when the government organized its own institution. Such collaboration with the government was unusual at that time and would completely disappear in the last decade of the 19th century.

THE STATE AND RELIGIOUS CONGREGATIONS
IN NINETEENTH CENTURY FRANCE

In the century following the French Revolution, France's spasmodic political climate did nothing to deter vocations to religious life. Sisters of St. Joseph regrouped and founded new communities in spite of the rise and fall of the anti-clerical political philosophies that came into vogue with the Revolution. The sisters gradually learned to manage the general precariousness resulting from religion's role in every political change. French historian Maurice Agulhon explains that at that time, "No ecumenical spirit existed…The 'war of religion'…had a bitterness which we can no longer imagine. Everyone's convictions were tinged with intransigence and passionate feelings."[8]

After the fanatical harassment and persecution of the Church between 1789 and 1801, Napoleon's Concordat with the Vatican allowed the return of exiled clergy, restored the freedom of worship and reinstated state salaries to clergy, including those of some women religious. While the Concordat did not restore confiscated property, it did recognize Catholicism as the religion of the majority of the population. After Napoleon's defeat in 1814, a conservative monarchy supportive of the Catholic Church came into power. Nevertheless, the Church's monopoly on education was beginning to fall apart. Between 1830 and 1870,

---

7 *Bourg,*77. Unless otherwise noted, the information about the growth of the Congregation comes from *Bourg.*
8 Maurice Agulhon, The French Republic, 1879-1992, (Translated by Antonia Nevill, Cambridge: Blackwell, 1993)

there were three revolutionary changes in the French government, each of which legislated changes in status for the Church and its institutions. The Third Republic (1870-1940) finally brought some political stability and established a series of measures that would have long-lasting, detrimental effects on the life and ministry of the Congregations of St. Joseph in France.

After the Revolution, the official Catholic Church in France had remained closely associated with monarchists and much of the hierarchy continued to be drawn from families that had belonged to the nobility. The memory of persecution and martyrdom consolidated Catholic loyalty to tradition and suspicion of liberal ideas.[9] Those attitudes played a role in the growth of vocations to the religious life: if the blood of martyrs is the seed of the church, ongoing persecution can act as fertilizer to embolden and intensify devotion. As anti-clericalism inspired increasingly restrictive laws, the communities of Sisters of St. Joseph in France continued to grow.

The most serious legal restrictions on Church activity began in 1879, with legislation that excluded the clergy from the administration of hospitals and boards of charity. In 1880, the government removed women religious from hospital work and replaced them with lay women. In 1881, flouting the 1801 Concordat between France and the Vatican, the state refused to pay the salary of priests they labeled "non-compliant." In 1882, the "Law of 28 March" declared that primary schooling was obligatory, free and secular. This law forbad all religious instruction in school, instituting Thursdays as a free day for those students whose parents wished them to receive religious education. The legal attempt to remove all religious symbols from schools, including the schools founded under the auspices of religious congregations, encountered too much popular resistance to make forced compliance worthwhile.[10]

---

9 The French experience of revolution and instability had its counterpart in Rome as well. The Papal States were lost and restored various times. In 1791, France annexed some papal lands, then a Napoleonic invasion annexed all the Papal States until Napoleon's fall in 1814. After much back and forth, the final blow to the Papal States came on September 20, 1870, when King Victor Emmanuel of Italy successfully took the city of Rome and destroyed papal imperial power. Victor Emmanuel's victory took place just two months after Pope Pius IX had won the First Vatican Council's ratification of his supreme spiritual jurisdiction over the Catholic Church through the definition of papal infallibility.

10 Many of the communities' problems with the government came from the loss of centuries-old privileges that could appear curious compared to the U.S. experience. For instance, the 1850 "Law of 25 March" recognized a letter of obedience as the equivalent of a state-issued teaching diploma. Much to the distress of the congregations, that privilege was revoked in 1882. Other laws were more obviously odious for the religious, including 1886 legislation which gave mayors or inspectors the right to prevent the opening of any school on

In 1888, the state withdrew all funding of private or denominational education, suddenly creating a situation which undercut not only the select schools, but also much of the education offered in the villages where sisters had been teaching the poor for decades. Another highly effective strike against religious congregations and their ministries came with the taxation of all "movable and immovable property." The rate of taxation was up to 20% of the property value, retroactive to 1885. In 1889, the Bourg community lost possession of their boarding school when the government seized and sold it for non-payment of taxes; the sisters had refused to pay those taxes because they considered them unjust.[11] The culmination of the anti-clerical education laws came in 1904, when members of the congregations were forbidden to teach in the schools. Women religious had to leave their congregations if they wished to continue their ministry. That law closed 14,404 schools in one fell swoop.

Like the French Revolution itself, the overall effects of the process of secularization and separation of Church and State in France turned out to be far more drastic for Catholics in France than the American Revolution or separation of Church and State had been in the United States.[12] In sum, while persecution and other factors were leading to an increase in religious vocations, state policies were increasingly constricting religious women and men's opportunities for ministry. With such a wealth of personnel and a dearth of opportunity, French religious and priests were driven to massive emigration. That displacement transformed itself into an immense contribution to Catholic world mission in the late 19th century. The Church in the United States, classified as a mission territory until 1908, was a major beneficiary of that movement.[13]

"moral or hygienic grounds," a poorly defined category that could leave the existence of a school to the whim of authorities. (See Goyau, Georges. "France." *The Catholic Encyclopedia*. Vol. 6. New York: Robert Appleton Company, 1909. 28 Sept. 2016, http://www.newadvent.org/cathen/06166a.htm)

11 See "Happenings," the annals of the New Orleans province of Bourg, under entries for the year 1889.

12 The disestablishment of religion in the United States sometimes actually worked in favor of the Catholics who were a minority in a Protestant dominated nation and culture. The difference between the two revolutions and their effects was something Europeans, and particularly the Vatican, did not understand well, leading to great difficulties for the Church in the United States. Rome tended to judge U.S. events and philosophies on the basis of European experience rather than the reality of the U.S.

13 On June 29, 1908, Pope Pius X issued the Apostolic Constitution Sapienti Consilio removing Great Britain, the United States, Canada, Holland and the Duchy of Luxemburg from the jurisdiction of the Congregation for the Propagation of the Faith, indicating that they were no longer considered mission territories but areas in which the Church was securely established with all its hierarchical functions.

FROM BOURG TO BAY ST. LOUIS

As in so many events in the history of the Sisters of St. Joseph, the Bourg Congregation's first foundation in the United States began with what might be considered providential happenstance. In 1844, Rev. Stanislaus Buteux, a French missionary who had been serving in Indiana, was visiting home in Paris and chanced to board the same trolley as Monsignor Georges-Claude Chalandon, the Vicar General of the Diocese of Metz.[14] Seeing the young Father Buteux dressed in his long black coat and tie, the older priest thought he must be a Protestant minister. They struck up a conversation and the two became friends. As time went on, Father Buteux regaled the older priest with tales of the adventures, rigors and poverty of mission life in the American wilderness. The detail of which Father Buteux was proudest was that he had obtained the special privilege of carrying the Blessed Sacrament with him as he traveled. He explained that because he could not afford a pyx, he carried the host carefully wrapped in his handkerchief. Monsignor Chalandon was sufficiently impressed to give the priest some gold coins with which to purchase what he most needed for his mission.

Rev. S. Buteux

Ten years later, Father Buteux, now stationed in the Diocese of Natchez, Mississippi, was convinced that Catholic education was the greatest unmet need in his parish in Bay St. Louis. He arranged for three Christian Brothers to establish a school, but that plan did not work out. In addition to serious conflicts among the brothers and between them and the pastor, the school suffered an outbreak of yellow fever; the boarders had to be sent home and the school was closed.[15] That disappointment led Father Buteux to France to seek the help of the Brothers of the Sacred Heart whom he

---

14 Stanislaus Buteux was born in 1808 in Paris. His ancestral family included Rev. Jacques Buteux, S.J., martyred in Canada in 1652. French-born Bishop Simon Bruté recruited Buteux while he was a seminarian in Paris and brought him to the Diocese of Vincennes, Indiana, in 1836. Buteux recruited Mother Theodore Guerin and the Sisters of Providence to Terra Haute in 1840 and worked with the laborers to help build St. Mary of the Woods. (See: http://www.stmarybasilicaarchives.org/archives/biography/buteux.html)

15 In addition to reported conflicts between the brothers and Father Buteux, there were three different brother directors in one year, three brothers left the community from Bay St. Louis and one died of yellow fever. See Xavier Werneth, S.C., "A Brief Biography" [of Louis Stanislaus Buteux], http://www.stmarybasilicaarchives.org/archives/biography/buteux.html.

successfully recruited to open a boarding school in Bay St. Louis.[16]

While in France on his recruiting trip, Father Buteux called on his one-time benefactor, now Bishop Chalandon, who by then had replaced Bishop Devie as Bishop of Belley.[17] This time, instead of seeking funds for a pyx, Father

Buteux hoped to recruit sisters for his educational projects. Bishop Chalandon turned him down. When Father Buteux insisted, the bishop sent him to Mother Claude, the Superior General at Bourg. After consultation with her council and having read a letter of support from Bishop James Van de Velde of Natchez, Mother Claude approved the founding of a mission in Mississippi.[18]

In October, 1854, Mother Claude wrote a circular letter asking for volunteers for Mississippi. One of the first to volunteer was Mother Eulalie Thomet, the superior of the community at Ceyzériat, a town of fewer than 1,000 residents about ten kilometers southeast of Bourg. She wrote to Mother Claude, saying that all the sisters in her local community

Mother Eulalie Thomet

shared her missionary desire. She was 56 years old when she volunteered for the Mississippi mission. Although Father Buteux was counting on welcoming four sisters, the community decided to send only three: Mother Eulalie

---

16 The Brothers of the Sacred Heart were founded in Lyon in 1821, by Andre Coindre, a priest of that archdiocese. In 1840, the brothers decided that the congregation should be led by a brother rather than a cleric. By 1859, they numbered more than 400 brothers in France serving in 70 schools. The community came to the U.S. in 1847 to establish a school in Mobile, Alabama. In 1854, they came to Bay St. Louis where they established St. Stanislaus College. The Sacred Heart Brothers' French motherhouse was near to that of the Sisters of St. Joseph in Lyon.

17 Buteux's timing was amazingly fortuitous; Bishop Chalandon had been named to Belley in 1852; he served for only five years before being named Archbishop of Aix. If Father Buteux had come a few years earlier or later, Bishop Chalandon would not have had Sisters of St. Joseph of Bourg in his jurisdiction.

18 Bishop James Oliver Van de Velde was a Belgian Jesuit, born in 1795. As a diocesan seminarian he was recruited by Father Charles Nerinx, the founder of the Sisters of Loretto at the Foot of the Cross. Due to illness, Van de Velde studied at Georgetown instead of going to Kentucky with Nerinx. He became a Jesuit and taught in various institutions including the Jesuit College of St. Louis where, in 1840, he became president of St. Louis University. In 1848, he was appointed Bishop of Chicago and was consecrated in St. Francis Xavier Church by Archbishop Peter Richard Kenrick. By 1852, failing health forced him to ask to retire; instead of granting his request, Rome sent him to the milder climate of Natchez, Mississippi. He died there two years later of yellow fever. Bishop Van de Velde's successor was Bishop William Henry Elder who assumed responsibility in the diocese in 1857 after being consecrated by Archbishop Francis Patrick Kenrick of Baltimore. Elder would later become Archbishop of Cincinnati.

who would be the superior, Sister Anatolie Charton, also from the local community at Ceyzériat, and Sister Gonzague Navatier, a nurse who had been serving in the Hospital of Bourg and may have been a lay sister.[19] On November 16, 1854, the sisters at Bourg held a farewell ceremony for the missionaries and three days later they left France on the sailing vessel, The John Hancock. On December 30, 1854, after a 41 day journey, the sisters arrived in New Orleans. Like so many other women religious arriving in the U.S. at that port, they gratefully accepted the hospitality of the Ursuline Sisters.[20] Mother Eulalie wrote to Bourg praising the hospitality the Ursulines extended to missionary sisters who arrived in their city. She said:

> Their courtesy was only surpassed by their generosity. Not only did they provide assiduously and attentively for all our needs during the eight days…but fearing that upon arriving at our post we would be in want, they filled a box with assorted provisions…[21]

The three sisters from Bourg finally arrived at their new home in the parish of

Our Lady of the Gulf on Saturday, January 6, 1855. The following day Bishop Van de Velde presided over a formal ceremony to install them in the parish. They described their new home as a "modest frame cottage" in which the one main room functioned as classroom, dining room, and kitchen. The sisters began their ministry in two different schools, one in Bay St. Louis and the other in Waveland, a spot about four miles away.[22] By April, 1855, the sisters decided they needed to

The Frame Cottage in Bay St. Louis

---

19 Mother Eulalie had entered the Sisters of St. Joseph at St. Etienne and made her novitiate under Mother St. John Fontbonne. She began her ministry in Brou before the Congregation separated from Lyon.
20 The French Ursulines had arrived in New Orleans in 1727. They were the first women religious in what became U.S. territory. The famous Ursuline Convent in the New Orleans French Quarter was the home of those Ursuline sisters until 1823. They moved out of that convent for a more secluded spot and the bishop took over their building in the heart of the city. The Sisters of St. Joseph who arrived in 1836, 1837, and 1854 would have been received at the Ursuline's second home, a convent no longer in existence.
21 "Happenings," letter entry dated 1/5/55.
22 In 1890, Waveland's first census counted a population of 328.

withdraw from the Waveland mission and by August, they had about 50 students at Bay St. Louis where sewing classes augmented the regular curriculum and the sisters' income. They had also accepted their first five boarding students.

Adjustment to their far-away mission cost the sisters more than they could have imagined. Mother Eulalie had expressed brave hopes when she volunteered, telling Mother Claude "In spite of my age, I still have the strength needed to make the voyage...God has granted me the courage."[23] If the idea of the journey to America seemed daunting but surmountable, the sisters had no idea of the challenges life in Mississippi would bring. They discovered varieties and quantities of bugs they had never imagined. The heat made wearing the habit a daily penance. Then there were the children, most of them absolutely unfamiliar with the concept of regular class attendance. The food available to the missionaries was very different from what they were used to and the boarding students found the sister cook's offerings just as unpalatable as the American cuisine was to the French sisters. Mother Eulalie wrote to Mother Claude about the challenges:

> Cholera epidemic...Yellow fever every year during three months of summer...From October to May we have no meat. Must live on salt pork. During winter, no milk; in summer, milk in two coffee cups for ten cents...
>
> This country certainly inherited some of the plagues of Egypt. Constantly we are harassed by flying insects...a little martyrdom...[24]

Father Buteux had not prepared them for what would later be labeled as culture shock. Like other missionaries of the era, they had no way to imagine how much they would have to adapt and accept as they replanted themselves in American soil. Within a year, Father Buteux understood that they were facing serious problems. In August, 1855, he wrote to Bishop Chalandon in Belley explaining the difficulties of culture, language and age and the effects they had on the sisters' ministry.

> The classes are suffering. Certain American customs which the Brothers felt they should adopt...are not acceptable to Mother Eulalie...she opposes them...

---

23 *Bourg*, 84.
24 "Happenings," dated 7/15/1855. Mother Eulalie was apparently anticipating the meatless winter as the sisters had not yet been in the country for a full year.

I know too well that she is aged, too aged to adjust...to the customs of the country, to the strange and rude manners of many of the country people.[25]

Father Buteux confided in Mother Claude at Bourg as a friend. He wrote to her, acknowledging encouragement she had given him and letting her know that they needed her help in the form of additional personnel as well as her prayers:

Two expressions in your letter comforted me very much...In truth, you say, 'the devil is very jealous and very furious against our work"... he does all he can to harm it. I hope our Sisters will not become discouraged...that they will be all the more fervent..."
We feel the necessity of sending other Sisters. Help us with your fervent prayers...I know Mother's health is poor....she is too aged to adapt to a new life...This can be remedied by giving her an Assistant who would be well instructed in reference to this country.[26]

From Father Buteux's letter we can see that Mother Claude knew that generous hopes were not enough to equip a missionary for a new culture. Refusing to be too alarmed by the problems of the mission, she assumed that every good work would encounter resistance. But she also realized that the sister superior was unable to make the necessary adaptations. Shortly after receiving that letter, Mother Claude received the news that Sister Gonzague had requested a dispensation from her vows.[27] Faced with what could have easily been sufficient reason to bring her sisters home, Mother Claude decided to send additional sisters to the mission.

As superior, Mother Eulalie struggled but wanted to continue the mission. She too expressed the need for additional sisters. In October, 1855, she wrote to Mother Claude, thanking her for a promise of help and insisting that she needed the new sisters as soon as possible. Having spent nearly a year in the U.S., she could now explain the needs and the hardships of the mission.

I was very happy that you informed me that you wanted to keep this establishment...I would not want to abandon it either, even though we

---

25 "Happenings," under dates of 8/18 and 8/20, 1855.
26 "Happenings," dated 8/20/1855.
27 "Happenings," has differing explanations of Sister Gonzague's decision under the dates of 8/18/1855, 9/25/1855 and a "Note" referring to July of 1855

are experiencing very great trials…We find ourselves here, two unhappy persons in a land half wild, with a handful of children, half of whom are black, and who can learn nothing. The announcement that you were sending two sisters gave me much pleasure, but it did not satisfy me for two reasons. First you are delaying too long in sending them… Moreover, you want to send only two…

My good Mother, is it possible to send the Sisters immediately… we have need for them, but the most pressing reason is that during the summer there is fever in New Orleans…which is terrible for foreigners. This year 13 Religious died in one house alone. Two of the priests who came from France in the beginning of the summer also died, as did our bishop of Natchez.[28]

While Mother Eulalie's description of trials and disease might not have seemed the greatest inducement to send additional sisters, the annals for May, 1856, indicated that her hopes for additional sisters were fulfilled, even if they arrived in the summer:

Three more sisters arrive from France: reach Bay St. Louis July 16, 1856: Sister Esperance Granger, named Superior to replace Mother Eulalie who is ill. Sister Esdras and Sister Isidore Bouvier (lay sister) accompanied Mother Esperance.[29]

Mother Esperance quickly assessed the situation and, trusting that Bourg would continue to send missionaries, she wrote to Mother Claude saying:

This country needs solid vocations with happy, strong and generous dispositions to be able to bear the pains and deprivations we have to endure…It is a life of sacrifice. The sisters destined to share our mission must be well-informed, completely convinced so that they will not regret having embraced it.

---

28 "Happenings," dated 10/21/1855. Bishop Van de Velde died of Yellow Fever in November, 1855, just 23 months after he became Bishop of Natchez. He was succeeded by Bishop William Henry Elder, who remained in the diocese from 1857 until 1880 when he became Archbishop of Cincinnati where he would continue in relationship with the Sisters of St. Joseph of Bourg.
29 "Happenings," Chronological List of Events 1856.

Then, having described the special qualities of spirit necessary in future members of the community in the U.S., she went on to explain the community's immediate practical needs:

> The choir Sister will be for the classroom, and especially for handicraft. She should provide herself with patterns of designs, supplies of flowers, etc. …Probably the lay Sister would be put in charge of a small class of black children…She will have charge of the kitchen, of the bread, of the garden, and going to market. If there are no boarders, it is because of the food we would not give according to the exigencies of the locality… If there are boarders, a lay Sister will not be able to care for little black children, therefore another choir Sister will be necessary…[30]

In December, 1856, a few months after the arrival of the new missionaries, Mother Eulalie left Bay St. Louis and opened a home for the Aged Infirm and Orphans in New Orleans, the sisters' first mission in the city that would be the home of their first province in the United States.

Opening the New Orleans mission left only two sisters in Bay St. Louis. Bishop Elder, the newly named Bishop of Natchez, saw that as a mistake and let Mother Claude know exactly what he thought. He wrote:

> I have just begun my pastoral visitation. Bay St. Louis was my starting point. There I experienced a great mixture of pain and of edification: pain at finding in that institution only two Sisters operating a school whose income was not even sufficient to pay their upkeep, and edification on seeing the courage, the resignation and the joyfulness of these two heroic women.

After expressing his admiration and concerns, the Bishop went on to ask for more help.

> I am writing you today to thank you and your community for all this good which your sisters have done for the faith in this country, and to beg you to send them two or three more Sisters so that they might be

---

30 "Happenings," dated 12/6/1856.

able to establish themselves more solidly and spread the good they are doing now.[31]

Bourg accepted the requests sent by the sisters, Bishop Elder and Father Buteux. The Congregation's willingness to send missionaries was undoubtedly buttressed by the fact that they had 110 postulants in 1855. Such an abundance of personnel would all but compel them to share, especially with their own sisters serving the foreign missions in their name.[32]

THE SISTERS AND THE CIVIL WAR

The American Civil War began on April 12, 1861. The Union forces captured New Orleans on April 29, 1862, not only cutting off the sisters' communications with France, but making interaction between the sisters in New Orleans and Bay St. Louis difficult and dangerous.[33] Food became scarce. Sister Stephanie Niogret described the situation in her memoir:

> The Civil War destroyed the greatest hopes. The panic was such that in a moment everything that could be of use to the enemy was destroyed: sugar, coffee, rice, etc., were thrown into the river…
>
> The Sisters in New Orleans were never without bread, which is almost unbelievable. This is the explanation. A baker…would serve Sister Isadore first…and he had her enter from the rear so that no one would see her.[34]

The annals explain that in Bay St. Louis,

> Mother Esperance rowed boat alone at night to enemy fort (Fort Pike), begged for food for Sisters and boarders. Request generously accepted,

---

31 "Happenings," dated September 13, 1857.
32 "Happenings," dated 12/15/1855
33 The states of South Carolina, Mississippi, Florida, Alabama, Georgia, Louisiana and Texas declared themselves the Confederate States of America on February 4, 1861, a month before Abraham Lincoln took office as President. They were joined later by Virginia, Kentucky, Arkansas, Tennessee and North Carolina. Fifty counties in the western part of Virginia declared themselves an independent state and were admitted to the Union in June, 1863, as the State of West Virginia.
34 "Histories – The Establishment of the Congregation 1854 – 1892 in the United States (America) & Powers of the Visitatrix" by Sr. Louise Stephanie Niogret," (Archives CSJoseph). Sister Stephanie arrived in New Orleans from Bourg on December 21, 1865.

soldiers rowed her back home. They invited her to return when again in need of food.[35]

The French sisters recorded very little about their impressions of the issues underlying the War. During Reconstruction, Sister Stephanie commented that the emancipation of the slaves had contributed to the ruin of the country and made rebuilding impossible because there were no more laborers.[36] At the same time, the sisters were teaching children of European, African and Native American heritage with no apparent distinction among them beyond the segregation demanded by law.[37] The sisters' status as foreigners left them highly vulnerable to censure should they be outspoken about slavery or related issues.

Race riot in New Orleans, 1866

The Civil War and its aftermath must have been both frightening and confusing to the French sisters. They had known class distinctions in France, but those had nothing to do with the concept of "race." New Orleans did not suffer the violent destruction of other defeated southern cities; it had been taken by the Union in April, 1862 without a battle in the city itself. Nevertheless, military occupation brought odious martial law. Then, little more than a year after the close of the war, a race riot in New Orleans left 44 Black protesters dead and hundreds wounded from an outburst that manifested the racial tension permeating a city where half the white men were veterans of the Confederacy and half the Black men had served the Union Army.[38]

While there was nothing the sisters could do about legally established racial segregation, they had been teaching black children from their earliest

---

35 "Happenings," under 1861, Chronological List of Events...Bay St. Louis.
36 "Histories."
37 The sisters taught the children of black, white and Native American families in free, but separate schools.
38 See Caryn Bell, Revolution, Romanticism, and the Afro-Creole Protest Culture in Louisiana, 1718-1868, (Baton Rouge: LSU Press) Picture: Theodore R. Davis, engraving: Public Domain, https://commons.wikimedia.org/w/index.php?curid=3474480.

days in Bay St. Louis. In 1868, the community opened a school and accepted the administration of an orphanage in Baton Rouge, 80 miles northwest of New Orleans.[39] The sisters at that mission also taught black and white girls and boys in free schools. A history of the Catholic Church in Baton Rouge tells the story of the community's involvement with the school for black children saying:

> It was...Mother Albina Thollot, to whom the Catholics of Baton Rouge owe so much that we must trace the beginning of the school for colored children in our city. It was Mother Albina...who bought the house and two lots on Florida Street and thither Sister Antonia Orgen went every morning, teaching the little band that had gathered at the call of Mother Albina.[40]

The community annals note that after they left that school, the Sisters of St. Joseph were contracted to teach African American boys in the public school in Bay St. Louis, an opportunity the Brothers of the Sacred Heart had declined.[41]

By 1872, continuing the tradition of their French sisters in Lyon, the sisters in Baton Rouge began ministering to people in prison. Sister Eugenia Veglia described the conditions in the prison near the convent:

> The prisoners were huddled together in dark, dingy cells, like cattle. Fresh air and sunshine were unknown...Cruel and brutal treatment was added to their lot as was also the insufficiency of wholesome food. The Sisters, not limiting their devotedness strictly to spiritual things, soon won the hearts of these unfortunate men by bettering their material conditions. Pardon for minor offenses and shortened terms for major crimes were obtained by the Sisters...All the persons for whom they hadobtained any pardon later lived exemplary lives and died holy

---

39 In 1895, the orphanage was turned over to the Sisters of the Holy Family, the second religious U.S. congregation of African American women religious. The congregation was founded in New Orleans in 1837 and officially established in 1842. The foundresses, Venerable Henriette DeLille, Juliette Gaudin and Josephine Charles, received help in religious formation from the Religious of the Sacred Heart and financial help from Marie Jeanne Aliquot, a Frenchwoman who, as a white woman, could not legally join a congregation of women of color. The sisters' main ministries started as education and care for orphans. There is lore that the Sisters of the Blessed Sacrament first adopted a habit copied from that of the Sisters of St. Joseph, but changed their habit, lest the communities be mistaken for one another.

40 "Happenings," under "Chronological list of Events," 1895.

41 "Happenings," under "Chronological List of Events" 1889.

deaths... many a Catholic prisoner went to the gallows after having made his peace with God.[42]

That ministry would continue as a hallmark of the community's contribution to forming the conscience of both prisoners and society at large.

THE STRUGGLES OF BEING A FRENCH COMMUNITY
IN THE UNITED STATES

The fact that Bourg continued to send sisters to America was the best indication of the congregation's commitment to their U.S. mission, a venture they seemed to envision as an outpost of the French Congregation. During the early years, the superiors assumed that aspirants would make their novitiate in France, but the sisters in America quickly saw problems with that policy. Twenty terse words in the community annals summarized the problem of old world formation in a new setting:

Irish novice presented herself. Required to say prayers in French, of which she understood not a single word. Novice left.[43]

Travel restrictions during the Civil War forced an end to the requirement that sisters go to France for formation. In 1863, Bishop Odin of New Orleans obtained Mother Claude's approval to open a novitiate in New Orleans. Sister Stephanie Niogret explained the new arrangement and described Louise Gauthreaux, the first candidate received in the novitiate in New Orleans.

Mother Eulalie was appointed Superior of the Novitiate with the title of Provincial. From now on, we may receive native subjects, which was absolutely necessary because of the English language...The first postulant who presented herself was almost completely blind. She was received because she could teach music...she renders us great service, not only for music and singing, but also and especially so for formation of subjects and the preservation of religious spirit. [44]

---

42 Sister Eugenie Veglia, "The Sisters of St. Joseph in Louisiana" a thesis submitted to Loyola University of the South, 1936, updated in 1990. Cited by S. Jane Aucoin, CSJ in "Sisters of St. Joseph of Médaille, Prison Ministry." (Archives CSJoseph)
43 "Happenings," under the date 8/6/1855.
44 "Histories."

Miss Louise Gauthreaux entered the congregation on January 1, 1862. She received the habit on May 16, 1863 and was given the name Sister Philoméne.[45] The majority of the women to enter the community in the early years had French surnames: Sisters Agnes Couevas, Clotilde Duvernbet, Teresia Delair, and Estelle Astier, but the reception of Sisters Marie Joseph Summer and Anne Finlay demonstrates that women from other ethnic backgrounds did enter, although they could expect to remain the minority.[46] Even with local vocations and additional sisters from France, the community struggled to respond to growing needs, a situation made worse by the loss of many young sisters to yellow fever.[47]

The three missions in Bay St. Louis, New Orleans and Baton Rouge became stable in spite of the sisters' constant struggles with material poverty and the unavoidable impoverishment of speaking in a foreign language and adapting to the cultural differences.[48] In the early years both Father Buteux and Bishop Blanc communicated with Bourg about difficulties in the community.

In 1858, Bishop Blanc wrote to Reverend Mother Claude in Bourg saying:

> Recently I made a visit to our good Sisters at the asylum for widows. I found them in good health and busy beyond what they should be…they make up for their small number by doubling in devotedness…However it is evidently too much for three sisters…
>
> In the supposition (and it is only a supposition) that you foresee that the impossibility of coming to their assistance will be prolonged for a long time, they begged me, my Reverend Mother, to ask if you…would

---

45 "Happenings," in "Chronological List of Events" 1862. Later dated 5/5/1866 is the notice that Sister Philoméne pronounced final vows in 1866 and that three novices received the habit and one sister made first vows. Dated 11/12/66, "Happenings" mentions that Sr. Philoméne asked the Reverend Mother for prayers for the restoration of her sight, "She believes that all the Novitiate united will do violence to Heaven." No miracle is recorded.

46 "Histories," Sister Marie Joseph's name is variously spelled Sommer or Summer.

47 Of the first 18 Sisters of St. Joseph of Bourg to die in the United States, only three were more than 35 years old. "Happenings," lists the ages of sisters who died between 1860 and 1886 as 24, 43, 68, 33, 29, 42, 24, 22, 21, 21, 19, 26, 50, 34, 24, 30, 35, 46, and 25. Mother Eulalie, who died in 1865, was the oldest. She died after serving 11 years in the U.S.

48 The letters quoted in "Happenings," mince no words in describing the difficulties the sisters faced, giving us more of an idea than anything communicated by the Carondelet sisters about just how difficult it was for well-educated and prepared French sisters to adjust to the poor living conditions in frontier areas of the United States. Also, as at Carondelet in the early days, intra-community problems compounded the sisters' struggles. If Sister Delphine Fontbonne's young age may have led her to a rigid dependence on the rule, the fact that Mother Eulalie was 56 when she left France seemingly made it harder for her to be flexible in relation to both the new culture and the younger sisters.

approve that, solely for the good of the work entrusted to them, they would take steps to know if they could be affiliated to the Congregation of St. Joseph of Lyons whose Mother House for this country is at or near St. Louis…

Perhaps I should have drawn your attention to the fact that in the Diocese of Natchez where your two Sisters of Bay St. Louis are, there is a community of Sisters of St. Joseph of Lyons, coming from St. Louis.[49]

Father Buteux wrote a similar letter, mentioning the possibility of joining with the St. Louis sisters and adding that sending additional sisters from Bourg would do a great deal to alleviate the problems they saw. Bourg continued to send sisters to the U.S. missions, but even so, cultural tensions continued and the question of separating from France never fully disappeared. The superiors from Bourg did not make an official visitation of the communities in America until 1876, twenty-one years after the first sisters had arrived. At that time, Mother Esperance Granger, the Provincial Superior in Bourg who had been superior at Bay St. Louis from 1856-1869 came on behalf of the General Council. Even though the sisters in America had hoped that Sister Coeur de Marie Chavant, the Superior General, would make the trip, the sisters expressed their appreciation for the visit. The community continued to grow, opening and closing missions in much the same pattern as Sisters of St. Joseph in other parts of the country.

NEW VENTURES: CINCINNATI AND SACRED HEART HOME

The Sisters of St. Joseph of Bourg had concentrated their U.S. ministries in the areas of Bay St. Louis, New Orleans and Baton Rouge until the 1890s brought an immense change that began in a deceivingly unanticipated way. In 1892, Reverend Mother Eugenie de Jesus, the Superior General in Bourg, asked Mother Louise Stephanie, the superior in New Orleans, and Mother Albina from Baton Rouge to come to France. While the two sisters were at the motherhouse, Mother Stephanie was appointed as superior of a community in France. Mother Albina was to return to the United States with a novice as a companion.

---

49 Letter from Bishop Blanc to Mother Claude, February 12, 1858, cited by Sr. Jane Aucoin in "Government Structures and the Question of Separation from France." (Archives, CSJoseph) From 1855 to 1861, the Carondelet community had a school in Sulphur Springs (now Camden) Mississippi. It is also notable in this context that by 1858, the Carondelet sisters had been in the U.S. for 21 years without additional personnel from Lyon and were in the early stages of planning to become a U.S. congregation, a fact that was no secret among them.

Mother Albina, already noted for her initiative in both education and prison ministry, made her return trip via a land route rather than sailing directly to New Orleans. From the East Coast she and her young sister companion traveled by land as far as Cincinnati from where they could continue to New Orleans via riverboats. When they needed a place to stay in Cincinnati, Mother Albina was somehow led to Sacred Heart Home, a residence for working women. Sacred Heart Home had been established around 1882 by Miss Margaret McCabe as a response to the problems young working women confronted when they were alone in the city. In the 1890s, women's major sources of income-producing employment were domestic service and factory work. Although work in a private home purported to provide a safe environment, steady wages and no expenses for room and board, factory jobs generally brought many times more applicants than could be hired while domestic workers were

Shoe Factory Workers

not always easy to find.[50] Depending on their experience and skill, working women would earn as little as forty cents a day as machine hands or as much as $2.06 per day as supervisors in clothing and glove manufacture; women always earned less than men doing similar work.[51] The working girl who found a boarding house with a good name could safeguard her reputation as well as have access to room and board and companionship. Seeing working women's needs as a vocational call, Margaret McCabe and two companions, Miss Madden and Miss Cooney, formed the "Sacred Heart Home for Working Girls." The three women offered a safe place for single working women and their apostolate proved so attractive that they soon had 14 co-workers. These women, pioneers of lay ecclesial movements, cultivated a deep religious spirit and took a private vow of chastity. Their work came to the attention of Archbishop

---

50 See Claudia Goldin "The Work and Wages of Single Women, 1870-1920" (*The Journal of Economic History*, Vol. 40, #1) http://nrs.harvard.edu/urn-3:HUL.InstRepos:2643864. Picture is from the Library of Congress, http://www.loc.gov/pictures/item/2006681286/, "No known restrictions on publication." http://www1.assumption.edu/ahc/1920s/modern%20woman/Sadiedefault.html
51 See "Sister Carrie and Women Wage Earners in The 1890s," http://www.incontext.indiana.edu/2006/may/5.asp.

Elder who had come to Cincinnati in 1880 after 23 years as bishop of
Natchez.[52] The archbishop was not interested in seeing the women of Sacred Heart
form a new religious congregation but encouraged the women who felt they had a
vocation to consider joining an existing community. Unfortunately, no community
in the area was open to the ministry these women saw as their special apostolate.

 Given Bishop Elder's previous connections with the Sisters of St. Joseph,
it seems plausible that Mother Albina's meeting the women at Sacred Heart in
Cincinnati had more to do with Archbishop Elder than with simple chance. While
staying at Sacred Heart, Mother Albina spoke with the community and let them
know that the Sisters of St. Joseph were involved in ministries similar to theirs. They
in turn were encouraged by the idea that the Sisters of St. Joseph could be open
to them and their apostolate. After consultations
with the superiors in New Orleans and France and
communications between the bishops, the Sisters
of St. Joseph of Bourg agreed to receive members of
the Sacred Heart community into the congregation
and to support their ministry.[53] In April, 1893,
Archbishop Elder presided over the ceremony in
which nine members of the "Association for the
Guidance of Youth," the formal name of the lay
association founded by Margaret McCabe, were
welcomed as postulants in the Congregation of the
Sisters of St. Joseph of Bourg. A postulant director
and three additional sisters came to Cincinnati
from New Orleans so that the women would not
have to abandon their apostolate as they began
their religious formation.[54]

Sacred Heart Home

---

52 William H. Elder (1819-1904) had succeeded Bishop Van de Velde as Bishop of Natchez in 1857, and was
named Archbishop of Cincinnati in 1880. He also had a cousin who was a Sister of St. Joseph in New Orleans.
Mother Albina was missioned in Bay St. Louis in 1861. (See Happenings, 1861, Letter from Mother Esperance
to Mother Assistant 4/23/1861.)
53 Unless otherwise noted, the information about the founding in Cincinnati is based on Sister Mary Colette
Baumgartner, SSJ, "History of the Sisters of St. Joseph in Cincinnati From 1892 to 1946," (Thesis submitted to
the Faculty of the Teachers College of the Athenaeum of Ohio, 1947). Archives CSJoseph.
54 "Happenings," under the title "Cincinnati, Ohio, April 1893."

The New Orleans sisters gradually took over the work of the home which came to be known as Fontbonne Home.

Miss Margaret McCabe, who did not become a Sister of St. Joseph, transferred the Sacred Heart Home and its $26,543 mortgage to the Sisters of St. Joseph and went on to establish The Fenwick Club, a home for newsboys and bootblacks. Within a few months, the sisters in Cincinnati purchased additional property. Beginning with a nine-room house and a few cottages, they opened "Cedar Point," a vacation spot and farm about 20 miles from downtown Cincinnati, reachable by a horse and buggy.[55] In 1893, the same year as the sisters purchased Cedar Point, the diocese opened Guardian Angels Parish in Mt. Washington, a few blocks from the sisters' new convent. In 1895, Guardian Angels, a parish of about forty rural families, opened a two room school where two sisters taught thirty-nine pupils. In an amazingly short period of time the Sisters of St. Joseph of Bourg had established themselves firmly in Cincinnati, a city 800 miles north of New Orleans and culturally almost as different from the South as both were from France.[56]

On February 15, 1895, the community lost its first member from the Cincinnati area, Sister St. Sebastian Madden, a 60 year old novice, one of the women who had entered the congregation from the Sacred Heart Home community.[57] By 1902, Sacred Heart Home was serving 60 women. In that same year the congregation received papal permission to establish a novitiate at Mt. Washington-Cincinnati.[58]

STRUCTURING AN INTERNATIONAL COMMUNITY
MIDST TROUBLES IN FRANCE

When Bourg first sent sisters to the United States, the congregation had not completed its process of securing Vatican approval for their *Constitutions*. They were a diocesan community with an international mission; the lines of authority

---

55 "Happenings," under the heading "Mt. Washington, April, 1894."

56 In 1890, Cincinnati had a population of nearly 297,000, making it one of the 10 most populous cities in the country. Its immigrant population was largely German and, before the Civil War, it had been an important stop on the Underground Railroad. The Diocese of Cincinnati was erected in 1821, and it became an Archdiocese in 1868. Archbishop Elder's appointment to Cincinnati could be interpreted as another of the providential happenstances that have marked CSSJ history. If Mother Albina had visited Cincinnati one year later, Archbishop Henry Moeller, a native Cincinnatian with no ties to the Sisters of St. Joseph would have been the local archbishop and it seems highly unlikely that the Sisters of St. Joseph of Bourg would have met Miss McCabe or taken on her apostolate.

57 "Happenings," under the headings "Mt. Washington 8/20/1893" and "Chronological List of Events, 1895."

58 The Sisters of St. Joseph would continue to use that home until 2017.

were not clearly articulated, leaving some uncertainty about the relationship among local superiors in America. When the community opened a novitiate in New Orleans in 1863, Mother Eulalie was referred to as the "provincial," even though the Bourg Congregation had no official provinces.[59] In 1895, the sisters in the U.S. lobbied for official recognition as the Province of New Orleans, but at that point the Congregation was in the process of obtaining approval for revised *Constitutions* and the timing seemed inauspicious. In 1901, the Congregation of the Sisters of St. Joseph of Bourg received a decree of approbation as an Institute and temporary approbation of the *Constitutions*.[60] In 1902, Mother St. Rose Thiberville was appointed as "Resident Visitatrix," for the sisters in the U.S. She was effectively a provincial superior although the congregation had not officially established provinces. Part of the difficulty in obtaining provincial status for the sisters in the U.S. was that the Vatican would not approve the establishment of a province in America if there were no provinces in France, and establishing French provinces would have required changes to the Congregation's civil status at a time when dealings with the government were extremely delicate.[61] The Sisters of St. Joseph of Bourg realized that regularizing the canonical/legal status of the Congregation had become extraordinarily important because of the French government's ongoing process of secularization and separation of church and state. Official status as an international congregation of papal right would provide safeguards against greater control by French authorities.

The French sisters in Louisiana followed the news of France's increasingly anti-Catholic laws with the unique anxiety that comes from being far from home; the French sisters on the American side of the ocean felt the pain of powerless solidarity with their distant, suffering homeland. The entries in the annals for the years from 1866 to 1914 are sprinkled with references to the losses the Congregation was experiencing in France. The following excerpts illustrate some of what they knew if not how it made them feel.

---

59 In 1856, when Mother Eulalie opened the home for the aged in New Orleans, she assumed that she would continue in her role as superior for all the sisters, telling Sister Esperance, the superior in Bay St. Louis, to send her additional help. (See Sr. Jane Aucoin, "Government Structures" citing Mother Esperance to Mother Claude, December 6, 1856.)
60 "Happenings," under the heading "Chronological List of Events 1901." In connection with the approval, "Happenings," mentioned that Rome stipulated that the novitiate had to be at least one full year entirely consecrated to religious formation.
61 "Happenings," under the heading "Chronological List of Events 1902." See also Sr. Jane Aucoin, "Ministry and Governance: The Little –Known Chapter of the Bourg CSJ Story in America, 1855-1977." (Archives CSJoseph)

* 1866: Trouble in France: French law stated that in all public schools, education would be exclusively confided to lay teachers...a period of adjustment was to be allowed;
* 1870-71: Franco-Prussian War: Bourg convent became a field hospital. More than 300 soldiers lodged in the novitiate during the excessively rigorous winter... cared for by the sisters;
* 1877: School secularized: Fifty (public) schools where the Sisters taught were secularized...Sisters opened a private school in almost every district where they had been dismissed;
* 1880: Fiscal laws placed taxes on revenues and extant assessments;
* 1881: Gratuitous education mandatory;
* 1881: Law of June 16: all teachers must be certified by the state and have a "brevet;"
* 1883: Education restricted to lay teachers;
* 1884-1885: Mental institutes secularized;
* 1885: Before the end of Mother Coeur de Marie Chavant's term, 72 institutes where the sisters had taught were secularized, 37 private schools had been opened;
* 1889: The boarding school property at Boulonge-sur-Seine was seized. The Sisters had refused to pay "Subscribers' Tax" because they saw it as unjust;
* 1889: Boarding school sold by the Government;
* 1890: Tax [levied] on all movable and immovable property owned by the Congregation, Subscribers' Tax to be paid in arrears from 1885;
* 1901: The Law of Associations (Restrictions on religious communities because they were governed by foreign powers)
* 1902: The beginning of the suppression of the schools
* 1904: Law of July 7: Religious orders and Congregations forbidden to teach in France.[62]

The French Law of July 7, 1904 seemed to toll the death knell for the ministries of women religious. Only by leaving their congregations in a way verifiable by the government could sisters continue to teach. As though participating in a domestic exile, the sisters came home to Bourg.

---

62 These measures are mentioned in "Happenings," in entries referring to 1866 to 1904. One might note that the government "allowed" the sisters to open their motherhouse as a hospital for wounded soldiers, but later secularized health care.

One by one the teaching establishments were closed, and all the Sisters arrived at the motherhouse. The first ones occupied the free rooms; the next set up living quarters in empty classrooms; finally, Sisters crowded together into corridors, their luggage heaped near the stairways... What would become of so many Sisters torn from an apostolate?
...The difficulty was not that of doing one's duty, but rather of knowing in what that duty consisted...Should one consent to secularization in order to save the schools? Or must one sacrifice the works of zeal in order to secure the perseverance of religious?[63]

Rejecting a forced choice between living as religious and carrying on ministry, Mother Marie Angele sought other settings in which the sisters could live out their charism.[64] In the early 1900s, France's anti-clerical laws impelled the Sisters of St. Joseph of Bourg to open missions in Belgium, England, the Austrian Tyrol and Italy. These were in addition to the extraordinary group of fifty sisters who arrived in America on June 2, 1903, calling themselves refugees from the persecution of the anti-clerical laws. The community annals explain that these sisters arrived in New Orleans to learn English after which some would remain in the South while others would open the houses of the "Northern Province."[65]

MISSION TO MINNESOTA - CROOKSTON

The Catholic Church in the United States, as in other places throughout Europe, India, Latin America and Africa, derived immense benefit from the exodus of priests and religious from France. Among the priests who emigrated from France in the 19th century and became bishops who worked with Sisters of St. Joseph in the U.S. and Canada we can count Bishop Cretin of St. Paul; Miège of Kansas; Charbonnel of Toronto; Verot of St. Augustine; Blanc, Odin, Perché, Leray and Chapelle of New Orleans; Salpointe of Arizona and Machebeuf of Colorado.

---

63 *Bourg*, 133. The sources do not indicate how many sisters were affected by the laws, but in 1866, when the late-19th century troubles began in earnest, the Congregation had been in existence for 42 years and numbered 1,600 sisters who were missioned in 256 local communities. ("Happenings," Under the title "France, Trouble in France 10/3/1866.")

64 Mother Marie Angele Morgera had become Superior General in 1897, she followed Mother Eugenie de Jesus Pelletier (1888-1897), Mother Coeur de Marie Chavant, (1869-1888), Mother Placide Megard (1843-1865), Mother Claude Monnet (1843-1865) and the foundress, Mother St. Benoit Cornillon (1823-1843).

65 "Happenings," dated June 2, 1903. The entry includes the list of sisters by name. Of the fifty sisters named, one was designated as a lay sister and two as superiors. Other details in the list include the years in which 11 of them returned or were recalled to France and the detail that a few of them studied English in Buffalo.

French missionaries could find fellow expatriates throughout nearly the entire territory of the United States with concentration in areas of strong French migration.[66]

At the same time as the Bourg Congregation sought ministry sites outside France, Father Joseph Barras, the pastor of St. Rose of Lima Parish in Argyle, Minnesota, was looking for sisters to staff his school. In 1903, the town of Argyle situated near the Canadian border, had fewer than 1,000 inhabitants. The resident Catholics, primarily French Canadian immigrants, had begun settling the area in the 1870s. Their first visiting priests had to travel by canoe to reach the town.[67] When St. Rose of Lima Parish was founded in 1879, Argyle was under the ecclesial jurisdiction of Bishop Rupert Seidenbusch, O.S.B., of the Vicariate Apostolic of Northern Minnesota.[68] In 1889, the area came under the jurisdiction of Bishop James McGolrick in the newly established Diocese of Duluth and in 1908 Rome created the Diocese of Crookston which included Argyle.[69]

The people of St. Rose of Lima Parish had wanted a school since at least 1894. Although they laid out plans for the Catholic school on the parish property, their follow-through was less ambitious than their hopes. The people took so little care of the parish that when Bishop McGolrick visited the town in 1894, he left strict orders that the people construct a decent residence for the pastor. When nothing happened Bishop McGolrick wrote to the parish leaders in September, 1894, giving them one month to rectify the situation:

I cannot and will not leave the priest in such a den as he now lives in. It is a matter of justice...Many places are crying out loudly for a priest and

---

66 The first major French-Canadian migration happened between 1755 and 1764 when the British expelled the "Acadian" (Cajun) people from the provinces of Nova Scotia, New Brunswick, and Prince Edward Island. Those migrants tended to create settlements around Maine, in Fall River, Holyoke and Lowell Massachusetts, as well as in New Hampshire, Rhode Island, Vermont, northern New York, Illinois, Kansas and Louisiana. Some of them migrated while territories in Michigan and Minnesota were still part of New France, others returned to France before migrating again to Louisiana. The Sisters of St. Joseph have served these populations particularly in the states of Louisiana and Maine and in cities and towns such as Concordia, Cahokia, Ste. Genevieve, Boston and Fall River.
67 Argyle is about 130 miles from Winnipeg, Manitoba and 370 miles from St. Paul.
68 Bishop Seidenbusch was a German-born missionary, a member of a Benedictine community Bishop Cretin invited to Minnesota. In 1866, he was elected the first abbot of St. John's Abbey and in 1875, he was named Bishop of the Vicariate Apostolic of Northern Minnesota which evolved into the Diocese of St. Cloud, the name of which is derived from the 6th century French saint, Clodoald.
69 Bishop McGolrick was Irish-born, studied for the priesthood at All Hallows Seminary in Ireland and was ordained in 1867 by Bishop Grace of St. Paul. He was named as first bishop of Duluth in 1889.

promise to build a house for the priest I send...I will remove the priest early in October if the suggestions made are not carried out."[70]

The bishop's letter moved the people to action and they built a rectory, but their hopes for a school would be deferred for at least another five years.

When Father Joseph Barras was named pastor of St. Rose of Lima Parish he instigated the building of a school and convent. He brought in the Sisters of St. Benedict from Duluth in 1900, but the poverty of the area and "other circumstances" caused the sisters to withdraw. Father Barras heard somehow that the Sisters of St. Joseph of Bourg had sisters in need of places for mission and he began correspondence with the Superior General, Mother Marie Angele. She agreed to send sisters and in August, 1903, Father Barras wrote to assure her of their welcome:

Argyle, August 17, 1903
Marshall County, Minnesota, U.S.
Very dear Mother,
I sent you a telegram telling you what had been worked out. Glory to God! I know you were anxious concerning your sisters...
Sunday from the pulpit I announced the arrival of our Sisters. The people are in joy. Flags fly from the towers of the convent.
Hoping, most Reverend Mother, that God will continue to bless our efforts and that we will always be worthy of them,
I sign myself Yours,
Very humble in Our Lord Jesus Christ,
J. M. Barras, Priest-pastor[71]

Unfortunately, Father Barras had more enthusiasm than care of details. When the sisters wired a message that they were in America and were soon to arrive, he wired back saying:

Go no further.

---

70 Letter from Bishop McGolrick to Mr. Geo. Morin of St. Rose of Lima Parish, September 13, 1894, quoted in "St. Rose of Lima Church History" (http://www.myerchin.org/StRoseLimaHistory.html). Hereafter: St. Rose of Lima History.
71 Quoted in "St. Rose of Lima History"

Go to one of your houses until the Bishop of Duluth shall have seen your Constitutions and shall have accepted you.[72]

The French-speaking Sisters somehow managed to get themselves to Ohio, where they stayed with other members of their Congregation until Bishop McGolrick invited the superior of the group to meet him in Duluth. Bishop McGolrick, an Irishman by birth was delighted to discover that they were Sisters of St. Joseph. He had studied in the Diocese of Belley before being ordained for the Diocese of St. Paul and was familiar with both French and U.S. Sisters of St. Joseph and happy to welcome them into his diocese.

When the émigré sisters arrived in Argyle they found a situation quite different from what they had been led to expect. The pastor had neglected to mention that another community had tried to establish a school and had left before they had been there even a full year.[73] Also, his jubilant welcome of "All is ready!" hadn't implied that the convent was equipped. The sisters arrived to a house without bed or table because the pastor had naively assumed that the French sisters would bring their own furnishings. The sisters had to delay the school opening for a week while they resolved the problems of a nearly dry well and a house and classrooms with no heating system. The parish's financial straits were such that the sisters had hardly settled in when they were asked to buy the convent building, thereby relieving the parish of major financial concern for their sustenance. In spite of it all, the Sisters of St. Joseph remained determined to make a new start, both for themselves as refugees and for the parish. They renamed the school "St. Joseph's" and announced that they would need to charge tuition. They also advertised the offer of private music, art, painting, handiwork and French lessons, all of which would supplement their income.[74]

The rough start didn't dampen the sisters' hopes or aspirations. Given that they had more personnel than income-producing ministries, Mother Marie Jeanne, the superior, consulted with Bishop McGolrick about opening a second school. The sisters hoped to go to Duluth, a port city with a population of 50,000. The bishop recommended that they investigate Crookston, a city of a little more

---

72 Sr. Jane Aucoin, CSJ, "History of the Sisters of St. Joseph: Part IV." (Partial manuscript, Archives CSJoseph.)
73 Annabelle Raiche, CSJ and Ann Marie Biermaier, OSB, They Came To Teach (St. Cloud: North Star Press, 1994) (21) explain that although they were Minnesotans, the Benedictines from Duluth were unable to withstand the cold of their home in Argyle and that they didn't have consistent access to water. The townspeople said they were surprised that all the sisters had survived their time there.
74 "St. Rose of Lima History."

than 5,000 inhabitants about 40 miles south of Argyle that had no Catholic school.[75] The Sisters of St. Joseph went to Crookston in 1905, and quickly began to build the convent and school that would be known as St. Joseph's Academy. They would eventually enlarge the building so that it could serve as their northern provincial house. The rough start didn't dampen the sisters' hopes or aspirations. Given that they had more personnel than income-producing ministries, Mother Marie Jeanne, the superior, consulted with Bishop McGolrick about opening a second school. The sisters hoped to go to Duluth, a port city with a population of 50,000. The bishop recommended that they investigate Crookston, a city of a little more than 5,000 inhabitants about 40 miles south of Argyle that had no Catholic school.[75] The Sisters of St. Joseph went to Crookston in 1905, and quickly began to build the convent and school that would be known as St. Joseph's Academy. They would eventually enlarge the building so that it could serve as their northern provincial house.

For some time, there was an easy exchange between sisters in the north and south. In 1900, sisters from the north and south had jointly opened a school in Salix, Iowa, a town of fewer than 400 inhabitants in in the northwestern edge of the state. In 1907, the sisters decided that the Iowa mission was simply too far away from their other convents and they needed the sisters in New Orleans where they were opening additional schools.

In 1910, Crookston was made a diocese and Timothy J. Corbett of Duluth was named the first bishop.[76] By 1912, the diocese listed two institutions under the care of the Sisters of St. Joseph: St. Joseph Academy and Boarding School in Crookston which had 10 sisters and 180 pupils and Villa Rose Academy in Argyle which had 12 sisters and 110 pupils.[77]

---

75 Duluth was about 250 miles southeast of Argyle, a formidable distance that in 1905 would have been made reasonable by rail travel.

76 Bishop Corbett was consecrated on May 19, 1910 in a flamboyant and ostentatious display of Catholic pride when Bishop John Ireland arranged for the simultaneous consecration of six new bishops all of whom would be under his leadership in the ecclesiastical province of St. Paul. The ceremony included fifty members of the hierarchy, including the Apostolic Delegate and 600 priests. "An immense gathering of the laity witnessed the procession, but owing to the fact that the chapel had seating capacity for only the priests, the public were not admitted." The six newly consecrated bishops were James O'Reilly of Fargo; John Lawler, Auxiliary of St. Paul; Patrick Heffron of Winona; Timothy Corbett of Crookston; Vincent de Paul Wehrle of Bismarck; Joseph F. Busch of Lead, S. Dakota (later, Rapid City). See The Sacred Heart Review, (Boston) May 28, 1910, Vol. 43, No. 23.

77 The only other Sisters in the diocese were 26 Benedictines who had charge of hospitals in Crookston and Bemidji and schools on The Red Lake and White Earth reservations. The 38 sisters who ministered in 6 institutions barely outnumbered the 35 priests who served the 53 churches, 20 missions and 7 chapels located in the diocese.

In that same year, 1907, the community annals state "School opened at Superior, Wisconsin." No additional details are given. This is the first announcement of the foundation of the Sisters of St. Joseph of Superior. Founded from Cincinnati, the Superior group would eventually become an independent congregation.

OFFICIAL STRUCTURES IN FLUX

The Bourg congregation's 1902 General Chapter established the office of "Resident Visitatrix" for the houses in America. The chapter's description of the role said:

> The Resident Visitatrix is appointed for three years by the Superior General in her Council. She must speak French and English sufficiently well. She is assisted by…two Councilors, appointed by the Superior General, from a list of five names presented by the Visitatrix herself with the assistance of the local house where she resides….
>
> She has the right to visit, in the name of the Superior General, all our houses in the South of America and to take the expedient and urgent measures required by the situation; then she shall render an account to the General Council.[78]

That Chapter decision was not codified in the *Constitutions* of 1920 or 1939. It was not until 1948 that a Chapter established 5 provinces: Bourg, Paris, and Verdun in France and New Orleans and Crookston in the U.S. Cincinnati remained a part of New Orleans until the General Chapter of 1962 established it as an independent province. Although the Congregation had opened a novitiate in New Orleans in 1863, the Crookston sisters made their novitiate in France until after World War II. With the Cincinnati sisters attached to New Orleans and the Crookston sisters operating so separately from them, the Minnesota and New Orleans sisters knew very little of one another and the Crookston sisters maintained a stronger French affiliation than did the southerners, especially as U.S. born women became the majority in the community. As the structures evolved, local sisters developed a stronger identity as provinces than as a Congregation, especially in the United States. The majority of the sisters in France had very little understanding of the culture of the U.S. or of how culturally different Louisiana

---

78 Aucoin, "Ministry and Governance."

and Mississippi were from Cincinnati and Minnesota. The latter quarter of the 20th century and the early 21st would see an evolution in the sisters' identity as dramatic and profound as were the changes brought by Vatican II. No other U.S. Congregation of St. Joseph has experienced processes of change comparable to those of the communities founded from Bourg beginning in 1854.

LE PUY LOOKS TO AMERICA
POST-REVOLUTIONARY LE PUY

The story of the Sisters of St. Joseph of St. Augustine, Florida, has its roots in the community reconstituted in Le Puy following the French Revolution. During the Revolution, the Le Puy motherhouse had been commandeered and used as a barracks where soldiers used convent furnishings for firewood and kept animals in some of the buildings. On June 17, 1794, Sisters St. Julien Garnier and St. Alexis Aubert of the Le Puy community were executed by guillotine in the city's Martouret Square.[79] Many of the sisters in the area went into hiding and most communities of religious women were dispersed. The 1801 Concordat between Napoleon and Pope Pius VII restored most civil rights to the Catholic Church, but many communities failed to recover their lost properties. It was not until November 6, 1814, that Louis XVIII returned the devastated hospice of Rue Montferrand in Le Puy to "les Soeurs hospitalières de St. Joseph."[80] By mid-January, 1815, Sister Anne Marie Grand and companions had begun the restoration of the Sisters of St. Joseph of Le Puy.

In 1824, the bishop of Le Puy, Louis-Jacques-Maurice de Bonald, approved the *Constitutions* of the Sisters of St. Joseph of Le Puy. As Mother Anne-Marie Grand led the sisters through the process of reorganization required by law, sixty previously dispersed and new communities came together under the auspices of a motherhouse-generalate. The organization of various communities under one general superior not only met Napoleon's requirements but offered the advantages of a greater sharing of personnel resources and the opportunity to have a common novitiate making it easier to fulfill Father Médaille's injunction to make the best use of the unique gifts of each sister. Under that model, the convent of Montferrand received ecclesiastical and civil approval to function as a Motherhouse for Sisters

---

79 A few weeks later, more Sisters of St. Joseph, Sisters St. Croix Vincent, Madelieine Sénovert and Toussaint Dumoulin of Vernosc were executed at the orders of the tribunal of Privas. (Information from the Archives of the Sisters of St. Joseph of Saint Augustine, ASSJSA)
80 "An Historical-Juridical Report on the Institute from the Time of its Origins" (ASSJSA)

of St. Joseph of the area, uniting the sisters in one Congregation that served the neighbor in schools, parishes, orphanages and hospitals. The Sisters of St. Joseph became well known in Southeastern France as servants of the poor and friends of anyone in need.

By the 1860s, the Church in France had gone through multiple transitions during which religious life grew beyond its pre-revolutionary stature. The flourishing of the Church and religious life was both cause and effect of France's great missionary zeal. The political restrictions on members of religious communities led French missionaries to venture not only to America, but to Africa, Asia, and the Middle East – in reality, all over the globe. The Sisters of St. Joseph of Le Puy were part of that renaissance both in religious vocations and in missionary spirit.

BISHOP AUGUSTIN VEROT OF LE PUY IN ST. AUGUSTINE, FLORIDA

One of the most influential missionaries to leave France for America was Augustin Verot. Born in Le Puy in 1803, he studied in Paris where he joined the Sulpicians after ordination. At the age of 27 he went to Baltimore to teach at St. Mary's, the first seminary in the U.S.[81] In 1858, after 24 years of teaching and pastoral work, he was ordained a bishop and named Vicar Apostolic of the State of Florida. In 1861, he was also named as the third bishop of Savannah, Georgia. At the time of

SLAVERY AND CATHOLICISM IN THE U.S.

The position of the Catholic Church in the U.S. took on slavery was ambiguous at best. In spite of the fact that since 1462, the papacy had repeatedly criticized slavery and condemned the slave trade, the U.S. bishops did not take an unequivocal position against slavery before the end of the Civil War. Many bishops perceived the abolitionists as fanatics, closely tied to the virulently anti-Catholic Know-Nothings. The Know-Nothings often compared Catholicism to slavery, claiming that both were fundamentally un-American. At the same time, Catholics tended to think of slavery as a social and political rather than a moral issue. They did not equate political bondage with spiritual bondage. As an alternative to abolitionism, Catholics like bishop Verot of St. Augustine tended to support a "gradualist" approach which hoped to prepare enslaved people for freedom rather than initiate a mass liberation that could leave great numbers of deliberately uneducated people without hearth or profession. Once the question was settled legally, Bishop Verot became one of the greatest champions of education for the freed slave and unsuccessfully lobbied to make care for the former slaves a priority of the U.S. Catholic Church.

---

81 Bishop John Carroll founded St. Mary's Seminary in 1791, in a former tavern. Until 1852, the seminary was staffed by Sulpicians who had fled the French Revolution.

Verot's nomination, Florida was home to a total of three priests and approximately 1,330 Catholics, more than a third of whom were of African descent. Not surprisingly, one of the new bishop's first activities was to travel to France seeking personnel and financial help.

So outspoken in favor of states' rights that he was known in Civil War times as "the rebel bishop," Verot sought to moderate, rather than immediately eliminate slavery.[82] When the Civil War came to an end, he became a relentless defender of human rights and tried to get others to share his conviction that service to the former slaves offered the Church an unprecedented opportunity for evangelization; his efforts in that area have been recognized as marking "the greatest involvement of Florida Catholicism in African American advancement up to the Civil Rights era."[83] Recognizing the incomparable importance of education as a path toward self-sufficiency and respectability, Bishop Verot returned to France after the end of the Civil War, this time to ask the Sisters of St. Joseph of Le Puy to take on the mission of the education of the former slaves of the territories under his jurisdiction.

LE PUY OPENS THE SAINT AUGUSTINE MISSION

After Mother Leocadie Broc, the Superior General of the Sisters of St. Joseph of Le Puy, promised to help him, Bishop Verot wrote a formal letter assuring her of the seriousness of his request for sisters. He told her:

I am unwilling to leave France without reminding you of the promises you made me in Le Puy. I am sending you a grammar and English dictionary so they may get down to work on it as a good start....I beg you to pray...for our favorable journey across the ocean...I send a blessing for all and I wish for all great courage and devotion in the service of the good God.

Bishop Augustin Verot, SSS
Born: Le Puy 1804 – Died, Saint Augustine, 1876

---

82 Verot shared the opinion that immediate and total emancipation would be disastrous because the slaves were not prepared for life in independence. He favored a gradual and well-planned process of emancipation that would not simply turn out homeless masses of ex-slaves.

83 Charles Gallagher & Kathleen Bagg-Morgan, *Cross and Crozier: The History of the Diocese of Saint Augustine* (Strasbourg, France, Editions du Signe, 1999) 39. In regard to the slavery question see Paul Giles, "Catholic Ideology and American Slave Narratives," *U.S. Catholic Historian*, v 15 n 2, 55-66.

Apparently, almost as soon as he arrived in Georgia he wrote again:

> I am in process of selecting the place where it would be the best to
> establish you...the liberated Blacks are scattered everywhere...no one
> cares for their spiritual needs; many die...What I ask of you above all is
> dedication, the virtue of obedience, and great love of our Savior and the
> souls he has redeemed.[84]

Bishop Verot's anxiousness to have the sisters was tempered only by his concern
that they needed a secure place to begin their ministry as well as safe travel
arrangements. Thus on February 21, 1866 he wrote:

> After long reflection, weighing carefully, and praying to God for His grace
> and light, I am writing to ask you to make all necessary arrangements in
> order to send a colony of your nuns...in the month of April...because of
> the ocean being disagreeable (not to say dangerous) during the winter...
>
> I have decided to have the Sisters come to Saint Augustine, Florida,
> where I have a suitable house to receive them...
>
> I wish you to understand clearly that it is for the Blacks and for them
> almost exclusively that I have the sisters of your Order come to my
> Diocese. I have between five and six thousand Blacks without education
> and without religion or Baptism for whom I would like to do something.
> Some Protestants from the North are coming to educate these poor
> unfortunates. Why couldn't we do something similar with devoted
> Sisters? There is an immense field open to the zeal of your devoted
> daughters and, if I am not mistaken, God is granting you a great grace
> in this choice. I hope that your House will cooperate faithfully in this,
> and that in the years to come many zealous workers will come from Puy
> to America under the guidance of Mary and Saint Joseph.
>
> For the time being I would like eight sisters...Send me those with a
> good head and solid virtue...[85]

Bishop Verot went on to explain that the sisters would be accompanied by a priest
of his diocese as they traveled. He added that he had asked the bishop of Le Puy

---

84 The first letter is dated August 6, and the second, September 18, 1865. (ASSJSA)
85This and a wealth of additional letters are found in Thomas Joseph McGoldrick, SSJ, *Beyond the Call, The
Legacy of the Sisters of St. Joseph of Saint Augustine* (XLIBRIS.COM, 2007). (39-40)

to take up a special collection and that the sisters should not travel with more than two or three locked trunks.

After some sixty members of the Le Puy congregation volunteered for the mission, eight were chosen: Sisters Marie Sidonie Rascle, Marie Julie Roussel, Josephine Deleage, Pierre Borie, Clemence Freycenon, Louise Joseph Cortial, Celinie Joubert and Julie Clotilde Arsac.[86] While the town of Le Puy was hardly a major metropolis, the majority of these sisters came from much smaller towns and, like most people of their time, had probably not traveled far from their homes; most likely they had never expected to see Paris, much less the other side of the Atlantic Ocean. The group from Le Puy sailed from Le Havre on August 2, 1866, and arrived in New York on August 18, 1866.

The relative speed of the journey did nothing to minimize the adventure or ameliorate its difficulties. They had hardly lost sight of France when Sister Sidonie wrote:

> All the passengers are polite, very solicitous…There is no inconvenience because of having kept on our religious dress…Sister Clemence was the first to be seasick; she felt the first symptoms after a quarter hour of crossing. Sister Saint Pierre as well as Sister Celinie did not wait long to be ill. No one has given in yet, thanks to Mother Agathe's excellent liqueur…[87]

Sister Sidonie Rascle

As time went on, a few of the younger sisters wrote to their novice director to share details of the trip and a good dose of the humor that made the misery bearable. Telling their friends how the journey was affecting their convent routine, they explained that they needed others to fast and pray in their stead:

> We are delighted to be able to write you from the middle of the ocean… our illness has disappeared, but happily it will return because without that we would have paid too good a bargain. Sister Marie Joseph and Sister Marie Clotilde had a little sleep of twenty-four hours without stirring either feet or hands…Our cabins are very dark, and our beds

---

86 McGoldrick, 38.
87 Sister Sidonie to Mother Leocadie, August 2, 1866 (McGoldrick, 45).

are...cozy like the shelves of a wardrobe; you have to be very skillful, even nimble, to get in there...

Have our dear companions hear Mass for us, especially on Sundays, and to do some abstinence for us too...we no longer recognize Friday or Saturday...

Permit us, dearest Mother, before closing, to ask you again for the help of your fervent prayers – we say so little ourselves! – and that little, we fear, may be drowned. Sister Clémence found herself so well off in her cradle yesterday that she said none of them that day; she contented herself with saying from time to time, "My God, I offer it to You."

Today we are joining together for this note. Please, Mother pardon our scrawl, for Sister Marie Joseph, who is our scribe, and Sister Marie Clotilde, the one dictating, have very heavy heads. Will you please be good enough to say something very affectionate to our companions, to all our sisters...[88]

The sisters arrived in New York on August 18 and stayed at St. Vincent de Paul Boarding School before embarking on a steamer for Savannah. On board they saw people of African descent for the first time in their lives and the religious with their habits and French language were as much a novelty for the black workers as the workers were for the sisters.[89] Instead of heading straight to Saint Augustine, the sisters were instructed to disembark and wait for the bishop in Savannah. Sister Julie wrote Mother Leocadie explaining:

We arrived here Sunday (August 23) at 8 p.m...[the bishop advised us to wait] until his return...Wednesday morning we had his visit; he had nothing more pressing than to ask us if we were progressing in English. Our negative reply disappointed him, for he thought some among us were quite fluent; he was hoping to keep at least three to open a class here in Savannah.

We are doing well, but if you saw [us]...we would make you pity us; one would say we had the mange...We attribute it somewhat to the bedbugs which are very abundant, to mosquitoes, more abundant

---

88 Letter of August 4, 1866. ASSJSA
89 This information comes from an anonymous manuscript ASSJSA.

still...We are en-route three weeks today and the kind of life we lead is a little different from what we followed in the convent. However...these are small annoyances...Our discomforts even contribute to our making a very happy recreation; without them we would not know what to do.[90]

The sisters' good humor impressed Bishop Verot so much that he commented on it when he wrote to the Bishop of Le Puy:

It gives me indescribable pleasure to report that the good daughters, or rather the glorious heroines, of your diocese arrived in Savannah...with an admirable enthusiasm to dedicate themselves to the service of the poor Black people, of whom they have already seen a large number...

They must learn English, and then their active life and their duties... will have commenced...It will be necessary to open an orphanage for the young Black boys and girls; that will be the means of doing much good. Unfortunately, the Black people are poor, and that enterprise will entail much expense; but Providence never is lacking toward its children, and I foresee that already in a short time I will have to request from Your Excellency another colony of Missionaries in veils.[91]

Bishop Verot wrote to Mother Leocadie on the same day, telling her that the sisters had already departed for Saint Augustine,

...where they have no doubt already established themselves. I thank Divine Providence that their trip was made without any accident...The Black people are delighted that Sisters from France have been brought over for them, and I do not doubt that they will come in large numbers when the Sisters open their schools...[92]

While the bishop shared the happiness of his people about the sisters' arrival, his confidence about the ease of their journey was a bit premature. He had no idea of the anxiety-producing adventure they would have as they neared Saint Augustine. The eight sisters had traveled on the steamer Caroline from Savannah to Picolata,

---

90 Sister Julie Roussel to Mother Leocadie, August 31, 1866 (McGoldrick, 53-54).
91 Bishop Verot to Bishop Le Breton of Le Puy, September 3, 1866 (McGoldrick 55).
92 Bishop Verot to Mother Leocadie, September 3, 1866 (McGoldrick, 56).

the mail coach landing that served Saint Augustine. On September 14, 1866, Sister Julie wrote to Mother Agathe in Le Puy recounting their experience at Picolata.

> Excellent and Dear Mother…
> We were having supper when all of a sudden Father left like a flash. We hardly left the dining room when he came to introduce two religious to us; he seemed very busy but as he was speaking English, we really did not grasp what he was telling us. However, from the few words in French which he sprinkled in from time to time we learned that four of us would be taking the carriage which had brought the religious and that the other four of us would wait for the next day at ten o'clock when someone would come for the others as well…
>
> Mother Sidonie, Sisters Josephine, Celine and Clotilde quickly left the boat with the good Father, and there we were, the four of us remaining with two good Sisters whom we thought would be going with us the next day to Saint Augustine. We expected the boat would be tied up for the night at Picolata, but scarcely had our Sisters gone when it started to move again. Just imagine our astonishment when we noticed that we were drawing away from the settlement. We were afraid we had misunderstood Father; we questioned the sisters and realized that they were not returning to Saint Augustine; our anxiety increased…
>
> At eleven, that evening, the boat stopped again. All the baggage was unloaded on the pier as we watched; thinking we recognized our own,

> we reasoned that someone would be coming for us there. The next day as soon as it was light, we went to see if our trunks were there; we couldn't find any of them. We spoke to this one and that one to find out whether we should disembark or remain aboard. We were not understood.
>
> At seven-thirty, the boat again began to move; we saw that all we could do was abandon ourselves into the hand of Providence…

At nine-thirty, the boat stopped and we recognized that we were once more at Picolata. A man whom father had brought from New York and who had slept aboard ship without our knowing it came to us and made a sign for us to follow him; he took us to a small house and withdrew. A lady tried to speak to us but in vain; we could not understand her; all we knew how to say were the words: "no speak English"…Father had told us someone would come at ten, and the carriage did not arrive until noon' we expected to leave immediately…

At two o'clock, our good lady came to indicate by signs that we must eat because the carriage would not be leaving until four and we would not arrive until eight-thirty. We accepted reluctantly because we had not money to pay her; however we decided to sit down at the table for we had eaten nothing since seven-thirty that morning. We were served, all on the same plate, some chicken, white beans, rice cooked in water, some beef in a red sauce and some potatoes, but not a bite of bread. At four we left thanking our hostess as well as we could and trying to let her understand that Father Aubril would pay her; she seemed offended by that!

…We reached Saint Augustine around eight-thirty…

I am your affectionate and grateful

Sister Julie Roussel[93]

While the four sisters on board were wondering where they were going and why, the sisters who had disembarked enjoyed their own set of adventures. From Saint Augustine, Sister Sidonie wrote to Mother Leocadie telling all about it, from the need to disembark, through the impossibility of entering the city at night. The only detail she omitted was the abundance of snakes and alligators in the river and along its banks.[94]

The big ships do not come as far as this town…we had to disembark just near Picolata, a town five long leagues distant[95]…the road which comes from there is extremely bad…in the forest; large carriages do not

---

93 Sr. Julie Roussel to Mother Leocadie, September 14, 1866 (McGoldrick, 63-65)
94 That detail about river life is recorded in a handwritten account written by Mother Lazarus L'Hostel who served in Saint Augustine and founded the Le Puy community in Fall River, Massachusetts. (ASSJSA)
95 A league was commonly understood to be about three miles. The distance from Picolata to the center of Saint Augustine is estimated to be twenty miles.

go that route...we did not find enough room in the stage coach...four of the sisters...stayed aboard ship...I was a little concerned...

[Arriving at Saint Augustine] Father Aubril presented himself to the watchman to obtain permission to enter the city. Permission was not accorded; it was too late; the health official had retired! "Is it possible," exclaimed good Father Aubril, "we must spend the night at the quarantine station!"

There we alighted...and [stayed] in the hospital. A soldier was already resting in the middle of the room; he did not stir 'of his sleep' in spite of the fact that people surrounded him. Sister Josephine and sister Clotilde went outside to laugh without restraint...

The proprietress of the Lazaret [quarantine hospital], as if by magic, arranged a vast bed for us; everyone retired wishing us "a good night." As soon as we were alone a fit of laughter overcame us while considering that enormous pad of at least three meters wide, and that little pillow which stretched almost from one end of the room to the other; fearing to burst laughing we went to sit in the garden...until two in the morning; the mosquitoes devoured us; we went to rest in that spacious bed completely dressed; all four of us...we could turn and turn over without touching; we did not have to fear falling from a height; the pad was on the floor.

We got up with the daylight...never had we seen one another so dirty. We had brought linen for fifteen days, and we were six weeks in route. We...went to make our meditation in the forest...It was not until three in the afternoon that we could leave for Saint Augustine...[96]

When the Sisters all had arrived in Saint Augustine, the Sisters of Mercy took them in and introduced them to the foods of the New World which included hominy and the potatoes that would take the place of French bread. They also helped the newcomers in their struggle to learn English. Within a few months, the sisters took possession of the "O'Reilly House" which would serve as their first convent and school. That house, built in 1691, was one of the oldest homes in the United States. In 1785, Father Miguel O'Reilly purchased it to serve as a parish house.[97]

---

96 Sister Sidonie (also referred to as Mother Sidonie) to Mother Leocadie, September 14, 1866 (McGoldrick, 57-62).
97 Father "Miguel" Michael O'Reilly was an Irish priest who studied in Salamanca during the epoch when

Within a few months, the sisters took possession of the "O'Reilly House" which would serve as their first convent and school. That house, built in 1691, was one of the oldest homes in the United States. In 1785, Father Miguel O'Reilly purchased it to serve as a parish house.[97] Although he died long before the Le Puy Sisters arrived in Saint Augustine, his will specified that the house should go to some unknown, unnamed, religious who would minister in education in the style of St. Francis de Sales, a condition unexpectedly but precisely met by the Sisters of St. Joseph.[98] The sisters moved into that house, their first U.S. home, on December 28, 1866, on the property that today houses the Motherhouse of the Congregation.

On January 1, 1867, Mother Sidonie wrote to Mother Leocadie about the sisters' progress:

> Dear and esteemed Mother...
> God be praised we have been in our own convent since Friday evening, the 28th of December...Feast of the Holy Innocents. Two days before, Father Aubril told us, "You must be settled before 'My Lord' Verot arrives, because he is bringing some postulants, you will welcome them into your home.
> Saturday, the 29th...the two priests knock; they bring us six aspirants. What a reception! What to give them? We had practically nothing; we were not expecting such a number!
> ...That was not all; beds were needed. The two good Fathers went into action. Either by borrowing or by gifts, before night we were able to make six beds. What do you think of this, Mother? Here we are fourteen in our little convent. America![99]

Within days of its inauguration, the O'Reilly House convent had become a novitiate. In January, 1867, the Sisters opened their school for black children on the same property. On February 17, 1867, Sister Sidonie wrote to Mother Leocadie.

----

seminaries were forbidden in Ireland. His missionary life in Saint Augustine began in 1784, just when the Treaty of Paris had returned Florida to Spain. In 1797, he was appointed parish priest of St. Augustine and began the construction of what would become the Saint Augustine Cathedral. Father O'Reilly died in 1812. (http://staugustine.com/interact/blog-post/olde-carriage-realty/2013-02-06/oreillys-st-augustine#.VZl0fvn551E)
98 For more information and a virtual tour of the O'Reilly house see http://www.oreillyhouse.org/.
99 McGoldrick, 133.

She spoke not only about their quickly expanding ministries, but offered new insights into the cultural challenges the sisters were facing. One can only wonder about their progress in speaking and understanding English as they heard the accents of their six American postulants and African Americans. The sisters' ability to adapt to English and local customs along with their quickly growing love of their new neighbors is evident in Sister Sidonie's letter:

> Our classes were opened January 29th, the Feast of St. Francis de Sales... at nine o'clock, Monseigneur was at the schoolhouse to wait for the children, bless them, encourage them; that day there were about twenty boys and girls. Each day the number increases, we have now about sixty...
>
> I was told three black women were asking for me; I went to the parlor, but not with pleasure, for I do not understand half of what is said to me...They ask me if I will admit them to night school; I tell them yes...I do not know how I did it, but I noticed I was speaking English, that the woman was understanding me...We separated after an affectionate 'good-bye" and at the same time a shaking of hands, which is an indispensable ceremony on leaving good friends.
>
> Our children are generally well disposed...we have only two who have made [first communion]. These children know nothing really about religious instruction. A little penny holy card, particularly if it is red, blue or green, makes them the happiest beings in the world.
>
> We have started evening school for adults; they call that "night school" – Monday, Tuesday and Friday for women; Thursday Saturday and Sunday for men; on Wednesday all Black people are welcome, men and women; they are taught songs; how I love to hear God's praise sung by all these poor people.
>
> Young and old shout, sing with all their heart and soul.
>
> We also have students for French, but these do not bring us consolation – only money![100]

By April of 1867, the overcrowding in the convent was relieved by the missioning of four Sisters to open an orphan asylum in Savannah. In September, 1867, the

---

100 McGoldrick, 136-137.

Saint Augustine sisters moved to a larger house nearby which had been the home of the Christian Brothers who had to abandon the area during the Civil War. That move took place just before the October arrival of four additional missionaries from Le Puy.

The incessant ministry and poverty of the community began to take a toll on the sisters. They had been more than fully occupied in teaching for two years when Sister Stanislaus Bertrand became superior in Saint Augustine. By then, the sisters were conducting five educational centers, but only the two sisters teaching boys were receiving remuneration for their work: a total of $60 per month. The sisters supplemented that income by making lace and offering private lessons in French, music, painting and drawing. Sister Stanislaus sought help from the ladies of the parish and they raised an additional $400 through a parish fair.[101]

The sisters' material poverty was exacerbated by the difficulties of life in a hot and humid foreign climate. The first sister to succumb to fatal illness was Sister Marie Joseph Cortial who was teaching in Savannah in 1867 when she began to cough blood. In spite of her illness, she continued to try to teach the 50 little girls in her class, but Mother Sidonie recalled her to Saint Augustine in December. There, her health continued to decline; she died on March 14, 1868, just five days before she reached her goal of dying on the Feast of St. Joseph. When it came time to celebrate her funeral, Mrs. Marie Pappet, one of the leaders of the black women in the community expressed her people's devotion to Sister Marie Joseph by taking charge of everything. She told the other women of the parish "Sister Marie Joseph came for us and not for you ladies, so it is right for us to take charge of her funeral and we are the ones who will walk first in the procession."[102]

Sister Marie Joseph was but the first of the Le Puy sisters to die in America. In the space of sixteen years, from their arrival in 1866 until 1882, twelve sisters died in Florida or Georgia. Two of them, Sisters De Sales Kennedy and Celinie Jourbert, were commonly hailed as "martyrs of charity" because when Yellow Fever was devastating the city of Fernandina, these two sisters who had been away on retreat, chose to return to the city to nurse the victims who were being abandoned by almost everyone else. The two sisters contracted the disease and died within eight hours of one another on September 21st and 22nd of 1877. They were accompanied in their last hours by others of their sisters who came to

---

101 McGoldrick, 131 & 378.
102 McGoldrick, Sister Louise Joseph Cortial was also referred to as Sister Marie Joseph.163.

continue their mission of nursing the sick and dying.[103]

THE COMMUNITY FINDS ITSELF IN TWO DIOCESES

The community founded at St. Augustine functioned like a province of the Congregation of the Sisters of St. Joseph of Le Puy in that it quickly established its own novitiate and the superior in St. Augustine received new members and missioned sisters to local communities. The sisters' first mission beyond St. Augustine was in Savannah where they began teaching in 1867. By 1868, the Savannah group had 120 children of African descent in their day classes along with a night school.[104] At first, Savannah seemed a great step forward, as Sister M. Josephine Deleage explained in a letter written in English to Mother Agathe in Le Puy:

> You know that we are in Savannah now. It is a very beautiful city where all that is wanted can be found, whereas St. Augustine is quite poor, nonetheless, I miss it now and then, the first separation has been very distressing.

Later in the letter Sister Josephine referred to their struggles with English. Displaying the good humor and ability to take herself lightly that seemed to be a specialty of this missionary group, she told the Le Puy superior:

> Father Dufau...told Mother "Forbid your sisters to speak French." As he should not be returning for three months, we have time to make progress, all the more so since our postulant is so eager to win all the "Ave Marias" that she exacts some from us every time she hears us speak French.
>
> What do you think of my English, good Mother? I think I hear you saying "You are not very skillful, Sister." That is surely true, Mother, I speak imperfectly, but I haven't time to notice whether I put my pronouns, adjectives and adverbs in their right place...the Sisters laugh at me; but that hardly bothers me.[105]

---

103 McGoldrick, 264-65
104 McGoldrick, 194.
105 Letter from Sister M. Josephine Deleage to Mother Agathe in Le Puy, Savannah, May 12, 1867. (McGoldrick, 195-6)

Although the sisters rarely alluded to it, their ministry to people of African descent was controversial in their new homeland. Many of the white citizens of St. Augustine and Savannah were less than pleased to have sisters teaching black students. If they whispered their displeasure inside the church, outside they felt free to use racist epithets to refer to both students and teachers.[106]

After making the foundation in Savannah, the sisters began to serve Anglo children as well. They opened schools in Mandarin (1868), Jacksonville (1869), Fernandina (1871) and Palatka (1876), all in Florida. The sisters enjoyed notable success in their educational efforts as attested in an article from the St. Augustine Examiner on August 17, 1867, which said in part:

> The Sisters of Saint Joseph have met with success in training the coloured [sic] children of Saint Augustine. The Catholic children belonging to the coloured population are now far above the level of their comrades of African origin belonging to other churches or no church at all; and we cannot give too much praise to these devoted Sisters…for having left their happy country and all the comforts of "la Belle France"…What they have done hitherto is a sure pledge of greater success for the future.[107]

Until 1870, those communities were all under the jurisdiction of Bishop Verot who was bishop of Savannah and Vicar Apostolic for St. Augustine.

All the available evidence indicates that Bishop Verot and the sisters enjoyed a warm, supportive and mutually respectful relationship. If the sisters felt any pressure from him, it stemmed from his desire that they quickly learn to understand and speak English well. The sisters frequently mentioned his genial concern for their well-being in their letters to France. One incident recalled by Sister Marie Julie gives a general sense of the rapport enjoyed between the sisters and bishop. Speaking of a surprise visit from the bishop, she wrote:

> We were sitting [outside] when we saw a carriage…We got up quickly… then we heard Father Delafosse's voice saying "You are afraid! Don't be frightened; we are returning," and soon he was beside us. Then… the usual greetings exchanged…we were preparing to say a word of

---

106 Barbara E. Mattick, "Ministries in Black and White: The Catholic Sisters of St. Augustine, Florida, 1859-1920" (Doctoral Dissertation: Florida State University, 2008: http://diginole.lib.fsu.edu/etd), 46.
107 Cited in McGoldrick, 84.

welcome to his traveling companion whom we thought to be the old gardener, when we recognized Bishop Verot. We let out a cry of surprise and joy, which should have let him know how happy we were to see him...the caretaker made some fried eggs and our two travelers sat down...After offering them three oranges, we went to prepare the beds. Monseigneur slept in the one which is in the black children's classroom... but we all stayed in the yard near the fire until 10 o'clock.

Monseigneur made us tell to the smallest detail what we had done the past fifteen days, what we had eaten; he seemed satisfied to see us cheerful and happy...

At the moment of leaving Monseigneur called me into his room and asked me several times if we needed anything – adding that he would send it to us...Then he gave me two $5 coins. How good he is, that holy Bishop![108]

Obviously, the sisters were at ease with the bishop and he demonstrated true personal care for them along with very simple taste in his accommodations. Unfortunately, that sort of relationship with the hierarchy would not last forever.

BISHOP PERSICO SEPARATES
SAVANNAH FROM SAINT AUGUSTINE

In 1870, the Vicariate of St. Augustine in Florida was raised to the status of a diocese and, given the necessity to choose between it and the diocese of Savannah, Bishop Verot chose to remain in St. Augustine and Bishop Ignatius Persico briefly replaced him as Bishop of Savannah.[109]

Although the sisters may not have enjoyed the same rapport with Bishop Persico as they had with Bishop Verot, their letters do not reveal any serious problems between them.[110] But for some reason Bishop Persico wanted the Sisters

---

108 Mother Julie to the Community in France, April, 1868 (McGoldrick, 170).
109 Ignatius Persico, was named Bishop of Savannah in 1870, but resigned three years later because of failing health. He returned to Rome and began a career in Vatican diplomacy and was made a cardinal in 1893, three years before his death.
110 One letter explains that the bishop "does not come to see us often; he is too busy, but he is all heart." (McGoldrick, 236) Another explains "Our saintly Bishop, cold as he seems, is nevertheless good. He does not often visit us because we are too far away...He does not go as Monseigneur Verot, for example." (McGoldrick, 243)

of St. Joseph in Savannah to be independent of Saint Augustine and, after consulting with Mother Stanislaus Bertrand, the superior in Saint Augustine, and with the motherhouse in Le Puy, he separated the sisters in Georgia from those in Florida, making the Savannah sisters directly dependent on Le Puy rather than part of one mission community centered in Saint Augustine.[111]

Various factors make Bishop Persico's decision difficult to understand. First, the beloved superior of the Savannah community, Mother Helene Gidon had recently died, leaving the Savannah sisters feeling like "poor orphans."[112] Secondly, according to a letter from Sister Josephine to Mother Agathe in Le Puy, vocations were far from abundant. She wrote: "It is difficult to find subjects in this country; humility and the spirit of sacrifice are not well developed among our Catholics."[113] Finally, the community had precious little in the way of material resources. Explaining rather than complaining, Sister Josephine wrote:

> When one lives on alms, one must often do what was not expected... we have just finished having a fair for our benefit; we had to work and go persuade the ladies to take an interest in us; I was hoping the priest would have the goodness to do that, but he was ill and it was thus quite necessary for me to initiate things; that was a terrible mortification, for I do not like to beg; nevertheless, I had to take my portion.[114]

If the creation of Savannah as a separate mission was an inexplicable surprise, the decision of Bishop Persico's successor to sever the Savannah community from France must have been an incomprehensible shock. When Bishop Persico resigned on account of his ill health in 1873, Bishop William H. Gross was appointed Bishop of Savannah. In May, 1874, Bishop Gross decided that the Sisters of St. Joseph in Savannah should become a diocesan congregation. He gave the sisters twenty-four hours to accept his decision or to leave his diocese, thereby unilaterally deciding to transform a mission of a religious congregation of pontifical right into a diocesan congregation. In response, Mother Josephine resigned her role as superior and sought refuge in Saint Augustine before returning to France. The bishop named

---

111 McGoldrick, 194.
112 In writing to the Reverend Mother in Le Puy of Mother Helene's death, Sister Josephine Deleage said "Mother, pray for us and think of us, your poor orphans of Savannah!" (Letter from Sr. Josephine, December 14, 1869, McGoldrick, 229-232) 113 Sister Josephine Deleage to Mother Marie Agathe Deschayeuz, January 15, 1871. (McGoldrick, 237-8)
114 Sister Josephine to Mother Agathe, April 30, 1870. (McGoldrick, 233-235)

a superior pro-tem until the sisters could hold an election. The new congregation under the leadership of Mother Clemence Freycenon could then boast of a total membership of six professed sisters, two lay sisters and seven novices.[115] It is worth noting that in spite of the legal severance, the sisters' communication with Le Puy conveys more unity than independence. As late as 1888, Sister St. John Kennedy, one of the first U.S. sisters to join the community and the first novice director in Savannah wrote to the superior in Le Puy. Her letter sounds as if she were writing to her own superior:

> My very good Mother,
> If I did not know how kind and amiable you are, I would despair of obtaining pardon for my long silence, and as it is, I expect a good penance, which I hope you will give me.

After explaining that she had reluctantly been persuaded to accept an additional term as superior of the congregation she went on to say that the bishop

> ...permitted me to ask Reverend Mother for a lay Sister to come to us, the next time some Sisters come from France, if she will be kind enough... and told me to keep up the friendly spirit of union between le Puy and Georgia, for Bishop Moore had spoken to him of the many advantages he derived from you – so you see, dear mother our good Bishop is very friendly disposed toward you now...[116]

Sister John's light hearted deference to Mother De Sales' authority and her explanation of how the she could work with or around the bishop demonstrate that canonical definitions notwithstanding, the sisters maintained their ties of affection and spiritual interdependence. The strength of their relationships was clearly more powerful than juridical constraints. Additionally, in spite of what seem to have been authoritarian and even unilateral decisions, Le Puy appeared to remain open to supporting the missions they had begun in the United States. Saint Augustine 1870- 1899

The correspondence between the sisters in the U.S. and Le Puy adds

---

115 McGoldrick, 248. A fuller account of the Georgia story follows, beginning on page 496.
116 Sister John (St. Jean) Kennedy to Mother de Sales, September 19, 1888, from Washington, Georgia. (McGoldrick, 249)

almost nothing to our understanding of the sisters' thinking about the separation of Savannah from Saint Augustine. There is one entry in the annals of the Saint Augustine community that hints at the sisters' feelings. An entry for 1871 reads:

> Up to this time our Sisters of Savannah had been united to us, but now to our great sorrow they are cut off from this diocese and are to depend on the Rt. Rev. Bishop of Savannah.[117]

Beyond that discreet statement, the sisters either did not mention the separation or they did not retain correspondence that did.

The Saint Augustine community continued to grow with native vocations, augmented by additional missionaries from Le Puy. There were even two lay Sisters of Mercy, Sisters Mary Ann Hoare and Monica Nicholson, who transferred to the Sisters of St. Joseph when their community left the diocese of Saint Augustine.[118] The sisters ministered primarily in education, first of black children and adults, then of others as well. In the period between 1867 and 1876, the sisters numbered between twenty-five and thirty-five with missions in Saint Augustine, Mandarin, Jacksonville, Fernandina, Mayport and Palatka, as well as Savannah until 1870.

In 1876, the local superiors in Florida gathered for a meeting with Mother Leocadie Broc, the Le Puy Assistant Superior General who had come to visit the mission. There, with the collaboration of Bishop Verot, the sisters received the documents from Rome that allowed for the establishment of Saint Augustine as an official province of the Congregation of the Sisters of St. Joseph of Le Puy. The sisters then needed to obtain their legal incorporation in the State, elect a Provincial Superior and formally establish a novitiate and common fund. They also decided to allow two sisters to return each year to France for retreat, and most likely for fundraising as well. Additionally, the Province was encouraged to establish a boarding house for invalids and make efforts to establish a religious group among colored females "similar to the "Soeurs Agrégées de Saint Joseph" whose ministry would be primarily to the sick.[119] It seemed as if Le Puy's mission in Florida had become firmly established. Le Puy continued to send sisters to Florida through 1897, with almost forty French missionaries coming in the space of thirty years. As time went on, the French sisters were well outnumbered by Irish immigrant

---

117 ASSJSA, Record Book: Vol. 1, pg. 7.
118 McGoldrick, 152.
119 McGoldrick, 188-190.

recruits and other U.S. born women.[120]

Bishop Verot died on July 10, 1876, and was succeeded by Bishop William Moore who was consecrated on May 13, 1877. For a number of years the sisters' relationship with the bishop seemed amiable and the community grew in numbers and ministries. The sisters' sense of their own progress can be seen in a letter Sister Julie Roussel wrote in 1886, responding to questions from a Sister of St. Joseph from the North. She said:

> In Florida we have six communities, we would have more had we subjects enough to send, but the vocations here are very scarce....St. Augustine is the principal house. Here in 1880 a regular novitiate was established under the auspices of Bishop Moore. The Sisters...have been placed in charge of four public schools...an academy for young ladies, a select day school...and two schools for colored children. In Jacksonville, Fernandina and Palatka our sisters have academies, day schools and colored schools. At Moccasin Branch...an academy and a public school... there are no colored people in that settlement. At Mandarin...a boarding school, a day school and a colored school...
> In this Diocese of St. Augustine we are only from 65 to 70 Sisters.[121]

In 1891, the sisters expanded their ministerial field to Tampa where the sisters worked with the poor and taught in Ybor City.[122] During the Spanish-American War in 1898, the Sisters of St. Joseph added care for sick and wounded soldiers to their ministries in Pablo Beach, Fernandina and Tampa; they turned their Pablo Beach summer cottage and the auditorium of their Tampa school into makeshift hospital wards.[123] In 1898, after presiding at the election of Mother Lazarus L'hostel as provincial superior, Bishop Moore visited the North. While traveling, he suffered a stroke. Everything changed upon his return to Saint Augustine. Years later, writing from Fall River, Massachusetts, Sister Mary Lazarus who had

---

120 McGoldrick, 367-369. Between 1866 and 1920, from a total 231 women who were part of the Sisters of St. Joseph of St. Augustine, 39 sister missionaries came from France, 70 women who entered the community were of Irish birth, 40 were born in Florida, 18 in Canada and 64 came from other places. For a variety of reasons some of the French sisters eventually returned to their homeland.
121 From Sister M. Julie Roussel, March 28, 1886. (McGoldrick, 282-284)
122 McGoldrick, 300.
123 McGoldrick, 311.

been the superior in St. Augustine, recounted the happenings of November 14, 1899. Writing to the Le Puy Superior General she said:

My Dear Mother,

You ask my dear Mother, that I recount for you how things came to pass when I was deposed and excommunicated. It costs me to do so, but obedience takes care of all.

Three or four years before the matter happened, Monseigneur Moore had ordered that in every community the Superior would read the Decree of the Holy Father on the Feast Day of St. Teresa…it was difficult to get together. I had explained this to His Lordship and asked to postpone that reading…Monseigneur was agreeable…saying "Provided that it be read once a year…" One year I forgot it, but every year at the retreat the Decree was read and explained by the Father who gave the retreat, which had been done three months before the deposition.

The morning of November 14, 1899, Wednesday, I received a note from Monseigneur saying that he would come to the convent at 3 o'clock, to have all the sisters assembled in the chapel….[he] gave no reason…

At three o'clock he came with the Pastor of the Cathedral; they went directly into the sacristy…Both of them went into the sanctuary, Monseigneur with a large paper in his hand.

[He announced to the sisters] "I had given orders to Mother Lazarus [about reading the decree]…This order has not been carried out. Mother Lazarus…is disobedient. In the presence of all the community she is deposed from her position and she is excommunicated…She will no longer fill any position in the community. I appoint Sister Eulalia Ryan in her place…"

After that he left the chapel…I followed them…I knelt down, asked him if it were forbidden to me to receive the Sacraments. His Lordship answered "Yes…but you will go to confession…"

I would have counted for nothing what had happened if the separation from our dear Motherhouse had not followed. I was fearing that at any moment. Ten days later I was called to the parlor. In the presence of the Superior and her Assistant, Monseigneur announced to me that we are no longer dependent on the house of Le Puy. You will let that be known to the French Sisters.

I was standing up before these three persons. That blow was more terrible to me than the first; I asked if we should leave for France. "No, you can stay." I think that he added, "You are free."

As I ought to stay in St. Augustine, I made the request to be assigned to Mandarin. But the order was that I go to Ybor, the house farthest from St. Augustine and from the others...

The 24th of November I left St. Augustine where I had spent 32 happy years, to go to Ybor, with orders not to stop in our houses which were on the way...The Superior had received orders to read all my correspondence...Our French Sisters urged me to return to France; the Superior in St. Augustine begged me to stay in Florida...I wrote to Mother Eulalie...His Lordship [told her] "Tell her that it would be better to leave and return to France."

...On May 3, 1900 we said our goodbyes to Florida. We arrived in le Puy about the 25th of the same month. You yourself, good Mother, with Sister Leocadie Broc were waiting for us at the station to wish us welcome and to accompany us to that well-loved Motherhouse; it is so good to enter there.

There we were received by open arms...[124]

In the course of the above letter, Sister Lazarus indicated that she had found Bishop Moore to be "a good and devoted Father to us." The sudden turn of events was as difficult to comprehend as it was to accept. Some speculate that the Bishop's illness had an extreme effect on his personality. Another possibility is that he was influenced by other bishops who were doing all they could to gain complete control over the religious in their dioceses and thus assure themselves of the teachers they needed for the parochial school system they wanted to implement throughout the country. Whatever the rationale or excuse, the bishop's authoritarian proceedings were probably illegal under Church law because, like his fellow prelate in Savannah, he was turning a province of a papal congregation into a diocesan congregation which seems to be a usurpation of papal prerogative by a local bishop. Unfortunately, the sisters had no one to plead their cause, to point that out or to help them rectify the situation. What still seems extraordinary, except when under the influence of the charism of unity and reconciliation,

---

124 From Sister Lazarus L'Hostel to the Superior General in Le Puy, September 28, 1908. (McGoldrick, 321-325)

is that in 1902, the Le Puy congregation opened another mission in the United States and Sister Lazarus herself took part in its foundation. That foundation became a Province of the Le Puy Congregation in Fall River, Massachusetts.

THE SISTERS OF ST. JOSEPH OF GEORGIA:
AS A DIOCESAN CONGREGATION

In 1867, less than a year after the first eight missionary Sisters of St. Joseph arrived in St. Augustine from Le Puy, Bishop Verot asked them to open classes in Savannah, Georgia, the diocesan see about 175 miles north of St. Augustine. In April, 1867, Sisters Mary Julia Roussel, Mary Josephine Deleage and Mary Joseph Cortial, together with Catherine Kennedy and Ellen Ronin, postulants who were born in the U.S., took charge of "the Colored Schools" in the rear of St. John's Cathedral where they had 120 students in night school by January of 1868.[125]

l/r:
Sisters
Mary Josephine Deleage,
Mary Julia Roussel,
Mary Joseph Cortial

---

125 "Annals of the Community of the Sisters of St. Joseph in Savanna Ga. and Washington Georgia" [sic] (Archives Carondelet) Hereafter, "Georgia Annals."
126 Photos Archives ASSJSA

Within seven months, Sister Julia, the superior, was recalled to Florida and replaced by Sister Helene Gidon who had recently arrived from France.[127] The work was an immense challenge, exacerbated by the fact that all of the professed sisters were French. Sister Helene wrote to Le Puy in February, 1868, trying to give the French sisters an idea of the busyness, the struggles and the joys of their mission:

> My Good Mother and dear Sisters...
> I thought I would not come to an end of getting myself into the study of English. The care of orphan boys which Monseigneur has confided to us is no small thing, above all when one cannot speak to ask one or another what one needs to ask and must make use of an interpreter... We have one of our new American Sisters, Sister St. John Kennedy, who writes very well and she understands French well enough so that I may communicate my thoughts.[128]
>
> There are lady patronesses here responsible for securing resources for the orphans, to cut and sew the clothing...they assemble to cut and to hold their meetings, which disorder is agreeable for me...
>
> We are having our orphan boys come to the community room to make their month of St. Joseph with us. They are singing a hymn to our Glorious Father with a fervor that would please you. I asked them to take as a special intention that I could speak English by the end of March, and Monday (the 2nd) some of them asked Sister Clemence if I didn't know how to speak already?...She is very busy with forty children...they have to be combed, to be bathed...to keep their clothing in order.[129]

The French missionaries who had not served people of African descent in their

---

127 The Le Puy congregation sent a total of 39 sisters to Florida between 1866 and 1897: eight in 1866; three; in 1867; one in 1869; three in 1872, 1874, 1879 and 1880; one in 1883; four in 1884, 1886 and 1894 and one in 1897. (See McGoldrick, 276-7)
128 As noted previously, Sister Josephine reported that the novice, Sister St. John Kennedy, earned an Ave Maria each time she corrected the French sisters' English. (McGoldrick, 195-6)
129 McGoldrick, 204-207 for this and the following quotes from the same letter, pictures from 129 and 68.

home country had never known the sort of racism that they encountered in the Reconstruction era South. Trying to explain the phenomenon to her French sisters, Mother Helene wrote and told them that the sisters who served the former slaves could not expect to live unscathed in an atmosphere permeated by prejudice. In March, 1868, she wrote:

> The colored people are disliked (hated!) in this country, and the aversion held for these poor people is quite naturally extended toward those persons who concern themselves with them...

But the sisters who had volunteered for the mission were ready to share Bishop Verot's commitment to the Americans of African descent. He had asked everyone working with him to "devote to this work their efforts, their time, finally, if possible, their lives."[130] Despite the challenges of language and culture, the sisters seemed to have had great success with their charges. Sister Helene explained that Bishop Verot, who had urged the sisters on in their struggles with English, was quite pleased with their teaching.

> Father Ryan who assisted at the catechism which Monseigneur gave those who were to be confirmed had been surprised to hear "Sister Josephine's black boys" respond so well. Monseigneur was very proud of it.

Although they did not focus on it in their correspondence, the physical adjustment to the Florida climate came at great cost to the sisters' health. In March, 1868, less than two years after arriving in the United States, Sister Mary Joseph Cortial died in St. Augustine. Speaking of her, Mother Helene pointed out how the bishop spoke at her funeral, telling the people about the sacrifices the French people had made on behalf of the mission of the Church in Georgia. It seems that the bishop wanted his people to know that the mission to African Americans was internationally known and supported.

---

130 Quoted in Gary Wray McDonogh, *Black and Catholic in Savannah Georgia*, Gary (Knoxville: U. of Tennessee Press,, 1993) 101.

Monseigneur gave the eulogy...he profited by the occasion to throw out into view that in France big sacrifices were made for the Sisters who came; he must have known the opinions of several persons who accuse him of sacrificing everything for the colored people...He spoke of her (Sister M. Joseph's) generosity, her humility, which made her embrace a work that was vile in men's eyes...He spoke of the generosity of her parents...which led them to bear all the expenses of their daughter's journey...we were grateful that Monseigneur profited by the occasion to have it brought to view that in France people had made great sacrifices for the Sisters who came...[131]

Scarborough House

This fragment offers the only kind of evidence we have of how the Le Puy sisters had to find creative means to finance their mission journeys and the emotional strain of facing prejudice and local rejection for their mission to people of African descent.

When the sisters had been in Savannah about seven months, Bishop Verot asked them to take responsibility for the children in the Barry Male Orphan Asylum. With this, the sisters and novices assumed responsibility for a day school, the orphanage, night school, catechetical work and "the linens and all things pertaining to the decoration of the Altars of St. John's Cathedral."[132]

In April, 1869, the Sisters of St. Joseph in Savannah celebrated the vows of their first U.S. born member, Sister St. John Kennedy, a native of Oswego, New York. Two novices received the habit at the same ceremony.[133] By September 1869, the sisters' original house could not hold all the inhabitants and Bishop Verot purchased the "Scarborough House," a local mansion that had changed hands multiple times and offered ample space for the sisters and the thirty-six boys

---

131 McGoldrick, 208-210. This includes the citations on the previous page.
132 Georgia Annals, January, 1868.
133 There is no record of how Sister St. John came to know the Sisters of St. Joseph in Savannah. Being from Oswego, she could have known the Carondelet sisters in her home town or other places in the Diocese of Albany, but she entered the Sisters of St. Joseph of Le Puy in Florida, being received in Jacksonville.

under their care.[134] By the end of the year, Mother Helene's health gave out and on December 3, she died of pneumonia, less than two years after arriving in America. Unanticipated Changes – Separation from St. Augustine

After Mother Helene's death, Sister Josephine Deleage acted as local superior for seven months until Mother Sidonie came from St. Augustine to visit and officially appointed her as superior of the community in Savannah.[135] In the meantime, the Vatican had made St. Augustine a diocese. Bishop Verot chose to be bishop of the smaller St. Augustine diocese leaving Savannah to Bishop, Ignatius Persico.[136]

Although the information from the annals is very sparse, the little they do convey offers hints and raises questions about the life of the pioneer sisters in Georgia and Florida. We might wonder why it took so long for Mother Sidonie to come to Savannah after Mother Helene's death. When she did come, the annalist mentions that she not only appointed Sister Josephine as superior but also named a first Assistant Superior and First Counsellor, thereby strengthening the governance of the Savannah community with officers they had not previously had in that locale. Perhaps Mother Sidonie's decision to give greater stability to the Savannah community was related to changes in the diocesan structures. In October, three months after Mother Sidonie's visit, Bishop Ignatius Persico made his first Canonical Visitation of the community. According to the annals, by March,

---

134 Picture of the house from http://www.shipsofthesea.org/scarbrough-house. In 1878, the Savannah Morning News reports that the Scarborough house had been purchased and "given to the Board of education on the condition that it be turning in a school for black children." (http://savannahnow.com/1800s-anniversary-stories/2010-03-26/savannah-morning-news-timeline-1800s)

135 Mother Sidonie Rascle had been the superior of the St. Augustine community since their departure from Le Puy. The Georgia Annals often refer to her as Mother Sidonia.

136 In 1870, the U.S. census records St. Augustine's population as 1,700, having declined by 10% in the past decade. In contrast, Savannah's census recorded over 28,000 inhabitants, with a growth rate of 25% in the same decade. Neither city had a great percentage of Catholics.

Bishop Ignatius Persico was a Capuchin Franciscan, born in Italy and consecrated bishop at the age of 31 as coadjutor to a bishop in India. Nearly losing his life in a persecution in India, he came to the United States and when Bishop Verot chose the Diocese of St. Augustine over Savannah, Persico was named as his replacement in Savannah. Persico remained only three years in the U.S., leaving in 1873, due to poor health and going on to a long diplomatic career. Before his death at the age of 73 in 1896, he had been made a Cardinal. Persico had participated in the First Vatican Council (Dec. 1869-Oct. 1870) and presumably came to Savannah after the final voting session in July, 1870. Some U.S. bishops who had expressed their disagreement with the proposal left before July 18 the vote on papal infallibility. The council was then suspended for a summer break and could not reconvene because on September 20, 1870, the Kingdom of Italy conquered the Papal States and took Rome, leaving Pius IX a "prisoner of the Vatican." (For additional information about Bishop Verot see: http://ufdc.ufl.edu/USACH00002/00007.

1871, Bishop Persico decided that he "would no longer permit the convent in Savannah to be a branch house of the Convents in Florida."[137] This meant that the Savannah house and those in St. Augustine, would relate directly to Le Puy rather than maintain the semi-provincial status which they had assumed during the nearly five years since they had come from France and their three years of presence in two states and two distinct ecclesial territories. Whatever Bishop Persico's rationale or motivation, his action abolished the juridical union of the Le Puy Sisters in America.

Bishop Persico's decision was a radical departure from Bishop Verot's practice with the sisters. Less than a year after the sisters arrived in St. Augustine, Mother Sidonie Rascle, the U.S. superior, explained the local clergy's thinking to Mother Leocadie Broc, the superior general in Le Puy:

> Father Delafosse asked us again if we would still be depending on Le Puy, if we would have a Superior General. I replied that we would continue to be dependent, on the Motherhouse which had sent us, which would be committed to give us subjects needed on the missions. I added that I would hope even to have the happiness of seeing you in Florida. "Very well, that is what I would like, a community dependent on a Motherhouse; these local houses are not worth anything."[138]

It seems clear that when Bishop Verot invited the Sisters of St. Joseph in Le Puy to his diocese he and his staff were aware of the implications and the advantages brought by sisters belonging to a congregation of pontifical right. When Bishop Persico demanded that the Savannah sisters be independent of the St. Augustine community, he effectively removed the Savannah sisters from any ecclesial

---

137 Georgia Annals. An entry for October, 1870 relates the mistaken information that Bishop Persico decided that the community should separate entirely from France. That did not take place in 1870. There are contradictory details in the Annals, giving the impression that the book has been preserved was copied from another source or sources. An entry for March, 1871, also refers to Bishop Persico's "first" canonical visitation and says that at that time he "finished up the business of making the convent in Savannah independent of the Mother House in Jacksonville." The St. Augustine Sisters had opened a mission in Jacksonville in 1869, but St. Augustine remained the "motherhouse." (The early missions of the St. Augustine community included St. Augustine, opened in 1866; Savannah, 1867; Mandarin, 1868; Jacksonville, 1869; Fernandina, 1871; and Palatka, 1876.) Unfortunately, the above-mentioned handwritten copy of the annals is the only primary source of information available for the period.
138 Sister Sidonie to Mother Leocadie, January 1, 1867. (McGoldrick, 133-4) Father Delafosse frequently worked with the sisters in Bishop Verot's stead.

protection Bishop Verot might have given them as a compatriot who understood and respected their congregational governance. The juridical decision complicated their life, making each place directly dependent on Le Puy for decisions and personnel, but it was powerless to affect the ongoing communication and mutual affection of the sisters themselves.

BISHOP GROSS SEVERS THE COMMUNITY FROM LE PUY

Bishop Persico who had come to the U.S. in poor health, soon found the Georgia climate too difficult for him. Within three years he resigned the see and became Apostolic Delegate to Canada. On April 27, 1873, Bishop William Gross was ordained as the fifth bishop of Savannah.[139] The following August he made his first canonical visitation of the Sisters of St. Joseph and reappointed Mother Josephine as superior.[140] The annals say nothing about the sisters' relationship with the new bishop. They do mention in passing that in May of 1874, Father Lewis who had been the community's ecclesiastical superior was recalled by his superiors to the great sorrow of the sisters and the orphans whom he had served. The loss of their clerical friend and superior would turn out to be more grievous than expected as, soon after his departure, Bishop Gross decided to sever the Savannah sisters' connection with Le Puy. It was a decision that would have been difficult to carry out had the sisters had an advocate versed in canon law or if they still had recourse to the protection of Bishop Verot. But without that kind of protection, the sisters in Savannah, French immigrants and young Americans, did not know their options. They were effectively powerless when Bishop Gross decided to carve a diocesan community out of a congregation of pontifical right. In reality, Bishop Gross may have set a precedent to be followed more than twenty years later when Bishop John Moore did the same to the St. Augustine sisters.[141] In a tremendously understated

---

139 William Gross was a Redemptorist. Immediately after being ordained by Archbishop F. P. Kenrick in his hometown of Baltimore, he became a Civil War chaplain and mission preacher. Named bishop at the age of 36, he spent eleven years in Savannah before being named as the third Archbishop of Oregon in 1885. He apparently met Bishop Persico while preaching a mission in Savannah and was nominated to the episcopacy at Persico's suggestion. (See http://www.redemptorists.net/images/upload/Bishop%20William%20H%20Gross. pdf) In a letter of September 10, 1867, Sister Julie Roussel told the Le Puy sisters that the Redemptorists were giving a mission in St. Augustine. The preaching team could well have included their future bishop, Rev. William Gross, who formed part of the traveling mission team at that time. (McGoldrick, 150)
140 Georgia Annals, entry for August 17, 1873.
141 Bishop McQuaid of Rochester did something similar when he separated the Sisters of St. Joseph in Rochester from their Buffalo diocesan congregation in 1864. It is quite possible that Bishop Gross knew of other

entry the Georgia annals state:

> May, 1875: The Rt. Rev. Bishop Gross held the 2nd Canonical Visitation…
> made some changes, accepted the resignation of Mother Josephine
> and appointed her Assistant, Sr. St. Peter, Sister Superior pro-tem. He
> announced his intention of having a new Superioress elected by the
> votes of the Sisters. Mother Josephine returned to Florida in June.[142]

What the annals do not divulge is that the bishop gave the sisters 24 hours to decide
if they would remain as part of a diocesan community or return to France.[143] The
sisters who remained in the Georgia community numbered
eight, including two lay sisters, plus seven novices. In July, the
sisters elected Sister Clemence Freycenon as the first superior
of the Sisters of St. Joseph of Georgia and Sister St. John
Kennedy was named director of novices. Sister Clemence
was one of the original missionaries who had arrived from Le
Puy in 1866, and in 1869, Sister St. John had been the first to
profess vows as a Sister of St. Joseph in Georgia. This began
the tradition that the Georgia sisters would elect both their
general and their local superiors.[144]

Sister Clemence
Freycenon

In spite of Savannah's size and prosperity, the Church
and the community struggled as a religious minority in a
staunchly Protestant region. As Sister Josephine wrote in 1872,

---

bishops who had instituted diocesan congregations by separating sisters serving in their dioceses from a mother
congregation in another diocese. Another famous case of a similar situation was the separation of the Sisters of
Charity in New York from Emmetsburg under Bishop Hughes.

142 Georgia Annals. McGoldrick cites the date as May of 1874, but gives 1875 as the date of the election,
which coincides with the Annals. (See McGoldrick, 248) Some sources indicate that Bishop Gross consulted
and communicated his intentions to the superiors in Le Puy. The U.S. archives have no evidence of such
consultation.

143 In discussing the paucity and circumspect tone of the information in the annals Sisters Loretta Costa, Laura
Ann Grady and Mary Ellen Jones, Carondelet sisters who entered the congregation in the Georgia Province in
1940, 1951, and 1955, respectively, noted that because the Georgia sisters were a diocesan community, the
bishops had access to all their records and the sisters would have been most circumspect in what they would
have recorded. The detail about the 24 hour decision period is mentioned in McGoldrick (248) and is a solid
part of the lore of the Georgia sisters. (Interview with Sisters Loretta Costa, Laura Ann Grady and Mary Ellen
Jones, January 18, 2017.)

144 The annals mention this almost as an aside, noting that in February, 1886, Sister Clemence was elected
as local superior at Sharon.

As to our financial resources, we are not exposed to a lack of poverty, for we have nothing of our own; we live from day to day. Monseigneur Persico…is seriously concerned for our position.[145]

Sanitary conditions were far from healthful in the city and mosquitoes were plentiful. Perhaps for that reason Bishop Gross decided that he needed the building occupied by the sisters as a healthcare center. In 1876, less than a year after changing the sisters' juridical status, he decided to move them and the orphans to Washington, Georgia, approximately 180 miles northwest of Savannah and 50 miles northwest of Augusta.[146] The annals' terse explanation of the move reads as follows:

> The Sisters of St. Joseph and the Orphan boys under their charge were removed from Savannah to Washington, January 25, 1876. Rev. Gross wanted to make an infirmary of the house occupied as an orphanage… he made Father O'Brien the superior and gave him the account books and financial affairs of the orphanage so that the Sisters had now only charge of the domestic departments and schools of the orphans. They have nothing more to do with pecuniary affairs of the Orphanage.[147]

Although that entry makes it sound as if the sisters were stripped of home and responsibility, their relationship with Father James M. O'Brien proved to be one of the best things that happened to the community in their 48 year history. Father O'Brien was one of those rare people gifted with strong business sense and an equal share of pastoral sensitivity and love for the orphans. He was stationed in Washington when the sisters arrived, became their friend and protector and although he was twice transferred to other parishes, he managed to return to serve in the Washington area at least twice more after his original term there.[148]

Rev. James
O'Brien

---

145 Mother Josephine Deleage to Father Superior in Le Puy, April 24, 1872. (McGoldrick, 246.)
146 This move doubled the distance between the communities; it was 175 miles by land or sea from St. Augustine to Savannah a land journey of 180 miles inland from Savannah to Washington.
147 Georgia Annals, January, 1876.
148 In February, 1889, when he was assigned to Augusta, the sisters wrote "we were loath to surrender our claims upon one whose very life seemed interwoven with our joys and sorrows. He bade a sad farewell to his children Feb. 16, carrying with him our grateful love and prayers…To him we owe, under God, the prosperity of

His help was so essential that when he was transferred to Atlanta in 1878, he was there only two years before he returned. The last line of the annals entry speaking of his death summed it all up by stating simply and clearly: "We shall never find anyone to replace him and his loss to the sisters of St. Joseph is more than words can tell."[149]

Although the sisters and others were told that the move to Washington was planned to give the orphans a healthier environment, that was not what they found when they first arrived. The annals avoid recording anything about the conditions the sisters found in Washington, but in the account of Father O'Brien's death they spoke of their first contacts with him saying:

> So ably and zealously did he discharge his varied duties that in 1876 Bishop Gross transferred the Boy's Orphanage from Savannah to Washington, the Sisters of St. Joseph retaining their care. The accommodations were wretched and no support provided, so Father O'Brien began his arduous task of begging for the orphans.[150]

Reading between the lines one gets the impression that without Father O'Brien the sisters and orphans would have been stuck, if not in squalor, at least in poverty and isolation. The account of the death of Sister Mary Joseph adds to the impression that Washington was no step up from the conditions the sisters left in Savannah.

> The community was called upon to make a sacrifice of one of our most promising subjects…Our dear Sister Mary Joseph gave up her pure soul to God on St. Matthew's day, Feb. 25, about five o'clock in the afternoon. She had almost completed her two years of Novitiate and when, before leaving Savannah, she was asked if she would not rather return to her home lest exposure to cold in the more Northern part of Georgia might hasten her death, she begged to be permitted to go and cheerfully made the sacrifice of her life. Twelve days previous to her death she had the happiness of making her vows in the hands of her Rev. Superior Father O'Brien. The profession hymn never sounded more sweetly solemn

---

St. Joseph's Orphanage and Academy and there remain as a monument to his self-sacrificing zeal." (Georgia Annals, Feb. 1889) 149 Georgia Annals July, 1899.
149 Georgia Annals July, 1899.
150 Georgia Annals, February, 1876.

than when its strains came to the dying bed...[she] clasped her cross and said, "O if I could only get up for a week, just to wear my profession cross![151]

In spite of the challenges, once in Washington, the sisters seemed to take on new life. If they were juridically separated from St. Augustine, they were also 180 miles from the bishop in Savannah. With Father O'Brien's incisive counsel, they seemed to understand that it was time for them to take matters into their own hands and secure some stability in their own right. In May, 1876, the annals report that:

> A two story frame house contiguous to the Orphanage was offered for sale and the sisters were very desirous to purchase in order to extend their sphere of usefulness.
>
> They had not however the purchase money. A plan was proposed, the Rt. Rev. Bishop and Rev. Father O'Brien immediately gave their consent that two of the sisters should go North to collect. Sister Mary Francis had many friends in the North who contributed generously. She and good Sister Agatha soon collected enough to pay for the House and lot to make the necessary repairs to fit it for a Convent and boarding school.

In some ways that entry raises as many questions as it answers. The sisters named here were both born in Ireland. Sister Mary Francis Burke was received in 1872, at the age of 28, and Sister Agatha Murphy was received at Jacksonville in 1870, went to Savannah as a novice and made her vows there in 1872. Where they lived and what they did before entering the congregation are not recorded, thus we have no hint as to how these immigrants knew wealthy northerners who would be able to help the community. Like Sister St. John Kennedy, they somehow found their way to the Georgia congregation and were unashamed to beg for help for the sisters' missions. It would not be surprising to think that these "home missioners" could have well touched the consciences of people who had supported the Civil War and abolition, asking them now to give practical expression to their commitments by supporting services to the freed slaves and their children. Whatever tactics the

---

151 Georgia Annals, February, 1876.

sisters used, they enjoyed significant success.[152]

The pride the sisters felt in having obtained their own home shone forth in the annals entry about the inauguration of their new endeavor:

St. Joseph's Academy for Young Ladies was opened on the 15th of October, 1876 with one young lady, Miss Lizzie Briody of Savannah. Sister St. Peter, Sister M Aloysius and Sr. Mary Rose were the first sent to this first Institution started by the Sisters as their own property. The Sisters were made very happy to be enabled to promote the greater glory of God and to increase their number under the powerful protection of their glorious Father St. Joseph.[153]

In May, 1877, seven months after the grand opening, the sisters obtained the legal incorporation of both the community and the academy. The entry that recorded the incorporation went on to say:

A school for colored children was opened in a house rented for that purpose. It is the intention of the sisters that this should be an Industrial School, where besides teaching the common English branches the girls and women will be taught to sew, cut and fit clothing. The colored ministers are bitterly opposed to the Sisters' school, still they come. There is not one solitary Catholic among all the colored people of Washington.

Mother St. John Kennedy
Born 9/24/1844, Oswego, NY
Received 12/28/67: Savannah
Novice Director: 1875 -1877
Superior General 1877 - 1899
Deceased: 3/11/1899

The sisters must have often felt caught in the crossfire as some townspeople disapproved of their mission to the African American and the ministers feared the dangers of Catholic influence on their black flocks. But the students came and the sisters continued to teach them the intellectual and manual skills that would help them live independently and well.

---

152 Of the first 25 women to enter the Georgia congregation, 8 were from the Savannah diocese; 8 were born in Ireland; 3 were born in New York State; 2 were born in Ohio; 2 were from near Wheeling; one each from the neighboring states of Georgia and South Carolina.

153 Georgia Annals, October, 1876. The entry about the collection was dated May, 1876.

In 1877, Mother Clemence, one of the original French missionaries and the first Georgia superior, suffered from health problems that forced her to resign from her office. Father O'Brien presided at an election in which the nine eligible sisters chose Sister M. St. John Kennedy as general superior. At the time of the election there were eleven professed sisters and seven novices in charge of the schools and 60 orphans. The following year the community opened Sacred Heart Seminary, an academy for boys in Sharon, Georgia, the area of the original Catholic presence in Georgia. This school gained such prestige that even some of the most outspoken anti-Catholic leaders of the area were proud to have their sons study there.[154] Sacred Heart flourished for nearly seven decades. It closed in 1946, when the town no longer had a viable population base.

In 1878, the sisters also began to build one of several additions to the Academy/motherhouse in Washington, an endeavor they could complete debt-free because of the generosity of a wealthy family from Savannah.[155] In July of that year, the bishop transferred Father O'Brien to Augusta, naming Father Colbert to take his place. In October, 1878, the community lost another American member to an early death: Sister Mary Joseph of the Sacred Heart died on October 22.[156] In that same year the sisters built a convent in Sharon and in January, 1879, they added a frame house on the Academy grounds to serve as the school house for their African American students. In January, 1880, when Sister St. John Kennedy's term of office came to an end she was reelected by the majority of the sixteen sisters eligible to vote. The community then numbered eighteen and had three novices.[157] Sister St. John would be reelected again and again, serving as superior for 18 years from 1877 until 1894.[158]

---

154 One of the most famous among these was Senator Tom Watson, who "launched vivid anti-Catholic, anti-Semitic, and racist drives through his newspapers in the early twentieth century. He pilloried the Catholic Church for repression, while conjuring the specter of the 'growing power and intolerance of popery in this country." (McDonogh, Black and Catholic, 79) Preston Arkwright, another alumnus of Sacred Heart, became the president of the Atlanta Street Car Service, and in gratitude for what the sisters had done for him, he instituted a policy of free transportation for any sister who wished to ride their cars.

155 Georgia Annals, entry for June, 1878. The family name recorded is Gilmartin, very likely a wealthy Catholic family whose daughter(s) may have been a boarder at the Academy.

156 Sister Mary Joseph was one of two blood sisters from Preston, W. Virginia. She had entered the community two years after her sister, Sister Clare Kinneavy and died at the age of 26.

157 The two sisters who did not have voting rights were lay sisters. The community stopped receiving women as lay sisters in 1880. (Dougherty, 97)

158 In 1894, Mother St. John was elected local superior at Sharon where she served until her death in 1899 at the age of 54.

BECOMING ESTABLISHED IN GEORGIA

It is hardly surprising that the Georgia community grew slowly. Catholics comprised no more than 2% of the Georgia population. Cut off from Le Puy, the community no longer received French missionaries. Even though the sisters ministered among local Catholics, many of the women who joined them were immigrants and/or came from other parts of the country. These women presumably learned of the community through friendly priests or from sisters who had already entered the community in the south, all companions among a minority willing to encourage women with a missionary spirit. Another attractive factor may have been the relative freedom of the lifestyle of the Georgia sisters.

The Georgia community's customs must have been inspired by the missionary attitude of some of the first sisters from Le Puy. The community practices reflect a culture of religious life uniquely suited to the South. Among the practices which differentiated the Georgians from many of their counterparts in other areas, one chronicler mentioned the following:

* "The silence was kept very well because there was not much of it." (The sisters spoke at dinner and on "white vestment feast days" they had recreation from the afternoon of the vigil until midnight of the feast day, including a lack of restriction on talking in the dormitories all through the vigil night. Silence at supper was dispensed with during the summer.)[159]
* The Office of the Blessed Virgin Mary was chanted on Saturday and Sunday. It was intoned by the chorister who was usually a novice...If the chorister was tone deaf, it was too bad.
* The sisters in this community never separated themselves from members of their families who visited the convent. It was thought particularly discourteous to have parents dine apart.
* Many sisters went home in the summers – in part because of poverty they couldn't keep large numbers of sisters in the convent at a time when no salaries were coming in.
* For two years after vows, a sister was referred to as a "professed novice." She recreated with the novices and did not have all the

---

159 A "white vestment day" was any day when the priest would wear white vestments. They included the Christmas and Easter seasons, many feasts of the Lord and the Blessed Virgin and the feasts of saints who were not martyrs. A good many days of the year could be counted as "white vestment days."

privileges of the other professed sisters. This took place before the institution of temporary vows to precede perpetual vows.[160]

In spite of the gentleness of their lifestyle, the sisters presented a spectacle in public and had to struggle to establish themselves in an area where Catholics were a very small but denigrated minority. At a time when communities in the north were growing prodigiously, vocations to the Georgia congregation were meagre and monetary support for Catholic efforts was sparse.

One of the northerners who brought a great deal to the congregation was Sister Sacred Heart (Ella) Trout, a cousin of Bishop Gross who entered the congregation in 1877, from Canton, Ohio. Sister Sacred Heart had been a teacher before entering the congregation at the age of 28. Even while she was a novice, she was directress of the sisters' Academy, and by 1910, she had obtained state accreditation for the school, making it the first in the State of Georgia to earn such an honor. She was also successful in affiliating the school with the Catholic University in Washington, D.C. Those accreditations assured that the graduates were recognized as fully prepared for university level work.[161]

In 1897, the first of two devastating fires struck the sisters' property in Washington. Although the orphanage was burned to the ground, no one was injured and, with Father O'Brien's help, the sisters successfully solicited the funds to rebuild. They were not so lucky fifteen years later when on November 20, 1912, another fire destroyed the convent and academy. Once again, no one was injured, but the sisters and students were suddenly homeless. At this point among a number of offers of help, the Chamber of Commerce of Atlanta made a proposal that the sisters couldn't refuse. In what was effectively an extraordinary tribute to the Sisters of St. Joseph, Mr. J. J. Farrell wrote to Mother Aloysius Bourke on behalf of the Augusta Chamber of Commerce. He did all he could to encourage the community to come to his city.

Augusta will give you all of Eastern Georgia and Western Carolina to

---

160 The list combines one made by Sister Rosaline Salome, CSJ, with a document entitled "Customs of the Georgia Community, 1867-1922." (Archives Carondelet)
161 Sister Sacred Heart spent most of her religious life at St. Joseph's Academy in Washington and then, after 1913, at Augusta. From 1894 – 1912 she was Assistant Superior General and from 1913-1921 directress of studies for the congregation. She died on April 28, 1921 when the process for union with Carondelet was nearing completion.

draw your scholars from and offers unsurpassed opportunities for a girls [sic] college, as there is none here or in any city near. Our climate is the best in the country in the winter and more wealthy Northerners spend the winter here than anywhere else in the south, except certain Florida points.[162]

Bishop Keiley, who had been bishop of Savannah since 1900, admitted to Mother Aloysius,

> I had never for a moment thought of Augusta, but it may be as well to consider their offer for as I understand it they not only propose to give you 5 acres of land on the hill in Augusta, but will also give money as well.[163]

The desperate sisters were only too happy to accept the city's offer and on December 26, 1912, Mother Aloysius, Sister Sacred Heart and two other sisters took over a "cottage" in Augusta. While the majority of their students had to return home, the sisters brought the 18 girls who were to graduate at the end of the school year so that they could finish their studies.

    The offer of land and financial help had been a godsend, but the people of Augusta were not planning to defray the entire cost of the sisters' new school. When the sisters secured a loan at 6% interest it was the beginning of their undoing. It was not the interest rate, but the fact that the Irish-American Bank of Augusta where they had deposited the loan failed. Although some of the sisters suspected thievery, or even the involvement of the Ku Klux Klan, the incontrovertible truth was that they had to take out a new loan to cover not only the cost of construction, but the loss of the original funds. Circumstances were forcing them into a financial hole from which they would not be able to escape easily and the once-generous populace did not appear to be able to come to their aid. Bishop Keiley did what he could to help, seeking financial support from outside the diocese and obtaining Vatican permission for additional loans, but no adequate

---

162 Letter from J. J. Farrell to Reverend Mother Aloysius, November 26, 1912, (Savannah Diocesan Archives) quoted in "A Journey of Dedication through Education: Sisters of Saint Joseph" by Father Pablo Migone. (http://www.patheos.com /blogs/labmind/2011/02/a-journey-of-dedication-through-education-sisters-of-saint-joseph.html)
163 Father Pablo, "Journey of Dedication."

solution came their way.[164]

Doubtless, part of the lack of support was based in the persistence of anti-Catholic prejudice.[165] In 1916, the Georgia General Assembly passed what was called the Veasey bill which appointed committees with the right to regularly inspect every convent and monastery for the purpose of "ascertaining what persons are confined...and by what authority such persons are held within the same. The implication, following the lurid tales of the previous century, was that Catholic institutions were centers of lechery and exploitation.[166] The Sisters of St. Joseph were subjected more than once to the intrusive but fruitless inspections.

When financial circumstances forced the sisters to give up their "Mount St. Joseph" in Augusta, Ms. Katie Flannery Semmes, the niece of Sister Gabriel Hynes and a graduate of St. Joseph's Academy, purchased a historic building known as "Chateau Le Vert," and gave it to the Sisters to serve as motherhouse and academy.[167] But even that gift was not enough to stabilize the sisters' situation. They began looking for help through affiliation with another congregation.

By heritage, the community was closest to the Sisters of St. Joseph of St. Augustine with whom they shared their founding stories in France as well as in the U.S. But that congregation was apparently not in a condition to help them out. In 1916, with the support of Bishop Keiley, the sisters began conversations with Mother Agnes Gonzaga Ryan, and then with Mother Agnes Rossiter, superiors general of the Carondelet congregation.[168] The process moved slowly, but by 1922 Bishop Keiley had personally communicated with each Georgia sister and the community was ready to vote on whether or not to join Carondelet. Fifty-five sisters were eligible to vote and forty-nine voted in favor, five against and one abstained. That was the final step necessary to ratify Rome's approbation, and on February 13, 1922, 48 years after being separated from the Congregation of the Sisters of St. Joseph of Le Puy, the Sisters of St. Joseph of Georgia returned to the status of being members of a congregation of papal right, now as Sisters of St.

---

164 Bishop Keiley's correspondence indicates that there may have been naiveté or mismanagement from the sisters' side as well. (Letter from Bishop Keiley to the Rector of the North American College, November 24, 1913, and a general solicitation letter from Bishop Keiley January 5, 1914. Archives Carondelet)
165 The sisters' major debt was to the Mercantile Trust Company in St. Louis. When the suggestion was made that the city of Augusta buy the sisters' indentured property for a school, some people apparently objected to the idea
166 See McDonogh, *Black and Catholic*, 79-80.
167 Mrs. Semmes was also a cousin to Flannery O'Connor who later became a friend of the Georgia sisters.
168 Mother Agnes Gonzaga was superior general from 1905-1917 and Mother Agnes from 1917 to 1936.

Joseph of Carondelet in the newly erected Province of Georgia.[169] On September 16, 1922, Mother Rose Columba McGinnis, the first provincial superior appointed for Georgia, arrived with her assistant, Sister St. John Hobbs, to begin the process of helping the sisters adjust to the changes implied in being part of Carondelet.[170] The sisters' awareness of the necessity of the move did not eliminate the pain of transition, but the spirit with which they entered into it is illustrated by their ceremonial acceptance of the Carondelet *Constitutions*. Knowing that it was necessary to accept the new rule, the sisters decided to build a bonfire and hold a solemn procession to put the old rule into the fire so that their hands were free to accept the new one.[171] The Georgia Province functioned as the youngest of the five provinces of Carondelet until 1961 when it became a part of the St. Louis Province.

LE PUY'S SECOND MISSION TO THE U.S.: THE FALL RIVER, MASSACHUSETTS PROVINCE

The Sisters of St. Joseph in Fall River have preserved a "black, ledger-style book" that has been translated and titled "History of Fall River: 1902-1908." The book is far from detailed and introduces the foundation of their mission very simply. Without great fanfare, the author, who at times speaks in the first person, begins the story as follows:

> In 1902, Father Giguère, pastor of St. Roch's Parish, Fall river, MA was in need of teaching sisters for his parish school. Divine Providence inspired him to share this need with a priest-friend, the Rev. Gaboury, pastor of the Sacred Heart Parish, New Bedford, MA who knew and appreciated the Sisters of St. Joseph already established in Florida. He did not hesitate to advise the Rev. Father Giguère to immediately get in touch with the Motherhouse of the Sisters of St. Joseph in Le Puy, France.[172]

---

169 "Records of the Augusta Province of the Sisters of St. Joseph, 1916-1930" (Archives Carondelet).

170 Among other things, the new provincial and assistant brought with them dozens of guimpes and other pieces of the habit as well as copies of the *Constitutions*, custom books and prayer books. The Carondelet sisters' habit was somewhat different from the Georgia sisters' and the community had to adjust to a new look as they became part of Carondelet.

171 This story comes from Sister Loretta Costa (reception of 1940) who heard it as a young sister from some of the participants. (Interview, January 18, 2017)

172 Anonymous, "*History of Fall River: 1902-1938*," Translated by Sister Irene Comeau, SSJ (Archives SSJS). Unless otherwise noted, the information in this section comes from this "*History*."

The "History" from which we have this account is one of two major sources about the life of the Le Puy sisters in Fall River. The other is entitled "Annals of the Fall River Foundation: 1903-1956."[173]

The Sisters of St. Joseph in Florida were the Le Puy congregation's 's first mission in America. The original Le Puy missionaries had gone to St. Augustine in 1866 at the invitation of Bishop Verot, himself a missionary from Le Puy. No one has recorded the Le Puy congregation's response to the bishops' decisions to separate the sisters in the U.S. from France. The complications of the situation included the fact that the French missionary sisters had come from a centuries-long tradition to a young country and Church. The Congregation of the Sisters of St. Joseph of Le Puy was over 200 years old when they first sent sisters to America and they had already developed their own way of working with their bishops. The Church in the United States was both foreign and new. Baltimore, the first diocese in the U.S., had been established in 1789, and until 1908, the country was still considered missionary territory. Among the bishops with whom the Le Puy sisters worked, the only one born in the U.S. was Bishop Gross of Savannah; Bishop Verot was French, his successor was Irish and Bishop Persico was an Italian.[174] But even if life was unpredictable in the Church in the U.S., circumstances in France were even more difficult for religious congregations. Referring to Father Giguère's 1902 invitation, the community historian explained:

> Reverend Mother Pélagie, the Superior General at the time, immediately and happily responded to the invitation and saw it as a way of safeguarding the sisters against the trials and tribulations that religious congregations were experiencing at that time in France.[175]
>
> In no time arrangements were made and Father Giguère, with the authorization of his bishop, Msgr. Harkins, traveled to Le Puy where he explained to Reverend Mother the needs of the Diocese of Providence, on which depended, at the time, the Catholics of Fall River.
>
> Once arrangements were made and accepted by both parties and approved by the Reverend Mother superior of the Congregation and Rev. Mounier, the foundation was established. A number of sisters

---

173 This document, hereafter referred to as "Annals LP ," was also translated by Sister Irene Comeau, SSJ. (Archives SSJS)

175 "*History of Fall River.*" Unless otherwise noted, all long quotes and general information are from this document.

spontaneously volunteered to be sent to the new mission. Nine were chosen.

The historian goes on to describe the missionaries' leave-taking as only a participant could do, saying that their thoughts were fixed on spreading the love of God and they found the necessary encouragement from "the prayers of the sisters who had not been chosen to go abroad." She summarizes their departure saying "No one could express the range of emotions we experienced during that final hour."

After arriving in New York, the sisters again boarded ship for the nearly 200 mile trip north to Fall River, arriving there at 5:00 a.m., on August 10, 1902. The highlight of their arrival was that they reached the convent in time for the Mass being celebrated by Father R. P. Pichon, S.J., who had been a spiritual director to Therese of Lisieux.[176] After staying a week with the French-speaking sisters at the Convent of Jésus-Marie, they stayed with a parish family for over a month until their "small, ordinary" house was ready for them. In the meantime, they opened school with six big rooms filled to capacity and not enough teachers. On October 8, they celebrated the arrival of two additional sisters from Le Puy. A month later they expanded their school to take in little girls. In April, 1903, three more sisters arrived from Le Puy. Included in this group was Mére Lazare, the former provincial superior of the community in St. Augustine who had been deposed and excommunicated by Bishop Moore.

With the additional sisters, they were able to accept a second school, St. Jean Baptiste, in Fall River. They opened this school on September 3, 1903, with 180 children in four grades. On September 14, three more sisters arrived from Le Puy and on October 14, the community received three postulants, all of whom returned home in the space of a few months for reasons of health.

The fact that the Sisters of St. Joseph in St. Augustine had been removed from the Le Puy Congregation seemed to have minimal effect on their relationships with the sisters in Massachusetts. Their documents record visits back and forth and even seem to indicate some sharing of personnel.[177] Although the history

---

176 The sisters were able to have Fr. Pichon as a retreat director in 1903 and 1904. Therese of Lisieux was beatified in 1923 and canonized in 1925, therefore her fame as a holy woman was well known, but she was not yet called St. Therese.
177 Those visits continued. An entry in the Annals LP dated August, 1908 says "Sr. Stephen from Florida who was visiting her father in New York came to Fall River to pass a few days in our houses. She, as well as Sr. Mary Joseph, was happy to see the Sister who had received them in the Congregation." The sister in question must have been Sister Lazare the provincial who had been deposed by Bishop Moore.

mentions one sister's extended stay in Boston for health reasons, there is no indication that the Fall River sisters visited with the Sisters of St. Joseph of Boston in their first year or two in the United States. The most obvious reason for that would be that the Fall River sisters were French and serving a largely French-speaking community. The majority of the Boston sisters were from an Irish heritage. The other community mentioned in the Fall River history are the Sisters of St. Joseph of Lyon. An entry in the history for December 21, 1904 says:

> Two of our Sisters of St. Joseph of Lyon, Sister Marie Benedict and Sister Marie Théophile have come to spend some time with us. They study the English language while waiting to go to their Mission.

The short annotations in the annals and history for 1903 deal with visits and school events. The only annotation that is out of the ordinary mentions that on December 28, "from the Pastor we receive 25 bottles of wine and a box of cookies," an indication that the pastor understood the French culture.[178] The first entry for 1904 gives an idea about the poverty of the school and the people's willing collaboration with the sisters: "Desks are placed in the 1st and 2nd grades. The children had sold $75 worth of tickets."[179] The other key financial entry for that year was dated August 1: "We bought a piano (Coté) for $135 – paid 25 dollars and took the piano with the promise of paying 10 dollars a month."[180]

In 1904, Fall River was made a diocese by removing Massachusetts territory from the Diocese of Providence, Rhode Island. The diocese's first bishop was William Stang, a 50-year-old German-born scholar and pastor who had served for years in the Diocese of Providence before being named to Fall River. When the Sisters of St. Joseph arrived there, two years before it became a diocese, Fall River was a growing manufacturing center nicknamed "Spindle City" because it was home to more mills than any other city in the world except for Manchester, England.[181] The people who came to work those mills were largely Irish and French-Canadian immigrants, thus increasing the need for Catholic schools and sisters who could speak French. The needs of the Sisters of St. Joseph of Le Puy

---

178 Annals LP, under the entry for December, 1903.
179 Annals LP, January, 1904.
180 Annals LP, August 1, 1904. Coté was a piano manufacturer in Fall River from 1890 until the time of the Great Depression.
181 Between 1870 and 1900, the population of the city grew from 26,766 to 104,863.

who were suffering under France's anti-clerical laws found a perfect match in the needs of the city of Fall River and its growing Catholic population.

In 1905, the sisters were invited to staff a third school, St. Mathew's, also in Fall River. For three years, the sisters who taught there commuted to the school because the parish had no convent. The fourth school the sisters took on was in Blessed Sacrament Parish where the community eventually established their Provincial House.

The sister-annalist's explanation of the process of acquiring the Provincial House came without pretense or even subtitle in the first entry for the year 1906. Mentioning only the date of the transactions, she told the story of the subterfuge necessary for the purchase and the ceremony with which they took possession of it.

Postulants express the desire to join the community.

Due to the great distance of the Motherhouse and difficulties imposed by such a long voyage, it became necessary that a small American novitiate be established. The purchase of a building became necessary.

Across the street, facing the Blessed Sacrament Church, on the summit of a hill dominating the city of Fall River on one side and Mont Hope Bay on the other, was a former residence surrounded by a vast enclosure. It was for sale!

His Excellency, Msgr. Stang, who was highly interested in the growth of this small mission, as well as the R.P. A. Pichon...and numerous friends thought that the former residence was exactly the place that was needed.

We immediately sent a telegram to the Motherhouse who immediately, by telegram, gave the permission to buy the property. However, the property was owned by a Protestant family! Of course, they would not want to sell their beautiful property to Catholics, even less to religious, or they would profit highly of this occasion.

We confided in St. Joseph! Msgr. Stang put the whole situation into the hands of a very charitable woman (Mrs. Nickerson) who bought the property in her name and later transferred it to the Community.

The sale was signed...on March 17, 1906. On the same day, the key to the house was in the hands of our Mothers who immediately took possession of the house. R.P. Delmare, in the name of St. Joseph, opened the door. Immediately following him was Mrs. Nickerson...Rev. Father P. M. Dagnaud (a Eudist), Mother L. Térèrsia, Sr. Louise Agnes and Sr.

Marie Anselme.

Immediately, R. P. Delmare sent someone to the rectory for a statue of St. Joseph! We placed it in a niche by the staircase and fell on our knees to thank our good and tender Father, who on the eve of his feast day gifted us with a house to live in![182]

One week later the community had the papers completed for incorporation. Bishop Stang was named as President of the corporation, Mother Lazare, as Vice President, Sr. Léocadie as Secretary and Mother Térèrsia as Treasurer. In June, 1906, the community moved into the motherhouse where, the history tells us "they had renovated the heating system, lighting and water!" In July, 1906, the community celebrated a ceremony of perpetual and temporary vows in the chapel of St. Roch's parish. Sister Cyprien made her perpetual vows and Sisters M. Gertrude, A. Celestine, Marie de la Croix, M. Euprhasie [sic], M. Justine, Louise Agnes and Marie Térèrse made temporary vows. On November 29, 1906, the community suffered the first death of one of their members, Sister Louise Josephine who was 25 years old and had been professed for three years. The annalist comments that on December 1st, she was given a "first class burial," and that Bishop Stang attended and sang the final prayer of absolution.

The memorable events of 1907 included the note that "Sr. L. Térèrsia and Sr. Marie Noel go to Springfield, Massachusetts in search of Postulants" and that "Sr. Théofrède and Sr. M. Térèrse go to our sisters in Boston to learn English."[183] The community's two historical documents go on recording details about sisters received, vows, school openings, etc. Rarely did they mention details that communicate the flavor of their life, their joys and struggles. Sisters continued to come to Fall River from Le Puy and the sisters maintained communications across the ocean. In 1907, the community received the first official visitation from Le Puy with the arrival of Mother Justine, the General Assistant. She remained among them for several months and on December 26, 1907, before returning to France, Mother Justine held a meeting with all of the sisters. The annals' account of that meeting gives us a rare glimpse of the life of the community in those days. It says:

---

182 "History." The Annals LP add the detail that the papers of sale from Mrs. Nickerson were made in the name of the Superior General, Mother Pélagie Boyer. That would have safeguarded the property from coming into the hands of any local authorities. Mrs. Nickerson seems to have been the wife of "Lawyer Nickerson" who did the legal work for the sisters.

183 In this, as in the above reference to "our Lyon sisters," the sisters express an easy identification with Sisters of St. Joseph from other congregations.

Our Mother Assistant calls all Superiors and Professed Sisters to St. Roch's. In the presence of all assembled, she reminds us of a few rules necessary for the good of all the Mission as well as for the unity of all the houses already established as well as for those to be founded in the future.

After the lecture on different topics, each one gave her opinion and approval or let know her own opinions according to what she deemed justifiable.

At the end of the discussion, the young Sisters left the assembly. The Superiors, the counselors of St. Roch and the three oldest of each house stayed. Our Mother Assistant named these last officers of each Community...[184]

The fact that the Superior from Le Puy met with the entire community is no surprise. The fact that the sisters remembered that she spoke of only a "few rules" implies that she was neither interested in placing a heavy burden on them nor had she found significant problems among them that she felt she had to address. The tone of her exercise of authority comes through without specific commentary by the mere fact that she invited every sister present to offer her own opinion or commentary on what she had heard. We could almost picture this as a meeting in which the sisters, continuing to act in the spirit of their founders, were invited to share their discernment and vision about their communal life and mission.

Finally, the superior named the local superiors who would be charged with maintaining the communal life and spirit. Each house was to have not only a local superior, but also a council that would share authority and the responsibility of discerning the best course of action in each local community. From the beginning of the meeting, it had been clear that the Congregation was committed to the mission in Fall River, not only in the already established communities, but, as the annals recorded "as well as for those to be founded in the future." From this and the fact that Le Puy continued to send sisters to the mission, it was clear that they felt they could now count on a stable future in the United States.

Although the community history and annals did not keep a strict accounting of the number of sisters in the local houses each year, the Catholic Directory of 1912 gives an overview of the state of the community as they neared the end of their first decade in the United States. The Sisters of St. Joseph

---

184 "Annals LP" dated December 26, 1907

were teaching in 5 of the 29 Catholic schools in the diocese. The largest number of sisters, 11, were at St. Roch's Parish, their first school in Fall River. The Directory lists a total of 32 teaching sisters, 10 in the provincial house along with 5 novices and 1 postulant. That number demonstrates both Le Puy's willingness to send missionary sisters as well as the response they were receiving in local vocations.

Fall River was certainly a more congenial place for the Le Puy sisters than had been St. Augustine and Savannah. In Fall River they were able to maintain their identity and become a province of the congregation. Because Fall River was home to a significant number of French-speaking Catholics, the sisters were able to be much more at home and it was far easier for them to serve their neighbors than it had been for the French missionaries working with the English-speaking former slaves and southerners. The women who joined the community in Fall River knew they were joining a U.S. branch of a French community and because they could be at ease with the local French customs, the French sisters had a much easier time of inculturation in their adopted land. All of those factors combined to allow the Sisters of St. Joseph of Fall River to grow as a province of Le Puy for the next seven decades. The 1970s would bring changes that no one could have foreseen in the early 1900s and those changes would result in the merger of the Fall River province with the Sisters of St. Joseph of Springfield. But in 1912, on the eve their second decade in the U.S., the 42 Sisters of St. Joseph in Fall River, had no idea of the morrow, not to mention how two World Wars, the Second Vatican Council and the needs of their Dear Neighbors would call them into a future of changing external identities and a deeper understanding of the charism shared by Sisters of St. Joseph in the United States and throughout the world.

THE SISTERS OF ST. JOSEPH OF CHAMBÉRY: ORIGINS OF THE COMMUNITY

The *Constitutions* of the Sisters of St. Joseph of Chambéry, published in 1862, contain a brief history of the Congregation. Like any history, it relates the sisters' story from a particular perspective, and includes some unique details and omits information found in other accounts. After describing the Le Puy foundation familiar to all Sisters of St. Joseph, the Chambéry authors focused the events of the early 1800s in their own way.

With the revolution of 1793, the Congregation suffered the same fate as all the religious institutions. When the storm came to an end, Msgr. Cholleton, the vicar general of the Lyon diocese gathered many virtuous young women in community. They deliberated about a choice of a rule until Cardinal Fesch, the archbishop of Lyon resolved the question. Deeply conscious of the needs of his flock, he wanted them to dedicate themselves to the care of the poor and sick, whether in hospitals or in their homes. Because of that he resolved to reestablish the Congregation of the Sisters of Saint Joseph.[185]

The history describes Mother St. John Fontbonne and her escape from the guillotine, explaining that she was the person the Cardinal chose to direct the new community. Without giving either their names or their number, the account records that on July 14, 1808, a group of women took the habit and then made vows under the direction of the venerable Mother St. John. It explains that very soon thereafter a community was founded in Chambéry to respond to the needs of young women in the resort town of Aix-les-Bains.[186]

In 1812, Cardinal Fesch accompanied the Empress Josephine, the Princess Leotitia and the Queen of Holland to Aix-les-Bains. His Eminence remarked that the girls of the city were very neglected in regard to religious instruction. He collaborated with Bishop Desolles, the bishop of the Diocese of Chambéry, to establish some Sisters of St. Joseph in Aix.

The princesses, relatives of the Cardinal, and especially Queen Hortense, frequently visited the little group of sisters and as long as the noble woman lived she never ceased to show signs of affection for the sisters of Aix-les-Bains and those in Chambéry where the sisters were called in the same year.

The history written in the *Constitutions* concentrates on governmental and royal officials and the community's legal establishment, surprisingly omitting details about Mother St. John Marcoux, the founding superior of the community.

---

185 *Constitutions Pour La Congrégation des Soeurs de Saint-Joseph de Chambéry*, (Chambéry: Imprimerie de Puthos Fils, Au Verney, 1862) "Préface" (v-xiv). All the citations from the Constitutions to follow are from this source, translation by the author.
186 Aix-les-Bains was a resort town of about 2,500 inhabitants and belonged to the Diocese of Chambéry which had been established in 1779 and was re-established under the terms of the Concordat of 1802 as a suffragan of the Archdiocese of Lyon. In 1817 it became an archdiocese, eventually including the suffragan dioceses of Aosta, Saint-Jean-de-Maurienne, Annecy, and Tarantaise. When the Duchy of Savoy was annexed to France, Aosta became a suffragan of the Archdiocese of Turin. All of these places became home to Congregations of Sisters of St. Joseph.

Born in 1785, Mother St. John Marcoux was among the first women to join with Mother St. John when she formed a community in Saint Etienne in 1808. From Mother St. John Marcoux's earliest days in community, Mother St. John Fontbonne trusted her to establish harmony and order in difficult situations. When Cardinal Fesch asked for Sisters of St. Joseph for Aix-les-Bains, he specified that he wanted Sister St. John Marcoux and to take on the mission with two additional sisters. While the Cardinal made that detail very clear, what apparently slipped his mind was the advisability of informing the bishop of Chambéry that he was sending sisters to his diocese. The bishop's surprise at the sisters' arrival was seconded by the municipal council who were less than enthusiastic about the arrival of religious women for whom they did not want to assume responsibility.[187] In the end, the sisters were given the use of a run-down chateau in which sick and wounded former soldiers had taken up residence as squatters. The sisters cared for their infirm boarders and tried to transform the palatial shambles into a home.[188]

In spite of that inauspicious beginning, the community grew steadily. When France lost control of the territory of Savoy, the Chambéry area was removed from the ecclesial jurisdiction of Lyon and came under the auspices of the newly elevated Archbishop of Chambéry. Because they were no longer in French territory, the Sisters of St. Joseph of Chambéry became an independent congregation. They obtained Lettres Patentes in 1816 and established their novitiate in 1817.[189]

---

187 This may not have seemed too serious to Mother St. John Marcoux who just three years earlier had been missioned to start a boarding school in another town and arrived before the priest had the house ready for the sisters. He invited them to stay with him, but their rule would not permit it. The sisters had started back to St. Etienne when some parishioners stopped them on the road and said they had a solution. "Wanting to save face for their good pastor [they] had found a stable and had arranged, not without difficulty, that the owner would put his horse elsewhere and cede to the religious the place that the animal would leave empty." The sisters used paper for windows and threw blankets over the straw for beds, scrounged some potatoes for dinner and "enjoyed thinking that their beginning was like that of Jesus in a stable." See: Léon Bouchage *(Chroniques de la Congrégation Des Soeurs de Saint-Joseph de Chambéry, Sous la Protection de L'Immaculée Mère de Dieu, De Sa Fondation a L'année 1885,* Tome I (Chambéry: Imprimerie Générale Savoisienne, 1911) 84-85, 108-109.

188 See Sr. Benedicte de Vaublanc, "Mother Saint John Marcoux, A Woman of Faith and Heart," (Archives, Sisters of St. Joseph of Chambéry). Sister Benedicte adds the detail that shortly after their arrival, the Cardinal visited the sisters at the chateau and was astounded that the sisters did not even offer to have him sit down. It did not take him long to realize that the reason was that they had absolutely no furniture. This so impressed the Cardinal that he told and retold the story with the result that "all the beautiful people hurried there to be impressed by the happy sisters in the midst of the indigent." One would hope they also donated what was necessary to provide a minimum of furnishings.

189 "Preface," Chambéry *Constitutions.* Chambéry was part of the Duchy of Savoy, a territory that originally belonged to the Kingdom of Sardinia and which changed hands multiple times over the centuries. When the Sisters of St. Joseph first went there, Savoy was under French rule and in 1815, it was returned to Sardinia, removing it from French civil and ecclesiastical jurisdiction until 1860.

Mother St. John Marcoux, the founder, served as superior for the next three decades. By the time she withdrew from office in 1849, she had opened multiple missions outside Chambéry including Saint-Jean de Maurienne and Moutiers in France and Turin and Pinerolo in territory that became part of Italy. Each of those became an independent congregation.[190]

The Chambéry *Constitutions* of 1862 include a short history of the *Constitutions* of the Sisters of St. Joseph in France. It says that for nearly 80 years every edition of the *Constitutions* was hand-written and subject to significant editing by the various congregations:

> For a long time, all the Sisters of St. Joseph of France, Savoy and Piedmont followed the primitive rule given at Le Puy by Bishop de Maupas which remained in manuscript form until 1729 when it was printed in Lyon under the authority of Bishop de Neville de Villeroy, the Archbishop of that city.[191]

Then the 1862 Preface puts its actual edition in its historical context, explaining the rationale for the changes made since 1729.

> Since that time, different needs, circumstances and the works undertaken by the Congregation have caused modifications to be made in these Rules. A great many editions have been made…all quite different from one another. Concerned that all these changes could alter[192] the primitive Rule, and above all lead to forgetfulness of its spirit, we thought it useful to make this new edition to establish the Rule as it is practiced today in the Diocese of Chambéry. While preserving not only the spirit but also the expressions of the primitive Rule, additions have been made which the necessity of time has rendered necessary.

The Preface goes on to say that for the sake of stability, the current Rule was sent

---

190 "Woman of Faith and Heart." The Congregation of the Sisters of St. Joseph of Annecy also traces its heritage to Chambéry, but came directly from Pinerolo with the help of the Countess Rochejacquelein. (*Chroniques*, 282 ff.)

191 This and the two following citations of the *Constitutions* come from the 1862 edition which can be downloaded from the address: http://gallica.bnf.fr/ark:/12148/bpt6k65186007. Other sources cite earlier printings of the *Constitutions*.

192 The Word translated as "alter" would be literally translated as "denature."

to Rome in 1856, and that Reverend Mother Félicité, the Superior General at that time, received a Brief of Approbation from Pope Pius IX on June 4, 1856. The Brief is published in both Latin and French. Perhaps the most notable feature of the Brief is what it says about the extension of the Congregation. Pope Pius IX wrote:

> It pleases us to learn that not only the countries of the lower Alps, but even the most distant regions enjoy the precious advantage of possessing houses of your congregation which, by virtue of the blessing of the Lord, continues to spread more and more.

The congregation, as it was approved in 1856, was already an international congregation with missions outside of Europe, the first of those being in India where the Sisters of St. Joseph of Chambéry worked in collaboration with the Sisters of St. Joseph of Annecy who had opened their first Indian mission in 1849. The Sisters of St. Joseph of Chambéry received the final approval of their *Constitutions* on March 22, 1861, and published them in 1862.

The structures of authority delineated in the *Constitutions* explain that the superior general is the highest authority in the Congregation. She is elected by the sisters who have been vowed for at least three years and by the local superiors in the diocese.[193] One of the unique features of the 1862 *Constitutions* is its treatment of communities founded outside the Diocese and in foreign mission territories. The Lyon *Constitutions* of 1858 had dealt with communities outside the diocese, but this was the first time *Constitutions* of the Sisters of St. Joseph mention international missions. The parts of the *Constitutions* dealing with foreign missions were among the additions "which the necessity of time" had rendered necessary.

While the Lyon *Constitutions* of 1858 went to great lengths to defend the new authority structure of a Superior General, a common novitiate, etc., the Chambéry *Constitutions* of 1862 seem to simply assume a congregational structure and go on to clarify the relationship that superiors in and outside the Archdiocese of Chambéry should maintain with the superior general and the Archbishop of Chambéry. They also delineated the organization of the congregation in foreign lands. Another first in these *Constitutions* is the question of how sisters can be

---

193 Chapter IV, 1. Although the *Constitutions* speak of the Archbishop of Chambéry as a superior of the congregation, the language has changed radically from the 1729 *Constitutions* which left nearly all authority in the hands of the local bishop. At least some of the Moutiers Sisters would have known these *Constitutions* as they were founded by Chambéry.

missioned to other countries. The Chambéry *Constitutions* specify that sisters who go to the foreign missions must do so as free volunteers and must be known well enough by the Superior General that she can feel assured that they have the maturity required by mission life.[194] By the time that the Sisters of St. Joseph of Chambéry were invited to the United States in the 1880s, they already had significant experience with missions outside of Europe. They had even already opened their first missions in America, having sent sisters to Sao Paulo, Brazil, in 1858.

JANE SEDGWICK AND CHAMBÉRY'S
MISSION TO THE UNITED STATES

In 1835, the pious French Catholic laywoman, the Countess Félicité de la Rochejacquelein, had been the driving force behind the mission of the Sisters of St. Joseph of Lyon to the Diocese of St. Louis. The Sisters of St. Joseph of Chambéry went to the United States at the behest of another laywoman, a convert to Catholicism and a native of Massachusetts, Miss Jane Sedgwick.

Jane Sedgwick came from a distinguished New England family. Her grandfather, a Colonel in the American Revolutionary Army, was a member of the Continental Congress, a judge and a lawyer who won a court case that led to the abolition of slavery in the State of Massachusetts.[195] Jane's biography says that as a young person "It is doubtful if Jane professed any definite religious creed. For Catholics, she felt only pity, considering them as adherents of a religion which held them in the bonds of superstition."[196] As a young adult, she began a close friendship with Mary O'Sullivan, a Catholic. That friendship, plus travel to Rome which brought Jane into Catholic churches with a beauty that enthralled her, ignited a fascination with the Catholic faith that led her to the decision to take instructions from Father Francis Knacksted, a German Jesuit who lived in Baltimore. Jane Sedgwick was baptized in May, 1853, at the age of 32. Like many new converts, her baptism led to a surge of apostolic activity which, in her case, lasted the rest of her life.

Jane's first great cause was to provide space for Catholic worship in her

---

194 The Congregation had sent sisters to India in 1851, more than a decade before this edition of the *Constitutions* was approved.

195 Sr. Mary Cornelia Sullivan, CSJ, "The Little Family: History of the American Province, 1885 – 1974. unpublished manuscript, (Archives CSJH).

196 Sr. Mary Cornelia Sullivan, CSJ, "A Miniature Portrait of Jane Sedgwick," unpublished manuscript (Archives, CSJH). Unless otherwise noted, information about Jane Sedgwick comes from this document. Only direct quotes will be noted. Hereafter referred to as "Portrait."

hometown of Stockbridge, Massachusetts. She arranged to rent a vacant blacksmith workshop. Unfortunately, when the owner discovered her plan for the place, he refused to rent it saying "he did not want his shop to be converted into a Catholic Cathedral."[197] She eventually succeeded in raising the money to build a parish church in Stockbridge and in 1860, she had her friend Father Isaac Hecker lay its cornerstone.[198] Her next project was to establish a Catholic school in the town, a cause that began well until her supportive pastor died and the next pastor was not interested in a school.

Jane inherited a fortune which was kept in a trust, thus leaving her wealthy but preventing her from spending it in a lump sum. Her wealth did allow her to travel extensively, and she returned to Rome frequently to escape the Massachusetts winters. In the course of those trips, she became friends with members of the Vatican curia including Cardinal Simeone, the Prefect of the "Propaganda Fide," the Vatican office in charge of the propagation of the Catholic faith among Protestants and in mission territories.[199] Jane made no secret of her plans for a Catholic school when she spoke to her friends in Rome, a fact that likely endeared her to them.

In 1870, the year in which the Springfield diocese was established, Jane made it a point to get to know the new bishop, Patrick Thomas O'Reilly, to let him know of her hopes. The bishop was impressed with her enthusiasm but tried to let her know that he had more pressing priorities. He was particularly in need of priests for the parishes of his diocese, and he worried that her plans for Catholic education were not financially feasible.

By 1873, Jane succeeded in getting the bishop's support in seeking help of the Sisters of St. Joseph of Carondelet in St. Louis. Mother Agatha Guthrie responded that she could not send sisters at that time, but left the door open until, in 1880, Mother Agatha wrote to Springfield saying that her congregation simply could not respond to their need. With that, Jane turned to the Sisters of St. Joseph of Brooklyn who had recently established a mission in the Springfield diocese. That community turned her down as well.[200]

---

197 "Portrait," 2.
198 Isaac Hecker was another famous convert who was baptized in 1844 and ordained in 1849. He became the founder of the Paulist Fathers and a biography published about him toward the end of the century became the catalyst for the "Americanist" controversy in the Catholic Church.
199 At this time, the Church in the United States was still classified a mission territory and remained under the authority of the "Propaganda."
200 The Brooklyn community had recently opened missions which evolved to become the Congregation of the Sisters of St. Joseph of Springfield. Miss Sedgwick felt that part of the problem with getting the help

According to her biographer, Jane was at the point of conceding that all her plans might be expressions of her own desires more than the will of God. Then an audience with Pope Leo XIII reinforced her passion for the cause. She described this catalytic event in her diary saying:

On the third of May, I was summoned to the Holy Father's presence and was accompanied by a Polish countess, much interested in my success…The rooms were crowded and we found ourselves among the last. The Holy Father was already very tired and when my turn came there seemed little hope that I could obtain anything satisfactory for the object I had at heart…

My prayer for some time had been, "If this be the will of God, may it prosper; if mine, may it perish." And this was on my lips as I was approaching his chair.

I knelt at his feet, being introduced by Monsignor Marchi as recommended by Cardinal Simeoni…

The Holy Father said playfully, "Behold the Mother of America." I told him that I had many…difficulties to encounter. He put his hand on my head…"This is the work of God, daughter," he said, "and I say to you, persevere in it in spite of all obstacles."

I left him greatly consoled and with the feeling that the perception of my trials and the state of the case was something almost miraculous."[201]

Jane continued to speak with Cardinal Simeone about her hopes for a school. In addition to being the Prefect of the Propaganda Fide, he was the Cardinal Protector of the Sisters of St. Joseph of Chambéry. In 1885, Cardinal Simeone wrote to Mother Félicité, the Superior General at Chambery:

March 26, 1885, Reverend Mother,
You already know that a pious lady, Jane Sedgwick, has labored much to establish a Catholic school in the mission of West Stockbridge…She has spared neither trouble nor money…she has begun to erect a new school

---

of the religious communities was a lack of whole-hearted support from Bishop O'Reilly. Unfortunately, she communicated that to friends in Rome and Bishop O'Reilly felt that she was putting him in a bad light with the Vatican. They eventually got beyond that problem, but for a time it created an uncommon situation in which a laywoman's influence brought Vatican pressure on a U.S. bishop.
201 "Biography," 34.

which will soon be completed. Nevertheless, she has not yet found teachers. I have been told that the Bishop of Springfield, convinced that the sisters of this Institute are very good teachers...has asked superiors to send some Sisters...but they have refused to grant his request.

It is for this reason that I urgently beg you to send some Sisters to direct this school...I am confident that you will do all in your power to support the desires of this pious lady, the Bishop of Springfield and mine.

Devotedly Yours in Jesus Christ,
John Cardinal Simeoni[202]

The Cardinal's letter was reinforced by another from Monsignor Ragonesi, Jane's spiritual director, who didn't hesitate to mention Pope Leo XIII's interest in the cause. These appeals arrived in Chambéry as Mother Félicité was dying. Her assistant and successor, Mother Hyacinthe, knew that Mother Félicité had been in favor of the project and wanted to continue her predecessor's initiative. At the same time she wanted to be certain that the sisters would have the necessary means of support and the apostolic freedom to which they were accustomed. After obtaining the permission of the Archbishop of Chambéry and after receiving all the necessary assurances, Mother Hyacinthe wrote Jane Sedgwick in Rome formally accepting the mission which was now to be situated in Lee, Massachusetts, a slightly more prosperous town about five miles from Stockbridge.

FROM CHAMBÉRY TO LEE TO NEW HARTFORD: FROM MISSION TO PROVINCE

On September 30, 1885, five missionaries, Sisters Mary of Jesus, Josephine of the Sacred Heart, Martha, Frances Henrietta and Honora, left Chambéry. They arrived in New York on October 12. There they were met by Father Smith, the pastor of the parish in Lee, and went with him to Lee the following day. Although Jane Sedgwick had provided a house for them, the pastor considered it too small and gave them his rectory instead.

The biggest problem then facing the sisters was that only two of them, Sisters Mary and Josephine O'Connor, had an adequate command of english

---

202 Quoted by Sister Mary Cornelia Sullivan in "The Way is Long" an unpublished biography of Jane Sedgwick, (Archives CSJH), 51.

and they spoke with a strong accent.[203] Given that they would not open their school until January, Father Smith arranged for the sisters to go to Springfield for a few weeks to learn from the sisters there about the teaching methods and the culture of their new country. When they opened the school in January, 1886, they had an enrollment of 150 girls and boys.

Within a year of opening the school, the sisters received their first candidates for the community. One, Mary Smith (Sister Frances Elizabeth), was a niece of the pastor, the other was Agnes Wrinkle (Sister Mary Aloysius). In 1888, Sister Mary O'Connor accompanied the postulants to France where they would enter the novitiate. In September, 1888, four additional sisters arrived from Chambéry: Sisters Louise Hermance, Louise Benedict, Mary Berchmans and Mary Antoinette. The year 1889 saw the arrival of three more French missionaries and the community's first foundation in Connecticut, in the town of Danielson. One year later, with six additional sisters who had arrived from Chambéry, the community opened its first mission in New Hartford, Connecticut. In 1891, three sisters made their final vows in the United States.

The need to send women who wished to join the community to France for formation proved to be a serious impediment to the community's growth. In July, 1895, Sister Josephine O'Connor wrote to Bishop Beaven of Springfield asking his permission to open a novitiate in Lee. She explained the community's situation saying:

> As time goes on, we feel more and more, the imperative necessity of finding subjects qualified for teaching in America, and therefore of multiplying vocations in this country. At present, the prospect of a voyage across the Atlantic is an insurmountable obstacle to many on account of the distance and the expense. We have some American Novices in France, but none of them have completed the required two years' novitiate. Had we a novitiate in America, they could even now begin to make themselves useful. The new establishment in Fitchburg we gladly accepted, though at the cost of many sacrifices to the existing communities. There is but one means of alleviating the pressure under which we are laboring, and it is to Your Lordship that your children

---

203 The two were blood sisters, born in England, but raised in various parts of Europe. Thus their reputed accent was either British or the result of their cosmopolitan background and ability to speak multiple languages.

have recourse...[204]

In 1896, the Chambéry Congregation created a United States province and named Mother Josephine, one of the original missionaries, as the first provincial superior. That demonstrated the Congregation's belief that the U.S. mission should become its own entity.

Believing that she understood the details of the U.S. situation and that she had Bishop Beaven's support, Chambéry's superior general applied to Rome for permission to open a novitiate in the United States. Sister Josephine, the provincial superior in Hartford, had to quickly explain to the bishop that the sisters were surprised to receive approval for their request and had not meant to circumvent his authority. She wrote to Bishop Beaven saying:

It appears that Reverend Mother, though doubtful of success, availed herself of your verbal permission to make to Rome the necessary application to open a novitiate. Contrary to her expectations, the reply was favorable...

As you will see, my Lord, in this document everything is referred in your hands [sic]. We may, therefore, I presume, in accordance with your previous permission, receive subjects, promising them that they may receive the Holy Habit in this convent after the necessary probation.

Of course, whilst the novitiate is located in Lee, all the conditions required cannot be strictly adhered to, our convent being so small; but I trust it will suffice for a beginning. For the future, we confidently look to that Divine Providence which has never failed us...

Humbly begging your Lordship's blessing
I remain,
Your obedient daughter,
Sister Josephine[205]

---

204 Letter from Sister Josephine O'Connor, local superior in Lee, to Bishop Beaven, July 20, 1895. (Archives, CSJH) Bishop Beaven came to the Springfield Diocese in 1892, after the death of Bishop Patrick T. O'Reilly, the bishop with whom Jane Sedgwick had worked to bring the sisters to Lee. In 1883, Bishop Beaven had asked Mother Teresa Mullen of the Brooklyn Sisters of St. Joseph to found a motherhouse and novitiate in the Springfield Diocese. By the time the Chambéry sisters were ready to open their novitiate in 1895, the Springfield sisters who had helped the Chambéry sisters in their early days in the United States, were well-established as a diocesan community.
205 Sister Josephine O'Connor to Bishop Beavens, December 5, 1895 (Archives CSJH).

Somehow, in the process of obtaining permissions in the United States, France and Rome, not only did the Superior General rely on Bishop Beaven's "verbal permission," but some mistaken information was passed on and the sisters' first pastor, Father Thomas Smith got involved in the question, thinking that the sisters were seeking permission to open a novitiate in Pittsfield, Massachusetts, where he had been sent after being in Lee. Father Smith suggested that the sisters had gone behind his own and the bishop's backs to seek Rome's permission for the novitiate.

The matter incited some very unpleasant communications, but in the end, the sisters opened their novitiate in Lee in 1896, in spite of the lack of sufficient space.[206] Three women received the habit of the Sisters of St. Joseph in the year that the novitiate was established. The community history includes an anecdote that indicates just how "foreign" the French Catholics and the new members of their community appeared to the general public in Lee:

On December 8, 1896, Bishop Beaven of Springfield presided at the ceremony of clothing, which took place in St. Mary's Church in Lee, since the convent chapel was too small. Never having witnessed such a ceremony before, the people of Lee, Catholic and Protestant, turned out in large numbers. A few days later, the three novices were taking a walk with their mistress when a lady approached them, saying that she wished to ask a question. Among her friends, Protestants like herself, there had been quite a discussion as to the meaning of the recent ceremony. The lady stated that one of her friends maintained that the three young women were being anointed, while she herself thought they were being ordained. Would Mother Ida please tell her which was right? The freshly "anointed" and "newly ordained" had a merry time relating the incident to the sisters when they got home.[207]

---

206 In December, 1895, Father Thomas Smith wrote to the bishop denying that he had invited the sisters to his parish in Pittsfield, intimating that the superior general in Chambéry, probably in league with Sister Josephine, had misrepresented his intentions. He concluded his letter saying, "I clearly perceive how undesirable such religious are in a diocese and what trouble and annoyance they are liable to cause." (T. M. Smith to Bishop Beaven, December 11, 1895, Archives CSJH). Ironically, one of the first U.S. women to join the Chambéry congregation was Father Smith's niece, Sister Mary Elizabeth Smith. On January 11, 1896, Mother Josephine wrote to Bishop Beaven explaining that there had been no underhanded intentions and that "we have looked to Pittsfield in the future, simply because we placed childlike confidence in him whom we have ever looked up to as to our Father and Friend, and who, very plainly and openly, told us his intentions previous to his departure from amongst us."

207 See Sister Cornelia Sullivan, "The Little Family: History of the U.S. Province, 1885-1974," unpublished manuscript, (Archives CSJH) 27.

Given the novitiate's difficulties in the small town which included tight quarters and misunderstandings with local clergy, it is not surprising that the community accepted the opportunity to move their motherhouse to Connecticut when the opportunity presented itself. Mother Josephine, the provincial superior, explained the sisters' desire to move to Bishop Beaven in a letter dated August 3, 1897. She wrote:

> My Lord,
> It is now nearly two years since we obtained permission to open a temporary Novitiate in Lee; with a view to transferring it to a more favorable position in your Diocese when circumstances would permit. No such opportunity has presented itself. On the other hand, our works are growing (we have four new foundations this year), our numbers are increasing and therefore it seems to me a duty to provide for future pressing needs. Divers [sic] providential events have seemed of late to indicate the Hartford Diocese as the spot most favorable for the foundation of a permanent Novitiate and Provincial House, and just recently an opening, such as we scarcely dared hope for, has been granted us in Hartford. May we venture to hope then, that under existing circumstances you will not blame me for humbly asking your Lordship's permission to take the necessary steps to transfer our Novitiate from Lee to Hartford?
>
> Such of our sisters as will still labor in Your Diocese will, I am sure, do their utmost to prove to you their devoted and respectful attachment. As for me, My Lord, I will leave the diocese with feelings of deep regret. But God's Holy Will be done. His ways are not like ours, and He knows best.
>
> Thanking your Lordship for your many acts of kindness in the past and requesting the favor of a reply, I remain,
> Your obedient Child,
> Sr. Josephine [208]

In 1898, the community was able to purchase a twenty-one acre plot of land in Parkville, now known as West Hartford, Connecticut. By the fall of that year the novitiate and provincialate were moved to the sisters' new home, the Convent of

---

208 Sister Josephine O'Connor to Bishop Beaven, August 3, 1897 (Archives, CSJH).

Mary Immaculate.

Miss Jane Sedgwick had died on February 12, 1889, having finally seen her dream begin to come to fruition. Little could she have guessed that within 25 years of their arrival, the Sisters of St. Joseph of Chambéry in the United States province would number over thirty and would have opened two hospitals and a school of nursing in addition to numerous schools. Without having known the charism of the community, she well fulfilled two of Father Médaille's maxims:

> Be courageous to undertake what God wants of you and constant to persevere in what you undertake, never giving up, whatever difficulties occur and whatever obstacles may be placed in your path unless you become totally powerless against them. Accordingly, pursue to the very end and with gentleness and vigor what you have once and for all resolved and what you prudently believe corresponds to the greater glory of God.[209]

Miss Jane Sedgwick, like the Countess Rochejacquelin and myriads of nameless men and women shared the zeal of the Sisters of St. Joseph and made it possible for them to exercise it on behalf of the Dear Neighbor.

THE SISTERS OF ST. JOSEPH OF LYON IN MAINE

A document displayed in the archives of the Generalate of the Sisters of St. Joseph of Lyon in France says:

> They aren't wanted in France!
> Then we will have them everywhere!
> In their soul they have too much life
> In the heart these Sisters of St. Joseph have
> too much fire for a human decree
>   To condemn them to die out.
> The One who guides everything wants
> them to continue living…
> From dusk to dawn; from the south to the
> north winds,

---

209 Translation of the Maxims 66 & 67 by Federation of the Sisters of St. Joseph International Research Team, 1975. Accessed through http://www.ssjfl.org/prayer/maxims-of-perfection/.

If on one point of his domain the sky becomes dark and the earth inclement...

He tells them: "Go everywhere!"

When, overflowing a too narrow France, the Sisters of St. Joseph sought to live elsewhere, it was on the land of Sem where they first stopped...and today we see them: at Odana, Caesarea, Sivas...Pushing further, all the way to the south of India...it's at Madura, in full Brahman country, that another swarm went to form their hive.

But the ancient world did not suffice the Sisters of St. Joseph, they needed the new world – America...land of hope and liberty...[210]

The document refers to the spread of the Congregation of the Sisters of St. Joseph of Lyon from their increasingly unhospitable home in France. They went beyond Europe to India and eventually made their second foundation in the United States.

At the end of the 19th century and the beginning of the 20th, life grew more difficult by the day for the Catholic Church and especially women religious in France. Ironically, while the government was curtailing and cutting out their apostolic works, French congregations of Sisters of St. Joseph continued to receive new vocations. While that was a formidable sign of faith and resistance, the practical reality was that there were more mouths to feed and far fewer salaries to spend in the market. The Church in France became more of a missionary sending church than ever before. Religious repression in France turned out to be a boon for local Churches, including in the United States.

SISTER MARIE BENEDICTE SETS
HER SIGHTS ON THE U.S. AND CANADA

In Lyon, Sister Marie Benedicte Nigay was particularly disturbed by the events taking place around her. She rebelled against the laws that forbad her to wear a religious habit while teaching. Her biographer says that when she returned to the motherhouse after the government had closed 100 of the congregation's schools she began to turn her gaze to other places.

Why shouldn't we look under another sky, for instance, in Canada, for a

---

210 "Jackman, Maine" poster celebrating the Lyon congregation's foundation in the United States. Although the document is Lyon's, the sentiment was common among the Sisters of St. Joseph and so many others for whom it was becoming impossible to carry out their apostolate in France. (Original translation by Sister Line Roux, CSJ, interpretation. M. McGlone.)

place to be free to do good and live our ideals?"

Thus, with an energetic gesture of contempt and farewell, she threw her hat on the table and declared that she would never be able to 'abandon these rags.'[211]

Sister Benedicte was ready to set out even if her destination was less than clear. Mother Henri-Xavier agreed to let her go and, like an advance guard for sisters who could come later, on December 8, 1904, Sister Benedicte and Sister M. Theophile left Lyon for Le Havre where they boarded the ship, *La Gascone,* headed for New York. From New York, the two sisters went immediately to Fall River to stay among and be oriented by the Sisters of St. Joseph of Le Puy who had opened their first mission in that city just two years earlier, in August, 1902.[212] Sister Benedicte's biography explains how well the sisters of the two French congregations fit together:

To Fall River where our Sisters from Le Puy have an important parish school, we exiles are always very fraternally welcomed. On their side, they are always satisfied and grateful, always marked by their natural joy and at the same time by their virtue. Sister Benedicte adapts quickly and looks for a way to be useful to the community…[213]

One of the Fall River sisters wrote about the visitors from Lyon in her correspondence with a superior in France. She said:

I can't resist the temptation to tell you about all the pleasure that we have in our dear sisters. They are so good, so gentle, so gay, so courageous. Real missionaries, real apostles. Yesterday I said to Sr. Marie Benedicte,

---

211 Quoted from the necrology of Sister Marie Benedicte Nigay (Archives CSJL). Some of the Lyon congregation's necrologies are extensive enough to be considered short biographies and will be referred to as either biography or necrology as appropriate to the context.

212 The archives of the Sisters of St. Joseph of Lyon in Maine have a number of informal documents recounting the adventures of their first sisters in the U.S. The sources for the information which follows comes from these, particularly, "Ile a La Crosse, Lac La Plonge, South Berwick," "The Sisters of St. Joseph of Lyons in Maine – 1906," "Mother Marie Philippine," the necrology of Sister Marie Benedicte, the necrology of Mother Mary Philippine Coupat, and Sister Janet Gagnon's compilation of the History of the Sisters of St. Joseph published in 1980 by the Diocesan newspaper *The Church World.*

213 In this section of the necrology/biography, the unnamed author makes it clear that she was among the sister missionaries in the United States, even if not Sister Benedicte's companion.

"Poor dear sister, I'm always afraid I'll find you in a corner crying." She replied, "O no, sister, It's too infant to cry!"[214]

The letter not only describes the spirit of the Lyon visitors, but shows the sensitivity of another French missionary who knew what it meant to miss her homeland. Sister Benedicte had made her choice and regrets were not going to plague her.

The Fall River superior, wrote to Mother Henri-Xavier of Lyon on March 3, 1905 and gave her an overview of how her sisters were faring in their new place:

> Your daughters are charming. Really apostles, always gay, always with even humor. Their douceur, their respect for one another edifies us greatly.

Her next remarks give additional insight into the character of Sister Benedicte, the sister who left home rather than abandon her "rags."

> If their English has hardly advanced, as Sister Louise Angela has hoped, it's because Sr. MB is actively pursuing another objective, knocking down castles, if not in Spain, but Canada where she thinks is the place designated by the Lord for a miraculous catch.
>
> In front of a map, she put her finger on Saskatchewan, where she might not have even known the name, she said one day to our Sister secretary, "It's there that I will go."[215]

Sister Marie Benedicte was actively looking for a mission for her sisters. She wrote to priests, religious, bishops, anyone she could think of. Her first offer was to help with a hospital – she was thrilled until she read that "English is absolutely necessary." Lamenting the sin of the architects of the Tower of Babel, she continued her search and finally found a possibility for work for her sisters with a parish in Jackman, Maine. She wrote to Mother Henri-Xavier in Lyon giving her the details. She was astounded when the reply she received from Lyon sent her not to Jackman, but to Canada.

---

214 S. Benedicte, necrology, quoting a letter of December 29, 1904 to Mother Angele Stephane.
215 S. Benedicte, necrology.

LYON FOUNDS NEW MISSIONS
IN THE UNITED STATES AND CANADA

It had been nearly 70 years since Mother St. John Fontbonne had sent the first French Sisters of St. Joseph to America. The Lyon missionaries who came in 1836 and 1837 had taken part in foundations from St. Louis to Philadelphia, to Toronto and St. Paul, and all variety of places in between. By the year 1900, the sisters who followed after them could be found from New York to California and from Northern Michigan to Florida and Texas. Now, in 1905, Mother Henri-Xavier decided to accept the mission in Jackman, Maine, and another in Canada. She was sending Mother Marie Philippine and a group of sisters to Jackman and missioned Sister Marie Benedicte to Prince Albert, Saskatchewan, Canada. Mother Henri-Xavier told Sister Marie Benedicte that she should go to the convent of the Ladies of Sion where she would meet the six sisters being missioned to be her companions in that place.

The background to that amazing piece of news was that Bishop Albert Pascal, O.M.I., the first Vicar Apostolic and then first bishop of Prince Albert, Saskatchewan, made a personal appeal to the motherhouse at Lyon. He was seeking religious women to serve in Ile a La Crosse, a remote part of his diocese.[216] Mother Henri-Xavier accepted the bishop's invitation to Canada at the same time as she accepted the invitation to Maine.[217] She then missioned six sisters from Lyon to go to that remote area of north-central Canada where they would meet Sisters Benedicte and Theophile.

Before going to Canada, Sister Benedicte visited the Sisters of St. Joseph in Philadelphia with whom she developed a great friendship. She let Sister Henri-Xavier know that those were the sisters to whom she should send future missionaries who needed to learn English. Sister Benedicte's biographer explained:

> The community of Chestnut Hill was, for us sister students, a true family. Mother MB…would write again and again to the motherhouse, send the sisters to Philadelphia to learn English…[we can] testify to their good spirit and the good pedagogical formation they will find there.[218]

---

216 Isle de la Crosse is the second oldest community in Saskatchewan. In 1846 Oblate priests established a mission in the area and the Grey Nuns from Canada joined their ministry in the 1860s.
217 In 1891, the Apostolic Vicariate of Prince Albert was removed from the Archdiocese of St. Boniface which began as the diocese encompassing all of the Canadian territory West and North from the Great Lakes to the Pole. It was established as a Diocese in 1907. Much of the territory was under the pastoral care of the Oblates.
218 S. Benedicte, necrology.

Sister Benedicte, although quite at home with the sisters from Le Puy, recognized the importance of what she and her fellow missionaries from Lyon could learn from the Chestnut Hill sisters, the majority of whose members were from the United States and native English speakers. Living with the French sisters in their French-language parish in Fall River may have been quite comfortable, but the sisters needed the inculturation and language immersion that only an English speaking American community could help them achieve.

Mother Clement Lannon the Superior General in Philadelphia who received the Lyon sisters and gave them a warm welcome is the same who helped the Cleveland community and offered a home to the Wichita sisters when their poverty seemed insurmountable. The Philadelphia community had a unique relationship and connection to Lyon through Mother St. John Fournier who had come from Lyon in 1837, and had been the superior in Philadelphia almost all the while from 1847 until her death in 1875. In 1905, Mother Henri-Xavier of Lyon wrote to Mother Clement in 1905 to ask for hospitality for the Lyon sisters who would be coming to Maine, asking if they could stay with the Philadelphia community until all was ready for them in Jackman. Her letter gives a quick glimpse of conditions in France and the sisters' response. Sister Henri-Xavier said:

> You have learned through the press, the storm has continued to rumble and to crush the French Congregations. Ours has not been spared. Nevertheless, our Communities possessing a legal decree of existence are still standing, although a considerable number have seen their schools closed. Some Sisters still in these houses are busy with the poor, visiting the sick, in the sacristy and parish work. The schools which are still functioning will close little by little, for teaching is henceforth forbidden.[219]

After more of that news, Mother Henri-Xavier explained where the French situation was leading the sisters and asked for the help of the Philadelphia community.

> Besides our missions in the Orient, we have made several foundations in Mexico.[220] A group left lately for l'Ile a la Crosse…where they will lack

---

219 This and the next selection are both from a letter from Mother Henri-Xavier to Mother Clement in Philadelphia, Oct. 12, 1905 (Archives SSJP).
220 Lyon opened their first mission in Mexico in 1903 and in Madurai, India, in 1906.

neither work nor privations…another group is preparing for Madura. Besides we are expected in September, 1906, in Jackman, Maine, where a schoolhouse is being built. These different foundations require the knowledge of English…would you be able to receive into your excellent community two or three of our sisters? They would stay in Philadelphia until the opening of the establishment at Jackman, to be able, if not to teach immediately, at least to observe the English teachers and establish connections. Although we regard this service beyond any remuneration, we do not intend to ask you to give it gratuitously. Besides, if it is agreeable to you, our Sisters would willingly undertake the teaching of French, for they are all certified and I believe would not cause you any annoyance…

Thus, the Lyon congregation had everything as well-arranged as possible to open two new missions in English-speaking North America, one in the northern United States and the other in the far northern part of Canada.

Sister Benedicte's biography says that she and Sister Theophile "left on a five-month trip" to arrive at Prince Albert in Saskatchewan. Although the journey was arduous, the amount of time they spent en route surely had much to do with the waiting period before the Lyon sisters would arrive and the visits they made along the way. One of those visits was to Bishop Pascal who "did not conceal the fact that they would have to suffer." The 360 miles distance from Prince Albert in Saskatchewan to their new mission in Ile a la Crosse was made more formidable by the fact that the roads would not take them there. Depending on the season, portions of the travel would always be by boat or sleigh, and the journey could not be made in less than 10 days. They were going to be in an isolated area, ministering to indigenous Native Americans as well as the Canadian settlers. Sister Benedicte learned from the bishop that she was to be the superior of the mission. Her biographer describes the sisters' arrival as follows:

On August 17, 1905, they arrived happily to Prince Albert, the little colony that had 8 members, the first American community of the Sisters of St. Joseph of Lyon. They just had time to catch their breath and they were to leave for Ile a la Crosse, where they debarked on September 8, 1905. This last stage was, by far the hardest. But to the end, Jesus was on their voyage…And he found them on their arrival, in the poor little chapel…

Their place was unhealthy where the wind came through their house, with a cold of 45 degrees below zero, poverty of furnishings, penury in everything. The most painful of all, the hostility of the population, who looked poorly on the newcomers.

From the material point of view, the sisters were dependent on the priests, where their undoubted goodness couldn't overcome certain details…With tact and good grace, Mother B knew how to do the best… and was finally able to get from the superior of the mission at least the minimum she saw as necessary for the mission and for the children. The village soon saw who it was dealing with; their sympathy flowed and at the same time, the demands. For these great children of the great lakes [sic] it took the remedy of everything, the illnesses, the clothing, douceurs of all sorts…The little [ones] became attached to their educators and were open to their influence. "At our arrival…the children didn't know how to laugh, they learned by seeing us. They quickly learned to pray, less so to obey…"

One sister spoke in the name of all saying "Our life is hard in its unending work, the temperature, the isolation, but is, one might say, the best from all other points of view. This is the family, and a very united and happy family…we have evening recreation excessively happy, we wouldn't miss them for anything in the world…"[221]

In 1906, three additional sisters joined the Canadian community and they opened a second mission at nearby lac La Plonge. The short history of the mission simply says: On September 7, 1908, they received notice from the Rev. Mother and her Assistants to leave la "La Plonge;" Mother Benedicte's biographer says simply, "it was for serious reasons."[222] The Canadian missionaries left their mission and joined their sisters from Lyon who were already established in Jackman, Maine.

LYON SETTLES IN MAINE

Lyon's first group to settle in Maine arrived in New York on September 10, 1906. There they were met by two sisters of St. Joseph from Chestnut Hill. There were eight sisters in the group, and, following the plans Mother Henri-Xavier of Lyon

---

221 The quotation marks are in the necrology/biography without an indication of whom they are citing.
222 The "short history" is a paper from the Archives entitled: "Ile A La Crosse, Lac La Plonge, South Berwick," (Archives, CSJL).

made with Mother Clement in Philadelphia, two of the group remained at Chestnut Hill when the rest departed for Maine. The travelers made the trip by ship as far as Boston and there boarded a train for Portland, Maine. In Portland, by some chance, they were met by a man who asked if they were the Sisters of St. Joseph destined for Jackman. When they said they were, he introduced himself as Father Forest, the pastor who had sought help from Lyon. His first question was "Why didn't you send me a telegram? I would have met you in New York!"[223] The sisters traveled with their pastor to Jackman, a town of about 80 families. According to their own account,

> The convent, a four story granite building which the priests had helped to build, was about ready for occupancy...The Superior, Mother M. Philippine, could write to France on September 26: "School opened on September 24, with a registration of 60 pupils, 24 boarders and 36 day pupils...November 21, Mass was celebrated for the first time in the convent chapel...
>
> The School grew by leaps and bounds. The pupils soon became attached to the sisters whom they gave the title of "Mothers."[224]

One of the factors that helped the sisters in their process of settling into their new homeland was that the population of the area was heavily French-Canadian. Thus the sisters could communicate easily with their students and the parents.[225]

The history of the mission continues:

> The fond hope of the Superior, Mother M. Philippine, was that religious vocations would one day develop in some of the children. She had not long to wait. In 1909, an Assistant of the Superior General came to visit the Sisters in Jackman. When she returned to Lyons, she was accompanied by a French-Canadian girl, Marie Louise Rancourt, who was the first postulant from Sacred Heart Convent. Another followed in

---

223 This information is in another short history titled "The Sisters of St. Joseph of Lyons in Maine – 1906," (Archives, CSJL)
224 This and the next citation about the history of the mission are from "Sisters of St. Joseph...in Maine."
225 Even in the 21st century, Maine has the highest percentage of French-speakers of any state in the Union, with Jackman listing 12% of its population as Francophone as measured by the U.S. census bureau in 2014. (See: https://en.wikipedia.org/wiki/New_England_French)

1911, and four others in 1912, when the Superior General herself visited the mission.

The superior of the Jackman mission, Mother Mary Philippine had received the habit in Lyon on September 8, 1887, at the age of 19.[226] At the age of 33, she was named superior for the first time in the convent in Dardilly, France. From her early years in the community she had volunteered for the missions, beginning with Armenia, but it wasn't until the school she directed was closed by the government that she received her opportunity to go beyond the French borders.

It was around the time her school closed that Sister Benedicte, already residing in Fall River, had been in touch with Father Forest, a Canadian missionary serving the small town and lumberjack population around Jackman, Maine. In advertising his town to the community he had described it as the "Switzerland of Maine," a description that doesn't do justice to Maine's winter weather which averages 20 degrees Fahrenheit colder than Zurich.

Mother Philippine approached the mission and her role as superior with creativity and zeal. She sought and won the bishop's approval to have Exposition of the Blessed Sacrament each Friday in the convent chapel and she used her influence to inaugurate the practice of 40 hours devotion in the area. On one occasion, hearing the story of the death of a young mother of three whose husband was a one-armed lumberjack, Mother Philippine went to the family home during the wake and told the bereaved widower that if he wished, the sisters could care for his children while he had to work in the woods. That afternoon, the convent became an orphanage.[227] On another occasion, she intercepted a woman about to board a train to abandon her husband and, in front of a crowd of onlookers, convinced her that she should return home to work out their difficulties. The biography also describes how, when the priests were away attending to the lumber camps, Mother Philippine would, "compensate...as best she could by reading the prayers of the Mass...comment on some of the passages and pray with the parishioners," making her perhaps the first Sister of St. Joseph in the U.S. to conduct "Sunday celebrations in the absence of a priest."[228] She was so well

---

226 Mother Philippine's biography mentions that her mother had entered the postulate of the Sisters of St. Joseph but had to leave for reasons of health. When she consulted the Cure of Ars, St. John Vianney, about her "lost vocation," he assured her that she would be called to marriage and would have a daughter who would become a religious. ("Translation of the Necrology of Mother Mary Philippine Coupat," Archives, CSJL)

227 Mother Philippine's biography mentions that one of the lumberjack's daughters later joined the Congregation.

228

received in that role that one parishioner said to her "Mother, you spoke very nicely to us, but it would have been even nicer if you had put on the vestments." Another woman who had attended her services came later and offered her a stipend to celebrate a Mass for her daughter, insisting, "I want you to say it." Mother Philippine tried to explain to her that only priests can say Mass. There is no record of whether or not the woman then went to a priest. Mother Philippine spent a total of 17 years in Maine, returning to France in 1923 when she was elected Assistant Superior General. She died in Lyon on January 17, 1926, at the age of 68.

During the time that Mother Philippine was superior, the community opened the mission at South Berwick. They began in 1909, under the leadership of Mother Benedicte and Sister Theophile, the first sisters who had come to the U.S., both of whom had opened the mission in Saskatchewan. The original community at South Berwick included 10 sisters to serve a school of 180 children.

When the Superior General visited Maine in 1912, the sisters began to make plans for a U.S. novitiate. Like the sisters in Fall River, they saw that the need to travel to France for a novitiate was an impediment to vocations. With Bishop Walsh's permission, the community opened a novitiate in South Berwick in 1913 and received three postulants in October of that year. In July, 1914, the Congregation of the Sisters of St. Joseph of Lyon gave the habit to the first three young women to enter the congregation in Maine: Sisters Rosa Benedicte (Marie Ange) Benoit, Louis Joseph (Angelina) Bolduc and Marie Denis (Alma) Pare.

The novitiate remained in South Berwick until 1949, when it moved to Auburn, then in 1965, it moved to Winslow. As the community grew, they took on new missions, always maintaining close contact with the Motherhouse in Lyon. The congregation would not establish Maine as a province until 1958, at which time the community had enough local vocations to be independent as a separate unit of the Congregation. That status would continue for 60 years before the Congregational Chapter of 2017 decided that the smaller number of sisters in Maine made it more feasible to consider the area a region rather than a province.

When the Sisters of St. Joseph of Lyon became established in Maine, the Lyon congregation had completed the unexpected task of supplying the first and the last of the French foundations of Sisters of St. Joseph in the United States. The first French sisters had come from Lyon in 1836. They were followed by sisters from Moutiers (1854), Bourg (1856) Le Puy (1866 and 1902), and Chambéry (1885). In 1904, Lyon opened a mission that would become a province of their international congregation. In between the first and the last of the Lyon foundations in America, at least 20 other congregations of St. Joseph were founded across the United States, not to mention those founded in Canada.

TOWARD THE FUTURE

The Little Design that had begun so quietly in small towns like Saint-Flour and Le Puy spread unobtrusively through France for 150 years. After the French Revolution it blossomed and changed in ways previously undreamed of. As a result of a century of anti-clericalism and persecution, the little French design spread throughout the world. From their earliest foundations, the Sisters of St. Joseph had responded to the call to "divide the city" and make the great love of God present among diverse peoples.[229] When they came to the United States, their growth as communities was occasionally well-planned out, often surprising and sometimes controversial. Marked by great diversity and willingness to move into the new, congregations of Sisters of St. Joseph in the United States would grow prodigiously during the twentieth century, offering the Church and society of the United States the gifts of anything of which women are capable to serve the dear neighbor. When the Sisters of St. Joseph of Lyon sent their 20th century missionaries to the United States, the Little Design had been growing in the country for nearly 70 years, but its greatest growth lay ahead in the dawning 20th century.

---

229 The Sisters of St. Joseph's Primitive *Constitutions*, Second part, includes the instruction that "Since their zeal should extend as far as possible to the prevention of any offense against God, they will divide the city into various sections and...they will work to learn all the moral disorders existing in each section in order to remedy them..." (See: Monica Flynn, Julie Harkins and Eileen Quinlin: The Little Congregation of the Daughters of St. Joseph, Primitive Texts in Translation (Wheeling, WV, 1984) 92

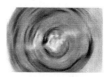

INDEX